Stalin's Police

Stalin's Police

Public Order and Mass Repression in the USSR, 1926–1941

Paul Hagenloh

Woodrow Wilson Center Press
Washington, D.C.

The Johns Hopkins University Press
Baltimore

EDITORIAL OFFICES

Woodrow Wilson Center Press
Woodrow Wilson International Center for Scholars
One Woodrow Wilson Plaza
1300 Pennsylvania Avenue, N.W.
Washington, D.C. 20004-3027
Telephone: 202-691-4029
www.wilsoncenter.org

ORDER FROM

The Johns Hopkins University Press
Hampden Station
P.O. Box 50370
Baltimore, Maryland 21211
Telephone: 1-800-537-5487
www.press.jhu.edu/books/

2 4 6 8 9 7 5 3 1

Library of Congress Cataloging-in-Publication Data

Hagenloh, Paul.
Stalin's police : public order and mass repression in the USSR, 1926–1941 / Paul Hagenloh.
p. cm.
Includes bibliographical references.
ISBN 978-0-8018-9182-3 (hardcover : alk. paper)
1. Political persecution—Soviet Union—History.   2. Police—Soviet Union—History.
3. Soviet Union—Politics and government—1917–1936.   4. Soviet Union—Politics and
government—1936–1953.   I. Title.
DK267.H22 2009
947.084′2—dc22   2008049892

Woodrow Wilson International Center for Scholars

The Woodrow Wilson International Center for Scholars, established by Congress in 1968 and headquartered in Washington, D.C., is the living, national memorial to President Wilson.

The Center is a nonpartisan institution of advanced research, supported by public and private funds, engaged in the study of national and world affairs. The Center establishes and maintains a neutral forum for free, open, and informed dialogue.

The Center's mission is to commemorate the ideals and concerns of Woodrow Wilson by providing a link between the world of ideas and the world of policy, by bringing a broad spectrum of individuals together to discuss important public policy issues, by serving to bridge cultures and viewpoints, and by seeking to find common ground.

Conclusions or opinions expressed in Center publications and programs are those of the authors and speakers and do not necessarily reflect the views of the Center staff, fellows, trustees, advisory groups, or any individuals or organizations that provide financial support to the Center.

The Center is the publisher of *The Wilson Quarterly* and home of Woodrow Wilson Center Press, *dialogue* radio and television, and the monthly newsletter "Centerpoint." For more information about the Center's activities and publications, please visit us on the web at www.wilsoncenter.org.

Lee H. Hamilton, President and Director

Contents

Tables

Acknowledgments

I have accumulated so many personal and professional debts in writing this book that a full account of them would likely take up a book of its own. It gives me great pleasure to acknowledge the individuals and institutions that have helped me, if far more briefly than they deserve.

Robert Moeller sparked my interest in European history many years ago, and Lynn Mally nudged me toward Soviet history and toward the University of Texas. In Austin I found an exemplary group of mentors and friends. Charters Wynn was and continues to be a model adviser; Joan Neuberger provided appropriate doses of intellectual guidance and moral support. Along with Joan and Charters, David Crew, Judy Coffin, and David Imhoof all gave their time generously and showed me how inspiring a community of scholars could be. Wendy Gerber suffered through the initial stages of this project but saw none of the results; I thank her for her support.

I am honored to have been associated with several exceptional institutions in the process of writing this book. I am deeply grateful for the support of Thomas Lindenberger and the Center for Contemporary Historical Research in Potsdam, Germany; Karen Dawisha and the Havighurst Center for Russian and Post-Soviet Studies at Miami University of Ohio; and Blair Ruble and the Kennan Institute of the Woodrow Wilson International Center for Scholars in Washington. I thank Jamie Durana, my research assistant at the Woodrow Wilson Center, for tracking down materials in the Library of Congress. I am particularly indebted to Blair Ruble, and to the Woodrow Wilson Center, for enabling me to continue to work on my manuscript in spite of difficult personal circumstances.

In Russia, my path through the archives was smoothed by the friendly staff at the State Archive of the Russian Federation, especially Galina Kuznetsova, and by the expert help of J. Arch Getty's Praxis International, especially Elena Drozdova and Leonid Vaintraub. Research for the book was supported by the International Research and Exchanges Board, the National Council for Eurasian and East European Research, the Social Science Research Council, the University of Alabama, and the University of Texas. The opinions expressed herein do not reflect the positions of any of the above-mentioned people or institutions.

At the University of Alabama, I have enjoyed the support of many current and past colleagues, including Margaret Abruzzo, Gregory Dorr, Michael Mendle, Scott O'Bryan, and George Williamson—the last, in particular, a model historian and mentor. I also appreciate the support of Robert Olin and Carmen Taylor in the office of the dean of arts and sciences.

I thank Golfo Alexopoulos, Stephen Bittner, Adrienne Edgar, Sheila Fitzpatrick, Wendy Goldman, James Heinzen, Yoshiko Herrera, Eric Lohr, Terry Martin, Amy Nelson, and Gabor Rittersporn for support at various stages of this project. Barbara Keys has long encouraged me to stay focused on the big picture, and her careful reading of the introduction improved it immeasurably. David Shearer deserves special mention for his unflagging professional and personal support, from the first time that we crossed paths in the Russian archives (both of us in the initial stages of projects on Soviet policing and Stalinist repression) to the current day.

Peter H. Solomon Jr. has shown an interest in my work that began with my first conference presentation as a graduate student, but my intellectual debt to him goes far beyond that. His work in the field of Soviet criminal justice is the touchstone for all that come after him. I have referred to his *Soviet Criminal Justice under Stalin* so many times that I long ago broke its spine (my apologies to the library of the University of Alabama). It is my hope that this book rises, in some fashion, to the standard that he has set.

At the Woodrow Wilson Center Press, Joe Brinley, director, and Yamile Kahn, managing editor, deserve thanks for guiding a long (too long) manuscript to publication. I am grateful to my two external reviewers (one of whom, to my great pleasure, identified himself as Peter H. Solomon Jr.) for insightful comments that made this book far better than it would have otherwise been. Alfred Imhoff provided expert copyediting. Any mistakes that remain are, of course, my responsibility alone.

Finally, Diane Williamson has read every word of this book more than once, cheerfully working far from her own field of expertise with a project that has consumed more of her time than it should have. Dedicating a book on mass repression to a loved one seems morbid, but to the extent that this book is dedicated to anybody, it is to her.

A Note on Translation

Russian terms, especially those pertaining to legal and police systems that do not correspond to Anglo-American traditions, present a certain amount of difficulty for an author attempting to produce text that is both readable and precise. I have chosen to use English equivalents for nearly all Russian terms, with a few notable exceptions. I reserve the original Russian for the notes. One exception is immediately obvious: I have retained the Russian term for the Soviet civil police, the *militsiia*. The proper English translation for the *militsiia* is simply "police," not the oft-used "militia," which implies a degree of volunteerism that disappeared from Soviet policing by the end of the Civil War. I use the term *militsiia* when referring to the civil police alone, "political police" when referring to the Bolshevik domestic security service (the Cheka, GPU, OGPU, or NKVD, depending on the time under consideration), and, when style requires it, the term "police" to refer to both institutions collectively.

Terms referring to the institutional divisions of the Soviet policing system cause numerous problems for translation, in part because they changed rapidly over the course of the early Soviet period. The People's Commissariat of Internal Affairs (NKVD) is perhaps the most confusing. In the early chapters of the book, the term "NKVD" refers to republic-level people's commissariats of internal affairs, such as the NKVD of the Russian Soviet Federated Socialist Republic (NKVD RSFSR), which were responsible for the *militsiia*, a portion of the Soviet penal system, and various lesser administrations such as fire departments. Each Soviet republic maintained its own internal affairs commissariat in the 1920s, but for the sake of simplicity I refer to the NKVD of the Russian Republic, which set policy for the nation, as "the NKVD" unless clarity requires otherwise.

The nomenclature for the Soviet political police is more complex. The original Bolshevik political police, the Cheka (an acronym for the full name of the organization, the All-Russian Extra-Ordinary Commission for Combating Counterrevolution and Sabotage), was renamed the State Political Administration (GPU) in 1922 and then the USSR-wide Unified State Political Administration (OGPU) in 1923. The Politburo restructured the entire Soviet criminal justice system in 1934, creating an Internal Affairs Commissariat at the USSR-level (NKVD SSSR) and subsuming under it all penal and policing institutions, including the civil and political police. The political police remained relatively unchanged in nature but became part of the larger bureaucratic structure of the NKVD, as the Main Administration for State Security of the NKVD (GUGB NKVD). Popular and scholarly works often refer to the political police after 1934 simply as "the NKVD" and to individual political policemen as "NKVD officers," usages that are imprecise and confusing. This book continues to refer to the State Security administration after 1934 as the "political police" (or the more cumbersome "GUGB" when necessary) and uses the term "NKVD" to refer to the entire internal affairs system. In addition, political police officers generally referred to themselves as "Chekists," even after the demise of Feliks Dzerzhinsky's Cheka; in several places I follow this practice, for the sake of style, to refer to political policemen in the 1920s and 1930s.

I have also translated into English numerous Russian terms for territorial units, juridical procedures, and institutions specific to Soviet judicial practices. Such terms often overlap in ways that English-speaking readers find confusing. In addition, slippages between terms like "arrest," indictment," and "detainment" were rife among the police themselves, sometimes quite intentionally. It is my hope that clarity and readability will make up for any loss of specificity in my translation choices; I have noted any inconsistencies in the notes. I have chosen not to italicize the term "troika," and to use the English plural "troikas," as most readers will be familiar with both the English word and the three-person extrajudicial commission to which it refers. The Council of People's Commissars of the USSR (Sovnarkom) appears frequently enough in this text to merit reference simply as the Sovnarkom. If a republic-level body is not specified (e.g., the Sovnarkom of the Russian Republic), then the term refers to the USSR-wide body. To make the text more accessible to the reader who does not speak Russian, I have omitted all hard and soft signs in the body of the book and used common spellings of well-known names, including those surnames usually spelled in English with a single "y" (Trotsky or

Vyshinsky, for example, instead of Trotskii or Vyshinskii). However, I adhere to a standard transliteration scheme in the notes.

Finally, any book that deals with issues of criminological categorization and social construction will invariably make use of terms that seem so tendentious that they demand some system of distance from the authorial voice. Terms like "socially harmful elements," "criminal elements," "class-alien elements," or the peculiar Soviet crime of "wrecking" are obvious cases. Upon closer consideration, similar cases abound; the crimes of "speculation" and "hooliganism," for example, appear as articles in all Soviet criminal codes but were so mutable, and entailed such dire consequences for the individuals to which they were applied, that they seem to demand the same treatment. Particularly contentious terms appear in quotation marks, but not every such term used in this book can be signified in this way. It is my hope that the text itself will make clear the difficult relationship between categorization and lived experience in Stalin's USSR.

Glossary

Central Inspectorate of the Militsiia under the OGPU. The secret central administration of the *militsiia* that was created in 1930 without public announcement and abolished in 1934.

Cheka—All-Russian Extraordinary Commission for Combating Counterrevolution and Sabotage. The Soviet political police from 1917 to 1922.

Detective Department. The Criminal Investigations Department of the Soviet civil police (Ugolovnyi Rozysk or the Operativnyi Otdel, depending on the year in question).

GPU—State Political Administration. The political police, 1922–23, formally part of the NKVD RSFSR, reorganized into the independent OGPU with the creation of the USSR; the institutional heir to the Cheka. "GPU" also refers to republican- and lower-level political police administrations. For the sake of readability, this book uses the term "OGPU" to refer to all political-police bodies between 1923 and 1934, even when the term "GPU" would be technically correct—for example, in the phrase "republic-level OGPU administration."

GUGB—Central Directorate of State Security of the USSR NKVD. One of several central administrations within the USSR NKVD after 1934; the institutional heir to the OGPU.

Gulag—Glavnoe upravlenie ispravitel'no-trudovykh lagerei. The acronym for the Main Administration of Corrective Labor Camps.

GURKM pri Sovnarkom RSFSR—Central Administration of the Workers' and Peasants' Militsiia attached to the Sovnarkom of the Russian Soviet Federated Socialist Republic. The nonsecret central administration of the civil police, 1930–34, created to mask the existence of the Central Inspectorate of the Militsiia under the OGPU.

Industrial Militsiia—vedomstvennaia militsiia. The branch of the police charged with guarding factories and other economic institutions.

Komsomol. Communist Youth League.

kulak. A relatively prosperous peasant, identified by the Stalinist regime as anti-Soviet and repressed during the drive to collectivize agriculture.

lishentsy. Individuals deprived of Soviet citizenship (voting) rights either due to their previous social position or because they were convicted of a crime.

NEP—New Economic Policy. The period of a limited market economy between the Russian Civil War and the First Five-Year Plan.

NKIu—People's Commissariat of Justice. The People's Commissariat of Justice of the Russian Republic or the USSR, depending on the sense; commissariats of justice existed only at the republican level until 1936.

NKVD RSFSR—People's Commissariat of Internal Affairs of the Russian Soviet Federated Socialist Republic. The commissariat in charge of the *militsiia* from 1917 to 1930. It was separate from and opposed to the political police until it was abolished in 1930.

NKVD USSR—People's Commissariat of Internal Affairs of the Soviet Union. The all-Union commissariat created in 1934, in charge of the *militsiia*, the political police, the Gulag, and various other aspects of internal security.

oblast'. The main administrative subdivision in the USSR below the republican level after 1929. Translated as "region."

OGPU—Unified State Political Administration. The all-Union political police, 1923–34. Reorganized from the GPU with the creation of the USSR. (See the note on translation above regarding the difference between the GPU and OGPU.)

Procuracy. The legal agency charged with prosecuting court cases and supervising the legality of police and court activity. Part of the Justice Commissariat before the creation of the All-Union Procuracy under Andrei Vyshinsky in 1933.

Rabkrin—Workers' and Peasants' Inspectorate. The supragovernmental body charged with supervising state administration.

Socialist Revolutionaries. A prerevolutionary populist political party.

soviet. A council; the basic administrative unit of the Soviet government from the local (village or urban district) level to the center.

Sovnarkom RSFSR—Council of People's Commissars of the Russian Soviet Federated Socialist Republic. The cabinet of the government of the Russian Republic; the de facto policymaking body, in many cases.

Sovnarkom SSSR. Council of People's Commissars of the USSR.

Troika (plural in Russian: troiki). A three-person police panel authorized to carry out extrajudicial repression. Several kinds existed at various times, including passport *troiki*, civil police *troiki*, and the notorious "special *troiki*" of 1937–38 that issued death sentences during the Great Terror.

TsIK SSSR—USSR Central Executive Committee. The executive arm of the All-Union Congress of Soviets.

VTsIK RSFSR—All-Russian Central Executive Committee of the Russian Soviet Federated Socialist Republic. The executive arm of the Russian Congress of Soviets.

Introduction: Soviet Policing, Social Categories, and the Great Terror

> Old prisoners claim to remember that the first blow allegedly took the form of
> mass arrests, striking virtually throughout the whole country on one single Au-
> gust night. (But, knowing our clumsiness, I don't really believe this.)
> —Aleksandr I. Solzhenitsyn, *The Gulag Archipelago 1918–1956: An
> Experiment in Literary Investigation, I–II*[1]

Aleksandr Solzhenitsyn, writing *The Gulag Archipelago* some two decades after Stalin's "Great Terror," could not believe the lore of the "old
prisoners" that a nationwide wave of mass arrests began suddenly in 1937,
"on one single August night." Neither, apparently, could anybody else, at
least not until the early 1990s, when the state and Communist Party archives in Russia began to yield documents that illuminated the shocking
events of that year. At the beginning of July, Joseph Stalin abruptly decided to launch a mass purge of Soviet society that extended far beyond
the purges of state and Communist Party elites already under way. Stalin
and his political police chief, Nikolai Ezhov, ordered local party bosses
and police chiefs to prepare for mass arrests of "criminals" and "former
kulaks"—the latter term referring to those peasants who were exiled from
their homes during the collectivization of Soviet agriculture in the early
1930s and had kept under surveillance by the local police ever since.
At the end of the month, Stalin and Ezhov provided local police chiefs
with arrest and execution quotas for every administrative region of the
USSR and instructed them to begin what were termed "mass operations
of repression of kulaks, criminals, and other anti-Soviet elements." These
operations were to begin on August 5, 10, or 15, depending on the region
of the country; Solzhenitsyn's "old prisoners" failed to make allowances
for the sheer size of the USSR.

1

Sixteen months of unrelenting mass arrests followed, carried out by the Soviet political police (the notorious NKVD State Security Administration) and the civil police alike, with little of the "clumsiness" that made it difficult for Solzhenitsyn to conceive of such a thing. In urban areas, the police targeted petty criminals or individuals who had spent time in the Soviet penal system. The Moscow police, for example, in the fall of 1937 arrested one A. I. Ul., who was gainfully employed in the construction trade but had previous convictions for theft and armed robbery and had been arrested five times for the crime of "hooliganism"; regional political police officials, citing his ongoing petty criminal activities, including purse snatching, sentenced him to death.[2] In the countryside, the police concentrated on "former kulaks," arresting hundreds of thousands of peasants deemed "anti-Soviet" for little more than their status as prosperous farmers in the precollectivization era. Once these operations began, Stalin also added numerous "suspect" ethnicities to the list of targets: Poles, Germans, Koreans, and others whom he feared would support anti-Soviet insurgencies in the event of war. The police responded by arresting what they termed "national elements" by the tens of thousands, targeting not only foreign nationals and members of suspect ethnicities but all Soviet citizens allegedly in contact with governments hostile to the USSR.

The initial waves of arrests in the fall of 1937 were expansive enough, but as the weeks of mass operations turned into months, local police made use of whatever means they could to fulfill the demands emanating from Moscow for continued arrests of "anti-Soviet elements." After local police administrations exhausted readily available categories of suspects, they swept up individuals in raids of public squares or open air markets and arrested them for lack of proper identification, or they arrested individuals known to them as petty criminals, vagrants, or individuals otherwise on the margins of Soviet society. To explain this dizzying expansion of arrests, local NKVD officials invented massive "anti-Soviet" conspiracies that purportedly united the "social base" of "kulaks" and ex-convicts with active diversionary organizations staffed by foreign spies and former White Army officers. NKVD troikas, three-person panels made up of regional NKVD and Communist Party bosses, sentenced these individuals without any supervision from higher police or legal authorities, while local NKVD authorities meted out sentences of execution on the spot.[3] As the local NKVD administrations filled the quotas set down for them by Stalin and Ezhov, they requested quota expansions, in part to show initiative but primarily because Stalin and Ezhov explicitly demanded such displays of vigilance from regional police administrations.

The mass operations were nothing like the well-known purges of Communist Party and state elites—the Moscow "show trials" of top party leaders, the purge of the party at large, and the devastating purge of the Red Army—which wracked the Soviet Union at the same time and which, for fifty years after they occurred, were synonymous with Stalin's "Great Terror." Stalin and Ezhov maintained tight control over these operations, but they approved continual expansions of arrests and executions throughout 1937 and 1938. By the time Stalin called off the mass operations in late November 1938, the NKVD had sentenced some 1.15 million people. Roughly 683,000 were shot, representing the vast majority of the individuals executed by the regime in these two appalling years of Stalinist terror.

* * *

Despite the sheer size of these operations, and despite the fact that they lived on in the collective memory of Soviet society—especially among prisoners of the Soviet Gulag, many of whom miraculously returned to Soviet society after Stalin's death in 1953—the mass operations disappeared from both Soviet and Western accounts of the Stalin years almost as soon as they occurred. Popular and academic accounts of the "Stalinist terror" focused instead on the public spectacle of the Moscow show trials, which featured top Bolshevik leaders debasing themselves in the name of the Communist Party, or on the purges of party, state, and military elites—events that seemed to defy rational explanation and to prove that Stalin was little more than a murderous tyrant.

The silence regarding the mass operations within the Soviet Union was the obvious product of censorship and, after Stalin's death, of the Communist Party's attempt to create a useable Leninist past while ignoring widespread repressions that called into question the legitimacy of the entire Soviet experience. Yet a broader intellectual process was also at work, in the Soviet Union as well as in the West, which turned on the place of Stalinist repression in the history of Soviet socialism. Leon Trotsky—not only a participant in the revolutionary events but, through his voluminous writings on the Stalinist system from exile, also perhaps the most important influence on at least two generations of commentators on the Stalinist regime—set the pattern for future accounts of Stalinist terror as early as the summer of 1937, when he argued that the ongoing party purges were a caesura in the history of Soviet socialism. "The present purge [of the party]," he protested, "draws between Bolshevism and Stalinism not simply a bloody line but a whole river of blood. . . . How can this not be seen?"[4] For Trotsky, the question was one of origins; if mass repression did not arise from the nature of Bolshevism itself, whence did it emerge?

Trotsky cast the entire phenomenon of Stalinism as a degeneration of Bolshevism in the context of domestic backwardness and the continued existence of international capitalism, but his specific answer to this question was political. He claimed that the Communist Party purges amounted to counterrevolution: they allowed Stalin to eliminate any genuinely socialist impulses within the party and to ensure that all opposition to his hold on power would be wiped out.[5] Trotsky's analysis identified the "purges" as the central event in a Stalinist Thermidor and in doing so made them into the pivotal moment in the history of Soviet socialism. It was the party purges of 1937 and 1938—not the "Red Terror" during the Civil War, not the repressions associated with the collectivization of agriculture in the early 1930s, and not the mass repressions of 1937 and 1938 that targeted broad swaths of the Soviet population—that represented an aberration in the Marxist historical narrative that underpinned Trotsky's analysis. Hence it was the party purges that required historical explanation in order to come to terms with the phenomenon of Stalinism itself.

The identification of the "purges" as the pivotal political event in the emergence of Stalinism made the "origins of the Great Purges" into the key question addressed by virtually every account of Stalinist repression that followed. Nearly all commentators from the 1950s to the 1970s, whatever their ultimate judgment of socialism, posited as the essence of the "purges" of 1937 and 1938 the perverse spectacle of Stalin destroying his own Bolshevik Party. Readers of Roy Medvedev's monumental history of Stalinist repression, *Let History Judge*, will find detailed analyses of the party purges, show trials, and repressions of intellectual elites, all of which made possible Stalin's triumph over Vladimir Lenin's supposedly more humane version of socialism; but they will search in vain for any sustained analysis of repressions in 1937 that struck outside these elites, save for a brief mention of arrests on collective farms and among church officials.[6] On the other side of the political spectrum, Robert Conquest, who popularized the term "the Great Terror" to refer to the Stalinist repressions between 1936 and 1938, argued that mass terror emerged from an inexorable expansion of Stalin's political purges—from the party elites, to their personal and professional contacts, to "all elements suspected of not being reconciled to the regime."[7] Even as balanced an observer as Merle Fainsod, in his pioneering study of Soviet rule in the city of Smolensk, argued that what he called the "Climactic Great Purge" of 1936–38 represented the culmination of repeated waves of party purges in the 1930s and resulted primarily in the decimation of the pre-Stalinist bureaucratic and intellectual elite.[8] For almost all commentators on Stalinism before the Gorbachev era, the non-elite victims of Stalinist terror fell prey to an expansion of party purges that were not initially aimed at them, and hence the causes of the "Great Purges" were identical to the causes of Stalinist repression in general in 1937 and 1938—except for scholars like Conquest and Solzhenitsyn, for whom repression was the inevitable outcome of Marxism itself and hence required no historical explanation at all.

This political account of Stalinist repression was surprisingly resilient, even as a new generation of scholars trained new methodologies on the question. Scholars in the 1970s and 1980s challenged the primacy of the political in existing analyses of Stalinism, questioning in particular the "totalitarian" model, which argued that Soviet society was so crushed by Stalin's dictatorial regime that it could not possibly have had any influence on the events of 1937 and 1938.[9] By the mid-1980s, numerous historians had cast Soviet "society" in a major role in the purges, arguing that tensions within the emerging Stalinist polity—conflicts on the shop floor, popular discontent with local bureaucratic satraps, peasant disaffection with the collective farm system—seeped up through the structure of the Soviet bureaucratic system and pushed the Communist Party and the NKVD toward mass purges.[10] Several historians took seriously Solzhenitsyn's idea of "clumsiness" as well, elevating it to a primary explanation of Stalinist repression; for them, the "Great Purges" became, rather than an expression of the complete domination of Soviet society by an all-powerful Stalinist state, the frantic and fearful reaction of a weak regime to its inability to control its own apparatus at the periphery.[11]

The explosion of archival access that occurred in the late 1980s and early 1990s had little immediate influence on these basic assumptions. The mass operations remained completely out of sight; if anything, the initial attempts by Western historians to mine the Soviet and post-Soviet archives produced accounts that amplified the stress on Communist Party and social elites (or former elites) as Stalin's chief victims. Historians continued to assume, following the pattern set by Trotsky decades before, that the origins of the "Great Purges" were to be found in political processes within the party and that the expansion of repression to Soviet society at large was the result of ancillary processes—such as a "snowball effect" of denunciations from one arrested individual to another, or the exercise of popular initiative within the party or the workforce, or the simple mean-spirited selfishness of individuals with something to gain by another's arrest.[12]

These accounts broadened our understanding of Stalinist repression and especially of the purges of Communist Party and bureaucratic elites, but they all continued to focus on the process by which the party purges expanded to become the "Stalinist terror."[13] In this respect, they were simply asking the wrong question. The mass repression of 1937 and 1938 was no mere expansion of ongoing purges within the Communist Party and the Soviet state; it was an explosion of police repression with roots in the histories of Soviet policing, social engineering, and state violence stretching back to the very beginnings of the Bolshevik regime.

* * *

The mass operations of 1937 and 1938, which remained so hidden from public view in the fifty years after they took place, suddenly became known to all in 1992, when the newspaper *Trud*—formerly the official Soviet trade union mouthpiece—reproduced parts of the Politburo's July 1937 decree that launched them, complete with quotas for arrests and executions.[14] Revelation after revelation followed, in both the academic and the popular press, detailing Stalin's incontrovertible role as the initiator of the mass operations and providing the first solid estimate of the number of individuals executed by the regime in 1937 and 1938—roughly 700,000.[15]

Historians in the West scrambled to make sense of this wave of new information, in most cases continuing to confuse the mass operations with the concurrent purges of Communist Party and state elites.[16] Some continued to argue that the mass operations were the direct product of the Great Purges—in one of the best-known formulations, presenting them as a "blind rage and panic" on the part of central authorities, who had found that their existing "discursive strategies" for controlling the party apparatus at the periphery were no longer effective.[17] Other historians began the arduous work of sifting through the massive amounts of newly available archival data and reconceptualizing the place of the mass operations in the overall constellation of repressive processes that made up the "Stalinist terror."[18] Several researchers began to draw analytic connections between the mass operations and Soviet "ethnic cleansing" in the 1930s, attempting to explain the targeting of "national contingents" during the mass operations as the product of a broader turn by the Stalinist regime toward an ethnocentric conception of the Soviet body politic—an issue that, as we will see in chapter 6, was crucial to Stalin's decision to launch mass repressions against broad sectors of Soviet society in 1937.[19]

Historians in the former Soviet Union, to the contrary, focused almost entirely on the role of Stalin and the top echelons of the Communist Party in the unfolding tragedy, attempting to prove beyond a shadow of a doubt that Stalin initiated and controlled both the party purges and the mass operations. These historians reveled in their ability, after years of silence, to relate the concrete details of 1937 and 1938: the execution lists containing hundreds, sometimes thousands of names of top party and state officials that were signed routinely by Stalin; the details of Stalin's interactions with his top lieutenants, including those who did not survive the decade; and the mechanisms of power within the Politburo.[20] For historians in the former USSR, the task of sorting through the archival materials of the party and the political police was motivated by far more than academic debate; many of the best studies of Stalinist state violence were produced after 1991 by individuals associated with Memorial, an organization dedicated to preserving the memory of the victims of Stalinist repression and protecting civic freedom in the post-Soviet era.[21]

A few commentators, including myself, began in the late 1990s to question the generally accepted link between the Communist Party purges and the mass repressions, focusing instead on the Stalinist regime's response to crime and social disorder during the 1930s and studying the mass operations on their own terms, as police operations that had precedents not in the history of party politics but in the history of the regime's attempts to control its populations through various means common to modern states: policing, internal registrations systems, surveillance, and law.[22] Yet despite the appearance in recent years of a vast amount of research on the mass operations, their precise nature, contours, and causes have still not been conclusively established, nor has the field produced anything approaching a consensus regarding their relationship to the larger set of events known as the "Stalinist terror."[23]

It is incontestable, however, that the repressions that began in August 1937 really were, as Solzhenitsyn's "old prisoners" described them, mass arrests, carried out by the Stalinist police and launched "one August night" on Stalin's direct orders. Explaining these horrific events, therefore, requires studying not only Communist Party politics but also the history of Soviet policing, broadly defined to include the regime's approaches to the surveillance of suspect individuals, attempts by the police to control the geographic mobility of the population, and the mobilization of state violence in the service of the overtly modernizing schemes of social engineering pursued by the Stalinist state.

* * *

This book is a history of Soviet policing between Stalin's rise to power and the beginning of World War II. It is the story of the emergence of a modern vision of Soviet policing during the era of the New Economic Policy (NEP) and the initial years of the Stalin era, and of the deformation of that vision under the pressures of Stalin's "revolution from above."[24] It is also the story of the connections between Soviet policing and mass repression, and especially of the expansion of police repressions of actual and merely potential lawbreakers in the mid-1930s that led directly to the mass operations of 1937 and 1938. I argue that a particular mode of thinking about crime and social disorder emerged within the Soviet policing system in the early Stalin period, one that revolved around the idea of preventing crime by controlling population cohorts that were deemed undesirable due to their supposedly criminal nature—cohorts identified as "contingents" (*kontingenty*) in Russian and defined by past criminal activity, sociological status, or geographic mobility. This criminological schema played a pivotal role in the genesis of the "Stalinist terror" of 1937 and 1938, but it emerged well before these events began; as early as the mid-1930s, Stalinist policing was fully predicated on the idea of identification, surveillance, and eventual excision from the body politic of those population cohorts identified by top Communist Party and police officials as "socially dangerous" or otherwise threatening to the regime.

Soviet policing in the first two decades after the Bolshevik Revolution has been studied far less than has Stalinist repression. The popular and scholarly literature on Soviet espionage, the Gulag, and the repression of political opposition—real or imagined—is vast, but little sustained analysis of the policing system itself existed before the collapse of the Soviet Union. Western studies of the domestic activities of the Soviet political police that were produced before the Gorbachev era tended to follow the "totalitarian" model, assuming that the political police served as Lenin's, and then Stalin's, personal praetorian guard, or that it represented a "state within state" that the Communist Party used to crush opposition inside or outside its ranks.[25] Recent studies of the political police in the formative years of the regime have complicated this picture substantially. The Bolshevik political police, despite their genesis as a revolutionary apparatus that employed virtually unchecked violence against civilians during the Russian Civil War, were surprisingly weak in the first years of the NEP, and their responsibilities were vast, including not only the surveillance of politically suspect individuals and groups but also the gathering of information regarding the population in general and the combating of internal insurgencies and organized criminal activity.[26]

Yet this literature, though rich regarding the first decade of Soviet power, has not pressed beyond the end of the NEP period, nor has it come to terms with the less sensational but equally important aspects of political police activity in the 1920s, such as the suppression of the illegal buying and selling of consumer goods, the control of criminal "banditry," and purges of urban areas of petty criminals and other individuals deemed "socially dangerous"—all of which constituted an extensive realm of political police activity directed at the control of crime and social disorder rather than at strictly "political" opposition to the Bolshevik regime.

Studies of the Soviet civil police, the *militsiia*, have been even more limited. A handful of Western accounts have focused on the *militsiia* during the revolutionary era and the NEP, painting a picture of an exceptionally weak administrative system that shared many structures and deficiencies with the Tsarist system that it replaced.[27] Studies of civil policing under Stalin that appeared within the USSR before 1991 were without exception produced by the Soviet Ministry of Internal Affairs; they were predictably adulatory and provided no serious discussion of the role of the civil police in Stalinist repression. Similar studies in the 1990s, still the exclusive bailiwick of scholars within the Russian Ministry of Internal Affairs, erred in the other direction, emphasizing the takeover of civil policing by the political police (the OGPU) in the 1930s and the resulting perversion of the institutional ethos of the civil police that made possible the participation of the *militsiia* in Stalin's purges. This argument is exaggerated but, as we will see, not completely without merit.[28] Nearly all accounts of civil policing maintain a strict analytic division between the *militsiia* and the political police, and hence between civil and political crimes, reinforcing the general assumption in the field that Stalinist repression was political repression, and that the civil police had little to do with it.[29]

This division is utterly artificial. From the very beginning of the Soviet period, civil and political policing were inextricably mixed, and both were part of a larger drive of the Bolshevik regime to "engineer" the populations under its control. Problems of public order, civil crime, and social stability were central to the activities of the political police, while the civil police were fully engaged in controlling behaviors deemed a threat—political, national security, or social—to the regime. The police themselves spoke freely of the "repression" of criminal activities, such as murder or armed robbery, in the same way that they spoke of the "repression" of sociologically defined population cohorts, such as "kulaks" or "socially harmful elements." Mass repression under Stalin entailed not only overt repression by the political police but also the surveillance of suspect populations; control of the geographic mobility of Soviet citizens; numerous informal systems for identifying, marking, and controlling "undesirable" individuals within Soviet society; and the manifold layers of the Soviet penal system, including the Gulag, the courts, administrative banishment or exile, and monetary fines meted out by individual officers on the street.

The interactions between Soviet statecraft, social engineering, and political violence in the early Soviet period have been the focus of several important studies in recent years, which have attempted to situate Soviet state violence in the context of pan-European approaches to population mobilization and social control.[30] This innovative body of scholarship places early Soviet statecraft in the context of an emerging "population politics" in nineteenth-century Europe, arguing that Bolshevik political violence was an example of the propensity of modern states to "garden" their populations using instruments as varied as the census, residence registration, cadastral mapping systems, and modern medical knowledge, as well as overt police coercion.[31]

These studies also draw explicit connections between Soviet political violence and the techniques used by the Tsarist and the early Bolshevik regimes to mobilize their populations under the pressures of World War I and the Russian Civil War. According to these accounts, mass repression in the early Soviet period was the product of the continued use during peacetime of modes of state violence that were forged in colonial conflicts and during World War I. The Bolshevik revolutionary moment, coming as it did in the midst of wartime mobilization, institutionalized these particularly modern forms of mass mobilization and state violence as the preeminent techniques of Bolshevik rule, and in so doing harnessed modern European modes of wartime population control to the particularly Bolshevik end of the total Marxist transformation of Soviet society.[32]

These lines of argument, grounded in solid research regarding the Tsarist and Bolshevik experience in World War I and the Civil War, are the most fruitful approaches to early Bolshevik repression to emerge since the opening of the Soviet archives. They have forced the field to return to the task of situating Bolshevik violence in the context of modern European state systems, where it certainly belongs, and they encourage us to understand state violence in the Stalin period as an unusual but not unique example of the propensity of modern states to use political violence to shape, rather than just to dominate, the populations under their control.

This book fits comfortably within this body of scholarship in many ways, stressing the overtly modern nature of the Soviet policing project, which was clearly visible even before the Bolsheviks gained complete control of the lands of the former Tsarist Empire. An ethos of "preventive policing" (*profilakticheskaia rabota*) emerged within the top levels of the Soviet police bureaucracies, both civil and political, well before the Stalin period. This ethos was expressed as a drive to perfect Soviet society by identifying, surveying, and excising all individuals deemed "socially harmful" or "socially dangerous." These trends moved to the center of Soviet policing ideology in the early 1930s, as the OGPU seized control of the *militsiia* and attempted to reshape civil policing in its own image.

Yet recent commentators on Soviet "population politics" have overestimated the constructive nature of this project, concentrating on the coherent sociological paradigms propounded by criminologists and top police or Communist Party officials and ignoring the far messier set of ideologies and ad hoc practices that defined Soviet policing at the local level.[33] The waves of state violence that pummeled Soviet society in the 1930s, I argue, emerged not from a modernist drive within Soviet policing but from the *failure* of the leaders of the Soviet policing system to implement the utopian projects that they dreamed of in the late 1920s. The inability of the OGPU to transfer their plans for the total transformation of Soviet society to the *militsiia* forced the local police to turn to far less utopian methods of identifying, categorizing, and controlling "socially dangerous" population cohorts: mass purges of urban areas, extrajudicial repressions of suspect populations, and the control of geographic mobility using the Soviet internal passport system. It was the failure of covert systems of surveillance and population control to mold the Soviet population that prompted the regime to turn to more drastic modes of identification and excision of undesirable "contingents" in the mid-1930s and, eventually, to their total elimination during the mass operations of 1937 and 1938. The mass repression of the early Stalin era was not an expression in the USSR of pan-European approaches to population politics; the Stalinist police system in fact engaged in little constructive "gardening" of the Soviet population at all in the 1930s. To the contrary, Soviet policing was dedicated to social quarantine, and to the "affixation" of suspect populations and "loyal" Soviet citizens alike to hierarchical positions in political and social space.

Nor was Stalinist repression a mere continuation of the forms of state violence characteristic of the Civil War, called back into action by the revolutionary impulses of the Stalinist regime. Continuities in Tsarist and early Soviet policing abound; connections of structure, ideology, and even personnel are clear over the first two decades of Soviet power. Yet competing visions of Soviet policing existed during the NEP period—within the civil police system, judicial agencies, and even the OGPU—and the eventual triumph of the more radical approaches to policing and social control that animated the Stalinist police system was not at all preordained. The nature of the mass repressions of the late 1930s, furthermore, differs fundamentally from that of the Civil War or the waves of repressions that accompanied the collectivization of agriculture in the early 1930s. The mass operations were not reprisals carried out in the heat of the Civil War between populations locked in deadly conflict; nor did they rely, as did the collectivization campaign, on chaotic popular activism among urban supporters of the regime, often barely controlled by the center. The mass repressions of 1937 and 1938 emerged from policing campaigns against "threatening" population cohorts in the mid-1930s, campaigns that involved little popular participation and relied instead on policing techniques developed in response to the immense social disorder created by Stalin's "revolution from above." Mass repression during the Stalinist terror was, in essence, police repression, carried out by officers who were completely capable of turning their activities toward the total elimination of "socially dangerous" and "anti-Soviet" population cohorts from the Soviet body politic.

* * *

The chapters of this book are arranged chronologically. Chapter 1 presents a history of Russian and Soviet policing from the eighteenth century to the beginning of Stalin's rise to power. The Bolsheviks inherited a particularly weak policing system from the Tsarist regime. Even into the early twentieth century, the autocracy relied on local political actors to maintain order in the countryside and treated urban policing as an extension of central administration rather than as a means of social integration and control. The influence of the Tsarist administrative system was plainly evident in the extreme decentralization and inefficiency of the early Soviet policing system, as well as in the relative criminological pluralism within the NEP-era criminal justice system. Open conflict between the Bolshevik civil and political police emerged almost as soon as the NEP era began. Although this conflict remained unresolved at the level of central politics until the end of the 1920s, in practice the balance of power gradually tipped toward the OGPU, which offered a vision of Soviet policing that corresponded to Stalin's intention to jettison the compromise with limited capitalism that underlay the NEP and to return to the revolutionary maximalism of the Civil War.

Chapter 2 examines Soviet policing during Stalin's "revolution from above." The preeminent role of the political police in the collectivization and industrialization drives of the late 1920s and early 1930s ensured that the OGPU would dominate Soviet policing under Stalin. In late 1930, in conjunction with Stalin's political victory over the "Rightists" in the Politburo, the OGPU gained control of all civil policing in the USSR. The leaders of the OGPU took this victory as authorization to restructure the Soviet police system entirely, implementing a far-reaching set of reforms based on contemporary European policing practices and on their own approaches to crime and national security. Top OGPU officials envisioned a Soviet policing system that relied on preventive, rather than punitive, policing tactics, including covert surveillance, the general registration of the population, and the nationwide tracking of suspect individuals. At their most optimistic, these police officials believed that proper implementation of their reforms would lead to the complete elimination of crime in the largest Soviet cities. These hopes were wildly exaggerated; OGPU reforms that relied on covert investigation and surveillance were an utter failure even before the First Five-Year Plan period had ended. Despite these failures, local *militsiia* administrations were instrumental in implementing the social and economic changes associated with the First Five-Year Plan. In the process, they expanded the methods of state control that made the Stalin revolution possible, and they shaped the repressive responses of the Stalinist state to social disorder in the years that followed.

Chapter 3 examines the regime's responses to crime and disorder during the shift from the maximalism of the First Five-Year Plan (1928–32) to the retrenchment of the Second Five-Year Plan (1933–37). Stalin and his ruling group, firmly in power but faced with overwhelming institutional and social chaos created by the First Five-Year Plan, retreated in several areas of criminal justice in 1932 and 1933, suspending police campaigns against the peasantry and attempting to restore a basic level of predictability to the Soviet legal system. At the same time, the regime called upon the police to restore "order" by repressing a wide variety of petty, violent, and economic crimes, using extrajudicial repression to control the most "threatening" of these behaviors, including armed robbery, the theft of public property, and the buying and reselling of scarce consumer goods for profit (termed "speculation" in the Soviet legal system). In the process of carrying out these campaigns in 1932 and 1933, the police often reverted to the same kind of lawless repressions that had characterized the collectivization drive, but they also began to rely on more regularized systems of coercion and control, including urban registration systems and, after 1932, the notorious Soviet internal passport system. This passport system, usually discussed in terms of controlling peasant migration away from collective farms, in fact emerged directly from attempts by the Soviet police to control crime and disorder in major cities after 1930. By mid-decade, it functioned as the basis of nearly all police operations in urban areas; the police conceptualized social disorder as the product of a discrete, identifiable category of "criminal elements," and they attempted to control this "criminal" cohort through increasingly restrictive systems of exclusion, social quarantine, and the "affixation" of suspect population cohorts into acceptable geographic, as well as social, locations in the Soviet polity.

Chapter 4 examines the mounting importance of questions of public order in the mid-1930s, focusing on major police campaigns against speculation, hooliganism, and juvenile delinquency. Far from being a respite between the upheavals of collectivization and the Stalinist terror of 1937–38, the mid-1930s saw several massive campaigns against low-level crime and marginalized urban populations.[34] Campaigns against hooliganism, the theft of public property, and speculation in consumer goods—the last intended to support a "normalization" of Soviet trade and the abolition of rationing in 1935—produced hundreds of thousands of arrests and expulsions of individuals from major Soviet cities, often carried out using the passport system, which by mid-decade functioned as a method for meting out extrajudicial sanctions as well as a way to control population migration. In 1935 and 1936, the regime launched a profoundly repressive campaign against urban juvenile delinquency and homelessness, problems whose scope reached grave proportions in the wake of the dislocations of the First Five-Year Plan. Top police officials understood youth criminality, much like social disorder in general, as a product of an identifiable number of incorrigible youth offenders, and they responded with mass campaigns intended not only to sweep homeless children off the streets but also to excise permanently all "socially harmful" juveniles from Soviet society.

Chapter 5 completes my analysis of the Stalinist policing system, arguing that the understandings of crime held by the police at all levels led to a radicalization of policing practice at mid-decade that prefigured the mass repressions of 1937 and 1938. By mid-decade, most of the ideas promulgated by the OGPU leadership regarding preventive policing had been completely abandoned in favor of less "modern" approaches, largely based on social quarantine and the mass purging of urban areas. The chapter concentrates on speculation and the crime of being a "socially harmful [*vrednyi*] element," both of which threatened the basic functioning of the Soviet system in the minds of top Communist Party and police officials. The expansion of the category of "harmful elements" was the pivotal development in the evolution of Soviet policing in the mid-1930s; although the police had long been accustomed to thinking in terms of policing populations instead of behaviors, it was in the mid-1930s that the category of "harmful elements" solidified into a sociological category, complete with an abbreviation (*sotsvredniki*) and, crucial in Soviet bureaucratic practice, an acronym (SVE).[35] Campaigns against "harmful elements" became the most important part of the Soviet policing system by mid-decade, expanding to include ever-larger categories of criminals: repeat speculators, passport violators, hooligans, and recidivist homeless individuals, both juvenile and adult. In 1935 and 1936, the police removed between 600,000 and 800,000 of these "socially harmful elements" from the USSR's major urban areas, condemning about 250,000 of them using extrajudicial procedures to lengthy terms in labor camps. These huge sweeps of "harmful elements," which virtually defined Stalinist policing in 1935 and 1936, formed the practical background for the far more deadly mass operations that Stalin would initiate in 1937.

Chapter 6 traces the connections between policing strategies in the 1930s and the Stalinist terror of 1937 and 1938, focusing on the genesis and implementation of the "mass operations." Although Stalin's decision to launch "mass operations of repression of kulaks, criminals, and other anti-Soviet elements" in the summer of 1937 was driven primarily by national security concerns, the implementation of these campaigns at the periphery was defined by existing policing practices and relied on a substantial amount of local autonomy. The operations were carried out by both the civil and political police—although civil police officers almost never had any role in the execution of victims—and the tactics and targets of these operations were heavily influenced by previous experiences with mass operations in the mid-1930s. The chapter pays particular attention to the interactions between the operations against "kulaks, criminals, and other anti-Soviet elements," which were fully consistent with Soviet policing practices during the 1930s, and those against "national elements," which were sui generis and required a substantial amount of experimentation on the part of local officials. The interaction between these two sets of mass operations allowed Stalinist repression to expand to the extent that it did in 1937 and 1938. By the time Stalin halted the mass operations in November 1938, the local police had seemingly accomplished the task toward which the entire Soviet police system had been building in the preceding years: the complete removal of all supposedly threatening, "socially harmful," or otherwise marginalized population cohorts from the body politic of the USSR.

Yet this victory over "anti-Soviet elements" was surely chimerical, as trends in the postterror period would show. Chapter 7 considers the evolution of Soviet policing between the end of the mass operations and the beginning of World War II, arguing that nearly all the trends that drove Soviet policing toward mass repression in the mid-1930s continued apace in the post-1938 period. Although the end of the mass operations in November 1938 was accompanied by a brief and halfhearted attempt by the center to halt all "mass arrests" and to eliminate extrajudicial repression entirely, the proclivity of the urban police to control social disorder by identifying, marking, and expelling "threatening" cohorts reemerged in the major campaigns of 1939 and 1940 against speculation, juvenile delinquency, and hooliganism. At the same time, the regime's policies regarding ex-convicts, dekulakized peasants, passport violators, and repeat offenders hardened substantially after 1938, signaling the end of earlier attempts by top justice officials to moderate the effects of Stalinist police violence on the populations that it displaced. The Stalinist regime, by the end of the 1930s, tended to attempt to solve public order problems of its own making by excessive use of the same tactics that had engendered those problems in the first place. This and the other defining aspects of the Stalinist police system were firmly in place by the beginning of World War II, and they would persist until well after Stalin's death in 1953.

1

Prerevolutionary Policing, Revolutionary Events, and the New Economic Policy

During the *transition* from capitalism to Communism, suppression is *still* necessary; but it is the suppression of the minority of exploiters by the majority of exploited. A special apparatus, special machinery for suppression, the "state," is *still* necessary, but this is now a transitional state, no longer a state in the usual sense. . . . *The people* can suppress the exploiters even with very simple "machinery," almost without any "machinery," without any special apparatus, by the simple *organization of the armed masses.*
　　—Lenin, *State and Revolution,* written in mid-1917[1]

It is completely obvious that speculators make use of and will continue to make use of the decline in production of textiles for their own speculative ends, both to stock up on reserves and to resell for tremendous profit. We should work up and implement a series of concrete measures, both of an economic character and using administrative pressure (including the OGPU). . . . I think we should send a couple thousand speculators to [the OGPU labor camps at] Turukhansk and Solovki.
　　—Feliks Dzerzhinsky, 1926[2]

Lenin, writing *State and Revolution* in the tumultuous year 1917, had reason to be optimistic about his chances of participating in the revolutionary uprising to which he had devoted his entire adult life. The Tsarist regime had collapsed only months before, and the teetering Provisional Government showed no signs of being any more capable than Nicholas II of dealing with the social dislocation and economic collapse caused by the Great War. Lenin's slim volume is best known for defending Marx and Engels's idea of the eventual "withering away" of the state, but it also outlined Lenin's understanding of state power during the "transitional" period from capitalism to communism, which he believed was imminent. Emphasizing time and time again that he and his Bolshevik compatriots held liberal

18

ideas of individual rights in utter disdain, Lenin stressed that the state, understood as a "special repressive force" for the oppression of one class by another, would remain necessary during a proletarian revolution as long as remnants of the bourgeoisie continued to exist, and that this simplified proletarian state would function primarily to repress the former oppressive classes.

Despite Lenin's certainty regarding the need for this transitional state, which he termed the "dictatorship of the proletariat," neither *State and Revolution* nor any other of Lenin's prerevolutionary writings contains a concrete discussion of the nature of this governmental apparatus, save certain polemical demands for the abolition of "the police, the army, the bureaucracy."[3] The Bolsheviks, when they came to power suddenly in late October 1917, possessed little notion of the kind of police, military, and judicial systems that would be necessary to administer their new "socialist" society. They believed, however, that such structures would be quite different from the Tsarist and "bourgeois" systems that preceded them, and they assumed that the creation of these systems would involve force, conflict, and overt violence.

The leaders of the fledgling regime disagreed on the contours of the "dictatorship of the proletariat" after October 1917, but none of them balked at the idea that they needed a strong state apparatus (including "the police, the army, [and] the bureaucracy") to survive. Many Communist Party officials retained at least some of the utopianism of Lenin's earlier writings regarding the self-administration of the proletariat, but Lenin's vision of the armed masses protecting themselves vanished in the face of the regime's drive to seize and hold power. The new Bolshevik government moved immediately to create its own systems of political and civil police. Yet no dominant vision of Soviet policing emerged in the first years after the 1917 Revolution, leaving top officials within the party, justice, and police systems to fight pitched ideological and political battles regarding the nature of the Bolsheviks' "special repressive force" in the era of revolution and civil war.

The Bolshevik ideology was not the only influence on early Soviet policing. Much of the institutional culture of the Tsarist civil policing system survived across the revolutionary divide, ensuring that the early Soviet police functioned as a nineteenth-century system of central administration rather than as a modern system of law enforcement.[4] The Russian Civil War of 1918–21 provided another vision of Soviet policing, enhancing centralization and militarization in the ranks of the police and allowing the political police, the notorious Cheka, to expand into the realm of civil policing. Pan-European approaches to policing played a role as well, as officers appropriated criminological theories that, even though they were products of "bourgeois" states, proved appealing to self-consciously modernizing police officials in the 1920s. The early Soviet policing system that emerged from this jumble of policy initiatives and historical forces was wracked by institutional and ideological conflict. At the same time, it contained the outlines of a Soviet statecraft dedicated to the same Marxist project of total social transformation that animated the Bolsheviks' drive to power.

The Tsarist Inheritance

The creation of a centralized civil police system in the Russian Empire occurred relatively late in the modern era. Initial efforts by Peter the Great and Catherine the Great notwithstanding, public order for most of the Imperial period was essentially a local matter, especially in rural areas, where peasant institutions and noble prerogatives provided the sole systems of social control well into the nineteenth century.[5] Tsar Nicholas I (1825–55) instituted the first coherent set of reforms aimed at creating a centralized police system, creating the office of rural constable (*stanovoi pristav*) and disbanding ad hoc night watches and municipal guards in urban areas in favor of full-time policemen who answered to a Ministry of Internal Affairs. His successor, Alexander II (1855–81), continued this process during the Great Reforms of the 1860s, removing district police chiefs in rural areas from the purview of noble assemblies and creating a network of sergeants (*uriadniki*) at the local level who were answerable to the police hierarchy rather than to local officials.[6]

Despite these reforms, the Tsarist police continued to rely on nonstate actors to maintain order in both the city and the countryside well into the twentieth century. In rural areas, so-called tenners and hundreders, elected by the corresponding number of peasant households, were responsible for most questions of public order. In cities, apartment-building concierges (*dvorniki*) and night watchmen (*nochnye storozha*) assisted municipal police with the collection of evidence and, under certain circumstances, the physical apprehension of individuals. Although Nicholas II (1894–1917) abolished the tenners, who numbered 67,000 in 1903, and replaced them with 40,000 appointed guards, such reforms could not compensate for the severe shortages of police officers that plagued late Tsarist policing.[7] At the beginning of the twentieth century, the Department of Police boasted a total complement of 47,866 officers (including political police, patrols on rivers, and office personnel), mostly concentrated in urban areas, which administered a population of roughly 127 million. Tsarist police officials met their own goals of fielding one patrolman for every 500 urban inhabitants in the years before the Revolution of 1905, but individual rural constables were often responsible for upward of 1,800 square miles of territory and between 50,000 and 100,000 inhabitants.[8] The local police also performed an immense array of administrative duties, including tax collection, enforcing local and municipal regulations, controlling beggary and homeless children, and overseeing the local activities of almost all the other central Tsarist ministries.[9] Even in urban areas and major provincial towns, the police devoted relatively little time to protecting public order and preventing crime before the end of the Tsarist era.

Even at the turn of the twentieth century, the Tsarist police system conformed to the essentially eighteenth-century European ideal of the police as an extension of the central system of administration rather than as officers engaging in the kind of population surveillance and control that became hallmarks of European policing systems in the second half of the nineteenth century.[10] Nearly all European policing systems, created by states as explicit responses to the social dislocation caused by industrialization and urbanization, sought to bolster their effectiveness in the late nineteenth century by promoting social integration and cohesion among mobile or marginalized populations. In most cases, European police officers became nascent sociologists as well, searching for scientific explanations of the causes of crime and attempting to implement crime control schemes based on this criminological knowledge.[11] The Russian police notably failed to participate in any of these developments. The reactive nature of Tsarist policing was obvious enough in the countryside, but even in the major cities police presence was usually limited to stationary posts located within sight of each other. Only in 1908 did the Ministry of Internal Affairs create the first detective departments at the city and county levels to extend the investigation and prevention of crime beyond the largest cities of the empire.[12] The basic model of civil policing changed very little from the eighteenth century to the end of the Tsarist era; stationary officers reacted to public violence only after the fact and spent little time with preventive measures of any kind.[13]

Tsarist political policing likewise changed surprisingly little in the last decades of the Tsarist Empire, despite the social upheavals caused by the Revolution of 1905. By the turn of the twentieth century, the Department of Police boasted extensive systems of covert surveillance, registration of suspect individuals, and internal exile of political offenders. Yet in the final years of the autocracy, both the covert security divisions and the uniformed gendarmes focused almost exclusively on the repression of political activism, especially the terrorist activities of populists and other radicals dedicated to overthrowing the Tsarist system. Even during the 1905 Revolution, the political police focused its energy on educated elites, who they incorrectly believed were responsible for fomenting discontent among the masses. The suppression of widespread discontent among the urban working classes and of the peasant jacquerie that engulfed the countryside in 1905 was, in the minds of police officials, a military matter, as were the "punitive expeditions" sent to the periphery of the empire to repress, ex post facto, those peasant populations that had been particularly unruly during the 1905 uprisings. These punitive expeditions, which were nothing less than military retaliation against subjects of the empire, blurred the lines between state violence in colonial, military, and civilian contexts and hence represented an innovation in Tsarist statecraft. Yet Tsarist political policing changed little in the years after 1905; modern approaches to surveillance, the molding of public opinion, and the direct shaping of mass society itself were largely foreign to the insular, conservative culture of the Department of Police.[14]

World War I, to the contrary, began a process of rapid expansion of both political and civil policing that would continue through the Bolshevik Revolution and into the Russian Civil War. The political police engaged in a broad array of activities in support of the war effort, concentrating not only on the repression of radical opposition movements but also on regulating the wartime economic system, controlling profiteering, and promoting the right-wing mass political movements that supported the war.[15] The police were also involved in large-scale deportations and internments of ethnic minorities that the Tsarist military deemed a threat to national security, especially German and Jewish subjects of the empire. In areas subject to martial law, including major cities like Moscow and Petrograd (as Petersburg was renamed once the war began), the Army coordinated these deportations, while the Department of Police controlled the "cleansing" of sensitive areas under civilian rule, including zones around important railways, defense-related factories, and waterways. The Tsarist army extended these practices to include individuals under active police surveillance for general criminal or political activity as well, further blurring the lines between military operations and basic policing activity. These operations, which were often termed "mass operations" or the "full cleansing" of suspect individuals, resulted in the internment or deportation of some 300,000 "enemy" Russian subjects during the war.[16] These repressions were part of a broader worldwide change in the conduct of war during the early twentieth century, which saw governments applying increasing levels of coercion to civilian populations in the course of what were seen as conflicts between citizenries. But they also served as the germ of a particularly Russian, and eventually Soviet, statecraft that aimed at radical social and demographic transformation, carried out by both the military and the police.[17]

These trends in Tsarist statecraft notwithstanding, the Tsarist political police focused throughout the war on the putative danger posed to the autocracy by political elites within the socialist and liberal political movements, a fact that played no small part in its inability to prevent the collapse of the regime. Although a handful of prescient police officials correctly identified the threat to the Tsarist system posed by mass politics during the war, none of them could conceptualize a policing approach that would combat, co-opt, or even diffuse the kind of mass protest that led to overt rebellion in early 1917.[18] The Tsarist political police remained a conservative organization to the end of their existence.

Revolution and Civil War

The collapse of the Tsarist regime in February 1917 shattered policing structures across the former Russian Empire. The new Provisional Government, which emerged from the liberal opposition to the autocracy, disbanded the Imperial police, both civil and political, in March 1917. Most political and many civil policemen had fled their posts by that time, attempting to blend into the revolutionary events and to evade marauding crowds. The Provisional Government declined to create a political police force of any kind, turning over the task of state security to the army. The government transferred the uniformed gendarmes to the military authorities for enlistment, and it encouraged covert policemen, most of whom were arrested during the February events, to follow them.[19]

The same cultures of antiauthoritarianism and local autonomy that contributed to the collapse of the autocracy shaped civil policing institutions in the tumultuous months after February 1917. The Provisional Government created a system of municipal police forces that were staffed by local residents, soldiers, and students who were loyal to the new regime, but these officers, nominally subordinate to provincial and district state administrations, insisted that they elect their own commanders and remain autonomous from higher authorities.[20] Workers' militias, which had appeared in urban areas even before the abdication of the tsar, stepped into the vacuum of power on the streets of major cities as well.[21] These militias were particularly important in Petrograd, where they enjoyed the vigorous support of the Petrograd Soviet, a spontaneous organization of radical socialists that challenged the authority of the Provisional Government. Yet, like the municipal police, the workers' militias resisted central interference in their affairs, even from the Petrograd Soviet. Relations between the municipal police and the workers' militias depended on local conditions. In some districts in Petrograd, for example, the militias disarmed not only the remnants of the Tsarist police but also the municipal officers; in others, the municipal police absorbed the workers' militias but remained loyal to the Provisional Government.[22]

This ad hoc system of policing and social control utterly failed to cope with the increasing levels of social disorder and revolutionary upheaval apparent in the summer and fall of 1917. The uneasy coexistence of the municipal police and workers' militias began to collapse after the unsuccessful revolt known as the July Days, in which impatient working masses and Marxist radicals attempted to rise up against the faltering Provisional Government. True to its origin, the Petrograd municipal police stood on the sidelines during the July Days, exercising authority only in explicitly nonpolitical cases such as public drunkenness and theft. The Provisional Government responded to this alarming passivity by attempting to abolish the election of officers and to subject local policemen to direct ministerial control, but the police and urban residents alike rejected both attempts at centralization. From this point forward, the workers' militias gained in popular legitimacy what the municipal police lost. The Provisional Government, in the fall of 1917 concerned primarily with suppressing radical activity in the capital, relied on the military for protection from political unrest and for basic policing duties on the streets, further weakening its tenuous hold on local police administrations.[23] When mass unrest gave way to insurrection in October 1917, those few municipal police officers loyal to the existing government could do little but stand aside.

The Bolshevik Revolution of October 1917, for all its importance as a pivotal moment in Russian history, initially did little to change the nature of civil policing in the lands of the former Tsarist Empire. After taking power, the Bolsheviks announced that all municipal police administrations would be replaced by volunteer militias, staffed by the existing workers' militias and augmented by members of the Red Guards, the spontaneous armed detachments that had played a major role in the October uprising. District-level soviets (councils), which took over the role of local administration from the municipal authorities of the Provisional Government, appointed commissars to coordinate these local militias, providing some amount of central coordination while bowing to demands for decentralization and local control from both police and population.[24] Yet the municipal police administrations were surprisingly resilient. In some locations, including Petrograd, they were unresponsive to the new regime and were abolished, sometimes forcibly, only after a period of several weeks. In others, like Moscow, the local soviets unified existing workers' militias and municipal police administrations into a single professional force rather than entirely abolishing either organization. Continuity in Moscow was substantial; the Detective Department, for example, remained completely unchanged during October 1917 in both structure and staff.[25] The Bolshevik regime, faced with its own institutional weakness, tolerated the continued existence of municipal police administrations in many areas for weeks or even months.[26]

This revolutionary model of decentralized local policing, so popular among urban residents and police alike, contradicted the drive of the Bolshevik regime to create a strong centralized state; hence, it did not last more than a few months. Immediately after seizing power, the Bolsheviks created a Commissariat of Internal Affairs of the Russian Soviet Federated Socialist Republic on October 28 (on the Julian calendar; November 10 on the Gregorian calendar), 1917, as one of thirteen commissariats—essentially ministries—in the new government. Although the internal affairs commissariats of the individual Soviet republics were guaranteed the right to conduct their own policing affairs, the Russian NKVD in most instances set policy for all areas under Bolshevik control.[27] Grigorii Petrovskii, named commissar of internal affairs in November 1917, quickly pressed Lenin's government to transform the volunteer police forces into a full-time, professional organization responsible directly to the center. In May 1918 Lenin, always a practical statesman, reversed his earlier stance regarding the self-administration of the armed masses and issued directives making the civil police into a full-time, paid institution.[28] The Bolsheviks restructured the detective system along the same lines, creating a centralized

Detective Department in Moscow in 1918 to coordinate complex police activities, such as the registration of criminals and covert investigative operations, across jurisdictional boundaries.[29] These changes settled the issue of volunteerism in Soviet policing. The police made liberal use throughout the Soviet period of volunteer detachments to aid in specific tasks, but the "Worker-Peasant Militsiia" itself was thereafter a professional police organization.[30]

Despite these changes, the early Soviet *militsiia* in many ways duplicated the structure and functions of the Tsarist police system. Although all police administrations nominally reported to the internal affairs commissariats of their respective republics, the police at the provincial and lower levels also reported to corresponding soviets, making them local administrators as much as professional policemen. The *militsiia*, like the Tsarist police before it, enforced central economic regulations, especially tax collection, assisted judicial officials in carrying out preliminary criminal investigations, transported prisoners to and from court appearances, and carried out sentences of banishment or compulsory labor (a reduction of pay at one's current place of employment for a set period of time).[31] The police in the countryside were often the only continuous representative of Soviet power in a given area; during the early years of Bolshevik rule, individual officers were responsible for setting up local soviets in the most remote areas as well.[32] Notwithstanding the genuinely populist strains in revolutionary-era Russian policing, the Bolshevik civil police system quickly reverted after October 1917 to a model of administration little removed from the era of autocracy.

The Russian Civil War of 1918-21, unlike the October Revolution, transformed virtually every aspect of Soviet policing, both civil and political.[33] At the top, Feliks Dzerzhinsky replaced Petrovskii as the Russian commissar of internal affairs in March 1919.[34] Dzerzhinsky also headed the Bolshevik political police—the Extraordinary Commission to Combat Counterrevolution, Speculation, and Sabotage, known by its Russian abbreviation as the Cheka—which was created in December 1917 to repress political opposition to the new regime. The Cheka, unlike the Tsarist Department of Police that it replaced, did not focus on political opposition alone. It functioned as an internal security service, responding with military force to mass uprisings against the Bolsheviks and meting out summary repressions against the regime's real and potential enemies.

Reprisals against suspect groups and individuals, carried out without regard to judicial or procedural norms, became Bolshevik policy after

September 1918, when the Cheka launched the "Red Terror" as a response to assassination attempts on the head of the Petrograd Cheka and on Lenin himself. The Cheka targeted not only those individuals who opposed the regime but also entire categories of the population deemed "counterrevolutionary" by nature, including Tsarist officials, members of the bourgeoisie, non-Bolshevik socialists, and Tsarist officers—repressions undertaken, in the words of one provincial Cheka newspaper, "as a measure of hygiene" to guarantee "the complete liquidation of all counterrevolutionary insurrections."[35] Such techniques became a central part of Bolshevik security operations during the Civil War, carried out by both the Cheka and military authorities to repress anti-Bolshevik uprisings and to cleanse society of "elements" deemed malignant or harmful to the body politic. In both spirit and implementation, they were a continuation of Tsarist campaigns of social cleansing carried out during World War I, intended as much to construct an ideal socialist society as to repress populations that posed a direct military threat.[36]

These constructivist notions were more prevalent during the Civil War in the Red Army than in the Cheka, in large part because continuities of personnel across the October divide, though strong in the military, were entirely absent in the Cheka.[37] For Chekists, the essence of the Red Terror was untrammeled class warfare tinged with a desire for revenge, an approach that corresponded to a political police filled with, in the words of one highly placed Bolshevik commentator, "criminals, sadists, and degenerate elements from the lumpenproletariat."[38] General surveillance of the population, a crucial aspect of any modern political policing system, emerged within the Cheka only well into the Civil War; until late 1920, information gathering and reporting on the "mood" of the population remained the task of intelligence agencies in the Red Army.[39] Dzerzhinsky's Chekists were primarily concerned with internal security rather than with the kind of constructivist statecraft carried out by Tsarist and Bolshevik military authorities between 1914 and 1921.[40]

Early Bolshevik civil policing was pervaded as well with notions of social transformation through "cleansings" of individuals deemed inherently "dangerous" (*opasnyi*) by nature. Although Russian criminologists both before and after 1917 rejected the biological determinism on which most Western understandings of inherent criminality were based, the concept of the social danger of a given individual was widespread among early Bolshevik legal theorists, criminologists, and top police officials.[41] For legal theorists, the idea of social danger was often part of a vision of a socialist judicial system free of legal codes and other "bourgeois" formalities, based instead solely on the nature of the criminal act and the class position of the perpetrator.[42] For the police, on the contrary, "dangerousness" was closely connected to the more prosaic question of recidivism among urban criminals. The police viewed repeat offenders and individuals without "defined places of residence" as the key cause of several categories of urban crime and hence as inherently dangerous to the socialist society that they were attempting to create.[43]

The local police during the Civil War often relied on the idea of social danger when engaged in mass campaigns against petty urban crimes, especially property crimes, categorizing repeat offenders as "dangerous elements" and subjecting them to judicial or, more often, extrajudicial punishment, even in the absence of a new offense. This practice was particularly widespread within detective departments, which were often staffed with Chekists. The Detective Department in Moscow, for example, organized a "Week of Thief Catching" in February 1921, during which the police arrested any individuals with past sentences for property crimes and sent their cases to special chambers of the Peoples' Courts, created specifically for the campaign, for sentencing based not on any new crimes committed but on their level of social danger.[44] The police also viewed the criminal populations released from Tsarist prisons as a key group of inherently dangerous criminals, suggesting that they made up a substantial portion of the professional criminal underworld.[45] The practice of labeling repeat offenders as "socially dangerous" and sanctioning them through the extrajudicial channels of the Cheka was widespread during the war; local *militsiia* administrations participated as well, helping to make the idea of social danger a central part of the justification for the widespread use of extrajudicial repression in the early Bolshevik policing system.

Dzerzhinsky's appointment as commissar of internal affairs in 1919 underscored the intention of the fledgling Bolshevik regime to expand the untrammeled state violence characteristic of the Cheka to the civil police system.[46] Borders between the work of the Cheka and that of the *militsiia* were porous during the Civil War; local *militsiia* administrations worked particularly closely with the Cheka to control speculation in scarce consumer goods, an area of policing in which mass arrests of people at open air markets, mass searches of apartment blocks, and summary repressions were the norm.[47] Although civil police officers were never authorized to carry out executions, the realities of local police work made this restriction moot. In Moscow, for example, the Detective Department sentenced individuals deemed "socially dangerous" to confinement in concentration camps without the approval of the Cheka, but detectives routinely transferred more serious cases to the city Cheka for adjudication and punishment, including execution.[48] The term "socially dangerous" continued to be used in a broader sense during the Civil War and the early years of the New Economic Policy (NEP); those deemed "socially dangerous" due to past criminal activity were a subset of the larger group of "socially dangerous" individuals that included political offenders, bandits, and other serious criminals. Nevertheless, the connection made during the Civil War between "social danger" and criminal recidivism resonated most with the activities of the local police and became the most durable of these concepts in the years that followed.

The convergence of civil and political police activity during the Civil War prompted Dzerzhinsky to attempt to unify the two branches of Bolshevik policing in name as well as in practice. Under Dzerzhinsky's tutelage, the Russian Internal Affairs Commissariat (NKVD) centralized control over local police administrations, while the Cheka gained an increasing amount of formal power over local *militsiia* officers. In April 1919, the entire *militsiia* was placed on the central government payroll, removing all funding and staffing questions from the purview of local soviets.[49] NKVD officials moved by 1920 to centralize several of the ad hoc policing systems that had emerged at the local level in the months after the October Revolution, including numerous "Industrial Militsiia" administrations that had sprung up to control theft and embezzlement in factories and retail organizations, and several separate systems of local railroad and water transport police.[50]

These changes were part of the increasing centralization of power associated with the policy of "War Communism," which substituted state control for the spontaneous forms of self-administration that had sprung after 1917, but they also supported Dzerzhinsky's explicit attempts to subordinate all *militsiia* activities to the Cheka. Dzerzhinsky flooded the Detective Department with Chekists between 1918 and 1920 to gain control of the organization and reduce its subordination to local police and soviet administrations.[51] He also expanded direct Cheka control over local *militsiia* administrations, creating political bureaus in county-level *militsiia* administrations in early 1920 and naming Chekists to staff them.[52]

This trend toward centralization during the Civil War peaked in regions of the country that saw active military conflict. The regime transferred direct control of all *militsiia* activity in these areas to the Red Army; it did the same in particularly important regions not directly affected by military operations, including Moscow, where *militsiia* officers were placed under military conscription regulations in February 1921.[53] By the end of the Civil War, any control that the local soviets enjoyed over the police was effectively broken, and in many remote areas the hierarchy functioned in reverse: local NKVD chiefs, usually Chekists, headed the administrative departments of the local soviets and ran the daily activities of the soviet in conjunction with the local Communist Party cell. Although the Tsarist political police had relied on the civil police for help with the surveillance of radical political groups, this level of coordination was new to Russian policing.[54] Dzerzhinsky's drive to create a "Chekist" civil policing system, although it would not survive the end of the Civil War, provided a conceptual model that, like War Communism itself, was available to proponents of radical visions of Bolshevik policing in the late 1920s, when Stalin began his climb to power.

Bolshevik Policing and the Transition to the New Economic Policy

By late 1920 the Red Army had defeated the last organized White forces, the loosely structured conglomeration of anti-Bolshevik armies that operated on the periphery of the new empire. Yet the conditions of civil war were far from over. Entire provinces remained under the control of anarchist armies or peasant rebellions, while popular rebellion in major cities threatened to undo the military gains made by the Red Army over the previous two years. The Red Army and the Cheka responded to these manifestations of popular discontent with massive force in early 1921, repressing uprisings among workers, soldiers, and peasants with the same brutality previously directed at the Whites.[55] Lenin, sensing that repression alone would not stabilize the situation, announced at the Tenth Communist Party Congress in March 1921 that the forced requisitioning of grain would be replaced by a "New Economic Policy" of limited market exchange and taxes in kind. Lenin's policy, which was unpopular with the more radical Bolsheviks in his ruling circle, was intended to reduce social tensions in the countryside and encourage peasants to deliver grain to the state; he viewed it as a temporary, but necessary, concession to the peasantry along the road to socialism.

The transition to the NEP posed grave problems for the Bolshevik policing system. Although the first months of the NEP were accompanied by continued repressions of political activists, discontented workers, and peasant rebels, Lenin and his moderate compatriots believed that a system of limited market exchange would ultimately require legal and administrative systems that restricted the exercise of arbitrary power by the Cheka. Once the wave of uprisings that prompted Lenin to institute the NEP had been repressed, the nature of Bolshevik policing under the new system could not be ignored. This question produced conflict throughout both the police and Communist Party apparatus, creating a tension between proponents of and opponents of moderation, the latter including most top officers of the Cheka, which destabilized Soviet policing through the end of the 1920s.

Lenin's announcement at the Tenth Communist Party Congress that a limited market economy would replace the grain requisitioning of War Communism was a major shift in Bolshevik economic policy, but the extent to which it was a shift in political and especially coercive policy has often been exaggerated by commentators searching for a humane variant of Soviet socialism.[56] Lenin's decision, which was prompted by the regime's inability to control simultaneous rebellions in the countryside and among workers and soldiers, who had been the most vocal supporters of the Revolution only months before, was accompanied by a tightening of the mechanisms of control at all levels of society and by expanded repressions against real or perceived internal enemies.[57] The Cheka, under orders from the Politburo, began systematic campaigns in 1921 against the Russian Orthodox Church, workers' strikes in Moscow and Petersburg, and the remnants of the Menshevik and Socialist Revolutionary parties. Military repressions of peasant rebels stretched into mid-1922, resulting in tens of thousands of internments and executions carried out by the most brutal methods—hostage taking, punitive executions of the eldest sons in rebel families, and the use of poison gas against "bandit" gangs in hiding.[58] That such actions continued into late 1922, a full eighteen months after the implementation of the NEP, shows that Lenin initially saw no contradiction between a limited market and the kind of unchecked administrative repression exercised by the Cheka.

Yet opposition to the continued use of administrative repression by the Cheka crystallized within the top echelons of Lenin's government in early 1922, especially among proponents of the Bolshevik judicial system. The repressions carried out by the early Soviet courts were often no less "extraordinary" than those meted out by the Cheka, but many Bolshevik legal theorists were concerned that the lack of defined legal procedures that characterized police work during the Civil War hampered the creation of a stable relationship between citizens and the state, and they began to press for some amount of rationalization and codification in the application of "revolutionary justice" as well as a substantial reduction in the extrajudicial powers of the police.[59]

Nikolai Krylenko, the chairman of the extraordinary court system known as the Revolutionary Tribunal and, after 1922, assistant commissar of justice for the Russian Republic, argued alongside Lev Kamenev, one of the leaders of the October Revolution, that the untrammeled use of repression by the Cheka was antithetical to the administrative and legal foundations of the NEP. Kamenev's position was clear: he had called for the complete liquidation of the Cheka in favor of revolutionary tribunals as early as January 1918, and he criticized the Cheka aggressively in January 1922, pressing for fundamental reform.[60] No major Communist Party or justice figures argued for an elimination of political violence, but Krylenko, Kamenev, and Dmitry Kursky, the Russian commissar of justice, attempted to convince the party leadership that the regime's interests would be best served if state terror were made part of a codified system of Bolshevik criminal law instead of remaining the prerogative of individual Cheka officers.[61]

The initial conflict was won by the opponents of the Cheka. In early February 1922, the Politburo restructured the political police, abolishing the Cheka and transferring control over political policing to a system of central political administrations (GPU) that were nominally subordinate, within each Soviet republic, to internal affairs commissariats. At the same time, the Politburo abolished the extrajudicial sentencing powers of the political police, forcing them to turn over all individuals to the court system for sentencing and making the GPU responsible for the policing of political subversion alone.[62] A good part of this change was fraudulent from the outset. The subordination of the GPU to republican internal affairs commissariats was a sham, intended only to conform to the constitutional requirement that all state institutions be subordinate to the Council of People's Commissars. In reality, the new GPU reported directly to the Politburo, and the Russian GPU continued to control the political police in the other national republics. Dzerzhinsky, furthermore, continued to head both the Russian GPU and the Russian NKVD. Yet the abolition of the extrajudicial sentencing capacity of the Cheka was a real, if short-lived, reform of the Soviet police system, which was reinforced by the promulgation of a unified Criminal Code in 1922 that, despite its reliance on nebulous legal concepts like punishment by analogy and class favoritism, was designed to bring some order into the chaotic system of Bolshevik criminal justice.

Representatives of the political police moved quickly to challenge these reforms, and within weeks the Politburo began to reauthorize the Cheka to use extrajudicial repression to control specific, pressing problems of public order. On March 9, 1922, the day after Dzerzhinsky's return from a two-month expedition to force grain procurements in Siberia, the Politburo authorized GPU officers to execute or exile individuals in areas of military conflict; to execute on the spot all armed robbers, bandits, and recidivist criminals carrying weapons in any region of the country; and to exile or send to concentration camps all anarchists, Left Socialist Revolutionaries, and "recidivist criminals."[63] In late April 1922, the Politburo authorized the GPU to send cases of counterrevolutionary activity not to the courts but to a Special Commission created within the NKVD system, which could issue sentences of internal exile of up to three years, or to the Presidium of the Central Executive Committee for harsher sentences.[64] These decisions made the extrajudicial repression of both political and civil crime a standard, if relatively limited, part of policing practices in the NEP era, despite the reformist impulses within the Politburo in early 1922.

Dzerzhinsky's hand was strengthened in his drive to regain extrajudicial prerogatives for the political police by the fact that local GPU officers often ignored the restrictions put in place in early 1922, meting out sentences on their own authority in the absence of any legal right to do so.[65] Still, such arbitrary police actions were often protested to state authorities in this period, usually by representatives of justice organizations; Dzerzhinsky's political police no longer enjoyed the absolute freedom of action that had defined Cheka activity during the Civil War.

The GPU also contended with a new institutional opponent in the first years of the NEP: the Commissariat of Internal Affairs of the Russian Soviet Federated Socialist Republic (NKVD RSFSR), which formally controlled all *militsiia* activities within the Russian Republic and in practice set policy for the rest of the country. In November 1923, in conjunction with the creation of the USSR, the Politburo separated the political and civil police systems, creating a Unionwide Unified State Political Administration (OGPU) but retaining republic-level internal affairs commissariats. The OGPU retained the functions and structure of the GPU but, as a

Unionwide body, it was completely separate from internal affairs commissariats, which continued to control all matters related to civil policing. The transfer of all funding for *militsiia* activities to local soviet budgets in October 1922 accentuated the division between political and civil policing, as local soviet officials used the power of the purse to establish control over civil policemen in their jurisdictions.[66] The Politburo appointed Aleksandr Beloborodov, who had served as assistant commissar of internal affairs after 1919, to the position of Russian commissar of internal affairs on Dzerzhinsky's recommendation. Existing scholarship provides little indication of Beloborodov's relationship with Dzerzhinsky and the Cheka before 1923, but his new position quickly brought him into direct conflict with the political police.

The NKVD challenged the leadership of the GPU in the realm of civil policing as early as July 1923, when it eliminated the position of political secretary in local *militsiia* administrations, which had been staffed by Chekists during the Civil War. The two organizations came into conflict in this period over control of the Soviet prison and labor camp system as well.[67] Dzerzhinsky's response was to revert to his earlier campaign to unify all civil and political policing in the USSR. The topic was widely discussed within the Russian Central Executive Committee at the end of 1923, where allies of the OGPU, especially the Worker-Peasant Inspectorate (Rabkrin), argued that most local officials supported the idea of unifying the two police forces and creating a single Commissariat of Public Order. Although this move failed, the Rabkrin continued to press for unification in early 1924, passing a resolution in April calling for the abolishment of the NKVD system and the devolution of its constituent parts to other commissariats, with the *militsiia* transferred to the OGPU.

The question was ultimately settled in mid-1924 by the Politburo, which resolved to remove the question of unification from discussion. The victory of the NKVD came only after vigorous lobbying by Krylenko and Mikhail Kalinin, the head of the Soviet government, both of whom opposed any further expansion of the power of Dzerzhinsky's political police.[68] Although this outcome was a major failure for Dzerzhinsky, the OGPU did not take this rebuff as the end of the conflict, instead beginning a long-term attempt to weaken the NKVD and to take over specific policing duties whenever possible. The Russian NKVD and the OGPU clashed openly from this point forward, struggling throughout the NEP for control over police bureaucracies and, in a broader sense, for the right to define the nature of Soviet policing in the postrevolutionary era.

By late 1923, the Soviet police system had settled into the basic bureaucratic form that it would hold until the end of the NEP era. The NKVD system emerged from the transition to the NEP as a viable institutional and political force within the Soviet Communist Party/state, an outcome that was not at all inevitable given the continued institutional and political power of its main rival, Dzerzhinsky's OGPU. Nevertheless, the structural and institutional contradictions that emerged in the process of creating the NEP-era police system made it unlikely that this more moderate constellation of policing forces would be permanent, and it ensured that the dissolution of the NEP, when it occurred, would entail a fundamental change in Soviet policing as well.

The NEP-Era Police

The relative weakness of the Soviet state during the NEP era was plainly visible in its police system. NEP-era *militsiia* officers were overworked, underpaid, and unresponsive to central authorities, resembling nothing so much as the ineffectual Tsarist police who preceded them. The OGPU was no less shaped by the conditions of the NEP; substantial reductions in funding and staff, along with political pressure from top Communist Party members who were eager to support the NEP experiment, curtailed the political and institutional strength of the OGPU in the mid-1920s and helped to create a short-lived period of institutional plurality within the Soviet criminal justice system.

The extensive decentralization of the Soviet state that accompanied the beginning of the NEP had drastic implications for the police system. The *militsiia* system retained nominal hierarchies of command that stretched from local police administrations to the Russian NKVD in Moscow, but the shift in 1922 of funding from central to local budgets placed the local police at the mercy of local soviets. Even in major cities, *militsiia* administrations cooperated as closely with regional soviets as with the NKVD hierarchy, while at the regional and district levels, police chiefs almost always served as members of soviet executive committees and usually served as the heads of their powerful administrative departments, positions that afforded them the power to control most daily activities of the civil police. As in the Tsarist period, internal affairs officials in regional capitals maintained only sporadic contact with most local administrations, ensuring that local officers would exercise tremendous latitude in making and implementing policy.

The failures of NEP-era policing were most obvious in the country-side. The NKVD set a goal of fielding one officer for every 5,000 rural inhabitants in the mid-1920s, but in reality individual policemen were often responsible for up to 20,000 residents, scattered across hundreds of square miles in villages that could not be accessed for large parts of the year due to spring rain and winter snow.[69] As in the Tsarist period, rural officers carried out a wide array of administrative duties and devoted minimal time to investigating crime. Not surprisingly, peasants turned to traditional means of enforcing local social order in the 1920s, resurrecting the prerevolutionary traditions of night guards and "tenners." Most rural communities preferred to handle their own affairs and wanted nothing from the Bolshevik regime but to be left alone.[70]

Urban policing during the NEP era suffered from many of the same problems. The leadership of the NKVD conceptualized the urban police system as an arena in which the relationship between state and society could be reformed; close cooperation between the police and urban residents, along with the inculcation of a tradition of respectful, professional behavior on the part of the officers themselves, would acculturate urban residents to the norms of the socialist society that they believed was coming into existence. Such ideals were difficult to put into practice. As in the countryside, nearly all the daily activity of the urban police involved administrative work, especially the enforcement of directives issued by local soviets. Police work was essentially reactive, as it had been in the Tsarist period; most officers worked in district substations or stationary posts in important public areas, responding to complaints from the population rather than cultivating covert contacts and carrying out daily patrols.[71] Even detective departments, which were better trained and had more resources at their disposal than the regular *militsiia*, engaged in only a modest amount of infiltration of the criminal underworld in the 1920s. Detectives in major cities claimed success in several high-profile cases involving notorious criminal gangs in the 1920s, and they worked to import modern policing technologies, like fingerprinting, into the USSR. Nonetheless, detectives, like the *militsiia* in general, were fundamentally disengaged from the kind of covert work that was necessary, in the minds of most contemporary criminal investigation specialists both inside and outside the USSR, for the effective policing of urban crime.[72]

Many of these problems were the product of severe shortages of officers during the 1920s. A systemwide purge in 1922 and 1923, along with drastic cuts in funding, resulted in a staff reduction of nearly 60 percent at the end of the Civil War. In the Russian Republic, the total staff of the *militsiia* dropped from more than 100,000 officers in 1923 to less than 45,000 by 1929.[73] Quantity was matched by quality; most rank-and-file officers in the 1920s had no formal training and little long-term policing experience. Most officers with prerevolutionary experience were purged between 1921 and 1923, after which only a statistically negligent number remained, mostly in the elite detective departments.[74] The pay levels for the police, furthermore, were well below the norm for workers throughout the NEP period, making the recruitment of qualified officers exceedingly difficult. Under such dire constraints, it is not surprising that the *militsiia* was viewed by most of the population as corrupt and inefficient.

As the size of the *militsiia* dwindled in the mid-1920s, a system of local industrial (*vedomstvennaia*) police forces emerged to fill the vacuum. In December 1921, for lack of funding, the NKVD abolished the centralized Industrial Police of the Civil War era, which guarded state property in major economic institutions such as factories and department stores. Individual factories and other economic concerns, now forced to find their own security arrangements, quickly began to collaborate with local soviets and *militsiia* administrations, paying local police administrations directly for the services of a set number of full-time officers. Central NKVD officials were not enthusiastic about this genuinely local initiative, because it bypassed central control altogether on questions of staffing levels and payment, but they consented, and in February 1924 they issued guidelines for contractual relations between the police and local economic administrations that required local branches of the Industrial Militsiia to operate under the jurisdiction of the local police administration.[75] In 1924, the first year that the Industrial Militsiia appeared in large numbers, roughly 6,300 officers guarded 520 individual economic concerns. By 1930, the Industrial Militsiia had climbed to roughly 58,000 officers, and by 1931 the police reported roughly 95,000 Industrial Militsiia policemen for the Russian republic, as opposed to 60,000 civil police (see table 1.1). Although the Industrial Militsiia system was popular enough to spawn an Industrial Detective Department organized along the same lines, it only accentuated the decentralized structure of the civil police during the NEP era.

The OGPU, despite its privileged place in the Soviet state, was no less affected by the budgetary constraints of the NEP. The size of the political police declined drastically in the early 1920s, from a height at the end of the Civil War of nearly 105,000 civilian employees, plus an additional 180,000 internal troops under the direct control of the Cheka, to roughly

Table 1.1. Civil Police Officers, Russian Republic and the USSR, 1923–1939

	Russian Republic					USSR	
Year	Regular Militsiia	Detective Department	Industrial Militsiia	Detective Administrative Staff[a]	Total	Regular Militsiia	Industrial Militsiia
1923	92,296[b]	10,500[b]					
1924	67,339[b]						
1925		5,151[b]					
1926	48,853[b]	5,190[c]	18,660[c]	3,871[c]	71,317[c]		
	43,696[c]						
1927	42,313[b]	5,109[c]	22,479[c]	3,679[c]	73,362[c]		
	42,095[c]						
1928	40,134[c]	4,552[c]	32,886[c]	4,481[c]	82,053[c]		
1929	37,800[c]	4,722[b]	37,606[c]	3,766[c]	83,894[c]		
	42,522[d]	4,722[d]	37,606[d]		81,128[d]		
1930	37,673[c]	5,014[c]	58,341[c]	3,640[c]	104,708[c]		
	44,433[d]		56,690[d]		101,132[d]		
1931	47,621[d]		81,961[d]		129,586[d]		
	59,977[e]		95,000[d]				
1932	60,733[f]					94,324[f]	
1933						120,498[g]	
1934							64,595[h]
1935						125,580[i]	28,381[h]
							(39,000[h])
1936							
1937							
1938						159,305[j]	
1939						181,995[k]	

Sources:

These figures come from a wide range of police, Sovnarkom, and Communist Party documents. They should be taken as indicators of trends or estimates of staffing levels rather than precise figures. Where two unrelated documents from different institutions provide information on the same year, I have included figures from both sources. The specific sources are as follows.

[a] The full title of this category is Administrativnoe Upravlenie Ugolovnogo Rozyska, or Administrative Directorate of the Detective Department.

[b] The 1923 (September 1), 1924 (May 1), 1926 (January 1), and 1927 (January 1) figures are given in *Politsiia i Militsiia Rossii: Stranitsy Istorii*, by A. V. Borisov et al. (Moscow: Nauka, 1995), 120. They represent a severe reduction in *militsiia* officers that accompanied the shift to local support in the early 1920s.

[c] From GARF, f. 1235, op. 72, d. 340, l. 81, report submitted to the All-Russian Central Executive Committee on January 3, 1931, by the head of the Central Police Administration (GURKM pri Sovnarkom RSFSR); these figures do not include autonomous republics.

[d] Totals from GARF, f. 1235, op. 141, d. 910, ll. 1–43. The Industrial Militsiia figure for 1931 contains two estimates: a lower one for May 1, 1931, and a higher one for August 1, 1931. Both numbers were given in the same report, suggesting an incredible increase of some 13,000 Industrial Militsiia officers in three months. The total includes the Detective Department.

[e] Figure from November 1931, based on GARF, f. 1235, op. 141, d. 1043, l. 1; includes both the *militsiia* and the Detective Department.

[f] GARF, f. 5446, op. 13a, d. 1320, ll. 6–8.

[g] GARF, f. 5446, op. 14a, d. 762, l. 9, including all militsiia employees for the USSR; figure provided by the USSR Commissariat of Finance. This figure includes 12,500 new police for the passport system and 12,000 new police for convoying prisoners, according to the USSR Finance Commissariat, as of November 11, 1933. This report also notes that, in addition to the above numbers, the *militsiia* still controlled "a significant number" of officers (approximately three to four thousand) that were supported by local budgets. The number of 120,498 officers for the USSR is confirmed by a separate OGPU request for additional staff; see GARF, f. 5446, op. 14a, d. 762, l. 11.

[h] These figures come from a report by Iagoda on the results of the Sovnarkom resolution no. 2330 from October 5, 1934, ordering a severe reduction in the size of the Industrial Militsiia. Iagoda reported the 1934 figure of 64,595, then stated that the Sovnarkom ordered a reduction for 1935 to 28,381. The figure of 28,381, however, refers only to the regular officers (*riadovoi sostav*) of the Industrial Militsiia. Iagoda's total request for Industrial Militsiia staff for 1935 was 39,000, which includes 5,676 officers (*nachsostav*), 1,200 administrative workers (*adminkhozsostav*), 1,419 individuals involved in training (*na podgotovku kadrov*), and 2,324 "reserves for the guarding of objects newly placed under protection." GARF, f. 5446, op. 16a, d. 1270, ll. 31–32.

[i] This number is an estimate that the USSR NKVD presented to the USSR Sovnarkom based on the accepted increase in budgets for 1935. The estimate refers to totals as of January 1, 1935, and includes all categories of the regular *militsiia*. GARF, f. 5446, op. 16a, d. 1270, ll. 12–17.

[j] See GARF, f. 5446, op. 22a, d. 130, l. 3, for a breakdown of these numbers, which include convoy troops (12,000), passport officers (12,000) and the railroad *militsiia* (20,000).

[k] Projected figure for 1939, based on a 1938 USSR Sovnarkom decision to increase the total number of *militsiia* officers in the USSR by 20,000. GARF, f. 5446, op. 22a, d. 130, l. 22.

26,000 civilians and 63,000 troops in 1925.[76] The OGPU was concentrated in major cities, with fully one-fifth of its personnel stationed in the Moscow region; political policing in the provinces generally involved sporadic visits by plenipotentiaries, along with military-style counterinsurgency operations in areas of ongoing uprisings against Soviet power, especially in Central Asia and the Caucasus.[77]

The OGPU was hemmed in as well by continued political attacks by top-level Bolsheviks in 1924 and 1925, including Krylenko and Nikolai Bukharin, a Politburo member and the chief proponent of the NEP after Lenin's death in early 1924. Dzerzhinsky mounted an aggressive defense of the political police, pointing to its extensive role in the control of banditry, political opposition, and "threatening" criminal activity, but the OGPU nonetheless continued to face challenges from moderates in the Communist Party, as well as from the NKVD and rival justice organizations, throughout the mid-1920s.[78] The OGPU was not a "state within a state," independent of any bureaucratic pressures and beholden only to the will of the Politburo.[79] To the contrary, it was forced during the NEP period to maneuver within a highly politicized state and party structure that provided room for its institutional rivals to challenge its dominance in the realm of Soviet criminal justice.

Extrajudicial Repression and "Socially Dangerous Elements" during the NEP Era

Extrajudicial practices were firmly rooted in all aspects of Soviet policing during the era of the NEP. The police engaged in aggressive campaigns in the 1920s against crimes deemed particularly threatening by the regime, including hooliganism, banditry, and speculation (i.e., the buying and reselling of scarce consumer goods for a profit), using the extrajudicial powers provided to them by the Politburo to bypass the court system as often as possible. The connection between "social danger" and recidivism that emerged during the Civil War survived into the mid-1920s as well, becoming the basis for widespread extrajudicial repressions of "socially dangerous elements." In practice, these campaigns pitted the *militsiia* and the OGPU against each other as both organizations were striving to gain the exclusive right to mete out extrajudicial sanctions. These conflicts clarified the vision held by the leadership of each organization regarding the proper nature of Bolshevik policing, and hence they became a struggle not only for control over specific aspects of Soviet policing but also for the continued existence of separate political and civil policing systems in the USSR.

The Politburo's decision in early 1922 to authorize the newly created GPU to repress certain categories of violent civil crime, including organized banditry and armed robbery, using extrajudicial means, signaled a lack of commitment at the top of the Communist Party hierarchy for a policing system based in codified law. For the reformers who supported restrictions on the Cheka in 1922, extrajudicial procedures represented a means to codify and regulate the repressive actions of the political police. These reformers believed that police repressions carried out on the basis of well-defined procedures, carefully set out in statues, would reduce the arbitrariness inherent in the summary repressions of the Civil War era and promote the acceptance of police actions by the Soviet population at large. Top officials within the Russian NKVD shared this vision of well-regulated police repression, but most OGPU officials, and many members of the Politburo, did not. The Politburo thus took several steps in the early NEP era to expand the rights of the *militsiia* and the OGPU to mete out extrajudicial sanctions and, in doing so, undercut the attempts of moderates in the party to ensure that repression, whether judicial or extrajudicial, would correspond to the legal foundations of the NEP system.

The Politburo followed its decisions in early 1922 to allow the GPU to sanction both political and civil crime by extending similar rights to the *militsiia* later in the year. In areas declared "beset" with crime by regional Soviet administrations, the civil police exercised the right to arrest repeat offenders or individuals otherwise identified as recidivists, to process them through the same NKVD Special Commission that handled the banishment of counterrevolutionary offenders arrested by the GPU, and to sentence them to three years of banishment, with specific prohibition against living in six major urban areas of the USSR—a system that came to be known as "Minus Six."[80] This practice focused on individuals with two or more past convictions, and hence it was a continuation of police approaches to "socially dangerous elements" during the Civil War.[81] The concept of "social danger" was written into Soviet law in 1922, as Article 49 of the Criminal Code of the Russian Republic, which gave the courts the right to sentence individuals deemed socially dangerous due to ongoing petty criminal activity and connections with the "criminal milieu" (*prestupnaia sreda*) to three years of banishment from certain major Soviet cities, including Moscow and Leningrad.[82] The courts did not make widespread use of this provision in the 1920s, but these judicial guidelines helped to shape similar extrajudicial sentencing procedures for both the *militsiia* and the political police in the years that followed.

Local *militsiia* administrations used their right to arrest and sanction "dangerous" criminal recidivists widely until March 1924, when the Politburo eliminated this right in conjunction with the creation of the OGPU. The Politburo abolished the NKVD Special Commission, replacing it with a panel called the OGPU Special Board (Osoboe Soveshchanie), which met in Moscow and sanctioned counterrevolutionary offenders and selected nonpolitical criminals who were arrested by the OGPU, including smugglers of contraband, counterfeiters, and speculators in foreign currency. Republic-level OGPU administrations maintained their own special boards as well, which were not permitted to sentence political offenders but could mete out sentences of three years of exile to several categories of criminals, including bandits, armed robbers, and individuals deemed "socially dangerous" due to past criminal activity, a lack of defined employment, or ongoing contact with the criminal milieu.[83] These regional special boards were provided with extensive lists of the kinds of activities deemed socially dangerous, which included various forms of gambling, trade in illegal drugs and alcohol, the solicitation of prostitution or pimping, speculation, and repeat hooliganism, all of which had been the subject of summary repressions during the Civil War.[84] Although this decision limited extrajudicial punishment to the OGPU special boards and hence was a major blow to the aspirations of the NKVD, it ensured the centrality of extrajudicial repression in virtually every aspect of policing activity for the rest of the NEP era.

From this point forward, the NKVD and the OGPU clashed bitterly over the right to use administrative sanctions, especially banishment, against "socially dangerous elements." In some areas, local NKVD officials attempted to ignore the new regulations, as in the Azerbaijan Republic, where republic-level NKVD officials continued to banish "criminal elements" on their own authority until Krylenko complained to central government officials that the practice violated the 1924 statute.[85] NKVD officials vigorously protested the methods employed by the OGPU in banishing criminal offenders, especially the widely used punishment of Minus Six, or banishment from the six most important cities in the USSR. Minus Six was the simplest of all punishments for local OGPU officials, and it was widely abused; OGPU officers often simply ejected offenders from their areas, sometimes abandoning them on the outskirts of second-tier cities and instructing them to register with local *militsiia* administrations.

This practice predictably resulted in the flooding of unprotected areas with recidivist criminals, prompting local *militsiia* and Communist Party administrations to petition the center to prohibit the police from other regions from sending exiles to them. Local officials could, on occasion, take matters into their own hands; in the fall of 1926, the police in Baku sent 170 exiles into the neighboring Astrakhan Province, provoking the Astrakhan police administration to send 190 exiles of its own back to Baku.[86] Although the NKVD campaigned aggressively between 1925 and 1928 to regain the right to repress "socially dangerous" recidivists, its complaints had little effect; as Stalin began to rise to power, criticisms of the OGPU became increasingly impossible to sustain.[87]

The NKVD nonetheless attempted to prevent the encroachment of the OGPU on the policing prerogatives of the *militsiia* whenever possible in the mid-1920s. The most overt of these challenges emerged in the context of campaigns against banditry, a term that referred to a panoply of organized criminal or anti-Soviet activities in the 1920s, ranging from criminal brigandage to explicitly political uprisings. The latter were most prevalent on the still-rebellious periphery, especially in Central Asia and the Caucasus, where insurgents (collectively termed *basmachi* by the Soviet regime) continued to resist Soviet power well after the conclusion of the Civil War.[88] As during the war, the Red Army and OGPU internal troops repressed armed uprisings during the NEP era, but the response to "nonpolitical" banditry was broadly shared between the OGPU, the *militsiia*, and border guards. In early 1924, the OGPU's leadership, fully understanding its superior political and institutional position vis-à-vis the *militsiia* in this situation, convinced the Politburo to expand the OGPU's extrajudicial rights in areas deemed "beset with banditry" by regional soviet officials; local OGPU administrations gained the right to sentence bandits to exile, terms in labor camps, or execution, and the Politburo placed them in direct control of all the police activity related to these campaigns. The Politburo also approved the formation of three-person panels, or troikas, in some areas to coordinate police activity against banditry and to mete out punishments on the spot, without preliminary approval from the Special Board.[89] The OGPU leadership interpreted these decisions as broadly as possible, sending instructions to local representatives to subordinate all *militsiia* activity to the local political police administrations in areas "beset with banditry." Local OGPU officials responded vigorously to the new regulations, in some cases actually taking over the direction of *militsiia* administrations at the provincial and district levels.[90]

NKVD officials immediately protested this ad hoc expansion of the Politburo decision, in the process pointing to some of the essential ideological differences between the *militsiia* and the OGPU. Evsei Shirvindt, the head of the NKVD Central Directorate of Prisons (GUMZ), suggested that the OGPU had no legal basis for dispensing sentences outside the Russian Republic, calling into question the compatibility of the OGPU itself with the constitutional basis of the NEP-era state. Beloborodov argued that the Soviet public understood the essential difference between the *militsiia* and the OGPU and that the *militsiia*'s participation in such campaigns sullied its reputation among the population and increased the Tsarist-style "police-mindedness" of its officers; he complained pointedly that "the GPU is conducting the struggle against banditry *with the methods of 1918*." The Communist Party ultimately resolved the conflict in favor of the NKVD, allowing the OGPU to control only those *militsiia* activities directly related to banditry in areas "beset" with the crime and halting, at least temporarily, the drive of the OGPU to take control of all policing activities in the USSR.[91] Even so, the OGPU retained the right to deal with banditry extrajudicially for the rest of the NEP period, including the right to carry out sentences in some areas without preliminary approval from Moscow.

Regime policies regarding speculation in consumer goods and the crime of hooliganism upset boundaries between civil and political policing in much the same way. Both the Cheka and the *militsiia* engaged in campaigns against speculation in consumer goods during the Civil War, but the move to a limited market during the NEP era made the control of speculation a daily police duty rather than an "extraordinary" response to a wartime situation. Both the OGPU and the *militsiia* began regular purges of petty speculators in urban areas, often carried out with particular vigor in preparation for public celebrations of major holidays. In November 1923, for example, the OGPU exiled some 2,400 individuals from Moscow for speculation, almost 1,800 of whom were sent to the Solovki labor camps for terms of one to three years.[92] Likewise, in two separate operations in February and July 1924, police exiled 4,500 "thieves, persistent offenders, and *nepmen* [petty traders]" from Leningrad and Moscow.[93] In March 1924 the OGPU was instructed to arrest and sentence extrajudicially all individuals who bought and resold bread products, and in November 1925 speculators in consumer goods were placed in the same category.[94] Dzerzhinsky's personal approach to controlling speculation is clear in the March 1926 letter to Soviet economic officials with which this chapter began; widespread shortages of textile goods, in his view, were caused primarily by speculators and could be best addressed by sending "a couple thousand speculators" to labor camps.[95] By the mid-1920s, individuals sanctioned for speculation represented a substantial portion of those exiled or banished by the OGPU, and the extrajudicial repression of petty speculators was a standard part of daily policing practice in most urban areas.[96]

Police responses to hooliganism—a crime defined in the Russian legal tradition as violent, often drunken public behavior that exhibits a lack of respect for social norms—created similar tensions within the Soviet criminal justice system in the 1920s. The Politburo launched a major campaign against hooliganism in 1926, targeting hooliganistic behaviors that threatened production on the shop floor as well as general public order.[97] Plans for the campaign, discussed in the Council of People's Commissars (Sovnarkom) of the Russian Republic, included the expansion of extrajudicial sanctions against hooligans by the *militsiia*; but the OGPU protested the idea of allowing the *militsiia* to sentence hooligans directly to prison or exile, suggesting that it instead be allowed to declare certain areas "beset by hooliganism" and follow the same procedures set out for banditry.[98] The NKVD balked at this suggestion, and the Politburo concurred, instructing the police and the courts to work together to sentence hooligans in open judicial proceedings in order to have an educative as well as punitive effect on the Soviet population. The judicial campaign against hooliganism that followed was intense; the number of sentences meted out by the courts increased about 900 percent in 1927, and prison sentences replaced fines or suspended sentences as the principal judicial punishment for hooliganism.[99] At the same time, most petty cases of hooliganism were handled outside the court system altogether, by fines levied by individual policemen and often collected on the spot. Hundreds of thousands of fines were meted out by the *militsiia* during the campaign, encouraging local officers to understand extrajudicial repression, albeit mild repression, as a standard part of civil policing activity.[100]

The extrajudicial repression of civil crime, and especially of "socially dangerous elements," became a fundamental part of Soviet policing practice during the NEP era. By the mid-1920s, both the OGPU and the courts enjoyed the right to sanction individuals on the basis of their potential "social danger."[101] Although the *militsiia* was prohibited from the independent use of extrajudicial sanctions, local *militsiia* officers often operated according to the same assumptions as the OGPU, arresting "dangerous" criminals and transferring them to the OGPU for sentencing. The category of "dangerous elements" remained fluid into the late 1920s, because it was more a reflection of policing practices than a precise theoretical definition of crime, but by the end of the NEP era, the term was generally applied to specific cohorts of criminal offenders; political crime was identified not as "socially dangerous" but as "counterrevolutionary," especially after the delineation of fourteen separate categories of counterrevolutionary crime in the infamous Article 58 of the 1926 Soviet penal code. Top Soviet legal theorists continued to debate about the nature of the legal system in a socialist society, sparring over issues of law and class consciousness, rehabilitation versus the isolation of offenders, and the proper relationship between law and political power.[102] But by the middle of the NEP era, both the OGPU and the *militsiia* had settled on an approach to "dangerous" criminal cohorts that assumed that they were the proper target of extrajudicial repression and that the still-fragile Soviet polity required complete isolation from them. Although local police officers in the mid-1920s were not able to define the nature of these cohorts with any theoretical precision, they were quite willing to repress them through all available channels, in effect creating both the category and the cohort itself.

As we will see in chapter 2, the extrajudicial repression of "dangerous elements" accelerated substantially in mid-1927, when the Politburo approved the creation of local OGPU troikas to repress speculators, grain hoarders, and other economic offenders in the countryside as part of a broad effort to pressure peasants to deliver grain to the state.[103] These large-scale campaigns signaled the end of the NEP era, but they were not simply precursors to future repressions under Stalin. Rather, they were an expansion of the kind extrajudicial repression that was a central part of Soviet policing under the NEP.

Conclusion

In late 1927, as Stalin removed his main rivals for power from the Politburo and directed widespread purges of the "Trotskyite" opposition throughout the country, the OGPU seemed poised to take over all aspects of policing and penal policy in the USSR. Continued support for the NKVD came only from moderate supporters of the NEP, whose influence was waning throughout the Communist Party in 1927 and 1928. Yet the extent to which the NKVD and the OGPU represented competing systems of Soviet policing—one moderate, the other the precursor of the "Stalinist" police—should not be overestimated. The trends in Soviet statecraft that would become defining aspects of Stalinism were indeed visible in many aspects of Soviet policing in the 1920s, especially the propensity of police at all levels to identify and repress "socially dangerous" individuals as a cohort, a practice that links the prophylactic "cleansing" campaigns of World War I and the Civil War to the waves of state violence that Stalin would launch in the 1930s. Yet these trends were only incompletely developed in the 1920s, and it would be a mistake to consider Stalinism the inevitable outcome of them.

As Stalin rose to power, however, the range of historical possibilities narrowed substantially. The OGPU, on the defensive for much of the NEP, regained its preeminent place in the Soviet criminal justice system as the NEP era drew to a close, in large measure because Stalin relied on the political police in his fight with his political opponents in the Politburo, who included critics of the OGPU like Kamenev and Bukharin. The death of Feliks Dzerzhinsky in 1926 was no hindrance to the increasingly close relationship between Stalin and the OGPU: Dzerzhinsky's replacement, Viacheslav Menzhinsky, was a staunch Stalinist, as was Menzhinsky's assistant, Genrikh Yagoda, both of whom had been devoted followers of Dzerzhinsky since the Civil War. Although the OGPU did not promote any aggressive attempts to abolish the NKVD between 1925 and 1928, it received nearly all of the prerogatives that it desired in this period, in part because Stalin took its side in conflicts with all institutional opponents, save the Communist Party itself.

By the time Stalin launched the First Five-Year Plan in 1928, few contemporary observers expected the NKVD to survive for long. Yet the ultimate victory of the OGPU, which came over two years later, did not emerge from long-standing institutional conflicts with the NKVD. This victory was fundamentally political, resting on the desires and actions of Stalin himself.

2

"Chekist in Essence, Chekist in Spirit": The Soviet Police and the Stalin Revolution

I find it necessary to point out in writing that I considered and continue to consider inexpedient the transfer of the *militsiia*, places of confinement, and the administration of compulsory labor to the OGPU. . . . Unification [of the OGPU and the NKVD] will result in the transformation of the nature of the OGPU or the spread of the methods of the OGPU to the activities of the other above-named organizations, a situation that benefits neither the former organization nor the latter.

—The assistant procurator of the Russian Republic, Bespalov, 1930[1]

At this point, precinct inspectors are exclusively administrative, purely investigative officials, and struggle with events that have already happened. . . . If, on a given beautiful day, nobody wants to declare anything to the inspector, he can find himself unemployed, and if not unemployed, then idling. When the precinct inspector has an informational-denunciatory network—that is, a cadre of undercover individuals secretly recruited to denunciatory work—then he will be able to carry out work not only by halting this or that antisocial manifestation that has already occurred, but will be able to halt these antisocial manifestations before they arise, that is, to begin on the path of so-called preventive work [*profilakticheskaia rabota*].

—The chief of the regional detective department to a meeting of precinct inspectors in Sverdlovsk, 1932[2]

During a meeting in the Kremlin in August 1942, Winston Churchill sat down for dinner with Joseph Stalin and, in the midst of careful negotiations regarding the war, asked whether the ongoing conflict with Nazi Germany was worse than the years of collectivization of agriculture in the USSR. "Oh, no," Stalin responded, "the Collective Farm policy was a terrible struggle." According to Churchill, Stalin called it a "fearful" and "difficult" period, during which Soviet peasants were either forced to participate in the Soviet system or were "wiped out."[3]

Stalin's response to Churchill, fantastic as it seems, was no exaggeration. When Stalin and his supporters in the Politburo decided in early 1928 to jettison the New Economic Policy (NEP), they called into question virtually every aspect of the compromise between the Bolshevik regime and Soviet society that had made possible the gradual social and economic recovery of the mid-1920s. Forced industrialization, a resurgence of radical cultural and social policies, renewed attacks on the prerevolutionary elites known as "former people" and on "bourgeois" industrial specialists—across the board, Stalin's policy initiatives at the beginning of the First Five-Year Plan period proclaimed that cooperation with the remnants of the old regime had ended and that massive state-driven social transformation was again the order of the day. Stalin's plans for the collectivization of agriculture, in particular, entailed a direct reversion to the practices of the Civil War; from his policy of forcing Soviet peasants to join collective farms flowed, almost inevitably, the mass repression of prosperous peasants "as a class" and the forced resettlement of broad swaths of the rural population. He and his compatriots intended these campaigns, which stretched into the mid-1930s, to reshape the demographic nature of the peasantry, to eliminate what they viewed as the last major impediment to the "construction of socialism" in the USSR, and to complete the revolutionary process begun in 1917.

All parts of the Soviet state were involved in these campaigns, none more directly than the police. The political police spearheaded repressive campaigns in the countryside and expanded repressions in cities against "former people" and the petty traders known as "NEP men." Civil police officers, for their part, struggled to control burgeoning levels of crime and social unrest in the cities and aided in the collectivization of peasant agriculture, often assisting teams of urban activists sent to the countryside to force peasants onto collective farms. Local officers understood these tasks as an expansion of the kind of violent statecraft practiced by both the OGPU and the *militsiia* in the 1920s, focusing much of their attention on the categorization and control of "dangerous" strata within the Soviet peasantry in the pursuit of social order as well as the total social transformation of the countryside. The drive to collectivize Soviet agriculture engaged officers in waves of mass repressions that far exceeded the boundaries of NEP-era policing, straining both the *militsiia* and OGPU administrations to their limits.

The era of the First Five-Year Plan also saw the widespread acceptance within the Soviet police system of a new set of explicitly modern approaches to policing, crime prevention, and social engineering, based on the idea of preventive policing (*profilakticheskaia rabota*) and on the identification and control of "contingents" (*kontingenty*) of inherently criminal populations. Both preventive policing and the identification of contingents as the object of police work reinforced the primacy of the political police in the Soviet criminal justice system, leading to the eventual takeover of all policing activity by the OGPU in late 1930. These two trends interacted under the pressures of Stalin's "revolution from above" to produce, by the end of the First Five-Year Plan period, a policing system that contained the cornerstone of a quintessentially Stalinist approach to law enforcement and social control.

Soviet Policing and the Onset of the "Revolution from Above"

In 1927 and 1928, Stalin abandoned the NEP in several steps, each designed to mobilize his supporters within the Communist Party and to bring the Soviet state one step closer to a complete break with the existing system. The police responded to these policy cues, likewise, in steps, using existing extrajudicial practices to increase pressure on individuals and, eventually, on entire social groups that they identified as hindrances to the changes demanded by Stalin. Such steps by the police were generally ad hoc responses to general policy formulations set down by the center; until late in the First Five-Year Plan period, central party and police officials had no coherent plan for a complete reformulation of Soviet policing to match the social and bureaucratic transformations taking place throughout the country.

The NEP's collapse was plainly visible in the rising number of arrests by the political police from 1927 to 1930. From a low for the NEP period of roughly 63,000 arrests in 1926, more than 32,000 of which were for nonpolitical crimes, the OGPU went on to arrest almost 77,000 individuals in 1927 (more than 28,000 for nonpolitical crimes), nearly 113,000 in 1928 (more than 40,000 for nonpolitical crimes), more than 162,000 in 1929 (30,000 for nonpolitical crimes), and more than 330,000 in 1930 (nearly 65,000 for nonpolitical crimes).[4] Much of the expansion in 1927 and 1928 involved arrests of "dangerous elements" in both rural and urban areas, as the OGPU repeatedly requested and gained from the Politburo the right to apply extrajudicial sanctions to disparate groups of threatening "recidivist" or "dangerous" individuals using its Special Board.

In mid-1927, the Politburo authorized local OGPU administrations in all areas to carry out summary repressions, including executions, of individuals accused of counterrevolutionary crimes or banditry; these sentences were eventually approved by the OGPU Special Board in Moscow, but local OGPU officials understood that they were authorized to carry out sentences on their own authority, in a return to the practices of the Cheka era. The police were also accorded the right in 1927 to repress as "socially danger-ous elements" all individuals convicted for hooliganism three times, even in the absence of a new criminal act.[5] Under explicit instructions from the center, local political police administrations began in early 1927 to clas-sify suspect individuals in the countryside as "anti-Soviet and socially dangerous elements," and in the fall the police began widespread arrests of them.[6]

These trends continued into 1928. In July, the OGPU received autho-rization to remove all "dangerous elements" from gold-producing areas, focusing on speculators and individuals with demonstrated connections to the criminal milieu; and in August the OGPU began a series of operations to remove homeless adults, beggars, and "hooliganistic elements" from major urban areas, banishing them or, for individuals deemed to have on-going contacts with the criminal underworld or past sentences, sentencing them to exile or to labor colonies.[7] The police generally referred to these large-scale campaigns as "mass operations" (*massovye operatsii*), a term that was widely used by the end of the 1920s, as it had been during the Civil War, to describe one-time sweeps aimed at "dangerous" individuals, including sweeps of major cities of "hooliganistic and homeless elements" in preparation for public holiday celebrations.[8]

The OGPU also increased its ability to incarcerate "socially danger-ous elements" on the basis of biographical or sociological considerations, rather than on the basis of concrete criminal activity. As early as 1925, the Politburo authorized the OGPU to sentence individuals who had com-pleted sentences in concentration camps or exile but were still deemed "socially dangerous" to up to three additional years of banishment under the provisions of "Minus Six" (see chapter 1) in order to protect major cities from cohorts of ex-convicts.[9] The OGPU expanded this practice over the next several years to include preemptive sanctions of "dangerous elements." In 1926, the political police in Moscow mounted a citywide sweep of speculators and currency traders, sentencing those arrested to three years in concentration camps, plus an additional, preemptive three years of banishment. The Politburo ignored protests from top justice officials that this practice violated existing statutes that limited extrajudicial sentences to three years, and in February 1928 it authorized the OGPU to sentence all individuals who had completed terms in labor camps to three additional years of exile to a specific location, and all individuals who had completed terms of exile to three additional years of "Minus Six."[10] The OGPU requested an expansion of this practice in early 1929 to include individuals identified as "hardened recidivists" who were serving sentences in the NKVD prison system for serious nonpolitical crimes, who upon release would immediately be considered "dangerous elements" based on past convictions and ongoing ties with the criminal milieu. Central Communist Party and state officials acquiesced in March 1929, standing only on the principle that the regulation applied only to individuals already in custody.[11]

These moves were part of the OGPU's long-standing drive to control all prison and labor-camp populations in the USSR, which stretched back to the reformulations of the Soviet policing system at the end of the Civil War, and hence they were precursors to the infamous July 1929 Politburo order that transferred all inmates with sentences of three years or more to the OGPU's labor camp system.[12] At the same time, they were part of a broad drive on the part of the OGPU, evident as early as 1925, to identify certain categories of individuals as inherently "dangerous" and isolate them from Soviet society altogether.

In early 1928, Stalin decided to respond to widespread difficulties in the harvest and grain procurement campaigns with overt coercion, jettisoning the NEP-era compromise with the peasantry and returning to the requisitioning practices of the Civil War. Stalin's policies, which included the dispatch of teams headed by top Politburo members to grain-producing areas in order to oversee the repression of "kulak" resisters, began a process that would lead within two years to the collectivization of Soviet agriculture and to the policy of the "elimination of kulaks as a class." Top OGPU officials responded to Stalin's policy changes in 1928 with much of the same millenarian vigor that drove radicals within the Communist Party, but they also understood these initial campaigns against "kulaks" as a continuation of actions against speculators and private traders during the NEP, and they carried them out accordingly.[13]

In January 1928, the OGPU launched a major wave of "mass operations" against small-scale private traders, manufacturers, and speculators in consumer goods in the countryside, especially grain and leather products, which were designed to prevent rural populations from offering products on the open market instead of to state procurement agencies. Local OGPU officers initially targeted private grain traders and small-scale manufacturers per se, much as they had during the NEP era, but the Politburo in mid-January specifically added the category of "kulaks" to the list of targets, instructing the police to arrest "kulak elements" who supposedly used the confusion created by the mass operations to purchase grain for speculative purposes and who agitated against the procurement campaigns in general. By early February, OGPU officials reported that mass operations against speculators had resulted in the arrest of some 3,000 private bread producers (*chastnye khlebniki*) in major grain-producing areas, along with 216 "kulaks" arrested in "antikulak operations" in the Siberian and Urals regions; by April, nearly 6,800 "speculative elements" had been arrested, most guilty of trading in grain or leather products in the countryside.

Operations against "speculators" and "kulaks" were conceptually separate at the center: Genrikh Yagoda, the assistant OGPU chief, instructed local officials in February to sanction private traders and speculators using the Special Board but to hide the OGPU's involvement in cases related to the repression of "kulaks," making use of local *militsiia* and procuracy officials to carry out these arrests and sending the resulting cases to the court system for public adjudication.[14] At the periphery, however, such distinctions were difficult to sustain. Local OGPU administrations, often unsure of the difference between simple speculators and "kulak elements" participating in speculative activity, made uneven use of extrajudicial repression in the following months, some sentencing both speculators and "kulak elements" internally and others relying more heavily on the court system.[15] Local OGPU officers distinguished between repressions of "kulak elements" and repressions of speculators and other economic criminals for the next several months, as they continued to attempt to support Stalin's muddled policies of forced grain requisitioning and the repression of "kulak" resisters through the difficult planting and harvest seasons of 1928 and early 1929.[16]

Stalin's response to these agricultural difficulties wrecked the fragile truce between city and countryside that had held throughout the NEP period, provoking a widespread crisis in Soviet agriculture. His ability to react to this crisis with overt repression was strengthened by his political victory in mid-1929 over the Rightists in the Politburo, including Nikolai Bukharin, who favored continued cooperation with the Soviet peasantry as the best method to support the industrialization drive. With the Right purged from the top echelons of Soviet power, Stalin responded to harvest problems in mid-1929 with a policy of the rapid collectivization of Soviet agriculture that was intended to abolish small-scale farming and force the Soviet peasantry onto collective farms, from which the state could procure grain more easily than from individual households. By the end of the year, Stalin and his ruling clique had thrown aside all caution, calling for the complete collectivization of Soviet agriculture and the "elimination of kulaks as a class."[17]

The Soviet police at all levels were thrown into this campaign, deemphasizing their standard duties in order to support Stalin's policies of radical social transformation in the countryside. Even before the beginning of "total collectivization" in early 1930, the OGPU expanded its repressions of "kulak elements," making use of extrajudicial practices honed in ongoing campaigns against speculators and grain hoarders. The police in numerous localities began in mid-1929 to repress "kulaks" as a social category, exiling "dangerous elements" en masse from productive farmland or from sensitive border areas in order to prevent any resistance from this cohort of relatively prosperous peasants.[18] This transition to the repression of "kulaks" as a social stratum preceded any specific Politburo instructions on the matter; local police and Communist Party administrations made use of the same tactics that had been employed against all categories of "socially dangerous elements" in the late 1920s, categorizing and exiling what they viewed as a threatening population cohort as a matter of standard extrajudicial procedure.

Although the Politburo took no specific action regarding the "repression of kulaks as a class" in late 1929, it did respond to the OGPU's requests for expanded extrajudicial rights against individual peasant resisters, authorizing the OGPU in October 1929 to carry out "rapid methods of repression, including execution" against peasants who committed terrorist acts or participated in mass uprisings.[19] Local OGPU administrations, freely mixing repressions of individuals peasants with repressions of the cohort of "kulak elements," seized the initiative in this campaign; by early November 1929—that is, nearly three months before Stalin officially launched the dekulakization campaign—the OGPU reported that it had arrested more than 28,300 individuals in support of grain procurement campaigns, with slightly fewer than half accused of counterrevolutionary crimes and the rest of economic crimes such as speculation and violations of the rules of trade.[20]

After several weeks of internal debate, the Politburo published legislation in early January 1930 calling for the complete collectivization of agriculture in the most important grain-producing regions of the country by the fall of 1930, and in all other grain-producing areas within the following year. At the same time, Stalin demanded that this wholesale collectivization be supported by "dekulakization," or the expropriation of the property of prosperous "kulaks" and their arrest or exile, depending on their level of opposition to collectivization. Central and local OGPU administrations alike played a major role in shaping the dekulakization drive, devising plans in January 1930 that combined the extrajudicial repression of "counterrevolutionary" peasant resisters with the kind of wholesale repression of entire social strata that harkened back to the Civil War. Local OGPU administrations launched campaigns to exile, arrest, or resettle "kulak" populations within their jurisdictions across the month of January, stepping up measures against "kulak elements" in order to protect the collectivization campaigns and making operational preparations for much larger operations to come.[21] By the time the Politburo issued specific instructions on dekulakization in early February, the process had been under way in nearly all areas for weeks.

Once launched, the dekulakization campaign quickly became the most fundamental task undertaken by the political police since the Civil War. Local OGPU administrations were charged with identifying three categories of "kulaks": peasants placed in the first category, deemed "most dangerous," were executed or sent to concentration camps, while the remaining two categories were exiled to special settlement camps maintained by the OGPU or to villages administered by local soviet officials. Initial plans called for the repression of 60,000 kulaks of the first category and 150,000 of the second; in the end, nearly 2 million peasants were deported in 1930 and 1931 as part of this drive to reshape the demographic nature of the Soviet countryside.

Much of the operation was ad hoc, devised by local OGPU officers who found themselves in charge of operations that had little precedent in NEP-era policing. The OGPU understood the repressions of first-category kulaks, at some level, as an extension of existing practices, targeting a wide range of individuals generally subject to extrajudicial repression in the 1920s—not only peasant resisters but also bandits, insurgents, and speculators, as well as "counterrevolutionaries" like white guards and religious figures. The individuals subject to extrajudicial repression were sentenced by OGPU troikas, which functioned under the auspices of the OGPU Special Board, and they were usually charged with "counterrevolutionary" activity, maintaining a semblance of procedural integrity.[22]

These operations, however, extended far beyond existing extrajudicial practices. The logistical requirements of dekulakization were immense, stretching even the robust OGPU to its limits; local administrations were forced to rely on reserve forces made up of *militsiia* officers, workers, and Communist Party activists. Local *militsiia* officers played a major role in these campaigns, but they remained subordinate to the OGPU throughout.[23] Although the NKVD leadership attempted to exercise some control over the resettlement of deportees, it made no attempt to wrest overall operational control from the political police.[24] Individual *militsiia* officers took orders directly from local political police administrations, even though they often found themselves on the front lines of the collectivization and dekulakization campaigns, especially once OGPU officers and party activists left an area that had been collectivized. *Militsiia* officers often faced unremittingly hostile peasant populations who rose up by the hundreds to demand the return of their property, especially cattle, from collective farms; in the process, the peasants often attacked police officers and justice officials directly, who found themselves in the precarious position of the only armed representatives of Soviet power in the countryside. In such situations, local officers usually abandoned all pretense of cooperation with peasant populations and resorted to overt force, calling on OGPU forces to handle situations that threatened to burst into open rebellion.[25] Ultimately, the OGPU proved more adept at carrying out these operations than the other state and party organizations that were originally involved, and by mid-1931 it had seized control over virtually every aspect of the expropriation and resettlement process.[26]

By the beginning of 1931, the tasks of the First Five-Year Plan, especially the dekulakization drive, had reshaped the basic institutional and operational nature of the entire Soviet police system. Although the political police carried out numerous mass campaigns against other categories of "dangerous elements" in 1928 and 1929, including massive repressions of traders, "bourgeois elements," and "former people" in major Soviet cities, the dekulakization campaign had the most fundamental effects on the police system itself.[27] The OGPU gained institutional and political strength at the expense of state and even Communist Party organizations in the process of carrying out these campaigns, increasing the Politburo's propensity to rely on the political police when launching major campaigns for the remainder of the 1930s. Just as important, dekulakization encouraged the police at all levels to turn to "mass operations" against population cohorts deemed inherently "criminal" or "socially dangerous" as part of their basic strategy for maintaining public order, basing their actions on an emerging informal criminology that linked the control of "criminal" behaviors to the repression of specific criminal "contingents" that were defined, like "kulaks," in socio-logical terms. This understanding of criminal contingents predated the deku-lakization campaigns, especially within the local OGPU administrations, yet it was the overt attack on the countryside that brought this criminology to the forefront of local policing practices.

This development emerged from within the Soviet police system it-self, and not all top police officials were comfortable with it. Yagoda com-plained in early 1930, for example, that local OGPU administrations were treating the dekulakization campaign as an opportunity to target broad social strata rather than individual "kulaks" guilty of anti-Soviet activity, and he demanded that they instead "take [the kulaks] according to the case [*delo*] and not [according to] social signs."[28] His comments contra-dicted both the general line of the Politburo and overall trends in Soviet policing, but they were completely consistent with an understanding of the OGPU as an institution dedicated to repressing the enemies of the re-gime, rather than serving as a tool to reshape the Soviet population. Yet the extrajudicial practices of the Soviet police before the end of 1930 made this distinction increasingly moot, as the conceptually separate processes of dekulakization and crime control began to converge into a single ap-proach to controlling disorderly and threatening "contingents" of "socially dangerous elements."

The End of the NKVD

The spread of mass campaigns into all areas of police work during the First Five-Year Plan period prompted a collapse of the conceptual and practical distinctions between civil and political policing and accelerated the OGPU's expansion into all areas of criminal justice. Top OGPU offi-cials clamored at the end of the decade for the abolition of the Russian NKVD, and for the transfer of control over all aspects of Soviet policing, including direct control over the *militsiia*, to their organization. The NKVD resisted this trend for a surprisingly long time, but it eventually fell victim to political pressure from the OGPU, from justice organiza-tions, and ultimately from Stalin himself.

The strains of the collectivization and dekulakization campaigns stretched local *militsiia* administrations to the breaking point, lending support to claims by top OGPU officials that the NKVD was unable to cope with the demands of the new era. High levels of social and geographic mobility and low unemployment after 1927 compounded ongoing staff shortages; the number of officers in the Russian Republic declined from roughly 42,000 regular officers and 5,100 detectives in 1927 to 37,600 officers and 5,000 detectives in 1930. Some of the shortfall was made up by the Industrial Militsiia, which expanded from 22,500 officers in 1927 to 58,000 in 1930 and at least 95,000 in 1931 (see table 1.1 in chapter 1). Yet Industrial Militsiia officers, who were paid by individual factories or other economic institutions, were completely unaccountable to the center and hence only exacerbated the problems of high turnover and poor discipline that plagued the *militsiia* in the late 1920s. Central NKVD officials complained consistently that the *militsiia* was poorly staffed in the first years of the First Five-Year Plan, with less than a quarter of all officers identified as "working class" and no more than 15 percent members of the Communist Party or the Soviet Youth League. Labor turnover accelerated during the period, reaching an average of 64 percent for the regular *militsiia* and almost 80 percent for the Industrial Militsiia by 1930. Turnover in certain areas, especially in the countryside, was as high as 100 percent, meaning that a given police position was occupied by a different officer each year; peasants reportedly treated the position as seasonal labor, taking the job to bridge slow periods between planting and harvest in the countryside.[29] Central NKVD officials attempted to improve staff shortages in March 1928 by ordering local administrations to recruit women into the lower ranks of the force, but this move contradicted the male institutional culture of the organization and made little headway; by 1931, women made up only 3 to 5 percent of the *militsiia*, and the problem remained acute.[30]

Central criminal justice officials likewise complained that corruption, drunkenness, and abuses of power were rife in local *militsiia* administrations in the late 1920s. Central NKVD officials received a continuous stream of reports from the periphery regarding drunkenness among local officers; the police drank while on duty, abused and beat detainees, and demanded vodka as "payment" for their services. Corruption, which had already been identified as a problem in local policing in the 1920s, became a major concern in this period as well. Criminal justice and police officials at the center argued that the social and bureaucratic dislocations of the First Five-Year Plan produced an epidemic of corruption among the local police, who reportedly extorted bribes and seized personal property at will, threatening to launch criminal investigations against those who complained.[31] Central officials focused on moral depravity among local officers, complaining that drunken parties, orgies, and rapes of prostitutes were common in local precincts across the USSR in 1929 and 1930.[32] Even when the local police carried out their duties to the best of their abilities, most commentators agreed that the quality of police work, especially investigation, was poor in the late 1920s and hampered the basic functions of the criminal justice system. The local police were unable to complete investigations in a timely manner or to gather sufficient evidence to support prosecution and trial in the majority of cases that they handled, leaving local justice agencies to attempt to compensate even as they themselves participated in Stalin's industrialization and collectivization drives.[33]

Widespread criticisms of the *militsiia* in the late 1920s drew on clichés, already strong within Soviet political culture, regarding the difference between "honest" Chekists and corrupt local bureaucrats, and they were often transparently exaggerated by top officials within the OGPU. Yet complaints about corruption and poor investigative practices also reflected fundamental ideological differences between the leaders of the OGPU and the NKVD in the late 1920s. Reformers within the NKVD pressed consistently for a *militsiia* that encouraged integration between the Soviet state and society, drawing on European and American models of policing that placed individual officers within local communities to engage citizens in the maintenance of public order. The OGPU, on the contrary, promoted a model based on its own practices, in which officers were isolated from local communities to encourage scrupulous attention to procedural integrity. The integration of the police into local communities might improve law enforcement but, in the minds of top OGPU and Communist Party officials, it also encouraged fraternization between the police and local notables and provided numerous opportunities for corruption and the abuse of power.[34] Such relationships did exist and were valuable to itinerant rural policemen in the 1920s, but they put *militsiia* officers on the defensive in 1929 and 1930 as the regime redefined rural elites as enemies of the state and forced the local police to repress them in the process of collectivization.

The ability of the NKVD to resist pressure from rival organizations crumbled when Aleksandr Beloborodov, its chief since 1923, was ousted for Trotskyite sympathies in 1927. Beloborodov was hardly a democrat, but his position regarding the corrosive effects of untrammeled OGPU power on the Soviet criminal justice system was consistent across the 1920s, and his leadership was one of the reasons that the NKVD survived as long as it did.[35] V. N. Tolmachev, Beloborodov's replacement, was an undistinguished career Communist Party functionary whose most important previous position had been deputy chair of the Executive Committee of the North Caucasus Soviet. The NKVD survived the change of leadership, but the ensuing turmoil weakened the institution substantially. Many local OGPU officials quietly closed local NKVD administrations and placed local *militsiia* officers under their direct control; in several republics, OGPU officials actually managed to abolish republic-level NKVD administrations by mid-1927. NKVD officials protested such moves to Union-level state organizations, arguing that they hampered policing at the periphery and violated the USSR Constitution, and in mid-1928 these republic-level governments were forced by the center to reinstate their NKVD administrations. Nonetheless, these events undermined the institutional power of the Russian NKVD, leaving it with little ability after 1928 to halt its overall decline.[36]

The Politburo provided no clear policy line regarding the NKVD between 1928 and 1930, leaving the door open for bitter, sometimes public conflict among all the institutions interested in dismantling the existing system. The Worker-Peasant Inspectorate (Rabkrin) carried out a series of investigations of the *militsiia* in early 1928, and in June it produced a particularly harsh set of criticisms of the leadership of the NKVD and the state of local police forces.[37] Likewise, justice officials attacked the NKVD openly in the legal press in 1928 and 1929, complaining that the *militsiia* was unresponsive to the working class and contaminated with "anti-Soviet elements." The *militsiia* was subjected to sweeping membership purges in 1929, as part of a general purge of the Soviet state apparatus. Although global figures are not available, scattered reports indicate that these expulsions were substantial, compounding the chronic labor shortages of the era.[38] Suggestions for reorganizing the policing system circulated freely in the press and within state and Communist Party bodies, ranging from proposals to turn over all policing and penal organizations to the OGPU to calls for the unification of all aspects of criminal justice under the umbrella of the Justice Commissariat. The NKVD defended itself vigorously throughout this conflict, but the victory of the Stalinists over the proponents of the NEP in the Politburo in late 1929 left the NKVD with few supporters at the top and no way to oppose its political marginalization.[39]

The only concerted response by NKVD officials to these criticisms in 1929 and 1930 involved the promotion of popular participation in daily policing activity, a move that represented a reversion to the ethic of self-governance that had defined Bolshevik policing during the revolutionary era. The most comprehensive such scheme, termed the "militia system," was the personal creation of the Russian commissar of internal affairs, Tolmachev, who in 1928 ordered urban police administrations to organize detachments of factory workers, who were released from their work with full pay for one week per month to patrol city streets. Tolmachev couched this plan in Leninist language about the "withering away" of the state, but he was primarily concerned with improving urban police systems at a time of limited resources and dire shortages of officers.[40] Although the plan received support from higher Communist Party and state institutions, most local police administrations participated without enthusiasm, viewing the plan as a distraction from more pressing issues or, at best, as a way to gain free assistance for mundane bureaucratic tasks. In Moscow, only two police districts implemented the plan, and the participants were reportedly less interested in patrolling the streets than in the municipal privileges awarded to volunteers, including free use of the public transport system and reduced rent in city-owned housing.[41] Police administrations across the Russian republic reported similar experiences, and the militia system, although it remained an official part of Soviet policing until the end of 1930, was largely abandoned in practice by the beginning of that year.

Local police enjoyed somewhat more success in the late 1920s with less utopian forms of popular participation, especially volunteer detachments that were loosely coordinated by local *militsiia* administrations and that carried out specific policing duties in a given area. Volunteer detachments were quite common during the NEP period, but they were usually organized by local Communist Party, Komsomol, or trade union officials and hence had little contact with individual police officers. Central NKVD officials moved to standardize these detachments in May 1930, renaming them "Societies for Assistance to the Militsiia" and placing them under the direct control of local officers. Individual society cells, made up entirely of volunteers, were usually assigned to patrol specific locations after working hours were over, but they also served as guards in police stations or convoyed prisoners to and from court appearances. Society members were allowed to carry firearms at certain times, such as when they were convoying prisoners, even though the central authorities were well aware of the extent to which arming these poorly trained volunteers was dangerous not only to the public but also to the volunteers themselves.[42] By mid-1930, central officials counted nearly 8,500 cells in the Russian Republic with a total of some 130,000 members, each connected to a specific factory, police administration, or village soviet. Three-quarters of the members were located in rural areas, underscoring the extent to which central officials viewed these volunteers as a means to compensate for the paltry police presence in the countryside, where an officer was often responsible for 7,000 to 8,000 inhabitants.[43]

As with the militia system, the central authorities promoted the Societies for Assistance to the Militsiia in the language of the First-Five Year Plan. One January 1931 circular described them as a method of "drawing society into the task of defense of public order, so that after a particular period of time the defense of public order and safety will become the direct right of workers themselves, therefore fulfilling the behest of the Great Leader and Teacher V. I. Lenin regarding the militia system."[44] Yet, as with the militia system, individual officers generally understood societies as a means to relieve pressure on local administrations, freeing up the police to deal with the more pressing tasks associated with the collectivization and industrialization drives. Despite the centrality of popular activism to the vision of social change promoted by the center during Stalin's "revolution from above," the local police operated within an institutional culture that stressed centralized administration and hierarchy instead. Such utopian visions did not spread deeply into the policing system during the First Five-Year Plan period, and they failed to reverse the institutional decline of the Russian NKVD after 1928.

Behind the scenes, most top policymakers in Moscow agreed on the need for a reorganization of the NKVD by the first months of 1930, but conflict on the issue continued through the end of the year, as all sides pressed for the creation of a policing system that corresponded to their particular vision of Soviet criminal justice. In early January, representatives from the Worker-Peasant Inspectorate, the OGPU, and the NKVD produced a plan, commissioned by the Russian Sovnarkom, that recommended the abolishment of the NKVD and transfer of the Detective Department to the OGPU, the prisons to the Justice Commissariat, and the general *militsiia* to a small central Directorate created to set policy for that organization alone.[45] The Politburo took an additional step toward making the NKVD redundant in April 1930 by making public its 1929 decision to transfer most inmates of the Soviet penal system to OGPU labor camps, renaming the OGPU's labor camp system the Main Administration of Corrective Labor Camps (*Glavnoe upravlenie ispravitel'no-trudovykh lagerei*, popularly known by its infamous acronym, the Gulag) and reiterating the general rule that all inmates sentenced to more than three years of confinement would serve their sentences in these camps rather than in penal institutions run by the NKVD.[46]

Although the overall trend was plainly obvious, the Politburo took no decisive action in the first half of 1930, and NKVD officials continued to oppose the abolition of their organization, often on highly principled grounds. Many top NKVD officials, including Tolmachev, were quietly sympathetic to at least part of the platform of the "right opposition." Most believed that the transfer of the *militsiia* to the OGPU would disrupt the work of local police administrations and turn individual officers into second-rate helpmates of the political police. Tolmachev himself spoke in these terms during one of the commission meetings in early 1930 that discussed the reorganization of the NKVD, arguing that the *militsiia*, unlike the OGPU, worked in close contact with society and that its subordination to the OGPU would cut it off from "everyday direct work with the masses" and prevent it from carrying out its basic duties of preservation of public order.[47]

Despite such opposition, a joint meeting of the Worker-Peasant Inspectorate and the Communist Party Control Commission on April 3 supported the earlier Sovnarkom decision, approving the abolition of the NKVD and the creation of a new Commissariat of Communal Services to handle those duties that could not be transferred to existing commissariats. Yet Stalin intervened unexpectedly at the April 5, 1930, meeting of the Politburo, ordering the inspectorate to delay any action on the NKVD for six months.[48] NKVD officials viewed this decision as a major victory, and they issued numerous circulars intended to boost morale and reverse the OGPU's recent inroads into *militsiia* activity. Taking Stalin's decision as a sign of triumph over the OGPU was certainly premature, but it allowed the leadership of the NKVD system to continue to fight for its institutional and political survival through the end of the year.[49]

In the end, the NKVD was undermined by the opposition of its leaders to the OGPU's expanding control over penal populations in the USSR. In mid-1930, Tolmachev was named to a Politburo commission charged with reviewing the sentencing practices of the OGPU during the dekulakization drive. In this capacity, he began to complain that the OGPU troikas had sentenced massive numbers of peasants incorrectly, estimating that at least 15 percent of those peasants identified as "kulaks" and deported to special settlements in the North did not merit that designation and that, in some areas, up to 60 percent of the individuals thus sentenced were likely innocent. He argued that these individuals deserved to be released and returned to their former homes—a proposal that Yagoda, for the OGPU, strenuously opposed and that Stalin chose to ignore.[50] In addition, Tolmachev attempted in mid-1930 to roll back the gains that the OGPU had made in 1929 regarding control over labor camp populations. He and his deputy, Evsei Shirvindt, gained the support of Aleksei Rykov, the chairman of the USSR Sovnarkom, which in late August 1930 resolved that the NKVD should regain control over inmates sentenced to three or more years of confinement, in complete contradiction to the 1929 Politburo decision on the subject.[51]

Stalin eventually intervened in the conflict, in part because Rykov represented the last vestiges of support for the discredited "Right opposition" within the leadership of the Soviet state. In a letter to Viacheslav Molotov, dated September 7, 1930, Stalin wrote: "These [maneuvers of the NKVD] are the machinations of a thoroughly corrupted Tolmachev. . . . I think that it is necessary to carry out the decisions of the Politburo, and to close the NKVD."[52] On Stalin's orders, the Politburo promulgated a decision on October 5 that reiterated the OGPU's control over prisoners sentenced to three years or more, and another on November 5 that abolished the internal affairs commissariats of all Union republics, transferred control of the *militsiia* and the detective departments to the OGPU, and handed over the NKVD's network of labor colonies and other places of confinement to the Justice Commissariat—all effective January 1, 1931.[53] Tolmachev, assigned to a commission that included OGPU, justice, and Communist Party representatives, was ordered to assist in the dismantling of his own commissariat, after which he was arrested and disappeared from the top levels of the Soviet state.[54]

Although Stalin's personal intervention ensured the victory of the OGPU, his decision did not immediately halt the political struggles between supporters of the two organizations. Opposition to the Politburo decision arose from the same Worker-Peasant Inspectorate commission that had discussed the issue throughout 1930. Even though the Politburo had specifically awarded all existing NKVD penal institutions to the Justice Commissariat, some members of the commission persisted in suggesting that they be transferred instead to the OGPU and added to the Gulag system, in part because a large proportion of individuals then incarcerated in prisons were there on cases originated by the OGPU.[55]

From the opposite point of view, one member of the commission, the assistant procurator of the Russian Republic, Bespalov, questioned the wisdom of Stalin's overall policy direction with the words with which this chapter began. Bespalov argued that the OGPU was an organization dedicated to "the battle with particularly socially dangerous elements," whereas the *militsiia* relied in contrast on "the widest popular activity" and on contact with "society at large"; the unification of the two, he concluded, would result in "the transformation of the nature of the OGPU or the spread of the methods of the OGPU to the activities of the other above-named organizations, a situation that benefits neither the former organization nor the latter."[56] Bespalov's prescient viewpoint, however, became politically impossible to sustain in December 1930, when Stalin removed Rykov as chair of the USSR Sovnarkom and replaced him with Molotov, his trusted lieutenant. On December 5, 1930, the Politburo ordered the USSR Central Executive Committee to promulgate legislation, made public on December 15, that abolished the NKVD system, transferred the NKVD's penal institutions to the Justice Commissariat, and created republic-level central police administrations that were nominally subordinate to state institutions but were, in reality, directly controlled by the OGPU.[57] With this decision, the decade-long struggle between civil and political police officials was over, settled by Stalin himself to the advantage of the OGPU.

The OGPU Takeover

Stalin's decision to transfer all policing activity to the OGPU prompted immediate changes at the center, as OGPU administrations co-opted existing *militsiia* hierarchies and brought regional administrations under their direct control. The changes at the periphery, however, were more confused. Local OGPU officials underestimated the difficulty of coordinating extensive police bureaucracies at a time of extreme demographic and social mobility, and they struggled to seize control of police activity from local police and soviet administrations. The OGPU officers in charge of the *militsiia* also found, to their surprise, that they were unable to overcome the same problems of minimal training, staff shortages, and poor discipline within the force that had stymied the leadership of the NKVD in the late 1920s. The OGPU succeeded in dismantling much of the centralized bureaucratic structure associated with the NKVD but failed to replace it before the end of the First Five-Year Plan, leaving local *militsiia* administrations with even more latitude to formulate policy and act independently than they had enjoyed during the last years of the NEP.

In the wake of Stalin's intervention in late 1930, the Politburo moved immediately to restructure the existing police administrations, placing the OGPU in direct control of police activity at both the central and local levels. The Politburo concealed the OGPU's control over the *militsiia*, creating republic-level central police administrations that were nominally in control of policing in the individual Soviet republics. In reality, a new Central Police Inspectorate within the OGPU set policy for most of the USSR, with parallel OGPU special police inspectorates in control in several Caucasian and Central Asian republics. This new system also retained token linkages between local *militsiia* administrations and their corresponding soviets, but the Politburo ordered individual officers to subordinate themselves directly to local OGPU administrations rather than soviet officials.[58] For the next two years, two parallel administrative systems controlled local police forces, maintaining a rough division of labor between them: republic-level police administrations coordinated with government agencies and were responsible for budgets, provisioning, and other strictly bureaucratic issues, while the OGPU, out of public view, set all operational policy from the center.

The OGPU officers in charge of the *militsiia* also promulgated a series of regulations in 1931 intended to improve the force itself, often referring to their goal as the "militarization" of the *militsiia* system. To reduce labor turnover, the OGPU standardized pay between localities and increased the provisioning of *militsiia* officers to match that of the military; it also made refusal to serve out the two-year contract signed by all new recruits into a military crime, punishable by military tribunals.[59] Local funding of police administrations, a perennial problem during the NEP, was abolished in a series of steps in 1931 in favor of central budgeting and provisioning for the regular *militsiia* (excluding the Industrial Militsiia), and by the end of the year all personnel and budgetary decisions were in the hands of regional police administrations instead of local soviets.[60] In January 1931, the OGPU unified city-level police administrations in major cities with regional-level administrations in order to eliminate the influence of local soviets and, in the words of one central police report, to prevent the *militsiia* from acting as the "technical assistant to local city, party ["party" is crossed out by hand in the draft of the document], and soviet organizations."[61] Finally, the OGPU created Political Departments within local *militsiia* administrations in January 1931 and launched a secret purge of "anti-Soviet, free-loading, trouble-making," and "kulak elements" within the police that stretched through the end of the year, recruiting replacements from OGPU border guards and internal OGPU troops.[62]

This process of bureaucratic consolidation was largely complete, at least at the center, before the end of the first Five-Year Plan period. In late 1932, the regime used the announcement of the new nationwide internal passport system (discussed below in chapter 3) as an opportune moment to create a single All-Union Central Inspectorate of the Militsiia under the OGPU's overt jurisdiction, abolishing republic-level police administrations and abandoning any pretense of control by local soviets.[63] *Militsiia* chiefs, now openly appointed as assistants to local OGPU bosses, continued to sit on the executive committees of the local soviets and often had a spot on the local Communist Party committee as well, but by the end of the First Five-Year Plan local soviets and party committees had little direct input into the daily activities of the *militsiia*.

Despite these aggressive moves at the center, local OGPU administrations encountered substantial difficulties, and sometimes outright resistance, as they attempted to consolidate the new regime at the periphery after 1930. Local political establishments often balked at the organizational changes handed down by the OGPU; some simply continued to direct local police activity, referring to the legislation promulgated in late 1930 that guaranteed the role of local soviets and republic-level central police administrations in the realm of law enforcement.[64] Regional and local OGPU officials, for their part, found it difficult to push the local soviets out of policing, especially in rural locales. The chain of command from center to periphery, though carefully defined in numerous circulars in 1931 and 1932, barely existed in many areas; a lack of administrative experience among the OGPU officials now in charge of the *militsiia*, poor communication technology, and even a simple lack of paper during the First Five-Year Plan period meant that directives failed to reach local administrations for months, and sometimes not at all.[65]

Centralization also faltered on poor information flow in the reverse direction; central officials complained almost unanimously in 1931 and 1932 that, despite repeated requests, local *militsiia* administrations generally failed to send adequate information to them regarding staffing, local crime trends, and even operational work.[66] Rural precinct inspectors in particular were almost entirely independent after the OGPU takeover, touring large areas of the countryside and administering justice to their own standards.[67] Central OGPU officials could force compliance on these issues only through threats to fire individual officers, a step they were reluctant to take because of the severe staff shortages that continued to plague local *militsiia* administrations in 1931 and 1932.

Problems of funding and staffing within the *militsiia*, in fact, continued unabated after the OGPU takeover, confounding top political police officials, who assumed that such problems were the product of incompetence on the part of the NKVD's outgoing leaders. Although financing for the local police was centralized in 1931, the OGPU leadership quickly realized that, in the chaotic economic context of the First Five-Year Plan, it had little chance of providing even the most basic provisions to local officers, including uniforms and shoes. In February 1931, financial planners in Moscow noted that the central *militsiia* hierarchy failed to supply the local police with automobiles. Some regional and territorial police administrations were so underfunded that they could provide firearms to only 50 to 60 percent of their policemen in 1931.[68] Funding for the finer points of police work was almost nonexistent; the Detective Department in Moscow, for example, complained that its meager budget did not allow for purchasing the foreign-made microscopes necessary to investigate crime scenes.[69] Uniforms were in particularly short supply, especially after the new leadership decided to redesign them in April 1931. The exchange of uniforms, planned for May of that year, so taxed the central provisioning authorities that it was postponed until January 1, 1933, and even then it focused initially on urban police alone; rural officers continued to use old uniforms well into the middle of the decade.[70]

The recruitment and training of new policemen were likewise little better under the OGPU than under the NKVD, in large part due to the demographic and employment pressures caused by the First Five-Year Plan. The *militsiia* continued to suffer from constant shortages of policemen, while the quality of recruits, according to central reports, actually declined after the OGPU takeover. D. V. Usov, the head of the Central Militsiia Administration after May 1931, complained in 1931 that recruits, most of whom came from the countryside, had neither experience nor any military background; being "not particularly valuable for industry or construction trades," they usually "join[ed] the *militsiia* while waiting for better work to appear."[71] Labor turnover continued to be a problem at all levels of the force. Central officials complained that those few policemen who received training, in preparation for careers in the officer corps, were prime candidates for better-paying positions in industrial or Communist Party bureaucracies, and that lower-level policemen often took better-paying jobs in the very same organizations, factories, or department stores at which they had been stationed as policemen.[72] OGPU officials were generally satisfied with their efforts to improve party representation within the *militsiia*, which by 1932 reached almost 25 percent, but they deemed deficient virtually all the other characteristics of the civil police system that they now controlled.[73]

The OGPU leadership complained constantly in 1931 and 1932 that these deficiencies led to disciplinary infractions, poor work habits, and outright corruption at all levels of the *militsiia*. Local officers lacked basic policing skills, especially in the countryside; most low-level policemen had little weapons training, were only vaguely familiar with their specific duties or the characteristics of the areas that they patrolled, and possessed virtually no understanding of Soviet law. The problems of poor performance and disciplinary infractions were particularly pronounced in the industrial *militsiia*, whose officers, like the police in general, often left their posts, fell asleep on duty, or failed to show up for work at all.[74] Some local districts reported levels of administrative sanctions for crimes on duty in 1932 that reached as high as 100 percent of the staff.[75] Central OGPU authorities were particularly concerned with what they termed a lack of "Chekist spirit" within the *militsiia*, manifest in the widespread abuse of prisoners, high levels of crime within the force, drunkenness on the job, and rude behavior toward the public in the process of carrying out daily policing duties.[76]

Top OGPU officials understood such acts as proof of counterrevolutionary tendencies within the force; central reports from 1932 are rife with charges of "anti-Soviet activity" among "class-alien and unfit elements" within the *militsiia*, ranging from simple acts of bribery to organized criminal activity that reached into local soviet and Communist Party administrations.[77] Alarming levels of corruption in the policing system after 1930 underscored the lack of control exercised by central authorities over local policemen in the aftermath of the OGPU's takeover, making it increasingly clear to top police officials that the transition from NKVD to OGPU control had exacerbated, rather than solved, many of the problems of the NEP-era policing system.

For top OGPU officials, such problems were not merely a sign of poor training or a lack of resources; they were a concrete manifestation of the OGPU's initial failure to transform the *militsiia* into a modern, efficient police system. One 1932 OGPU circular made the point clearly, complaining that local *militsiia* officers continued after 1930 to work "by the book" and acted as "passive watchguards [*budochniki*] of the old times or, at best, blind executors of policy," instead of seeing themselves, as did the OGPU officers, as the "master [*khoziain*] of the street."[78] Complaints about corruption and a lack of "Chekist spirit" among civil policemen seem peculiar, coming as they did from the leaders of an organization that was responsible for the mass repression of hundreds of thousands of Soviet citizens. Yet such criticisms were genuine; these OGPU officials believed that the ethos of the Cheka, based on a vision of the incorruptible political police officer in service of the Communist Party and the Revolution, could counteract years, if not decades, of institutional inertia within the civil police system. That such notions were naive, and indeed inaccurate, as they applied to political police officers does not detract from their conceptual power among the OGPU officials who were attempting to create a Soviet policing system capable of completing the Revolution begun in 1928.

Covert Policing and Crime Prevention under the OGPU

OGPU officials brought to civil policing in 1930 a coherent vision of reform, one that took as its chief goal the prevention of criminal activity through the surveillance of suspect populations and the preemptive removal of "criminal elements" from society. The new leadership of the *militsiia* focused its efforts on improving the covert policing activities of local detective departments, attempting in particular to create widespread networks of informants, within both the criminal milieu and the population at large, who could assist detectives in scrutinizing the population.[79] Attention to covert policing, in the minds of OGPU officers, would transform what they viewed as a passive NEP-era policing system into a constructive institution—one engaged in preventive policing and, ultimately, in actively shaping the Soviet population itself. OGPU officials patterned these reforms on contemporary European policing practices, but they also based them on their own practices regarding the suppression of political opponents and organized crime in the 1920s. Local *militsiia* administrations, on the contrary, had little experience in the 1920s with covert investigation, surveillance of the population, and preventive policing, and they were utterly unprepared for the changes forced upon them by the OGPU. As a result, these reforms failed in the early 1930s, and the OGPU was unable to create a functional covert civil police system at any time in the era before World War II.

The OGPU concentrated its efforts in 1931 on detectives, attempting to remake them into expert investigators who used covert tactics but dealt with nonpolitical crimes. The OGPU leadership abolished the detective departments as separate bureaucratic entities in 1931, renaming them operational departments and stressing their place within local police administrations. The OGPU also transferred a substantial number of political policemen to the new departments, ensuring that virtually all the chiefs of the new operational departments were also OGPU officers.[80] This change represented the culmination of Feliks Dzerzhinsky's drive to transfer control of the detective departments to the political police in the 1920s, but it was also an attempt to erase what OGPU officials saw as an unnecessary division between investigative and policing practices within the *militsiia* as a whole. Detectives were expected to coordinate their covert work with the daily patrols carried out by lower-ranking policemen, mimicking the investigative practices of the OGPU.[81]

At the same time, the OGPU leadership created an entirely new hierarchical structure for operational departments, one that corresponded to the structure of the OGPU and that reflected central understandings of particularly threatening categories of crime. At the USSR and regional levels, the Operational Department handled active investigations of major crimes, and a Secret Informational Department coordinated general undercover surveillance of crime-ridden areas, such as train stations, criminal "lairs" (*pritony*), hotels, and open air markets. A Scientific-Technical Department gathered and analyzed information sent in from localities. At the center, the Operational Department was further divided into three subgroups, each of which coordinated police responses to what were deemed important categories of crime: violent, organized crime and banditry; major economic crimes involving state property; and petty property crimes committed by "professional" criminal elements. Each subgroup overlapped substantially with the corresponding OGPU departments, reflecting the tendency of OGPU officials to view violent and especially organized civil crime as "anti-Soviet" activity by the early 1930s.[82] At lower levels of the police hierarchy, the operational departments, now directly subordinate to *militsiia* chiefs, investigated all three areas of crime and generated recommendations for crime-fighting tactics in their jurisdictions.[83]

The OGPU leadership backed up these institutional changes with a major change in covert policing tactics, ordering local operational departments to create networks of undercover informants to assist in the investigation and prevention of crime. Informants were new to the civil police of the 1930s; few officers, save the OGPU functionaries who were transferred to operational departments, had any experience with them at all.[84] The detective departments in a handful of major cities in the 1920s maintained a small number of informants, but reports from the early 1930s unanimously claim that the NEP-era *militsiia* made little use of these informants, in part because detectives viewed them as a Tsarist or bourgeois tactic that had no place in a socialist policing system.[85] The OGPU, to the contrary, displayed no such scruples, ordering detectives to create a three-tier system of informants, patterned on the practices of the political police, that engaged both average citizens and suspects themselves in the surveillance of the criminal milieu. The most common category, that of "general" informants, was organized in groups of five to ten individuals and reported on specific locations such as public parks, markets, and major department stores. Detectives generally identified a single individual, termed a "resident," as a liaison, and maintained contact only with that person rather than with all members of the group. Although technically volunteers, residents received monetary rewards when their information proved particularly valuable.[86]

"Special" informants, by comparison, followed particular groups of professional criminals, uncovered evidence for important crimes that had already been committed, and monitored the criminal underworld. Detectives maintained direct, secret contact with these informants and paid for their information. Although OGPU officials initially assumed, quite correctly, that detectives lacked the expertise to cultivate useful contacts with the criminal informants, the OGPU's experience had demonstrated the value of "double agents" within the surveillance system in the 1920s, and by 1932 OGPU officials ordered detectives to recruit freely from within the criminal milieu, allowing these informants to remain at large as long as they provided useful information.[87] Finally, detectives recruited "assistant" informants from Communist Party or state officials, members of the Communist Youth League, and other official groups, who were expected to report any useful information they obtained directly to local police administrations. This category of informants provoked substantial disagreement among top police officials in the early 1930s, because many expected such individuals to inform as a matter of course, without formal status as an informant. By late 1932, the Operational Department eliminated the category of "assistant" informants altogether.[88]

Information gathered through covert policing activity was useless without the ability to collect it and make it legible to central authorities, and hence the OGPU created extensive reporting systems that were designed to funnel raw data, and the criminological implications thereof, directly to

Moscow. Detectives were ordered to maintain files of their work with informants, organized into card catalogs that contained records of each transaction and summaries of the information gathered. The detectives forwarded compilations of this information to the center, at least in theory, every three days, focusing on areas prone to criminal activity and on the activities of recidivists who they deemed likely to reoffend. This kind of enforced information flow from periphery to center mirrored the reporting system of the OGPU itself, but it also served as a means to ensure that individual detectives refrained from establishing personal and corrupt relationships with criminal informants.[89] For the OGPU, the connection between covert policing, informants, and information flow to the center was the key to the entire reformulation of the Soviet policing system in which they were engaged; informants were not only a crucial source of contact between the police and the population but also the source of knowledge about the criminal milieu itself as well as the direct lever that would allow operational departments to repress the most threatening categories of violent, anti-Soviet crime.[90]

Restructuring of the Detective Department after 1930 was relatively successful in Moscow and a handful of other major Soviet cities, but in most areas it was either resisted by the detectives themselves or, more often, proved beyond their abilities. Local OGPU officials and detectives misunderstood the overall sense of the reforms, moving instead to amalgamate civil and political police at the periphery and expand the covert operations of the OGPU itself into the realm of civil crime. D. V. Usov, the head of the Central Militsiia Administration, warned police chiefs against this tendency during a 1931 meeting of the leaders of regional police administrations; he insisted that the ongoing reforms were meant to separate, rather than merge, the work of the OGPU and the *militsiia*, and he demanded that local police chiefs maintain a conceptual and practical distinction between the two. "Our general task in this matter," he stated bluntly, "is to make the agencies of the *militsiia* into Chekist agencies in essence, Chekist in spirit, in methods of work, in forms of work, but not in any sense to replace the agencies of the GPU with the *militsiia*."[91]

Despite such clarity of vision from the center, the local police generally took steps that corresponded instead to particularly local understandings of Soviet policing during the First Five-Year Plan period. OGPU officials often treated detectives as technical or administrative staff, ordering them to handle the bookkeeping duties of OGPU officers rather than creating their own informant networks. Conversely, particularly energetic chiefs of the operational departments, who were usually OGPU officers of long standing, used the departments to repress peasant resistance and other forms of "political" crime, easing demands on local OGPU administrations.[92] In many cases, OGPU officers simply ignored covert work in the *militsiia* altogether after 1930, especially in rural areas; as late as 1932, central officials complained that many regional OGPU administrations made little effort to supervise *militsiia* operations at all.[93]

The informant networks created by detectives suffered from many of the same problems. Local detectives demonstrated little enthusiasm for complex surveillance systems and the extensive paperwork they entailed, often taking months to create even the most rudimentary networks of informants. Even in Moscow, according to one 1932 report, informant networks "with rare exceptions are in a poor state and in several districts are completely nonexistent"; district police chiefs assigned the task to inexperienced detectives who "likewise did nothing, as one would expect."[94] The police in the Leningrad region set up informant networks only in mid-1932, and they generally limited their undercover activity to placing informants in major state economic institutions within the city itself; informant networks were expanded into the collective farm system only in conjunction with the infamous August 1932 law on the theft of state property (see chapter 3 below).[95] Once undercover networks were created, they performed far below the levels expected by the OGPU leadership. Local detectives often set up informant networks on paper but made little effort to integrate them into daily policing practice, and most informants provided little or no useful information to the police.[96] Even those detectives who created informant networks failed to use them to prevent crime or to identify potential offenders, as demanded by the center; most simply used them to aid investigations of crimes that had already been committed, a practice that made sense to local police but vitiated the entire point of the system in the minds of top police officials.[97]

The failures of the OGPU's plans to create informant networks within the *militsiia* promoted a shift in focus in 1932 and 1933, as local police administrations began to create systems of informants that relied not on voluntary contact between police and population but on much smaller groups of paid, full-time police agents. Local police administrations, under pressure to create informant networks and to arrest "professional" members of the criminal underworld, began to turn to paid, full-time informants in late 1932. Central officials acquiesced to suggestions made by the local police that paid informants were the best way to solicit information from within the population and, by mid-1933, endorsed this system over the idea of voluntary informant networks. Even so, relatively few paid informants worked in the civil police system in the early to mid-1930s.[98] The *militsiia* leadership simply did not have the funding to blanket the country with paid agents, nor could it find enough qualified cadres to implement effectively the small system of undercover policing that did exist.[99] Local police administrations sent reports to the center touting the kind of successes that they knew were expected of them, yet central OGPU authorities had little difficulty discerning the true nature of the situation: local detectives were unable to create the kind of preventive policing system envisioned by OGPU officials when they took over the *militsiia*.[100]

Policing the Street: Precinct Inspectors and Popular Assistance under the OGPU

At the same time that the new OGPU leadership attempted to reform the undercover operations of the *militsiia*, it introduced a full-scale revision of urban policing systems. These changes focused on daily police patrols, moving officers out of the stationary posts from which they surveyed the population in the 1920s and encouraging them to become part of the communities they policed. OGPU officials attempted to invigorate popular participation in daily policing practices as well, building on the experiences of the recently abolished NKVD. Like the reforms of covert activity, the OGPU's plans for a new model of outward policing faltered almost immediately; poor training, a lack of qualified officers, and a lack of interest in volunteers among most urban policemen doomed these reforms to failure, in some instances within months of their introduction.

The OGPU leadership began to reorganize the outward patrolling system as soon as it took over the *militsiia*, dividing major cities into precincts and assigning a "precinct inspector" (*uchastkovyi inspektor*) to each. These urban precincts, which covered thirty to thirty-five apartment buildings, were small enough that an inspector could patrol the entire territory on foot each day.[101] OGPU officials intended this Soviet version of the European "constable" to change the nature of civil policing in Soviet cities, eliminating the division between police and population that was so prevalent during the NEP period. The OGPU instituted no comparable reform of the rural police system; itinerant rural policeman were renamed "inspectors" but left in charge of an area that was far too large to allow for more than a handful of visits to a given location each year.

Urban precinct inspectors also maintained small networks of informants, chosen from trustworthy residents and low-level municipal employees, especially apartment stewards (*dvorniki*). These stewards had been uniformed, paid officials of the Ministry of Internal Affairs in the Tsarist period, and NEP-era *militsiia* officers resisted using them as informants for that reason. OGPU officers, on the contrary, viewed stewards as a major source of information in the 1920s, and the OGPU officials in charge of the *militsiia* after 1930 ordered the local police to cultivate relations with them.[102] These informant networks, though separate from the networks maintained by detectives, had the same primary goal: to make it possible for inspectors to identify "criminal elements" and remove them from their jurisdictions before they were able to commit crimes—an approach generally termed, as in the second epigraph at the start of this chapter, "preventive" or "prophylactic" work.[103] The urban precinct inspector, in the minds of top OGPU officials, unified the investigative and patrolling functions of the *militsiia* and served as a point of connection between the daily activities of the *militsiia* and the OGPU.[104]

OGPU officials reinforced the precinct system by restructuring all forms of popular participation in urban policing in 1931 and 1932. OGPU officials condemned the variegated nature of popular participation in the 1920s and the utopianism of Tolmachev's "militia system," but they understood the need for additional officers in major cities, as well as the ideological affinities between such schemes and the ethos of social activism that pervaded the First Five-Year Plan. The police leadership reorganized existing systems of participation, beginning by subordinating volunteers to individual police officers in mid-1931 and concluding with the creation of a uniform set of "Brigades for Assistance to the Militsiia" in 1932. Like volunteers in the 1920s, brigades patrolled those streets and public areas known for petty criminal activity, but they worked under the direct control of *militsiia* officers. Brigade members were authorized to use force if necessary to halt crimes in progress and to apprehend offenders; the OGPU leadership even made provisions to issue weapons to them in particularly demanding situations. OGPU officials also expected volunteers to coordinate with detectives and precinct inspectors, maintaining contact with apartment stewards and carrying out their own covert work to prevent crime.[105] The Assistance Brigades were particularly important in Moscow,

where the police and Communist Party officials widely publicized a campaign to bring the number of members up to 30,000 by the end of 1932.[106]
The brigades, in the minds of top OGPU officials, were not simply a
means to enhance popular participation in policing. Like precinct inspectors, they were a way to expand the reach of covert surveillance systems
and to integrate police presence on the streets with the kind of preventive
work that top police officials believed was the hallmark of modern policing systems.

Neither the urban precinct inspectors nor the Assistance Brigades met
these expectations. The inspectors, who were generally far less qualified
than detectives, found it particularly difficult to cope with the complex tasks
of cultivating informants in the chaotic context of the early 1930s. One inspector from the city of Sverdlovsk complained to a regional conference of
OGPU and *militsiia* officials that undercover work was appealing but impossible, given the existing work conditions: "It is necessary to give the Inspectors the possibility to work normally. We don't have separate rooms in
which to conduct our most secret work—there are no theft-proof lockers,
there is nowhere for us to store our secret information. On top of that, we've
piled up a large quantity of inquires, roughly 270, and there is nobody to
investigate them, no officers; staff positions are vacant."[107] Local officers
complained that work with informants was new to them and that, with the
exception of occasional conferences, central authorities took little interest in
it. The tendency of detectives to treat inspectors as extra hands for mundane
work compounded the overlap between the two types of officers. In some
areas, understaffed detective administrations even turned over some of the
responsibility for their own informant networks to precinct inspectors, much
to the chagrin of central police officials.[108] These problems forced central
police officials to jettison the goal of making precinct inspectors into qualified covert policemen who used the same tactics as detectives in the pursuit
of preventive work. Instead, within two to three years after the OGPU takeover, the precinct inspectors had sunk to the level of the urban officers they
had replaced; they were midrank administrative officers who patrolled the
city streets, higher in stature than regular patrolmen but unable to carry out
effective covert work of any kind.

The Assistance Brigade system faced many of the same difficulties.
Central officials complained in 1932 and 1933 that local Communist Party
and trade union organizations paid little attention to the task of recruiting brigade members and that local police administrations consistently
undervalued their utility.[109] A major police report on the work of the brigades,

prepared in 1934, argued that the institution was completely incapable of assisting *militsiia* administrations in any meaningful way. Local police conducted only "campaign-like" work with volunteers, recruiting large numbers of participants but failing to make them a regular part of police practice; more than 40 percent of registered brigade members did not participate in daily practical policing work at all. Worse yet, according to the report, local brigade cells were often infiltrated with people deemed "socially alien" or "criminal elements," including individuals with previous criminal convictions. Investigators found that brigade members in several districts in the Moscow region illegally arrested citizens and stripped them of money and valuables; the members reportedly colluded with gangs of thieves and hooligans to extort money from city residents, especially at open air marketplaces.[110] By roughly 1934, the local and central police generally agreed that the Assistance Brigades were ineffective and, in many cases, detrimental to the task of maintaining public order.

As a result of these failures, the OGPU leadership jettisoned the idea of integrating popular participation into daily policing in any substantial way and began to rely on more professionalized forms of "popular" assistance. This transition emerged first in Moscow, where the district police administrations organized teams of volunteers to patrol the city streets after dark, in groups of two or three, as early as March 1931.[111] By April, 150 men patrolled the streets at night, and by July the patrols had grown to 367 members, 80 percent of whom were recruited from the ranks of demobilized OGPU border guards. These Night Patrol Teams (Komandy Nochnoi Okhrani), as they came to be called, were divided into seven divisions in Moscow, six of which patrolled the territories corresponding to detective administrations; the seventh responded to emergency situations in the city as a whole.[112]

In 1932, the Moscow police organized similar groups, termed "socialist auxiliaries," to aid precinct inspectors in their daily patrols of city streets. These auxiliaries worked under more concretely defined regulations than did Assistance Brigade members and exercised many of the powers of inspectors, with the exception of covert duties, which were never passed along to them.[113] Both types of police assistants were paid for their efforts, making them essentially part-time professional policemen rather than volunteers. The Night Patrols in particular were touted as examples of popular participation in policing, yet in reality they were usually hired detachments of demilitarized soldiers, former OGPU internal troops, or off-duty policemen. The Night Patrols were not without their problems, but they proved to be the most successful of these localized forms of policing assistance in Moscow, and the city police administration enthusiastically endorsed their continued place in the policing system in the mid-1930s.[114]

By roughly 1934, this trend had spread to most major Soviet cities. Brigades continued to exist throughout the decade, but central police officials left the supervision of brigades to individual officers, who generally paid attention to them only when they were required to do so during specific campaigns. In 1935, for example, local police focused significant attention on the brigades during an aggressive campaign against hooliganism (see chapter 4 below), but they continued to view the brigades as both corrupt and inefficient, and they quickly settled back into a pattern of apathy once the campaign was over. By the mid-1930s, the police paid only cursory attention to the brigades and concentrated instead on tactics that they deemed more efficient.[115]

The Assistance Brigades and the precinct inspectors were closely interconnected aspects of the OGPU's attempt to reform the overt Soviet policing system after its takeover of the *militsiia* in late 1930. Volunteerism, for top OGPU officials, was less a goal in and of itself than a means to engage the Soviet police with society at large, to erase the division between state and society, and to make information flow effortlessly from the latter to the former. State violence in the era of the First Five-Year Plan was hardly the exclusive prerogative of the police, but the kind of social activism that animated most other areas of administration during this era never ran deep in the institutional culture of the OGPU. None of the utopian visions of decentralized policing and volunteerism that had emerged in the revolutionary period, and that had persisted in muted form throughout the NEP period, survived the OGPU's takeover of the *militsiia*. OGPU officials continued to pay a certain amount of lip service to these ideas after the end of the First Five-Year Plan, but a genuine emphasis on volunteerism disappeared rather quickly after 1932, leaving the local police to create what they deemed to be more effective methods of "preventive" policing in urban areas.

Surveillance and Geographic Mobility in the Wake of Collectivization and Dekulakization

The initial waves of dekulakization were well under way by the time the OGPU took over the *militsiia*, but top OGPU officials had hardly begun to understand the implications of the forced resettlement of hundreds of thousands of peasant families for the Soviet policing system. The flood of peasants fleeing the upheavals in the countryside stretched thin the fabric of urban life in major Soviet cities; urban crime became more rampant, more violent, and in the minds of police more threatening to "socialist" norms of public order. Crime in the countryside was on the rise as well, especially cattle theft, rural hooliganism, and banditry. Central police and Communist Party officials understood many of these crimes as overt resistance to the policies of the Stalinist regime, pointing to the role of "kulaks" and "bourgeois elements" in those crimes deemed most "dangerous." For the local police, however, concentrating on the role of "kulaks" or other "class-alien elements" provided little explanatory power. It was plainly evident to all policemen that the burgeoning levels of crime and disorder evident across the USSR in the early 1930s were the result of the social upheavals caused by forced industrialization and collectivization, rather than the work of "kulak elements" bent on opposing the Soviet system.

The police responded to this conceptual conundrum by drawing on familiar ideas about the political nature of certain criminal acts and about the inherently "dangerous" nature of certain population cohorts. The application of these concepts, however, was shaped by the extreme geographic mobility characteristic of the era of Stalin's "revolution from above." Top OGPU officials combined an analysis of crime based on social class with one based on the danger posed to Soviet society by the mobility of "dangerous" individuals; "criminal elements" and "socially dangerous elements" became sociologically defined population cohorts, their social identities as essential and immutable as those of "kulaks" or "workers" no matter what their physical location in the Soviet polity. Once this conceptual connection between "social danger" and geographic mobility was made, local and central police moved to control the mobility of "socially dangerous" populations through overlapping systems of surveillance and registration. As the era of the First Five-Year Plan came to a close, the drive to identify, categorize, and "fix in place" (*zafiksirovat'*) populations deemed "socially dangerous" became a defining aspect of the Stalinist policing system.

When the OGPU took over the civil policing system, its top officers brought with them a coherent set of explanations of the nature and causes of those types of crime deemed particularly threatening by the regime. This set of concepts diverged substantially from the ideas promoted by

professional criminologists in the 1920s. OGPU officials were openly con-
temptuous of the premier criminological research organization in the USSR,
the Institute for the Study of Criminality, which was part of the NKVD in
the 1920s and became associated with the Justice Commissariat after
1930. Top OGPU officials claimed that the institute concentrated too
much on individual and psychological influences on crime, ignoring the
political nature of certain crimes and underestimating the need to isolate
offenders from Soviet society. Most local officers, in addition, found that
criminological schemas based solely on social class, an approach prevalent in Soviet criminology in the 1920s, provided them with little guidance for predicting the identities of "criminal elements" and controlling
those populations that they deemed prone to criminal activity.[116] Once the
OGPU reorganized the operational departments of the *militsiia* system,
top police officials generally ignored the institute altogether, relying instead on detectives, many of whom were OGPU officers, for explanations
of crime and policy recommendations alike.[117] The criminological schemas that served as the basis for police activity in the early Stalin period
hence emerged not from within the legal or criminological profession but
from within the police system itself.

The approach to crime brought to the *militsiia* by the OGPU concentrated, at one level, on a relatively simple definition of the political nature
of certain crimes. Top OGPU officials encouraged local police officers to
seek political meanings in several categories of violent crime, especially
rural crimes that were committed by "kulak elements" or other "class-
alien elements." This explanation was most pronounced in the OGPU's
responses to crimes that had provoked conflict between the political and
civil police in the late 1920s, such as crimes in office, banditry, and the
theft of state property. Given that OGPU officials had pressed before 1930
for control over all policing of banditry, for instance, it is not surprising
that those officials in 1931 and 1932 explicitly instructed the local police
to seek political undertones in virtually all instances of violent rural
crime.[118]

Yet the problems faced by the local police in 1931 and 1932 greatly
exceeded the explanatory capacity of a criminology focused exclusively
on political crime. Top local police officials more often pointed to the
issue of geographic mobility, and in particular to the role of populations
of vagrant recidivist criminals (*gastrolery*, literally "touring" criminals) in
the most worrisome categories of criminal activity. Reports compiled for
central police officials identified "vagrant criminal elements" as the key

cause of several kinds of violent or organized crime, including swindling, armed robbery, and major thefts of state property—usually with the added assumption that such individuals were likely dekulakized peasants or "former people." For the local police, however, the sociological origin of these populations was less important than their identity as a "vagrant recidivist," and the latter identity was as essential as the former.

The importance of mobility became particularly clear in discussions in the early 1930s of "swindling" (*moshenichestvo*), a crime defined as the act of deceiving, cheating, or stealing from an individual or the state, often by impersonating a government functionary. Many swindling cases were particularly local, such as cases of peasants obtaining blank Communist Party cards and distributing them to friends who could use them to gain access to rationed consumer goods. Central police officials were particularly concerned, however, with cases in which their failure to track suspect individuals allowed criminals to roam freely across the USSR, committing the same kinds of criminal acts over and over again.[119] The police insisted that such offenders, once captured, almost always turned out to be criminal recidivists with numerous previous arrests and convictions who had simply managed to hide their identities by constantly moving around the country. "Professional" crimes like qualified theft—major robberies of banks or other state institutions, often by means of planned break-ins using technical means such as tunneling or lock picking—were almost always attributed by police to "vagrant recidivists." The police believed that these categories of crime were the work of a finite group of recidivist criminals that could be controlled by increasing both hierarchical and lateral flows of information within the police system in order to find these touring criminals as they moved around the USSR.[120]

OGPU officials in the 1920s were already prone to conceiving of certain sections of the population as inherently "dangerous," but such populations were generally deemed dangerous because of their potential political unreliability or because they were part of a relatively small cohort of recidivist or professional criminals. In the early 1930s, to the contrary, OGPU officials began to identify all individuals who committed crimes as "criminal elements," positing an essential social identity that overrode the identities of "workers" or "peasants." Usov clearly pointed to this issue in 1931, exhorting his police chiefs to categorize individuals as "criminal elements" rather than workers or peasants: "We know that industrial workers, not fake workers [*lzhe-rabochii*], don't carry out acts of banditry or speculation, reselling of goods [for profit], etc."[121] He knew full well that this was not the case, because numerous reports on crime in the early 1930s that were prepared for the center showed that workers in urban areas represented substantial portions of those arrested for petty crimes, especially speculation and hooliganism. Yet this idea allowed central police officials to continue to address the issue of social class while devising a practical response to the problem of "criminal elements" who were impossible to identify in any way other than by their criminal actions.

This conception of crime retained none of the idea of rehabilitation popular in the 1920s among justice, NKVD, and even certain OGPU officials; nor could it possibly explain all instances of crime in the USSR. It did, however, allow top police officials to begin to construct a set of explanations for social disorder that maintained a focus on social class and, at the same time, provided local police officers with an explanation of crime that resonated with their experiences regarding vagrant and "socially dangerous" criminal cohorts.

If crime serious enough to threaten the stability of the Stalinist economic and social systems was the product of mobile populations of incorrigible criminals, the solution, for top OGPU officials, was clear: find ways to halt the movement of "criminal elements" altogether. Carrying out this task was not simple, because the issue touched on several related problems in Soviet administration in the early 1930s. Extensive systems of population registration and surveillance of suspect individuals already existed in 1930, both within the OGPU and the *militsiia*, but they were highly inefficient and overlapped in ways that made it virtually impossible for police to track suspect individuals as they moved across the USSR. The police in major urban areas maintained a system of required residence permits (*propiska*), which was created in 1925 largely to protect urban welfare systems but which served as the basis for later attempts to control migration into Soviet cities.[122] *Militsiia* administrations also maintained extensive but disorganized registration systems that targeted ex-convicts and suspects in a given area, usually organized into card files containing information on individuals released from penal institutions, known recidivists, and wanted criminals still at large.[123]

Finally, both the *militsiia* and the OGPU maintained registration systems in the 1920s of individuals sentenced to banishment from major urban areas (*vysylka*) or to exile to a specific location (*ssylka*), placing these individuals under "open" (as opposed to covert) surveillance and, in the case of banished individuals, tracking their mobility to ensure that they did not enter restricted urban areas. Although the exile of convicts to a specific location presented little conceptual difficulty for the local police, the punishment of banishment from the most important cities in the USSR ("Minus Six" and, later in the 1920s, "Minus Ten") was more problematic. The police allowed banished individuals to choose their place of residence from nonrestricted cities; these individuals were then instructed to travel to their place of banishment and report to the local police administration. Local police found it virtually impossible to maintain any sort of accurate count of banished populations in the late NEP period, even before the explosion of geographic mobility caused by the First Five-Year Plan.[124]

The mass expropriation of peasant households after 1930, and the resulting surge in demographic mobility across the USSR, wrecked the already limited ability of the local police to track the migration of suspect individuals, provoking substantial consternation among top OGPU officials. Escapees, especially individuals who had escaped from the disorganized systems of exile and banishment, were a particular concern because they were nearly invisible to existing registration systems. Central police officials complained in early 1931 that individuals who escaped from places of exile and banishment often returned to their former places of residence but were not discovered by local officers until they committed several crimes.[125] The OGPU attempted to respond to this problem in February 1931 by creating a single institution in Moscow to coordinate all populations of exiles across the USSR; local police administrations sent to the center estimates of the exile populations that their areas could handle, and in return they received authorization to exile prisoners to specific locations.[126] Such a system was understandably a headache for local police, who evaded it as much as possible and continued to send exiles to whatever region suited them. It also did little to control the escape and flight of exiled and banished individuals, who had no trouble disappearing along the way to their places of incarceration.[127]

One possible response to these problems, long used by the OGPU, was simply to lengthen the sentences of individuals in suspect categories. In February 1931, the OGPU requested the right to impose additional extrajudicial sentences of exile or terms in labor camps, using OGPU troikas or the Special Board, to "kulak, former traders, former landowners, and other nonlaboring elements" who completed terms in labor camps.[128] The Communist Party leadership acquiesced in mid-1931, giving the OGPU the right to subject dekulakized peasants who had completed their terms of exile or hard labor to an additional five-year term of exile.[129] As we will see, this step was the first of a series of progressively harsher restrictions on the geographic mobility of ex-convict populations in the 1930s.

Such drastic steps were necessary, according to the OGPU, because of the weakness of the registration systems that were intended to control the mobility of these ex-convict populations. One March 1931 circular complained that local practices were so chaotic that the center was unsure which local police administrations even maintained registration systems.[130] The registration of offenders was made more difficult by the rapid expansion in 1930 and 1931 of the number of areas prohibited to individuals sentenced to banishment (*vysylka*); by September 1931, the "Minus Six" system had grown to thirty-seven cities, plus the entire Crimean Republic, the North Caucasus Territory, the Moscow and Leningrad regions, and all areas in contact with the Soviet border.[131]

In 1931, the OGPU launched a major reform of registration and surveillance, building on existing *militsiia* practices as well as on their own experiences with the surveillance of politically suspect individuals. The OGPU created a uniform nationwide registration system, administered by both the political and civil police, which tracked all suspect populations but focused on recidivist criminals still at large. Registration was based on a standardized set of card catalogs, maintained by newly created registration bureaus within local police administrations, which contained entries on every person in a given administrative area with past criminal convictions, current sentences, demonstrated recidivist tendencies, or connections to the criminal underworld. Registration cards were alphabetized and cross-referenced to a card catalog of fingerprints, if local police administrations had the expertise to maintain them, and to an additional catalog of criminal aliases (*klichki*).[132] Local registration officials compiled information regarding "well-known vagrant criminals" for inclusion in centralized catalogs maintained by the Detective Department in Moscow; central registration administrations in turn distributed lists of particularly important vagrant criminals to all local police administrations, which checked the identities of local criminals against the central lists.[133] OGPU officials imagined that a constant process of local registration and central compilation would keep these lists current and provide the local police with the information necessary to uncover threatening populations of mobile criminals as they attempted to move about the USSR.[134]

The ultimate goal of this registration system was not simply to identify escaped convicts but also to make the criminal milieu itself transparent to the police. In the words of the resolution of a conference of detectives in

1931, the new system was intended to track "the more socially dangerous leaders of the criminal underworld on a republic-wide scale in order to control the location and movement of such individuals" and "to fix in place [*zafiksirovat'*, also to record] recidivists, as the most dangerous part of the criminal world."[135] The idea of "fixing" populations—identifying them and preventing their geographic mobility—was central to police discussions of the registration system in the early 1930s. OGPU officials specifically spoke in terms of putting criminal populations "on the registry" (*na uchet*), a term that duplicated the surveillance practices of the OGPU regarding politically suspect populations.[136] The new registration system, in the minds of the OGPU officers, unified covert surveillance practices with the mass purges of criminal elements that were already widespread in police work at the beginning of the 1930s, and hence they served as the focal point for nearly all policing activity in a given administrative area.

As with many of the OGPU's reforms of the *militsiia*, plans for this extensive registration system were wildly optimistic and completely out of touch with the capacities of the local police administrations. Registration bureaus were severely understaffed, even according to plan; the entire staff of the bureau for a city with a population of more than 200,000 was nine, including two inspectors to deal with the catalog and two fingerprinting experts, whereas cities with 100,000 residents boasted only two registration officers.[137] Shortages of staff, especially of officers sufficiently qualified to administer these complex registration procedures, made it difficult for most local police administrations to keep accurate catalogs or make use of the "most-wanted" lists provided by the central authorities. The Moscow regional Detective Department was the only police administration in the nation with anything that approached the kind of global registration system that the OGPU had intended to create in the early 1930s. Coordination between administrations across the USSR was virtually nonexistent.[138]

Such difficulties notwithstanding, the creation of new registration systems in the early 1930s shaped the evolution of Soviet policing in several important ways. The initial goal of this new registration system was not simply to increase pressure on a particular group of criminals but also to imbue the police system with an ethos of rationalization and efficiency. At the beginning of the 1930s, the OGPU leadership understood the registration system as a way to tie together all police work, to make information flow more easily from one *militsiia* administration to another, and to connect covert activity with the outward patrolling undertaken by police officers on the streets. The stress on registration and surveillance also strengthened the tendency of the local police to attempt to control categories of suspect elements rather than specific criminal behaviors. As we have seen, many of the reforms of the *militsiia* implemented by the OGPU after 1930 failed because they were incompatible with the institutional realities of Soviet policing. Registration systems, on the contrary, were compatible with local policing practices and, at the same time, reinforced preconceptions at the center regarding the causes of crime and social disorder. These compatibilities ensured that the registration and surveillance of suspect population cohorts would become one of the most important aspects of the Stalinist policing system in the years to come.

Conclusion

The takeover of the *militsiia* by the OGPU in late 1930 indeed brought "the methods of the OGPU" firmly into the realm of nonpolitical crime, but this change had already begun during the NEP's last years. Civil policing in the late 1920s took on the contours of the OGPU project, focusing on the extrajudicial repression of entire cohorts as the basic approach to maintaining public order. Although many in the NKVD leadership resisted the expansion of the OGPU into the policing of nonpolitical crimes before 1930, they embraced the rough-and-ready criminology promoted by top OGPU officials and engaged in their own campaigns to identify and repress "criminal elements."

Despite these strong continuities, Stalin's massive collectivization and dekulakization drives revolutionized the nature of Soviet policing. Local practices and central policies interacted in a reciprocal manner during these campaigns; the local police brought their own approaches to the repression of "socially dangerous elements" to the dekulakization drive, while the center's demands for the "elimination of kulaks as a class" encouraged the local police to expand their relatively limited definitions of "social danger" to include, by 1932, potentially every form of serious crime and social disorder. The campaigns associated with the First Five-Year Plan also helped to obliterate the boundaries between political and civil crime, and political and civil policing. Local police administrations, under the tutelage of OGPU officers, increasingly viewed broad categories of crime as essentially "anti-Soviet" activity, regardless of the social background of the perpetrators, and turned to the "methods of the OGPU"—surveillance, categorization, and extrajudicial repression—to control them.

That such trends contradicted the reform efforts of the OGPU in the realm of regular policing after 1930 is not surprising. The OGPU, despite its authority within the Soviet Communist Party/state at the beginning of the 1930s, was unable to reverse years, if not decades, of institutional inertia within the Soviet civil police system; nor was it able to overcome the pressures of Stalin's "revolution from above" as it attempted to create a new regular Soviet policing system. Top OGPU officials engaged in their own sort of utopian planning in 1930 and 1931, attempting to create an omnipresent system of both overt and covert interaction between the modernized Soviet police and a conceptually "fixed" citizenry that would make the population instantaneously legible to the state. Such schemes, however, were far beyond the capacity of even the OGPU in the early 1930s. Failures were most evident in the areas of covert activity and prophylactic work among the local police, which together formed the crux of the OGPU's vision for a modern Soviet policing system, but they were visible in virtually every aspect of the organizational and bureaucratic changes implemented by the OGPU after 1930.

The failures of the specific plans promoted by the OGPU in 1931 and 1932, however, did not dull the overall effects of the concepts themselves on police work after the end of the First Five-Year Plan. The criminological ideas that emerged within the police system before 1932, including the focus on the inherent social danger of specific criminal "contingents" and the connection between geographic mobility and crime, became the core of a quintessentially Stalinist approach to understanding and controlling crime after 1932. These ideas survived in new models for the registration and surveillance of suspect populations—models that did not necessarily translate into effective policing practice in the first years of the decade but that resonated with virtually every aspect of both civil and political policing practices and hence quickly moved to the center of daily policing activity. As during the dekulakization campaign, local conceptual models and central fears regarding the nature and effects of crime reinforced one another, ensuring that preventive policing tactics that relied on the overt practices of registration and "open" surveillance, rather than on the covert practices like informants and denunciation, would quickly become the most important aspect of police work in the USSR. These models of policing emerged within the "revolution from above" itself, becoming the basis of the Stalinist policing system for the rest of the 1930s.

3

The New Order, 1932–1934

Without these (and similar) draconian *socialist* measures, it will be impossible to establish a new *social* discipline, and without this discipline—it will be impossible to defend and to strengthen our *new* order.
  —Stalin to Lazar Kaganovich, July 20, 1932, outlining measures that would become the August 7, 1932, law on the theft of state property[1]

We have to battle against kulaks, against speculators, against thieves, against those antisocial elements who, when it comes to their own private property—even if it's a single button, any sort of trifle, but their own—they look after it, they will throttle anybody in order to protect their little bit of personal property. But state property— . . . a horse, factory machinery—that's worth nothing, that's "not mine," it's "public." Let it break down. That planted tree isn't mine—go ahead and ruin it, pull it out by the roots. The train car—it's not mine, break it, break it! . . . Comrades, this kind of person is an inveterate class enemy, even if he hides in the skin of a member of our class. No, comrades, even if he has wormed his way in among the peasantry, among the collective farmers, among the working class, he is our enemy, because he is ruining everything for which we have spilled our blood. He is ruining our society, our socialist society, our proletarian workers', peasants', and people's property.
  —Lazar Kaganovich, explaining the significance of the August 1932 law on the theft of state property to an assembly of policemen in Moscow, August 11, 1932[2]

By the end of 1931, the "revolution from above" had produced dizzying achievements along Stalin's road to socialism. Industry expanded exponentially, as the state poured money into massive industrial projects like Magnitogorsk, the famed steel city that emerged from the empty steppe in the Urals to rival Gary, Indiana, in size. In the countryside, 2 million members of the "enemy" class—those "kulaks" who supposedly exploited their fellow peasants and resisted Soviet power—had been dispossessed of their

89

property and deported from their homes, while millions of individual peasant households had been forced into collective farms, a process that was not complete but was certainly irreversible by this time. The "workers' state" became increasingly urban, as peasants fled Marx's "idiocy of rural life" and poured into cities in search of jobs and refuge from repressions at home. Stalin's famous boasts in 1931 that there were "no fortresses that the Bolsheviks cannot storm," and that the Soviet economy would catch up with the industrial countries of Europe within ten years, seemed like more than mere rhetoric to the dedicated in the Communist Party.

Yet the Stalin revolution also created massive social upheaval and led to repeated economic and political crises in 1932 and 1933. Despite the threat of dekulakization, peasants were no more willing to accept collectivization of agriculture in 1932 and 1933 than they had been two years earlier. The regime responded once again with force, especially during the yearly harvest drives, creating a series of shortages in the winters of 1931–32 and 1932–33 and, ultimately, leading to famine and the starvation of some 6 million people. The situation was little better in cities: massive in-migration strained urban society to its limits and produced waves of armed robbery, hooliganism, and petty theft that seemed beyond the control of standard police approaches to crime. The Stalinist administrative system had emerged in a context of chaos and crisis, and it bore the imprint of its birth. Mass mobilization, campaigns to "storm the heights" of not only heavy industry but also of virtually every aspect of local administration, and a tremendous amount of barely controlled social violence masquerading as legitimate governmental action—these were all hallmarks of Stalin's "revolution from above," and they created a Stalinist state in the early 1930s that was capable of astonishing levels of social transformation only at the expense of rational planning and central control.

Beginning in late 1931, Stalin began to turn to the task of consolidating his "new order"—reeling in some of the worst bureaucratic excesses of the dekulakization and collectivization campaigns, and imposing a semblance of discipline both on urban social life and on the sprawling administrative system that had just come into existence. This general policy direction required a reduction of the arbitrariness that had characterized local Soviet administration between 1929 and 1931. It also required force, including the overt repression of recalcitrant peasants and "draconian measures" applied to broad sectors of the Soviet population who, in Stalin's mind, had shown themselves, by their propensity to commit acts like hooliganism or theft of state property, to be enemies of Soviet socialism no matter what their class background. Forcing compliance in the countryside involved harsh judicial and extrajudicial campaigns, including Stalin's infamous August 1932 law on the theft of state property, which made the offense punishable by death. It also involved the overt repression of kulaks and, indeed, of the peasants "as a class," including restrictions on mobility and continued resettlement campaigns, which showed that the Politburo was more than willing to allow the police to exercise coercive power outside any predictable judicial or even extrajudicial framework in order to support its policy goals. In cities, forcing compliance required massive campaigns against hooligans, speculators, and homeless children, making the kind of "mass operations" that had been used by the OGPU and the *militsiia* as extraordinary policing tactics in the late 1920s into a regular part of Soviet policing under Stalin's "new order."

Stalin's attempt to instill "social discipline" in his populace took place not during a period of calm but during the most chaotic and dire years of the early Stalin period. Unfolding famine, crisis conditions in major cities, and horrific conditions, verging on collapse, within the penal system were pivotal moments for the leaders of the Stalinist regime. The "draconian measures" with which Stalin responded set the parameters of policing, and state repression in general, for the rest of the 1930s.

Moderation, Repression, and Order, 1931–1932

By the middle of 1931, Stalin's Politburo sought a new approach to the administration of the systems of collectivized agriculture and forced labor that were created during the "revolution from above." The "breakthroughs" of 1929 and 1930 had been accomplished through a chaotic process of state-sponsored mass activism; in order to transform rural society, the regime relied on not the only power of the state apparatus but also the power of spontaneous revolutionary activity among Communist Party radicals and pro-Communist urbanites. Stalin learned the dangers of this approach in early 1930, when massive peasant resistance forced him to call a temporary halt to "total collectivization" with his famous March 1930 "Dizzy with Success" speech. This speech, widely publicized and disseminated to collective farmers, blamed the supposed "excesses" in collectivization on local officials and stressed the "voluntary" nature of the collective farming system. Peasants responded by streaming out of collective farms and, more ominously for the regime, by rising up en masse to demand the return of confiscated property. This tactic rescued a faltering collectivization policy in the countryside and, just as important for the regime, encouraged peasants to participate in the spring sowing campaign. It also undermined the spontaneous and anarchic administrative practices that had made possible the first waves of collectivization and dekulakization, while doing little to improve central control over local Soviet officials.

In response, Stalin and his ruling group began to demand that local officials, especially the police, take control of local administration and reduce the chaotic application of violence to the population by authorized and unauthorized local representatives of "Soviet power." This goal resulted in seemingly contradictory policy directions in 1931 and 1932: waves of comparative moderation in the countryside, usually accompanied by calls for increased attention to "socialist legality" and restrictions on the unhampered use of force by local officials, alternated with waves of repression. Although most accounts of this period stress the contradictions in these policy directions, such policy swings were complimentary, as the Politburo attempted to force local officials, especially the police, to complete the inherently chaotic processes of collectivization and dekulakization even as it demanded that local officials bring a semblance of order to their administrations.

Central authorities were aware as early as mid-1930 that the forced resettlement of hundreds of thousands of "kulaks" occurred without sufficient transportation, housing, or basic supplies of food and water, resulting in disastrous conditions, mass flight, and starvation among deportees once they reached their destinations. The Politburo took up the issue in May 1931 and responded with a series of measures designed to bring some amount of order to the process. In May, the Politburo attempted to reassert central control over the dekulakization process, restricting the rights of local OGPU troikas to sentence peasants for counterrevolutionary crimes and requiring them to bring cases to the OGPU Special Board in Moscow for adjudication rather than handing down (and carrying out) sentences themselves. These changes resulted in a decline, by almost half, in death sentences meted out by the political police in 1931 in comparison with 1930.[3]

Yet Politburo discussions in mid-1931 also led to the transfer by July of the entire system of deportation and special settlements for dekulakized peasants to the OGPU. This change was intended to produce a more rational and less chaotic system of deportation, and it allayed fears at the center regarding the threats posed to Soviet society by the peasant deportees themselves.[4] The change was not, however, primarily designed to moderate the repression of the "kulaks." Instead, it supported a second wave of dekulakization, which was already in the planning phases in early 1931 and was designed to support a renewed push for "total collectivization" in the aftermath of the "Dizzy with Success" speech. In numerical terms, dekulakization peaked in the spring and summer of 1931, when a major wave of planned deportations struck well over half the roughly 2 million peasants deported in the early 1930s. The Politburo declared that the era of mass dekulakization was over at the end of this campaign, in late July 1931, but it did not order a halt to repression in the countryside; instead, it instructed the OGPU to carry out further repressions against peasants who resisted the ongoing collectivization and harvest campaigns in an individual and controlled manner, rather than as a mass campaign against the kulaks "as a class."[5]

The Politburo took similar steps in the area of OGPU arrests of technical specialists and state elites in mid-1931, restricting the ability of local officers to act independently but stopping short of measures that would reduce overall levels of repression. In late June 1931, the Politburo rehabilitated some of the 138,000 civil servants and "bourgeois specialists" who had been stripped of their jobs during the initial years of the industrialization drive.[6] At the same time, it forbade the OGPU to arrest Communist Party members or technical specialists without the approval of the Central Committee or the appropriate People's Commissariat, to hold any individuals on suspicion of political crimes for more than three weeks without charging them formally, or to execute any individuals without prior approval of the Central Committee itself.[7] These restrictions applied only to the arrest of elites; in early August 1931, the Politburo issued explicit instructions to the effect that local OGPU troikas retained the right to carry out executions without the approval of the Central Committee in all cases related to nonpolitical crime (in the words of the Politburo, "bandits, counterfeiters, etc."). These categories excluded peasants charged with resisting collectivization but were elastic enough to allow the OGPU to sentence several thousand individuals to death in 1932 and 1933.[8] Restrictions on the ability of the OGPU to arrest party and state elites, and to execute peasants in support of the collectivization and dekulakization drives, were intended to curb the worst excesses of OGPU activity but not to reduce overall levels of arrests, which actually increased between 1930 and 1932.[9]

Stalin reinforced this new policy direction with a series of personnel changes at the top of the OGPU. In late May 1931, Stalin replaced Kashirin, head of the Central Militsiia Administration since the OGPU takeover, with D. V. Usov, and in July he demoted or transferred out of the OGPU several Chekists of long standing, including Efim Evdokimov, head of the OGPU's Secret Operational Department, and Stanislav Messing, the assistant chair of the OGPU under Yagoda. At the very top, Stalin demoted Yagoda, who had essentially headed the OGPU for several years due to the poor health of its de jure chief, Viacheslav Menzhinsky, to the rank of second assistant, bringing in I. A. Akulov, deputy head of the Worker-Peasant Inspectorate (Rabkrin) and an Old Bolshevik of substantial tenure, to take control of the organization. Several lesser personnel changes in the OGPU followed within days, along with new regulations intended to prevent top-ranked Chekists from building up their own power bases within regional OGPU administrations.[10] Taken together, these changes amounted to an influx of Communist Party representation into the upper levels of the political police and represented a censure of the activities of the OGPU in the first phase of the Stalin revolution; they were intended not to reduce overall levels of repression but to signal Stalin's intention to regain control over the untrammeled repressions carried out by the OGPU.

Gaining control of repression at the periphery, however, was not as easy as making leadership changes in Moscow. Even into late 1931, dekulakization was carried out by local Communist Party and soviet officials in ways that the OGPU was aware of but unable to control. Representatives of local soviets continued to deport peasants en masse, often concentrating on fulfilling quotas in a given location rather than concentrating on any specific policy goal.[11] Local *militsiia* officers, nominally under control of the OGPU but in reality exercising a substantial amount of autonomy in the countryside, continued to arrest both dekulakized peasants and technical specialists on their own authority and according to their own standards.[12] Basic issues of local police activity remained ill defined as well, especially those related to protecting the property of newly created collective farms. Local police administrations often created Industrial Militsiia teams for this purpose, formed in agreement with individual collective farms, but just as often they ignored the issue completely, leaving the protection of collective farm property to the farmers themselves. The use of Industrial Militsiia officers to protect collective farm property was such a drain on scarce resources that in July 1931 the center forbade the local police to enter into any such agreements, ordering collective farms to guard their property at their own expense, using private hired guards or social organizations such as Militsiia Assistance Societies (known as OSMs).[13] Local *militsiia* organizations, however, continued to create Industrial Militsiia teams for the protection of collective farms for the next several years, in part because contracts with local agricultural organizations made up for the lack of provisioning that was endemic to local police administrations in the early 1930s.[14]

Reports from central OGPU authorities and from representatives of the Procuracy, the agency charged with prosecuting court cases and supervising the legality of the actions of the police, uniformly condemned these ad hoc policing strategies, but the local police had few other means with which to respond to the realities of administration in the collectivized countryside in 1931 and early 1932. Such difficulties notwithstanding, Stalin and the Politburo generally perceived the outcome of collectivization and dekulakization in positive terms in late 1931, believing that the peasants generally approved of the recollectivization of agriculture during that year and that the successful grain collection campaign of that fall signaled the end of major difficulties in the countryside.

Events in the winter of 1931–32, however, gave the regime cause to reassess this conclusion. Despite the ongoing threat of dekulakization, millions of peasants fled collective farms in late 1931 and early 1932, driven by hatred of collectivized agriculture and by the widespread famine already apparent in Kazakhstan and Ukraine. The peasants' rebellion again reached proportions that the regime deemed threatening to state security and, as in 1930, it was suppressed by the OGPU and military force.[15] Central discussions of collectivization and famine in early 1932 also focused on more mundane expressions of peasant dissatisfaction, such as theft or embezzlement of collective farm property and speculation in foodstuffs in urban and rural areas alike. Such "criminal" actions were natural responses of a rural population reeling under the new collective farm system, but central police officials, already accustomed to repressing petty economic crimes as "anti-Soviet" activity in the course of grain procurement campaigns, took them as overt attacks on the new Stalinist system.[16] The fact that the collectivization of agriculture had been carried out more gradually after mid-1930 than during the first wave of "total collectivization," and that the dekulakization campaign had removed from the countryside hundreds of thousands of the "class-alien elements" that were supposedly responsible for such disturbances, made the peasants' actions in early 1932 all the more unintelligible to top Communist Party and police officials.

Stalin responded to this set of problems in ways that were consistent with his earlier patterns, mixing moderation with extreme harshness. That the regime would respond to peasant unrest with overt repression was a foregone conclusion; the OGPU arrested tens of thousands of peasants for counterrevolutionary crimes in the first half of 1932, concentrating on organized "kulak resistance" and the distribution of anti-Soviet propaganda.[17] At the same time, the regime promulgated several moderate moves that were intended to soften the worst effects of collectivization. In the spring of 1932, the Politburo launched a series of measures, sometimes referred to as a "neo-NEP [New Economic Policy]," that were intended to increase the production of grain and cattle by allowing peasants some freedom to trade in agricultural products once they met their obligations to the state.[18] These steps were cynical and, in any case, largely ineffective, because they applied to peasant populations that were starving and hence hardly could be expected to meet state obligations, much less market substantial amounts of food products to the rest of the country; yet they signaled the regime's desire to avoid the levels of social disruption that forced Stalin to concede, if temporarily, to the peasantry in March 1930.

Along the same lines, in late May 1932 the Politburo began a discussion of measures intended to reduce arbitrary repression in the countryside, which in late June culminated in a major edict titled "On Revolutionary Legality."[19] This edict, usually discussed in terms of long-term trends in extrajudicial sentencing, was not concerned with the activities of the police (neither the OGPU nor the *militsiia*) but instead concentrated on the chaotic application of force to the peasantry by local soviet and Communist Party officials in support of the collectivization process.[20] The edict took no concrete steps to limit the ability of the police to carry out arrests, but it did reflect a determination on the part of the Politburo to control abuses of power within the local state apparatus and to bring the most chaotic aspects of the collectivization campaign to a halt.[21]

These decisions in mid-1932 marked the conceptual boundary, for top Communist Party leaders, between the revolutionary upheavals of the first years of the Stalin revolution and a new period of forced consolidation of the economic and social systems that it had created. The worst effects of the Stalin revolution were still to come, as we will see, but Stalin and his ruling group believed that the paramount tasks at hand were the consolidation of the collective farm system and the imposition of order on Soviet cities swelled with immigrants from the countryside. However, Stalin's policy choices in 1932 regarding the countryside must be understood as part of larger central and local trends regarding crime and social disorder that were beginning to appear in the postcollectivization period, to which we will now turn.

Economic Crime and the Stalinist System

Stalin responded to problems of continued disorder in major Soviet cities and disruptions in the collective farm system in mid-1932 with a series of repressive acts directed not at "kulaks as a class" or counterrevolutionary "elements" but at the behaviors of Soviet citizens attempting to cope with Stalin's version of "socialism." Chief among Stalin's concerns in 1932 was the threat posed to the Soviet trade system by economic crimes, including speculation, the theft of private and public property, and various forms of embezzlement and bribery within Soviet economic institutions. Economic crimes interfered with the fragile relationship between city and countryside, and they called into question the essential difference between Stalin's understanding of socialism and the NEP: the abolition of private property in favor of public.

Yet the interests of central Communist Party leaders, central police officials, and local police regarding the protection of public property diverged substantially in this period. Central party and police officials were most concerned with the large-scale theft of state property made possible by the extreme administrative chaos of the First Five-Year Plan, such as robberies on railroads and water transport, massive accounting scams, and organized speculation in consumer goods. Stalin was also anxious about individual behaviors that challenged the Soviet economic system, such as the buying and selling of scarce goods by individual consumers and petty theft of collective farm property, including food, by peasants themselves. Local police administrations, however, were generally unwilling to repress individual cases of petty theft or speculation in the early 1930s, because they had neither the desire nor the practical capacity to do so. They were, on the contrary, more than willing to increase pressure on "organized" economic crime, an issue that correlated with the concurrent reforms of covert policing discussed in chapter 2. As a result, most police pressure on economic crime in 1932 and 1933 fell on crimes committed by "recidivist" or "professional" criminals, categories that formed the conceptual basis for police approaches to speculation and theft for the rest of the decade.

The regime's initial responses to problems in the state trade sector in the difficult winter of 1931–32 targeted the large-scale theft of manufactured goods and foodstuffs, areas that were particularly susceptible to the chaotic conditions prevalent throughout the entire Soviet administrative system during the First Five-Year Plan period. Information reaching the Politburo focused on large-scale, organized criminal operations that embezzled or stole goods worth hundreds of thousands of rubles; central officials were particularly concerned with organized "channels" of theft and massive accounting scams within Soviet trade organizations that damaged the flow of goods from the countryside to cities.[22] The Politburo launched campaigns against these categories of organized crime in early April 1932, authorizing local police administrations to sentence offenders extrajudicially and ordering didactic show trials in four major cities, which were to end with sentences of execution for several lawbreakers.[23]

Local police responded to these orders in mid-1932 with covert operations, carried out by detectives and OGPU officers, that generally targeted scams within collective farm and transport administrations. The police in Leningrad, for example, detained 217 individuals and confiscated substantial amounts of food products and more than 20,000 rubles in cash during the campaign, arranging show trials in twelve exemplary cases (and in the process substantially overfulfilling the Politburo's instructions, which called for only one such trial per city).[24] The OGPU concentrated on the organized theft of state property on railroads in early 1932, carrying out a purge of railroad workers caught participating in theft and speculation in April and May.[25] The police in the Moscow and Leningrad regions both reported substantial successes in controlling organized economic crime in April and May 1932, stressing that all investigations were carried out by careful covert work within the trade sector, usually by detective departments and not with mass sweeps or operations of any kind.

Stalin, however, became increasingly concerned with the effects of economic crime committed by individual Soviet citizens, especially collective farmers, in early 1932. The reaction of peasants to the first major waves of famine, in the winter of 1931–32, was understandably to steal collective farm property; Stalin and the Politburo were aware of this behavior, traced by OGPU reports that were transmitted to them.[26] Stalin's personal concerns about the issues of theft and speculation were intensified by his decision to lift restrictions on trade in farm products in May 1932, allowing a small amount of market exchange in order to improve peasant responses to the spring sowing campaign. This step, though unavoidable in

Stalin's mind, nonetheless represented a threat to the collective farm economy, and in June he instructed Lazar Kaganovich, a Politburo member and one of Stalin's top lieutenants, to work out measures to prevent the peasants from taking advantage of the relaxed trade rules to speculate or steal public property.[27] In Stalin's understanding, the organized theft of state property and individual theft of collective farm property were manifestations of the same anti-Soviet tendencies—both were threats, in Stalin's words, to the "new order" (*novyi stroi*) from individuals who were essentially hostile to the Soviet state, and both required "draconian" actions to prevent the disruption of the new Soviet trade system, including judicial and extrajudicial executions.

Stalin's intervention produced the notorious August 7, 1932, law regarding the protection of state property and, just as important, an August 22 edict titled "On the Battle against Speculation."[28] The law of August 7, which mimicked Stalin's recommendations to Kaganovich in late June, called for the execution, using judicial sentences, of individuals guilty of the theft of state property on railroads and water transport, and in collective farms and state cooperatives of all sorts; reduced sentences of ten years in a labor camp were permissible only under extenuating circumstances. Instructions to local justice and OGPU administrations on carrying out the law made it clear that the Politburo intended the campaign to target primarily large-scale, organized theft or embezzlement, especially within the trade and transport system. These instructions ordered the police to arrest "socially alien elements," such as kulaks or former traders, who stole any amount of state property or speculated in any amount of stolen goods, and local justice officials were to sentence individual peasants or collective farmers who stole small amounts of collective farm property to ten years in a labor camp.

The force of the law of August 7, however, was directed at the same kind of organized theft and embezzlement that had been the target of OGPU activity in the first half of the year. Sentencing was primarily carried out by the judicial system; the OGPU adjudicated those cases that involved theft in conjunction with mass rebellion, overtly violent or terrorist acts, or thefts involving large-scale criminal organizations, but all other cases, including individual theft by collective farmers, were heard by the courts.[29] The law on theft was an exercise in Stalin's vision of repression carried out in an orderly fashion. He was not opposed to extrajudicial sentencing by the OGPU during this campaign but chose to promote the educative functions of a codified legal campaign, which he believed taught Soviet citizens, especially peasants, the proper respect for Soviet institutions.

The August 22 edict on speculation, to the contrary, was intended to launch police repressions against economic crime, and it specifically instructed the OGPU, as well as justice agencies, to sentence those guilty of speculation in consumer goods to five to ten years in labor camps.[30] The resulting OGPU campaign focused on speculation by individuals in bread and grain products, the sale of which the Politburo banned on the open market until January 15, 1933, in an attempt to head off shortages and prevent price inflation during the harvest campaign. The Politburo instructed the *militsiia* and procurement agents to seize all grain products offered for sale by individuals at markets and to undertake "serious operational measures" against individuals offering prepared bread for sale, in hopes of uncovering speculative organizations providing flour to them. Indiscriminate repression, however, was not the Politburo's goal; terms in labor camps were explicitly reserved for nonfarmers guilty of systematic speculation, and the police were instructed only to confiscate the property of collective farmers selling their own products, referring them to their own collective farms for punishments of a "social" nature. Even individual farmers (*edinolichniki*) guilty of a repeat offense were subject only to confiscation of property and a fine. Local police were instructed to carry out the campaign "without excesses or distortions" and to target the "class-enemy" among speculators, refraining from wasting time with "trifles" or seizing small amounts of flour ("10 to 15 to 20 pounds") from individuals not guilty of systematic speculation.[31]

True to the spirit of the August Politburo decisions, the police arrested tens of thousands of individuals in 1932 and early 1933 for economic crimes, processing most of those charged with theft through the court system but sentencing most speculators extrajudicially. As of March 15, 1933, the police had apprehended some 127,000 individuals for theft of state and public property; roughly 55,000 of them were detained for theft within the consumer goods distribution system, while 72,000 were detained for theft from state and collective farms, most during the harvest campaign. Of the nearly 74,000 individuals sentenced for these crimes, only 14,056 were sentenced by the OGPU, most of whom were, according to the OGPU, guilty of large-scale or organized theft.[32] Speculation, however, was a different matter; the OGPU reported that it had apprehended more than 54,000 individuals for speculation in roughly the same period (up to April 1, 1933), of whom more than 32,000 received either a judicial or extrajudicial sentence. The OGPU itself sentenced 16,636 of these individuals, including 7,124 to between five and ten years in labor camps and the remainder to less than five years.[33]

Neither justice nor police officials responded to these orders in the ways intended by the center. There is ample evidence that justice officials attempted to blunt the repressive nature of the law on theft, refusing to sentence individuals to death for simple theft of collective farm property.[34] The police, for their part, responded actively to both campaigns, but they generally did so in ways that corresponded to ongoing approaches to economic crime. OGPU reports from August and September 1932 touted the increasing numbers of individuals arrested for economic crimes; the OGPU in the North Caucasus Territory, for example, reported that it had detained some 830 speculators in the ten days after August 10 alone, and that it had detained nearly 2,200 individuals involved in speculation and the theft of public property in the first twenty days of the month.[35] Yet a report from the Leningrad region on police activity in August noted that the undercover surveillance of institutions and locations where trade took place, especially collective farm markets and retail locations, remained the predominant approach to dealing with speculation and theft. The patrol police were instructed to improve their own supervision of public markets in order to address the issue of individual speculation as well, but the local police focused most of their efforts on improving their surveillance networks. The Leningrad Detective Department explicitly discussed the new campaigns against theft in the context of ongoing operations against embezzlement in the state banking system, showing that they understood the campaigns as extensions of ongoing operative campaigns (although they admitted that, outside the city of Leningrad itself, surveillance networks in state trade agencies were nonexistent and had to be set up in the process of fulfilling these directives).[36] Covert surveillance, as we have seen, was exceptionally weak among *militsiia* administrations in 1932, but local officers were nonetheless more inclined to rely on it rather than on widespread repression of individual Soviet citizens in order to police low-level economic crime.

Although urban police administrations could claim some level of success in response to these campaigns, the rural police were unable to comply in any manner other than episodic arrests. The *militsiia* was so poorly represented outside major cities, according to central police officials, that most of the day-to-day work of protecting "socialist property" on collective farms in 1932 was carried out by Industrial Militsiia officers or guards hired by the collective farms themselves. Collective farm property was usually protected by one or two local peasants who had been hired for the position because they were not qualified to do much else and who themselves often participated in theft and speculation.[37] Justice officials, after several months of processing cases related to theft of collective farm property, came to the same conclusion: collective farm property was stolen so often because it was virtually unguarded.[38] Likewise, the OGPU had little role in the daily policing of theft and speculation in the countryside, largely due to the paucity of OGPU officers and the lack of any sort of functioning network of informants outside the most important collective and state farms.[39] Most rural police activity in support of these campaigns, then, was undertaken by the OGPU during the harvest and grain procurement drives, often under the direct control of commissions to top Communist Party leaders that were sent by the Politburo to crucial agricultural areas to enforce grain collection in what would be the most difficult harvest season of the decade. The OGPU identified peasants engaged in speculation or theft as "antisoviet" or "kulak" elements who were resisting the harvest campaign and repressed them accordingly, making it impossible to separate precisely the number of individuals arrested by the OGPU and the *militsiia* in 1932 and early 1933 in conjunction with the law on theft and the edict on speculation from those arrested as part of what were, by this time, standard repressions in the countryside in support of the fall harvest campaign.[40]

Top justice officials deemed the entire campaign a failure. Aron Solts, as part of a discussion in July 1933 of judicial application of the law on theft in the Leningrad, Urals, and Central Black Earth regions, argued that the campaign had failed to target organized, large-scale thieves but had fallen instead on "incidental ordinary criminals."[41] For the police, this failure was the fault of justice organizations alone. Top police officials generally deemed their role in these campaigns a success, pointing to ongoing covert operations against organized criminal activity as evidence that the OGPU-dominated policing system was capable of protecting the Stalinist economy from economic malfeasance. Such claims were a vast exaggeration, because covert policing was of dubious value in the early 1930s and was completely incapable, in any case, of controlling individual behaviors, like speculation or petty theft, that were carried out by average Soviet citizens. Police campaigns against property theft and speculation would become much more repressive when central dictates corresponded precisely to local approaches to policing—which happened, as we will see, not in 1932 but 1934 and 1935.

Hooliganism and Urban Life

Although campaigns in the countryside consumed much of the attention of central OGPU officials in 1931 and 1932, control of disorder in the cities was never far from their attention. The end of the bulk of the dekulakization campaign in late 1931, along with Stalin's increasing concern with crime and public order in early 1932, refocused police attention on urban policing, especially the protection of cities from peasants uprooted by waves of rural repression. Central police officials conceptualized this task explicitly in terms of the creation of inherently Soviet urban spaces; the police were responsible, in the words of a 1932 police circular, for "transforming cities and workers' settlements into genuinely socialist cities" and for dealing with the effects of "arriving populations including large quantities of immigrants from the countryside, the pouring in of criminal elements, the low level of amenities, etc."[42] Yet this focus on protecting "socialist cities" from rural influences gave way after 1932 to approaches that better resonated with understandings of crime among the police themselves, including a renewed focus on the role of "socially dangerous elements" in crimes, such as hooliganism, that threatened the stability of urban society.

During the First Five-Year Plan, central officials pressed local police administrations to improve urban services and to create the conditions necessary for "normal" city life, focusing on sanitation, the regulation of automobile traffic, the control of hooliganism on city streets, and patrols of city streets at night.[43] Such solutions were difficult to put in place, because the local police were stretched thin throughout the First Five-Year Plan period. Police coverage was especially poor in new industrial cities, where one policeman for more than 3,300 residents was the norm. In some cases cited by central police authorities, such as Krasnouralsk, the ratio dropped as low as 1 to 15,400; in other cases, especially smaller workers' settlements, there was no *militsiia* representation at all in the early 1930s.[44] At the same time, rapid urbanization exacerbated aspects of urban life that had always been difficult to police; the newspaper of the Moscow *militsiia* administration, for example, reported that peasant in-migration made it exceptionally difficult to control petty crime at the infamous Sukharevskii market, which had been the focus of police attention for decades.[45]

Hooliganism was the most prominent of crimes blamed on peasant migrants, especially in the new industrial cities. A typical 1932 report noted that hooliganism had increased substantially in the Russian Republic in the previous months and blamed the problem on "the uncultured mass of population arriving from the countryside."[46] Such explanations coincided with police approaches to hooliganism in the 1920s, when hooliganism was seen as a direct product of the petit bourgeois mentality of the peasant class. Although this kind of low-level disorder was ubiquitous before 1932, it was not a major concern for central police officials in the initial years of the Stalin revolution. Prosecutions for hooliganism climbed rapidly in both the court and extrajudicial systems after 1928, yet before 1932 most petty hooligans were sentenced to either fines or short jail sentences.[47] For most of the First Five-Year Plan period, police maintained that the solution to urban hooliganism was more police supervision of public places or better integration of social organizations, such as the police Assistance Brigades and trade union cells, into the project of controlling hooliganism among working populations.

Conceptual definitions of hooliganism began to change late in the First Five-Year Plan, as the term began to refer to more violent actions that were deemed threatening by top Communist Party and police officials to the fabric of urban Soviet society. Kaganovich, in a speech to an assembly of *militsiia* officers in Moscow quoted at the beginning of this chapter, hinted at these differences; in addition to identifying as enemies those individuals who cared little for the achievements of Soviet power, he returned repeatedly to the ideas of protecting cities from disruption, protecting "revolutionary order," and defending workers and peasants against, as he termed them, "hooligans, against thieves, against people who want to disturb our normal life" and "want to prevent us from building socialism."[48] The impetus for this change came, in part, from Stalin himself. In early August 1932, he called attention to the issue of hooliganism on railroads, as part of ongoing discussions of how to protect public property from theft and speculation. He claimed, in a letter to Kaganovich, that hooligans were responsible for "outrages" on rail transport, disrupting normal travel and especially rail shipments of scarce food items; railroad workers, he wrote, were "being raped and terrorized by hooligans and homeless children." Stalin associated hooliganism on transport with the ongoing campaigns against theft and speculation, discussed above, and he demanded that the OGPU deal with the issue by shooting hooligans on trains "on the spot."[49]

The OGPU reacted to Stalin's demands immediately. The Transport Department of the OGPU accelerated the formation of transport brigades made up of OGPU officers, transport workers, and Communist Party and

Komsomol members, reporting that by August 1932 nearly 900 such brigades were patrolling important transport corridors. The OGPU apprehended more than 14,700 people for hooliganistic activity on transport in August 1932, compared with slightly more than 10,000 in April and roughly 7,500 each in May and in June. Even more striking were police detentions of homeless and hooliganistic juveniles on transport, which jumped from just under 1,100 in July to almost 7,700 in August. Fines levied by the police on individuals traveling without tickets or breaking other rules of transport also jumped markedly in August 1932, from some 47,000 in July to almost 85,000. The OGPU handled the majority of these cases itself, either through extrajudicial sentencing or by simply ejecting individuals from the locations where they were found.[50]

These campaigns against hooliganism on transport continued at least through the end of 1932, and they were matched by campaigns against hooliganism in major urban areas, which were invigorated by Stalin's intervention as well. Central instructions for these campaigns corresponded closely to the ideas held by both central and local police officials regarding the nature and causes of hooliganism in the early 1930s, and hence the police responded vigorously, making these campaigns against hooliganism much more dynamic than the concurrent campaigns against the theft of public property. In reporting on the causes of hooliganism in Leningrad, for example, the Leningrad Detective Department in 1932 concentrated on the intertwined issues of youth, drunkenness, group crime, and recidivism. Hooliganism, according to the detectives, was the product of drunken youth, most between seventeen and twenty-two years of age, who gathered in groups and attacked inebriated city residents. Nearly half of all youth who participated in such activities, furthermore, had previous sentences for hooliganism or theft.[51] Hooliganism, in this view, was not predominantly a problem of an influx of peasant cultures; rather, it was a violent challenge to urban life, increasingly linked to the criminal milieu and to recidivists and "dangerous elements," which were becoming more central to police conceptions of crime in this era.

This definition of hooliganism placed it squarely within the categories of crimes that were understood by the police as the proper targets of extrajudicial repression, and hence central police officials pressed for expanded extrajudicial powers to deal with urban hooliganism at several points after mid-1932. On August 1 the Presidium of the Moscow Soviet, following the instructions of the Moscow Communist Party Committee, requested that the USSR government provide the Moscow *militsiia* with the right to detain "hardened violators of city regulations and malicious hooligans" for thirty days.[52] The Politburo seems to have declined to approve explicit extrajudicial actions in urban areas against hooligans in 1932, but it did approve continued arrests by the OGPU of hooligans on transport, including train stations in major Soviet cities; the OGPU also retained the right in 1932 to sentence any hooligans deemed recidivists as "dangerous elements."

As a result, OGPU campaigns against hooliganism expanded in late 1932, despite the absence of any specific authorization for extrajudicial action outside the transport system. The OGPU reported that more than 8,400 individuals had been arrested for hooliganism on transport in September and October, of whom nearly 2,100 were sentenced by the OGPU to three or more years of labor and 361 were sentenced to death. During the same two months, the OGPU apprehended nearly 37,000 individuals on the territory of transport lines (as opposed to transport itself) as "socially dangerous and juvenile-homeless elements," as part of what one OGPU report termed "extremely important preventive [*profilakticheskii*] measures" against hooliganism. Some 6,000 of these individuals were sentenced by the OGPU to terms in labor camps as "dangerous elements," and the rest were exiled or banished. In addition, the police handed out fines in these two months to almost 594,000 individuals, worth a total of 3.75 million rubles. Menzhinsky, in forwarding his report on this activity to Stalin, noted that these measures had produced substantial decreases in hooliganistic activity across the USSR and recommended that the "extraordinary authorization" of the OGPU to sanction "declassed hooliganistic-bandit elements" be extended through February 1933.[53] Stalin evidently concurred, because in late December 1932 the USSR Central Executive Committee approved a request submitted by Yagoda to allow the OGPU to sentence hooligans, individuals guilty of "debauchery," and individuals breaking regulations on railroads and other similar areas of state importance to terms in labor camps as a matter of standard extrajudicial practice.[54]

Even though the most aggressive campaigns against hooliganism in 1932 took place on transport, the crime of hooliganism became increasingly important to all aspects of urban policing in this period. The explicit connection made by Stalin between hooliganism and attacks on state property on railroads signaled to the local police that the Politburo had accepted the idea that hooliganism was closely related to issues of criminal recidivism and social dangerousness, reinforcing the tendency of local officers to deal with hooligans in extrajudicial order, not only with troikas but also through fines and simple ejections from the location in question. Campaigns against hooliganism would become much more public, and virulent, at mid-decade, but already in 1932 the basic connection had been made, by local and central police officials alike, between urban social disorder, threats to the Soviet economic system, and widespread (often low-level) extrajudicial repression by the police themselves. The police were hardly passive actors in this process. Local police strove to control definitions of urban crime in ways that gave them the most latitude to use extrajudicial sanctioning powers, ranging from fines to executions. In the process, they reinforced the overall tendency of top police and Communist Party officials alike to see "dangerous elements" as the basic cause of urban crime.

Juvenile Delinquency and Homelessness

Harvest difficulties, mass repressions in the countryside, and expanding famine produced another threat to "normal" urban life in 1932 and 1933: throngs of homeless and neglected children, who were ubiquitous in virtually every major Soviet city in these years. The regime responded to this situation with police campaigns against juvenile lawbreakers and by building a system of juvenile labor colonies to house homeless children deemed "difficult to rehabilitate"—actions that represented, for many contemporary and later observers, the worst failures of the emerging Stalinist system. The Soviet response to juvenile homelessness in the 1930s is particularly appalling when compared with the progressive reaction of the regime to the same problem just after the Civil War, when the 7 to 9 million homeless waifs that wandered the USSR were the object of largely positive interventions by numerous welfare and justice agencies.[55]

Yet the repressiveness of the early 1930s was not simply the product of Stalin's personal approach to the question of juvenile affairs, cruel though it was. Police responses to youth issues were part of larger campaigns to control crime and protect "socialist life" in Soviet cities. The local police, generally acting on their own initiative, developed explanations of juvenile homelessness and crime in the early 1930s that resonated with their general understandings of violent urban crime, focusing in particular on the idea that inherently "dangerous" juvenile criminals were the root cause of both homelessness and delinquency. By mid-decade, the police were subjecting juvenile delinquents to the same harsh measures that they used against adult vagrants, hooligans, and other enemies of Stalin's "new order."

For most of the 1920s, welfare, police, and justice organizations shared responsibility for juvenile affairs. At the center, a Children's Commission, operating under the All-Russian Central Executive Committee, coordinated efforts to reduce homelessness and delinquency, while local representatives of the Education, Health, and Social Welfare commissariats oversaw orphanages for various categories of homeless children, ranging from infants to older juveniles deemed "difficult to educate." The responsibility for removing homeless children from the streets fell both to the police and to juvenile affairs commissions (*komonesy*), which were supervised by local administrations of the Commissariat of Education. The police, including both the *militsiia* and the OGPU, often apprehended the homeless during preparations for holiday celebrations, but the commissions were responsible for most local aspects of juvenile affairs.[56] The judicial system only rarely became involved, and punishments were generally minimal; the courts heard cases concerning children over the age of sixteen years (fourteen for several serious crimes), but as a rule they handed out reduced sentences for young offenders. Most children younger than sixteen had their cases heard by the commissions, which were exceptionally lenient. Soviet juvenile jurisprudence was therefore consistent with progressive European practices for most of the 1920s.[57]

Although welfare organizations struggled in the late 1920s with inadequate funding and neglect from central state agencies, this progressive model of juvenile affairs held its ground in the initial years of the Stalin revolution. By the beginning of the 1930s, welfare officials claimed, with some justification, that the problem of child homelessness was generally under control. The local police from nearly all areas of the Russian Republic reported in mid-1931 that levels of juvenile delinquency and homelessness had fallen over the previous several years, and the All-Russian Children's Commission claimed that only about 7,000 street children remained at large in the entire republic in 1931.[58] Central welfare officials realized that the system of orphanages in the Russian Republic was in abysmal condition and that the roughly 130,000 children living in them in 1930 experienced terrible conditions, but they nonetheless looked forward to what one report called a "complete liquidation" of the problem of street children by 1931.[59]

Hopes for the disappearance of child homelessness at the beginning of the 1930s were premature. Homeless children flooded into major Soviet cities in the winter of 1931–32, seeking refuge from the disruptions of collectivization and localized famine. In Moscow, where increases in the population of homeless children were always felt first, police officials began sounding the alarm about climbing rates of child homelessness in the fall of 1931.[60] As famine conditions worsened across the USSR, reports flooded into the center regarding the inability of local officials, especially Education Commissariat officials, to deal with the problem.[61] The commissar of education of the Russian Republic, A. S. Bubnov, and the head of the Children's Commission, N. A. Semashko, blamed the situation on the poor conditions in orphanages, especially lack of food and winter clothing, and they estimated that, by October 1932, 4,000 children were living on the streets of Moscow at any given time.[62] Welfare authorities campaigned for additional funding for orphanages and for the work of local juvenile affairs commissions in late 1932, but on the whole they did not propose fundamentally new approaches to the problem until the situation became critical.[63]

The police at all levels were fiercely critical of the work of welfare agencies in 1931 and 1932, blaming delinquency and homelessness almost entirely on the inability of the orphanages administered by the Education Commissariat to reform, or even to hold, "difficult" homeless children. The police argued that juvenile detention centers (*priemniki*) and orphanages had become home bases for gangs, locations where children could get some food, find a reasonably safe place to sleep, and store stolen goods.[64] Severe overcrowding in all juvenile institutions, furthermore, meant that the police often had nowhere to deliver the homeless and delinquent children they swept off the streets. Children languished in *militsiia* jails for weeks or even months, and detention centers, which were designed to hold children only temporarily until they could be transferred to orphanages or the court system, essentially functioned as prisons.[65] The police argued that their work regarding juvenile delinquency, which was limited to arresting children for concrete crimes and participating in periodic mass sweeps of homeless children, could not be effective as long as orphanages were unable to prevent the children from returning to life on the streets. Top OGPU officials hence campaigned vigorously in 1931 and 1932 for the replacement of a large part of the orphanage system with a system of closed labor colonies, run by the OGPU.[66]

The police also blamed burgeoning levels of delinquency and home-lessness on the appearance of "dangerous" behaviors among homeless children, especially among children deemed "difficult to rehabilitate." This explanation was transparently related to emerging police approaches to crimes like hooliganism and speculation, and it allowed the police to understand delinquency in the context of their ongoing campaigns against violent urban crime. L. Vul, the head of the Moscow Detective Depart-ment, noted in May 1932 that juvenile crime had taken on a "threatening form"; juveniles were responsible in Moscow for not only petty theft, which was the most common form of juvenile crime in the 1920s, but also murder, armed robbery, cattle theft, and arson, among other serious crimes.[67] Roughly half the crimes committed by juveniles in 1931 and 1932 were minor property crimes, but 5 percent were classed as hooliganism, and a substantial number of those juveniles arrested were picked up for being "socially harmful" (39 percent for the second half of 1931, 49 percent for the first quarter of 1932).[68] As with adult offenders, the police identified "socially dangerous" children primarily as recidivists, and they believed that most juvenile crime was caused by a core group of permanent delin-quents who maintained active contacts with the adult criminal under-world.[69] In Moscow, nearly 70 percent of the children detained by the police in the first half of 1931 were repeat offenders; Vul, in reporting this figure, argued that these children were "candidates for entry into the world of adult criminals" and hence were the proper targets of extraordinary police measures.[70]

Not only recidivism but also homelessness itself was evidence of the "dangerous" nature of juvenile delinquents, as it was for adults. Numer-ous police reports in 1931 and 1932 claimed that most children appre-hended for committing crimes had escaped multiple times from orphanages. In 1931, 69 percent of the children detained by the police in Moscow had previously been charged with petty crimes, and 66 percent had previously spent time in orphanages, leading the police to speak of a "defined contin-gent [*kontingent*]" of criminal youth making Moscow their home.[71] Local police assumed that both homelessness and delinquency were essentially urban problems, despite the fact that both were widespread in rural areas, and they focused nearly all their attention on male offenders.[72] Homeless girls were, to some extent, protected from police actions by the welfare system, which treated them differently than boys, but the differential is primarily explained by the fact that the police made connections be-tween male culture and youth violence, which were both central to the

definitions of crimes like hooliganism, when apprehending both homeless and delinquent children. These conceptual connections allowed the
police to attribute homelessness to the same causes with which they
explained urban crime in general: homeless children were recidivist
criminals, in touch with the adult criminal world, and were not apt to
respond to rehabilitation in orphanages due to their inherently criminal
natures.

Local police moved aggressively in 1931 and 1932 to take control of
juvenile affairs from welfare agencies, often making use of their extrajudicial prerogatives in order to ensure that children removed from city
streets would not return. The police in Moscow, warning in the summer of
1931 that existing approaches would not prevent the situation from wors-
ening in the fall, launched a one-month campaign against homelessness
timed to coincide with the October Revolution holiday. The operation
began on October 10 and followed a strict schedule: police teams concentrated on specific areas of the city during the initial weeks of the campaign, followed by a "mop-up" period during which each police precinct
removed the remaining homeless children from their areas. The Moscow
Juvenile Affairs Commission, stationed in the Danilov Monastery, processed the cases, but welfare organizations were entirely shut out of the
daily aspects of the campaign.[73] In the end, 2,811 children were apprehended during the October sweep, which was repeated in major cities
across the USSR.[74] Although the Juvenile Affairs Commission participated in the Moscow sweep, it could be bypassed when necessary, especially because police responses to delinquency were coordinated by OGPU
officers in local detective departments; of the 4,454 juveniles arrested by
the Moscow police for specific crimes from January to early October
1931, 2,131 were sentenced by the Moscow OGPU troika to some form
of deprivation of freedom.[75]

Major sweeps in October 1931 notwithstanding, the police across the
USSR reported that delinquency and homelessness worsened in early 1932.
In Moscow, Vul complained again that ongoing police actions against
homelessness faltered on the inability of welfare organizations to place
children in orphanages and the inability of orphanage staff to keep them
there. The Moscow detention center functioned as a permanent juvenile
prison rather than, as was intended, a distribution point; 250 to 500 children lived in the center permanently, and most children spent several
months in the facility. The Moscow police could only respond by carrying
out repeated sweeps of city streets, often, according to Vul, detaining the

same children again and again.[76] Local police across the USSR forwarded similar complaints to Moscow in 1932.[77] The police in the Ivanov industrial region, for example, in 1932 put under surveillance a number of the most "dangerous" juvenile lawbreakers, sending fifteen of the most hardened "recidivists" from Ivanovno-Vosnesensk to a juvenile labor colony in Iaroslavl, but they complained to the center that further removals were impossible because the colony was filled with children from Moscow; hence, more than 100 "recidivist" children remained at large.[78] The police in the Nizhegorodskii Territory offered largely the same complaint in July 1932; although they were capable of removing children from the streets through ongoing searches and sweeps, they had no way to hold juvenile delinquents, who escaped from local orphanages and returned to criminal activity immediately.[79]

Central police officials argued explicitly that the liquidation of the juvenile affairs commissions and the complete transfer of all responsibilities for juvenile delinquents and homeless children to the police were necessary to improve the situation in the streets. In addition, the police leadership in April 1932 recommended reorganizing the existing orphanage system so that the Education Commissariat retained control only over standard orphanages, while all institutions for the rehabilitation of "difficult" children were transferred to the OGPU.[80] By early 1933, many top justice and welfare officials had accepted the basic assumptions of this analysis. In April 1933, for example, Russian commissar of education A. S. Bubnov and Russian commissar of justice Nikolai Krylenko appealed directly to Stalin and Molotov for the creation of a set of closed labor colonies in remote locations in the Northern Territory, well away from populated areas, to house various categories of "difficult" homeless children. Although Bubnov and Krylenko suggested that these colonies be operated by the Education or Justice commissariats, they shared the assumption that the child welfare system was paralyzed by the existence of a core group of "particularly neglected children, ruined by lengthy life on the streets, connected to the criminal underworld," who required more stringent measures than those associated with the orphanage system.[81]

These increasingly strident analyses of the situation, which focused on repeat offenders and dangerous populations among juveniles, were swept away by the realities of the massive famine that gripped the nation in 1933.[82] The orphanage system expanded continuously, climbing from 200,000 children in December 1932 to 246,000 by April 1933. The following months saw staggering increases in homeless children; some 120,000 children entered the orphanage system in the Northern Caucuses alone in 1933, and the nationwide orphanage population climbed to 400,000 by the end of the year.[83] Nearly half the children in orphanages in early 1934 were reported to be of preschool age, a major downward shift in age distribution that was obviously caused by the deaths of their parents during the 1933 famine. This change temporarily muted suggestions that delinquency among the homeless was caused by repeat offenders and escapees.[84]

None of the institutions responsible for juvenile affairs were prepared for such a situation. Orphanages were unable to provide for the children already under their care, especially in famine-stricken regions. Local officials in many areas abandoned all attempts to control homelessness, in some cases instructing hungry children to flee to major cities such as Kiev and Kharkov instead of attempting to prevent such migration, as the Politburo demanded.[85] The only concerted policy efforts at the center that were possible in such a context were the same measures taken against starving peasant populations in general: Politburo orders in early 1933 to limit the influx of peasants into cities, and in particular to force starving peasants in Ukraine and the Northern Caucuses to stay in their native areas instead of seeking food elsewhere, applied to children as much as to adults. Ultimately, the crisis was solved neither by the police nor welfare institutions but by the easing of famine in late 1933 and 1934. The number of children in orphanages fell to 282,000 by mid-1934, 82,000 of whom were located in the Northern Caucuses and 40,000 of whom were housed not in orphanages at all but in special settlement villages with deported peasants.[86]

The understandings of delinquency and homeless that emerged within the police system in the early 1930s persisted after the end of the famine. As we will see in chapter 4, in mid-1935 the regime launched the most repressive set of campaigns against juvenile lawbreakers in the entire Stalin era. This second wave of attention to juvenile issues unfolded under direct central pressure from Stalin himself, but harsh policies regarding juvenile offenders had been discussed and implemented by local police officials from the beginning of the 1930s. Local officers, acting on emerging ideas regarding the centrality of recidivism and social dangerousness to all forms of disorder among youth, developed the tactics and criminological approaches that shaped severe police actions against delinquency and homelessness in the years that followed.

"Harmful" and "Dangerous" Elements

Increased central and local concern with urban social order brought the issue of "socially dangerous elements" back to the forefront of local police activity at the end of the dekulakization drive. The very idea of "social danger" changed substantially in this period, expanding to encompass broad categories of urban criminal and marginalized populations that far exceeded the cohorts of "professional" or "recidivist" criminals targeted in the 1920s. Local police administrations began to rely on extrajudicial repressions of "dangerous elements" to sanction a wide range of urban offenders without having to turn to the court system. Between 1931 and 1933, the police began to use the term "socially harmful" (*vrednyi*) alongside "socially dangerous" (*opasnyi*) to describe this increasingly inclusive "contingent" of urban undesirables. By mid-decade, the repression of "socio-harmfuls" (*sotsvredniki*, often referred to simply by the acronym "SVE") was the single most important aspect of Soviet policing, unifying police approaches to surveillance, the control of geographic mobility, and the extrajudicial repression of virtually all categories of crime.

Police actions against "socially dangerous elements" were a limited but important part of policing practice during the era of collectivization and dekulakization. The police continued to sentence a narrowly defined cohort of recidivist or "professional" criminals as "dangerous elements" in 1930 and 1931, even though police actions against "kulaks" in the countryside and "vagrant" criminals in cities, discussed in chapter 2, tended to blur the distinction between "socially dangerous elements" and threatening population cohorts in general. Local police paid little systematic attention to the control of "socially dangerous elements" in urban areas in these years, largely because the statutory requirements that had to be met in order to sentence them (Article 35 of the Criminal Code, or corresponding guidelines for republic-level OGPU special boards, which required the police to compile case histories showing two prior convictions or four prior detainments) proved difficult for officers overwhelmed with the collectivization and dekulakization campaigns. Local officers instead exercised a far more simple option, dealing with recidivist criminals using OGPU troikas as part of ongoing campaigns against kulak uprisings or banditry. As a result, the OGPU sentenced relatively few individuals specifically as "socially dangerous elements" before 1932. In 1931, the OGPU sentenced only 7,457 individuals as such, identifying them as "swindlers [*aferisti*], members of the criminal underworld, and recidivists," out of

180,696 individuals sentenced and 479,065 arrested.[87] Justice officials viewed police practices regarding "dangerous elements" as a relatively minor issue before 1932; in one major report on OGPU activity, for example, P. Krasilkov, the procurator of the USSR Supreme Court, argued that the majority of those individuals sentenced by OGPU troikas in 1931 as "dangerous elements" were indeed "declassed elements, professional thieves, and professional criminals"—the same categories targeted in the 1920s—who generally deserved the sentences to labor camps that were meted out to them.[88]

The turn toward policing cities that began in early 1932 brought the concept of "dangerous elements" to the forefront of policing activity once again. Across the board, police reports from 1932 and 1933 identified recidivists or "dangerous elements" as the primary cause of most urban crime, especially economic and violent crime. Detectives in Leningrad, for example, reported that over one-third of the property crimes committed in the city in August 1932 were the work of "unemployed declassed elements and recidivists" and argued that the best way to combat such crimes was to use the criminal registration system to identify individuals prone to reoffend.[89]

Central OGPU officials reinforced these conceptions among the local police by sending to the periphery numerous requests for information and demands for the standardization of local practices, which transmitted to local officials complex criminological assessments of the nature and causes of crime. Central OGPU officials were particularly concerned with the connection between "dangerous elements" and populations of former exiles or ex-convicts, arguing that ex-convicts usually formed the core of dangerous populations in urban areas.[90] "Vagrant" criminals, likewise, were a major concern, prompting the OGPU in October 1932 to order local police to collate all the existing information about recidivist or professional criminals and to forward it to Moscow for inclusion in a central card catalog. All professional or recidivist criminals, whether at large or currently serving time in forced-labor institutions, were included and divided into three groups: "active" (currently at large and involved in crime), "passive" (former criminals who had served out sentences but were gainfully employed and not involved in crime), and all those currently serving sentences, including exile and banishment.[91] The distinction between active and passive recidivists duplicated OGPU practices regarding the surveillance of politically suspect populations; the entire structure, furthermore, mirrored police instructions on the division of kulak populations into

three categories during the dekulakization drive.[92] Similar ideas prolifer-
ated within OGPU and *militsiia* administrations before 1932, but they became virtually universal as the center began to seek theoretical justifications
for the mass repressions in the post-dekulakization era.

As we have seen, local police during the First Five-Year Plan period
generally attempted to control "professional" criminals by restricting the geographic mobility of suspect populations, rather than relying on the covert approaches promoted by central OGPU officials. In 1932, central police
authorities began to agree, coordinating a series of nationwide campaigns
intended to purge urban areas of "dangerous elements." These campaigns—
carried out by both the OGPU and local detective departments—relied on
registration systems and overt sweeps of city streets rather than covert
work of any kind. They resulted in the expulsion from major cities of substantial numbers of "dangerous elements," who were either sentenced by
the OGPU Special Board or, more frequently, simply expelled by the registration bureau of a given *militsiia* administration. In Leningrad, for example, the Detective Department arrested some 439 "socially dangerous,
criminal and parasitic elements" in November 1932 and sentenced them
using the Special Board to terms in labor camps, colonies, exile in Kazakhstan, or banishment from the major cities of the USSR, bringing the
total arrested in the course of this operation in Leningrad to 6,412. At the
same time, the police detained 3,712 additional individuals with criminal
backgrounds or alleged connections to the criminal milieu in Leningrad in
November 1932 alone, deporting them from the city and recording their
names in the Registration Bureau in order to prevent their return.[93] No
nationwide figures are available regarding these urban purges of "socially
dangerous elements" in 1932, but, based on fragmentary data, the number
must be in the tens of thousands; expulsions by the registration bureaus
were likely even more considerable but, because they were technically
neither judicial nor extrajudicial punishment, they appear in none of the
available statistical compilations of court or OGPU sentencing practices
in 1932 and 1933.

The administrative ejection of "dangerous elements" from urban areas
was particularly vexing to those justice officials who attempted to maintain some level of oversight over police activity in the early 1930s. The
"removal" (*iz"iatiia*) of "dangerous elements" often escaped even the
minimal procedural controls associated with extrajudicial punishment; individuals so removed were not technically even arrested (a step that eventually required approval, even if pro forma, by local Procuracy officials),

and they were completely at the mercy of individual police officers. An early 1932 Procuracy investigation of police activity in the Central Black Earth region, for example, complained of substantial excesses (*peregiby*) in the area of police sweeps of "socially dangerous elements [recidivists]," including detainments of individuals who did not fit the strict definition of dangerous elements but were simply unregistered in a particular location or had no permanent place of residence.[94] Local police could choose to transfer these individuals to the OGPU Special Board for sentencing to labor camps, but they could just as easily subject them to de facto banishment by ejecting them from a given city, circumventing the OGPU's extrajudicial system of punishment altogether.

Even as police campaigns against "dangerous elements" expanded to include individuals with minor past offenses, the concept of "socially dangerous elements" itself expanded to include numerous categories of marginalized or otherwise undesirable urban residents. In the early 1930s, the concerns voiced by central Communist Party and police officials regarding the detrimental effects of urban criminal contingents on the building of Stalin's "new social order" began to resonate with police approaches to marginal urban populations, such as prostitutes, beggars, the adult homeless, chronic alcoholics, and drug users. In the 1920s, the police had generally referred to these individuals as "socially harmful elements"—a usage that corresponded to the theoretical distinctions between "harmful" and "dangerous" criminal activity promoted by radical jurists during the NEP. Into the first years of the 1930s, the distinction between "harmful" and "dangerous" elements was clear to police and justice officials alike; "dangerous elements" fell under the long-standing statutes on OGPU extrajudicial punishment and were characterized by multiple past infractions, whereas "harmful elements," such as prostitutes, beggars, and drug addicts, might have ties to the criminal underworld but could not be considered career criminals according to the letter of the statutes on "socially dangerous elements" and hence were subject to intervention by the welfare system rather than to extrajudicial repression.

This distinction between harmful and dangerous elements began to break down in the early 1930s, as both the local and central police began to mix terminology and to view both categories as part of the same larger cohort of urban criminals. A 1932 police report on trends in urban crime, for example, concentrated on the role of individuals who were properly within the purview of welfare organizations. Homeless children, "declassed elements," and other "social anomalies," according to the report, were drawn to major urban areas in the postcollectivization era and created "a real threat of befoulment [*zagraznenie*] of our cities [and] the growth of hooliganism and criminal activity." The report claimed that the welfare system in general was incapable of dealing with the problem, and it argued for the transfer of all aspects of the "fight against social anomalies" to the police; a new system of labor colonies for those who could be rehabilitated would be paired with an "energetic purge [*ochistki*] of cities of socially alien and socially dangerous elements who have connections to the criminal world."[95] High-ranking OGPU officers in charge of detective departments echoed many of these sentiments at a national meeting in late 1932, praising local detectives for ongoing campaigns against "criminal professionals and socially harmful elements" in urban areas but noting that further progress would require a the transfer of responsibility for "harmful" elements—beggars, adult homeless people, the juvenile homeless and delinquents, alcoholics, and prostitutes—to the OGPU.[96]

Central police authorities drew direct connections between these "harmful" populations of urban marginals and the pressing problems of social disorder in mid-1932, blurring technical distinctions between "harmful" and "dangerous" offenders and connecting them both to the issue of geographic mobility. In August 1932, the OGPU instructed the local police to produce estimates of "criminal and social-parasitic elements" in their areas, dividing them into three categories: Category I, including bandits, armed robbers, murders, train robbers, swindlers, and professional criminals of all types who had not found permanent work and who had continuing contacts with the criminal milieu, who were subject to incarceration in labor camps; Category II, including individuals having contact with the criminal underworld, former criminals who were employed but still maintained contact with the criminal underworld, recidivist hooligans, and "declassed and parasitic elements" (prostitutes, beggars, etc.), subject to exile or banishment to the periphery of the USSR; and Category III, including juvenile criminals of all sorts, subject to rehabilitation in closed labor colonies.[97] A January 1933 response to the circular from the North Caucasus territorial OGPU administration counted 2,800 Category I, 5,009 Category II, and 1,300 Category III "criminal elements," noting that most Category I criminals were "professional" thieves and swindlers and that most Category II criminals were "declassed" elements such as prostitutes and beggars.[98] Although the local police could count these individuals, they argued that existing practices were not capable of controlling them. Much as in the case of homeless children, criminals reappeared almost as soon as they were swept off the streets of major cities in "mass operations" directed against them; in Rostov on the Don, for example, the police swept some 900 individuals off the streets in one twenty-four-hour "mass operation" in February 1932, but by April the police estimated that more than 2,000 new "criminal elements" had appeared.[99] Like the August OGPU order on "vagrant recidivists," this three-part criminological schema was identical to the criteria that guided local OGPU administrations during the dekulakization drive. It also equated disparate criminal and marginalized cohorts—prostitutes, organized bandits, and juvenile delinquents—which therefore became targets of extrajudicial repression. By the beginning of 1933, police officers at all levels assumed that the mere existence of diverse categories of "criminal elements" threatened "normal" urban life.

These conceptual connections were reinforced in early 1933, as Yagoda made plans to create a new system of "special settlements" in Western Siberia and Kazakhstan, originally slated for 500,000 inmates each, and as the OGPU began to send "criminal elements" to them alongside populations of dekulakized peasants.[100] The police never spoke of eliminating criminals "as a class," as they did of "kulaks"; instead, by 1933 the language of class had been replaced by the language of "contingents" in the case of resettled peasants and criminal elements alike. The dekulakization drive did not merely set the pattern for police actions against "criminal elements" in the early 1930s. Rather, both actions emerged from the same set of assumptions among top Communist Party and OGPU officials regarding the desired form of state-driven social transformation, and from the same set of criminological understandings held by local police officers regarding the nature of population "contingents" and local problems of social order.

Policing Soviet Cities: The Internal Passport System

The Stalinist regime's attempt to impose order in Soviet urban spaces unfolded against the backdrop of a widespread famine, which began in late 1932 and by the end of 1933 had claimed at least 6 million lives. The famine threatened virtually every aspect of the Stalinist system, even in areas that were far removed from the affected areas. Peasants fled collective farms by the millions, pouring out of Ukraine, Kazakhstan, the northern Caucasus, and the Black Earth region and streaming into major cities in search of food. In late 1932, Stalin and the Politburo resolved to protect Soviet cities from this influx of hungry peasants by creating an internal passport system and by forbidding peasants from entering major urban areas.[101] Although the passport system was conceived in an atmosphere of crisis, it must be also understood in the context of ongoing attempts by the police to control the movement of criminal and marginalized populations, as well as systems designed to regulate legal geographic mobility during the First Five-Year Plan period. Whatever the intentions of the Politburo, the passport system was put in place by local urban police administrations, which had a broader set of concerns in the early 1930s than fleeing peasants alone. Local police used the passport system to target "dangerous" or "harmful" criminal populations, ejecting them from major cities without interference from the court system. Hence the passport system emerged, in the space of only several months, as one of the most important policing techniques in urban areas across the USSR.

The Politburo began to attempt to control peasant migration as soon as it became clear that peasants were rejecting the collective farm system in large numbers. The police in cities, for example, were ordered on January 1, 1932, to halt in-migration of dekulakized peasants by increasing attention to the documents of in-migrants and by expanding the covert surveillance of hotels, flophouses, and railroad stations.[102] For most of 1932, however, controlling migration was seen as a routine part of police activity. The Leningrad regional *militsiia* administration, for example, reported no major influx of fleeing peasants in the first nine months of 1932 and hence carried out no large-scale operations against them, reporting only several hundred cases of apprehension of fleeing "kulaks" for the entire period.[103]

By the fall of 1932, poor harvests and difficulties with the grain procurement campaign prompted the Politburo to prepare for the widespread shortages that would inevitably follow. In late November, the Politburo set up a commission to recommend legislation to clear Moscow, Leningrad, and other major cities of what were termed "kulaks, criminals, and other anti-Soviet elements," along with all individuals not connected with production or industry.[104] The commission members agreed on several general points: dekulakized peasants and other "class-alien" individuals would be ejected from all major urban areas, Moscow and Leningrad would be protected first and other urban areas would be added as quickly as possible, a uniform internal passport would replace all existing systems of identification and labor books, and the new passport system would function in tandem with existing urban registration systems (*propiska*).

Other aspects of the pending legislation, however, provoked substantial debate, especially the questions of past behaviors that made individuals ineligible for passports and punishments for violators. The OGPU recommendations on both counts were extraordinarily harsh: OGPU representatives suggested that individuals arriving in cities without proper documentation be subject to thirty days in jail or a 500-ruble fine, followed by ejection from the area in question, and that prior conviction for a vast array of crimes be grounds for refusal of a passport, including any theft committed by an individual without defined employment or place of residence and any crime whatsoever committed by a "recidivist." OGPU representatives also suggested that the police be authorized to deny passports to individuals involved in gambling or street swindling and to individuals having any contact with illegal sales of alcohol, narcotics, or other aspects of the urban criminal underworld—a blatant attempt to expand the extrajudicial authority of local officers, directed not at ex-convicts but at suspects still on the streets.[105]

By the time the commission's recommendations were forwarded to the Politburo, the most aggressive OGPU suggestions had been rejected: all mention of expulsions of urban criminals without prior convictions had been removed, and punishment for first offenders was set at 100 rubles and ejection from the city in question.[106] The top OGPU officials were highly dissatisfied with this outcome, because they assumed that the passport system would function as a way to control criminal populations in cities as much as to purge them of "kulak elements," and they began to campaign for broader authority to use the passport system to police urban areas immediately after the legislation was promulgated in late December.

Stalin was not completely satisfied with the recommendations either. Impatient with the pace of deliberations, he personally changed several items in the draft legislation, making the system more strict and increasing punishments for violations. Some of these changes made little administrative sense and would present major problems for the police in the future. Stalin decided, for example, that passports would be valid for three years instead of the five recommended by the commission, and he decided that Soviet citizens would have to pay a fee of 3 rubles for their new passports. He also decided to allow individuals arriving in a location covered by the passport system a rather short forty-eight hours to register their passports with the local police, after which they were subject to a 100-ruble fine. By the time the legislation was promulgated, that requirement had been lowered to twenty-four hours.[107]

The legislation defining the passport system, approved by the Politburo on December 14 and published on December 27, 1932, foresaw the issuance of passports to all urban residents of the USSR, along with all residents of construction sites, state farms, workers' settlements, transport corridors, border zones, and other areas of particular state importance. Most rural residents, including both collective and individual farmers, were not issued passports of any kind.[108] By the end of December the city of Kharkov, in Ukraine, joined Moscow and Leningrad as the first targets of passport distribution, which was to begin on January 15; the published legislation also listed Kiev, Minsk, Rostov on the Don, and Vladivostok as secondary priorities, with all remaining urban areas of the USSR slated for passport distribution by the end of 1933. All permanent residents over sixteen years of age in these areas received three-year passports; seasonal workers received three-month documents that could be renewed by the local police as long as the workers proved that they had a place of residence and officially approved employment. Registration (*propiska*) of these passports with local police administrations, carried out through apartment building administrations or directly with the police, began on February 1 and was to be completed by May 1, 1933.[109]

Published instructions only vaguely defined the categories of individuals who were ineligible for passports in regime cities, stating that the goal of the passport system was to purge urban areas of individuals not connected with production or education, not carrying out "socially useful labor," and "threatening kulak, criminal and other antisocial elements."[110] Secret instructions provided to the police were more specific. The police were to deny passports to several categories of "unnecessary" individuals, including fleeing "kulaks"; the unemployed; any individuals arriving after January 1, 1931, without an official invitation for work; "labor shirkers"; individuals who had been fined for disorganization of production; those deprived of voting rights (*lishentsy*); and refugees from other countries. In addition, the police were to refuse passports to all individuals who had served sentences of imprisonment, exile, or banishment for a specific list of crimes, which included all counterrevolutionary and state crimes (Articles 58 and 59 of the Criminal Code) and a slew of lesser crimes such as speculation, aggravated hooliganism, embezzlement, bribe taking, and several categories of theft. This list, arrived at after substantial debate, was intended to be exhaustive and unchangeable, and local police were ordered to obey the exact letter of the instructions. However, the police were also authorized to refuse passports to any "anti-Soviet elements who had contact with criminal individuals," an exception that provided local officers with substantial latitude in the expulsion process.[111]

Despite extensive central discussions of the passport system in the months before its implementation, important aspects of the system required improvisation as they were put in place. The most important such improvisation concerned the status of individuals expelled from Moscow, Leningrad, and Kharkov in the first wave of passport distribution. The initial instructions, promulgated on January 14, 1933, contained specific provisions for individuals who were refused a passport in these three urban areas or who were refused registration, in the case of individuals arriving from other locations once the passport system was in place; these individuals were explicitly accorded the right to live in *all other* locations in the USSR and to receive a passport in those locations, even if that location was subsequently brought under passport restrictions.[112] Central officials, in discussing the passport system in late 1932, had assumed that the major cities, like Moscow and Leningrad, would be off limits to the various categories of individuals identified as "unnecessary," but they made no provisions for ejecting these individuals from all the lesser urban areas of the USSR. The records of the commission's debates in December 1932 suggest that OGPU officials hoped that the passport legislation would allow them to eject such individuals from all urban areas, rather than just from Moscow, Leningrad, and Kharkov, but none of the initial legislation or instructions to the police during the initial wave of distribution made any mention of this idea.

The next set of published instructions, covering passport distribution to the remainder of the USSR and dated April 28, 1933, added a list of twenty-five additional urban areas in which passports were to be refused to individuals on the same basis as Moscow, Leningrad, Kharkov, and the 100-kilometer zone at the Soviet border. Any individual refused a passport in any of these locations was forbidden to live in all of them but was authorized to move to any other urban locale and receive a passport there. In all urban locations not on the list, passports were to be issued without restrictions and without any prejudice regarding social position or past convictions (with the exception, of course, of fleeing "kulaks" and other fugitives).[113] The restricted areas eventually came to be referred to as "regime" (*rezhimnyi*) areas. The division of urban areas into "regime" and "nonregime" locales was an ad hoc adjustment to problems with the distribution process, and it was made in response to the realization that the original regulations, if implemented to the letter, would have forced hundreds of thousands of suspected criminals and other "unnecessary elements" into the Soviet countryside—precisely where the OGPU and *militsiia* administrations were least developed and had little chance of maintaining any kind of surveillance of them.

The essential outlines of the regime system were not new to the police or to Soviet jurisprudence; in effect, it was the same system of banishment (*vysylka*) that had been used by the courts and police alike since the early 1920s and was still often called "Minus Ten" or "Minus Twelve" (for the number of restricted cities) in the early 1930s. For the local police, the connection was clear: the passport system provided them with the ability to subject Soviet citizens to permanent banishment for a variety of reasons, including prior criminal convictions or ongoing contact with the criminal milieu. In fact, once the first wave of passport distribution was complete, covering twenty-eight specific cities and Soviet border zones, the police began to refer to banishment as "Minus Thirty." Yet the existence of the passport system made banishment redundant as a specific punishment, because conviction for any number of crimes was cause for automatic refusal of a passport in regime locations, which was, in effect, a permanent sentence of "Minus Thirty." The distinction between regime and nonregime passport locations unified police systems of banishment and registration with police approaches to "socially harmful and dangerous elements"; as such, it became one of the most dynamic aspects of policing practice for the rest of the 1930s.

The initial distribution of passports in the most important Soviet cities was carried out in an atmosphere of crisis.[114] Stalin's personal response to the crisis was made clear by his order in late January 1933 instructing regional Communist Party and OGPU officials to prevent all movement of starving peasant populations out of the North Caucasus and Ukraine and subjecting all migrating peasants detained by the OGPU to repatriation to their places of residence or, for the "counterrevolutionary elements" among them, terms of forced labor.[115] In the following month, OGPU administrations detained nearly 220,000 of these starving peasants, arresting some 34,000 and returning the rest to their famine-stricken homelands.[116]

In this atmosphere, passport distribution proceeded with amazing speed. The operation commenced in Moscow and Leningrad on January 25, 1933, and in Kharkov on February 1.[117] By February 10, the police had issued 407,324 passports in these three cities; by February 20, 886,374.[118] In mid-February, the police prepared to distribute passports in Magnitogorsk,

Kuznetsk, Gorkii, Stalingrad, and Baku, none of which was listed as among the first locations to be targeted in the original passport legislation.[119] By March 20, the police had issued 2.9 million passports in the three original regime areas, plus an additional 133,838 as part of the second wave of distribution in five additional regime locations.[120] By April 20, they had issued 6.6 million passports in eleven major urban areas (now including Minsk, Odessa, and Kiev, though still not including Vladivostok, which had been listed among the original seven cities in December 1932).[121] In May, the police began to distribute passports in the remainder of the twenty-eight regime cities; they then distributed passports, without restriction, in all nonregime urban areas during the remainder of 1933 and 1934 (see table 3.1).

By August 1934, the police reported that they had issued roughly 27 million passports in the Russian Republic, including 12 million in regime locations and almost 15 million in nonregime locales; at this point, the operation was largely complete, although it stretched on for several months in other national republics.[122] These levels of speed and comprehensiveness were possible only because passport distribution built on existing systems of registration maintained by both the OGPU and the *militsiia*, and because the OGPU, which had now been in charge of policing for more than two years, was fully involved in every aspect of the process.

Although the Politburo intended the passport system primarily to prevent the migration of peasants to cities, it also expected the new regulations to solve several related problems, including the regulation of seasonal labor flows between city and countryside, control of the size of the largest cities in the USSR, and ejection of unwanted categories of individuals from urban areas. The police concentrated on five major groups targeted by the legislation: individuals arriving in cities without the proper labor recruitment documentation, dekulakized peasants fleeing the countryside, individuals with criminal convictions, those "not engaged in socially useful labor," and individuals deprived of voting rights (*lishentsy*), plus the dependents of those individuals ejected due to their prerevolutionary social identities (see table 3.2). Instructions to the local police stressed that wholesale purges of suspect individuals were forbidden, likely in anticipation of the kind of chaotic police actions that characterized the dekulakization drives.[123] Yet the rates of passport refusal as reported by the police themselves were surprisingly low, hovering around only 4 percent in the largest cities of the USSR in 1933, although the rates in some areas, including Baku and Kiev, climbed as high as 10 percent in the initial weeks

Table 3.1. *Cumulative Total Passports Issued in the First Eleven Cities Passportized in the USSR, 1933*

Location	As of February 10, 1933[a]	As of February 20, 1933[b]	As of March 20, 1933[c]	As of March 31, 1933[d]	As of April 20, 1933[e]	As of May 4, 1933[f]	As of May 8, 1933[g]
Moscow city	177,312	332,185	812,665	1,206,789	1,951,037		2,392,642
Moscow region	64,780	200,512	794,897	1,008,014	1,308,586	1,421,471	
Leningrad City	147,660	301,189	1,067,403	1,365,905	1,785,093		
Leningrad region			81,846	160,165	294,266		
Kharkov	17,572	52,688	186,505	302,813	600,242		
Magnitogorsk			39,889	64,370	74,314		
Stalingrad			38,465	79,324	159,246		
Gorkii			42,313	100,743	239,903		
Stalinsk			12,251	30,604	63,443		
Baku			920	6,641	48,287		
Minsk					13,235		
Odessa					52,816		
Kiev					6,046		
Total:	407,324	886,374	3,077,154	4,325,368	6,596,514		

Sources:

[a] GARF, f. 3316, op. 64, d. 1227, ll. 77–83 (*Svodka #1 o passportizatsii*).
[b] GARF, f. 3316, op. 64, d. 1227, ll. 84–91 (*Svodka #2*).
[c] GARF, f. 5446, op. 14a, d. 740, ll. 89–99 (*Svodka #5*).
[d] GARF, f. 5446, op. 14a, d. 740, ll. 82–88 (*Svodka #6*).
[e] GARF, f. 5446, op. 14a, d. 740, ll. 71–81 (*Svodka #7*).
[f] GARF, f. 1235, op. 141, d. 1517, ll. 17–18 (Procuracy figures, Moscow region only, includes temporary labor documents).
[g] GARF, f. 1235, op. 141, d. 1517, ll. 17–17ob (Moscow city only, includes temporary labor documents).

Table 3.2. *Cumulative Total Reported Reasons for Passport Denials in the First Eleven Cities Passportized in the USSR, 1933 (number of reports and percentage of total)*

Reason	As of February 10[a]		As of February 20[b]		As of March 20[c]		As of March 31[d]		As of April 20[e]	
	Number	Percent	Number	Percent	Number	Percent	Number	Percent	Number	Percent
No invitation	3,401	39.8	9,208	39.1	35,158	31.3	49,612	29.4	76,670	28.8
Fleeing kulaks	2,701	31.6	6,698	28.5	26,185	23.3	38,965	23.1	60,508	22.8
Ex-convicts	896	10.5	2,542	10.8	14,371	12.8	21,870	13.0	34,338	12.9
Lishentsy	645	7.5	1,740	7.4	9,591	8.5	14,248	8.4	21,926	8.2
Not engaged in socially useful labor	563	6.6	1,140	4.8	12,430	11.1	20,055	11.9	34,851	13.1
Refugees (*perebezhchiki*)	55	0.6	172	0.7	873	0.8	1,231	0.7	1,949	0.7
Dependents of above categories	275	3.2	966	4.1	11,156	9.9	18,054	10.7	28,379	10.7
Kulaks and criminals uncovered via "operational means"									7,310	2.7

Note: All percentages are calculated. Columns may not add up to 100 percent because of rounding and because a small number of denials were not categorized in any of the above categories.

Sources:

[a] GARF, f. 3316, op. 64, d. 1227, ll. 77–83 (*Svodka #1 o passportizatsii*).

[b] GARF, f. 3316, op. 64, d. 1227, ll. 84–91 (*Svodka #2*).

[c] GARF, f. 5446, op. 14a, d. 740, ll. 89–99 (*Svodka #5*).

[d] GARF, f. 5446, op. 14a, d. 740, ll. 82–88 (*Svodka #6*).

[e] GARF, f. 5446, op. 14a, d. 740, ll. 71–81 (*Svodka #7*).

of distribution (see table 3.3). By August 1934, 384,922 people had been denied passports in the Russian Republic, compared with 27 million passports issued, roughly a 3.3 percent refusal rate. According to police reports, the relatively low rates of refusal were attributable to the massive flight of individuals who knew that they would not receive passports in regime cities, but the police provided no solid estimates of the total numbers of such individuals.[124] The flight from cities was indeed massive, and the resulting reversal of population trends was clear and immediate. Moscow police reported that the city's population fell steadily over the course of 1933; by January 1934, it was 3,613,000, down from a height of 3,663,000 in 1933 (although still higher than the 1932 figure of 3,135,000). Leningrad saw a similar overall reduction of 176,000 people over the course of 1934.[125] In virtually every category that concerned central Communist Party officials, the passport distribution process was an unqualified success.

In the course of the initial distribution of passports, the local police generally focused their energy on uncovering the categories of individuals targeted by the center, but they often applied these categories flexibly in order to shape the process to their own benefit. At times, local police could simply be overvigilant; central officials complained, for example, that the police denied passports to "toilers, many young workers, specialists and white-collar employees, even to Komsomol members and Communist Party members solely because they [were] by social origin children of former nobility, traders, clergy, etc." or that they relied on denunciations from state or social institutions, such as local housing administrations, to deny passports to individuals who were eligible for them but deemed "not ours, alien elements, or former people."[126] Yet the police applied the instructions most liberally to those categories of individuals that related directly to their daily work, especially individuals with prior convictions. The local police regularly denied passports to individuals with any sort of past judicial or administrative arrest or with convictions that led to fines or short terms of compulsory labor, ignoring specific instructions that only convictions that led to deprivation of freedom were grounds for refusal. Some local administrations went so far as to deny passports to individuals who had been arrested for crimes listed in the instructions but had been acquitted in court. The police in Moscow had a particular tendency to deny passports to the families of individuals who were serving sentences in prisons or labor camps and hence were "connected with the criminal milieu," a practice with no basis in the legislation.

Table 3.3. Cumulative Number and Percentage of Total Passports Denied in the First Eleven Cities Passportized in the USSR, 1933

Location	As of February 10, 1933[a]		As of February 20, 1933[b]		As of March 20, 1933[c]		As of March 31, 1933[d]		As of April 20, 1933[e]	
	Number	Percent	Number	Percent	Number	Percent	Number	Percent	Number	Percent
Moscow city	4,057	2.3	8,839	2.7	30,641	3.5	45,857	3.6	70,814	3.5
Moscow region	1,934	3.0	6,939	3.5	33,469	4	42,455	4	57,231	4.3
Leningrad city	2,533	1.7	7,638	2.5	34,638	3.1	51,120	3.6	73,620	4.1
Leningrad region					2,553	3.02	5,095	3	9,628	3.2
Kharkov	25	0.1	99	0.2	4,264	2.2	9,158	2.9	18,896	3.1
Magnitogorsk					2,620	6.1	2,909	4.3	3,872	5.2
Stalingrad					1,977	4.8	6,605	7.6	13,230	8.3
Gorkii					1,765	4	3,984	3.8	8,388	3.4
Stalinsk					272	2.1	1,129	3.5	2,011	3.1
Baku					37	3.8	438	6.1	4,967	10.9
Minsk									674	5
Odessa									1,978	3.7
Kiev									622	10.2
Total	8,549	2.8	23,515	3.9	112,236	3.5	168,760	3.7	265,931	4

Note: Percentages for February 10 and February 20 are calculated; all other percentages are found in the original documents.
Sources:
[a] GARF, f. 3316, op. 64, d. 1227, ll. 77–83 (Svodka #1 o passportizatsii).
[b] GARF, f. 3316, op. 64, d. 1227, ll. 84–91 (Svodka #2).
[c] GARF, f. 5446, op. 14a, d. 740, ll. 89–99 (Svodka #5).
[d] GARF, f. 5446, op. 14a, d. 740, ll. 82–88 (Svodka #6).
[e] GARF, f. 5446, op. 14a, d. 740, ll. 71–81 (Svodka #7).

Local officers also applied the regulations in more creative ways; the police in Moscow, for example, interpreted the orders to deny passports to individuals "not engaged in socially useful labor" to mean all individuals without a job, including career workers who had recently quit or were between jobs, and they interpreted instructions on denying passports to individuals "connected with the criminal milieu" as applicable to individuals who wrote letters to friends who were in prison.[127] By August 1933, individuals classed as ex-convicts or "not involved in socially useful labor," the two most flexible categories targeted by the passport regulations, had climbed to just over 30 percent of the total rejections in regime areas. Central police officials railed against these abuses, but a certain amount of "excesses" were inevitable in a project as massive as the distribution of 27 million passports to populations as mobile as those in Soviet cities in the early 1930s.[128]

The overt repression of "active" criminal elements was central to the passport distribution process as well. In Moscow, the OGPU Operative Department worked closely with *militsiia* officers in order to conduct coordinated "purge operations" (*operatsii po ochistke*) of the city of "criminal elements." Individual OGPU and *militsiia* administrations provided the Operative Department with lists of individuals who were under surveillance by detective departments or registered (*na uchet*) by one of the numerous overlapping registration systems. These secret lists guided *militsiia* officers as they refused passports to individuals under investigation or even suspicion, and they allowed the police to identify and arrest wanted criminals if they attempted to obtain a passport.[129] Passport distribution took place during ongoing campaigns to purge major Soviet cities of harmful and dangerous elements, which, as discussed above, made use of extrajudicial repression under both the OGPU troikas and the actions of local registration bureaus. The local police naturally extended these operations, ongoing in 1932, into 1933 as part of passport distribution, targeting the same categories of individuals that had been the object of earlier sweeps. Individual officers could send "criminal elements" directly to OGPU troikas, but they could also simply refuse to issue a passport, a practice that extended the reach of the registration bureaus, and hence of extrajudicial sanction, to virtually every urban resident of the Soviet Union in 1933.

Once the implementation of the passport system was complete, the police turned to preventing the migration of individuals without passports to regime areas and to uncovering and sentencing those "criminal elements" who continued to live in regime cities. The Politburo expanded the ability of the police to sentence these offenders in mid-August 1933 by creating OGPU troikas dedicated to sentencing violators of the passport system. These "passport troikas," composed of the assistant OGPU chief in charge of the *militsiia* for a given administrative area and the corresponding heads of the OGPU Passport and Operative departments, were authorized to mete out sentences ranging from banishment for first-time offenders who were unemployed, or "labor shirkers," to three years in a special settlement for "*lishentsy*, kulaks, and dekulakized peasants," to three years in labor camp for "criminals and other antisocial elements" and all second offenders. Like all OGPU troikas, the passport troikas nominally functioned under the supervision of the Procuracy, although the fact that cases were to be heard and sentenced within forty-eight hours suggests that expediency, rather than proper procedure, was paramount.[130]

Local police used these extrajudicial prerogatives aggressively after mid-1933. The administrative troikas in the Leningrad region, for example, heard 24,369 cases of passport violators between August 1, 1933, when the passport troikas were created, and January 1, 1934; 16,809 of these individuals were eventually freed, attesting to the continued tendency of local *militsiia* officers to expand expulsions beyond the intentions of the center, but 6,692 were sentenced to deprivation of freedom, mostly to camps, special settlements, or banishment. The majority of those condemned were identified as "not engaged in socially useful labor" or "criminal elements," the two categories that became most prevalent once the initial distribution process was complete (see table 3.2).[131] According to a report compiled by the police leadership in mid-1934, from early 1933 to August 1934 the local police focused a massive amount of daily attention on uncovering such individuals, carrying out more than 600,000 individual searches of public areas frequented by criminal elements and uncovering more than 630,000 violators of the passport regime. Of these offenders, the OGPU sentenced just under 66,000 individuals through the troikas, sent 3,596 to court, fined 185,000, and ejected nearly 176,000 more from the regime cities.[132]

By mid-1934, the passport system seemed to have succeeded in promoting the kind of social stability demanded by the Politburo in the post-dekulakization period. The populations of major cities had stabilized, and by the summer of that year the number of passport violations was decreasing from month to month.[133] The local police, however, predominantly viewed the passport system as a way to bypass the court system and to target urban criminal populations with a minimum of effort. In 1933, the police at all levels found that this particular method of policing was far more effective than covert approaches to controlling "dangerous elements," and they embraced it energetically. The right to mete out extra-judicial repression using the passport troikas was a major part of this appeal. As we will see below, even as the Politburo reduced most of the OGPU's extrajudicial sentencing capacity in mid-1933, it left untouched the local police's ability to sanction passport violators. The local police, not surprisingly, focused their attention on repressing passport violators in the years that followed, and extrajudicial repression in connection with the passport system skyrocketed between 1934 and 1936. The dynamism of the passport system ensured that extrajudicial sanctions and campaigns against "dangerous" and "harmful" criminals would continue to animate Soviet policing in the years that followed.

Institutional Consolidation and Central Control

The relative success of passport distribution attests to another major trend in policing in the mid-1930s: the gradual assumption of administrative control over the local police by the OGPU leadership in Moscow. Under the tutelage of the OGPU, the *militsiia* benefited from more officers, supplies, and financial support in the early 1930s than in any previous period of Bolshevik rule. After sharp declines from 1924 to 1930, the number of officers rose dramatically between 1930 and 1935. The most rapid expansion occurred from 1931 to 1933, as the OGPU campaigned for additional forces in order to support Stalin's policy initiatives. In addition to the dekulakization drive, the passport system required additional *militsiia* officers; the Politburo added 12,500 positions to the force specifically for that purpose in early 1933. Similarly, the Politburo responded to OGPU complaints in early 1933 that local *militsiia* administrations were overwhelmed with duties related to prisons, especially convoying prisoners, by approving an increase of 12,000 officers to deal with transfers of prisoners in areas not served by convoy troops.[134] Top Communist Party officials did not always acquiesce to such requests; in December 1933, for example, the Central Control Commission rejected a request from the OGPU itself for 2,546 more officers for the calendar year 1934, allowing an increase of only 1,150.[135] Expansion of the *militsiia* slowed after 1934, yet by 1935 roughly 125,500 civil policemen (not including the Industrial

Militsiia) served in the USSR, likely more than double the levels during the NEP (see table 1.1 in chapter 1).

The OGPU took a series of steps in 1932 and 1933 to improve control over local *militsiia* administrations, focusing on personnel issues and on structural changes that helped to streamline connections between the center and the periphery. Problems of funding and provisioning continued throughout this period, in part because of nationwide shortages caused by the famine in 1932 and 1933, yet the transfer of all police to the USSR budget in mid-1931, and the creation of a single OGPU administration for dealing with funding issues later in the year, allowed the OGPU to coordinate issues of pay and rank across jurisdictions and to reduce disparities between locations.[136] In 1932, the OGPU took over several aspects of local administration completely, including the selection of cadres. Pay scales for the highest-ranking *militsiia* officers were equalized with those of officers in the OGPU in 1932, in part because many of them were in fact OGPU officers. In early 1933 the OGPU gained the right to use troikas to sentence the officer corps of the *militsiia*, as well as all undercover operatives employed by the Detective Department, for crimes in office.[137] Finally, the very top of the OGPU and *militsiia* hierarchy was reorganized during the implementation of the passport system, when the Politburo created a new Central Militsiia Administration within the OGPU (GURKM pri OGPU), named G. E. Prokofev its new head, and announced publicly for the first time that the OGPU was directly in charge of all policing in the USSR. This announcement ended two years of "secret" control of *militsiia* functions by the OGPU and in the process abandoned the pretense that individual republics controlled their own police systems.[138]

According to central police reports, the quality of *militsiia* personnel improved after 1932 as well. The OGPU takeover resulted in immediate increases in Communist Party membership; in mid-1932, party members and candidates made up nearly 45 percent of the *militsiia* officer corps and nearly 75 percent of the upper ranks, and by late 1932 party or Komsomol members made up nearly 30 percent of the overall force. Levels of disciplinary infractions stabilized in this period, and those infractions that still existed were usually caused, according to the center, by poor working and living conditions and by provisioning difficulties rather than by inherent deficiencies in the police cadres themselves.[139] The OGPU reported a substantial reduction in labor turnover in the *militsiia* as a whole as early as February 1932, especially in the officer corps; although in mid-1932 nearly 18 percent of the *militsiia*'s officer corps had been on the force for less than a year, more than 30 percent had between one and three years of service and nearly half had been on the force for three years or more. Part of the improvement was due to the fact that the new OGPU leadership could call up cadres from the party, and especially the OGPU itself; nearly 7,000 of the new *militsiia* officers added to the force in 1931 and 1932 were called up from the party, and more than 500 OGPU officers were transferred to the *militsiia* between January 1931 and July 1932, most to leadership positions or detective departments. The OGPU also instituted a policy of frequent transfer of top members of the *militsiia* officer corps from one administration to another, duplicating their own leadership system in order to prevent local police officials from developing close working relationships with local party and soviet administrations.[140]

These improvements notwithstanding, the Soviet police system suffered from numerous administrative problems through the middle of the decade. Training remained completely inadequate. The OGPU in 1933 complained that the existing system of schools for the *militsiia* officer corps was so insufficient that it would take nine years to put eligible officers through the program, assuming that none of them quit in the meantime. Training for the rank and file, especially for rural officers, was generally nonexistent, as it had been before the OGPU takeover.[141] The sheer lack of a police presence in the countryside and at the periphery was a more fundamental problem. The police remained concentrated in major urban areas, even after the end of the First Five-Year Plan period; rural policemen in Western Siberia, for example, were generally responsible for upward of 10,000 rural residents scattered in villages up to 100 kilometers apart.[142]

In areas without substantial *militsiia* representation, the Industrial Militsiia grew to become the most widespread form of police presence; by the end of 1931, it was already 150 percent the size of the *militsiia* itself, and it continued to grow until 1933 (see table 1.1). The OGPU took steps to improve control over the Industrial Militsiia immediately after the takeover in 1930, attempting to make individual units answerable to standard police hierarchies rather than to local factories or other economic institutions.[143] In February 1932, central OGPU officials, complaining that the system had drained provisions, supplies, and weapons from the police as a whole, forbade local officials from setting up new contracts without the explicit approval of the center and, to drive home the point, ordered local police administrations to reduce their own officer staffs to compensate for the increased drain on resources whenever a new contract was put in place.[144] In late 1932, the OGPU leadership categorically refused to provide any provisions, supplies, or weapons to local police forces organized by local soviets or factories without the explicit consent of the center.[145] None of these moves, however, could overcome the propensity of local police administrations to broker lucrative contracts with individual factories or retail establishments, nor could they halt the drain of central resources to Industrial Militsiia administrations at the periphery.

The problems of rural policing and the Industrial Militsiia were made plainly obvious by the failure of the policing system in the countryside to deal adequately with the issue of theft of collective farm property, especially in conjunction with Stalin's August 1932 law on theft. Officials from all concerned commissariats in early 1933 agreed that the existing system was completely inadequate to protect the industrial, distribution, and especially collective farm systems from theft and embezzlement. Most protection of public and state property was not even the responsibility of the Industrial Militsiia but fell to guards hired directly by individual factories, collective farms, or other state institutions. Such guards numbered several hundred thousand and represented the largest group of "police" forces in the USSR in 1933. These guards were generally of even worse quality than Industrial Militsiia officers; according to central police reports, they were usually made up of "socially alien elements," individuals unfit for full-time labor, or the elderly, and only 7 percent were armed in any way. Hired guards were popular with economic officials because they were far less expensive than Industrial Militsiia officers; many commissariats moved in this period toward reducing existing contracts with the *militsiia* and relying almost entirely on hired guards because it saved them millions of rubles each year.[146] This trend, however, did little to protect these institutions from increasing levels of theft.

The issue was discussed at the USSR Sovnarkom level in April and May 1933. Representatives from several commissariats, especially the Agriculture Commissariat, called for the assumption of policing duties within state agencies by the OGPU; agricultural officials noted that the military-style defense of collective farm property by the OGPU had proven to be the most effective solution in 1932 and 1933, and they suggested that the OGPU take over the majority of policing activity in the countryside.[147] Justice officials, including Andrei Vyshinsky, resisted this call for expanded OGPU activity in Soviet economic life, suggesting instead that the commissariats themselves take increased responsibility for improving the qualifications of their hired guards and that the OGPU concentrate only on improving the performance of its own local administrations.[148] All participants, however, understood the inadequacy of rural police systems and their inability to prevent crimes against state property. This debate was halted by the instruction of May 8, 1933, which attempted to bring some order to the rural policing system by other means (see below), but the issue continued to vex central and local police officials through the end of the decade.

The "End" of Dekulakization and the Clearing of Prisons, May 1933

The passport system and purges of urban areas may have protected major Soviet cities from the worst effects of the famine in late 1932 and 1933, but these strategies had little effect on the famine itself. The Politburo's initial response to this widespread hunger, as discussed above, was to continue to apply extrajudicial pressure to the countryside to force grain collection, and, when the situation became so serious that no amount of coercion could maintain order, to close the borders of the affected areas and to force starving peasants to meet their fates without disrupting other parts of the country.

In the face of such obvious policy failures, in the spring of 1933 the Politburo began to consider fundamental administrative changes in the countryside, calling into question the entire existing system of mass deportation of dekulakized peasants. After weeks of debate, Stalin launched a major policy initiative, which was communicated to the public by the May 8 instruction titled "On the Halting of Mass Banishment of Peasants, Regulation of the Carrying Out of Arrests, and Clearing Out of Places of Confinement." This instruction is generally seen as a turning point in Stalinist criminal justice, as a measure that halted indiscriminate repression in the countryside and signaled the beginning of several years of moderation in the mid-1930s.[149] Careful consideration of this instruction's genesis and exact implementation, however, shows that Stalin intended it primarily to bring order to the prison and special-settlement systems, which had virtually collapsed during the famine, rather than to initiate any changes in the practices of the *militsiia* or OGPU. Despite a serious discussion of reforms within the Soviet criminal justice system at the top of the Communist Party hierarchy in early 1933, Stalin ultimately chose order over moderation, as he had in every instance since the "Dizzy with Success" speech in March 1930.

The destabilizing effects of ongoing repression in the countryside were real, and by the end of 1932, top Communist Party and especially justice officials understood the dangers of continuing the current course. Vyshinsky, in particular, campaigned consistently in 1932 and early 1933 to restore the authority of the Soviet legal system and, based on the recommendations of the June 1932 edict "On Revolutionary Legality," to bring some order to the yearly planting and harvesting campaigns. In late 1932 and early 1933, justice officials forwarded to the center reports of widespread violations of even the most basic procedural norms in the countryside, stressing familiar themes of police brutality and abuses of power (*proizvol*) by local soviet officials.[150] Justice officials added to their complaints in late 1932 the problem of overcrowding in police and Justice Commissariat prisons, which was reaching crisis proportions in many areas. The system of police lockups, maintained by local *militsiia* administrations and intended to hold prisoners only for several days, was particularly overcrowded; random checks by Procuracy officials found that massive numbers of individuals were arrested by the police or local soviet officials and held while their cases languished in local police stations, often without any ongoing investigation.[151] This issue of prison overcrowding was discussed vigorously in early 1933 among police and judicial officials at the center; nearly all the participants in these discussions argued that something had to be done about this truly dire situation, which was likely to worsen as a result of the ongoing famine.

Police officials also provided a substantial amount of detail on the conditions in the prison and camp system to top Communist Party officials in early 1933. Prokofev, the OGPU's assistant chief in charge of the *militsiia*, argued in a February 22, 1933, letter to Avel Enukidze, the secretary of the All-Union Central Executive Committee, that a crisis in short-term police prisons was imminent. The closing of numerous prisons within the Justice Commissariat in 1931 and 1932, he argued, had occurred at the same time that arrests increased substantially due to collectivization campaigns, resulting in the severe overcrowding of police jails that were intended only to hold individuals for short periods but had effectively become long-term prisons.[152] Prokofev based his report on information sent to him only days before by regional OGPU officials, which painted an even more dire picture of the situation. According to the OGPU, the local police lacked the labor power to run the prison system and the financial ability to support these prisoners, who were not provided for by any state budget resources because they were technically not in prison at all. Cells meant for 15 to 18 people were overfilled by up to 800 percent; one jail in Moscow, with a capacity of 350 individuals, was filled with 2,341 people as of January 31, 1933. The situation in the North Caucasus Territory was even worse: the police held nearly 35,000 prisoners in short-term jails, many with 500 to 1,000 prisoners each, and almost 11,000 of these prisoners had already been sentenced but could not be transferred to long-term prisons for lack of space.[153] The results, Prokofev argued, were widespread epidemics, escapes, and starvation within the prison system, especially in Kazakhstan and the North Caucasus, where the famine was most severe. The police at all levels were being diverted from their regular patrols and operative duties to deal with this crushing problem.[154]

Yagoda attempted to address these problems in early 1933 in conjunction with a major plan for an expanded system of "special settlements" (*spetsposelki*), which he intended to make into the backbone of the Soviet Gulag. His plan, sent directly to Stalin and dated February 13, 1933, called for the creation of new settlements in Western Siberia and Kazakhstan containing a million individuals each. These new settlements would incarcerate not only peasants arrested during the dekulakization, sowing, and harvest drives but also what was termed a "new contingent" of urban criminals and marginals sentenced during passport distribution and extrajudicial purges of major cities in 1932 and 1933. Yagoda proposed that all individuals sentenced to five years or less, by either the OGPU or the courts, be transferred to the new special settlements in order to relieve pressure on the prison system. Stalin agreed with Yagoda's plan in principle but added that the issue of overcrowding in prisons should be addressed immediately.[155]

The Politburo acted quickly on this information, forming a commission on February 23, headed by Krylenko and including Yagoda and Anastas Mikoyan, to discuss the "immediate clearing out [*razgruzka*] of prisons."[156] Two weeks, later, on March 8, 1933, the Politburo issued a major instruction titled "On the Clearing Out [Razgruzka] of Places of Confinement," which contained a detailed set of instructions to regional OGPU, Communist Party, and justice officials intended to reduce prison populations in both police lockups and Justice Commissariat prisons. The OGPU in Ukraine, for example, was to move 25,000 prisoners, sentenced to three years or more, from prisons to OGPU labor camps; to move all prisoners sentenced to between two and three years of deprivation of freedom to special settlements; and to sentence to compulsory labor in labor colonies in Ukraine all convicts within the prison system who did not warrant deprivation of freedom (the latter two categories were to total roughly 40,000 individuals). The Politburo ordered similar transfers in the North Caucasus Territory, the Central Black Earth region, and the Lower Volga Territory, totaling roughly 150,000 individuals, and it instructed Yagoda and Krylenko to prepare quotas for all other locations. Justice officials were also instructed to check the cases of all individuals awaiting trial in jail and to halt all cases that they deemed incorrect, while the OGPU was ordered to complete all ongoing investigations of individuals currently held under their auspices, which the order put at some 77,500 in the above-mentioned four areas alone.[157]

Yet the March 8 instruction did not order the police or justice officials to arrest fewer individuals, underscoring the limits of Stalin's desire to reform the criminal justice system in early 1933. The instruction was issued in the midst of ongoing campaigns against urban criminals and passport violators, which, as we have seen, relied heavily on extrajudicial repression. The Politburo also reversed its prohibition of extrajudicial executions at this time, authorizing an OGPU troika in Belorussia to execute "counterrevolutionary" peasants in early February 1933; it accorded the same right to an OGPU troika in Ukraine on March 10, only two days after approving the instruction. Yagoda's initial plan for new special settlements, now officially termed "labor settlements" (*trudposelki* or *trudposeleniia*), was likewise approved on March 10, despite resistance from the West Siberian Communist Party boss to the idea of additional settlements in his area.[158] The demonstrated goal of the instruction was to alleviate some of the most egregious difficulties in the Soviet penal system and to blunt the effects of the famine on the Soviet administrative system, but it did not signal any fundamental change in Soviet criminal justice.

The "clearing" of prisons, which began under Krylenko's supervision in mid-March, did not go as smoothly as planned. Local police received the order on March 22, and by March 31 the head of the USSR Convoy Troops, who was responsible for the transfer of prisoners to labor camps and colonies, reported that most of the 56,500 inmates in the above-mentioned four areas slated to go to OGPU labor camps had been transferred. However, convoy troops were unable to transfer inmates in the Central Black Earth region; many were under quarantine, and local OGPU and prison officials were unprepared to carry out the transfers. Nearly all transfers to labor colonies had been delayed, partly because of difficulties in scheduling the transport of rail cars, and partly because many of the prisoner convoys were ravaged by epidemics, especially typhus, resulting

in sickness and death in railway cars along the way.[159] Krylenko complained to Molotov on May 7, 1933, that the March instruction was not
being fulfilled correctly and that it, in any case, did not adequately deal
with the realities of the situation. Transfers out of the prison system, he
argued, were not keeping pace with the influx of new prisoners, and the
March instruction did nothing to change this situation. By the beginning
of May 1933, he estimated, the number of inmates in prisons, not including open labor colonies under the Justice Commissariat, would surpass
400,000.[160]

Although many central officials were concerned with this situation,
reducing coercion was not among the options preferred by Stalin in the
spring of 1933. OGPU repressions in the countryside continued in areas
still beset by famine, and on April 16 the Politburo extended the right to
issue extrajudicial sentences of execution to the OGPU troika in Leningrad.[161] In Ukraine the famine's effects were still dire, leading its Communist Party officials in early May to launch major extrajudicial sweeps
in Kharkov, Odessa, and Kiev of homeless beggars and to instruct local
police and soviet officials to force them into work detachments on local
building sites or state farms.[162] At the same time, the Politburo continued
with ongoing plans to expand the OGPU special settlement system in
Western Siberia and Kazakhstan, in mid-April instructing the OGPU to
begin building these settlements and authorizing OGPU and justice officials to send to them all individuals sentenced to three to five years of
hard labor, along with their families—a practice that was prevalent in the
dekulakization process but that had not previously been applied to individuals sentenced by the courts or the OGPU for specific crimes.[163]

All these issues played a role in the Politburo's decision to issue, only
two months after the order on "clearing" prisons, the most important instruction on sentencing procedures in this period. On May 7, 1933, the
Politburo issued an abrupt order forbidding all OGPU troikas to issue
death sentences (with the notable exception of the Far Eastern Territory),
and it approved an instruction titled "On the Halting of Mass Banishment
of Peasants, Regulation of the Carrying Out of Arrests, and Clearing Out
of Places of Confinement," which was issued as a joint Central Committee and Sovnarkom document the next day.[164] The instruction of May 8
announced the end of the regime's full-scale attack on the countryside;
the Bolsheviks, it stated, had triumphed over kulak and other anti-Soviet
forces in the countryside, making possible a halt to banishment and other
"acute forms of repression" against peasants. The instruction also focused

on the abuse of power by local officials, complaining that arrests were carried out by unauthorized soviet and Communist Party officials and that the OGPU and the *militsiia*, for their part, had "lost all sense of proportion" and had carried out unfounded mass arrests. The instruction specifically ordered a halt to all mass deportations in the countryside, and to all arrests by individuals other than *militsiia*, OGPU, and justice officials.[165]

Despite the laudatory tone of the instruction regarding the supposed end of "acute forms of repression" in the countryside, little changed in the short term; mass dekulakization had ended, in essence, in late 1931, whereas extrajudicial repressions in conjunction with the yearly sowing and harvest campaigns were ongoing in early 1933 and would continue throughout the 1930s. The more pertinent goals of the instruction involved Stalin's decision to bring order to the countryside's criminal justice system and to restore some of the authority of legal procedures that had been lost during the collectivization and dekulakization campaigns.[166]

Although the May 8 instruction complained of mass arrests by *militsiia* and OGPU officials in the countryside, specific policy changes regarding the police were decidedly limited. The instruction ordered both the OGPU and the *militsiia* to submit to prosecutorial oversight; the OGPU in particular was to obey existing legislation regarding the right of local prosecutors to supervise and overrule arrests. The instruction, however, included numerous exceptions to these requirements. The OGPU was not required to seek preliminary approval for arrests for a number of specific crimes, including terrorism, counterrevolutionary organizations, counterrevolution, and "wrecking," all of which were widely abused by the OGPU, as central Communist Party officials well knew. In addition, implementation of the measures regarding prosecutorial sanction was delayed for six months in the Far Eastern Territory, Central Asia, and Kazakhstan. *Militsiia* officers were required to seek approval from local procurators within forty-eight hours of an arrest, but only for cases that were to be processed through the court system; cases that were bound for extrajudicial hearings required only the approval of corresponding OGPU chiefs.[167] In practice, the police continued to arrest massive numbers of individuals without any form of prosecutorial sanction, including "harmful and dangerous elements," individuals subject to repression by the OGPU troikas (at least one of which was still authorized to sentence individuals to death), and violators of the passport regime. The restrictions placed on the police by the instruction were minimal, especially when compared with the restrictions placed on the activities of local Communist

Party and soviet officials, and they did not interfere with the ability of the police—both the *militsiia* and the OGPU—to process the majority of cases of concern to both organizations using extrajudicial means.[168]

Restrictions on police activity were limited, in part, because the most important aspect of the instruction was the reduction of prison populations. In this area, the instruction expanded on the March attempt to reduce prison populations; in some instances, the language was in fact identical, suggesting that the Politburo was simply attempting to force implementation of the original March instruction. The May instruction, however, was more extensive. Police and justice officials were ordered to cut prison populations from more than 800,000 to less than 400,000 in the space of several weeks. To accomplish this immense (and, for the OGPU, rather novel) task, the Politburo ordered a set of specific transfers that followed many of the outlines of the March instruction. Individuals in prisons sentenced to five or more years were to be transferred to OGPU labor camps, those sentenced to between three and five years were to be sent to the new OGPU special settlements in Siberia and Kazakhstan, and those serving sentences of less than three years were to have their sentences commuted to one year of compulsory labor. Finally, all peasants sentenced to between three and five years in the course of the dekulakization drive were to be moved permanently to special settlements.[169] No quotas were provided for specific regions of the country: Krylenko was left to work out the details in the course of the operation.

The second "clearing" of prisons was rapid and dramatic. Krylenko reported to Molotov on May 20 that more than 99,000 individuals had already been removed from prisons; roughly 8,350 had been transferred to camps or colonies, and an additional 34,400 were being prepared for transfer. By late May, Krylenko had established quotas for all areas of the USSR; and by June 20, nearly 325,000 individuals had been removed and just over 38,000 had been transferred to camps and labor colonies.[170] By mid-July, roughly 400,000 inmates had been removed and over 68,000 transferred, bringing the current totals in OGPU, *militsiia*, and Justice Commissariat prisons, and in labor colonies, to 397,284 individuals, which, according to Krylenko, both met the requirements of the May 8 instruction and provided a "reserve" of some 40,000 spaces for future arrests. The clearing of additional spaces in preparation for the arrests that would accompany the upcoming harvesting campaign, Krylenko noted, would be the responsibility of the Procuracy, a comment that hardly suggests that top Communist Party officials expected an end to "acute" repression in the countryside after May 1933.[171]

The Politburo had no intention of simply releasing 400,000 prisoners into Soviet society, even in the face of deadly overcrowding. At least 133,400 individuals, plus their families, were transferred to the new OGPU labor colonies in Western Siberia and Kazakhstan.[172] The rest, at a minimum, found their sentences commuted to one year of compulsory labor, a punishment that kept them under police surveillance and forced them to move to nonregime locations, where they were attached to a specific job and worked for a reduced salary. Some of them were released from jails while their cases worked their way through the court system, only to be sentenced later. Simple release, with no further legal restrictions, was not among the options provided by the May 8 instruction.

Certain aspects of the May 1933 instruction contradicted the basic nature of the Soviet policing system and were jettisoned almost immediately by the Politburo, often under pressure from local OGPU officials. The tendency of the Politburo to accord local OGPU troikas the right to apply the death sentence in "exceptional" situations had become so strong by 1933 that the general prohibition of extrajudicial executions lasted scarcely two months. In late June, Communist Party officials in Western Siberia requested that the Politburo authorize an OGPU troika to carry out death sentences in the area in order to control high levels of banditry, murder, and robbery committed by criminal recidivists who had been sent to the new OGPU special settlements in the region; the Politburo agreed on July 15.[173] On August 11, the Politburo provided the same right to the OGPU troikas in Ukraine, the Lower Volga Territory, the Far Eastern Territory, Belorussia, Kazakhstan, the Urals, and again Western Siberia, signaling a wholesale return to pre-May 1933 practices.[174] The Politburo also quickly jettisoned the stricture against the mass deportation of peasants, in late June authorizing the resettlement of 5,000 peasant families in the Far Eastern Territory for use as labor at gold- and timber-producing operations and, in early August, the resettlement of 20,000 peasant families, identified as "particularly malicious kulak elements" from across the USSR, to the territory of the newly completed White Sea Canal.[175] Instructions regarding these and other resettlement operations for the rest of 1933 stressed that they were to be carried out in "individual" order as much as possible, but the realities of ongoing campaigns in the countryside, especially the harvest campaign of 1933, meant that mass resettlement and extrajudicial repression in the countryside would continue as part of standard regime policy.

The contours of police activity in the period after the May instruction were also complicated by changing systems of banishment and exile, both of which were closely connected to police campaigns to purge urban areas of criminal offenders in 1933. In early June, in the middle of the "clearing" of prisons, the Politburo abolished the punishment of exile (*ssylka*) without compulsory work, and banishment (*vysylka*) of any kind, for sentences handed down by the courts. The implementation of these sentences had become increasingly difficult in the early 1930s; the burden of controlling these populations had fallen on local *militsiia* administrations, which were unable to track individuals who were not attached to specific labor camps or colonies.[176] The OGPU replaced this punishment with sentences, often extrajudicial, to the new system of special settlements in Kazakhstan and Western Siberia, sending large cohorts of urban criminals, along with substantial numbers of teenage homeless children, to them beginning in early 1933.[177] The "new contingent" of urban criminals and passport violators was resettled separately from peasant populations, usually far to the north in order to prevent escapes, a practice that caused immediate problems. Most of these prisoners lacked the skills required to support themselves, and many were ill, often with syphilis. Local officials in the areas of resettlement, complaining that this new group was completely incapable of any kind of farming or industry and engaged instead in criminal activity at the expense of both local residents and resettled peasants, requested in mid-1933 that no further resettlement of urban criminal elements be allowed and that these individuals be directed instead to the OGPU labor camp system.[178] Yet the central police and Communist Party leadership continued to see the OGPU special settlement system as a major part of police attempts to purge urban areas of "dangerous" elements in 1933, and the OGPU continued to send urban criminal populations to them in large numbers through the end of the year.[179]

These difficulties led the Politburo to attempt once again to reduce pressure on the prison and special-settlement system by changing one of the basic assumptions of the Soviet penal system. On August 14, 1933, the Politburo ordered justice and police agencies to send all individuals sentenced to two or more years of deprivation of freedom, without exception, to OGPU labor camps. This order was a substantial departure from existing practice, under which individuals sentenced to three or more years went to OGPU labor camps, and it was a major reversal of several of the sentencing guidelines of the May 8 instruction, including the provision that invalids, pregnant women, women with nursing children, and the elderly were not to be sent to camps.[180]

This move was a substantial victory for the OGPU over the Justice Commissariat, which lost control of a substantial number of inmates, but it was also a repudiation of Yagoda's plan to make special settlements in Kazakhstan and Western Siberia into the backbone of the Soviet forced-labor system. Justice officials would challenge this transfer in 1934, in the context of a major reform of the political police system, as we will see below. In 1933, however, the move was a necessity, based as much on real problems within the Soviet penal system as on any long-term plan held by the Communist Party leadership.[181] Despite two attempts at "clearing" Soviet prisons in 1933, trends in Soviet criminal justice ensured that problems of overcrowding in them would remain acute through the end of the decade and that the Gulag would thereafter become the defining institution of the Stalinist penal system.

Conclusion

By the end of 1933, Soviet policing had taken on the form that it would hold until the beginning of World War II. Extrajudicial campaigns against specific categories of crime, carried out in conjunction with the daily functioning of the internal passport system, had become a standard part of policing practice, whereas the centrality to police work of ideas of "social danger" and "social harm" reinforced the tendency of local officers to equate disorder with the existence of the "criminal contingent," and hence to equate policing with the prophylactic removal of this "contingent" from the body politic. This approach to crime control had little to do with the reforms of covert policing promoted by top OGPU officials in 1931 and 1932, discussed in chapter 2; rather, it represented the triumph of a competing vision of policing, promoted most aggressively by the local police themselves, which relied on overt surveillance and the "fixing" of suspect contingents in order to make the population overtly, as opposed to covertly, legible to the state. The internal passport system, and the entire edifice of registration and extrajudicial procedures that surrounded it, became the institutional centerpiece of this approach to crime control; local officers made use of the myriad opportunities for extrajudicial repression that were inherent in the passport system, ranging from the drastic to the mundane, to bring their particularly local visions of policing to fruition. In the process, the local police brought the criminology of prevention and "social danger," which was promoted within the top echelons of the

OGPU in the early 1930s, to the center of daily policing practices by 1933, but they did so in a way that resonated with local, rather than central, ideological concerns.

The policy choices made by Stalin and his ruling group played a major role in the emergence of this approach to crime and social order in the early 1930s. None of Stalin's policy initiatives in this period deserve to be called moderate; his cyclical attempts to reorient chaotic repressive practices toward more orderly forms of administration were always matched with strident calls for "draconian measures" that prevented the Soviet populace from taking advantage of the situation. Law, like proper administration in general, was for Stalin a method for instilling respect for Soviet officials in the minds of simple citizens. "The peasant (*muzhik*) loves legality," he wrote to Kaganovich in July 1932, to explain why the public handling of impending measures against theft and speculation should occur, in his view, within the court system rather than through the extrajudicial channels of the police.[182] Rather than evidence of confused or competing policy initiatives within Stalin's inner circle, the Politburo's cyclical demands for repression and order in 1932 and 1933 were complementary aspects of an overall policy designed to enforce social stability and "normal" life through repression.

4

The Police and the "Victory of Socialism," 1934–1936

Hooligans, thieves, robbers, and other declassed elements operate unpunished in our socialist cities and workers' settlements. . . . The chiefs of our detective departments do not understand that petty thieves, hooligans, and homeless children grow up to become robbers, bandits, and serious thieves, who are much more difficult to control. . . . I warn all OGPU chiefs and chiefs of territorial and regional *militsiia* administrations that they will be judged on the work of the *militsiia* in tearing out banditry, robbery, and hooliganism by the roots; on their support of the passport regime; and on the state of revolutionary order in [their] cities and regions.

    —Yagoda, to all OGPU and *militsiia* chiefs, March 26, 1934[1]

For us the most honored matter is the battle with counterrevolution—this is absolutely correct. But in our current situation, a hooligan, a bandit, a robber—isn't this the most genuine counterrevolutionary? . . . The role of the old, obscene criminal has moved to the background, and this is natural, because most of them have been executed or are now in labor camps. Today's criminal (hooligan, thief, robber) exists under the guise of a worker, a collective farmer, a student, a Komsomol member, etc. . . . In our nation—a nation where the construction of socialism has been victorious, where there is no unemployment, where every citizen of the Soviet Union is presented with the complete possibility to work and live honorably, any criminal act by its nature can be nothing other than a manifestation of class struggle.

    —Yagoda, to a meeting of regional *militsiia* chiefs, April 16, 1935[2]

At the beginning of 1934, Stalin decided that the time was right for a new approach to local administration and, in particular, local policing and criminal justice. The most chaotic events of the "revolution from above" were behind him: the famine had eased, the worst problems in the OGPU's system of special settlements were over, mass migration to major cities was under control, and collectivization and dekulakization were complete in almost all regions of the country. Yet complaints about local administration were still rife, especially complaints from top officials of the Justice Commissariat and the Procuracy regarding the chaotic nature of the 1933 harvest campaign and continued violations of "revolutionary legality" in the countryside. Stalin's response to this constellation of problems was to announce, at the Seventeenth Party Congress in January and February 1934, that the building of "socialism" had been victorious and that the period of forced social transformation was over: repressions of entire socioeconomic classes were things of the past, and the Soviet Union could settle into the maturation of the "socialist" system that had been created during the First Five-Year Plan period.

The "Congress of Victors," as the event came to be known, is usually seen as the beginning of a "Great Retreat" from the utopian revolutionary impulses of the early Bolshevik regime in realms as diverse as art, family policy, and international politics. In law and criminal justice, likewise, Stalin decided in early 1934 to make good on some of the promises of earlier policy shifts—for example, the promotion of "revolutionary legality" in 1932 and the May 1933 instruction on the clearing of prisons—by restructuring the judicial system, prohibiting almost all extrajudicial sentencing by the police, and launching a wide array of policies designed to raise the stature of law in Soviet society. This broad change in Soviet criminal justice—termed a "conservative shift" by the premier scholar of the Soviet legal system, Peter H. Solomon Jr.—involved moderating some of the most repressive aspects of local administration during the early Stalin period. Just as important, it entailed promoting a more traditional legal culture among justice officials, a step that Stalin believed would make the Soviet criminal justice system more predictable and hence enhance the Soviet population's compliance with the dictates of the regime.[3]

These attempts to reform the legal system did not produce comparable reforms of the police system. No conservative shift took place in the structure, culture, or practice of Soviet policing in the mid-1930s. Instead of a shift from "radical" to "conservative" policing, the mid-1930s witnessed the culmination of trends toward the more stable and consistent bureaucratic functioning of the police system as a whole, as well as the continued ascendance of the political police in the overall bureaucratic structure of the USSR. The most important event in this trend was the formation of the Unionwide Commissariat of Internal Affairs (NKVD USSR) in 1934. The creation of the USSR NKVD has long been viewed as a watershed in the history of Soviet criminal justice, a major reform of Soviet policing that reduced the extrajudicial prerogatives of the political police. In reality, it was more important as a victory for the OGPU in its decade-long drive to gain control over all aspects of policing and penal policy within the borders of the USSR. The moderate aspects of this reform were merely temporary, in some cases lasting no more than a few months, whereas the structural aspects were permanent and would last until the end of Stalin's rule.

The changes in policing that were implemented by the Politburo in 1934 had little chance of overcoming long-standing local approaches to crimes like hooliganism, speculation, and "socially dangerous" behavior. By the mid-1930s, police actions against these categories of urban crime relied almost entirely on mass purges of the "criminal contingent," a practical reality that reforms of the police system did little to change. The local police, fully aware of the power of extrajudicial policing structures like the internal passport system, strove to convince the center that mass purges of urban areas were the most effective policing strategies available; the Politburo generally agreed, launching massive campaigns in 1934 and 1935 against speculators, hooligans, passport violators, and juvenile delinquents, all of which relied on widespread purges of "threatening" population cohorts. Extrajudicial repression was so thoroughly intertwined with the everyday operation of the police system by the mid-1930s, even regarding relatively petty crimes, that reforms of the judicial system ultimately made little difference in the overall direction of Soviet criminal justice.

Political Conflict and the Creation of the USSR NKVD

Problems within the Soviet policing system in 1933, including the difficulties experienced in "clearing" the prison system, convinced Stalin late in the year that fundamental change was necessary. The tipping point occurred in late December, when problems with public order in Moscow prompted Stalin to command the Moscow OGPU to deal with a number of violent and public urban crimes using immediate extrajudicial purges. The Politburo instructed the Moscow police to execute all individuals caught participating in armed robbery; to expel from the city any individuals who had two or more sentences for theft or had been detained two or more times for hooliganism in the previous year, regardless of whether or not they were guilty of any new offence; and to banish all beggars and "declassed elements" or sentence them, if necessary, to terms in special settlements or labor camps.[4]

Stalin reinforced these orders with a change in the *militsiia*'s leadership on January 3, 1934, replacing Prokofev as head with L. N. Belskii, who had previously served as head of OGPU administrations in Central Asia, the Moscow region, and the Lower Volga Territory but had been removed from the OGPU during the leadership shakeup in 1931. At the same time, Stalin ordered Yagoda to present to the Central Committee a concrete plan of activity for the *militsiia* and its Passport Department for 1934.[5] The Politburo followed up on January 20, in a point initiated by Stalin himself, by instructing the OGPU, "under the personal responsibility of com[rade] [D. V.] Usov [the former *militsiia* chief, now head of the Moscow *militsiia*], to bring order to the streets of Moscow and to cleanse them of filth."[6] These changes were the first substantial censure of OGPU activity since the change of leadership in May 1931, when Stalin brought Akulov into the OGPU and demoted Yagoda to second assistant, and they expressed Stalin's profound displeasure with the direction of Soviet policing in the post-dekulakization era.

Stalin reiterated his determination to reform Soviet administration at the Seventeenth Party Congress. He took the opportunity to connect the "victory" of socialism with the need to reform Soviet administration, railing at the Congress against abuses of power and disregard for laws by local officials, a trope that was familiar to justice and police officials from previous campaigns for "revolutionary legality."[7] Stalin was serious about these reforms, as the events of the following weeks would show, but he had not decided on specific policy initiatives in early 1934, and he allowed police and justice officials to present radically different suggestions for change to the Politburo over the next several months.

Yagoda's plan for the activities of the *militsiia* in 1934—which was forwarded to Molotov on February 4, 1934, and then on to Stalin—shows that the OGPU had little indication that the rhetoric at the Congress of Victors threatened the power of the police system in any way. Yagoda responded to Stalin's evident displeasure with calls for harsher extrajudicial repression of banditry, hooliganism, and juvenile homelessness and delinquency. He proposed particularly harsh punishments for public-order crimes, such as a mandatory ten-year sentence to labor camps for all cases of hooliganism and "knife fighting." He also offered a range of suggestions regarding juvenile affairs, all of which increased the role of the OGPU in sweeping children off the streets; he recommended that the Gulag system organize labor colonies to incarcerate 10,000 "particularly malicious juvenile homeless children" from Moscow and Leningrad, and he suggested, in the event that the orphanage system was unable to handle the quantity of homeless children detained by the police, that the OGPU simply banish them to nonregime cities. He offered substantial self-criticism in the report as well, much of it focusing on the failures of the passport system to control migration to regime cities, especially Moscow and Leningrad. Once passports had been handed out, he admitted, poor daily police work threatened to turn the passport regime into what he called an "empty formality." He recommended that patrol officers expand their contacts with municipal officials, like apartment managers and concierges, who could ensure that all arriving and departing individuals were accounted for. Despite this self-deprecation, none of Yagoda's numerous recommendations suggest that he saw Stalin's request for a plan of action as a fundamental attack on the OGPU's institutional power.

Ivan Akulov, the USSR procurator since Stalin had elevated the Procuracy to Unionwide status in June 1933, better understood Stalin's mood in early 1934 than did Yagoda. Akulov, responding to Yagoda's plan, did not oppose increased repression against troublesome categories of crime; he agreed that punishments for hooliganism and "knife fighting," for example, were too low and that harsher laws were needed regarding juvenile delinquency and homelessness. He did oppose, however, any expansion of extrajudicial sentencing by the police in order to deal with urban crime; he rejected Yagoda's suggestions that individuals living in regime locations without passports should be subject to terms in concentration camps and that individuals convicted of any form of hooliganism should be banished automatically from regime cites.[8] Akulov's response reinforced Stalin's belief that the police system required reorganization in the context of the "victory of socialism," and it clarified the claims made by justice officials for the previous several months that substantial changes were necessary regarding the OGPU's extrajudicial prerogatives.

Yagoda's report and Akulov's response led, at least in part, to Stalin's decision in early February to reorganize the OGPU and to create a Unionwide Commissariat of Internal Affairs (NKVD) in its place. Stalin initially appointed a commission of Yagoda, Lazar Kaganovich, and Valerian Kuibyshev to draft a resolution on the nature of the new commissariat within five days, but vigorous disagreement among interested parties prompted him to expand the commission on March 8 to include sixteen of the leading figures in the criminal justice system.[9] Stalin's decision to open the matter to broader discussion immediately invigorated ongoing attempts by justice officials, especially Vyshinsky, Krylenko, and Akulov, to increase the bureaucratic strength and the cultural authority of Soviet law. Top justice officials had been arguing since the instruction of May 8, 1933, that greater attention was needed to the strict observance of law by local officials. Yet, before early 1934, they generally refrained from complaining directly about the actions of the police, concentrating on local soviet and Communist Party officials instead.[10] In early 1934, justice officials took the opportunity presented by Stalin to expand their attack on the extrajudicial functions of the OGPU itself.

Akulov took the lead in this criticism, reprising the role that he had assumed in 1931, when Stalin promoted him as assistant OGPU chief, above Yagoda, to serve as a trusted Communist Party representative within the political police. In late February 1934, Akulov sent a blistering attack on the OGPU's extrajudicial activities to Stalin, charging that the actions of the local OGPU troikas far exceeded any demonstrable need on the part of the police to sentence individuals without turning to the court system. The OGPU troikas, he argued, adjudicated too broad a range of cases, sentencing individuals for any and all crimes that were investigated by the OGPU, and a fair number that were investigated by the *militsiia* as well. He also stressed the abysmal quality of the troika investigations and included examples of outrageous troika prosecutions for minor offenses to prove his point. He differentiated between what he called the judicial and the administrative sentencing functions of the OGPU, and he maintained that the police should retain only the latter, which pertained to nonpolitical offenders. He suggested that the police be allowed to mete out sentences of three years of banishment or five years of exile for criminal offenses, but he insisted that all cases of a political nature should be heard within the court system. Finally, he suggested that a reform of the penal system should also be part of the creation of the USSR NKVD, including a transfer of all prisons and labor colonies currently part of the Justice Commissariat to a reorganized NKVD Gulag system.[11]

Nikolai Krylenko, the head of the Justice Commissariat, echoed many of these same concerns in his suggestions to the first commission meeting on the new NKVD. Like Akulov, he accepted the idea that the NKVD would retain the rights to the administrative sentencing of "dangerous" criminals, but he suggested that the NKVD be accorded only the rights that the GPU enjoyed in 1922, when the Special Board could apply maximum sentences of three years of banishment, exile, or hard labor. He also agreed that transfer of most penal institutions to the new NKVD was the only reasonable option, given that the OGPU generally sent able-bodied prisoners to its own camps and directed the feeble, infirm, or young to the institutions of the Justice Commissariat. Finally, he argued that the current caseload of the OGPU troikas, which he identified as "counterrevolutionary crimes, speculation, crimes of office, contraband, counterfeiting, etc.," could be handled easily by the existing court system, with far greater assurance of correct sentencing practices.[12]

These initial responses, especially those of Akulov, set the basic parameters for further debate on the reformulation of the political police system. The general outlines of the impending restructuring were accepted by all parties as early as March 1934. That the OGPU would lose most, and perhaps all, of its extrajudicial capacity regarding counterrevolutionary and state crimes was a given. Yagoda attempted to salvage as much sentencing capacity as he could, but it was clear even to him that the court system would handle the majority of offenses. All participants in the debates made a clear distinction, as did Akulov, between the "judicial" and the "administrative" sentencing powers of the OGPU; the former, which pertained to adjudication of serious political and state crimes, were hotly contested, whereas the latter, which pertained to OGPU repression of criminal, hooliganistic, and "dangerous" population contingents, were never in question. Kaganovich, Yagoda, and Kuibyshev sent a short draft instruction to Stalin on March 26, which simply stated that the new NKVD should enjoy all the rights and be subject to all the same responsibilities as the OGPU, with the exception of judicial functions regarding counterrevolutionary or state crimes. Stalin may have been unhappy with the vagueness of this document and likely demanded more detail, but he did not challenge its overall conclusion.[13]

Despite this general accord, discussions of the OGPU in early 1934 exploded into acrimonious debate about virtually every aspect of the Soviet criminal justice system. Krylenko, on the defensive for most of 1933 against the encroachments of the Procuracy and the OGPU on his Justice Commissariat's sphere of activity, seized the opportunity to challenge several trends in Soviet criminal justice. He wrote to Stalin at least twice in February 1934, recommending fundamental changes in the justice system and going so far as to suggest that, should Stalin not support these suggestions, he should consider abolishing the republic-level justice commissariats altogether.[14]

Stalin responded in late March by creating another Politburo commission to examine the role of the courts and the Procuracy in the criminal justice system. This commission overlapped in membership with the commission on the NKVD, but it was chaired by Kuibyshev and included Nikolai Ezhov, the rising Communist Party functionary and Yagoda's future replacement as head of the political police.[15] Kuibyshev's commission met throughout mid-1934 and discussed a wide range of judicial issues, but the question most pertinent to the reform of the police was the nature of the courts that would hear cases taken away from the OGPU. The commission recommended in mid-April that special courts be created to hear all state crimes and crimes against administration and that all political crimes (counterrevolution, terrorism, and sabotage) be heard by military tribunals.[16] This set of recommendations became the basis for a new system of courts, created along with the new USSR NKVD, which were staffed not by existing judges but by officials from the Procuracy and from the OGPU itself.[17] This set of personnel changes, which represented a clear defeat for Krylenko, suggests that the Politburo intended to ensure that the new NKVD would retain a substantial amount of control over the sentencing of counterrevolutionary crime, whether through judicial or extrajudicial means.[18]

Although the basic outlines of the NKVD reforms were set by April, Stalin remained profoundly ambivalent regarding the extent to which the political police should exercise extrajudicial sanctions. Stalin added himself and Ezhov to the commission on the NKVD on April 1 in order to handle sharp disagreements about the exercise of extrajudicial powers by the political police.[19] On April 11, the Politburo moved to restrict these powers by forbidding the OGPU Transport Department to arrest railroad employees without the express agreement of the Commissariat of Transport, a step that could have only been seen as a threat by Yagoda.[20] Yet in Stalin's mind, specific extrajudicial repressions were a necessary part of Soviet administration, even in the midst of overall reforms. On June 1, the Politburo ordered the same OGPU Transport Department to carry out a ten-day purge of railways that targeted "professional hooligans, criminals, and homeless children"; the OGPU was authorized to sentence all "malicious hooligans" to three years in a labor camp and to send hooliganistic homeless juveniles to "special camps" set up for that purpose. In addition, the Politburo ordered the OGPU to arrest all individuals caught hitching rides in transport cars and to sentence them to six-month terms in labor camps, a provision that violated both the existing stricture against sentences of deprivation of freedom for less than a year and the practice of sending individuals sentenced to less than two years to labor colonies of the Justice Commissariat.[21] The Politburo authorized an OGPU troika to hear cases arising from these campaigns on transport in Ukraine; this troika functioned continuously, throughout the period of the NKVD reforms, until February 1935.[22]

Akulov encountered the same propensity of top Communist Party officials to choose security over reform in May 1934, when he forwarded a complaint to Molotov regarding extrajudicial repression and the passport system. Akulov charged that the police in major cities were using the passport system for extrajudicial punishment, purging their areas of unwanted individuals by seizing their passports and, in effect, banishing them permanently from all regime cities without any procedural hearing. He documented numerous abuses of the passport system by the local police, yet the Sovnarkom flatly rejected his request that local Procuracy officials be allowed to suspend administrative expulsions until they could be reviewed by local soviets. Likewise, the Sovnarkom rejected his rather meek follow-up request for a circular simply instructing Procuracy and police officials to cooperate on the issue. Yagoda's response to Akulov's request for the circular, written in mid-June, underscored the helplessness of the Procuracy on this issue. Yagoda stated, with evident relish, that the Sovnarkom's original rejection was clear and that Procuracy officials already had the right to "acquaint themselves" (*oznakomit'sia*) with police materials regarding passport refusals.[23] Although the passport system easily represented the most widespread use of administrative sanctions by the police in 1934, it was not a matter for discussion in the Politburo commissions discussing justice or NKVD matters; restricting it would have been unthinkable for top party and police officials, including Stalin.

When the Politburo finally promulgated legislation that abolished the OGPU and created the new USSR NKVD, on July 10, 1934, these conflicts remained largely unresolved. The regulations subsumed the OGPU into the NKVD as the Central Administration of State Security (GUGB) and created separate central administrations for the *militsiia*, border and internal troops, the fire department, labor camps (the Gulag), civil registrations, and administrative-economic concerns.[24] Convoy troops, previously part of the Justice Commissariat, became part of the NKVD in early September.[25] Yet the instructions omitted any discussion of the extrajudicial powers of the police or the new NKVD Special Board, both of which were still the subject of active debate within the Politburo.

Yagoda's suggestions for the Special Board make clear the extent to which these debates did not fundamentally challenge the nature of police activity regarding nonpolitical crime. In late August, Yagoda asked that the legislation on the board be considered as quickly as possible because a "large quantity" of individuals had been arrested and awaited sentences as part of ongoing "purging operations in cities and on transport of socially harmful [*vrednye*] elements." Such purges continued even in the absence of extrajudicial bodies to sentence those arrested; the police simply arrested individuals and waited for the opportunity to sentence them, which they assumed would be forthcoming. Yagoda, to drive the point home, recommended that NKVD administrations in areas far from the center, including the Far Eastern Territory, Eastern Siberia, and Kazakhstan, be allowed to form special commissions, composed of two NKVD functionaries and a Procuracy representative, to process cases of dangerous elements on the spot, sending the cases to the Special Board for final approval. Yagoda refrained from using the term "troikas," but it was unlikely that anybody was confused as to the nature of these "commissions."[26]

In the end, the Politburo's instructions about the NKVD Special Board restricted the administrative sentencing powers of the police regarding criminal populations but did not abolish them. The Special Board was authorized to sentence "socially dangerous" individuals to five years of banishment, exile, or hard labor, and to banish "dangerous" foreigners from the USSR. The instructions made no provisions for sentencing by local troikas; all such cases, once prepared by local NKVD officials, had to be approved by the Special Board in Moscow.[27] The retention by the NKVD of these extrajudicial sentencing prerogatives is the clearest proof that Stalin did not intend the creation of the USSR NKVD in 1934 to limit the overall repressive capacities of the police regarding nonpolitical crime.

Yagoda and the political police also triumphed over rivals in justice organizations in 1934 regarding control over the Soviet penal system. Yagoda began to connect the restructuring of the OGPU with the question of control over prison populations in late March 1934, claiming that the transfer to the OGPU in late 1933 of prisoners sentenced to two years or more (see chapter 3) was a permanent, rather than one-time, measure.[28] He expanded this claim in early April, informing Molotov that a commission headed by Akulov and including himself and Krylenko had agreed to transfer all individuals sentenced to any term of deprivation of freedom to the OGPU camp and colony system. Under this plan, the Justice Commissariat would retain only individuals under investigation or appeal.[29]

In early May, Molotov, likely acting for Stalin, took up the issue by requesting a report from Akulov on the situation in the prisons. Akulov answered with a lengthy condemnation of the prison system maintained by the Justice Commissariat. He argued that the Politburo directive from May 1933 regarding the "clearing out" of prisons had been thwarted by overcrowding, difficulties in convoying prisoners promptly, and the inability of local courts to hear cases within the time limits prescribed by law; he also noted that police were sentencing "dangerous elements" in excess of the limits set for them in the prison system.[30] Yagoda brought up the issue again in early June, forwarding essentially the same suggestion to Kuibyshev, the head of the Politburo commission on judicial matters, and arguing that a transfer of all prisoners to the OGPU would reduce "colossal" labor shortages in the camp system.[31]

The principal opposition to this plan came from Krylenko, whose Justice Commissariat had the most to lose from a transfer of prison populations to the new NKVD. Sounding a note of personal offense, Krylenko in mid-July sent a note to Stalin and Akulov complaining that Yagoda's plan deviated from the compromise that had been reached earlier in the year.[32] He made the same complaint to Kaganovich in early August, stating that he was "categorically opposed" to the transfer of all penal institutions to the NKVD and that doing so would violate the recent decision of the Politburo to retain the Justice Commissariat.[33] Yet the change took place anyway, largely per Yagoda's suggestions, in October 1934, with the complete transfer of all prisons, labor colonies, and compulsory labor administrations to a new Department of Places of Confinement within the Gulag system, effective December 1, 1934.[34] This change was a defeat for Krylenko, but it was completely consistent with the overall direction of Soviet penal policy following Stalin's original decision in late 1933 to transfer all inmates sentenced to two or more years to the OGPU. By the end of 1934, all decisions regarding the use of prison labor, prison releases, transfers between penal institutions, and the regulation of the lives of ex-convicts were firmly under control of the new NKVD.

The restructuring of the OGPU and the creation of the USSR NKVD in 1934, while reducing the ability of the political police to sentence individuals charged with political and state crimes, left most major aspects of Soviet policing almost untouched. It did nothing to restrict the administrative sentencing of "dangerous elements" or passport violators, categories that became the most important aspect of policing activity in 1935 and 1936. Viewed in this context, the changes in policing that took place in 1934 are better understood as a culmination of centralizing trends that began in 1930, with the takeover of the *militsiia* by the OGPU, than as part of an attempt to encourage a "conservative shift" in Soviet criminal justice.

Policing and Public Order: Central Debates, 1934–1935

The debates surrounding the creation of the USSR NKVD were part of a series of conflicts within the top levels of the Communist Party regarding the nature of law enforcement and criminal justice in the USSR in 1934. Stalin's determination to restructure the Soviet police system brought into question virtually every aspect of Soviet criminal justice, including the nature of Soviet jurisprudence, extrajudicial repression, the passport system, and police responses to crimes like hooliganism, juvenile delinquency and speculation in consumer goods. The Politburo created overlapping commissions to consider these issues, which focused on reforms of the police system and, in some cases, attempted to limit the actions of the police along the lines set down by Stalin at the Congress of Victors. Yagoda and other top police officials defended their organization vigorously throughout these debates, pressing throughout 1934 for an expansion of extrajudicial repression against hooligans, passport violators, and other marginalized groups in the population. As the year wore on, many of the participants in these debates followed suit, and by 1935 general agreement emerged at the top of the party hierarchy that drastic measures were once again required to protect the Soviet system from the threat of violent urban crime.

Yagoda found himself on the defensive on these issues between April and August 1934, as the Politburo debated the restructuring of the OGPU. Yet he understood the nature of Stalin's call for order better than most top Communist Party officials, and he responded with a series of measures in mid-1934 intended to improve the basic functioning of local police administrations. In late March, 1934, he took local police administrations to task for failing to control crime in major cities, complaining that they allowed "hooligans, thieves, robbers, and other declassed elements" to terrorize urban residents and that they sat, "filling out forms," in administrative offices or stationary posts instead of patrolling the streets. He was particularly critical of the detective departments, demanding that they improve covert policing tactics, but most of his policy recommendations focused on the passport system, which he claimed provided local police with the capacity "to free [regime cities] completely of the criminal-hooliganistic element" and to "uncover criminal and suspect elements and make substantially easier the working over [*prorabotka*] of these groups" in nonregime areas. He ordered the local police to institute the strictest possible passport regime, coordinating the activities of constables, apartment concierges, and housing administrations to ensure that nobody resided in cities without passports, and to sentence individuals without passports using OGPU passport troikas. He finished by warning all local police chiefs that they would be "severely punished" if they were unable to eliminate banditry, robbery, and hooliganism in their areas and instill a strict passport regime.[35]

Yagoda returned to these issues in mid-August 1934, after the creation of the NKVD, criticizing local administrations for not following his previous order regarding the passport system. He again railed on the failure of local detective departments to take preventive measures regarding hooliganism and thievery, waiting instead for citizens to report crimes to them. He complained that such passivity would never result in the suppression of these types of crime, and he demanded that local police repress "SVEs" [socially harmful elements] more systematically. He listed several regime cities, including Baku and Sochi, in which he claimed the police had not arrested a single individual for violation of the passport system in the preceding months, and he added several more in which the police had made only a handful of such arrests during that time. Nonregime cities, he claimed, were even worse; the police had "completely forgotten" about the passport and registration systems in these areas, in which thousands of individuals lived without registration or passports. The work of the *militsiia*, he concluded, was as valuable in the current period as that of the political police; he demanded that the police across the USSR approach issues of public order with the same gravity directed toward counterrevolutionary crime.[36]

Once the basic outlines of the reformulation of the new NKVD were set, the Politburo took up these questions directly, creating several interrelated commissions to study policing and public order. On May 25, 1934, the Politburo created a commission to consider the issue of juvenile delinquency, headed by Vlas Chubar, deputy chair of the Sovnarkom, and including Yagoda, N. A. Semashko, and several others.[37] On July 14, Kaganovich was put in charge of ongoing discussions of the work of the *militsiia* and instructed to generate policy recommendations.[38] Finally, in August the Sovnarkom created a commission to consider the problem of speculation in consumer goods, under the leadership of Ian Rudzutak, the Sovnarkom's deputy chair, and including several justice and NKVD officials.[39] All three commissions shared members, and they overlapped with the concurrent commissions regarding the NKVD and the justice system. In November, the Politburo tied together all these discussions by creating a large commission to take over Kaganovich's work regarding the performance of the *militsiia*. The commission, chaired by Rudzutak and containing Prokofev and Belskii as representatives of the OGPU, was ordered to meet on December 15 and to answer the overarching set of questions raised by Stalin's censure of the police almost a year before.[40]

Yagoda sent his recommendations for improving police performance to the Sovnarkom in late November, challenging many of the changes that had occurred in Soviet criminal justice as a result of the May 1933 instruction on the "clearing" of prisons. Yagoda recommended again that the Criminal Code be revised to provide punishment of up to ten years for hooliganism, and he suggested that the police be authorized to mete out ten-day prison sentences for violators of public order and repeat traffic offenders. He suggested that thieves and malicious hooligans be held in jail until their cases were heard at trial, and that the limits on prison and labor colony populations set by the May 1933 instruction be ignored for these two categories of criminals. He also addressed juvenile delinquency, suggesting that the age of criminal responsibility for "serious crimes" be lowered to twelve, that delinquents guilty of these crimes be sentenced to closed colonies for the "difficult to rehabilitate," and that parents of juvenile delinquents be subject to judicial punishment for crimes committed by their children, including banishment of the entire family from regime cities.[41] These suggestions were as aggressive as anything Yagoda had proposed earlier in the year, and they show that he had by the end of 1934 regained any nerve that he had lost during the debates that had accompanied the creation of the NKVD.

Rudzutak's commission prepared its materials in late November 1934, but it met for the first time on December 15, just after the infamous December 1, 1934, murder of Sergei Kirov, a Politburo member and the head of the Leningrad Communist Party organization. Yet despite the atmosphere of crisis that followed the Kirov murder, the commission declined to expand the administrative sentencing rights of the police in any fundamental way. The commission agreed that the police should be authorized to arrest and hold individuals who committed any kind of theft in cities, if it could be established that they were "harmful" or "dangerous" elements without a defined place of residence and a place of employment, and it approved Yagoda's suggestions that the age of criminal responsibility be lowered for several serious crimes, settling on the age of thirteen, and that special colonies be created for these young lawbreakers.[42] But to the contrary, it rejected out of hand Yagoda's suggestions that hooligans be punished with ten-year sentences to labor camps and that families of delinquent children be banished from regime cities.

Despite this outcome, NKVD officials continued to press for expanded extrajudicial rights to handle urban crime in early 1935, fully aware that Stalin and the Politburo would make the final decision on any proposed legislation. Belskii, the head of the *militsiia*, simply ignored the conclusions of the commission in the draft report he prepared for the Politburo, including many of Yagoda's harsh suggestions and adding several more for good measure. Belskii's draft, forwarded to Rudzutak on February 25, 1935, recommended that the police arrest all individuals not only for theft but also for hooliganism, if they had no place of residence or employment, and that recidivist thieves, robbers, bandits, and "especially dangerous hooligans" be kept in jail until trial, notwithstanding set limits on prison populations. He largely repeated the commission's recommendations regarding juvenile delinquents, but he suggested that the age of criminal responsibility be lowered to thirteen for all crimes, rather than a specific list, and he suggested that the police be allowed to hold juvenile delinquents in their own police jails, isolated from adult offenders. He also suggested that the parents of juvenile delinquents be subject to compulsory labor for up to a year for not preventing their children from being drawn into the "criminal and immoral milieu."[43] The recommendations from the Procuracy, sent to the Sovnarkom on March 8, concurred with most of these suggestions, arguing only that individuals charged with hooliganism and theft not be held without trial for over a month and that parents of juvenile delinquents not face any criminal responsibility.[44]

Top NKVD and Procuracy officials correctly understood that Kirov's murder substantially increased the likelihood of drastic responses to problems of public order. In early 1935, the Politburo preempted the discussions occurring in Rudzutak's commission and launched massive campaigns against hooliganism and juvenile delinquency, which will be discussed below. These decisions were not the result of the Kirov murder alone, nor were they the product of Stalin's whims. What seemed like abrupt policy moves were actually products of months of ongoing discussions at the highest levels of the Communist Party, and they represented a broad consensus among both NKVD and Procuracy officials that "threatening" urban crimes again demanded drastic responses from the police.

Geographic Mobility, "Criminal Elements," and the Passport System, 1934–1935

In early 1934, Stalin and his top advisers launched a series of policy initiatives that were designed to normalize the legal status of broad categories of common citizens who had been banished or exiled in the previous years. In conjunction with the restructuring of the OGPU, top justice officials convinced Stalin, perhaps for the last time in the 1930s, that some amount of relaxation of pressure on these individuals would reduce social disorder and improve the overall stability and security of the country. The top NKVD officials strenuously opposed these policy changes, while the local police struggled to respond to the Politburo's attempts to relax passport restrictions and restrain administrative sentencing and at the same time protect important urban areas from suspect individuals. As central debates on crime and social disorder turned toward repressive solutions late in the year, these reformist impulses gave way to harsh policies designed to ensure that "threatening" population cohorts remained permanently isolated from Soviet society.

By the spring of 1934, passport distribution was complete in most areas of the USSR. Central police officials encouraged local administrations to halt widespread purges of Soviet cities in favor of more methodical approaches to controlling geographic mobility, often referred to as the "filtration" of migrating populations moving to and from regime areas. In February 1934, the local police ceased issuing passports in areas under passport restrictions, forcing individuals to apply for passports in their home locations before traveling.[45] The police in Moscow and a handful of other major cities also took steps to ensure that individuals ejected from their areas could not return or migrate to other regime areas, compiling and exchanging lists of those expelled. In late February 1934, the center extended this practice to all regime areas and ordered the local police to add information on passport violators to their card files.[46] The goal of this process of "filtration" was to uncover undesirable individuals and ex-convicts among immigrants without disrupting legal migration patterns, especially the seasonal migration of peasant workers to urban areas that was central to the Soviet economic system.

In April and May 1934, the Politburo—prompted by criticisms raised by Vyshinsky and Akulov during the restructuring of the OGPU—also softened passport restrictions for several categories of individuals no longer deemed "threatening" to the regime. Local police began to issue regime passports to individuals released from prisons under one of the many amnesties that took place in the mid-1930s, and individuals who had completed sentences for minor crimes and had previously been residents of regime areas were granted passports valid in regime locations.[47] Although these policies pertained to only a tiny fraction of the hundreds of thousands of Soviet citizens prohibited from living in regime areas, they represented genuine attempts by top justice officials to reduce the number of Soviet citizens living with the permanent stigma of passport restrictions.

Most local police administrations, however, found it difficult to cope with the bureaucratic difficulties involved in using the passport system to "filter" migrating populations rather than as a means to carry out mass purges. In particular, the police balked at central demands to incorporate the passport system into covert surveillance operations; local officers instead continued to use the passport system throughout 1934 to support sporadic purges of criminal populations, targeting recidivists, professional criminals, and "declassed elements" almost exclusively.[48]

Long-standing patterns of peasant migration, especially seasonal labor migration (*otkhod*), also wrought havoc on police attempts to keep criminal and ex-convict populations out of regime cities. During the initial process of passport distribution, seasonal laborers received three-month passports, issued by the police in the cities where they worked; once the passport system was in place, laborers were required to obtain one-year passports from police officials in their rural places of residence before departing for seasonal work.[49] The urban police were required to demand from rural inmigrants both passports and documentation attesting to the goal of their move, ensuring that criminals and individuals with prior convictions could not legally migrate to areas under passport restrictions.

This system, though rational in theory, faltered on the voracious appetite of urban construction and industrial sites for labor in the early 1930s. Factory administrations, operating under continual labor shortages, ignored organized labor recruitment systems and hired individuals "at the factory gate," often requesting passports from local police administrations after the fact. According to central police officials, this practice destroyed the ability of the passport system to prevent criminal or marginal contingents from entering regime cities.[50] In cities under nonregime passport restrictions, the police generally ignored this aspect of the passport system altogether, allowing hundreds of thousands of individuals to work in major factories without proper identification.[51] Although such practices made perfect sense in the local contexts in which they operated, they interfered with what were, in the minds of top police officials, the main goals of the passport system: the isolation of regime areas from threatening criminal cohorts and the registration and surveillance of those same cohorts in nonregime locales.

As a result, the populations of most regime cities began to climb again in the fall and winter of 1934. Central police officials blamed this growth on the overly charitable actions of local officers, especially regarding the relatives of authorized residents; one circular complained that "the police expel socially alien elements from cities with one hand, while with the other hand they legalize, using registration practices, unnecessary categories of the population and hence emasculate the essence of the passport regime."[52] Central NKVD officials likewise warned in early September 1934 that the situation regarding escaped prisoners had reached "threatening proportions" and that the passport system did nothing to prevent escapees from flooding into regime cities.[53] Such complaints were entirely plausible from Moscow's point of view, but they ignored the difficulties faced by the local police as they attempted to control massive levels of geographic mobility, much of it legal, in the post-dekulakization era.

The Sovnarkom began to address this problem in September 1934, ordering factories in regime cities to refuse to employ collective farmers who did not receive passports in their home areas in advance of their move.[54] Peasants reacted rapidly to this new regulation by requesting passports in their home locations en masse in the fall and winter of 1934, even if they were not planning to travel in the short term. The NKVD responded in turn on January 1, 1935, ordering rural police administrations to cease issuing passports to peasants unless they showed intent to leave and to seize passports from all peasants who requested them but did not leave their home villages.[55]

The resoluteness of the January 1935 instruction likely made it all the more surprising to both police and rural residents when the NKVD reversed itself two months later. In December 1934, Yagoda sent a request to the Sovnarkom for a major change in passport procedures. The practice of issuing passports to peasants only when they moved to urban areas, he argued, allowed "criminal elements" in the countryside who wished to escape detection simply to move to another rural location, where they were not known by the police or soviet authorities. After a short time, Yagoda claimed, such individuals could receive a passport that authorized them to migrate to regime cities in search of work. Yagoda suggested that all rural residents who wished to leave their homes for any length of time, even if they were planning to visit another rural area not under passport restrictions, be required to receive a passport from local police officials before they left.[56] Grigorii Leplevskii, Vyshinsky's assistant, responded for the USSR Procuracy on December 19 with no objections, agreeing that existing regulations "make it possible, as has been shown in practice, for a criminal element to receive a passport after moving to a location in which he is not known."[57] The Sovnarkom approved the suggestion, and the NKVD issued the corresponding instructions in mid-March 1935: all individuals in rural locations were henceforth required to receive one-year passports from local police officials before moving anywhere.[58] This policy was not primarily intended to fasten Soviet peasants to collective farms. Rather, it was the last in a series of attempts on the part of the NKVD to improve the ability of the local police to "filter" migrating populations and to reduce the ability of suspect individuals to evade registration and surveillance.[59]

The geographic mobility of dekulakized peasants and "criminal elements" who reached the ends of their sentences posed similar problems for local police administrations. Control over the mobility of these populations became particularly important in early 1934, when the first cohort of peasants who were arrested during the dekulakization drive began to complete their sentences. The initial reaction of the regime to the possibility that these marginalized populations would return to Soviet society was genuinely moderate. In May 1934, the Politburo ordered the restoration of citizenship rights to several categories of resettled individuals upon the completion of their sentences, in an attempt to encourage them to settle permanently in their areas, forge economic and social connections with local populations, and create new communities that would eventually become stable settlements.[60]

In early January 1935, however, Matvei Berman, the head of the Gulag system, warned Yagoda that most resettled individuals assumed that their rehabilitation entailed freedom of movement and left the special settlements immediately. Many returned to their previous places of residence. Berman recommended that mass reinstatements of civil rights for resettled populations be halted, and that any individuals restored in their civil rights be fixed permanently to their places of resettlement.[61] Yagoda immediately authorized Berman to inform all Gulag officials that the restoration of citizenship did not entail the right to leave special settlements, and he followed up with a series of emergency orders to local NKVD administrations in mid-January 1935 that were designed to "affix" these individuals permanently to the settlements.[62]

The issue had legal implications, insofar as it concerned the right of the NKVD to apply coercion to individuals who had completed their sentences, and so on January 17, 1935, Yagoda requested that the Politburo take up the matter. The May 1934 decision to restore voting rights to this group of individuals, he argued, had "without question encouraged the [permanent] settlement of such individuals in the locations of their resettlement," a statement that was absolutely false and that was disproved by Berman's report. Because the decision provided no specific guidelines regarding the right to leave, Yagoda noted that many of these people returned to their former places of residence, a situation that he dryly termed "politically undesirable."[63] Stalin evidently agreed, because in late January 1935 the Central Executive Committee issued an order stating that exiled kulaks whose civil rights were reinstated did not thereby gain the right to leave their places of exile. The NKVD handled the mechanics of the order through the passport system, instructing Gulag officials to issue passports to dekulakized peasants who regained their citizenship rights with a specific notation to the effect that the passport was valid only in a given special settlement. The police across the USSR then arrested any individuals who carried such passports and returned them to the settlements.[64]

The Politburo's willingness to provide the police with expanded administrative rights to control suspect populations had its limits in early 1935. In February and March, for example, the Politburo rejected a request from Berman to extend the January 1935 directive on exiled peasants to "criminal elements" in special settlements, likely because such a move would have, in effect, expanded the ability of the police to sentence individuals to permanent exile status through the extrajudicial operation of the passport system.[65] Yet mass resettlement was standard policy again by early 1935; in February, Yagoda sent to Molotov a plan for a major wave of resettlement operations targeting 36,000 individuals—including 12,000 "counterrevolutionary nationalist elements and kulaks" from Ukraine, who were to be sent to resettle the territory of the White Sea–Baltic Canal; 20,000 "remnants of kulak farms" from the North Caucasus Territory; and 4,000 "begging elements" in Moscow, who were to be sent to labor colonies in Northern Kazakhstan.[66]

This turn away from the moderate policies of 1934 was certainly related to Stalin's response to the Kirov murder, which included broad purges of urban areas, especially Leningrad, and increased attention to the covert surveillance of suspect populations by the NKVD.[67] Yet these changes were, more fundamentally, a reaction by both central and local police officials to the difficulties they faced in implementing the policies demanded by the Politburo. The realities of local police work were impossible for the center to ignore after 1934; local administrations made it clear, through numerous channels, that only those tactics that relied on mass purges of urban areas had any effect on overall levels of social disorder.

Speculation, Theft, and the "Normalization" of Soviet Trade

The end of class warfare and the "normalization" of Soviet life, as announced at the Congress of Victors in early 1934, prompted dramatic changes in the Soviet economic system. After several years of privation and rationing, Stalin embarked on a gradual relaxation of trade restrictions, culminating in early 1935 in the abolition of the rationing of bread products and, later in the year, of all consumer goods. Stalin's goal was to create a "cultured" system of retail trade, unfettered either by rationing or shortages, that would serve as the basis for a truly socialist trade system.[68] Yet these policy changes quickly produced an expansion of market activities, both legal and illegal, which threatened to overwhelm the Soviet trade sector. The regime responded in late 1934 and 1935 with widespread campaigns against speculation, focusing in particular on small-scale speculation in consumer goods in major cities. The local police, for the first time in the 1930s, responded positively to central demands to repress individual petty speculators, most of whom were average individuals trying to make ends meet within the confines of the Stalinist economic system. By the end of 1935, local police were fully engaged in the daily policing of urban speculation, and the definition of the crime itself had grown to encompass a wide spectrum of economic behaviors that had previously been condemned by the center but tolerated, in practice, by local officers.

Little in the regime's response to trade and speculation in early 1934 suggested that major changes were imminent. Although the Politburo announced in late 1933 that peasants would be allowed to market grain and bread products in 1934 in those areas that had fulfilled their grain procurement targets, this move was unexceptional; alternating cycles of repression and moderation had been part of every previous planting and harvest cycle since the abolition of the NEP. Likewise, every Politburo decision in the early 1930s to allow some level of free trade in grain products entailed substantial police repression of speculation, and early 1934 was no exception. In early January, the OGPU ordered local *militsiia* administrations to increase pressure on speculators at collective farm markets and urban bazaars, focusing in particular on "juvenile homeless, begging, and general vagrant elements" who were supposedly taking advantage of the decision to allow limited free trade. The police were to apply the August 1932 law on speculation to arrested individuals, but they were warned not to resort to "mass searches and arrests" in the markets themselves. Central police officials, correctly understanding the policy cues emanating from the Politburo in early 1934, took pains to avoid the kind of mass operations that might frighten the population and hamper small-scale trade by collective farmers in advance of the spring planting campaign.[69] The local police remained generally unconcerned with widespread petty speculation in early 1934, concentrating on "professional" speculators and ignoring petty behaviors that were, as was becoming increasingly clear to top Communist Party and finance officials, the real cause of difficulties in the trade sector.

In early 1934, top finance officials began to respond to this reality, arguing to the Politburo that petty speculation by average Soviet citizens directly compromised the integrity of the Soviet trade system as much as, or perhaps more than, the "professional" buying and reselling of goods. In late January 1934, Grigorii Grinko, the USSR commissar of finance, complained to the Sovnarkom that insufficient police attention to small-scale speculation was producing elevated market prices and, just as important, substantial losses in tax revenue. The local police, he argued, virtually ignored petty speculation at open air markets, concentrating instead on organized embezzlement and resale; local *militsiia* administrations sometimes went as far as refusing to launch investigations in cases of petty speculation that were transferred to them by local finance officials, suggesting that such problems be dealt with using the tax system instead. Grinko, alluding to the August 1932 law on speculation, suggested that the Sovnarkom order the police to intensify their repression of petty speculation, subjecting speculators at a minimum to fines (with half the proceeds going to local budgets) in order to, in his words, "tear out by the roots, once and for all, resellers and speculators who are attempting to get fat at the expense of workers and the laboring peasantry."[70]

Yagoda responded to these complaints in late February with characteristic reluctance to engage the issue of petty speculation. Writing to Molotov, Yagoda argued that Grinko's complaints "did not correspond with reality." The local police, he noted, initiated some 10,000 criminal cases a month regarding speculation in early 1934, and they deported a substantial number of urban speculators in the process of ongoing campaigns against "parasitic and alien elements." Yagoda's concern, as head of the police, was with public order rather than tax revenue, and he declined to expend much energy targeting speculators who were not otherwise part of the criminal milieu. The Sovnarkom dropped the question from consideration in early March, and it languished for several months as the Politburo focused its attention on restructuring the OGPU.[71]

Nonetheless, the economic effects of speculation remained paramount in the eyes of economic planners in mid-1934, especially as troubles with the grain procurement campaign began to appear in the summer and fall. The 1933 harvest had been relatively full, but in mid-1934 local officials began to sound the alarm about mounting problems with the upcoming harvest campaign. In preparation for the June–July Central Committee Plenum meeting, which was concerned exclusively with the state of agriculture in the USSR, Grinko managed to get the issue of speculation back on the Politburo's agenda, and in late June, Stalin agreed to create a commission, consisting of himself, Kuibyshev (head of the state economic planning agency, or Gosplan), Kaganovich, and Grinko, to examine "the battle with violations of retail prices."[72] Local trade officials also reported, through various channels, that the expansion of the collective farm system had slowed and in some areas even reversed in early 1934, as peasants realized that they could live better, even in the face of economic pressure by the state, by skirting trade regulations and making their way as individual rather than collective farmers.[73]

The Commission for Soviet Control came to similar conclusions regarding urban speculation in a July 1934 report on theft and embezzlement in the cooperative trade sector. According to the report, economic losses from these crimes amounted to nearly 150 million rubles in 1932 and more than 211 million in 1933; the trend continued to accelerate into early 1934, in part because the local police did little to halt this hemorrhage of goods, most of which ended up on the open market.[74] These ongoing concerns with the economic effects of individual trade and petty speculation ensured that, when the issue arose in late 1934 in conjunction with the fall harvest campaign, central Communist Party officials would be inclined to expand their focus beyond the limited targets of earlier campaigns.

Events at the June–July Central Committee Plenum suggested that a major policy change was under consideration. The plenum resolved to halt all trade of bread and grain products by individuals and collective farms as of July 15, 1934, with the exception of the Far Eastern Territory and eastern parts of Eastern Siberia. Although this restriction was an established part of grain procurement campaigns, the orders sent to local NKVD administrations on carrying it out stressed moderation over expediency, instructing local officials to arrest only repeat speculators and peasants who had not yet fulfilled their grain procurement quotas.[75] The plenum also prompted broader consideration of the proper response to speculation and theft in late 1934, as both the Sovnarkom and the Council of Labor and Defense created working commissions to consider the issue and create policy recommendations for the Politburo.[76]

Opinions within these commissions diverged along well-established lines, between finance officials, who were concerned with the effects of petty speculation on the trade system, and the police, who remained more concerned about the existence of the "criminal contingent" than with the petty reselling of individual items. Grinko reprised his calls for additional police action with a lengthy report on trade practices in Ukraine, arguing that private trade in both manufactured goods and foodstuffs was widespread in urban areas, especially Kiev. Several thousand traders a day filled markets in Kiev; nearly 30 percent of the goods on sale were originally purchased from the state retail sector, and a good portion of the rest was purchased from peasants or handcraft workers for resale. Ukrainian finance officials estimated that unauthorized trade amounted to some 500,000 to 1 million rubles worth of goods per month in Kiev alone. They recommended that these speculators should either be repressed by the police or legalized and taxed.[77]

Yagoda in turn defended the position of the NKVD, reiterating his contention that speculators were a concern for the police only when they disrupted public order or were connected with organized crime. He reported that the police "brought to responsibility" some 58,000 individuals for speculation in the first half of 1934 and expelled from major cities 53,000 more who "did not have any defined employment, who gathered in markets, who speculated, but who were impossible to sentence according to the law of August 22, 1932." Nonetheless, he admitted that markets in urban areas were "flooded" with petty speculators, most of whom were workers, housewives (*domokhoziaiki*, although the majority would have been employed as well), dependents of workers, or white-collar employees.[78] His claims were typically self-aggrandizing, yet he correctly identified the key problem with ongoing approaches to speculation: the behaviors that disrupted the Soviet trade system were the responsibility not of organized "speculative elements" but of average Soviet citizens attempting to cope with shortages, and the NKVD, while capable of repressing these citizens, did not consider the task central to its mandate to preserve order in major cities. Although the Sovnarkom commission met in mid-August and generated policy suggestions, the Sovnarkom declined to take action and in early October removed the issue from consideration for the rest of the year.[79]

The recalcitrance of central authorities on this issue was related to fundamental impending changes in the Soviet trade system. Discussions at the November 1934 Central Committee Plenum returned to the issue of retail trade and rationing in consumer goods, and on December 7, 1934, the Politburo decided to abolish the rationing system for bread products entirely as of January 1, 1935, setting strict prices for the sale of bread nationwide and promulgating a host of regulations for the sale and purchase of these products.[80] At roughly the same time, the Politburo began to encourage preparations for the upcoming planting campaigns, issuing standard instructions that approved free trade in grain products by collective and individual farmers in numerous areas of the USSR where grain procurement campaigns had been fulfilled.[81] Allowing free trade in grain by collective farmers was by itself not an unusual step, but when coupled with the abolishment of the rationing system in bread products, it signaled Stalin's intention to replace the existing state trade system with a commercialized version of "socialist" trade based on the unrestricted purchasing of all consumer goods.[82]

The response of the population to these decisions was immediate. Soviet citizens, unconvinced that the experiment in "free trade" would last and worried about future shortages, took the only reasonable course of action and began to purchase as much bread as they could find. Peasants were the most active purchasers, streaming into urban areas to buy bread from state-run stores at artificially low prices. The first week of the unlimited sale of bread was crushing for local trade officials, who saw their entire January allotment sold off within days. Trade officials across the USSR responded with ad hoc restrictions on the sale of bread, but the Politburo refused to permit any sort of localized rationing systems for fear of disrupting the transition to "free" trade, and it instructed Procuracy officials to arrest local retail administrators who attempted to create them.[83]

Most of the responsibility for preventing excessive purchasing of bread products, by common citizens and "professional" speculators alike, therefore fell to the police and to Procuracy officials, who were to maintain order in retail trade after January 1, 1935, solely by repressing all forms of speculation. Local officials were instructed to focus not only on resale but also on the "systematic" purchase of products above allowable norms (originally 2 kilograms of bread per person), which was defined as more than a two days' or three days' supply. Both the police and Procuracy officials, however, were instructed to charge average citizens who purchased bread above the allowable norms with violations of the rules of trade (Article 105), which usually entailed only a simple monetary fine. Harsher judicial and extrajudicial forms of repression, including the provisions of the August 1932 edict on speculation, were reserved for professional speculators or individuals demonstrating a clear intent to resell items for a profit.[84] These instructions were, in essence, self-contradictory; local police had virtually no chance of preventing shortages of grain products through the policing of speculation alone if they were unable, or unwilling, to arrest Soviet citizens for simply purchasing too much bread, a behavior that nearly all trade officials knew was the true cause of the problem.

Given the contradictory policy directives emanating from the Politburo, the NKVD responded with the policing tactic most familiar to them in the mid-1930s: purges of urban areas of "speculative elements." In late March 1935, the Politburo launched a major campaign against speculation, paralleling similar moves against hooliganism, robbery, and juvenile delinquency that began at almost the same time (see below). A joint instruction from the NKVD, Procuracy, and Supreme Court warned local criminal justice officials that speculation was on the rise and ordered them to arrest all speculators and resellers; the police were to complete their investigations within three days, while the courts were to hear cases in an additional three days, publishing the results of particularly important or instructive cases in local press outlets for the edification of the population. The repression of purchasing behavior was the real innovation of this campaign, building on restrictions put in place earlier in the year. The simple purchase of 80 kilograms or more of bread for any purpose was proof of speculative intent, while the purchase of 32 kilograms of bread was a "socially dangerous activity," sufficient to charge the offender with violating the norms of trade (Article 105 of the Criminal Code). The local police were explicitly ordered not to create any kind of volunteer detachments to patrol markets or to carry out any mass searches and arrests as part of this campaign. Nonetheless, local police administrations tended to approach this campaign as an expansion of ongoing operations against "dangerous elements" and violators of the passport system, arresting individuals who bought and sold even small amounts of consumer goods if they could be identified as "dangerous" criminals based on previous criminal infractions or ongoing "connections with the criminal milieu."[85]

The local police also continued to ignore the issues that were most important for finance officials, refusing to suppress those behaviors that were financially ruinous but had relatively little effect on urban public order. For example, a comprehensive report on markets in Moscow, Kharkov, Rostov, Minsk, and Leningrad carried out by the Commission for Party Control in mid-1935 concluded that crowded markets in major cities had become "their own type of department store," offering a wide variety and quality of goods in an unregulated, but completely open, manner. The infamous Iaroslavsky market in Moscow maintained organized spaces for only 100 registered handicraft workers, yet some 2,000 registered traders crowded the market each day, selling openly without any stationary storefront. Speculation in Kharkov was, according to the report, "legalized" by the daily payment of fines to the police; petty traders treated the daily 2-ruble market registration fee and the 5- to 10-ruble daily fine to the police as simple business expenses.[86] This problem of petty speculation by individuals not otherwise identified as criminals, often carried out by employees with privileged access to goods through trade union or employment channels, was obvious to finance officials, yet the police continued to ignore such issues in everyday practice, focusing instead on repressing the "speculative contingent."

These problems were further exacerbated by the Politburo's decision, in October 1935, to deepen the transition to "free" Soviet trade by eliminating rationing in numerous other consumer items, including extraordinarily scarce items like meat, sugar and, after January 1, 1936, manufactured goods.[87] Grinko doggedly pursued the issue of the economic effects of speculation in late 1935, arguing in a letter to Molotov that speculation in manufactured goods had reached threatening levels and required immediate action. Grinko's suggestions were aimed predominantly at preventing organized speculators from operating as registered traders, but he also included several recommendations that suggest that he was beginning to accept at least some of the NKVD's focus on the role of the "criminal contingent" in urban speculation. He suggested that finance officials be given the right to fine speculators up to 500 rubles (the same request that Yagoda had made for the benefit of the police in mid-1934), and that former traders, "exploiters of hired labor," and those deprived of civil rights because of past social status (*lishentsy*) be prohibited from trading at markets altogether. He recommended as well that the NKVD be authorized to banish, for up to four years, any individuals carrying out "systematic" speculation in regime locations in order to control the problem.[88]

Top police officials, for their part, began to accept some of the arguments of top finance officials as a result of their activity against speculation in 1935. Yagoda, in an early 1936 report on police actions against speculators, noted that the sheer number of individuals involved in reselling consumer goods continued to climb in late 1935 and early 1936, despite the arrest of nearly 105,000 individuals for the crime in 1935. According to Yagoda, the persistence of speculation was due to the changing nature of the crime, which was increasingly characterized by the individual buying and selling of small quantities of scarce consumer goods, which the sellers themselves had purchased legally by standing in long lines.[89] By early 1936, his comments suggest, top police officials were beginning to conceptualize speculation as one of many daily responses by the working masses to the realities of the Soviet economic system, rather than the result of "professional" criminals alone.

The Politburo's attempts to promote "normal" economic life and "free" socialist trade in 1934 and 1935 ultimately caused a fundamental change in the understandings of speculation held by the central and local police alike. Local police had long insisted that petty reselling by average Soviet citizens did not constitute "socially dangerous" behavior, even during Stalin's aggressive campaign against economic crimes in 1932. Yet the system of "cultured" socialist trade, as envisioned by Stalin, forced the local police to respond to individual behaviors that threatened the distribution of scarce consumer goods. By early 1936, local officers generally accepted the idea that urban speculation could no longer be blamed solely on "organized" criminals. The local police did not respond by jettisoning their approaches to the "speculative elements," with which they were quite comfortable; on the contrary, they began a process of widening the definition of "social danger" to include far broader cohorts of the population. As we will see in chapters 5 and 6, once the local police made the connection between the everyday behaviors of Soviet citizens and extrajudicial repression, they were more than willing to arrest average citizens taking part in speculation, violations of retail trade rules, or numerous other strategies for coping with the unrelenting shortages in the Soviet trade sector.

Hooliganism, Armed Robbery, and Urban Public Order

March 1935 was a busy month for the Soviet police. In addition to the campaign against speculation, at midmonth the Politburo launched a major campaign against armed robbery, ordering the police and justice officials in twenty cities to sentence robbers to death within five days of their crime. Late in the month, the Politburo expanded this order to numerous locations across the USSR and ordered local officials in all areas to begin a similar campaign against hooliganism, sentencing individuals guilty of malicious hooliganism (Article 74-2 of the Criminal Code) to five years in prison.

This campaign against hooliganism, which was widely propagandized in the press and discussed in criminal justice journals, is often taken as a sign of an abrupt decision on Stalin's part to return to a more traditional, and certainly more repressive, approach to regular criminal justice. On the contrary, these campaigns were no surprise to top police and justice officials, as they emerged from months of debate within the Politburo and the Sovnarkom regarding the nature of Soviet criminal justice in the post-dekulakization era. The local police likewise understood them as an expansion of ongoing operations against "dangerous elements" and as a culmination of their efforts to control crime in cities that began with the implementation of the passport system in early 1933. From the Politburo's point of view, these campaigns were an almost unqualified success; by the beginning of 1936, violent hooliganism and armed robbery in major cities had receded to almost negligible levels, and the police could boast with some justification that the more menacing aspects of these problems had been "solved," whatever the means required to do so. These campaigns increased the tendency of the local police to equate rowdy or disorderly behavior with "social danger" and counterrevolutionary crime, lending a distinctly political hue to the offense of hooliganism. Such conceptual connections played a major role in the expansion of repression against "dangerous" population cohorts in the years that followed.

As we have seen, by early 1934 hooliganism was understood by central police and Communist Party officials as a particularly threatening category of crime, characterized not only by flagrant disrespect for public order but also by violent physical assault. Stalin's irate censure in early 1934 of the Moscow police regarding violent crime on the city's streets was consistent with his orders regarding hooliganism on rail transport in June, and with Yagoda's suggestions early in the year that hooligans and "knife fighters" be punished with ten years in a labor camp. For Stalin, as for top police officials, violent acts of hooliganism were by 1934 tantamount to banditry or even diversionary activity and demanded severe repression. The political police leadership vigorously propagandized this understanding of hooliganism to local officials in 1934, using circulars, direct orders, and even the judicial press. Yagoda lambasted the local police in a March 1934 circular, for example, for failing to respond to the threat; he deemed it "impermissible" that "hooligans, thieves, robbers, and other declassed elements operate unpunished in our socialist cities and workers' settlements," and he exhorted the *militsiia* to "pull out banditry, robbery, and hooliganism by the roots."[90]

L. Vul, the Moscow police chief, scolded his officers in the same manner in an article published in the newspaper of the Moscow police force in late February, complaining that by sentencing hooligans to simple fines or compulsory labor rather than sending them to court, they failed to recognize such criminals as "class enemies."[91] Top judicial and police officials echoed this characterization of hooliganism in published journal articles in early 1935, focusing on the question of class struggle; hooliganism represented a form of opposition from petit bourgeois elements, especially former property owners from within the peasantry, and was therefore similar in essence to the theft of public property or "wrecking."[92] Urban hooliganism represented a major part of police work throughout the early 1930s, yet by 1935 central officials were inclined to view it as much more than simple drunken brawling by peasant youth on religious holidays.[93]

The local police were far less alarmist regarding the causes of hooliganism before 1935, in part because explanations based on social class continued to provide little explanatory power. Most urban residents charged with hooliganism in 1934 were, in fact, workers, and most were guilty of the same kind of drunken public activity that had defined hooliganism in earlier years.[94] The local police maintained a completely different calculus: they tended to levy fines for behaviors that might be considered "dangerous" enough to warrant criminal prosecution, especially street fighting and other personal assaults, simply because fines required less paperwork; but at the same time, they handed out fines liberally for petty acts that could not be considered "dangerous" but nonetheless threatened norms of public order, such as public drunkenness, verbal insults, and, according to one report on fining practices in Moscow in December 1934, incidents as trivial as a driver honking his horn excessively on a busy Moscow street.[95] Even into early 1935, investigations in Moscow suggested that most incidents of hooliganism were simply drunken "scandals" and fights, rather than the extreme violence that concerned central officials.[96] The urban police did expend a substantial amount of effort in controlling hooliganism; the Moscow police, for example, issued more than 100,000 fines for hooliganism alone in 1934, representing some 25 percent of the total number of fines handed out for the year, and they sentenced more than 23,000 hooligans to terms of compulsory labor, representing some 30 percent of the total such sentences for the year.[97] Nonetheless, for local police administrations, petty urban hooliganism remained predominantly an administrative issue in 1933 and 1934, as local officers directed harsher repressions toward crimes that seemed more immediately threatening to the Soviet system.

Major changes in regime policy regarding hooliganism emerged in late 1934, from within the Sovnarkom commission that considered the overall performance of the *militsiia*. The proper response to hooliganism was a major issue of contention within the commission. Its members rejected Yagoda's request that hooligans be punished with ten years in a labor camp, but police and justice officials did agree that a "simplified and accelerated" procedure for hearing all cases of hooliganism was necessary, and they instructed Belskii and Leplevskii, for the NKVD and the Procuracy, to prepare a draft of suitable legislation for the Politburo's consideration.[98] The two officials were unable to come to agreement after two months of argument, and they submitted competing recommendations to the Politburo on February 25, 1935. The draft presented by the NKVD violated both the spirit and the letter of the commission's debates, suggesting that police be given wide-ranging powers to incarcerate hooligans and other violent, dangerous criminals before trial, notwithstanding the limits on prison populations set down by the instruction of May 8, 1933. Procuracy officials continued to oppose the most drastic NKVD suggestions in early 1935, but, in the changed political atmosphere after Kirov's murder, they acquiesced on the need to arrest and incarcerate even first-time hooligans and thieves until their trials.[99]

Whatever the details of the debate within this commission, top police and justice understood that a major campaign against hooliganism was likely in the near future, and in early 1935 they began to instruct local officials to increase attention to the crime within the framework of existing regulations. The Procuracy of the Russian Republic, for example, called meetings of regional and local officials in early 1935 to discuss the issue, and on February 14 the Russian Supreme Court ordered local judges to sentence malicious hooligans, as a rule, to deprivation of freedom rather than to fines.[100] Central justice officials prompted local judges in February and March to increase punishments for violent crimes and to qualify as many cases as possible as either "malicious hooliganism" or banditry, both of which entailed prison or labor camp sentences.[101]

The response from local officials was immediate. In Moscow, the number of court cases for hooliganism doubled in March compared with January, and the number of administrative fines increased by 150 percent, well in advance of any central decision to launch a campaign.[102] Local police expanded the extrajudicial repression of hooligans as well in early 1935, despite the fact that the NKVD exercised no general right to sentence hooligans or any other criminal offenders using troikas in this period. The police did sentence hooligans using the NKVD Special Board as "dangerous elements," and they could also eject hooligans from regime areas using the passport system.[103] Limited evidence from Moscow also suggests that, despite the general restriction on extrajudicial sentencing that accompanied the creation of the NKVD, the police repressed malicious hooligans alongside "dangerous elements" during the first three months of 1935, using an NKVD troika created specifically to handle such cases.[104] Hooliganism and violent urban crime, then, were an increasingly pressing issue for local criminal justice officials in the months before March 1935, one that the local police dealt with using every judicial and extrajudicial means available to them.

When the Politburo intervened in this situation in mid-March, it was initially concerned not with hooliganism but with armed robbery. On March 13, the Politburo discussed a news story, published that day in *Pravda*, about a particularly brutal armed robbery and rape that had been carried out by a group of four young criminals in Moscow at the end of February. All four perpetrators, according to the news story, had previous convictions or ongoing contacts with the criminal milieu, and all four qualified as professional criminals.[105] The Politburo immediately ordered police and justice agencies in Moscow, Leningrad, and eighteen other major urban centers to launch a campaign against armed robbery, hearing all cases within five days in court and sentencing all guilty individuals to execution. Local newspapers were to publish accounts of such cases, relating the details of the crime and emphasizing that the sentence of execution had been carried out. At the end of the month, the Politburo added to the campaign several more specific urban areas, plus all the industrial areas in the Donbass region, all the cities in the Kuzbass region, and all the districts bordering on Moscow and Leningrad.[106] At the same time, on March 29, Stalin launched a major, public campaign against hooliganism; malicious hooliganism (Article 74-2) would henceforth be punishable by five years in prison, and the possession of certain kinds of knives was prohibited under the same rules that pertained to firearms.[107] Although Stalin had the final word on the nature of these campaigns, all the policy changes they entailed had been discussed in explicit terms by the commission on the *militsiia* in the preceding months, and local police had stepped up the suppression of violent urban crime well in advance of his intervention.

For top police and justice officials, hooliganism and violent urban crime were not merely a threat to "normal" urban life. By 1935, they were viewed as an assault on the fabric of Soviet urban society, as a conscious affront to socialism, and hence as counterrevolutionary activity. Soviet criminologists made these connections in an outpouring of essays about hooliganism in the judicial press in mid-1935, arguing that hooligans often committed serious and potentially political crimes, such as organized robbery and banditry.[108] Vladimir Antonov-Ovseenko, reporting on Procuracy activities in the Russian republic for the first five months of 1935, likewise noted that hooliganism was the cause of nearly 30 percent of the murders committed in the Russian Republic, and that hooliganistic acts in many areas had "grown into" banditry and counterrevolutionary activity; he portrayed hooligans as terrorists on city streets, targeting workers, women, and national minorities with violent attacks.[109] Yagoda was most aggressive in this regard, demanding that the *militsiia* approach the policing of public order with the same vigor directed at political crime. In the April 1935 speech quoted at the beginning of this chapter, he declared that hooligans, bandits, and robbers were "genuine" counterrevolutionaries, and he instructed local *militsiia* chiefs to look "behind the hooligan, the bandit" in order to find counterrevolutionaries and therefore aid the work of the political police. His conclusion—that "any criminal act by its nature can be nothing other than a manifestation of class struggle"—accurately summarized the conceptual connections prevalent among top criminal justice officials between issues of social order, the "victory of socialism," and extrajudicial repression by 1935.[110]

Despite such rhetoric, local officers initially reacted to these campaigns with the same tactics directed at hooliganism earlier in the decade. Local officers continued to maintain that most urban hooliganism was committed by drunken workers, especially among groups of men who had just received their pay, and usually occurred in pubic places such as parks or workers' clubs. Simple fistfights predominated in public, and the police reported that "hooliganism" in private spaces often occurred in the context of marital conflict. Serious violence, including "knife fighting," remained relatively rare.[111] Local police therefore responded with proven tactics, including extra patrols in public areas, fines, and extrajudicial sentencing in the most egregious cases. The NKVD specifically allowed for the administrative sentencing of malicious hooligans as part of this campaign, but the limited available evidence does not suggest that the police responded with a substantial increase in extrajudicial sentences specifically for hooliganism.[112] Local administrations also rejected orders to involve the public in these campaigns. Individual officers dutifully organized volunteer Assistance Brigades to patrol parks, workers' clubs, and movie theaters as part of the campaign, but they placed little emphasis on daily work with volunteers, complaining that brigade members were usually young, members of the working classes, and often drunk (much like the hooligans they were supposed to police).[113] Urban officers continued instead to issue fines, sometimes in amounts of 100 rubles or more, as their primary response to hooliganism, even for repeat offenders who clearly fell under the guidelines of the March decree. Such practices violated the intent of the Politburo's order, and central Communist Party organizations complained in the late spring and summer of 1935 that the local police failed to understand the political importance of the Politburo's directive, and that hooliganism, as a result, was increasing with the approach of the summer months.[114] But for local officers, the extensive use of fines, along with the extrajudicial repression of the most troublesome cases, was the best means of controlling a behavior as widespread as hooliganism, even in the face of substantial central pressure to do otherwise.

Local police claimed that the poor performance of the judicial system made their work against hooliganism essentially worthless, leading them to search for solutions to the problem that ignored the court system entirely. The police in the Moscow region, for example, complained that slow investigations by the courts and local procurators hampered the effectiveness of their actions against hooliganism and vitiated any educative effect of the campaign. Communist Party reports on the work of justice organizations in the Moscow region echoed these charges; local procurators participated only nominally in investigations of hooliganism, while judges continued to sentence malicious hooligans to compulsory labor instead of deprivation of freedom.[115] Yagoda broadened these complaints in mid-July 1935, railing on the performance of the court system in a letter to Stalin and Molotov. Yagoda complained that the courts ruined ongoing police work against bandits, thieves, hooligans, and robbers by handing out "criminally lenient sentences" and taking too long to complete investigations. The courts, he argued, issued sentences of compulsory labor to "declassed, hooliganistic, and thieving elements," who often had no defined place of residence and who had multiple past arrests for petty crimes; such individuals simply moved to a neighboring area and continued their criminal activities.[116]

These complaints were certainly unfair. Data from the court system of the Russian Republic show that judges did in fact apply increasingly harsh sentences to robbers, bandits, and hooligans in 1935 and 1936. This trend was particularly pronounced for robbery and banditry, as what one Russian Supreme Court official referred to as "merciless judicial repression" produced a wave of executions for these crimes.[117] The courts increased punishment for hooliganism as well, sentencing 42 percent of individuals convicted of hooliganism in the Russian Republic in the first half of 1935 to terms in prison or labor camps, up from only 10 percent in the second half of 1933.[118]

Despite this increasingly severe judicial repression of violent crime, local police were more inclined to connect the policing of hooliganism to ongoing sweeps of "dangerous" or "harmful elements" and passport violators, and to process them using their own extrajudicial institutions, than to pursue these cases through the court system. Individual officers maintained lists of "known hooligans" in their areas, in addition to the unemployed, ex-convicts, administrative exiles, and juvenile delinquents; repeat hooliganism was one of the crimes specifically identified in police regulations by 1935 as evidence of a "dangerous" or "declassed" social identity.[119] By placing individuals suspected of hooliganism under surveillance, the police in effect removed them from the sphere of the hooliganism campaign proper and added them to the cohort of "dangerous elements," making them the subject of ongoing urban extrajudicial purges of Soviet cities.

The first evidence that the 1935 campaigns against armed robbery and hooliganism were having an effect on violent urban crime appears, in fact, not in trends pertaining to court cases but in police reports on declining levels of crime in late 1935 in the 120 largest urban areas in the USSR, all of which were protected under the regime rules of the passport system.[120] Yagoda repeated this argument several times in early and mid-1936, claiming that banditry, armed robbery, arson, murder, and cattle rustling decreased dramatically during 1935; in one report, he crowed that there were more armed assaults and robberies in the city of Chicago alone in July and August 1935 than in all the cities in the USSR combined.[121] By early 1936, Yagoda maintained that nearly half of all individuals arrested for hooliganism, theft, and speculation were "socially harmful [*vrednye*] elements," and he insisted that further reductions in crime would come only through the elimination of this cohort of "socially harmful elements" from urban society altogether.[122]

In this assessment, Yagoda was absolutely correct. "Success" in the policing of violent crime in 1935 had come not from specific judicial campaigns against hooliganism or armed robbery, which were drastic enough but were limited in scope when compared with ongoing extrajudicial campaigns against urban crime. Nor had success come from fundamental changes in the way that the police went about patrolling the streets; the numbers of police officers remained relatively constant in this period, and new techniques promoted by the center, such as the reinvigoration of volunteer brigades, had little impact on police operations themselves. Rather, the real innovation in Soviet policing of the mid-1930s was the police's propensity to deal with violent crime by repressing as a cohort those urban lawbreakers deemed "recidivists" or "socially dangerous elements."

Campaigns against Juvenile Delinquency, 1934–1936

Juvenile delinquency, much like hooliganism and speculation, became a focal point for discussions about "normal" Soviet urban life in the months after the Congress of Victors in early 1934. Although the number of homeless children on the streets of major Soviet cities declined as the famine eased in late 1933, police and Communist Party authorities became increasingly concerned about the effects of juvenile delinquency (*beznadzornost'*—literally "unsupervisedness") on the fabric of urban life in 1934. By 1935, the local police generally identified delinquency as the product of a core group of hardened juvenile criminals who had been in and out of orphanages for years, rebuffing all attempts at rehabilitation by welfare officials and exercising a corrupting influence on other children.

This explanation of juvenile crime, which appeared in muted form in the early 1930s, resonated with the assumptions held by both local and central police officials regarding the role of "socially harmful elements" in urban crime, and it prompted aggressive attempts by local police administrations to solve the problem on their own terms, pushing welfare agencies to the periphery of juvenile affairs. Conflicts over juvenile issues simmered throughout 1934 and early 1935, leading to the notorious Politburo decision in April 1935 to lower the age of criminal responsibility to twelve years for several specific crimes and to launch a major judicial campaign against delinquency. This Politburo decision was only the most visible part of a general takeover by the police of nearly all aspects of juvenile policing, sentencing, and incarceration, most of which had been the responsibility of Soviet welfare or educational institutions before 1935.

Although the end of the famine in late 1933 produced an immediate decrease in homeless children on the streets of major Soviet cities, in 1934 homeless populations continued to stretch the orphanage system beyond its limits, complicating efforts by the police and welfare agencies to control the "difficult" among them. Central Communist Party officials reported in early 1934 that, although the number of homeless children under state care had dropped from 400,000 to roughly 282,000, the USSR's budget provided funding to support only 220,000 children, resulting in systemwide shortages of clothing, supplies, and, in some areas, food.[123] Local welfare organizations, still overwhelmed by the situation, devoted little attention to their traditional tasks of controlling delinquency on the streets and preventing escapes from the regular orphanage system in early 1934.

According to the local police, this breakdown in the welfare system led to increased levels of juvenile crime in early 1934, especially among children who were truant from school or who, because of the maximum four-hour working day for children, were left to their own devices for much of the day while their parents were at work. The police estimated that some 2,500 such children spent time on the streets of Moscow each day, gathering at markets and around schools, where they sold cigarettes, begged for money, and fell under the influence of adult criminals. The police deemed juvenile delinquents between the ages of twelve and sixteen a particular problem, because they were capable of overtly criminal acts but were not held criminally accountable for their actions, even if they were repeat offenders. By mid-1934, the discussion of these issues had filtered up to the top of the Communist Party hierarchy in Moscow, where general agreement emerged that delinquency among the "unsupervised" was a growing problem and that existing approaches to controlling it had little effect.[124]

Central consideration of this issue emerged in mid-April 1934, in conjunction with ongoing debates at the center regarding the nature of the police and the creation of the NKVD. On April 11, Semashko, the head of the Russian Children's Commission, brought the problem to the attention of Mikhail Kalinin, noting that threatening forms of juvenile crime, especially hooliganism, were on the rise among the unsupervised, and asking that the issues of homelessness and delinquency be placed on the Politburo's agenda.[125] Procuracy reports echoed the same complaints: serious crimes among juveniles, including hooliganism, robbery, murder, and rape, were on the rise in major cities in 1934, and were often committed by children who had been expelled from school for poor behavior. Working parents had little time to supervise such children, and welfare organizations, including the juvenile affairs commissions, did not have the resources to adequately handle this group of offenders, who were invariably pulled into petty criminal activities on the streets.[126]

Responding to these complaints, the Politburo created a commission to consider the issue of juvenile delinquency on May 25, 1934, headed by Chubar and including Yagoda, Semashko, and several others with an institutional interest in the issue.[127] Chubar's commission met in early June and generated a relatively moderate set of policy suggestions, largely under the influence of its members from the welfare and educational commissariats, which concentrated on improving the orphanage system. The only radical change recommended by the commission was the creation of special children's courts at the regional level and in major cities for hearing cases of lawbreakers between the ages of twelve and sixteen, a move that suggested but did not require lowering the age of criminal responsibility.[128]

The Politburo took no action on these suggestions until late in the year. Meanwhile Chubar, likely responding to the obvious trend toward the harsher repression of urban criminals, reconsidered his initial policy suggestions, and in mid-September 1934 he forwarded a much more severe set of recommendations to the Politburo. He suggested that "difficult recidivists" among homeless children, down to twelve years of age, be sentenced to terms in special "closed" institutions created by the Justice Commissariat for that purpose. He also outlined plans for a ten-day sweep of all major Soviet cities and railway stations, to begin on October 15, that he expected to net some 40,000 homeless and delinquent children.[129] The Politburo again declined to approve Chubar's suggestions, but in late October it instructed Kalinin to "familiarize himself" with Chubar's work, effectively announcing that Kalinin would be taking over the discussion of juvenile affairs.[130] The Politburo's evident lack of faith in Chubar notwithstanding, the policy suggestions he made in September 1934 contained many of the essential aspects of the changes that would occur in juvenile affairs in 1935.

Despite a lack of direction from the center, the local police implemented major changes in their approach to juvenile affairs in the last months of 1934 and the first of 1935. In October 1934, Semashko and M. Epshtein, the assistant commissar of education of the Russian Republic, sent orders to local education and child welfare officials announcing a relatively standard one-day sweep of homeless children in preparation for the Revolution holidays. Child homelessness, they wrote, had declined enough in the preceding months so that a short-term campaign, "without any especially exceptional measures," would allow for the "complete liquidation" of homelessness in all major cities and workers' settlements.

Once it began on the evening of November 2, 1934, this sweep of homeless children entailed several exceptional practices. Children under the age of sixteen were removed from city streets by welfare and police officials and sent to local detention centers, where special troikas, comprised of representatives of local educational, child welfare, and police organizations, decided their fates based on age, criminal activity, and previous escapes from orphanages. The troikas sent most "normal" homeless children to regular orphanages, but the "difficult" among them were sent to juvenile labor colonies. In flagrant violation of existing law, the troikas sent all children fifteen or older who were identified as "malicious lawbreaking recidivists" directly to closed labor colonies of the Justice Commissariat.[131] The campaign turned into not a one-day but at least a four-day affair. When it was over, local officials had detained more than 10,300 children in the Russian Republic, including nearly 1,800 in the city of Moscow. Despite the fact that this campaign made no provisions for arrests of children who were not homeless, more than 2,000 of these children were identified as "unsupervised," pointing to the growing propensity of local police officials to view underage lawbreakers and the homeless as part of the same larger problem.[132] Although the effective reduction of the age of criminal responsibility to fifteen was the most obvious innovation during this campaign, the ability of the local police and justice officials, rather than the courts, to sentence children to labor colonies pointed to fundamental changes still to come.

Central debates regarding the issue of delinquency continued through the winter of 1934–1935. The same Sovnarkom commission that discussed the work of the *militsiia*, chaired by Rudzutak, addressed the issue of juvenile delinquency, using much of the same vocabulary that pertained to hooliganism and other violent urban crimes. As we have seen, Yagoda recommended to the commission that the age of criminal responsibility for "serious crimes" be lowered to twelve, that recidivist juveniles be punished by terms in closed labor colonies, and that parents of children found guilty of crimes be fined or, if necessary, banished from regime cities.[133] In contrast to the disagreements regarding hooliganism, the Procuracy and police representatives on this commission came to striking agreement on the issue of juvenile delinquency: on February 25, 1935, both Belskii and Leplevskii forwarded to Rudzutak draft resolutions that set the age of criminal responsibility at thirteen, authorized special juvenile labor colonies to house delinquents, and gave the NKVD the general, but as yet undefined, right to adjudicate the cases of more "serious" juvenile offenders.[134]

As with the issue of hooliganism, the Sovnarkom declined to act on these recommendations for several months, in part because Stalin, unsatisfied with Chubar's work, in late December 1934 put Kalinin in charge of an entirely new Politburo commission on the issue and ordered him to propose additional policy recommendations. Kalinin's commission was staffed by the most senior Communist Party officials, including Stalin, A. S. Bubnov, Semashko, Yagoda, Commissar of Defense Kliment Voroshilov, Nadezhda Krupskaia (Lenin's widow), a young Nikita Khrushchev, and a half-dozen others of similar stature.[135] The composition of the commission, and the intense debate that took place within it over the next four months, attest to the importance that Stalin placed on homelessness and delinquency in the mid-1930s.

In advance of the commission's meetings, its members prepared extensive surveys of the situation regarding delinquency and homelessness that echoed the concerns with delinquency, urban crime, and "social danger" expressed by the police and justice officials earlier in the year. One report estimated that some 13,500 homeless children roamed the streets of various cities of the Russian Republic in early 1935, and an additional 13,400 lived in other republics; a slightly later report put the total at 45,000 homeless boys and 15,000 homeless girls.[136] The problem of "unsupervisedness" (*beznadzornost'*), all participants agreed, was growing worse. Police and welfare officials in Moscow, for example, estimated that more than 20 percent of the children swept from city streets as homeless in 1934 were eventually returned to their parents, and that 5 percent of the school-age population had quit school and spent their time on the streets instead.[137] A substantial portion of homeless children on the streets in 1934 reportedly had escaped from orphanages ten to twelve times, and nearly half, according to a May 1934 report, had escaped at least once, whereas unsupervised children often fell under the sway of these "hardened" juvenile criminals.[138] These trends, according to commission materials, resulted in an increasingly "threatening" situation: juvenile recidivists "terrorized" urban populations in lines and at open air markets, while young delinquents moved from petty to serious crimes in the course of their lives, leaving simple theft and hooliganism behind for "malicious, organized armed robbery, murder and rape." Delinquency and homelessness, according to commission materials, created "important sources of cadres for criminal activity" and required immediate and serious action.[139]

Kalinin's commission met twice in March 1935 and prepared a draft of a forthcoming Central Committee edict, to be titled "On the Liquidation of Juvenile Homelessness and Delinquency." Although the commission members agreed on the basic outlines of the edict, they disagreed on several key points, forcing Kalinin to forward to the Politburo a qualified set of suggestions. They agreed on measures designed to improve the orphanage system and provide better social services to homeless and unsupervised children, and they agreed that parents should be held accountable for the criminal actions of their children. But they disagreed on the issue of punishment; the NKVD recommended that parents be banished from regime cities, but the commission eventually accepted only a 100-ruble fine. The commission recommended that the age of criminal responsibility should be lowered, but it failed to agree on an age. It did propose, however, that cases involving lawbreakers under the age of sixteen be heard not by juvenile affairs commissions but by judicial boards consisting of a judge, an educator, and a doctor (essentially an administrative "troika," insofar as such a board was not provided for in the Criminal Procedural Code). The commission approved the idea of NKVD labor colonies for juvenile lawbreakers, with a "special labor and pedagogical regime" for recidivists. Finally, it suggested that there be a separate law to prohibit several categories of knives and that parents be held responsible if their children used these types of weapons (a suggestion that was shortly thereafter incorporated into the Politburo edict on hooliganism, as we have seen above). By the time Kalinin forwarded these suggestions to the Politburo on March 27, all the commission's members understood that a major policy change was imminent, even if the details remained undecided.[140]

Although Kalinin's commission placed numerous options on the table, the ultimate decision belonged to Stalin.[141] On April 7, 1935, some two weeks after Kalinin forwarded his recommendations to the Politburo,

Stalin cut short the discussion and issued a brief edict titled "On Measures in the Struggle against Crime Among Juveniles."[142] This instruction contained only three essential points. It lowered the age of criminal responsibility for juveniles from sixteen to twelve years for a short list of specific crimes—theft, assault with battery, bodily injury, mutilation, murder, and attempted murder—and it sent juveniles accused of these crimes to trials at court rather than to hearings by the juvenile affairs commissions.[143] The edict also subjected adults who made use of children for criminal purposes, such as speculation or prostitution, to five-year sentences in labor camps. Finally, the edict abolished the section of the Criminal Code that provided for reductions of penalties for juveniles, making all individuals over sixteen years of age juridically equivalent to adults and eliminating the ability of judges to issue reduced sentences for children under sixteen.[144] The list of crimes for which children over twelve could be prosecuted was not exact in juridical terms, but it corresponded to Stalin's concerns regarding violent urban crime; the campaign against armed robbery had been launched some three weeks earlier, and the campaign against hooliganism only a week before.

The April 7 edict provoked an immediate response from local officials in charge of controlling juvenile homelessness and crime, but it left the majority of the issues raised by Kalinin's commission undecided.[145] The day after Stalin issued the April 7 edict, the USSR Procuracy and Supreme Court instructed local justice officials to create separate people's courts specializing in juvenile affairs, sending all cases regarding juveniles to them. Until such courts could be created, cases involving children were to be heard in the regular chambers of local courts. This move was a blatant attempt by justice agencies to increase the likelihood that all cases involving juveniles offenders would be heard by the court system, an idea that was supported by some of the participants in Kalinin's commission but was not addressed in the text of the April 7 edict.[146]

The issue of juvenile courts, however, was still under active consideration by Kalinin's commission, which returned to work after April 7 and attempted to salvage what was left of its draft recommendations. Despite continued conflict between the police and welfare officials, the commission drafted measures to improve the orphanage and child social services systems, instructed the police to pay more attention to juvenile hooliganism in the streets, and, per Yagoda's suggestions, forced orphanages to accept homeless children delivered to them by the police and authorized police to fine the parents of delinquents up to 200 rubles.[147] In late April, the commission forwarded its recommendations to the Politburo, which approved the text with only minor changes and promulgated it on May 31 as a Sovnarkom and Central Committee instruction titled "On the Liquidation of Juvenile Homelessness and Delinquency."[148]

The May 31 instruction, and secret instructions to the police and justice agencies that accompanied it, clarified almost all the issues left unclear in Stalin's original edict, shifting most of the responsibility for juvenile affairs away from the welfare and court systems and to the police. The Politburo transferred all juvenile labor colonies and temporary detention centers (*priemniki*) in the USSR to the NKVD.[149] Children younger than three were transferred directly to orphanages once they were swept off the streets, but all older children were evaluated at detention centers by a panel comprising the center's NKVD chief, a doctor, and an educator. These panels forwarded all "normal" homeless children between the ages of three and fourteen to orphanages, but they were authorized to send directly to NKVD juvenile labor colonies all homeless children between the ages of twelve and sixteen who had previous convictions, had been detained by police before, or had fled from orphanages or labor colonies. All homeless children between the ages of fourteen and sixteen, even if they had no history of escapes or convictions, were sent "without exception" to NKVD labor colonies.[150] Finally, all homeless children between sixteen and eighteen were treated juridically as adults and sent to regular NKVD labor camps rather then labor colonies, despite vigorous protest from Vyshinsky.[151]

These decisions put the NKVD in control of a substantial population of juvenile offenders. Yagoda estimated in June 1935 that the May edicts would result in a total population of 85,000 children in NKVD institutions, including 260 detention centers with 23,000 children transferred from the Commissariat of Education, 22,000 children in the NKVD's existing communes and colonies, and some 10,000 children currently held in prisons and labor camps who were awaiting transfer to juvenile labor colonies once space could be found for them.[152] The Politburo left in the hands of the Commissariat of Education the orphanages for "normal" children under the age of fourteen, and the orphanages for those deemed "difficult to reeducate" but who had no previous convictions or escapes, but virtually all other aspects of juvenile affairs, including the initial process of assigning children to colonies, camps, or orphanages, were in the hands of the local police after May 1935.[153]

Although the April and May instructions concentrated on juveniles younger than sixteen, in practice they had as much impact on police and judicial responses to children between the ages of sixteen and eighteen. According to an explanatory circular issued by the Politburo in mid-April, Stalin's April 7 edict, in eliminating preferential sentencing for juveniles, effectively abolished those sections of the USSR and republican Criminal Codes that prohibited the death penalty for children under the age of eighteen. Death sentences were henceforth allowable for juveniles between the ages of twelve and sixteen for crimes listed in the April 7 edict, and for individuals sixteen and older for all capital crimes. This change had little effect on executions of children under the age of sixteen, because none of the crimes listed in Stalin's edict carried the death penalty, with the exception of the 1932 law on the theft of public property, which had fallen out of use by 1935.[154] Children over sixteen years of age, however, were henceforth subject to the same range of punishments as adults for all crimes. Consequently, when local Procuracy officials in November 1934 requested guidance regarding the sentencing of juveniles between the ages of sixteen and eighteen with counterrevolutionary crimes and crimes against the state, Vyshinsky insisted that no reductions in sentencing based on age be allowed and that the death penalty, if warranted, must follow.[155] Extrajudicial procedures followed suit. Although those memoir sources that claim that the Stalinist regime responded to the problems of child homelessness in the mid-1930s by shooting children en masse are completely false, the May 1935 instructions did subject juveniles above the age of sixteen to the same extrajudicial punishments as adults.[156] In practice, children older than sixteen were subject after May 1935 to all forms of extrajudicial repression, including execution at the hands of the notorious NKVD troikas in 1937 and 1938.

The Politburo's instructions in April and May provided local police administrations with expansive powers to sweep children from the streets and to return them to their parents, send them to court, or transfer them to detention centers. Yagoda encouraged aggressive action in a series of circulars to the local police in June and July 1935, calling for a "complete liquidation" of homelessness and ordering officers to concentrate on begging, speculation, and a range of lesser "hooliganistic" offenses against public order such as fighting, harassing citizens, hitching rides on trams or cars, and playing on train and tram tracks.[157] The local police carried out these campaigns on their own, without the aid of welfare organizations, Assistance Brigades, or local soviets; they generally detained as many children as they could, even for violations not listed in the edict, issuing fines or warnings in cases where parents could be found and sending cases regarding children older than sixteen directly to the NKVD Special Board for extra-judicial sentencing.[158] After the officers finished processing cases, they sent all youths between the ages of three and sixteen whose parents could not be located to detention centers; the cases of those who committed crimes listed in the April 7 edict were immediately transferred to the court system.[159]

The police officials in detention centers, after years of reluctantly sending delinquent and "difficult" homeless children to orphanages, took every opportunity to make sure that the children who passed through their hands in 1935 would go to an institution run by the NKVD. The police falsified the ages of children they apprehended in order to send homeless children younger than fourteen to labor colonies, children under twelve to courts as adults, or children younger than sixteen to hard-regime labor camps. They exaggerated information on past infractions in order to ensure harsher penalties for recidivism, and they ignored information given by children about their parents, especially parents living outside the city where a child was detained.[160] The police often sent homeless children above the age of fourteen, and "recidivists" above twelve, to labor colonies directly from *militsiia* stations, because their instructions made it clear that such children would end up there anyway; the hearing in the detention center, in these cases, was often treated as a mere formality.

Cases that were transferred to the court system fared little better. The justice officials who were supposed to supervise these cases were generally unable to cope with the demands of the campaign, whereas investigations were almost always carried out by the police themselves.[161] Local procurators, who were required by law to provide preliminary approval for all arrests and indictments, were often bypassed completely; in July 1935, Yagoda specifically ordered policemen to obtain preliminary approval for arrests from local police chiefs rather than from the Procuracy, as was required by law.[162] Court cases were often heard with the utmost speed and a complete lack of proper procedure, especially early in the campaign, when most were completed in a single day in a so-called duty chamber (*dezhurnaia kamera*), an ad hoc courtroom set up to process petty criminal cases; such cases were often heard by a single judge and were based solely on information provided by the *militsiia*. As a result, court cases against children younger than twelve were common in 1935, as were cases for crimes not listed in the April 7 edict.[163] Both published and internal discussions of the campaign are rife with such complaints; the Politburo's decision to abolish the juvenile affairs commissions, and the fact that justice organizations were already overburdened with campaigns against hooliganism, robbery, and speculation, made it nearly impossible for local justice officials to meet the high standards demanded by central justice officials.

The overall number of juveniles detained during these campaigns is difficult to determine, but the available data make it clear that more children were incarcerated in the second half of the 1930s using extrajudicial means than through court cases initiated under the April 1935 edict. Courts in the USSR sentenced roughly 58,000 juveniles in 1935, and between 43,000 and 54,000 a year for the following three years. More children between the ages of sixteen and eighteen years of age were sentenced in the first half of 1935 (i.e., before the April and May instructions took full effect) than in any of the following six-month periods, largely due to campaigns against hooliganism and speculation; but the proportion of children under sixteen climbed to 18 percent in the second half of 1935 and to more than 40 percent by 1938.[164] Despite the clear requirements of Stalin's April edict, judges continued to hand out lenient sentences to children younger than sixteen in 1935, most of whom were guilty of nothing more serious than petty theft.[165]

The police, on the contrary, applied these instructions vigorously, especially regarding children between sixteen and eighteen. According to summaries created by labor camp officials, at least 155,000 juveniles spent time in labor colonies from 1935 to 1940, only 68,927 (44 percent) of whom had been convicted of a crime in a judicial proceeding; these figures would not include children over sixteen, who were often sent to labor camps with adults.[166] A more comprehensive report on homelessness and delinquency in the post–May 1935 period, compiled by the NKVD Department of Labor Colonies in November of 1937, counted 319,801 juveniles passing through NKVD detention centers between May 1935 and August 1937. Some 37,600 of these children were transferred directly to NKVD labor colonies, while 2,119 were listed as transferred to "prison."[167]

Yagoda, in reporting on the work of the *militsiia* in the USSR for 1935 and early 1936, provided similar figures for 1935, stating that the *militsiia* had removed from the streets in the final eight months of 1935 a total of just under 160,000 children; just under 76,000 were homeless, roughly 80,600 were unsupervised, and just under 3,200 were simply lost. Of these, roughly 74,100 were returned to their parents, 14,700 were sent to orphanages, and 61,900 were forwarded to the NKVD system of detention centers; only 10,000 were "arrested and sent to court."[168] Although the judicial portion of the 1935 campaigns received the most coverage in newspapers and legal journals in the mid-1930s, the broad range of police actions, as with campaigns against hooliganism and speculation, dwarfed it in size.

The 1935 campaigns produced immediate reductions in homeless populations in major Soviet cities, prompting numerous commentators to agree in 1936 and early 1937 that juvenile homelessness in the USSR had effectively been eliminated.[169] Yagoda argued as well that the April and May 1935 edicts had resulted in substantial reduction in theft, hooliganism, and unarmed robbery among children.[170] "Unsupervised" delinquents, however, remained a major problem and, according to the police and justice officials, continued to threaten public order in the largest Soviet cities in 1936. Of the almost 33,000 children apprehended by the Moscow police in the first half of 1936, for example, only 2,942 were homeless; more than a third were detained for petty hooliganism, a crime that could not be prosecuted in court under the 1935 edict but that evidently constituted grounds for detention anyway. Roughly half of these children were simply released by the Moscow police to their parents, but almost a fifth saw their parents fined by the *militsiia* without the benefit of any legal proceedings, and almost a tenth were sent to the Danilov detention center, predominantly for thievery or begging.[171]

The trend was similar across the USSR; even in early 1936, the police continued to remove 7,000 to 8,000 children from the streets of urban areas every month, and the number of children sent to detention centers across the USSR climbed steadily in 1936 and into 1937.[172] Homeless children, like armed robbers and hooligans, could be controlled by overtly repressive campaigns that swept them off the streets, but juvenile delinquency, like speculation and petty hooliganism, was far more resistant to such tactics and would continue to pose problems for the Soviet police through the end of the decade.

Police actions against delinquency and homelessness in 1935 exhibited all the essential aspects of the concurrent campaigns against violent crime, hooliganism, and speculation. Central Communist Party authorities, unwilling to accept long-standing problems of public order in the context of the "victory" of socialism, turned responsibility for these problems over to the police almost entirely, disrupting ongoing attempts by welfare and education agencies to ameliorate them through more gradual means. The 1935 campaigns against juvenile delinquency and homelessness were not simply a product of Stalin's desire for more drastic solutions to problems of public order. The local police had already taken control, from welfare and educational agencies, of most of the responsibility for sweeping children off city streets by mid-decade; the 1935 campaigns only completed this process. Central and local police officials brought to the realm of juvenile affairs the same conceptual focus on recidivists and "dangerous elements" that animated their approaches to all urban crime.

This approach produced an entirely successful campaign against homelessness, given the demands of the Politburo; but it proved far less effective in explaining and controlling juvenile delinquency after 1935. Yagoda's assertions that a "corrupted" core group of recidivist juveniles was the key cause of both homelessness and widespread delinquency did not correspond to the reality of the situation, as many of the participants in Kalinin's commission understood. Such an assertion was, in any case, more and more difficult to support in 1936 and early 1937, as it became clear to top party officials that "unsupervised" children, often schoolchildren whose parents were members of the working classes, were the source of most crime among urban youth. The failure of the 1935 campaign to control these more widespread forms of petty urban disorder was puzzling to central party and regime officials alike. These failures reinforced the regime's tendency to turn to an absolute quarantine of important urban areas from all "marginal" population contingents in 1936 and 1937.

Conclusion

The campaigns against robbery, hooliganism, speculation, and juvenile delinquency between 1934 and 1936 were interrelated parts of an attempt by the Stalinist regime to repress all forms of urban crime in the period after the Congress of Victors. Stalin's announcement in early 1934 that socialism had been "victorious" signaled the beginning of several months of genuine debate within the highest levels of the Communist Party regarding the proper relationship between law, order, and repression in Soviet society; but it also forced local police administrations to confront the continued existence of widespread criminal activity, especially in major cities, where exceptionally repressive policies in 1932 and 1933, in the minds of top party members, should have removed the "objective" causes of crime altogether. Politicized explanations of urban crime came naturally to top police and party officials; criminologists had long argued that crimes like hooliganism and banditry were the product of remnants of a petit bourgeois ideology among the peasantry, while top regime officials, especially Stalin and Yagoda, by 1935 understood urban violence and economic malfeasance of all sorts as overt threats to the Soviet system, and hence as essentially political behaviors.

Yet such claims mattered little at the periphery, where officers found that the concept of threatening population "contingents" was the key to making the center's policy demands intelligible in particularly local contexts. This stress on cohort, rather than class, harmonized with the rhetoric of the "victory" of socialism, which claimed that the transformation of Soviet society was essentially complete. No longer a matter of "class-alien elements" (i.e., kulaks or former bourgeois), the crimes of speculation, hooliganism, and juvenile delinquency became the work of "career speculators," "hooliganistic elements," and "socially harmful juveniles" who demanded repression not "as a class" but as a sociological category nonetheless.

This vocabulary of "contingents" and "elements" was particularly powerful at the local level because it corresponded perfectly to the policing tactics that had emerged, under the tutelage of the OGPU, to control social disorder in urban areas in the early 1930s. Yagoda had pursued the expansion of these forms of policing—especially the internal passport system and related mass sweeps of cities of "harmful" and "dangerous elements"—for the previous several years, but his vision of urban policing had lost ground, if only temporarily, during the restructuring of the political police system in 1934. The campaigns in 1935 against hooliganism, speculation, and delinquency therefore represented a victory for the kind of Stalinist policing system that had been promoted by Yagoda and the OGPU since its takeover of the *militsiia* in 1930. These campaigns reinforced the ability of the police to act on their own against criminal "contingents," and they ensured that, in the future, the center would see massive campaigns against these entire population cohorts as a viable response to pressing problems of public order and national security.

5

The Stalinist Police

The precinct inspector should proceed from the idea that every person without a passport, every nonregistered person is already a suspicious individual, he has either committed a crime, or escaped from prison or a camp and is covering his tracks, or he is a person who is preparing to commit a crime.
  —Printed instructions to urban precinct inspectors, 1936[1]

As a rule, in those places where [the police] do not fight against socially harmful elements and do not send them to camps using troikas, but limit themselves to various registration procedures and other driveling half-measures, robbery and theft increase constantly. . . . [I order you to] halt the absurd practice of allowing a registered thief, who is arrested for a concrete crime, to get off with compulsory labor [a judicial sentence of reduced salary at one's current place of employment], while at the same the very same thief, detained in the process of removal of S[ocially] H[armful] E[lement]s (according to Order 00192) without evidence of any concrete crime, is locked up in a labor camp. Thieves and recidivists who are caught committing concrete crimes are to be sentenced by troikas [and sent to labor camps].
  —Yagoda to republican and regional NKVD chiefs, March 17, 1936[2]

Although police campaigns against hooliganism, robbery, and juvenile delinquency in 1935 were largely a success from the point of view of the Politburo, they wrought havoc on nearly all other aspects of the Soviet criminal justice system. A policing system based on purges of criminal elements could control certain acute forms of disorder, such as armed robbery, banditry, or juvenile homelessness, but it was incapable of controlling the low-level disorder that was inherent in the everyday functioning of the Stalinist system, such as juvenile delinquency, petty hooliganism, and especially speculation in consumer goods. Major campaigns in 1935 notwithstanding, these expressions of disorder continued into 1936 and early 1937, much to the bewilderment of top police and Communist Party officials.

The response of the Stalinist regime to this situation was to demand a virtual quarantine of urban areas from "threatening" population cohorts of all types, enforced by unrestricted administrative sentencing and by rigorous implementation of the internal passport system. Urban police forces engaged in unrelenting purges of "socially harmful elements" (often identified as "socio-harmfuls" (*sotsvredniki*, or simply the acronym "SVE") between 1935 and early 1937, which struck hundreds of thousands of Soviet citizens and which aimed at removing the "criminal contingent" from Soviet society altogether. These urban purges were the broadest application of extrajudicial repression in the USSR since the end of the dekulakization campaign, sending several hundred thousand individuals to the Gulag. They also marginalized ever broader swaths of the Soviet population as potentially "harmful" individuals, especially outside the most important Soviet cities, where the existence of cohorts of ex-convicts and suspect criminals was officially tolerated but hardly welcome by the local police. As a result, top Communist Party and police officials agreed in 1936 and early 1937 that the level of danger posed to Soviet society by the "criminal contingent" was actually rising, despite the virtually unlimited authority vested in the local police to repress this cohort of petty offenders, ex-convicts, and passport violators. Several attempts by prescient party and justice officials to halt this trend in 1936 failed completely, faltering on the structural realities of the Stalinist policing system as well as the growing political strength of the NKVD.

Policing and Social Control at Mid-Decade

The ability of Soviet police to carry out massive purges of urban areas between 1935 and 1937 hinged on substantial improvements in the basic bureaucratic functioning of the police system after the end of the dekulakization drive. Many of these enhancements were direct results of the creation of the USSR NKVD in mid-1934, which entailed a series of bureaucratic changes that were intended to complete the process, begun in 1930 with the takeover of the *militsiia* by the OGPU, of making the *militsiia* into a "Chekist" institution without entirely obliterating the difference between regular and political policing. This overall trend was nonetheless complicated by countervailing tendencies within the Soviet police system, especially the continued inability of local *militsiia* administrations to create any sort of functioning covert policing systems that could carry out the surveillance of the population alongside the political police.

The reforms of Soviet policing in 1934, including the creation of the USSR NKVD, elevated the position of the *militsiia* within the overall structure of the Soviet policing system. Within the USSR NKVD bureaucracy, a new Central Militsiia Administration directed police activity nationwide, making the *militsiia* nominally equal to the new Central Administration of State Security (GUGB) rather than subordinate to the political police as it had been since 1930.[3] The Politburo retained L. N. Belskii, who had been in charge of the OGPU's Central Militsiia Administration since January 1934, to head the NKVD's Militsiia Administration, suggesting that upsetting existing hierarchies was not Stalin's primary goal.[4] Yet the formal bureaucratic parity of the *militsiia* and the political police within the USSR NKVD enhanced Belskii's ability to maneuver for the benefit of the *militsiia*; he successfully lobbied Communist Party and NKVD officials for improvements in living and working conditions for the *militsiia* in 1934, such as pay increases for the officer corps and for midlevel policemen working in major cities.[5]

New regulations tightened disciplinary requirements for *militsiia* officers. In late 1934, Yagoda created a centralized system of inspectorates to handle all disciplinary infractions within the *militsiia* force; and in March 1935, he placed the entire officer corps under the same service regulations that covered the political police officers, making it nearly impossible for an officer to quit without the approval of his superiors.[6] He supported these changes with strong demands to regional and local NKVD chiefs to improve the qualifications, training, and "Chekist spirit" of the officers under their control.[7] At the central level, these changes were relatively successful; the *militsiia* officer corps was generally viewed as an integral part of the NKVD leadership, and the organization as a whole gained much more stature within the NKVD system than it had enjoyed under the OGPU.[8]

These policy changes encountered substantial resistance at the local level. Regional and local NKVD administrations, still headed after 1934 by the same cadre of career OGPU officers who oversaw the absorption of the *militsiia* by the political police after 1930, generally rejected Yagoda's demands that they treat civil policemen as equals, often with good reason.[9] Repeated purges of the ranks of the *militsiia* in the early 1930s notwithstanding, bribery and corruption remained widespread among local police in the mid-1930s, and certain aspects of local practice remained little better than they had been during the New Economic Policy era. Investigations of local *militsiia* stations, for example, found that they were often staffed by officers who had no training, responded to the public with overt rudeness, and instilled little respect for the police in those law-abiding Soviet citizens who appealed to them for help.[10] The illegal or negligent use of weapons by off-duty officers was so widespread that, in late December 1934, the NKVD forbade all *militsiia* officers below the senior officer rank to carry weapons while not at work.[11] Experienced political police officers simply refused to see such ill-trained, unqualified policemen as members of the "Chekist" system of state security.

Despite such problems, Yagoda's overall drive to improve the qualifications of the civil police produced significant results by the mid-1930s. The number of police continued to climb in this period; by 1935, roughly 125,600 full-time policemen served in the USSR, not including the Industrial Militsiia, an increase of more than 30,000 from just three years before (see table 1.1 in chapter 1). The end of passport distribution allowed central police authorities to redistribute some 10,000 passport officers to patrol duties on the streets in 1934 and 1935, increasing the number of precinct inspectors stationed in major cities and allowing most inspectors, for the first time, to patrol their entire administrative areas every day.[12] Urban policing saw the greatest improvements; an internal investigation of the Moscow *militsiia* in mid-1935, for example, depicted a relatively professional and disciplined force, especially within the officer corps and the Detective Department, which responded proficiently to ongoing campaigns against armed robbery and hooliganism.[13]

The greatest single improvement in police work in the mid-1930s came with a drastic scaling down of the troublesome Industrial Militsiia system after 1934. Yagoda viewed the Industrial Militsiia as the most inefficient and uncontrollable aspect of Soviet policing. Using budgetary issues as a wedge, he maneuvered during the creation of the USSR NKVD to rid his institution of almost all responsibility for controlling disorder and theft in factories and other economic concerns.[14] He managed to cut the Industrial Militsiia from almost 65,000 to just over 28,000 officers between 1934 and 1935; the number of police guarding institutions of the Commissariat of Heavy Industry fell even more steeply, from more than 31,300 officers in 1934 to just over 11,500 in 1935.[15] The NKVD continued to allow local police administrations to conclude individual contracts with local institutions, but beginning in 1935 all planning for these agreements was controlled by the center, even though Yagoda insisted that the central budgets would pay for none of the officers or provisions required to support such contracts.[16] By 1936, the Industrial Militsiia system had shrunk to only 22,481 officers. Although local police administrations remained concerned with theft, embezzlement, and other economic crimes in factories and on collective farms alike, Yagoda had succeeded in shifting the bulk of the responsibility for guarding economic institutions to the economic administrations themselves.[17]

Urban police forces received the most support from the center in the mid-1930s, and it was in major Soviet cities that Yagoda's plans for improving the *militsiia* produced the greatest results. By mid-decade, the precinct inspectors usually patrolled their areas twice a day, at least in the largest Soviet cities, and they were qualified enough, and stable enough, to cultivate the kinds of ongoing contacts with local residents that was the hallmark of the OGPU's plans for reforming the *militsiia* early in the decade.[18] The precinct inspectors continued to carry out numerous administrative duties—including oversight of trade, urban sanitation, and traffic control—but their primary task was to maintain public order, receiving complaints from city residents and resolving conflicts, if possible, without involving the judicial authorities.[19] Many such complaints concerned unsanitary living conditions and other petty issues of urban life, as the local police assumed a greater part of the duties previously handled by welfare and municipal administrations, but the precinct inspectors were also fully involved in the surveillance of "criminal elements" and the control of petty crime.

One inspector, working in Moscow's Thirtieth Precinct, described this balance of educative and punitive functions in some detail to a meeting of his district soviet in 1936. The officer patrolled an area in the heart of Moscow, covering some 3,900 individuals and centered on the famous Patriarch's Ponds neighborhood. Complaints from residents, he noted, were mostly genuine, like the complaint he received in early 1936 regarding one resident, Sk., who was unemployed, drank heavily, and fought with his neighbors. Sk. had a wife and three children, but he also had four past convictions for hooliganism and petty theft—more than enough to qualify as a "dangerous element" and subject him to administrative sentencing. The inspector described this difficult case:

> I figured that he had three children and a wife, and I decided that he needed to be helped. I tried to find him work, but the guy didn't want to work. I approached him in the spirit of comradely relations, but he even tried to get into a fight with me once. We, of course, sent him to court [after that]. Such people do exist in my area—seven people who simply have not responded to education

The Stalinist Police

(*vospitanie*). [My] area . . . is a very old area, a handicraft area, where the majority of the population are old handicraft workers, traders, old moneyed people, people who still have old habits—drinking and hooliganism.[20]

This inspector, like most policemen at mid-decade, attempted to balance the need for social stability and a certain amount moderation of approach with the policy dictates of the center. Yet systems of police surveillance and judicial, or extrajudicial, repression were never far from the surface of police activity in major urban areas.

Even with such improvements, urban policing at mid-decade continued to rely almost exclusively on overt systems of population surveillance and control rather than the covert systems promoted by the police leadership throughout the early 1930s. Yagoda identified the covert work of the detective departments as the single weakest aspect of policing in urban areas in early 1935, charging that detectives were completely incapable of using informants, including those within the criminal milieu itself, to identify and remove potential criminals.[21] His complaints were well founded. A mid-1935 investigation of the Moscow *militsiia* showed that detectives carried out little direct work with undercover operatives; only 15 percent maintained any direct contacts with informants, the rest relying on information gathered by paid "residents," which was both scarce and unreliable. In the first half of 1935, only 7 percent of the cases investigated by the Moscow Detective Department were based on information gained from informants; for the entire Moscow *militsiia*, the figure was a paltry 0.7 percent.[22]

Yagoda began to respond to the realities of this situation as early as mid-1935, reversing several years of consistent policy and suggesting that local police chiefs deemphasize covert policing and informant networks, especially outside the most important detective department administrations. Local officers, he told a meeting of regional *militsiia* chiefs in April, 1935, "don't need massive lists and files on hundreds of thousands of new names;" instead, "every officer and precinct inspector needs to report on what he sees and hears," relying only on trusted municipal employees for information about hooligans, thieves, and individuals without passports.[23] After 1935, the central authorities continued to demand that detective departments use informants as a method of investigation, but they gave up almost entirely on the idea that precinct inspectors, and the rest of the urban police force, would make use of informants as part of any sort of preventive policing system.

There was good reason for Yagoda's shift of emphasis. As we have seen, the local police, including both regular officers and precinct inspectors,

proved during the campaigns against hooliganism, delinquency, and speculation in 1934 and 1935 that they were far more capable of controlling
urban crime and disorder using overt means, especially the passport system, than using undercover surveillance networks. Yagoda, after Stalin
removed him from the NKVD in 1936, would be blamed for these failures
in covert policing, but the trend was hardly his fault. Rather, it was the
product of several years of expansion of police systems designed to control population cohorts overtly rather than to restrain individuals and prevent specific criminal behaviors.

The Passport System and Mass Repression of "Socially Harmful Elements" at Mid-Decade

The relatively successful campaigns against urban crime in late 1934 and
1935 brought urban purges and extrajudicial repression to the heart of
policing activity in major Soviet cities. Central police officials encouraged
local administrations to cleanse urban areas of all "criminal elements,"
making use of the internal passport system in order to repress suspect
population cohorts on an ongoing, rather than sporadic, basis. Local police were more than willing to comply, because the passport system provided them with substantial freedom to deal with local issues on their own
authority, without deference to the court or welfare systems. By the end of
1936, the urban police saw the passport system as the single most important technique available to them, and they understood their basic task as
enforcing a strict social quarantine against all "dangerous," "harmful," or
otherwise threatening population cohorts through whatever judicial, extrajudicial, or simply administrative means available to them.

Yagoda took several steps in 1935 to expand the ability of the passport
system to protect regime areas from ex-convicts and other suspect population cohorts. In mid-1935, he ordered the police to expel from regime
areas all individuals released from labor camps or colonies, no matter
what their crime, a move that flatly contradicted existing passports regulations but was made possible by the standard police practice of marking all
past convictions in passport documents themselves. Later in the year, he
ordered police administrations to issue passports to all ex-convicts immediately upon their release from imprisonment and to include notations regarding their past sentences, rather than waiting for them to move to an urban
location and request a passport there, in order to reduce the possibility that

bureaucratic mistakes might result in a "clean" passport being issued to an ex-convict in a regime locale.[24]

The Kirov murder played a role in this process as well, because the NKVD followed the expulsion of politically suspect individuals from Leningrad in 1935 with a general tightening of residence restrictions in all regime cities.[25] The purging of cities in 1935 was also aided by a nationwide exchange of passports handed out in 1933, which began in mid-July; in the process of providing all current passport holders with new documents, local police were instructed to uncover and expel from regime cities any "socially alien and criminal elements" who managed to hide from the authorities during the initial distribution.[26] By the end of 1935, central NKVD officials expected the police in all regime locations to prevent the migration of any suspect individuals to their areas, using systems of residence registration and card catalogs developed earlier in the decade to ensure that in-migrants were not ex-convicts or members of other unwanted population cohorts.[27]

For most local police administrations, these activities only diverted scarce resources and labor power from the more pressing tasks at hand. The most appealing aspect of the passport system, for the local police, remained the ability it gave them to eject petty criminals from their jurisdictions and to sentence repeat offenders, or more serious criminals, to labor camps on their own authority, using the passport troikas. The passport troikas were a supposedly temporary aspect of passport distribution in 1933, but top police officials, including Yagoda, campaigned vigorously throughout 1934 and early 1935 to retain them, arguing that judicial punishments of passport violators were wholly inadequate and that only extrajudicial sentencing at the local level could cope with the volume of cases created by the system.[28] Stalin and the Politburo concurred; despite the limitations on extrajudicial sentencing associated with the creation of the USSR NKVD, the police in several regime cities sentenced passport offenders to up to three years in labor camps, using passport troikas, without pause in 1934 and 1935.[29]

The police in regime locales also used the basic functioning of the passport system as a means of punishment, illegally seizing passports from individuals and ejecting them from regime areas for petty crimes that would not provoke comparable judicial or extrajudicial sanctions. The center strengthened this tendency in early 1935 by authorizing the local police to refuse passports to individuals who, although they had no past sentences, had been taken into custody previously and who maintained

connections with "criminal individuals."[30] In practice, the police confiscated passports liberally from individuals suspected of hooliganism or
theft by referring to these supposed "connections" with criminals: the
Leningrad police confiscated some 25,000 passports from such individuals in 1935; the Moscow police, 15,000.[31] Such conceptual connections
between passport violators and "dangerous" population cohorts were easy
for the local police to make, allowing them to use the passport system to
repress individuals who were merely suspected of being part of the criminal milieu.

These practices, in conjunction with campaigns against urban crime,
produced notable increases in the number of individuals sentenced using
the passport system in 1935. Yagoda, reporting on police activities for the
year, noted that the police had sanctioned 1,370,000 violators (515,000 in
regime areas and 855,000 in nonregime areas), of whom 944,00 were
fined and 90,000 were sent to court; all were subject to ejection from the
cities in question.[32] Even though the police had sent large numbers of
cases to the court system, they continued to complain that the courts were
handing out lenient sentences to passport violators and hence placed little
emphasis on the investigation of such cases. In fact, the most serious sanctions handed down for passport violations in 1935 were meted out by the
police themselves. The procurator of the Russian Republic, Vladimir
Antonov-Ovseenko, made this claim explicitly in September 1935, reporting by way of example that the Moscow passport troika handed out 10,199
sentences in the first five months of 1935, compared with only 340 cases
tried by the court system; most sentences handed out by the passport troikas were for terms in labor camps or for permanent banishment from regime areas.[33] The passport system, by the end of 1935, relied almost
exclusively on extrajudicial punishments, including prison and labor camp
sentences, fines, and administrative expulsions from regime cities.

Purges of regime areas, as we have seen, were not the only goal of the
passport system as conceived by the center. The registration and surveillance (*nadzor*) of suspect populations in nonregime areas, where all Soviet
citizens were authorized to live, were equally important.[34] The increasingly obvious failure of local *militsiia* administrations to create covert
surveillance systems in the mid-1930s left the passport system as the primary means for the surveillance of suspect populations in chaotic nonregime locales. The process of counting and surveying suspect cohorts in
these areas began with the implementation of the passport system; by
August 1934, central passport officials reported that passport distribution

had "uncovered" nearly 425,000 ex-convicts and "socially alien elements" in nonregime locations, more than 275,000 of whom were employed. Such individuals were placed under "open surveillance" by the police and were allowed to live and work normally, but they were recorded as "suspect elements" in card catalogs by local passport officials.[35] Central police officials, for their part, were concerned that these individuals could slip through the porous barriers between nonregime and regime areas and commit crimes in important Soviet cities; but by 1935, they believed that this cohort was the primary cause of crime and disorder in nonregime cities as well.

Like so many other policing systems in the mid-1930s, the system of "open surveillance" was far less effective in practice than in theory. Putting an individual "under surveillance" (*na uchet*) entailed little more than recording relevant biographical details in the card catalog maintained by a given city police administration.[36] Local precinct inspectors maintained lists, usually incomplete, of all individuals under surveillance in their areas, but most found it impossible to coordinate their records with citywide passport catalogs, much less the nationwide compilations of suspect individuals distributed by NKVD officials in Moscow.[37] Regional police administrations were unable to coordinate these registration systems across jurisdictional boundaries; one central police official complained repeatedly in 1935 and 1936 that registration systems were incapable of following the movements of individuals within the same city, much less across the USSR.[38] The passport system, then, increased the overall ability of the NKVD to measure suspect population cohorts, but by mid-decade it had failed to improve the ability of the local police to track and control them in the manner desired by the center.

The expanding use of extrajudicial sanctions by local police administrations in 1935, especially the use of passport troikas by local NKVD administrations to incarcerate "criminal elements," prompted the USSR Procuracy to challenge the sentencing practices of the NKVD once again, in March 1935.[39] Ivan Akulov brought his complaint directly to the Politburo, arguing that the NKVD was, in practice, gradually reversing the 1934 decisions regarding the restrictions on extrajudicial sentencing that the Politburo had put in place with the formation of the NKVD. Akulov complained that the NKVD Special Board, and the various troikas that functioned under its jurisdiction, heard mostly criminal cases, such as swindling, escapes from prisons, and speculation, all of which presented no particular difficulty during court hearings. The Special Board, he argued,

should be restricted to cases for which evidence had been gathered by covert means and was hence classified, or in which the accused was clearly
"socially dangerous" according to the statute.[40]

The Politburo not only was not swayed by Akulov's argument; it resolved to do the exact opposite, creating standing NKVD troikas in May
1935 within all regional-level NKVD administrations in order to sanction
criminal offenders of all types. These "police" (*militseiskie*) troikas, as
they were termed, were authorized to sentence repeat passport offenders
and individuals who returned to areas where they had been refused passports, as well as all "socially harmful elements" (specifically "harmful"
rather than "dangerous," showing that the earlier distinction between the
two had disappeared in practice by this point). "Harmful elements" were
defined as individuals having previous detainments and ongoing contact
with the criminal milieu; unemployed individuals with ties to the criminal
milieu, even in the absence of previous detainments; and professional beggars.[41] In practice, these instructions permitted the local police to sanction
virtually all individuals deemed criminal, dangerous, or harmful by nature, including passport offenders, to up to five-year sentences in labor
camps, exile, or banishment. Like the previous NKVD troikas, the police
troikas functioned under the authority of the Special Board, and all their
decisions were nominally approved by the board itself. Yet this change
represented a substantial expansion of the local police's ability to sentence
criminal offenders, and it signaled a resolute end to Stalin's moves, begun
in mid-1934, to restrict the extrajudicial sentencing power of the NKVD.
Once in place, the existence of the police troikas was largely taken for
granted by top justice, Communist Party, and police officials.[42] The police
troikas functioned continuously, alongside more notorious forms of extrajudicial sentencing like the Special Board and the later "special" NKVD
troikas, from mid-1935 to the end of 1938.

The expulsion of suspect and ex-convict elements from regime cities
during passport distribution placed tremendous stress on police administrations in nonregime locations, especially those located close to regime
areas. Most local police administrations in nonregime areas were unprepared for the influx of "undesirable elements" arriving from regime cities,
especially in the context of ongoing campaigns against hooliganism, juvenile delinquency, and violent crimes, which sapped the already-thin investigative and patrolling strength of local police forces. Not surprisingly,
police officials in nonregime localities often balked at the idea of accepting
expellees from regime cities, and they often flatly refused to issue passports

to them, even though they were required to do so by the passport regulations. The contradiction in the passport regulations was clear to local officials; central instructions drew direct connections between public order and purges of urban areas, yet the police in nonregime locales were denied the right to expel the "criminal element" and were instead forced to control it with troublesome, and inefficient, surveillance and registration systems.

As a result, local police administrations clamored in 1935 and 1936 for inclusion in the list of regime areas. Central NKVD officials were generally willing to approve their requests, although they did deny petitions that might upset the balance between urban and rural policing in a given region or present enforcement difficulties.[43] The overall trend, nonetheless, was clear. By October 1935, the list of regime cities had expanded to 120 locations, plus border zones, and by April 1938 some 517 cities and individual districts (*raiony*) fell under regime restrictions throughout the USSR.[44] This expansion of the regime system caused constant movement of individuals with criminal pasts from regime to nonregime locations in the mid-1930s, because any individual under "open surveillance" who refused to leave cities as they gained regime status faced sentences to labor camps through a police troika. As the regime system expanded to cover more and more urban areas, an ever larger group of individuals was marginalized and ejected not only from their home cities but, in effect, from Soviet society altogether.

Understandings of crime among top police and Communist Party officials now matched local policing practice more closely than at any other time in the early Stalin period. The local police were authorized to sentence all urban recidivists, passport violators, beggars, prostitutes, and other marginalized individuals using extrajudicial means. They viewed the existence of these categories of criminals as the root cause of crime in their areas and strove to remove them as efficiently as possible. After mid-1935, internal police and Procuracy documents generally referred to "harmful" rather than "dangerous" elements, often using the shortened "socio-harmfuls" (*sotsvredniki*) or the acronym "SVE." The term was no longer a strict juridical definition of repeat petty offenders, as it had been in the 1920s, nor was it a general description of urbanites living on the margins of society, such as the homeless or prostitutes. In the minds of local police officers, it signified a concrete cohort of urban criminals who disrupted normal social life and hence demanded complete removal from Soviet urban space.

Once the police troikas were in place, the police engaged in mass sweeps of SVEs in regime locations, which included virtually every urban area of any size in the USSR. Central police reports referred to these actions as "campaigns of removal of harmful elements" or "purges of cities of declassed and criminal elements," suggesting that central officials conceptualized them as a permanent extension of campaigns against urban crimes and "dangerous elements" in 1934 and 1935.[45] Between the creation of the police troikas in May 1935 and the beginning of November, the police removed 266,000 "socio-harmfuls" from major urban areas across the USSR, almost 65,000 from Moscow and Leningrad alone.[46] An NKVD source suggests that the police troikas sentenced 119,000 individuals as "harmful elements" in 1935, 141,000 in 1936.[47] The total number of individuals swept off the streets across the USSR during these campaigns in 1935 and 1936, then, was likely in the range of 600,000 to 800,000.[48]

These extrajudicial sentences represent a substantial portion of the sentences to prison and labor camps meted out by the Stalinist regime in the mid-1930s. Although the courts sentenced far more individuals in this period, reaching nearly 923,000 in 1935 in the Russian Republic alone, they also handed out far more lenient sentences than did the police troikas. The courts, furthermore, generally preferred short-term sentences for non-political offenses, usually between one and two and a half years, whereas most sentences meted out by the police troikas were for terms in labor camps, usually three to five years.[49] In addition, Procuracy officials complained that the police troikas consistently sentenced "harmful elements" to ten-year sentences, in complete violation of central instructions.[50] "Harmful elements" were the only category of offenders whose relative and absolute weights increased in the NKVD labor camps between 1934 and 1936, when they equaled the number of individuals in camps for counterrevolutionary crimes.[51] Police actions against socially harmful elements represented the most repressive aspect of Soviet criminal justice in the mid-1930s, overshadowing the activities of justice agencies and even of the political police regarding strictly political offenders.

By the end of 1936, the police in major urban areas had fully internalized the assumptions of the political police leadership regarding the role of "socially harmful elements" in urban crime. They also accepted central demands to use the internal passport system to control this cohort of urban marginals and criminals, even if the specific tactics they used did not always meet the approval of top police officials. One-time "campaigns" against specific categories of crime gave way to continuous purges of urban areas of "socio-harmfuls," who were defined not by their actions or their socioeconomic class but by their criminological biographies. These approaches to population "contingents" and extrajudicial sanctions formed the crux of a truly Stalinist policing system. Little that occurred in Soviet policing and mass repression in the following years strayed far from these assumptions about the nature of public order and state coercion in the USSR.

Political Conflict and the Stalinist Police, 1935–1936

Top justice officials did not acquiesce to the increasing importance of extrajudicial sanctions in the Soviet criminal justice system without a fight. The expanding extrajudicial repressions in 1935 and 1936 prompted strenuous debate between the police and justice officials, some of which were as fundamental as the conflicts that surrounded the creation of the USSR NKVD in 1934. Personal conflict played a role in these debates, especially conflict between Yagoda and Andrei Vyshinsky, who obviously detested each other by 1935 and made no attempts to hide their mutual scorn. A new actor appeared on the scene as well: Nikolai Ezhov, the rising Communist Party functionary who would become Stalin's trusted lieutenant in all matters related to the NKVD in 1935 and who would eventually take Yagoda's place as head of the political police. Vyshinsky's formidable political skills notwithstanding, the nature of the Stalinist policing system was largely settled by 1936, and reformers within the upper echelons of the party and justice system could do little to change it.

The political conflicts regarding Soviet criminal justice in 1935 were shaped by the increasingly bitter feud between the NKVD and the USSR Procuracy, and in particular between Yagoda and Vyshinsky. Both Vyshinsky and Akulov, the USSR procurator before March 1935, opposed the NKVD on numerous issues in 1934 and 1935, but Akulov bore less personal animosity toward Yagoda than did Vyshinsky, and as the latter rose in political stature across the middle of the decade, his tendency to clash with Yagoda and the NKVD increased as well. Vyshinsky's open clash with Yagoda began in December 1934, while Vyshinsky was still Akulov's assistant. In that month, the Politburo heard a Procuracy report, organized by Vyshinsky, on the activities of the police and justice officials in Azerbaidzhan. The report directly criticized the political police, pointing to falsified evidence, the use of torture to extract confessions, and the tendency of local officers to fabricate large-scale conspiracies from unrelated local incidents to bolster the appearance of their own effectiveness. Further consideration of this issue by the Politburo was shunted aside by the regime's response to the Kirov murder, but Yagoda did not take the criticism lightly, and he ordered local NKVD organizations to gather compromising information on the activities of local justice organizations in order to prepare for political retaliation.[52]

In late June 1935, Yagoda, perhaps emboldened by Vyshinsky's failure to halt the creation of the police troikas in May and June of that year, launched a blistering counterattack on the judicial system. In a letter sent directly to Stalin and Molotov, Yagoda railed on the performance of the courts in the period after the creation of the USSR NKVD. He complained of lenient sentences handed down by the military tribunal system for what he viewed as counterrevolutionary activity in the wake of the Kirov murder, and he blasted courts in the countryside for lenient sentences handed out to the "counterrevolutionary saboteurs and thieves" who interfered with grain procurement campaigns. Finally, he complained that lenient court responses to hooliganistic, bandit, and thieving "elements" ruined the work of the *militsiia* and political police against these cohorts of criminals, and he made the stunning recommendation that all cases of crimes that could result in sentences of three years or more of deprivation of freedom, which entailed the vast majority of criminal cases by mid-1935, be removed from the competence of the court system altogether and transferred to the police troikas or, for more serious crimes, to the Special Board itself.[53] His attack was not out of character, but the scope of his recommendations suggests that he believed that the time was right, in mid-1935, to attempt to halt the ascendance of the USSR Procuracy and to tilt the balance of Soviet criminal justice resolutely in favor of the NKVD.

Vyshinsky's response to this attack, sent to Stalin and Molotov only days later, was uncharacteristically meek. Vyshinsky, who became the USSR procurator in early March, admitted that the court system was experiencing problems, adding only that poor work in the court system could be traced directly to the poor quality of investigation by the police.[54] Vyshinsky seems to have been surprised by Yagoda's condemnation and offered no real criticisms of the police system, but from this point forward he and Yagoda were open enemies.[55] All further debate regarding policing and Soviet criminal justice in 1935 and 1936 took place in this context of this bitter feud between the heads of what were, by that time, the two most powerful criminal justice institutions in the USSR.

For the next several months, Vyshinsky's drive to reshape Soviet criminal justice was muted, in part because his control over the court system was not yet assured. He supported two major policy moves in 1935 and early 1936 that were designed to moderate police pressure on the "loyal" sectors of the Soviet peasantry. First, the Politburo in late July 1935 ordered justice officials to grant amnesty to the farmers who had been sentenced during the collectivization campaigns to five years or less of deprivation, as long as they had served out their sentences and returned to productive work on collective farms.[56] This action was not intended to reduce penal populations, because it did not apply to any individuals still serving sentences; rather, it allowed a large group of peasants, mostly men of working age, to regain Soviet citizenship, take positions in collective farm administrations, and obtain internal passports so they could migrate to manufacturing or construction jobs. Although the operation encountered problems in the early months of its implementation, by April 1936, Vyshinsky was able to report to Stalin that nearly 769,000 collective farmers across the USSR had been absolved of past sentences.[57]

In the second major policy move, along the same lines, in January 1936 the Politburo ordered a review of all sentences handed out before December 1, 1935, under the auspices of the August 1932 law on theft of public property. This campaign, driven by Vyshinsky's complaints that the law had targeted members of the working or peasant classes for petty infractions, resulted in the immediate release of at least 40,000 individuals from the Soviet penal system.[58] Both campaigns were intended less to reduce police pressure on suspect population cohorts than to mitigate the effects of chaotic police repressions of the peasantry, which were still a major part of the yearly planting and harvest cycle, but they did signal Vyshinsky's determination to bring the police repressions of average Soviet citizens under control. Neither of these two policy initiatives, however, restricted the ability of the police to sanction Soviet citizens by extrajudicial means.

Vyshinsky's only successful move in 1935 to restrict the sentencing powers of the NKVD came in June, when the Politburo ordered the local police to obtain preliminary approval from the Procuracy before making arrests.[59] In practice, however, this instruction pertained only to arrests of important military, Communist Party, and state officials and to the operations of the court system. The instruction, coming as it did just weeks after the creation of the police troikas and in the midst of major campaigns against violent urban crime, did not restrict the rights of police to carry out administrative arrests and mete out extrajudicial punishments to "harmful elements" in any meaningful way. The willingness of the Politburo to consider moderate moves of any sort was severely limited in 1935, forcing Vyshinsky to rein in his criticisms of the NKVD itself for most of the year.

In 1935, Vyshinsky also had to contend with extensive Politburo censure of the work of the courts, much of it driven by political maneuverings at the highest levels of the Soviet state. Molotov, responding to complaints from the NKVD, in early May ordered the Commission for Soviet Control to carry out an investigation of the court and Procuracy systems. Yagoda's June 1935 broadside against the judicial system, delivered to the Politburo in the middle of this investigation, was an attempt to shape the debate to the advantage of the police, but it was hardly necessary. When the report was forwarded to the Politburo in September, it railed on the court system, agreeing with Yagoda on the tendency of local courts to issue lenient sentences for the very crimes that were the subject of the 1935 campaigns—hooliganism, armed robbery, and speculation, among others.[60] The harshest criticism was reserved for Krylenko's Justice Commissariat, a fact that aided Vyshinsky in his drive to elevate the Procuracy in the Soviet criminal justice system but placed the entire judicial system on the defensive vis-à-vis the police.[61]

Although the Committee for Soviet Control's report on the courts spawned extensive discussion of police activities as well, the NKVD avoided serious censure, in part because of the protection of Ezhov, the rising Communist Party functionary who oversaw the investigation of the Kirov murder and who, by mid-1935, was serving as Stalin's personal representative within the political police. After Stalin considered the committee report in September 1935, he chose to forward it, along with Krylenko's letter on the subject, to the Organizational Bureau (Orgburo) of the Central Committee.[62] Stalin's decision to turn over the issue to the Orgburo, a sprawling party bureaucracy that sat just below the Politburo, effectively placed the issue in the hands of Ezhov, who had cochaired the Orgburo, with Andrei Andreev, since mid-1935. Ezhov was charged with drafting a closed letter to local party bodies regarding deficiencies in the work of judicial organizations, much like the famous letter he sent to local party leaders in May 1935 in order to breathe life into the ongoing party purges.[63] Ezhov and Stalin created a large commission within the Orgburo in early 1936 to draft this letter, which included Ezhov, Osip Piatnitskii (head of the Political-Administrative Department of the Central

Committee), Vyshinsky, Krylenko, and several other representatives of the police and justice agencies; Yagoda was conspicuously omitted from these deliberations.[64]

The initial drafts of the closed letter were wide-ranging in scope and concentrated on the inadequacies of the court system and, to a limited extent, of police work as well. An early draft, for example, complained that in 1935 the *militsiia* completed 1.59 million investigations but halted 30 percent of those before they reached the court system; an additional 25 percent were halted by either the Procuracy or the court system in the process of trial. The early drafts also contained the demand—often repeated by Vyshinsky—that all arrests be approved by the Procuracy, a requirement that was nominally in place already but generally ignored by the local police.[65] Still, none of the participants directly criticized the sentencing practices of the police troikas or of the Special Board.

Ezhov's control of the NKVD was increasingly evident in early 1936, and he began to protect the organization from attacks by justice agencies by gathering compromising materials on local justice administrations gathered by local NKVD administrations. He commissioned "special reports" from regional administrations during the committee discussions, often bypassing Yagoda and the standard NKVD hierarchy in the process, that provided him with proof that local courts were lenient regarding counterrevolutionary crime and resistance to the harvest and grain procurement campaigns. Local NKVD administrations provided him with recommendations for improving local judicial affairs, including thorough purges of the court and Procuracy administrations in their areas.[66] The mere existence of these reports suggests that Ezhov was preparing himself for the political conflict that he would face once he took over the organization later in the year.

The ultimate fate of the draft closed letter on the courts was a slow death by orchestrated neglect. The commission forwarded a completed draft to Ezhov in early March 1936, but Ezhov, unhappy with the result, ordered the commission to rewrite it, omitting reference to the police altogether.[67] Public discussion of the proposed text of the USSR Constitution was under way by this point, as was the final maneuvering that put Vyshinsky's Procuracy on top of the Soviet judicial system, pushing the letter to the background of judicial affairs.[68] Piatnitskii forwarded a final draft to Andreev in late June 1936, adding minor changes that brought it into line with the new USSR Constitution, which was completed in May.[69] The letter was never sent; as we will see below, by the fall of 1936, the political situation had shifted substantially, making any kind of reformist moves in Soviet criminal justice virtually impossible.

In the midst of these criticisms of the court system, Vyshinsky launched his most direct attack on the extrajudicial sentencing capacities of the NKVD since its creation in 1934. As a member of the commission drafting the closed letter on the court system, he understood that the letter would ultimately focus on the shortcomings of justice organizations alone; but as a member of the commission drafting the new USSR Constitution in 1935 and early 1936, he also sensed the possibility of limiting the extrajudicial powers of the NKVD in conjunction with the promulgation of a document that promised, prima facie, extensive citizenship rights to all free residents of the Soviet Union and full judicial independence for the courts.[70] In early February 1936, he forwarded a letter to Molotov and Stalin that strongly criticized the NKVD Special Board. The board, he noted, concentrated on three major categories of crime: counterrevolutionary agitation, terrorism or conspiracies to commit terrorism, and cases of "socially harmful and socially dangerous elements," which he identified as "recidivists, individuals connected to the criminal milieu, those leading a parasitic lifestyle, etc." The first two categories, he argued, suffered from intolerable deficiencies of investigation and case preparation, including the widespread practice of oral hearings of cases without the presence of either witnesses or the accused. He argued that the NKVD should be prohibited from sentencing either category of offender and that all cases of terrorism or anti-Soviet agitation should be transferred to the court system. In addition, he suggested that local procurators should be granted expanded powers to halt cases investigated by the NKVD that they deemed unfounded.

Vyshinsky crowned this argument by noting that the sentencing practices of the Special Board had played a major role in expanding the NKVD labor camp, colony, and prison system to more than 1.25 million inmates by October 1935, a trend that contradicted concurrent Politburo attempts to reduce pressure on "loyal" collective farmers.[71] No challenges to the NKVD this fundamental had been broached at the center since the Kirov murder; this was a bold move by Vyshinsky at a time when his political victory over his rivals within the justice system seemed assured.

Yagoda's response, submitted less than a week later, was furious and condescending, even by his standards. He ridiculed Vyshinsky's selective use of statistics, arguing that the Special Board was responsible for only 33,823 convictions in 1935 and that counterrevolutionary agitation and terrorism, the offenses with which Vyshinsky was concerned, amounted to no more than 12,000 to 15,000 of those sentences. The vast majority of the nearly 300,000 cases investigated by the political police in 1935, Yagoda argued, were transferred to the Procuracy and the courts for judicial review; Vyshinsky, in demanding that the court system hear the majority of cases investigated by the NKVD, was "knocking on an open door." Yagoda noted that the Procuracy already exercised the right to protest decisions handed down by the Special Board, and he claimed that the hearings carried out by the board were completely reasonable, given the nature of the cases under consideration. He then turned the tables on Vyshinsky, arguing that the growth in camp and prison populations after 1932 was attributable to the court system; he estimated that extrajudicial sentences of the OGPU and the NKVD Special Board accounted for only about 292,000 of the total penal population of 1.25 million—not including the activities of the police troikas, which he deemed entirely proper. Finally, Yagoda argued that Vyshinsky's criticisms were a veiled suggestion that the Special Board should be abolished altogether and that the NKVD should lose all rights to administrative sentencing, a suggestion that Yagoda termed "completely incorrect." In broadening his response beyond Vyshinsky's original complaint, Yagoda made it clear that the NKVD would not accept any expansion of the powers of the USSR Procuracy that extended beyond the court system or that limited the extrajudicial sentencing practices of the police.[72]

Vyshinsky, in response, expanded his attack even further, criticizing the activities of the Special Board, police troikas, the *militsiia*, and the political police itself. He argued that the NKVD was ultimately responsible for increasing penal populations because the vast majority of criminal cases were investigated by the police rather than justice agencies. The *militsiia* was particularly guilty of applying unnecessary repression to the population: it had initiated criminal investigations on more than 2.4 million people in 1935 but ultimately charged only 590,000 of them. The administrative sentencing practices of the Special Board, he continued, did indeed have a fundamental influence on the size of penal populations, especially when the tendency of the police troikas to mete out lengthy sentences was considered; he noted that more than 35 percent of the NKVD camp, colony, and prisons populations, as of October 1935, were the result of sentences meted out by the OGPU or NKVD. Finally, Vyshinsky returned to the central issue, arguing that Yagoda's response was an attempt to prevent the Procuracy from exerting an influence over the sentencing practices of the NKVD, a direction that Vyshinsky claimed contradicted Politburo instructions reaching all the way back to the May 1933 instruction on the clearing of prisons.[73]

Vyshinsky was supported in this conflict, somewhat surprisingly, by his political rival Krylenko, who in late March forwarded to the Politburo a lengthy condemnation of NKVD sentencing practices regarding the crime of counterrevolutionary agitation (Article 58-10). This article of the penal code, Krylenko argued, was widely abused by local NKVD officers, who expanded the definition of the crime to include all sorts of public complaining about essentially local issues.[74] Vyshinsky picked up this line of attack in mid-April, warning Molotov that by February 1936 some 87 percent of all political cases heard by the court system were for counterrevolutionary agitation—many for mere critical remarks regarding specific governmental policies.[75] Vyshinsky returned to the issue again in late May, complaining that case files prepared by the political police for both courts and the Special Board contained only vague references to supposed counterrevolutionary proclamations by the accused rather than specific accounts of the offenses. Iakov Agranov, Yagoda's assistant commissar, responded for the NKVD by arguing that inclusion of this kind of evidence in case files would turn investigative paperwork into a "catalog [*sbornik*] of unprintable jokes." The possibility of abuse in such a system was clear to all involved, but the issue was shelved by Molotov in late June, only days after he received Agranov's response.[76]

Although Stalin's initial reaction to Vyshinsky's complaints was favorable, the procurator's complaints ultimately failed to produce any restrictions on the sentencing power of the NKVD. Stalin, after reading the exchange between Vyshinsky and Yagoda, decided in late March to distribute it in full to all members and candidate members of the Politburo, adding a notation on his own copy that read: "It seems to me that c[omrade] Vyshinsky is correct. The question should be decided at [the or a] meeting [*soveshchanie*]. I. Stalin."[77] Yet it is unclear exactly what part of Vyshinsky's complaint with which Stalin agreed, and the question was never discussed formally at the Politburo level; it may very well have been discussed within Ezhov's commission on the court system, or within the commission drafting the new USSR Constitution.

The evident trend at the Politburo at the beginning of April was indeed toward a rejection of any expansion of the extrajudicial powers of the NKVD. In early April, Molotov, acting on Stalin's orders, rejected a request from the NKVD and the USSR Procuracy that would have authorized the NKVD Special Board to confiscate the property of individuals subject to repression as a matter of course.[78] Yet Vyshinsky's complaint produced no response from the Politburo, which issued no instructions after April 1936 that limited the extrajudicial capacity of the NKVD. Vyshinsky's failure was likely related to the growing power of Ezhov at the center, but it was also the result of his surprising decision to focus his complaints on strictly political cases and to omit criticism of the police troikas. These troikas sanctioned far more individuals than the Special Board itself in 1935 and 1936, and they had been the subject of Vyshinsky's complaints in the past; yet he, like all other top police and justice officials, seems to have accepted their existence as part of the Soviet criminal justice system by early 1936.[79] His recalcitrance to attack the work of the police troikas wasted the only real opportunity he would have to resist the expansion of extrajudicial repression for the next two years.

At the same time that Vyshinsky attacked the hearing of political cases by the Special Board, he attempted to force reform in one of the most central aspects of Soviet policing: the passport system, and especially the use of passports to purge cities of ex-convicts. As with his attack on the Special Board, this move was not prompted by external events but seems to have been an attempt to question the extrajudicial practices of the NKVD while the time was right.[80] Vyshinsky wrote to Molotov in March 1936 with several complaints about the passport system. He complained that the passport regulations in effect subjected individuals to lifetime sentences of banishment from regime cities for a wide range of crimes, some relatively petty; he proposed that the list of crimes that resulted in banishment from regime cities be reduced substantially, and that individuals who served out sentences be restricted from living in regime areas for three or five additional years, depending on the severity of the crime. He also suggested that local Procuracy officials be allowed to supervise the seizure by the police of supposedly fraudulent or unregistered passports, a practice that was essentially an administrative sentence of lifetime banishment carried out by an individual police officer on the street with no hearing and no prosecutorial oversight at all.[81] He added several other lesser criticisms, in sum questioning a set of practices that, although they were quite harsh and often arbitrary, were seen by the police by early 1936 as a central part of their attempts to control the "criminal contingent" in major Soviet cities.

Vyshinsky's suggestions were opposed vigorously by the NKVD when they were discussed by the Sovnarkom in late March. During these discussions, Yagoda both defended the passport system and brought up a long-standing request for a change in the system of registering and tracking suspect elements in nonregime areas. In the course of the debates about the police system in 1934 and early 1935, Yagoda had repeatedly requested that the police be allowed to place a notation on the passports of "socially alien and criminal elements" in nonregime areas to the effect that they were forbidden to live in regime cities. He argued that this practice would make it easier for the police in regime areas to identify ex-convicts and other individuals under "open" surveillance if they attempted to move to regime locations.[82] The issue had disappeared from central discussions during the campaigns against violent crime in mid-1935, but Yagoda took it up again with Molotov in December 1935, and he returned to it in March 1936 when Vyshinsky's complaints about the passport system were heard by Molotov and the Sovnarkom.[83]

Top Communist Party officials initially responded negatively to Yagoda's request for this change in passport regulations, but as Procuracy and NKVD officials exchanged opinions in the spring and summer of 1936, Yagoda's position gradually won out. Molotov expressed doubt about Yagoda's request in March, and Grigorii Leplevskii, the assistant USSR procurator, followed suit, noting that the idea of differing marks in passports had been discussed when the passport system was created in 1932 and rejected because many of the conditions that could result in refusal for a passport in a regime area, such as unemployment, were temporary by nature. Leplevskii suggested that the Procuracy would not oppose a notation in the passports of ex-convicts, but he added that even this limited option would be difficult to implement, because criminal sentences changed constantly due to appeals and one-time amnesties.[84]

Vyshinsky reiterated his original position in mid-April, preparing a draft instruction for the Sovnarkom's consideration that included all the reforms he had suggested to Molotov in mid-March; in principle, Vyshinsky accepted Yagoda's request for a passport notation, but he insisted that it apply only to ex-convicts.[85] Yagoda, in turn, responded immediately to Vyshinsky's draft by rejecting all his suggestions, save the idea of shortening the list of crimes that resulted in refusal of a passport in regime cities. He claimed that permanent banishment of "criminal" and "harmful" cohorts was central to the ability of the NKVD to protect public order, and he insisted that the proposed notation in nonregime passports apply to all individuals who were forbidden to live in regime areas.[86] The positions of the NKVD and the Procuracy were completely opposed in all important aspects, and the concurrent conflict regarding the Special Board made it unlikely that the two sides would come to an agreement without pressure from above.

Debate on this issue at the Sovnarkom level was delayed for several months in mid-1936, for largely the same reasons that slowed discussion of Ezhov's closed letter on the courts. In late July, the Sovnarkom, under Vlas Chubar's guidance, agreed on a draft instruction to forward to the Politburo, which in early August accepted the recommendations without change. Vyshinsky won certain concessions from the NKVD: the list of crimes that resulted in the automatic refusal of a regime passport was shortened substantially, and individuals who were sentenced to banishment by the NKVD Special Board as a primary means of punishment were freed from further restrictions once their sentences had been served. Yet the NKVD gained far more. The instruction ordered the police in non-regime areas to place a notation in the passports of all individuals ineligible for regime passports to prevent an influx into major cities of "the criminal element," individuals deprived of citizenship rights, and noncitizens.[87] Both the text of the Politburo decision and the NKVD instructions to local passport officials, which followed on August 16, make it clear that the notation was to be placed as quickly as possible in the passports of all individuals either refused or ineligible for regime passports. The Sovnarkom rejected Vyshinsky's suggestion that the expulsion from regime areas last only three or five years, as well as his request that the Procuracy supervise the confiscation of passports.[88] All three decisions signaled that the central Communist Party authorities, by mid-1936, would tolerate no meddling by the Procuracy in the functioning of the passport system or the purging of regime cities of "the criminal element."[89]

The determination of the Politburo to allow the police to repress social disorder using extrajudicial means after mid-1936 is plainly evident in regime responses to speculation in consumer goods. As we have seen in chapter 4, by the end of 1935 the police were beginning to understand speculation as an individual behavior, carried out not by "professional" criminals but by average Soviet citizens who were willing to stand in lines to buy consumer goods legally and then resell them to those not fortunate enough to secure a good position in line. The emergence of this conception of speculation among the police was the logical result of the Politburo's decision in 1935 to eliminate rationing in food and consumer goods, but it did not sit well with Soviet judges; according to Yagoda, the court system in early 1936 disrupted police work against speculation by refusing to prosecute individuals who sold individual items purchased in the retail trade sector.[90] Vyshinsky, still able to contradict the NKVD on issues of substance at this point, responded in May by arguing that Yagoda's conception of speculation, much like his understanding of anti-Soviet agitation, was overly broad and that the NKVD was "inclined to view as speculation every case of sale by a worker at a market of things he doesn't need"; such an approach, he argued, repressed loyal Soviet citizens unnecessarily and did not address the causes of speculation in urban areas.[91]

Vyshinsky's complaint was reasonable, but suppression of individual buying and selling of even single items was regime policy by mid-1936. In addition to restrictions on the amounts of food one individual could purchase, the Politburo announced in December 1935 that individual trade in most manufactured items would be illegal in open air markets as of January 1, 1936, in conjunction with an end to the rationing of all manufactured goods. Petty trade at markets was to be suppressed by the police, but, as in 1935, it was impossible for local officials to halt entirely. Finance officials in Moscow, for example, complained in May 1936 that petty speculation went largely unpunished, especially at the famous Iaroslavskii market, where the police dedicated only three detectives and ten to fifteen regular officers to what was the largest open air market in the capital.[92] As shortages of consumer goods deepened in the spring of 1936, local finance officials attempted to deal with the situation by creating ad hoc rationing systems, much as they had in early 1935 when "free" trade was first introduced. As in 1935, the Politburo ordered NKVD and Procuracy officials to prevent local trade officials from creating rationing systems, averting shortages instead by enforcing restrictions on maximum purchase amounts for a single individual and by repressing any attempts at speculation.[93]

Nevertheless, these approaches could not cope with expanding shortages of consumer goods in 1936, nor could they halt the appearance of huge lines in front of major department stores, which often formed hours before opening time. These problems prompted Stalin, in June 1936, to create a commission, headed by Chubar and including Ezhov and Anastas Mikoyan, the head of the Trade Commissariat, to recommend measures to improve the distribution of consumer goods and to effect an "elimination" (*unichtozhenie*, often translated as "annihilation") of lines at major retail stores.[94] The commission made its recommendation to the Politburo in mid-July, blaming the long lines on the poor distribution of goods across the USSR and, more directly, on the failure of the Procuracy and police administrations to repress individuals speculating in petty amounts of goods.[95]

The Politburo responded immediately, launching a major campaign against speculation on July 19, 1936. Trade organizations were ordered to expand the network of stores in Moscow, Leningrad, Kiev, and Minsk, and to institute pricing controls and drastic restrictions on the amount of goods sold to one individual—a single pair of shoes or galoshes, or between 4.5 and 10 meters of cloth, depending on the type. The Politburo also ordered police and Procuracy officials to charge individuals, as a rule, with violating Article 107 of the Criminal Code (i.e., speculation, which carried a minimum sentence of five years) for any resale of manufactured goods for profit, even without clear proof of intent to speculate, instead of Article 105 (violations of the rules of trade), which was generally applied to petty offenses before 1936.

In comparison with previous campaigns against speculation, the 1936 campaign involved several novelties. The Politburo provided the NKVD with a quota for extrajudicial repression; the police were to expel administratively a total of 5,000 speculators from the four cities that were the focus of the campaign. The sale of any amount of manufactured goods at inflated prices by individuals with previous police detainments for speculation, or of quantities of goods that suggested speculation (e.g., several pairs of shoes), was automatically treated as speculation; such cases, if not dealt with by the police themselves, were to be heard by the court system within ten days, with automatic confiscation of property. In addition, the Politburo ordered the USSR Procuracy to stage several show trials of speculators in the four cities in question, complete with wide press coverage.[96] Arrest quotas were part of the dekulakization drive earlier in the decade, but this campaign represents the first time that the Politburo provided the local police with quotas in response to a specific public-order issue, rather than allowing the local police to define the scope of the operation themselves.

In carrying out this campaign, urban police officers demonstrated that they still operated under an essentially local set of assumptions about the nature of speculation and the proper responses to it. The police continued to sentence individuals to fines, rather than arresting them, for activities that clearly qualified as at least violations of trade, if not speculation; despite pressure from the center, they remained unwilling in 1936 to arrest and jail otherwise noncriminal urban residents for merely reselling a single item purchased at a state retail store.[97] At the same time, the local police were more than willing to move against repeat petty speculators, even if they were dealing in inconsequential amounts of goods. The police in Kiev, for example, targeted individuals speculating at markets with the utmost haste and a total lack of consideration for any concerns of proper investigation or formulation of cases. Procuracy officials in Kiev protested nearly half the sentences handed down by the NKVD troika in the process of carrying out this campaign, but such protests were generally futile because the individuals were immediately exiled from the city.[98]

In any case, the police had little trouble filling their quotas. As of early September 1936, little more than a month after the campaign began, the police troikas had sentenced 4,003 individuals for speculation in the four cities in question, compared with 1,635 individuals sentenced by the courts.[99] Even though the parameters of local police activity differed from the understanding of the crime held by top Communist Party officials, by mid-1936 the local administrations were nonetheless fully capable of utilizing the entire array of policing tactics and extrajudicial sentencing practices, which had emerged in the mid-1930s in the context of mass campaigns against urban crime, to produce the results demanded by the Politburo.

At the end of the summer of 1936, the window of opportunity for reform of the Soviet policing system closed rapidly. As the Exchange of Party Documents, begun in December 1935 under Ezhov's direction, drew to a close in the summer of 1936, Ezhov began to turn his full attention to the work of the NKVD. Operations against suspected foreign spies and saboteurs began in earnest in mid-1936; in February the Politburo, following Ezhov's suggestions, ordered the NKVD to begin to register all suspect political émigrés, with the intention of exiling as many foreigners as possible, and by the summer mass exiles and arrests of Poles and Germans were under way.[100] The first of Stalin's famous show trials was under way; the August 1936 trial of Zinoviev, Kamenev, and others, scripted by Stalin and staged by Ezhov, signaled the beginning of the deadly purges of the Communist Party, which would continue through late 1937. These purges also struck directly at the justice agencies; materials collected by the NKVD and forwarded to Ezhov in August 1936, for example, spoke of the "infiltration" of the courts and local Procuracy administrations by "socially harmful elements, former kulaks, nationalists, former active whiteguardists, former priests, etc."—a clear sign that local NKVD officials were beginning to settle conflicts that had simmered since 1934.[101]

Finally, in early August, at exactly the time of the decision regarding the passport system, the Politburo authorized the courts to sentence "the most dangerous criminals" to prison rather than to labor camps, and the NKVD to sentence individuals who had served out sentences in labor camps but had violated camp regulations or attempted to escape, to additional two-year terms in prison.[102] Taken together, these decisions made clear that, by August 1936, the Politburo was determined to allow the NKVD, and Ezhov, all the latitude they needed to carry out Stalin's unfolding purges of the Communist Party, of state elites, and, eventually, of Soviet society at large.

In this rapidly changing political atmosphere, Vyshinsky's last major attempt in the mid-1930s to alleviate the effects of police repression had little chance of success. Vyshinsky wrote to Stalin in late July 1936 with a request that the Politburo consider an amnesty for individuals sentenced to ten years for hooliganism on railroads in the early 1930s—a campaign that had been carried out on the basis of instructions dictated by Stalin himself (see chapter 3). He argued that hooliganism had receded in importance and that the continued incarceration of these individuals was unnecessary, but he offered no compelling argument of the benefit to be gained by releasing them.

Yagoda's reply to Vyshinsky was concise, arguing that "increased repression" of hooligans had reduced the crime to manageable levels and that a "mass revision" of sentences would lead to an increase in hooliganistic activities on transport.[103] There is no record of any reply from the Politburo, nor of any campaign to amnesty hooligans; Vyshinsky's suggestion was far out of step with Stalin's approach to criminal justice after mid-1936. Vyshinsky continued to send circulars to local procurators in late 1936, exhorting them to attempt to control local police actions, to ensure that arrests took place only with their sanction, and to monitor and improve the situation in local places of confinement. Yet his instructions were increasingly unenforceable, as local NKVD administrations began to translate Ezhov's rise to power into complete freedom of action in their jurisdictions.[104]

In the end, central policy debates regarding the criminal justice system in 1935 and 1936 produced little in the way of reforms of Soviet policing. Despite far-reaching discussions of the court system, the Criminal Code, the relationship between the Procuracy and the Justice Commissariat, and implications of the 1936 Soviet Constitution in the realm of law, none of the participants in these debates questioned the tactics employed by local police forces, the structure of the NKVD itself, or the application of extrajudicial repression using police troikas to the "criminal contingent."

The handful of attempts by top justice officials, especially Vyshinsky, to broach the issue of extrajudicial punishment, limited though they were, failed to result in any policy changes, because the Politburo made it clear that it would not support any moves that interfered with the mechanisms of control that had been created by the police in the preceding years.

Top Communist Party officials did not conceptualize these conflicts between justice and police agencies as a choice between an orderly, conservative vision of law, promoted by Vyshinsky, and an arbitrary, revolutionary ethos of policing, promoted by the NKVD. Rather, the dichotomy between order and arbitrariness (*proizvol*) ran through the work of all the criminal justice agencies. The Politburo, and Stalin himself, were willing to consider restrictions on NKVD responses to political crimes when the chaotic actions of local officers threatened to disrupt central policy initiatives, but they were unwilling to criticize police efforts to control urban crimes and "harmful elements," which relied on interlocking systems of population surveillance and extrajudicial sanctions and were central to the entire Stalinist system of repression and social control. Reform efforts that concentrated on narrow issues, such as the police's handling of counterrevolutionary agitation, could have little impact on the overall contours of the Stalinist police system by 1936.

Conclusion

By the end of 1936, a fully Stalinist police system had emerged in the USSR. Police hierarchies stretched from local officers directly to NKVD officials in Moscow, altogether bypassing local soviets and justice agencies. The NKVD was responsible only to the top state and Communist Party bodies, and ultimately to the Politburo itself. Close cooperation between the regular and political police at the local level, a product of the OGPU takeover in 1930, encouraged a merging of definitions of political and regular crimes and ensured that political police officers were fully engaged in issues of crime and public order by mid-decade. Most important, the entire Stalinist police system, from Yagoda down to the individual patrol officer on the streets, employed a conceptual apparatus that focused almost exclusively on identifying, cataloging, and controlling population "contingents" in pursuit of social order.

Although the chaotic years of the First Five-Year Plan had been replaced by forced normalization in the mid-1930s, the Soviet police continued to pursue a coherent vision of social transformation, viewing the complete removal of "harmful" and "criminal" cohorts from Soviet society as a prerequisite for the success of the Stalinist system. These assumptions regarding population cohorts were widely shared throughout all levels of the government and the Communist Party by mid-decade, making them seem almost second nature to policymakers at the time. Despite the political conflicts that erupted at mid-decade regarding specific aspects of the extrajudicial practices of the NKVD, the ultimate goal of identifying and eliminating "socially harmful elements" was never in question. Finally, the police exercised a massive amount of coercive power against these categories, using several overlapping extrajudicial systems.

These systems were particularly dynamic after 1935 because they were inherently local. Stalinist surveillance targeted population contingents based not on race or class but on an individual's correspondence to categories that had been created through years of interaction between criminology, local policing practices, and transformative regime policies. Top police officials, dreaming of modern preventive policing in 1929 and 1930, would have imagined a police system that made unnecessary the kind of purges of urban areas that defined Soviet policing by 1936. By 1936, top police officials could imagine nothing else.

Ironically, as the Stalinist policing system was taking its full shape, the tenure of the individual most responsible for the direction it took in the 1930s was coming to an end. Yagoda's position as the head of the NKVD weakened during 1936, as Ezhov, on Stalin's orders, took a greater role in the administration of the political police. Ezhov, while coordinating the August 1936 show trial of Zinoviev and Kamenev, began to amass charges against "Trotskyites" in the NKVD and, by association, against Yagoda himself. Although Ezhov complained to Stalin in late 1936 that the NKVD needed "restructuring," Stalin's decision to remove Yagoda in late September 1936 did not arise from any specific failures in policing in the previous years. By late 1936, Stalin had lost trust in the Yagoda's willingness to support harsh repressions of the "Trotskyite center" and the "Rightists" after the Kirov murder.[105] Yagoda's removal, when it came, was an essentially political act.

The appointment of Ezhov as head of the NKVD was seen by most high-level Communist Party officials as a positive change in the political police system. Not only inveterate Stalinists like Kaganovich and Sergo Orzhonikidze but also Nikolai Bukharin and a number of other top officials believed that Ezhov, as a representative of the Communist Party, would return a "party atmosphere" to the NKVD.[106] Such hope, of course, was worse than fiction; it willfully ignored the fact that Yagoda had faithfully fulfilled the instructions of the Politburo, and of Stalin himself, throughout his time as head of the political police. After taking control of the NKVD, Ezhov did indeed attempt to change the atmosphere of the policing system, in part through purges of Yagoda's supporters. As we will see, his overall program, both political and bureaucratic, had more in common with policing trends in the final years of Yagoda's career than is usually assumed. The Stalinist policing system was fully in place before Ezhov took control of it, and it would outlast his brief tenure as head of the NKVD.

6

Nikolai Ezhov and the Mass Operations, 1937–1938

> Very good! Continue to dig up and clean out this spying Polish filth. Crush it in *the interests of the USSR*.
> —Stalin to Ezhov, responding to reports on the initial course of the "Polish operation," September 1937[1]

> The Constitution [of 1936] wasn't written for swindlers. You've been sentenced before for robbery and theft, which means that you're a thief and a robber and you are subject to isolation and exile.
> —The Moscow police to an individual sentenced by the Moscow NKVD troika in November 1937 to eight years as a "socially harmful element" because of prior sentences[2]

Nikolai Ezhov, after taking over as head of the NKVD in late 1936, presided over a wave of state repression that has become emblematic of the Stalin era.[3] The NKVD, under Ezhov's control, carried out repressions in 1937 and 1938 against the Communist Party, the Soviet military, the Communist International, industrial and governmental elites, ethnic minorities, dekulakized peasants, criminals and ex-convicts, and masses of ordinary Soviet citizens who had the misfortune to be swept up in the "whirlwind" of Stalinist terror.[4] The police were involved in all aspects of these repressions, but they were directly in control of the most widespread and, in terms of numbers of victims, the most devastating of these processes: the "mass operations" of 1937 and 1938. In August 1937, Stalin ordered the NKVD to launch a series of police repressions that were termed "mass operations of repression of former kulaks, criminals, and other anti-Soviet elements." Shortly thereafter, he ordered the police to expand these operations to include individuals deemed a threat to national security due to their ethnicity or potential contact with hostile foreign governments. Local political police administrations carried out these mass operations with the help of *militsiia* officers, sweeping defined geographic areas and targeting specific categories within the population based on precise instructions from the center. Stalin and Ezhov provided NKVD administrations with arrest and execution quotas, by geographic region, for some but not all the target categories of these operations. By the time Stalin halted the mass operations in November 1938, the NKVD had sentenced some 1.15 million individuals, and executed just over 683,000, as part of this set of police actions, accounting for the majority of sentences and executions carried out during these two years of Stalinist terror.

The scope of these repressions was unprecedented in the post–Civil War era, but the nature of police activity in 1937 and 1938 was hardly unique. Police actions during the mass operations emerged from existing approaches to population cohorts deemed threatening in the mid-1930s, especially those related to "socially harmful elements," passport violators, and dekulakized peasants. When Ezhov took control of the NKVD in 1936, he actually sought to reverse this trend, promoting a series of reforms of covert surveillance and investigation that attempted to make Soviet policing less reliant on mass arrests. Yet his reform attempts found little support at lower levels of the NKVD, and they contradicted the structural realities of the Soviet policing system. They were jettisoned without fanfare in August 1937, when Stalin decided to launch the most expansive round of mass repressions to date.

Ezhov and the Nature of the NKVD

Nikolai I. Ezhov, head of the USSR NKVD from September 1936 to November 1938, came to power in the NKVD as an outsider, a nonpoliceman who was sent to the organization by Stalin in order to ensure that it followed his wishes during the unfolding purges within the upper ranks of the Communist Party. Upon taking office, Ezhov made use of his position as Stalin's trusted lieutenant to institute a wide range of changes, drawing on ideas that he had developed in the short time he spent as Stalin's lead investigator in the Kirov murder. Much of his attention focused on improving surveillance and covert investigation, but he also promoted a coherent set of reforms of Soviet policing in general, attempting to separate the work of the political police from that of the *militsiia* in order to improve the ability of political police officers to uncover and investigate the "counterrevolutionary" conspiracies that he, and Stalin, viewed as the chief political threat to the regime. These policy directions corresponded to many aspects of the original vision of Soviet policing promoted by the OGPU in 1930 and 1931, but they contradicted long-term trends in Soviet policing. Ezhov's plans were also constrained by an emerging focus within the Politburo on the threat of diversionary activity among certain ethnic minorities, and the threat posed by these "national contingents," as they were termed, in the event of war.

Ezhov was not cut from the same cloth as the career policeman who he replaced; he was, at heart, a Communist Party functionary. Having worked as a metalworker in Saint Petersburg before World War I, he joined the Bolshevik Party in the months after the February 1917 Revolution and played at least some role in the October events in Belorussia. His Communist Party career began in the Red Army, but in the early 1920s he began a series of positions in regional party administrations, and by the end of the decade he had held several high-level appointments in central party and commissariat personnel offices. These positions afforded him access to the highest-ranking party officials and schooled him in the exercise of political power within the Stalinist bureaucracy. By the early 1930s Ezhov, although not a Politburo member, was thoroughly engaged in the daily work of the Politburo. He became even more important when Stalin entrusted him with directing the membership purges that dominated party affairs between 1933 and 1936. By mid-1935 Ezhov's rise was complete: he occupied several leading positions in the party, including Secretary of the Central Committee, cochair, with Andrei Andreev, of the Organization Bureau (the Orgburo), and head of the Department of Leading Party Organizations.[5] Ezhov's importance for Stalin's plans for the NKVD became clear after the Kirov murder in late 1934, when Stalin placed him in direct control of the investigation of the crime, the initial January 1935 trial of Grigorii Zinoviev and Lev Kamenev, and the resulting purges of the city of Leningrad—moves signaling that Ezhov, and not Yagoda, was in charge of the most politically important policing issues of the day.

Ezhov's role in investigating the Kirov murder smoothed his promotion to head the NKVD, but it also gave rise to several themes that would reappear in his attempts to reshape the organization after he took over. In the wake of the murder, he directed an investigation of the NKVD, focusing on Leningrad, where the murder took place. He identified several long-term trends that he deemed detrimental to political police work: he claimed that political police officers spent too much time investigating and repressing nonpolitical crime and that the training and investigative practices of NKVD officers remained inadequate and prevented them from uncovering counterrevolutionary conspiracies. Most of his attention focused on the possibility of infiltration of the NKVD by "counterrevolutionary elements" and foreign intelligence agents; he concluded that the NKVD was filled with "alien" elements, former White officers, members of the nobility, and Trotskyites, who could, he reported to Stalin, "betray us at any moment."

Ezhov also deemed NKVD informant networks wholly inadequate to the task of protecting the country from internal counterrevolutionaries and foreign spies. He claimed that informant networks, which included some quarter-million unpaid "general" informants and tens of thousands more trusted but still voluntary "residents," were poorly organized, worked without any direct contact with officers themselves, and were easily infiltrated by unreliable elements or outright "double-dealers" and spies.[6] Informant networks depended entirely on the "taste" of local NKVD officials, and recruitment was carried out either by unpaid informants themselves or by low-level NKVD officers. Ezhov recommended to Stalin that the NKVD reduce the size of the informant network and limit the recruitment of informants to high-level officers, and he suggested that a thorough purge of the Leningrad NKVD be followed by a broad purge of all NKVD staff, officers and informants included.[7] His focus on membership purges within the NKVD mirrored his ongoing involvement with the Communist Party purges, and it resulted in substantial purges of the membership of the political police and the *militsiia* alike.[8] These purges, however, did little to respond to the concrete deficiencies of local police activity identified by Ezhov, many of which had been the subject of reform attempts by Yagoda for the preceding several years.

Despite these concerns with deficiencies in the police system, Ezhov focused on political matters in 1936 because Stalin directed him to do so, and it was his political reliability that led to his promotion to head of the NKVD. In mid-1936, Ezhov concentrated on actions against foreigners suspected of espionage, including foreigners within the NKVD itself, and on the fabrication of the first of the three great show trials of the late 1930s, the August trial of Zinoviev, Kamenev, and the "Trotskyite-Zinovievist Center." The evidence regarding Stalin's ultimate motives for replacing Yagoda with Ezhov in September 1936 is incomplete, but it is likely that Stalin saw Ezhov as more capable than Yagoda of carrying through the expanding campaign against "Trotskyite-Zinovievist" oppositionists within the Communist Party and, just as important, against the Rightists, including Nikolai Bukharin, Mikhail Tomskii, and eventually Yagoda himself. When the decision came, it was swift and absolute: Stalin replaced Yagoda via telegram from his vacation house in Sochi, refusing to grant an audience to the disgraced commissar and rapidly replacing his top assistants with Ezhov's men.[9] Ezhov thus became, in public, what he had been in private for the past several months: Stalin's personal representative within the NKVD.

Upon taking over the NKVD from Yagoda, Ezhov initiated several structural reforms in the policing system, concentrating on separating the work of the regular and political police in order to improve the ability of the latter to prevent diversionary activity and espionage. Ezhov complained consistently in 1935 and 1936 that the political police expended more effort on civil crime, especially economic crimes such as the theft of state property and embezzlement, than on political crimes such as diversion and wrecking—semantic differences for local officers, to be sure, but for Ezhov a clear indication that the NKVD spent too much time on issues of public order and not enough uncovering counterrevolutionaries and spies.[10] The limited available evidence suggests that Yagoda supported, or at least did not oppose, this policy direction. In mid-June 1935 Yagoda transferred the covert surveillance of retail trade and open air markets, and all investigation of crimes of the theft of public property, speculation, and abuse of office in the trade sector, from the economic departments of the NKVD to the detective departments of local *militsiia* administrations.[11] Ezhov and the Politburo reinforced this change in November 1936 by abolishing the central NKVD Economic Department altogether, as part of a general reorganization of the political police. The control of "wrecking" and diversion (i.e., strictly "political" crimes) became the exclusive responsibility of the Counterintelligence Department within the State Security Administration, while economic crimes like speculation, bribery, and embezzlement were transferred to the aegis of the central Detective Department.[12] At this point, perhaps the most politicized of civil crimes, the theft and embezzlement of state property, was, in theory at least, completely out of the hands of the political police.

Ezhov broadened this policy shift in early 1937, as Stalin's purge of the Communist Party began to unfold. During the notorious February–March 1937 Central Committee Plenum, at which Stalin essentially launched the repressions that engulfed the party in 1937 and 1938, Ezhov complained that more than 80 percent of the individuals repressed by state security agencies in 1935 and 1936 were guilty of "petty criminal acts" that should be handled by the *militsiia* rather than the political police. This criticism, of course, ignored the fact that the repression of "criminal elements" by the political police had been regime policy, handed down in some cases by Stalin himself, since the early 1930s, but it was consistent with Ezhov's attempts to force political police officers to focus on the tasks of the day.

Ezhov and the Politburo followed up these complaints in March 1937 by creating a "Department for Combating Theft of Socialist Property and Speculation" (OBKhSS) within the Central Militsiia Administration and shifting to it all surveillance of state trade systems, grain procurement and distribution systems, and banks. The Speculation Department handled the investigations of all crimes committed within these institutions, including any uncovered by the political police but exhibiting a purely criminal nature, but it was ordered to transfer all cases exhibiting signs of terrorism, espionage, or other counterrevolutionary activity to the political police.[13] Ezhov initiated a parallel reorganization of the policing of rail and other transport systems in early 1937, reversing earlier attempts by Yagoda to involve the political police more directly in the suppression of crime on railroads by transferring all police work regarding hooliganism, theft, and juvenile delinquency to a newly created Railway Police.[14] The Railway Police, which was subordinated directly to the Central Police Administration of the USSR NKVD, was to have 11,500 officers in place by January 1938 in order to handle all nonpolitical crimes on rail lines and stations; crimes like wrecking, diversion, and spying in all transport systems remained the purview of the State Security Department of the NKVD.[15] These changes ran counter to several years of consistent regime policies regarding the suppression of particularly "threatening" categories of urban and violent crime by the political police, and they had little chance of creating a meaningful division between political and civil policing in 1937. They did, however, underscore Ezhov's determination to force local NKVD officers to focus on counterrevolution and diversionary activity in the months that followed his ascension to power.[16]

Ezhov's focus on exposing counterrevolution and diversion paralleled the most important conceptual development in NKVD activity in the first months of his tenure: the increasing tendency of police leaders to equate internal political opposition with foreign intelligence activity among ethnic minorities within the USSR. Ezhov gained experience with this issue through his supervision of purges of foreigners, especially Poles and

Germans, in Communist Party and state administrations in 1935 and 1936, but broader waves of ethnic cleansing were well under way before he took over the NKVD. In early 1935 the NKVD deported nearly 50,000 Poles, Germans, and Ukrainians from the western Ukrainian border zone in a process related to the implementation of the internal passport system in those areas; and in 1936, almost 64,000 Poles and Germans were deported from regions along the western Ukrainian border and resettled to agricultural colonies or collective farms in Kazakhstan, a process that had no basis in passport regulations.[17] Ezhov, under Stalin's orders, took a series of steps in 1936 and early 1937 that signaled a growing willingness at the center to target ethnic populations that were deemed a security threat, including the placing under surveillance of all foreign citizens living in the USSR; the expulsion of all foreign citizens, especially Japanese, Germans, and Poles, from Western Siberia; and the expulsion from the USSR of all German citizens and all foreigners suspected of intelligence activity.[18] Ezhov and Stalin were concerned not with a general sense of danger emanating from these cohorts of "foreign elements" but with the specific possibility of diversionary activity and rebellion among them in the event of war.[19]

The supposed connection between foreign powers, domestic opposition, and wartime rebellion was a central topic of discussion at the February–March 1937 Central Committee Plenum. The plenum signaled the beginning of Stalin's offensive against the Communist Party at large, rather than just former oppositionists: Stalin stressed that counterrevolutionaries were now more dangerous because they were hidden inside the party, "with a party card in their pocket," and that the campaign against them had to turn to new tactics of "tearing them out by the roots."[20] Stalin's speech to the plenum also emphasized the connection between political opposition and internal rebellion, arguing that the Moscow show trials proved that internal oppositionists were preparing for diversionary acts and open rebellion in the event of war with either Germany or Japan.[21] Ezhov's report to the Plenum stressed many of the same themes: he concentrated on the connections of the Rightists to foreign intelligence services in order to prepare the ground for their eventual trial, and he criticized cadres within the party and the NKVD for allowing the infiltration of foreign agents and traitors into the highest ranks of those organizations.[22]

In the weeks following the Central Committee Plenum, the NKVD moved to collect information on potential foreign agents, and the domestic populations that could be expected to support them, in preparation for broader actions to follow. The Third (Counterintelligence) Department of the Central State Security Administration (GUGB) instructed local NKVD administrations to prepare materials on populations most suspected of possible collaboration, including foreigners; Soviet citizens of Polish, German, Korean, or other "hostile" ethnic backgrounds; "former people"; dekulakized peasants; and a host of other categories of internal "alien" elements. The instructions stressed that Polish, German, and Japanese agents working within the USSR had already created large networks of counterrevolutionaries and were planning to launch internal rebellions in the event of war.[23] The NKVD gained a substantial expansion of extrajudicial authority in the wake of the February–March plenum as well, when in April the Politburo authorized the Special Board to sentence individuals suspected of spying, "wrecking," diversionary activity, and terrorism to five to eight years "in prison."[24] The ideas that a connection existed between internal political opposition, remnants of the "kulak" or bourgeois classes, and foreign intelligence operations, and that these connections posed a grave threat in the event of war, were thus fully in place in central political rhetoric by the beginning of 1937. Local police administrations would respond to this rhetoric with their own versions of "counterintelligence" activity in the months that followed.

The structural changes initiated by Ezhov when he took control of the NKVD in late 1936 were, on paper, fundamental in every way. His chief goal was to reorient the political police toward the surveillance and repression of foreign intelligence agents and internal counterrevolutionaries. In the process, he intended to turn over all aspects of the policing of nonpolitical crime to the *militsiia*. This goal was completely consistent with Ezhov's, and Stalin's, political aims in early 1937; nearly all political trends at the center pointed toward an expansion of police repressions against "foreign elements" and the criminal, "kulak," or otherwise marginalized domestic populations that could be expected to support them in the event of war with Germany or Japan. Ezhov's attempts to separate the regular and political police, however, were incomplete: although he adamantly ordered the political police out of the business of dealing with regular crime, the reverse was hardly true, as the *militsiia* in 1937 was charged with controlling several categories of overtly politicized crimes. The mixing of cadres, duties, and targets between the regular and political police was, by 1937, a constituent part of the Stalinist policing system, one that a handful of structural reforms by a new NKVD chief was unlikely to change.

Ezhov and the Suppression of "Socially Harmful Elements"

Ezhov's policy initiatives regarding the repression of suspect foreigners and the restructuring of the political police, though central to unfolding policy initiatives within the Politburo, had little relationship to the realities of police work in 1936 and 1937. The concrete problems faced by local officers in this period had nothing to do with "foreign elements"; they included harvest shortages, flight from collective farms, speculation in food and consumer goods in cities, and the geographic mobility of several hundred thousand people who, based on the text of the 1936 Soviet Constitution, attempted to exercise their newly granted right to move about the country without reference to their previous social status as "ex-kulaks" or "disenfranchised" individuals. Ezhov, upon taking over the NKVD, had no experience with these issues, and he initially left them to his subordinates, but he could hardly ignore them, because controlling social disorder remained one of the central tasks of the NKVD in 1937. His responses to these issues were constrained by the nature of the Soviet police system; the realities of local administration mitigated against his attempts to separate political and criminal policing, and his focus on counterrevolution only reinforced the propensity of local officers to conflate civil and political crime. By the summer of 1937, Ezhov, like Yagoda before him, equated the "social danger" posed by ex-convicts, "socially harmful elements," and dekulakized peasants with counterrevolutionary activity, and he moved, with Stalin's approval, to repress it accordingly.

Ezhov's initial moves in the area of regular policing were tepid at best. He expected the *militsiia* to assist the political police in controlling "petty wrecking" in the trade system and anti-Soviet agitation in the countryside, but he did not view the organization as central to his mandate to protect the country from foreign intelligence agents and domestic insurgents. He retained L. N. Belskii, who had served as head of the USSR-wide Central Militsiia Administration since January 1934. This decision contradicted Ezhov's general policy of replacing Yagoda's top assistants, and it ensured substantial continuity in the NKVD's work regarding crime and social disorder in 1937.[25]

Ezhov's first major move regarding the *militsiia*, once he became fully acquainted with the state of civil policing, was a simple request for 10,000 additional officers. Ezhov complained to Molotov that expanded police duties in 1935 and 1936—including dealing with juvenile homelessness and delinquency, convoying prisoners to and from court appearances, and searching for nonpayers of alimony in conjunction with the 1936 law that outlawed abortion—had sapped the strength of local administrations even as Yagoda had reduced the size of auxiliary police forces such as the Industrial Militsiia. Ezhov's request, with an estimated cost of 45 million rubles a year, was more in keeping with his previous role as Stalin's exceptional representative in the NKVD than with his new role as commissar of internal affairs, which entailed working within the bureaucratic pressures of the Sovnarkom. Molotov, following the advice of the USSR Finance Commissariat, flatly rejected it, forcing Ezhov to return to the issue of staffing levels several times in 1937 and 1938.[26]

Ezhov quickly found that issues of public order demanded his full attention, especially ongoing problems of shortages of consumer goods and speculation in major urban areas. Widespread shortages of manufactured goods in 1935 and 1936 (discussed in chapter 5) were exacerbated in the fall of 1936 by serious shortfalls in the harvest, leading to a crisis by the end of the year. Provisioning difficulties in the countryside in November and December were severe enough in many areas to cause the mass slaughter of cattle and flight from collective farms; famine, particularly in the southern areas of the USSR, caused at least several thousand deaths. Although conditions were in place for far greater losses, the regime intervened, in contrast to 1932 and 1933, in order to limit damage to the Soviet agricultural system.[27] Nonetheless, shortages of manufactured consumer goods expanded to the food sector in late 1936, and long lines, already a stable part of the Soviet urban landscape, appeared in front of bread stores, which were open for only a few hours each day. Customers in some regions were restricted to purchasing only 1 kilogram of bread per visit to a store, but the Politburo once again refused to permit local trade officials to create rationing systems, attempting to mitigate shortages by controlling the distribution of scarce resources and carefully timing the release of products onto the market.[28] Such measures could hardly deal with the reality of shortages and the resulting rise in prices on the open market in early 1937. As in 1935 and 1936, the primary responsibility for controlling speculation hence fell on the local police.

Local officers, responding to central calls for increased pressure on speculation in early 1937, continued to address urban speculation in much the same manner as they had under Yagoda, incarcerating "registered" petty offenders using police troikas but subjecting average citizens only to fines for selling their own property or single items purchased from state-run stores. The police were willing to sentence petty speculators as "harmful elements" if they were repeat offenders, but they rarely carried out any substantial investigation of such crimes, charging individuals simply on the basis of excess amounts of goods.[29] These approaches to speculation did not rely on the highly politicized rhetoric emanating from the center regarding the role of spies and internal "oppositionists" in the difficulties of the trade system, which provided local officers with no real guidance in targeting speculators, either petty or organized, in their jurisdictions.[30] Yet the understanding held by the local police of the importance of the "speculative contingent" in petty economic crime did resonate with central demands to search for cohorts of hidden internal enemies in early 1937; local officers had little difficulty making the transition to categorizing these "speculative elements" as part of a larger cohort of anti-Soviet populations later in the year.

Ezhov also quickly became engaged in the issue of controlling the geographic mobility of exiled "kulaks" and ex-convicts, a long-standing part of Soviet policing that resonated with his concerns about the security threat posed by ethnic minorities and marginalized individuals in the event of war. The question of geographic mobility was brought to the fore by the promulgation of the USSR Constitution in December 1936, which guaranteed civil rights to all Soviet citizens and abolished the social category of *lishentsy* (those deprived of citizenship rights due to their social background, e.g., social origin, previous property ownership, or past occupation). By the time of its promulgation, the Constitution was purely propagandistic; the substantive internal debates regarding the nature of the Soviet criminal justice system that had accompanied its drafting had been superseded by Ezhov's rise to power, the first Moscow show trial, and the beginning of mass purges within the Communist Party.

Yet the Soviet population took the new Constitution quite seriously, especially Article 135, which nominally removed all residence and employment restrictions from individuals who regained their citizenship rights. Although Article 135 explicitly did not apply to ex-convicts—who as a rule lost citizenship rights when they were sentenced to terms of exile, banishment, or deprivation of freedom—ample evidence shows that the hundreds of thousands of individuals who were subject to residence restrictions because of past criminal convictions believed that the Constitution applied to them anyway. Local police and judicial organizations reported that these individuals, along with "ex-kulaks" and the formerly disenfranchised, applied en masse for passports, and for permission to move from their places of exile to regime locations, in the months after the publication of the Constitution.[31] Allowing all ex-convicts and special settlers to move freely about the country was inconceivable for local and central police officials alike in early 1937, as it would have contradicted the essence of the expanding passport regime and, with it, the entire edifice of the Stalinist policing system. Yet local officials were confused as well by the text of the Constitution, requesting guidance from the center as to how to handle the massive number of requests for identity documents from individuals who believed that the Constitution had awarded them the right to unrestricted geographic mobility.[32]

The regime moved quickly to quash the idea that the Constitution provided the right of geographic mobility to the reenfranchised, especially those dekulakized peasants and ex-convicts living in the special settlements of the NKVD. Stalin had already decided in January 1935 that special settlers were permanently ineligible to move from their locations of resettlement, and there is no evidence that he or any other central officials intended the Constitution to change this restriction. Vyshinsky and Ezhov, responding to requests from local officials in early 1937 regarding the implications of the Constitution for individuals who had served out their sentences in special settlements, quickly came to an agreement that all settlers would remain fastened to their locations of resettlement until 1939 and be allowed to leave the regions where they lived only in 1940; Article 135 of the Constitution, in practice, would apply only to the right to vote and not to the supposed right to move.[33] No further instructions on the issue seem to have been issued during Ezhov's tenure, but none were necessary. In the absence of complete amnesty for all special settlers and ex-convicts, the passport regulations already in place made it impossible for the vast majority of them to move about the country, even after their sentences were complete.[34] A certain number of individuals deprived of voting rights because of their social background (the *lishentsy*) did gain the nominal right to move about the USSR as a result of the 1936 Constitution, but passport regulations placed numerous obstacles in their paths as well, especially if they attempted to migrate to one of the hundreds of areas under regime passport restrictions. The Constitution, in practice, did not expand the right of geographic mobility substantially in late 1936 and 1937; on the contrary, the concurrent expansion of regime passport restrictions to hundreds of cities and towns further restricted the mobility of ex-convicts, former kulaks, and other marginalized categories of Soviet citizens.

The mobility of marginalized individuals was not an inherently "political" problem, in Ezhov's understanding of the term, but it became politicized in late 1936 and 1937 as the central police and Communist Party authorities made conceptual connections between resettled "kulaks," harvest difficulties and famine in the countryside, and the threat of rebellion in the event of war. Flight from collective farms was a completely rational response to conditions of shortage and starvation in the countryside in the winter of 1936–37, yet local NKVD reports sent to the center focused instead on the role of "kulak agitation" and wrecking by "anti-Soviet elements" within collective farms. The social category of "kulak" was no longer part of the official lexicon, because the 1936 Constitution had announced the disappearance of the class itself; yet increased attention to illegal migration away from special settlements prompted central police and justice officials to identify "kulak elements" who had migrated back to their homelands as the central cause of the difficulties in the agricultural sector.[35] The events of 1936 and 1937 in the countryside proved to central officials that "kulak elements" were willing to disrupt the agricultural system in times of difficulty and were inherently disloyal to the collective farm system, and that existing restrictions on formerly dekulakized peasants, including the internal passport system, were inadequate, paving the way for expanded repressions of "kulak elements" later in the year.

The Politburo took several steps to ensure that expanding repressions in 1937 did not disrupt the basic functioning of the Soviet economic system, especially in the countryside. These moves were supported primarily by Vyshinsky, who continued to attempt to limit extrajudicial repressions in favor of what he deemed a more orderly application of coercion by the court system. In early 1937, Vyshinsky and Krylenko shepherded through the Sovnarkom a limited plan to grant amnesty to collective and individual farmers who had been repressed in 1936 for failing to meet their procurement quotas, in order to encourage those collective farmers in famine-stricken areas to participate in the new planting season and reduce the possibility of a repetition of the events of the fall of 1936.[36] In October 1937, well after the beginning of mass repressions, the Politburo approved a similar amnesty for collective farmers who had been charged after 1934 with malfeasance in local offices; this campaign stretched into 1940 and resulted in the overturning of convictions for roughly 450,000 individuals.[37] These policies underscore the extent to which the center saw the repressions that were unfolding in 1937 in differentiated terms, targeting the "enemy" cohorts among the population while promoting the participation of loyal citizens in Soviet economic and political life.

Vyshinsky and Ezhov found a surprising amount of common ground on these issues, but they came into open conflict in early 1937 regarding the rehabilitation of ex-convicts who had been released from the Soviet penal system. In early 1937, Vyshinsky returned to his earlier attempts to promote the reintegration of ex-convicts into Soviet society, directly challenging the new NKVD chief for the first time. On March 19, he sent a letter to Molotov reporting on the appearance at the USSR Procuracy office in Moscow of a group of career criminals who had decided, based on a series of carefully staged newspaper articles about recidivists who had given up their criminal activities, to present themselves to the authorities and ask for amnesty and for honest work.[38] Although the articles, published in the daily newspaper *Izvestiia*, stressed the capacity of habitual criminals to repent and to refashion their criminal consciousnesses into true proletarian identities, Vyshinsky's report to Molotov was more subdued, noting simply that the twenty-seven career criminals who had appeared had been placed in factory jobs in various cities around the USSR. Vyshinsky suggested that this "spontaneous movement among the criminal element" would likely continue, and he recommended that a permanent institution be created to place ex-convicts into jobs as they were released from labor camps or colonies. With his request to Molotov, he included several letters from recidivist criminals attesting to their desires leave the criminal milieu, stressing the capacity of at least some ex-convicts to become loyal Soviet citizens. Molotov's initial reaction, penciled on Vyshinsky's request by hand, was that the quantity of recidivists in question was insignificant, but he ordered Ezhov and Vyshinsky to discuss the question and arrive at a policy recommendation.[39]

Ezhov responded to Molotov on April 9 with an aggressive refutation of Vyshinsky's position on this group of recidivists in particular and on ex-convicts in general. Ezhov argued that recidivists and ex-convicts were the most pressing public order problem facing the USSR; he claimed that most "threatening" (*derzkie*) crimes, including robbery, brigandage, murder, and qualified theft, were committed by what he called the "contingent" of ex-convicts, especially those who had recently completed their sentences and been released. Ezhov pointed out that, by mid-1937, over 60,000 individuals were released from places of confinement each month, of whom only 6,000 to 7,000 were placed in employment by the NKVD; the rest "spread out across the USSR in search of work, beginning to commit crimes even on their initial journey away from the camps." Ezhov acquiesced to part of Vyshinsky's proposal, agreeing that ex-convicts who had truly been rehabilitated could be placed in jobs in nonregime locales by trade unions, with the assistance of local NKVD administrations. At the same time, he suggested that the NKVD be accorded the right, using the courts or special NKVD troikas, to sentence all "unreformed recidivists" who had served out their sentences but were identified by camp officials as "troublemakers [_otkazchiki_], hooligans, violators of labor discipline, etc." to additional three-year terms in labor camps. Ezhov noted that Vyshinsky was in agreement with his suggestions with the exception of the point on additional sentences; this point was the only one that mattered, because both experienced politicians understood that the creation of a job placement program was far less probable in mid-1937 than was the creation of NKVD troikas to sentence recidivists to additional terms in camps.[40]

The issue of ex-convicts was debated for the next three months between representatives of several commissariats and members of the Politburo. Trade union officials objected to Ezhov's suggestion to turn over responsibility for ex-convicts to them, noting the practical difficulties of creating a nationwide job-placement system. Krylenko and Vyshinsky, for their part, objected to the extrajudicial sentencing of recidivists in camps for unspecified crimes, arguing that the NKVD already exercised the right to sentence camp inmates to additional terms of exile or banishment for specific offences.[41] Representatives of the NKVD stood firm on the need to keep ex-convicts out of regime areas and to sentence the "troublemakers" among them to additional terms in labor camps. The Sovnarkom eventually generated a set of policy recommendations that ordered the trade unions to create a system to place ex-convicts in jobs and declined to create NKVD troikas to sentence recidivists but did suggest that existing courts in labor camps be accorded the right to sentence unreformed "criminal-recidivists" to three additional years in camps.[42]

The bulk of this discussion regarding ex-convicts took place before the meeting of the June Central Committee Plenum. Discussions at the Plenum, as we will see, made the point moot. By the time the above recommendations were forwarded to Molotov, on July 2, Stalin had already decided to launch the waves of mass repressions that engulfed the Soviet Union in late 1937, ensuring that "recidivists" and ex-convicts would meet a far different fate than being placed in a job set up by local trade union officials.

These debates regarding recidivists and ex-convicts represent a turning point in Ezhov's approach to policing and the maintenance of public order, signaling a dramatic end to his lack of attention to regular crime and a shift in focus toward the administrative repression of the "criminal contingent." Ezhov's position was wholly compatible with the direction of policing during the previous several years, and it was strikingly similar to the analyses of the causes of crime promoted by Yagoda in 1934 and 1935. The ideas that recidivism was the key cause of most crime, that the majority of serious crimes could be traced to a professional core of "criminal elements," and that effective policing action required repression of the entire "criminal contingent" were central to every aspect of police work by mid-decade. Ezhov brought to the NKVD a particular focus on connections between these "socially harmful" cohorts and the threat of rebellion in time of war, and his leadership encouraged the local police to categorize existing groups of ex-convicts, expellees from regime cities, dekulakized peasants, special settlers, and petty criminals in the increasingly politicized language emanating from the center. Still, the response of the local police to these trends ensured that mass repressions, when they began in mid-1937, would be directed at the same groups of ex-convicts, dekulakized peasants, and "socially harmful elements" that had been the targets of police actions in the preceding years.

The Launching of the Mass Operations

By mid-1937, several overlapping trends pointed toward an impending expansion of police repression to broad swaths of the Soviet population. Purges of state elites, including former oppositionists and current Communist Party members, were well under way; the NKVD had moved to put foreigners under surveillance and to purge particularly sensitive areas of suspect nationalities; and strong conceptual connections existed at the center between threats to national security and the existence of cohorts of former kulaks and ex-convicts. The decision to launch mass repressions, however, was Stalin's alone. The available evidence suggests that Stalin decided to begin a series of repressions against "former kulaks, criminals, and anti-Soviet elements" in the summer of 1937 specifically because he viewed them as a potential threat in the event of war with Germany or Japan.[43]

Stalin's decision was abrupt, but it was not a radical turn in policy, coming as it did on the heels of large-scale operations against "harmful elements" and ethnic minorities over the previous two years. His understanding of the threat evolved rapidly in mid-1937 under the influence of top party and police officials, including Ezhov, and in dialogue with local NKVD administrations, which promoted their own definitions of "anti-Soviet" activity in the initial weeks after Stalin's decision. As central police officials coordinated Stalin's demands with the desires and capacities of their local organizations, Stalin and Ezhov expanded the scope of planned repressions to include not only former kulaks and ex-convicts but also former "oppositionists," religious figures, foreigners, individuals formerly disenfranchised (*lishentsy*), and eventually a vast number of individuals who supposedly belonged to active anti-Soviet insurgent organizations. Local NKVD administrations were not as concerned as Stalin about the possibility that these populations might rise up in time of war, but years of policing campaigns against them had conditioned officers to view "harmful" and "kulak" populations as general threats to the Soviet political and economic systems. Hence the local police had little difficulty translating Stalin's demands into action in the fall of 1937.

By the summer of 1937, Stalin and Ezhov were in control of several widespread purges of state and Communist Party elites. The February–March 1937 Plenum marked the beginning of widespread party purges, a process that combined local initiative with direct central pressure: the Politburo encouraged local party cells to criticize and purge their superiors in the name of "party democracy," but all decisions regarding party secretaries were ultimately made at the center. These party purges were accompanied by a campaign against supposed "wreckers" and saboteurs in industry, who were allegedly responsible for accidents, failures to meet plan targets, and all other possible problems in the industrial and agricultural system; by mid-1937, the Soviet judicial system was noisily involved in prosecuting such cases as political crimes.[44] Ezhov presided over purges of the NKVD after the plenum as well, removing more of Yagoda's lieutenants and replacing them with Chekists loyal to him and with several hundred party members approved by the Central Committee. He also directed a purge of military intelligence and, beginning in May, of the Red Army command itself.[45] These purges targeted the upper echelons of the Soviet bureaucracy, but they reflected Ezhov's general concern with foreigners and saboteurs in state and party institutions and suggested that broader purges of "foreign elements" were still to come.

Stalin's exact motives regarding the launching of mass repressions may never be known, but the existing documentation allows us to piece together the general contours of his decision. Discussions at the June 1937

Plenary meeting of the Central Committee presaged the impending change. The main issue at the plenum was Ezhov's stunning report on the progress of the ongoing purges within the Communist Party, the Soviet government, and the military. Ezhov outlined the existence of a vast conspiracy within these bodies, which he claimed were connected via a "United Center" made up of representatives of all the political groupings previously targeted by Stalin's purges, who were working to overthrow the Soviet government in the service of Germany, Poland, and Japan. Although Ezhov reported that many of the ringleaders of these organizations had been uncovered and arrested, he stressed that entire sectors of Soviet administration were contaminated with "anti-Soviet elements," including not only the party and the military but also the defense industry, the transport system, and agriculture. He argued that the diversionary and wrecking activities of these foreign agents had been responsible for widespread industrial and economic difficulties in the preceding months, and he charged that foreign and counterrevolutionary agents had organized huge groups of rebels among "former people, White-Cossack partisans, kulaks, special settlers, criminals, and others" in order to carry out armed uprisings in the event of war.[46] His charges were consistent with his explanations of internal difficulties in administration in the preceding months; they also clearly suggested that additional purging was to come, and that such purging would take place not only among the rank and file of Soviet institutions but also among marginalized groups within the population at large.

The events at the plenum, however, were not the cause of Stalin's decision. Central Committee plenums generally communicated major policy shifts to regional Communist Party officials, and the June Plenum was no exception: signs of an impending move toward mass repressions of "anti-Soviet elements" were visible before the plenum began. In early 1937, regional NKVD administrations responded to Ezhov's rhetoric regarding counterrevolutionary conspiracies by "uncovering" numerous large-scale organizations within their areas, arresting hundreds of supposed conspirators and submitting reports on their actions to Moscow as proof of their vigilance.[47] In mid-June, however, the NKVD in Western Siberia altered this rhetorical exchange. The regional NKVD chief, S. N. Mironov, reported to Ezhov and Stalin that he had uncovered a "Constitutional-Democrat/monarchist/Socialist Revolutionary" organization under the direction of Japanese agents, which had established military-style branches in several cities in the region and was preparing to launch an uprising against Soviet power. Mironov argued that this conspiracy was particularly dangerous because it united anti-Soviet activists among former elites with the counterrevolutionary social "base" of kulaks and special settlers that populated West Siberia. Mironov pointed to the 208,400 exiled kulaks who were settled in the Narym area and in the cities of the Donbass, and to the 5,350 former White officers and other former "oppositionists" who had been exiled to the area, arguing that the extent of the danger was clear.[48]

Mironov's report was not sui generis, because it echoed Ezhov's contentions regarding the connections between foreign agents and domestic counterrevolutionaries, including former kulaks and special settlers.[49] Yet his report exhibited a new level of urgency, and it drew direct connections between anti-Soviet conspiracies and the population cohorts that had been the target of police work on the periphery for the preceding decade. Stalin moved on this report on June 28, during the plenum, authorizing NKVD officials in Western Siberia to execute all participants in this particular "counterrevolutionary insurrectionary organization" and approving the formation of an NKVD troika to process cases and mete out sentences on the spot.[50] Stalin specifically instructed the NKVD in Western Siberia to focus on the "insurgent organization among exiled kulaks," underscoring his concern with the spread of insurgency to the "social base" of exiles.[51] Mironov's report, although it fit comfortably within ongoing rhetorical trends regarding the nature of domestic and foreign threats, was crucial in convincing Stalin that broader action against exiled peasants and criminal populations was necessary to ensure domestic security.

Whatever Stalin's decisionmaking process, his intent became clear in early July 1937. On July 2, Stalin approved a telegram, sent to regional and republican Communist Party leaders the next day, instructing them to prepare to begin mass repressions of exiled peasants and criminals. According to the text of the telegram, individuals who had been sentenced to exile in various areas of Siberia and the north were, after the end of their sentences, illegally returning to their former places of residence, where they had become the "principal instigators of all sorts of anti-Soviet and diversionary crimes" in collective and state farms, on transport, and in several areas of industry. Stalin ordered local party and NKVD administrations to place all "returning kulaks and criminals" under surveillance and to prepare to arrest the "most hostile" among them, who would be immediately tried by NKVD troikas and sentenced to execution. The remaining "less active, yet still hostile elements" were to be registered in preparation for exile. Stalin ordered regional party committees to prepare separate estimates of the numbers of "kulaks" and criminals in each category within five days and to recommend to the Politburo the composition of the troikas.[52] The categories targeted by Stalin's instruction had precise and specific meanings for regional NKVD administrations, and they conformed exactly to the categories of marginalized individuals with which central and local NKVD officials had been concerned in the previous months. In fact, the Sovnarkom recommendations on the issue of criminal recidivists, discussed above, were forwarded to Stalin on July 2, 1937. Stalin's telegram was not intended to launch a process of indiscriminate repression by the NKVD; it was, rather, aimed specifically at cohorts of resettled peasants and criminals that, in Stalin and Ezhov's minds, might support a "fifth column" in the event of war.[53]

The initial reaction of local NKVD administrations to these orders, and the recommendations they made to the Politburo regarding the cohorts to be repressed, show that the local police generally understood Stalin's telegram as a signal to expand ongoing repressions of "criminals" and "kulak elements" rather than as a drastic change of course. Communist Party and NKVD administrations submitted the required estimates to the Politburo in early July, generally providing exact numbers for each of the four categories under consideration.[54] The relative weight of the categories to be repressed depended entirely on local circumstances; "kulaks" dominated the estimates in predominantly rural areas or areas that had been the destination of special settlers earlier in the 1930s, while "criminal elements" were the main target in urban areas. The Moscow Party Committee, for example, informed the Politburo that some 2,000 "kulaks" and 6,500 criminals in the region qualified for execution, and 5,869 "kulaks" and 26,936 criminals qualified for exile; the West Siberian Party slated 6,642 "kulaks" and 4,282 criminals for execution and 8,201 "kulaks" and 6,853 criminals for exile; and the party in the Avoz-Black Sea Territory targeted 5,721 "kulaks" and 923 criminals for execution and 5,914 "kulaks" and 1,048 criminals for exile. Forty out of sixty-four NKVD administrations were prepared to send such estimates to the Politburo immediately, suggesting that they had correctly understood previous policy signals regarding the registration of suspect population cohorts and had generated such estimates before Stalin's telegram arrived.[55]

At the same time, local NKVD and Communist Party officials began to influence the unfolding operations by making specific requests to Ezhov regarding the repression of categories that did not appear in Stalin's telegram. Party officials in the Far Eastern Territory, for example, requested authorization to sentence unruly camp inmates to execution; in

Azerbaidzhan, in addition to separate quotas for exile and executions of criminals and "kulaks," party officials requested the right to execute 500 and exile 750 individuals involved in "counterrevolutionary insurgent organizations" and to send to labor camps 150 "family bandit groups" (*semeistv bandgrup*). In the Orenburg region, the NKVD troika was authorized to exile the families of those "kulaks" and criminals that it repressed, a right generally not accorded to the NKVD in the initial weeks of the operation, while the troika in Uzbekistan was authorized to hear cases of "nationalist-terrorists" in addition to "kulaks" and criminals.[56] The most direct and pertinent request came on July 10 from the West Siberian NKVD chief, Mironov, who asked the Politburo to expand the authorization of the existing regional troika, which was already sentencing to death members of the "conspiracy" discussed above, to include "not only kulaks, but also all former people and White Guard/Socialist Revolutionary activists who are the organizers of this conspiracy"—that is, individuals beyond the strict categories of "kulaks" and "criminals" set down by Stalin's telegram.[57] These requests were specific and local, but they were generally approved by the Politburo and they eventually found their way, often using identical language, into the operational orders issued by the Politburo to local police administrations in the following months. Regional party leaders were willing and able to repress cohorts of kulaks and criminals but also had specific concerns that they wished to address with the same means; Stalin and Ezhov, almost without exception, were willing to comply.

In light of these developments, Stalin and Ezhov altered the nature of the impending operation substantially during the month of July. The Politburo approved the forty estimates sent in by regional Communist Party administrations before July 11, but on July 12, M. P. Frinovskii, Ezhov's deputy commissar, issued an order to all local NKVD chiefs forbidding them to begin the operations and summoning them to Moscow for an operational conference.[58] The delay was likely related to central concerns, including Ezhov's, that local officers were preparing to repress the wrong cohorts; estimates of registered kulaks and criminals suggested that regional NKVD administrations were targeting broad groups of criminals and rural marginals rather than "counterrevolutionary insurgent organizations," a charge that resonated with Ezhov's concern in the preceding months that the NKVD generally targeted "criminal elements" instead of spies or counterrevolutionaries. Ezhov sought to correct this misconception among regional NKVD chiefs in person, on July 16, exhorting them to target anti-Soviet groupings and insurgent organizations among kulaks, criminals, and ethnic minorities, including Poles and Germans. The operations, according to Ezhov, would target counterrevolution and insurgency, of which kulaks and criminals were the "social base," rather than targeting criminals and kulaks per se, as had the mass operations against "harmful elements" of 1935 and 1936.[59]

Once this operational conference was over, Stalin, Ezhov, and Frinovskii worked through the estimates sent in by the regional NKVD administrations, preparing final quotas for an operation that was set to begin at the end of the month. Although the Politburo initially approved the exact quotas sent to them by the regional administrations, in the process of reviewing the operations Stalin and Ezhov reduced the execution quotas for several regions, especially those that proposed comparatively high quotas for "criminals"—for example, Moscow from 8,500 (including 6,500 "criminals") to 5,000, and Western Siberia from 10,800 (including 4,200 "criminals") to 5,000. By the beginning of August, the Politburo had reduced the total number of approved executions for the forty regions that had sent in initial estimates before July 12 from 67,510 to 48,350; the number of proposed exiles, although increased in some areas and decreased in others, remained roughly the same (although these individuals were now to be sent to labor camps rather than exiled).[60] By changing these quotas, Stalin and Ezhov sought to make clear to local officials that the operation would be strictly controlled by the center; by reducing the number of executions in regions that had initially suggested comparatively high quotas of "criminals" and resettled peasants, they sought to bring the operation in line with their original intent, which was to target population cohorts that they deemed a threat in the event of war.[61]

The change in focus in mid-July 1937 was also the product of Stalin's concurrent decision to repress ethnic minorities that he deemed an immediate national security threat. At a Politburo meeting on July 20, just after the NKVD conference in Moscow but before final quota decisions were made, Stalin ordered Ezhov to arrest all Germans working in the defense, electrical, chemical, and building industries in all regions of the USSR, launching what became known as the "German operation." Five days later, Ezhov alerted NKVD administrations to the supposed existence of a conspiracy of German spies within the Soviet industrial system, coordinated by the German General Staff and the Gestapo, and he instructed the police to arrest all German citizens working in sensitive industrial agencies as well as all Soviet citizens and foreigners from other countries that had ties to German nationals. The beginning of this operation was set for July 30; after a week of arrests, Ezhov reported to Stalin that the NKVD had arrested 340 Germans, along with 95 Soviets and others involved in espionage.[62] As we will see, this "German operation" eventually expanded, as one of several operations against "national contingents" in 1937 and 1938, to target tens of thousands of individuals, German or not, suspected of spying and preparing for rebellion in the case of war. The fact that it was launched in late July, while Ezhov and Stalin were still working out the quotas for the upcoming operations against criminals and kulaks, underscores the importance of national security in Stalin's decision to turn to mass repressions in mid-1937.[63]

On July 30, 1937, Frinovskii, Ezhov's assistant, presented to Stalin a draft of an NKVD operational order, titled "Regarding Operations of Repression of Former Kulaks, Criminals, and Other Anti-Soviet Elements."[64] The Politburo approved Frinovskii's draft the next day, authorizing Ezhov to send the order, identified by its NKVD operational code 00447, to regional NKVD and Communist Party administrations and to begin the mass repressions that had been under preparation for the previous month. Order 00447 began by repeating the language of Stalin's telegram of July 2 regarding "escaped kulaks," but it expanded the target categories to include members of numerous other supposedly anti-Soviet political movements, church officials, former White officers, repatriates, and a range of other "anti-Soviet elements," all of whom, according to the order, remained "nearly untouched" in the countryside and, in many cases, had infiltrated industrial, transport, and construction sites as well. The order also expanded targets among "criminal elements," noting that substantial numbers of horse and cattle thieves, recidivists, and robbers had escaped from Soviet penal institutions and carried out criminal activity with impunity in both the countryside and in major cities. The order repeated Stalin's earlier claim that such individuals were the "chief instigators of every kind of anti-Soviet crime and sabotage" in all areas of Soviet industry and agriculture, and it ordered regional NKVD administrations to begin a four-month campaign that would "put an end, once and for all," to the counterrevolutionary activities of these suspect cohorts. The order then described in detail the procedures that local NKVD officers were to follow in arresting and sentencing individuals subject to repression. Finally, the order presented revised quotas of individuals subject to either execution ("Category I") or eight to ten years in a labor camp or prison ("Category II"); the latter category represented a fundamental change from the intentions outlined in the July 2 telegram, which referred only to execution or exile.[65] The separate regional quotas added up to a total of 268,950 "kulaks, criminals, and other anti-Soviet elements," including 75,950 executions, all of whom were to be processed through the local troikas that were approved by the Politburo in the month of July. Sentences of execution were to be carried out immediately. Regional Communist Party administrations were instructed that quotas could be raised only with the specific approval of the Politburo but could be lowered by NKVD chiefs. All existing evidence suggests that Stalin intended to maintain full control of the course of the operations, which were to last for exactly four months.[66]

The decision to launch the mass operations was Stalin's alone.[67] Existing archival documentation does not make clear at what point, or for what exact reasons, Stalin decided to order the NKVD to carry out not only mass arrests but also mass executions of "anti-Soviet elements"; this decision may well remain one of the mysteries of the twentieth century.[68] What is clear is that Stalin's turn toward mass repressions was related to several interconnected concerns regarding national minorities, "returning kulaks," "criminal elements," and prerevolutionary elites. Stalin decided to launch repressions against "German elements" precisely at the same time he was reconsidering the nature of the pending operation against "kulaks" and criminals in July 1937; he himself penned the blunt Politburo directive ordering the NKVD to arrest "all Germans." The explanation best supported by the available evidence is the one that corresponds to the goals expressed in Order 00447 itself: Stalin was concerned with the activities of a wide range of population groups in the event of war with Japan or Germany, and he launched the mass operations in 1937 to rid the country of the potential "social base" of insurrection, in the words of the order, "once and for all."

Despite the importance of Stalin's decision, the text of Order 00447, even with its apocalyptic descriptions of the dangers posed by "anti-Soviet elements," did not represent a fundamental change in police approaches to "kulaks" and "criminal elements." The structure of the operation was hardly new; it duplicated aspects of both the dekulakization drive and the repressions of "socially harmful elements" in the mid-1930s. Neither the Politburo nor local police administrations were confused regarding the targets of Order 00447; to the contrary, the text of the order referred to specific categories of suspects that were completely familiar to local NKVD administrations.[69] Much of the language of the order, furthermore, mirrored specific requests made by local NKVD and Communist Party officials in the process of submitting quota estimates in early July. Even the planned scale of the operation—entailing almost 270,000 arrests and 76,000 executions—was, though shocking on a humanitarian level, comparable to previous waves of Stalinist repressions.[70] Ultimately, the text of Stalin's order regarding "kulaks, criminals, and other anti-Soviet elements" was completely consistent with the nature of the Stalinist policing system as it existed in mid-1937. The local police, when they received the order, knew exactly what to do.[71]

The Mass Operations: Initial Implementation

NKVD Order 00447 marked the beginning of more than sixteen months of unrelenting police repressions of ex-convicts, dekulakized peasants, ethnic minorities, and other population groups deemed threatening by Stalin and Ezhov. In addition to the operations against "kulaks, criminals, and other anti-Soviet elements," Stalin launched a series of operations against Germans, Poles, and several other "national contingents" in late 1937 and early 1938. By the end of November 1938 these operations, taken together, resulted in the executions of some 683,000 individuals and the imprisonment of some 470,000 more.[72] Although Stalin began several of the "national operations" at roughly the same time that he issued Order 00447, the operations against "kulaks, criminals, and other anti-Soviet elements" initially exercised the most influence on the overall makeup of the campaign.[73] The operations against "anti-Soviet elements" took the form of previous mass operations against criminal and "socially dangerous" population cohorts; in urban areas, they relied on existing registration systems, including the internal passport system, while in rural areas they reprised aspects of the dekulakization drive of the early 1930s and mirrored the repressions of "kulak elements" that accompanied yearly harvest campaigns. These operations required little prompting or explanation from the center in their initial months of implementation. Local police quickly identified and repressed individuals who had been the targets of police surveillance and repression for the preceding several years, using tactics that were familiar to them from years of campaigns against the same "threatening" populations.

The month of planning and interaction between the center and the periphery in July 1937 allowed local NKVD officials ample time to prepare for the impending operations. Regional NKVD chiefs, after being briefed during their meeting with Ezhov in mid-July, returned home, recalled any policemen on leave, and organized conferences of city and district NKVD chiefs to discuss the structure of the campaign.[74] Regional NKVD administrations then gathered estimates of "kulak" and "criminal elements" from their subdepartments, a task that often involved little more than collating existing lists of individuals ineligible for a regime passport. Local *militsiia* officers also strove to expand their lists of suspects in the days before the operations began, categorizing petty criminals and ex-convicts as "anti-Soviet" and placing them under active surveillance. The Speculation Department (OBKhSS) of the West Siberian Territory, for example, reported on July 8 that it had identified 400 to 450 "hostile and criminal elements" working in the grain collection system, including suspect nationalities, former small-scale traders, former White officers, individuals previously deprived of voting rights, and ex-convicts sentenced for theft; 259 more such individuals had already been expelled and were under active surveillance. The Speculation Department also identified 200 ex-convicts in the city of Tomsk, released early from labor camps for good behavior and placed in jobs, as part of the cohort to be repressed.[75] The NKVD of the Western Region reported that, as of August 1, it had registered and was prepared to arrest 11,000 individuals, almost double the 6,000 arrests approved by Order 00447; the NKVD chief promised Ezhov that even more "counterrevolutionary elements" would be found with further investigation.[76] Local NKVD administrations were not overwhelmed with the requirements of the pending operations; to the contrary, they were generally prepared by the beginning of August to begin arrests and to meet, and in many cases to surpass, the quotas set out for them.

Order 00447, when distributed to regional NKVD and Communist Party administrations in early August, specified not only the targets of the operation but also the precise procedures to be followed and the structure of the local apparatus that was created to carry them out. The order instructed the regional NKVD chiefs to divide their areas into "operational sectors" and to create "operational groups" to implement the campaign, made up as a rule of experienced Chekists from regional NKVD administrations. These operational groups were in charge of planning, compiling lists of those to be arrested from information provided by local police administrations, and issuing arrest orders; they also coordinated investigations after arrests took place, extracting confessions and preparing case files for consideration by troikas.[77] Finally, the operational groups were responsible for finding suitable sites for mass graves and for carrying out executions once troika decisions were made, taking care to maintain the complete secrecy of the place and time of the executions, even from the rest of the NKVD apparatus.

These operational groups, which were the primary structural innovation in the NKVD system connected with the mass operations, were generally not responsible for identifying targets or carrying out initial investigations, although as we will see they did so in some cases, especially in the latter months of the campaigns. This structure separated the work of operational groups from the general work of NKVD administrations and, in the initial months of the operations, kept the bloodiest aspects of the mass operations separate from much of the daily work carried out by low-level NKVD and *militsiia* officers.[78]

In major urban areas, the mass operations in the fall of 1937 generally targeted "criminal elements" directly. Order 00447 provided an extensive list of the criminal cohorts to be repressed, including bandits, armed robbers, pocket thieves, and all professional or recidivist criminals; the police were to consider the extent to which individuals were "connected with the criminal milieu" when deciding whether to send their cases to the NKVD troikas. On August 7, as the mass operations began, Frinovskii ordered local police administrations to transfer all ongoing cases involving armed robbery, recidivism, organized criminal activity, and several other crimes characteristic of "socially harmful elements" to the new NKVD troikas. He also ordered local *militsiia* administrations to increase pressure on criminal cohorts as a whole, organizing additional patrols and sweeps of urban areas and sentencing "harmful" individuals to five years in labor camps using the standing police troikas, if they did not merit harsher punishment by the new NKVD troikas.[79]

Similarly, Belskii, the head of the *militsiia*, in early August ordered the railroad police administrations to create "operative groups" to purge the railways and train stations of "criminal elements." Belskii instructed the rail police chiefs to select young and energetic *militsiia* detectives or precinct inspectors to staff these teams, which were ordered to apprehend criminals and homeless children on the rail system, especially those involved in theft, robbery, and hooliganism, and to send their cases to the nearest territorial NKVD "Operative Sector" for sentencing by the NKVD troikas.[80] The repression of "criminal elements," then, was not a product of local concerns or a diversion of the campaign toward targets important only to local police; it represented a primary part of Stalin and Ezhov's goal to repress "threatening" population cohorts in all sectors of Soviet society, and it engaged the *militsiia* directly in the mass operations alongside local political police officers.

Urban police administrations carried out repressions of "criminal elements" in the fall of 1937 in ways that duplicated earlier mass operations, especially the operations against violent criminals and "socially harmful elements" of 1935 and 1936. The police in Moscow, for example, responded aggressively to Order 00447, arresting 2,271 "criminals" out of a total of 3,668 individuals by August 15. The Moscow NKVD chief, S. F. Redens, took pains, in reporting his progress to Ezhov, to show that the repressions of "kulak elements" had broken up organized insurgencies that were actively preparing to rebel against Soviet power, yet he made no similar attempt to justify the arrests of "criminal elements."[81] The Moscow police continued what they referred to as a "removal [*iz'iatie*] of socially harmful elements" from the region through the fall of 1937, targeting individuals who had previous convictions but generally lived without incident since their release from penal institutions. The quotation with which this chapter began, for example, refers to an individual, K., who had worked in Moscow for the newspaper *Komsomolskaia Pravda* since his early release for exemplary behavior from a camp in early 1937. K. was called to a precinct police station on October 29 and charged with being a "socially harmful element" due to six prior arrests and two sentences for theft. His mother, appealing to the precinct police chief with information to the effect that K. had a job, a place of residence, and proper residence paperwork, reports that she was told: "He is a thief and a robber, and we are purging Moscow." K. was sentenced in late November 1937 to eight years in a labor camp for "connections with the criminal milieu."[82]

Anecdotal evidence from other areas shows the same basic pattern. In a case from Leningrad, a collective farm worker, who had been arrested and expelled from the city in November 1937 for failing to obtain the proper documents from her collective farm before traveling to the city, was apprehended by the Leningrad police in December of the same year, again without the proper documents. She claimed that she had returned only to collect her belongings, but she was apprehended at one of the city's open air markets attempting to sell a single item of clothing (a child's raincoat), and hence the Leningrad regional police troika sentenced her to three years in a labor camp as a "socially harmful element."[83] The police in the Chechen-Ingushetian Republic, according to a postterror Procuracy review, targeted individuals for crimes as petty as pocket theft or apartment burglary, even in the absence of any evidence of recidivism or connections to the criminal milieu; as a rule, the *militsiia* sent all criminal cases under its jurisdiction to the NKVD troika throughout the mass operations, most of which resulted in sentences of execution.[84] The assistant *militsiia* chief of the city of Saratov, under investigation in 1940 for his role in the mass operations, provided a similar picture of local police activity in an extensive explanation of his own actions in the fall of 1937:

> Among other work in 1937 we carried out a cleansing of the city and the region of criminal elements according to the NKVD Order No. 00447. It is necessary to note that not only did neither I nor my subordinates read Order No. 447 itself, but we did not even see it, we fulfilled the written and verbal orders, with references to the Order, that the head of the regional NKVD gave to us. . . . The basic instruction was to produce as many cases as possible, to formulate them as quickly as possible, with maximum simplification of investigation. As regards the quota of cases, [the NKVD chief] demanded [the inclusion of] all those sentenced and all those that had been picked up, even if at the moment of their arrest they had not committed any sort of concrete crime.[85]

The assistant chief also recounted in detail the investigative process in Saratov: the police sent cases from all areas of the region to the Detective Department of the *militsiia*, rather than one of the NKVD operative sectors that was created by Order 00447, where they were prepared for review, approved in batches, and sent to the Saratov NKVD troika for adjudication. Although the local *militsiia* administrations prepared individual case files, the Saratov Detective Department often rewrote the files to "improve" both their language and their content. The cases in question clearly pertained to criminals, although it is impossible to tell if they were sentenced under one of the commonly used sections of Article 58 of the Criminal Code, such as counterrevolutionary agitation or terrorism. The particular case about which the police chief was being questioned, for example, concerned an individual, K., who was arrested on August 23, 1937, as part of a sweep of Saratov of "criminal elements." K. had three previous sentences for hooliganism in 1935 and 1936, had "maintained connections with the criminal milieu," and was suspected of robbing drunks on city streets. A judicial review after the end of the mass operations concluded that police put little effort into determining the identities of the "unknown criminal elements" and that K.'s crime was not "concrete." As in Moscow, however, previous convictions were enough to qualify him as a "socially dangerous element," and the Saratov regional NKVD troika sentenced him to death.[86]

Throughout the fall of 1937, the police in urban areas freely mixed the mass operations with ongoing campaigns against "criminal elements," suppressing all categories of suspect criminals and sending their cases to NKVD troikas for rapid and absolute adjudication.[87] Local police targeted full-time traders and speculators in open air markets who were familiar from past investigations or personal experience on the streets, sentencing them through regional police troikas as a matter of course.[88] "Kulak elements" were swept up in purges of urban areas as well, as the police combed their lists of registered suspects and ex-convicts for individuals who had left the countryside and been accorded the right to live in nonregime locations but who were under surveillance. Yet such activity differed little from ongoing work by local police in support of the internal passport system, including the sentencing practices of police troikas in 1935 and 1936. Local police did attempt to shape the sentencing procedures to meet local needs; in some areas, NKVD chiefs funneled "criminal elements" to the police troikas in order to reserve execution and camp quotas for more serious cases, while in others NKVD administrations freely transferred individuals from the police troikas to the NKVD troikas for harsher sentences.[89]

The police troikas also sentenced between 200,000 and 400,000 individuals in 1937 and 1938 to labor camps (in many cases to terms longer than five years, even though they were not authorized to do so) alongside the NKVD troikas, a number completely consistent with the work of these extrajudicial bodies in 1935 and 1936.[90] Ultimately, the repression of criminal elements in the fall of 1937 represented the culmination of urban policing trends over the previous years: local police removed, "once and for all," the criminals and urban marginals whom they had viewed as the primary cause of urban disorder since the end of the 1920s.

Police activity in rural areas during the initial weeks of the mass operations naturally focused on "kulak elements," but it followed many of the same patterns as police actions in cities. Rural operations were complicated by the fact that the NKVD maintained a substantially smaller network of officers in the countryside, forcing operative groups to rely more heavily on local *militsiia* and Communist Party administrations to provide cases for regional troikas. The form of the operation, however, was largely the same: NKVD administrations identified "kulak and criminal elements" based on existing information, generally without substantial help from local residents or collective farmers themselves. Local NKVD organizations often targeted those "kulaks" who had been internally exiled during the dekulakization drive and remained in the area, either as individual or collective farmers. For example, NKVD officials from the

Western Region began a report on mass operations in early August with the statement that the original dekulakization drive had repressed only 5,000 of the 22,000 kulak households in the area; the remainder, exiled internally, were now disrupting local administration alongside the "return-ees" identified by Order 00447 as the focus of the campaign. Although the police claimed to have uncovered large-scale "kulak-insurgent" conspiracies of a hundred or more participants among dekulakized peasants, the mere existence of this group of "kulaks" in the countryside was enough to justify police actions against them; they were conceptualized as the potential social base of insurrectionary organizations and targeted as such.[91]

Ezhov himself, in a report to Stalin on the initial weeks of the mass operations, demonstrated this same combination of rhetorical stress on counterrevolutionary organizations and practical concern with the mere existence of marginal cohorts in the countryside. Ezhov provided lengthy explanations of the various diversionary activities in which former kulaks and anti-Soviet elements supposedly engaged, yet he also focused on the more mundane and concrete activities of these "active counterrevolutionary contingents" in the countryside, including the spoilage of grain, disruption of harvest campaigns, killing of cattle, and agitation against the collective farm system in general. Such problems, of course, were rife in the collective farm system in 1937, in large part because of the disastrous harvest season of the previous year. Ezhov, in attributing these problems to a specific, identifiable cohort of rural marginals, was both following the rhetorical script he had devised for the mass operations and repeating the explanations of difficulties in the agricultural system that had become commonplace among local NKVD administrations by 1937.[92]

The course of the mass operations in the village of Sokolskoe, in the Lipetskii district of the Voronezh region, underscores these issues, showing the way that *militsiia* officers worked alongside political policemen to select targets in ways that conformed to both local needs and central rhetoric. In June 1938 several women from Sokolskoe sent a complaint to Kalinin, protesting the false denunciation and arrest of seventeen men by the *militsiia* in the village in late 1937. A Procuracy team sent to investigate found that, to the contrary, the repressed individuals had been targeted by the police because of their personal histories, either as former kulaks or ex-convicts. Six of the men were investigated by the political police as "kulak elements"; all six, according to the Procuracy review, were former kulaks or children of kulaks who had been sentenced previously to exile or banishment and had returned after serving out their sentences.

All six were charged with "concrete" criminal activity in the form of "anti-Soviet agitation against the policies of the Soviet government," and all six were sentenced under Article 58 by the regional NKVD troika. The remaining eleven men were investigated by the *militsiia*, rather than the political police, as "socially harmful elements." The review concluded that these individuals were involved with "thievery, malicious hooliganism, led a criminal lifestyle," and that all had multiple past offenses, spent time in prison or labor camps, and retained "contacts with the criminal milieu"—in the context of such a small village, presumably with each other. Several of the repressed were related pairs, perhaps father and son but more likely brothers. The Procuracy's review concluded that the complaint that these sentences had been based on false denunciations was entirely unfounded, as they were not based on denunciations at all. The local *militsiia* and political police officers in Sokolskoe had followed Order 00447 to the letter, repressing the exact cohorts targeted by Ezhov's order.[93]

The police in rural areas, as in cities, began to mix the mass operations with ongoing administrative activities almost immediately after Order 00447 was promulgated, especially activities related to the harvest and procurement campaigns. Numerous areas of the USSR, still reeling from the effects of famine in the winter of 1936–37, experienced initial difficulties with the harvest in the late summer, prompting local officials to sound the alarm in July regarding the possibility of severe shortages to follow. Fearful of a repeat of the previous year, the Politburo intervened to support the collective farm system, releasing substantial quantities of grain to areas experiencing shortages in July and eventually reducing grain delivery targets in affected areas.[94] These measures initially failed to improve the harvest and collection campaigns; local officials continued to send dire reports to Moscow through the end of August, warning of failing procurement drives and burgeoning shortages of food in many areas. Stalin responded to these difficulties by launching widespread repressions of Communist Party and state officials in the collective farm and grain procurement administrations, ordering local NKVD and justice officials to stage show trials of "wreckers" within these administrations in all regions of the country in order to explain to the population the causes of yet another year of scarce consumer goods and to garner support from the rural population for the repression of these elites.[95]

Local show trials, like administrative pressure on the peasantry in general, were hardly new to the rural police in 1937, but the context of the mass operations changed local responses to the harvest campaign substantially. NKVD reports in July and August included numerous references to poor grain storage and transport, theft, and "kulak agitation" against the collective farm system—explanations of harvest difficulties that would not have been out of place during any fall harvest drive in the 1930s. For example, in August the West Siberian NKVD forwarded reports to R. I. Eikhe, the Communist Party boss of the territory, which carefully negotiated between the vocabulary promoted by the center and meaningful explanations of local conditions. According to the NKVD, shortages in the area were the result of an overly "bureaucratic" approach by regional grain procurement administrations, and of the fact that ongoing repressions produced "moods of panic" among local officials. Yet harvest difficulties were also supposedly the result of "counterrevolutionary activities of Trotskyites, Rightists, Socialist Revolutionaries, religious monarchists, kulak and other anti-Soviet elements" who sabotaged the gathering and delivery of grain in order to weaken the Soviet state.[96] As the mass operations unfolded, the Politburo and central NKVD officials promoted the latter explanation, positing direct conceptual connections between the harvest campaign and "diversionary activity" and encouraging the local police to situate their attempts to support the harvest in the context of ongoing campaigns to repress "anti-Soviet elements."[97]

Regional NKVD administrations, responding to these central cues, tied together the mass operations and the grain procurement campaign in the fall of 1937, targeting huge organizations that supposedly disrupted agriculture in the service of foreign governments. The NKVD in Western Siberia, for example, in late August reported uncovering a vast "Siberian church-monarchist counterrevolutionary conspiracy" that supposedly carried out direct sabotage of the collective farm system, disrupting the harvest campaign, wrecking farm machinery, and lowering labor discipline in order to aid foreign powers in the event of war. As of August 20, the NKVD arrested some 500 participants in this organization, plus another 300 connected to a similar organization called the "Council for the Salvation of Russia."[98] The West Siberian NKVD repeated this explanation of agricultural difficulties two weeks later, reporting the harvest was fulfilled only to 38 percent of the plan and denigrating the "counterrevolutionary theories" of grain procurement officials who suggested that the slow tempo was caused by objective conditions, like a lack of draft animals or gasoline, rather than by the organized diversionary activity of massive anti-Soviet conspiracies.[99] The center, in turn, reinforced the idea that the grain procurement campaign could be improved by repressing cohorts of "anti-Soviet elements." The Central Militsiia Administration, for example, warned local speculation departments in November 1937 that the cooperative grain-purchasing campaign was far behind schedule and ordered them to augment standard administrative pressure on the peasantry with broad purges of "anti-Soviet elements" in local procurement administrations.[100] These direct conceptual connections between grain procurement and the mass operations did little to improve the delivery of agricultural products to the state in 1937, but they ensured that local police would be able to identify and repress larger cohorts of the population as the fall wore on, even after the original lists of "kulaks" and "criminal elements" under police surveillance had been exhausted in the initial weeks of the campaign.

In both urban and rural areas, the mass operations of 1937 and 1938 were essentially police operations, exhibiting little of the reliance on denunciations or other forms of popular participation that were characteristic of concurrent Communist Party and elite purges, and of the dekulakization drive earlier in the decade. Mass operations in urban areas were carried out exclusively by the police, both civil and political, who generally did not seek help from the population in identifying and arresting targets.[101] Even the Police Assistance Brigades—the groups of volunteers that patrolled city streets and had been assigned specific policing duties during the 1935 campaigns against violent crime—were restricted to standard patrolling duties in public areas during the mass operations.[102] In the Turkmen Republic, for example, the Third Department of the NKVD, responsible for carrying out arrests of "anti-Soviet elements" in urban areas, responded to Order 00447 by initiating raids and sweeps of open air markets in major cities like Ashgabad; NKVD officers, according to a Procuracy review of their actions, took into account "neither the age, nor the past or current activities" of the individuals arrested but simply targeted everyone unfortunate enough to be at the market on a given day. "Suspicious" characteristics as petty as a long beard were enough to trigger arrest as a "mullah" (a term referring to an Islamic cleric). Beatings and torture often followed, as NKVD officers attempted to coerce confessions and provide sufficient paperwork to support subsequent troika decisions.[103]

Denunciations from the population at large played a relatively minor role in the process. Regional NKVD administrations often reported to the center denunciations from collective farmers of "kulak elements" as proof of the dubious assertion that the Soviet population responded positively to mass arrests in August and September 1937, but the police generally relied on more direct means of identifying targets—including, once the operations were under way, the common practice of coercing denunciations from arrested individuals by torture, which could produce dozens or even hundreds of names.[104] Local NKVD administrations encouraged popular participation in the rural show trials that were staged throughout the country in August and September 1937, but they generally declined to involve collective farmers directly in the process of selecting targets for the mass operations.[105] The sheer speed with which the mass operations took place—by August 15, over 100,000 individuals had already been arrested—suggests that denunciations and covert investigations were largely irrelevant.[106] Passive support for the mass operations, or a lack of overt resistance, was all that was required.[107]

Stalin and Ezhov did not intend the mass operations to rely on the initiative of local NKVD administrations any more than on popular activism, and they took several steps in the first weeks of the operations 1937 to ensure that local police followed their explicit or implicit guidelines regarding the cohorts to be targeted. Even though Order 00447 widened Stalin's original focus on "kulak and criminal elements" to include numerous categories of "anti-Soviet elements," local administrations understood that the order did not give them blanket authorization to repress all supposed "enemies." Most obviously, existing practices regarding the repression of Communist Party members and high-level state officials remained in place. Arrests of party members generally took place only after they were expelled by relevant party bodies, even at the local level, while any arrests of party officials appointed directly by the Central Committee took place only after Stalin gave his personal approval.[108]

Yet even outside the party elite, the local NKVD administrations did not expand their actions beyond the cohorts listed in Order 00447 without first seeking specific approval from the center, and Ezhov and Stalin did not always comply. Within days of the beginning of the operation, for example, NKVD officials in the Udmurt Republic requested permission from Ezhov to add religious figures (*tsirkovniki i sektanti*), as a category, to the targets of the operations. Ezhov demurred, citing the specific language of his operational order: "If religious figures in your area are carrying out counterrevolutionary activities, then they are subject to arrest in general order and transfer to the courts. . . . If, on the other hand, they belong to insurrectionary, terrorist, fascist or bandit groups (point 3 of part 1 of the Instruction [00447]), then they are subject to repression in the first or second category." Approvals, however, were more common. In mid-September, for example, Stalin and Ezhov approved a request by the NKVD in the Far Eastern Territory to repress "Trotskyites" serving sentences in labor camps using the regional NKVD troika; in mid-October, a request from the party secretary of Turkmenistan to repress some 2,000 "mullahs and bais" (the term *bai* was the equivalent of "kulak") who had joined collective farms after returning to the USSR from Iran and Afghanistan; and in mid-November, a request from Sverdlovsk to execute individuals guilty of diversionary acts on the Kaganovich railroad line.[109] In all these cases, the "anti-Soviet" nature of the individuals was not in question, but local NKVD administrations did not assume that such cohorts automatically fell under the jurisdiction of the NKVD troikas or the mass operations.

Such distinctions were particularly clear in a request made by Lavrentii Beria, the Georgian Communist Party boss and future head of the NKVD, to Stalin in late October. Beria complained that, although the Georgian NKVD had arrested more than 12,000 individuals over the course of 1937, nearly 5,000 of them were currently held in NKVD prisons, awaiting sentencing. The Georgian NKVD troika had already sentenced 5,236 individuals (just over the quota of 5,000 set at the beginning of August), and the Military Collegium of the USSR Supreme Court, the NKVD Special Board, military tribunals, and various other courts had sentenced 2,138 more. Beria complained that the Military Collegium, which generally handled "political" cases involving state and party elites, had sentenced only 910 individuals for the entire year, causing severe overcrowding in the prison system. He asked Stalin to approve the transfer of cases of participants in Trotskyite and "rightist" organizations—two distinct categories of offenders that did not fall under Order 00447—to the NKVD troika for sentencing, a request that the Politburo approved in early 1938.[110] The issue at hand was not whether these 5,000 individuals were likely to face repression but how quickly the repression would take place, whether they could be sentenced by the NKVD troika as part of the mass operations, and how long they would crowd Beria's prison system. Stalin and Ezhov had been careful to specify the nature of the operations and the categories to be targeted, and the local NKVD and party administrations responded by following orders as closely as possible.

Stalin and Ezhov likewise strove to maintain strict control over the number of executions taking place in the initial months of the mass operations.

Regional NKVD administrations correctly understood the quotas issued as part of Order 00447 as temporary limits on the sentencing ability of the NKVD troikas, yet they also knew that they were to act within these limits until they were increased by the center. Ezhov stressed this procedure even before the operations began, instructing local NKVD administrations to arrest the more "embittered, active kulaks and socially dangerous criminals" that were uncovered during the month of July, in the process of preparing for the mass operations, but to refrain from sentencing any of them until the Politburo formally launched the operation and approved the quotas.[111] Local NKVD administrations followed this basic pattern throughout the first weeks of the operations, arresting far more individuals than stipulated by their quotas but sentencing within the guidelines set by the center and, in many cases, immediately requesting additional quotas from Ezhov.

The Politburo approved some of these requests but delayed others for weeks or even months, underscoring Stalin's desire to control the overall number of sentences throughout the course of the operations. In Western Siberia, an area for which the Politburo initially approved 10,800 executions in early July but allowed only 5,000 under Order 00447, Mironov, the NKVD chief, wrote to Ezhov immediately after the operations began with a request to raise the quota to the original figure. Mironov noted that the NKVD in his region, as of August 5, had identified 12,686 individuals that warranted execution and had already executed 1,254 of them. Ezhov refused the request, ordering Mironov to continue to make arrests but to refrain from carrying out executions until higher quotas were approved by the Politburo.[112] Stalin did approve several substantial quota expansions in late August, including requests from the NKVD of the Omsk region for an increase from 1,000 to 8,000 executions; from the Krasnoiarsk region, from 750 to 7,350 executions; and from the Orenburg region, from 1,500 to 3,500 executions.[113] These quota expansions added to the total number of individuals repressed in the first wave of the mass operations but did not change their nature in any meaningful way.

The initial weeks of the campaign, from all the available evidence, occurred without confusion, chaos, or unintended consequences.[114] Ezhov, reporting to Stalin on the results of the first month of the campaign, sounded an entirely positive note. He informed Stalin that the "blow" against counterrevolution had been delivered accurately by the NKVD, striking the "most hostile elements" in agriculture, transport, and industry. He added that collective farmers greeted the "cleansing" of the countryside with

approval, and that urban purges had led to substantial decreases in robbery and theft. As of September 1, 1937, the police had arrested 146,225
individuals nationwide, including 69,172 former "kulaks," 41,603 criminals, and 35,454 "other anti-Soviet elements." The NKVD troikas had
sentenced 31,530 people to death and 13,669 to labor camps. Ezhov also
maintained that Category II arrests had taken place correctly in August,
even though he had not approved the beginning of operations against individuals slated for labor camps in all areas; individuals not deemed sufficiently dangerous to execute were held for future sentencing, proving, for
central officials, that the executions were correctly targeting the "most
hostile" counterrevolutionaries and that the local NKVD administrations
were following the center's directives. Ezhov concluded that the campaign
against the "most hostile" elements was an unqualified success: "In general, the operation has been carried out calmly, at this time with no excesses that deserve consideration."[115] The mass operations, as we will see,
were far from over, but Ezhov's conclusion that their first weeks had gone
according to plan was largely correct.

The mass operations against "anti-Soviet elements" were hardly models of bureaucratic efficiency, yet the Soviet policing system was, by 1937,
completely capable of carrying them out to the standards demanded by
the center. The implementation of these orders varied substantially from
region to region, and between urban and rural areas, but all the available
evidence suggests that local and central officials were in agreement about
the nature of the cohorts to be repressed and the procedures to be followed. The local NKVD and *militsiia* administrations were not at a loss as
to how to carry out these operations; the orders they received were consistent with long-standing policing practices, especially the use of passport
and registration systems to control geographic mobility and the mass operations in urban areas in the previous several years. The speed with which
the police were able to arrest hundreds of thousands of suspect individuals within weeks of the promulgation of Order 00447 shows that fundamental changes in the nature of police work were not required, in contrast
to the chaos and confusion that characterized initial OGPU efforts during
the dekulakization drive.

In both city and countryside, the local police conceptualized the mass
operations as the final stage of the social transformations that had begun
years before: the final purging from society of the "kulak elements" that
had been incompletely removed in the early 1930s, or the removal of inherently "dangerous" criminal cohorts that the police viewed as the primary

cause of urban crime throughout the mid-1930s.[116] Although central and local officials differed on the nature of the threat to society posed by these "kulaks, criminals, and other anti-Soviet elements," they agreed that their removal, "once and for all," was a necessary part of the drive to secure social and political order in the Soviet Union.

The "National Operations" and "Anti-Soviet Elements" in 1937

Although questions of foreign infiltration and insurgency were muted in the initial weeks of the operations against "kulak" and "criminal elements," Stalin's orders in late July to arrest German citizens working in defense and other key industries provided a hint of a new policy direction to come. In the fall of 1937, Stalin ordered the NKVD to begin mass arrests and executions of several specific "national contingents"—individuals who were connected, by ethnicity, citizenship, personal relationship or insinuation, to hostile foreign governments, especially Poland, Germany, and Japan. These "national operations," as they were termed, were carried out in several waves during 1937 and 1938, resulting in the arrest of roughly 335,000 individuals, 247,157 of whom were sentenced to execution.[117]

The "national operations," unlike the operations against "anti-Soviet elements," had little precedent in policing activity, and local administrations had little sense of what was required; hence, central NKVD and Communist Party officials were forced to provide detailed and repeated instructions to local administrations in order to control the course of these repressions. Although the two sets of operations targeted conceptually separate categories of the population, they overlapped substantially in implementation, sharing similar arrest mechanisms and, at times, sentencing procedures. As a result, local NKVD administrations utilized the familiar strategies associated with Order 00447 to deal with the unfamiliar task of purging population cohorts defined by nationality. The converse was true as well; the "national operations," once under way, shaped the nature of the operations against "anti-Soviet elements," bringing the issue of espionage and conspiracy to the center of police repressions of "kulaks" and criminals by the end of 1937. After several months of intertwined activity at the local level, the national operations made the anti-Soviet operations far more deadly; both continued well into 1938, pushing Stalin's initial quota of just under 76,000 executions upward into the realm of one of the most immense waves of mass repressions in modern European history.

Stalin's order targeting German citizens and refugees in mid-July 1937, discussed above, was the first sign that he intended to launch mass operations against specific ethnicities. On August 9, the Politburo authorized a much broader operation against "Polish diversionary-espionage groups," setting the pattern for the wave of "national operations" that followed. Ezhov's orders to the NKVD, sent out two days later, outlined a new kind of operation against populations suspected of having ties with Polish intelligence agencies. Ezhov reported that Polish intelligence agents, in contact with a widespread conspiracy calling itself the "Polish Military Organization" (POV), had carried out diversionary and intelligence work in the USSR "basically untouched" for two decades. He argued that, although the NKVD had recently arrested many of the POV's leaders, tens of thousands of spies and collaborators from within the Soviet population remained at large. Ezhov ordered the NKVD to begin a three-month operation against the POV that was to result in the "complete liquidation" of both the POV and, in Ezhov's words, the "principal human contingents of Polish intelligence in the USSR."[118] The focus on mass repressions within the Soviet population, both of individuals of Polish descent and of collaborators within the non-Polish population, was clear in Ezhov's order: he instructed the NKVD administrations to arrest, in addition to suspected participants in the POV, refugees from Poland, all former Polish prisoners of war remaining in the USSR since World War I, members or former members of Polish nationalist parties, and the "more active anti-Soviet and nationalist elements" in regions populated by Poles—categories similar in essence to the social "base" of diversionary activity that was targeted by Order 00447.

The arrest and sentencing procedures during the Polish operation duplicated many of the practices associated with Order 00447, with several important exceptions. Local NKVD administrations identified targets and carried out initial investigations, while "operative groups" coordinated investigations, carried out interrogations, and prepared cases for extrajudicial sentencing. Short descriptions of completed cases in a given operative sector were forwarded every ten days to a two-person panel, consisting of the republic- or regional-level NKVD chief and the corresponding procurator, who separated the cases into Category I or II sentences, as under Order 00447. These panels then forwarded lists of cases to Moscow for approval by Ezhov and Vyshinsky, a process referred to in internal police documents as the "album procedure," after the albums in which lists of cases were collected. The operative groups carried out the sentences at the periphery only after receiving approval at the center.[119] Stalin specified no quotas for the Polish operation; he intended the "album procedure," which resembled the lists of Communist Party members and state elites sent to Moscow for his personal approval before their executions, to maintain some degree of central control over an operation that was new to local and central police alike.

To carry out the Polish operation, local NKVD administrations required a substantial amount of explanation and prompting from the center regarding what was an entirely unfamiliar task. Most political police officers had little experience identifying the "human contingents of Polish intelligence in the USSR," save those that participated in the purges of western border regions in 1935 and 1936 as part of the implementation of the internal passport system.[120] The passport system provided some assistance to NKVD officers in uncovering "Polish elements," yet until April 1938 an individual's nationality was entered into their passport on the basis of their own self-identification, making it impossible for the police to rely on passports to uncover "hidden" enemies.[121] Most local NKVD administrations, furthermore, had no idea how to identify non-Polish collaborators, because this cohort, unlike "kulaks" or criminals, had been completely absent from their work in the preceding years.[122] Ezhov understood this problem, and he thus sent a lengthy letter explaining the history of the POV since 1914, and the efforts of the NKVD to combat it, to all regional NKVD chiefs at the beginning of the operation. This letter ran to thirty pages and undoubtedly made for dry reading in the provinces; it was clearly intended to explain to the local NKVD administrations the nature of an operation that had little precedent in the history of Soviet policing.[123]

The Polish operation became the basis for two additional major, and several lesser, "lines" of national operations (the term used to describe them in internal NKVD documents). In September, Stalin ordered an operation against "Kharbin returnees," that is, employees of the Chinese Eastern Railway who had returned to the USSR when the railway was sold to the Manchukuo authorities in 1935. The NKVD estimated that some 25,000 Kharbin returnees had re-immigrated to the USSR with the intention of spying and committing diversionary acts for Japan; by the end of 1938 almost 54,000 individuals had been arrested as part of this operation for supposed contact with Japanese espionage agencies.[124] Later in the fall of 1937, the Politburo expanded the "German operation" along the same lines, targeting not only German citizens but also Soviets of

German descent, former prisoners of war, employees of German firms, and others with direct or indirect contacts with Germans or Germany itself, and sentencing them using the procedures set out for the "Polish operation." Similar, though smaller, operations followed in late 1937 and early 1938 against Latvians, Estonians, Finns, Greeks, Romanians, Iranians, the wives of "traitors to the motherland," and others, each based on specific NKVD orders and each targeting populations deemed a threat in time of war.[125]

Local NKVD administrations initially responded to the national operations only haltingly. The head of the Orenburg regional NKVD, for example, reported to the center that, as of September 3, his officers had arrested 160 "Polish spies and insurgents," mostly Polish refugees. Although he provided a lengthy description of the POV activity uncovered in his area and promised that he could have 100 additional cases ready for Ezhov's consideration by mid-September, these figures hardly compare with the 3,500 sentences of execution that the regional troika had handed out against "kulaks, criminals, and anti-Soviet elements" by the end of August.[126] Ezhov reported to Stalin in mid-September that, as of September 10, the NKVD had arrested 23,216 individuals in the Polish operation across the USSR, including 7,651 in Ukraine and 4,124 in Belorussia. Stalin seems to have been pleased with the progress of the operation; his approving note to Ezhov regarding "Polish filth," with which this chapter began, was handwritten on Ezhov's report.[127]

Yet Ezhov complained to his subordinates at the same time that the operations had stalled, and he ordered them to speed up the investigation and sentencing of cases in progress.[128] On November 3, he chastised his regional chiefs for the same problems via telegram, complaining that the ongoing operations against "anti-Soviet elements, Germans, Poles, Kharbin returnees, and wives of traitors to the motherland," especially the German operation, were being carried out "at an extremely slow pace" in numerous regions. Shortly thereafter, he ordered the local NKVD administrations to repress the "German contingent" according to the same guidelines used for the Polish operation in order to speed up arrests and the processing of cases.[129] For most of these local NKVD administrations, the national operations in the early fall of 1937 were understood as an expansion of the operations against "anti-Soviet elements" and were secondary to the task of filling the quotas set for them by the Politburo.

The national operations, although less important for NKVD work in 1937 than they would be in 1938, were nonetheless crucial in shaping the nature of the unfolding mass operations in general. Even though the threat of contacts between foreign agents and domestic counterrevolutionary contingents had been key to central discussions of NKVD work since at least the beginning of 1937, such concepts played a relatively small role in the initial wave of operations against "anti-Soviet elements." Stalin's July 2 telegram made no mention of large-scale conspiracies, and the exchanges between center and periphery on the proposed quotas for the operation likewise concentrated on population cohorts deemed threatening in essence rather than in action. Order 00447, furthermore, contained no requirements, technical or conceptual, that forced local NKVD administrations to explain mass arrests in terms of huge nationwide conspiracies. It was the process of "scripting" the national operations, and in particular the exchange of narratives between center and periphery regarding the POV conspiracy, that prompted the local police to move from targeting suspect cohorts as potential supporters of insurgencies in time of war to targeting a much broader range of individuals as supposed active participants in counterrevolutionary organizations.

When the regional Communist Party and NKVD organizations received Ezhov's letter on the POV on August 11, they understood it as a template for their own efforts to repress the "Polish contingent," sending reports to the center in the following weeks that duplicated the form and content of Ezhov's account. The NKVD chief in the Urals region, for example, reported to Ezhov on August 16 that arrests of highly placed party and military officials in the area had uncovered a "Urals Insurrectionary HQ" that united Trotskyites, Rightists, Socialist Revolutionaries, White officers, and clergy in an organization that was preparing for an armed uprising. This report provided a history of the organization, dating back to 1925, and claimed that the conspirators had organized quasi-military divisions of insurrectionary troops and were prepared to launch biological and chemical attacks, including the spreading of cholera and anthrax, in the event of war. This NKVD chief apparently underestimated the extent to which his report conformed exactly to the issues that Ezhov and Stalin considered most urgent. Stalin, after reading the report, wrote a note on it to Ezhov to the effect that the NKVD was acting too "sluggishly" in this case, adding: "It is necessary to arrest *immediately* all (both minor and major) participants in this 'insurrectionary group' in the *Urals*."[130]

The NKVD administration in the Sverdlovsk region sent in a similar report in late August regarding a German insurrectionary organization that had supposedly carried out diversionary and counterintelligence operations since 1930, organizing small cells of agents that lived quietly in the USSR for years but were prepared to carry out attacks in the event of war.[131] By October, the Sverdlovsk NKVD had completed the narrative history of this organization, forwarding to Stalin a lengthy description of a long-standing fascist military conspiracy that maintained active connections to counterrevolutionary conspiracies in other regions and professed the goal of creating a Nazi-style military-fascist dictatorship in the event of war with Germany. The report ran to a dozen pages, duplicating the tone and nearly the length of Ezhov's letter on the POV, but it left out the most important information: the NKVD chief had failed to provide any arrest figures, an omission that evidently irked Stalin, who wrote to Ezhov that the report was "strange," did not provide any indication of who had been arrested and who had not, and gave the "impression of a newspaper article."[132]

The vocabulary of diversion and insurgency was common at the center from early 1937—for example, in Ezhov and Stalin's speeches to the February–March Plenum—but it was only after the launching of the national operations that local NKVD administrations began to produce the same explanatory tropes. These texts were not simply a means for local NKVD officials to provide Ezhov with the type of information he demanded; they were also part of an exchange between center and periphery that allowed local NKVD officials to be sure that they were carrying out the national operations correctly, and that allowed the center to make clear to officers at the periphery how operations that supposedly targeted "diversionary" activity could be directed at cohorts of ex-kulaks, ex-convicts, and other individuals living on the margins of Soviet society.

The conceptual connections between the repression of "kulak and criminal elements" and the supposed existence of foreign-controlled conspiracies were particularly clear in Western Siberia, where regional NKVD officials manufactured their own major "insurgent" organization in the summer and fall of 1937. It is quite possible that the region's NKVD chiefs—Mironov and, after mid-August 1937, G. F. Gorbach—were more sadistic than their colleagues, but it is also true that Western Siberia, with its substantial populations of exiles, ex-convicts, and fugitives, was fertile ground for the expansion of the campaigns against "anti-Soviet elements" and that Mironov and Gorbach were particularly adept at interpreting signals from the center in 1937.[133] The issue of a large-scale counterrevolutionary conspiracy in Western Siberia arose in advance of the mass operations. Mironov's June 1937 report, which prompted Stalin to send his July 2 telegram regarding "kulak and criminal elements," identified a

"Kadet-Monarchist Socialist Revolutionary organization" in the area that took orders from both Japanese intelligence agencies and a domestic group named the "Russian General Military Council" (ROVS).[134] Although Stalin's reaction to this report, as we have seen, focused on the repression of special settlers, ex-kulaks, and criminals, Mironov's innovation was to claim that this "social base" was controlled by "oppositionists" and foreign intelligence agencies.

Still, Mironov's understanding of various "counterrevolutionary" organizations in his region in early 1937 did not fit the model, provided by Ezhov in his letter regarding the POV, of a single, massive conspiracy directing all diversionary activity in the area.[135] Once the mass operations were under way, the regional NKVD began to assemble these organizations into a single counterrevolutionary conspiracy, eventually subsuming the entire range of putative organizations under the appellation "ROVS." Mironov and then Gorbach sent successive reports to the center regarding ongoing investigations, developing the idea that suspect elements who had been exiled from neighboring areas in the previous years, especially from the Far Eastern Territory, had united into a conspiracy in the service of Japan, Poland, and Germany.[136] Within weeks of the beginning of the mass operations, the regional NKVD officials had transformed this loosely connected group of counterrevolutionary organizations into the same kind of unified, quasi-military conspiracy that Ezhov outlined in his letter on the POV, bringing their local narrative into line with the script offered by the center.

This transformation was not simply conceptual; it was directly related to the sentencing capacities of the NKVD in the region. The NKVD troika in Western Siberia that was approved by Stalin in late June 1937 sentenced individuals throughout the course of the mass operations, alongside the troika created by Order 00447. These sentences took place outside the quotas set for "anti-Soviet elements." Although the ROVS troika, as it came to be called, was comprised of the same three officials as the troika dealing with Order 00447, it operated separately and sentenced individuals with no respect to quotas at all. As of October 5, 1937, 9,689 individuals had been arrested for participation in ROVS in Western Siberia and 6,437 had been sentenced to death by the troika, accounting for nearly 40 percent of the arrests and almost half the executions approved by NKVD troikas in the territory to that point.[137] The ROVS troikas ultimately sentenced 29,528 individuals in 1937 and 1938 in Western Siberia—24,853 (84 percent) to death.[138]

The importance of the ROVS organization was not limited to Western Siberia, as NKVD administrations in other regions made reference to branches of the organization in their own reports to the center. Yet only in Western Siberia was the NKVD authorized to sentence members of "counterrevolutionary" conspiracies in excess of the quotas stipulated by Order 00447. Insofar as it unified the practices of both the national operations and the operations against "anti-Soviet elements," the NKVD's actions against ROVS in Western Siberia formed the archetype for the expansion of the mass operations from targeting "kulak and criminal elements" to targeting massive and supposedly active counterrevolutionary conspiracies, in conjunction with the "national operations," in the fall and winter of 1937.

By the end of 1937, conspiracies and cross-border contacts, rather than the repression of population cohorts as such, had become the standard explanation provided by regional NKVD administrations of their actions during the mass operations. This language was prevalent at the center as early as the February 1937 Communist Party Plenum, but it was the launching of the national operations, and the extensive explanatory apparatus that Ezhov and Stalin brought to bear on that process, that changed the focus of mass repressions at the periphery by the end of the year. Such explanations were not part of the conceptual apparatus that had developed within the Soviet policing system during the 1930s regarding marginalized population cohorts. They were products, rather, of the campaign against "the human contingents" of diversionary activity as conceived and implemented by Ezhov and Stalin. The unfolding national operations allowed local NKVD administrations to make conceptual connections between foreign intelligence agencies and domestic marginal cohorts that otherwise made little sense to them; they also allowed the local police to justify fantastic levels of arrests that were part of both the national operations and the operations against "anti-Soviet elements" by the end of 1937. As 1937 ended and the planned four-month deadline for the end of mass operations passed, repressions of "anti-Soviet elements" and "national contingents" became largely indistinguishable. Both would continue, with increasingly deadly results, for almost another year.

Mass Operations and "National Contingents" in 1938

By early 1938, Stalin and Ezhov deemed the operations against "kulaks, criminals, and other anti-Soviet elements" largely complete in most areas of the USSR. They also understood, based on past experience, that Soviet society, especially the agricultural sector, could not long withstand administrative pressure of the type associated with the mass operations. The Politburo took several steps in early 1938 to bring certain aspects of these operations to a halt, expanding sentencing quotas in some areas but ordering the regional NKVD administrations to process existing cases and to prepare for an end of operations under Order 00447 before the beginning of the spring planting season. Nevertheless, mass repressions were far from over in early 1938. Stalin and Ezhov remained convinced that Soviet society had been infiltrated by "anti-Soviet" and "national elements," even after four months of unrelenting repression and well over half a million arrests. They therefore reinvigorated the national operations in early 1938, and they authorized continued repressions under Order 00447 in regions where "anti-Soviet elements" continued to pose a threat, in their minds, to national security.

Local NKVD administrations responded by attempting to fill quotas and arrest "national elements" using any available means, making operations against "anti-Soviet elements" and "national contingents" virtually indistinguishable by the spring of 1938. Previous conceptual distinctions between "kulak" and "criminal" cohorts, members of suspect nationalities, and supposed participants in putative anti-Soviet conspiracies disappeared; the mass operations lost any semblance of the instrumental rationality that they had exhibited in 1937 and devolved into utterly pointless arrests of individuals who could be identified as marginalized—by biography, genealogy, or past behavior—in any way. The mass operations also turned more deadly in 1938, as regional NKVD administrations executed increasing proportions of the "national contingents" and "anti-Soviet elements" arrested in the summer and fall. These trends culminated in the fall of 1938 in a wave of repressions of "national elements," which relied on techniques developed in the operations against anti-Soviet elements and which resulted in nearly 75,000 executions in under eight weeks. Stalin, still in charge of events, then brought the mass operations to an abrupt halt in November 1938, ejecting Ezhov from the NKVD and ending the "Stalinist terror" that, in the end, claimed the lives of nearly a million residents of the USSR.[139]

Mass operations against "kulaks, criminals, and other anti-Soviet elements" were originally scheduled to last four months, ending in early December 1937. Yet the Politburo never intended to limit the operations to the quotas handed out in early August, and it approved piecemeal quota expansions even during first two months of the operations, often on the initiative of regional NKVD administrations petitioning for the right to sentence individuals already arrested in the course of the operations. In mid-October 1937, Stalin expanded the operations in a more fundamental way, increasing quotas in all fifty-eight republics, regions, and territories by a total of 120,320 sentences, including 63,120 executions.[140] This increase was prompted, in part, by the concerns of local police and Communist Party officials that the upcoming elections to the USSR Supreme Soviet, set to begin in early December, would provide an opportunity for "anti-Soviet elements" to engage in counterrevolutionary agitation, especially within the collective farm system.[141]

In practice, these quota expansions, along with smaller individual expansions over the last two months of 1937, allowed regional NKVD administrations to sentence individuals already under surveillance or arrested, in some cases already sentenced to death but, in accord with Ezhov's specific instructions on the matter, held in prison pending authorization from the center. In November the Politburo approved a second broad set of quota expansions for most regions, specifically ordering NKVD administrations to sentence individuals already in custody and to prepare for the end of the mass operations; but in early December Ezhov extended the operations until January 1, 1938, both to allow the local administrations to carry out arrests during the elections and to complete the processing of individuals already in custody before the planned end of the operations.[142] With this last round of quota expansions, the majority of the arrests associated with Order 00447 were complete. As of January 1, 1938, the NKVD had arrested 555,641 individuals as part of this operation, plus an additional 22,108 supposed members of ROVS in Western Siberia, and had sentenced 553,362 individuals using the NKVD troikas, out of the more than 767,000 individuals eventually sentenced under Order 00447 in 1937 and 1938.[143] There is no indication that local officials pressed for substantial additional quota expansions in December 1937 or January 1938, suggesting that local officials, as well as Stalin and Ezhov, assumed that the operations associated with Order 00447 would end with the turn of the year.

Stalin reinforced his intention to moderate certain forms of repression at the January 1938 Central Committee Plenum, which was devoted to discussions of ongoing purges in all sectors of Soviet society. Stalin halted the wholesale purges of the Communist Party, which had resulted in upward of 100,000 expulsions in 1937 alone, communicating this decision to local party officials as a plenum resolution and ordering the arrest of party members deemed responsible for the "excesses" of the previous months.[144] None of the speakers at the plenum directly criticized the work of the NKVD regarding the mass operations. Ezhov, in fact, spoke approvingly of both the national operations and those against "anti-Soviet elements" in late January, at a conference of regional NKVD chiefs that followed the plenum, arguing that the operation against "kulaks, criminals, and anti-Soviet elements" had gone off "brilliantly" and should continue. The regional NKVD leaders at the conference agreed, calling for a continuation of the operations and further expansion of the quotas allotted to them.[145]

Stalin evidently had other plans. On January 31, the Politburo resolved to allocate additional quotas, totaling 48,000 executions and 9,200 sentences to labor camps, to twenty-two specific regions, territories, and republics—just over a third of the total number of administrative areas carrying out repressions under Order 00447 at the time. Stalin authorized the regional NKVD administrations in areas approved for additional quotas to extend operations until March 15 (April 1 for the Far Eastern Territory), but all other regions were ordered to complete all sentencing operations by February 15 and to obey existing quota restrictions.[146] The limited geographic scope and the heavy relative weight of executions in the new quotas suggest that Stalin intended this set of quota expansions to serve as a "mopping up" at the end of the campaign.[147] With only a handful of exceptions, discussed below, the Politburo did not approve major additional quotas for arrests under the auspices of Order 00447 for the rest of 1938. National operations would continue, but Stalin's decision made it clear that mass repressions of "kulaks, criminals, and other anti-Soviet elements" were to come to an end.[148]

Early 1938 also saw several restrictions on the ability of the police to sentence "criminal elements" using police troikas, which underscored the message that the mass operations were no longer to target merely "marginalized" individuals. The USSR Procuracy in late February ordered local Procuracy administrations to review the activities of regional police troikas, singling out the troika in the Gorkii region for sentencing workers in good professional standing for petty criminal violations and for conducting only cursory, and usually oral, case hearings, often hundreds at a single sitting.[149] Along the same lines, on May 20 Vyshinsky attacked the investigative practices of the *militsiia* directly with an instruction regarding a specific case of "wrecking," in which *militsiia* officers charged a factory worker with counterrevolutionary activity for allegedly ruining a single can of food in the production process.[150] Such practices were difficult for local procurators to control, especially at the periphery, where local justice officials themselves were the subjects of ongoing purges at the hands of the NKVD and where the entire system of local prosecutorial oversight had been wiped away in the previous months.[151]

Despite a substantial amount of foot-dragging by Ezhov and his subordinates, the NKVD eventually responded to these policy changes, issuing a circular in late May that ordered local administrations to halt all "mass operations" and "campaign-style activity" against criminals and to cease sentencing individuals as "socially harmful elements" who did not meet the strict criteria of recidivism and connections with the criminal milieu.[152] This circular, which superseded the original 1935 NKVD instruction creating the police troikas, maintained these troikas as part of the extrajudicial prerogatives of local police and authorized them to continue sentencing "socially harmful elements" to five years in a labor camp, but it underscored the Politburo's decision to halt the mass repressions of the "criminal" cohorts that had been one of Order 00447's original targets.

These moves in the spring of 1938 were intended to reorient, rather than moderate, the overall levels of repression in the USSR. Procurators were encouraged to reassert control over arrests carried out by the *militsiia*, but they were not given the right to interfere in the ongoing mass operations in areas where Stalin had approved their continuation. In mid-April Vyshinsky made this policy explicit by instructing local procurators to refuse to hear complaints from individuals sentenced by the NKVD troikas, allowing protests only in exceptional cases in which the accused could provide absolute proof of his or her innocence.[153] Furthermore, justice officials had absolutely no ability to intervene in what was becoming the most important part of NKVD work in early 1938: the national operations.

Although Stalin and Ezhov were initially pleased with the course of the "Polish operation," they became increasingly concerned in late 1937 that the national operations had fallen behind schedule. The Politburo took several steps to force the regional NKVD administrations to carry out repressions of "national contingents" with more vigor in late 1937, repeatedly extending the duration of the Polish "line" and launching additional operations against Finns, Estonians, Lithuanians, Bulgarians, Greeks, and others in areas of particular military importance.[154] Nonetheless, by the beginning of 1938, Stalin was well aware that the national operations had produced far fewer arrests than the operations associated with Order 00447.[155]

In response to this situation, Stalin moved to invigorate the national operations in January 1938, following the January Plenum meeting. On January 31 the Politburo instructed the NKVD to extend the national operations to April 15 and to target the entire list of ethnic "contingents"— Poles, Latvians, Germans, Estonians, Finns, Greeks, Iranians, Kharbin returnees, Chinese, Romanians, Bulgarians, and Macedonians—in all areas of the country; the Politburo added Iranians and Afghanis in separate orders shortly thereafter. At the same time, the Politburo ordered the NKVD administrations to target all foreign refugees (*perebezhchiki*) as potential spies, executing those "directly or indirectly" connected to espionage and sentencing the rest to ten years in labor camps, regardless of their motives for entering the USSR.[156] These orders not only expanded the scope of repressions but also made clear to local NKVD officials that wholesale repressions of "national" cohorts, regardless of any putative involvement in anti-Soviet conspiracies, was to replace repressions of "kulak" and "criminal" cohorts as the policy of the day.

This expansion of all national "lines" to all areas of the country provided some local NKVD administrations with entirely new cohorts to repress, especially in the border regions in the south and east. But in most areas the targets remained the same, forcing the local administrations to produce additional "national elements" from sectors of the population already thoroughly worked over by Order 00447. Stalin and Ezhov were aware of this issue, at times criticizing the regional NKVD administrations for repressing individuals on the margins of Soviet society instead of "diversionary elements" within national cohorts, and at other times encouraging the local police to arrest "counterrevolutionaries" no matter what their sociological origin.

Ezhov himself underscored this dichotomy during a trip to Ukraine in mid-February, where he installed a new republican NKVD chief and set about correcting "deficiencies" in the conduct of the mass operations. He complained to a conference of Ukrainian NKVD officials that they had substituted quantity for quality during the mass operations, arresting collective farmers and workers rather than the "ringleaders" of the conspiracies that they had uncovered. He demanded that they target "national contingents" in the upcoming months, but he also ordered them to repress the "leading cadres" of diversionary organizations among former "oppositionists," members of nationalist parties, religious figures, and any remaining dekulakized peasants who had not yet been repressed. This order could only have been interpreted as permission to continue arresting the same marginalized population cohorts targeted by Order 00447.[157] Upon Ezhov's return to Moscow, the Politburo authorized the Ukrainian NKVD troika to execute 30,000 additional "kulak and other anti-Soviet elements" (this in addition to the 6,000 approved on January 31). The cohorts to be targeted, Ezhov had made clear, differed little in practice from those to be targeted in the national operations.[158]

Local NKVD administrations responded enthusiastically to this policy change, in part by targeting individuals who had no contact with "national" cohorts but sentencing them using the "album procedure" in order to prove that they were responding adequately to central demands. The local NKVD administrations in areas like Western Siberia, the Urals, and the northern Caucasus that were far from the western border provided substantial numbers of "Polish" and "German elements," most of whom were not Polish or German.[159] In late March 1938, Ezhov's assistant, Frinovskii, castigated the NKVD chief of the Sverdlovsk region for this very practice. Frinovskii complained that, of the 4,142 individuals submitted to the center as part of the German operation by the Sverdlovsk NKVD, only 390 were Germans; of the 4,218 arrested in the Polish operation, only 390 were Poles; and of the 1,249 arrested in the "Kharbinite" operation, only 42 were Kharbin returnees. The majority of the 10,024 individuals arrested in the national operations in the Sverdlovsk region, according to Frinovskii, were either workers or "former kulaks and their children"; the NKVD simply targeted Russians and Ukrainians with compromised pasts, especially among populations of special settlers, and processed their cases as part of the various national "lines."[160] Frinovskii's charge was certainly correct, but most regional NKVD chiefs could hardly do anything else if they expected to produce enough "national elements" to satisfy Ezhov and Stalin.

The Politburo encouraged this mixing of categories by approving additional quotas for several specific areas under Order 00447 in the summer of 1938, usually in conjunction with the national operations and usually allowing for more executions than sentences to labor camps. The Politburo in mid-April approved 1,500 executions of "kulaks, S[ocialist] R[evolutionarie]s, recidivists, and criminals" in Leningrad; in mid-May it authorized the NKVD troika in the Rostov region to sentence 5,000 additional cases, including 3,500 executions, of individuals involved in "counterrevolutionary groups." The largest single addition came in late July, when Stalin authorized the NKVD in the Far Eastern Territory to execute 15,000 additional "counterrevolutionary elements" and imprison 5,000 more, but the Politburo continued to authorize smaller expansions through the end of August.[161] These quota expansions did not represent a return to mass operations against "anti-Soviet elements." Rather, they generally applied to areas where the national operations were particularly important, or where the local NKVD administrations successfully convinced the Politburo that a substantial number of "anti-Soviet elements," who might carry out espionage in the service of foreign powers, remained at large. For most regional NKVD administrations, however, these quota expansions were largely superfluous by mid-1938; the national operations provided them with ample opportunity to arrest and sentence any and all suspect individuals in their areas.

Local NKVD administrations responded to this pressure from the center by arresting tens of thousands of "national elements" a month in 1938. The sentencing procedures associated with the national operations, however, were far less efficient than the NKVD troikas associated with Order 00447, resulting in a massive backlog of cases by midsummer. Even in the best of circumstances, forwarding "albums" of cases to Moscow for approval by Ezhov and Vyshinsky took weeks. Ezhov and Vyshinsky had little time to review lists containing tens of thousands of cases in mid-1938, and the "albums" were usually processed by midlevel officials, who considered the task a burdensome waste of time. As cases piled up in Moscow, regional NKVD official sent complaints to the center regarding the difficulty and expense of housing prisoners who had already been, in effect, sentenced to death but whose executions had been delayed by unfinished paperwork. The Politburo resolved in May to extend all national operations to August 1 to allow for the processing of these cases, but this decision only compounded the problem. By the end of the summer, some 100,000 cases had accumulated at the center, with little prospect for immediate resolution.[162]

This backlog, along with the complaints of regional NKVD officials regarding the overcrowding of prisons in the summer of 1938, led Stalin to abandon the album procedure altogether in mid-September. On September 15, the Politburo ordered Ezhov to transfer all cases of individuals currently under investigation as part of the national operations to new "special" (*osobye*) NKVD troikas, which were comprised of regional or republican NKVD chiefs, Communist Party secretaries, and procurators. Special troikas were authorized to sentence individuals to death or to terms in labor camps according to the regulations pertaining to the Polish operation. No central approval of the sentences was required, and NKVD operative sectors were authorized to carry out sentences immediately. The Politburo stipulated no quotas for the special troikas, authorizing them to sentence as many individuals to death as they saw fit. The NKVD operative sectors were given two months to process all remaining cases, including the backlog of cases in Moscow, and to carry out all resulting sentences. Special troikas were authorized by position rather than name, and the Politburo did not retain the right to select the troika members as it had under Order 00447.[163]

In making this change, Stalin was doing more than transferring the national operations to demonstrably efficient local troikas, which had already sentenced nearly 700,000 individuals in the course of the operations against "anti-Soviet elements." He was unbinding the hands of local NKVD chiefs entirely, allowing them to repress any and all individuals in their areas who had been identified over the previous months as "anti-Soviet" or "national" enemies.

Despite the freedom this decision provided to local NKVD administrations, Stalin intended to retain ultimate control over the work of the special troikas, and he specified two important limitations on their sentencing powers. First, the troikas were authorized to sentence only individuals arrested before August 1, 1938; individuals arrested after that date were to be sent to courts, military tribunals, the Special Board, or other sentencing bodies that predated the mass operations. With this provision, Stalin signaled his clear intent to end the mass operations completely on November 15, with the conclusion of this wave of sentencing. This time limit also prevented, at least in theory, the local NKVD administrations from carrying out a rash of new arrests in order to sentence those individuals using the special troikas.[164] Second, the troikas were required to collect information on the ethnicities of those arrested and sentenced, and to send it regularly to Moscow, in order to ensure that "national contingents" were the predominant target.[165]

In practice, these restrictions did little to impede the actions of the special troikas. In less than two months, the troikas considered the cases of nearly 108,000 individuals and sentenced 105,032 of them—72,254 to death.[166] The number of cases depended entirely on local conditions. In some regions, the troikas heard only dozens of cases, but in others, including Leningrad, Novosibirsk, and Sverdlovsk, they processed thousands of cases, sometimes handing down several hundred sentences a day.

Even more so than in the previous phase of "national operations," the local NKVD administrations worked to include marginalized individuals and "criminal elements" in the hearings of the special troikas. Only two-thirds of the 24,471 individuals sentenced by the troikas under the "German line" were ethnically Germans, slightly fewer than the 75 percent characteristic of the earlier phase of the operation; only 55 percent of the 36,768 individuals sentenced by the troikas as "Polish elements" were ethnically Polish, compared with an estimated 70 percent for the earlier phase.[167] Yet such actions do not suggest that local NKVD administrations operated beyond the control of the center in late 1938, because Stalin and Ezhov knew from experience that the local officers would respond in this manner and approved the special troikas nonetheless. With this order, Stalin knowingly approved the extrajudicial repression of all individuals in NKVD custody, whether arrested as members of national cohorts or supposed counterrevolutionary organizations, as former kulaks, or for any other reason—as long as they had been arrested before August 1, 1938.

The Politburo made it clear that the operation was scheduled to end on November 15 and explicitly forbade any implementation of death sentences after that date. As a result, the NKVD operative sectors worked frantically and, on the whole, successfully to process cases and carry out the executions within the time limit set by the center.[168] In at least some areas, the operative sectors continued to shoot individuals after November 15, in order to complete the operations, but there is no indication that the local NKVD administrations continued mass arrests or executions in the weeks after the November instructions.[169] Although local officers attempted to take advantage of what they saw as their final days of freedom from the court system, the local NKVD chiefs who violated the September 15 instructions generally did so to avoid censure and arrest for failure to complete the operations, as demanded by Stalin, by the November 15 deadline.

The End of the Mass Operations

Stalin's decision to set up special NKVD troikas was not the only sign that the mass operations were coming to a close. Ezhov's position within the NKVD became increasingly weak in the summer and early fall of 1938, as Stalin prepared to blame him for supposed "distortions" of the mass operations and to remove him from office. In late August, Stalin promoted Lavrentii Beria, the head of the Communist Party in Georgia, to the position of first deputy of the NKVD. Stalin likely chose Beria because of his experience in party and NKVD work and because he was already in open conflict with Ezhov, providing a natural opponent to the commissar within the NKVD. Ezhov's trusted deputy Frinovskii was ejected from the NKVD within weeks of Beria's appointment. By mid-September, Beria was co-signing NKVD documents with Ezhov and had effectively assumed daily control over the organization.[170]

The impending end of the mass operations was no secret in the upper echelons of the Communist Party and the NKVD in late 1938. On October 8, Stalin assigned a commission composed of Ezhov, Beria, Vyshinsky, Justice Commissar Nikolai Rychkov, and Georgii Malenkov to draft a Politburo resolution halting all extrajudicial sentencing and returning the exclusive right to approve arrests to the Procuracy.[171] On November 15, exactly two months after the creation of the special troikas, the Politburo halted all hearings of cases by the NKVD troikas, the military tribunals, and the Military Collegium of the USSR Supreme Court.[172] The Politburo followed up two days later with a lengthy order, drafted by the above-mentioned commission, which forbade all the "simplified" arrest and sentencing procedures associated with the mass operations and abolished all NKVD troikas, including the police troikas that had existed since 1935. All arrests were to be approved in advance by local Procuracy officials, and most cases were to be forwarded to the applicable courts under the strict control of the Procuracy.[173]

Separate NKVD and Procuracy orders to local administrations followed within days, stressing that "mass arrests" of any kind were thereafter prohibited, that the Procuracy would be restored to its role as ultimate arbitrator of all investigations, and that all cases, as a rule, would be heard by the courts. The NKVD Special Board was retained, but its purview was limited to particularly important political cases in which the nature of the evidence made the case impossible to hear in open court.[174] Shortly after issuing these orders, Stalin replaced Ezhov with Beria as head of the NKVD, cementing the overall policy change.[175] The mass operations ended, as they had begun, under direct orders from the center.

The mass operations of 1937 and 1938 resulted, according to NKVD documents, in some 1.15 million sentences, including roughly 683,000 executions—roughly 818,000 sentences and 436,000 executions as part of the operations against "kulaks, criminals, and other anti-Soviet elements," and 335,513 sentences and 247,157 executions as part of the national operations.[176] The national operations were particularly deadly; nearly three-quarters of those sentenced as part of a "national contingent" were put to death. The mass operations against "anti-Soviet elements," to the contrary, were initially intended to result in the execution of a minority of those arrested. Stalin's original telegram of July 2, 1937, which first announced the impending operations, envisioned the execution of a certain number of suspects and the relatively lenient punishment of exile for the remainder of those repressed. Order 00447 itself, though replacing exile with labor camp sentences, originally called for an execution rate of roughly 25 percent of all arrests. That rate climbed to some 40 percent by the end of 1937, and by the end of the operations more than half those individuals arrested as "kulaks, criminals, and other anti-Soviet elements" had been executed. The increasing severity of the mass operations in 1938 was the result of the intertwining of police actions regarding Order 00447 with those regarding the national operations. Although trends within the history of Soviet policing made the mass operations possible in 1937, it was only when these operations were cut loose from the moorings of existing policing practices that they expanded to the extent that they did, driven by the disjuncture between central demands for national security and local attempts to complete the operations, whatever the means required to do so, to Stalin's satisfaction.

Conclusion

The mass operations were, first and foremost, police operations. This simple truth can easily be lost among the numerous factors that led to Stalin's decision in the summer of 1937 to repress broad swaths of the Soviet population. It can also be lost in the complexity of the operations as they were carried out, and in the confusing relationships between the mass operations and the other processes that, taken together, made up the "Stalinist terror" of 1936–38. Analyzing the mass operations as police operations removes them from the realm of the "political"—from the context of Communist Party purges and the public "campaign of vigilance" against state and party elites—and allows us to understand them in the broader context of the history of the Soviet policing system.

Seen from this perspective, the mass operations were not an abrupt change in policy on Stalin's part but rather the culmination of years of regime policies toward population groups deemed "dangerous" to the security of the state.[177] The responses of the Politburo in the mid-1930s to violent urban crime, "socially harmful elements," and cohorts of dekulakized peasants or ex-convicts whose geographic mobility was deemed a threat to the social stability of the country—these were the direct precursors to the mass repressions of 1937 and 1938. "Mass operations" against these groups virtually defined Soviet policing between 1934 and 1937, despite Ezhov's attempts to reduce their importance in the initial months after he became head of the NKVD.

That mass repression followed a period of relative moderation is not surprising. Signs of moderation were indeed visible in the Soviet criminal justice system in the mid-1930s; as we have seen, even in the last months before the mass operations began, top justice officials, especially Vyshinsky, attempted to soften the particularly harsh policies that isolated ex-convicts and "dekulakized" peasants from Soviet society in the mid-1930s. Yet throughout the 1930s, Stalin supported moderation when he believed that it would improve administration and jettisoned it when he believed that repression would produce better results. His choice to launch mass repressions of "kulaks, criminals, and anti-Soviet elements" in mid-1937 was abrupt, as were many of his major policy initiatives in the 1930s, but it was hardly novel. It was not particularly surprising to those police officers charged with carrying it out, nor should it be to historians attempting to explain it some seventy years later.

The mass operations were also police operations in the sense that they involved little popular participation and relied only tangentially on denunciations from the general public. Many aspects of the Stalinist terror, including the Communist Party purges and the "campaign of vigilance," did involve a substantial amount of denunciation, popular participation, and social activism.[178] The mass operations, however, required none; the identification of targets and the actual arrests were carried out exclusively by the police, and the regime called only for passive support from the rest of the population. The Stalinist police, like the entire Stalinist state, was of course a huge and sprawling apparatus, and the borders between state and society were porous, often by design. Yet the mass operations took place with none of the public fanfare or spontaneous social violence that had characterized earlier waves of mass repressions in the USSR, such as the dekulakization drive. Even denunciations extracted from prisoners through torture, though common enough, were largely superfluous. The mass operations were carried out by local police officers with the utmost speed precisely because their methods for identifying and targeting suspect populations required no broad mobilization of Soviet society.

Analyzing the mass operations as police campaigns also shows that they were not launched by Stalin from a position of institutional or political weakness. They were not a "blind terror" or a lashing out by the Politburo at enemies that the center could neither identify nor understand. They were not, as is sometimes argued, a fearful response on Stalin's part to the prospect of "free" elections to the Supreme Soviet; they were not, in fact, a product of fear at all.[179] Stalin and Ezhov were well aware of the weaknesses of the Soviet policing system in 1937, especially its inability to sustain any kind of covert surveillance of suspect populations. They were also well aware of its strengths, especially its demonstrated capacity to carry out massive purges of "dangerous" or "harmful" population cohorts. The initial repressions of "kulaks" and "criminal elements" in the fall of 1937 were quite precise, targeting suspect categories that both the Politburo and local police had deemed the most pressing problems of public order and national security for the previous several years. These mass repressions were understood by Stalin and Ezhov as a form of social prophylaxis, intended to remove "threatening" population cohorts in preparation for war. This goal was understood by police officials at all levels, and it was something to which they were ideologically and practically prepared to respond.

The question of war brings up the difficult problem of the relationship between the mass operations and the "Stalinist terror" as a whole. The idea that the repressions of 1937 and 1938 were part of Stalin's preparation for war has a long history in Soviet studies; Isaac Deutscher said as much several decades ago, and the point is now incontrovertible, based on the newest archival documentation. In the case of the mass operations, this concern with foreign infiltration is unambiguous and direct: Stalin and Ezhov both believed that domestic cohorts of "kulaks," "criminal elements," "former people," religious figures, and individuals connected in some way to hostile foreign powers would form the "principal human contingent," in Ezhov's words, of organized counterrevolutionary insurgencies in the event of war with Germany or Japan. This focus on national security united the separate parts of the "Stalinist terror" in the minds of top Communist Party and police officials. In Stalin's mind, traitorous party functionaries, state elites supposedly involved in "wrecking," Red Army officers, "national contingents," and "kulak elements" were all suspect because of their potential political unreliability during the great conflict with the capitalist world that he believed was inevitable.

These conceptual connections between marginalized domestic "contingents" and the threat of foreign infiltration may have been clear at the center, but implementing mass repressions based on them posed tremendous difficulties for the local police. Operations against "former kulaks" and "criminals," although straightforward for local NKVD administrations, were by nature limited: they did not exist "outside of time and space," as Ezhov had noted after the initial months of mass arrests, and police repressions of them could last only until these cohorts had been exhausted by the local police.[180] Stalin and Ezhov, however, demanded continued and expanding repressions in 1937 and 1938, forcing central and local police alike to find a way to make a transition to mass purges of "anti-Soviet elements" rather than "kulaks" and "criminals." The local NKVD administrations solved this problem by mixing existing methods of repression of "harmful" and "dangerous elements" with notions of national security. The exchange of information between center and periphery regarding the nature of anti-Soviet conspiracies in 1937 and 1938 (what this chapter has called the "scripting" of the mass operations) allowed the local NKVD administrations to conceptualize and carry out operations against "national elements" in a way that made sense to them and, in the process, provided a justification for the expansion of operations against "anti-Soviet elements" to several times the initial quotas set down by Stalin in August 1937.

It would be a mistake, however, to overestimate the coherence of these events as they played out across the USSR. In the early months of the operations, local police administrations worked to sweep off the streets all individuals who had been previously placed under surveillance as "kulaks" or "criminal elements"—a process that can be described as a rough kind of "social engineering." But once these sweeps were under way for several months, the mass operations devolved into utterly pointless mass arrests, devoid of any rational aims regarding population categorization and control. Even the national operations—which were specifically intended by Stalin and Ezhov to target precise strata of the population defined by ethnicity or contact with "enemy" governments—quickly devolved into the same kinds of mass arrests of any individuals who could be identified as marginal or suspect in any way. In the end, the mass operations were driven not by any kind of instrumental rationality but by the internal logic of the Stalinist policing system, pressed forward by the disjuncture between central demands for military security and local officials' need to complete the operations to Stalin's satisfaction.

Despite the numerous influences that shaped the nature of the mass operations in 1937 and 1938, Stalin bears the ultimate responsibility for them. Ezhov played some part in bringing the issue of foreign infiltration to the center of the Communist Party's internal discussions in 1936 and 1937, but the mass operations, much less the entire Stalinist terror, cannot be attributed to his influence. Stalin was the party leader with extensive experience launching "mass operations" earlier in the decade; Stalin was the leader who responded to perceived threats from the peasantry with the massive campaign to eliminate kulaks "as a class"; and Stalin was the leader who made all the crucial decisions in 1937 and 1938.

Nevertheless, the mass operations of 1937 and 1938 were possible only because the Soviet police had responded with "mass operations" to problems of public order and "threatening" population cohorts throughout the 1930s. The elimination of these cohorts "once and for all," in the words of NKVD Order 00447, was something that the entire Soviet policing system had been working toward since the OGPU had taken control of Soviet policing at the beginning of the decade.

7

Policing after the Mass Operations, 1938–1941

Immediately cease carrying out any sort of mass operations of arrest or deportation, understanding the term "mass arrests" to mean group arrests or deportations without a differentiated approach to each arrested or deported individual and without preliminary, thorough investigation of all existing incriminating materials related to that individual. . . . Arrests are to be carried out in strictly individual order.

> —Lavrentii Beria to all regional, territorial, and republican NKVD administrations, November 1938[1]

As soon as [nomadic Gypsies] appear in areas in which the passport system has been put into effect, they are immediately arrested and subjected to criminal prosecution (often the men alone are arrested, leaving free the women Gypsies with children, which does not lead to anything but beggary). . . . In this manner, the Soviet government will put all Gypsies into camps within six months. . . . If the traditional lifestyle of Gypsies has become a crime, then it seems to me that a special legal instruction on this topic is necessary.

> —an assistant procurator of the Uzbek Republic to Stalin, Molotov, and Bochkov, November 1940[2]

When Stalin halted the mass operations in November 1938, he took several steps to signal, to both the Soviet criminal justice system and to the population at large, that the era of unchecked police repression was over. He replaced Nikolai Ezhov with a new NKVD chief, Lavrentii Beria, and blamed Ezhov and his team for the "excesses" that had taken place during the preceding months. The police lost most of their extrajudicial sentencing powers; proper legal procedures and norms were to be applied to almost all political and criminal prosecutions initiated by both the political and civil police, carried out under the strict control of the Procuracy.

Stalin did not intend these changes to reduce the repressiveness of the police system per se. Rather, he promulgated them to halt an operation that had clearly run its course, to explain the abrupt policy change to the public, and to improve aspects of police work that had suffered during the chaotic campaigns of 1937 and 1938. Working through his new NKVD chief, Stalin implemented several reforms of Soviet policing in an attempt to improve the policing capabilities of the *militsiia*; to reorient the activity of the police toward predictable, regularized methods of crime prevention instead of mass operations; and to delineate more clearly the boundaries between civil and political policing, and hence civil and political crime. These reforms were not simply reversals of the repressive policies of 1937 and 1938. They must be understood in the longer-term context of Soviet policing, including the reforms promoted by the OGPU in the early 1930s and Ezhov's attempts in 1936 and early 1937 to replace "mass operations" of all kinds with more predictable forms of surveillance and covert police activity.

A number of issues complicated these attempts to reshape Soviet policing after 1938. The purges within the NKVD that followed the end of the mass operations hindered the process of reconstruction, because the few policemen with substantial tenure who had survived the period leading up to the mass operations were swept away by Beria's team. Deeper structural problems reappeared after November 1938 as well. The issue of controlling "dangerous" population cohorts remained central to police work after 1938, notwithstanding the supposed elimination during the mass operations of all "kulaks, criminals, and other anti-Soviet elements." The police continued to focus on controlling populations with the internal passport system, a tactic that was as fraught with contradictions as it had been in the years before the mass operations. Economic crime again became a crucial focus of police activity, as constant shortages of agricultural and manufactured goods in the years between 1938 and 1941 led to increasingly repressive police campaigns against speculators, thieves, and Soviet citizens forced to stand in line to purchase consumer goods. Juvenile delinquency again became a central focus of police activity, with the police and central justice officials alike blaming urban social disorder—especially street theft, hooliganism, and even more serious violent crimes such as banditry and rape—on the prevalence of "unsupervised" children within the criminal milieu. Finally, the regime returned to the issues of hooliganism and youth crime in the months before World War II, launching a campaign against urban disorder that was not intended to separate a "contingent" of hooligans from the rest of the population but that tended toward that tactic anyway.

These overlapping police campaigns against urban crime and "harmful" cohorts in the prewar years vitiated attempts by legal officials to strengthen the borders between judicial and extrajudicial prosecutions, and they weakened the November 1938 directives calling for a fundamental reduction in extrajudicial sentencing by the police. By 1940, extrajudicial repression was again a major part of the Soviet criminal justice system. The persistence of extrajudicial forms of repression in the most basic of police activities in the post-1938 period—the administration of the passport system, control of speculation in consumer goods, suppression of hooliganism in Soviet cities—underscores the importance of such tactics in the Stalinist policing system in the years before the mass operations of 1937 and 1938. The police campaigns of the immediate prewar years were all steeped in long-standing approaches to identifying, marking, and repressing population cohorts as a way to control social disorder. Hence, they signaled a return to the Stalinist model of policing that was only briefly disrupted by the end of the mass operations in November 1938.

Soviet Policing and the "End" of the Mass Operations

Ezhov's fall from power, Beria's promotion to head the USSR NKVD, and the November 1938 Politburo orders that called a halt to the mass operations are generally viewed as pivotal events in the history of Stalinist repression—not only an end to Stalinist terror but also an attempt by the Politburo to reorient the entire Soviet criminal justice system toward more traditional forms of policing and criminal law, and a realization of at least some of the promises of the 1932 edict "On Revolutionary Legality" and the May 1933 instruction on arrests and the "clearing" of prisons.[3] The short-term effects of Stalin's policy changes in November 1938 are clear: the Politburo abolished all NKVD troikas, eliminated most instances of extrajudicial repression, and placed the Procuracy at least nominally in charge of prosecutions for civil and political crimes alike. At the same time, these policy changes were part of a long-term attempt by the Politburo and the new leaders of the NKVD to eliminate mass arrests as a basic policing technique and to promote instead the kind of systematized, covert policing systems that had been the goal of the NKVD and OGPU leadership since the early 1930s. These reform attempts, which began in early 1938 and stretched well into Beria's tenure, were largely ineffective, because trends in Soviet policing were far more powerful than the often halfhearted policy changes dictated by the Politburo. Reforms of the policing system in 1938 and 1939, including the November 1938 instructions that ended the mass operations, did little to change the basic methods used by the police to investigate crimes, control social disorder, and define categories of suspect or marginalized individuals. Hence they did little to alter the overall contours of the Soviet policing system in the late 1930s.

The mass operations strained the Soviet policing system well beyond its limits, forcing local NKVD administrations to ignore virtually all policing duties that did not pertain directly to carrying out Stalin's campaigns. Local *militsiia* administrations had little time to investigate cases that were initiated by other organizations, including the Procuracy, generally ignoring such cases entirely or returning them to justice organizations on the grounds that they did not require covert investigation and hence were not a police matter.[4] Local police also ignored summonses from peoples' courts and failed to deliver prisoners to court appearances in 1937 and 1938, despite specific orders from the NKVD leadership in Moscow to the contrary.[5] Although Ezhov did focus his attention on these issues during the mass operations, Stalin generally ignored them in favor of matters directly related to the ability of regional NKVD administrations to carry out mass repressions—for example, adding 3,800 officers to guard the border with Iran and Afghanistan, or increasing the number of NKVD convoy troops from 18,800 to 28,800.[6]

Ezhov's most acute concern involved the extent to which the mass operations disrupted the ability of local police administrations to carry out covert investigations of both political and civil crime. As we have seen, local NKVD officers concentrated on mass arrests exclusively in 1937 and 1938, generally ignoring policing tactics based on patrolling, cultivating relationships with individuals within the criminal milieu, and tracking suspect populations using the passport system. Ezhov focused on these very deficiencies in his censure of regional NKVD administrations in early 1938 (discussed above in chapter 6), as he attempted to redirect the mass operations toward both "national contingents" and the "ringleaders" of supposed counterrevolutionary conspiracies. The Politburo reprised many of these same themes at the end of the mass operations, charging that the NKVD had ignored covert surveillance and investigation in favor of the "much simpler method of making mass arrests."[7] Such complaints can be attributed, in part, to Stalin's demonstrated proclivity to blame local officials for policies that he himself had devised—after all, the repression of population cohorts, rather than individuals as such, was his exact intention in 1937 and 1938—but they were nevertheless accurate. Covert work was woefully inadequate in most areas of domestic NKVD activity in 1937 and 1938.

In mid-1938, as the mass operations against "anti-Soviet elements" began to wane, Ezhov and the Politburo began to address these inadequacies directly. Ezhov requested 20,000 additional *militsiia* officers nationwide, citing expanded duties regarding the transport of prisoners, the involvement of civil policemen in the repression of anti-Soviet agitation and crimes against public property, and the need to strengthen police forces in the fifty largest urban areas.[8] The Sovnarkom (and Stalin) concurred, bringing the total full-time staff of the USSR *militsiia* up to 181,995 officers, which was substantially more than the just over 120,000 in place at the end of the collectivization era.[9] At the same time, Ezhov submitted a plan to the Politburo in February 1938 that repeated his earlier attempts to separate the work of the *militsiia* from that of the political police. He recommended that separate counterintelligence departments within the NKVD be created to combat "wrecking" and espionage in individual branches of the defense industry, heavy industry, agricultural production, and state trade organizations, and that all covert surveillance of "political" crimes in the economic sector become the responsibility of the political police rather than the *militsiia*.[10]

The Politburo implemented Ezhov's plan in several steps during 1938. In March it created three separate directorates within the NKVD of equal bureaucratic stature: State Security, Special Departments (related to the surveillance of the Soviet military), and Transport and Communications. In August, the NKVD transferred almost all covert surveillance of potentially "political" crime within trade organizations from the *militsiia* to the political police. A newly created Ninth Department of the USSR NKVD supervised all local efforts to combat economic crime, while local Speculation Departments lost control of policing of all economic crime—except the theft of state property, speculation, and counterfeiting—to local political police administrations.[11] In mid-September, at precisely the point when Stalin decided to bring the mass operations to a close, the Politburo completed this restructuring by removing the Economic and Transport subdepartments from the State Security Directorate (GUGB) and creating corresponding freestanding central directorates within the NKVD (technically equal to, rather than part of, State Security).[12] Taken together, these changes elevated the surveillance of railroads and commerce to the bureaucratic level of counterintelligence and antidiversionary activity, and they separated the work of the *militsiia* from that of the political police in the troublesome area of economic crime—a direct return to the early-1930s vision of a *militsiia* that would be "Chekist in essence" but separate in practice from the political police, allowing the two halves of the Soviet policing system to concentrate on the separate tasks of the preservation of domestic tranquillity and state security.

The Politburo reinforced these attempts to improve covert methods of investigation and surveillance as it replaced Ezhov with Beria and ended the mass operations in November 1938. The November 17, 1938, Politburo resolution that ended the operations, titled "On Arrests, Procuratorial Oversight, and the Conduct of Investigations," included numerous tropes intended to explain the accompanying policy and leadership changes to local Communist Party and NKVD administrations, such as the idea that Ezhov had allowed enemies to "worm their way" into the NKVD and thus failed to "fully unmask" spies and "oppositionists" within the country. Yet the resolution also focused directly on poor investigative work among local police administrations, charging that the NKVD had abandoned operative work altogether in 1937 and 1938 and preferred "mass arrests" over "meticulous, systematic work with agents and informants" and the careful investigation of individual cases. Regional NKVD administrations, according to the resolution, had "lost the taste" (*poteriali vkus*) for covert measures and had become so dependent on mass arrests that they continued to request additional quotas from the Politburo until only days before the operations were halted.[13] Both the resolution and follow-up instructions sent to regional NKVD officials by Beria several days later prohibited mass arrests or mass deportations of any kind. Beria, in the order quoted at the beginning of this chapter, forbade officers to carry out "any sort of mass operations of arrest or deportation," specifying that the term "mass arrests" meant "group arrests or deportations without a differentiated approach to each arrested or deported individual."[14] The abolition of the NKVD troikas was the most apparent part of the November 17 Politburo instructions, yet the prohibition of "mass operations of arrest or deportation" was more fundamental for daily police work. As we will see, it would also prove more difficult to make permanent.

Central and local police administrations quickly fell into line with the requirements of the November instructions, in part due to fear of the purges that inevitably accompanied leadership changes within the NKVD.

At the center, Ezhov's removal was accompanied by thorough purges of the upper echelons of the NKVD, as Stalin and Beria ruthlessly removed Ezhov's remaining supporters. By the end of 1938, more than 300 top NKVD officials had been arrested; by the end of 1939, more than 1,300 more.[15] Purges in the civil police system were substantial as well; in mid-December 1938, the head of the Moscow *militsiia* reported that more than 3,000 policemen had been purged during the year for lack of "political reliability," compared with 645 expelled in 1937.[16] In addition, the Politburo implemented measures to "revive" Communist Party control over the NKVD in late 1938 and early 1939, a move that elided the fact that regional party secretaries were fully involved in nearly all aspects of the mass operations.[17]

These measures were intended to force the local NKVD administrations to react swiftly to the policy changes that had accompanied Beria's appointment. The new party and NKVD chiefs sent to the periphery to replace the officials who had served under Ezhov largely complied, obediently reporting to the center on "excesses" that had taken place during the previous months and deferring, in the initial weeks of Beria's tenure, to local Procuracy officials regarding control over investigations.[18] All the available evidence suggests that the end of the mass operations was, from a bureaucratic standpoint, relatively orderly, and that it took place under the direct control of the center.[19]

A single Politburo instruction, however, could not transform the one-sided relationship between justice and police organizations, and within weeks of the November 1938 instructions both central and local NKVD administrations began to resist encroachments by the Procuracy on their ability to detain and arrest suspects. This problem was plainly visible in the failure of Vyshinsky, and his relatively weak replacement as head of the USSR Procuracy after June 1939, Mikhail Pankratev, to effect substantial reconsideration of sentences that had been handed down by the NKVD troikas in 1937 and 1938. A review of select cases of individuals sentenced by the troikas as "socially harmful elements," which had begun in early 1938, remained decidedly limited in 1939, in large part because the local procurators were required to submit their complaints directly to regional NKVD chiefs for consideration, rather than to local soviet or justice administrations.[20] The NKVD chiefs, many of whom were new to their jurisdictions in the immediate post-Ezhov period, were not always opposed to such revisions, because reversals in individual cases allowed them to demonstrate their vigilance in correcting the supposed "counterrevolutionary excesses" of previous NKVD officials.[21] Yet the Procuracy carried out no systematic review after 1938 of the sentences handed down by NKVD troikas; local procurators were simply instructed to accept protests from arrestees themselves and handle them to the best of their ability.

Not surprisingly, repeated Procuracy circulars in 1939 complained that tens of thousands of complaints languished for months without action, both because local procurators were overwhelmed by their expanded duties and because regional NKVD administrations controlled the case files necessary to consider complaints and were generally unwilling to cooperate.[22] Pankratev attempted to improve the situation in mid-September 1939 by ordering local procurators to address all outstanding complaints by the beginning of December, but the task was beyond the capacities of justice administrations. The Leningrad procurator, for example, reported that, as of December 1, exactly 12,855 complaints remained unconsidered, compared with 9,798 two months earlier.[23] The procurators in the Gorkii region, staggering under workloads that were made all the more difficult by the fact that paperwork regarding the vast majority of cases heard by the troikas had long before been sent to Moscow, reportedly handled protests in the only way they could: they simply forwarded complaints directly to the regional NKVD administration rather than undertaking any investigations themselves, a move that ensured that such complaints would be, at best, ignored.[24]

Pankratev's demand that local procurators complete all case reviews also ignored the reality that local Procuracy officials were at the bureaucratic mercy of the NKVD, which, under the strong leadership of Beria, quickly regained its institutional nerve after November 1938.[25] By early 1940, regional NKVD administrations rejected all protests from the Procuracy as a matter of course, likely under direct orders from Beria.[26] Reviews came to an official halt in August 1940, when Pankratev ordered local procurators to refrain from "indiscriminate protesting of the decisions of former [NKVD] troikas regarding cases involving criminal elements" and to operate on the assumption, still the basis of juridical understandings of "social danger," that individuals deemed "harmful" were subject to punishment regardless of their actual criminal activity.[27] Given the complexities of the review process and the active hostility of many regional NKVD chiefs, successful protests of troika decisions could have amounted to no more than a negligible fraction of the sentences handed down in 1937 and 1938.[28] In addition, there is no indication that Procuracy or NKVD officials ever undertook a review of the sentences handed down in the "national operations."

The policy changes of late 1938 did not emerge from any desire on the part of Stalin or Beria to force the NKVD to relinquish possession of the penal populations already under its control, nor could they overcome the structural inequalities between the NKVD and the Procuracy at the local level. The Procuracy, like the judicial system in general, had been far more decimated by the Stalinist terror than the police, and it was in no position to direct a total restructuring of the Soviet criminal justice system in 1939.[29] The nature of Soviet policing in the late 1930s, and the way that the mass operations were brought to an end, virtually ensured that these reform efforts, which were in many respects begun by Ezhov in 1938 and continued by Beria as he climbed to power in the middle of that year, would come to naught.

Passports and Population "Contingents," 1938–1941

Beria's attempts in 1938 and 1939 to counteract the tendency of the Soviet police to rely on mass deportations and arrests contradicted what continued to be the single most important policing structure in urban areas: the internal passport system. The mass operations intensified the propensity of local police to use passports in order to purge their jurisdictions of suspects and ex-convicts, ensuring that officers would continue to use "mass" arrests to police important urban areas after November 1938. Local police retained the power to exile or banish passport violators on their own authority from all major cities in the USSR even after November 1938, despite attempts by the Politburo in 1939 and 1940 to shift the responsibility of sentencing passport offenders to the courts. The passport system remained the most important extrajudicial system used by the local police to protect "Soviet" spaces from "threatening" cohorts of ex-convicts, ethnic minorities, and those "special settlers" whose geographic mobility was deemed by the Politburo to be a threat, after the mass operations as before, to national security.

The mass operations in 1937 and 1938 intensified the propensity of local police to use the passport system not as a means of covert surveillance but to identify and target suspect population cohorts using "open" surveillance techniques. As the operations began, L. N. Belskii, the USSR *militsiia* chief, specifically ordered local administrations to put their registration and passport systems in order so that political policemen could rely on them

when targeting "kulaks and criminal elements."[30] Local police administrations generally complied, but they continued to ignore demands from the
center to use the registration and passport systems to track and uncover
suspects and wanted criminals at large within their jurisdictions as well,
focusing instead on the registration of known ex-convicts and "former
kulaks"—something that one NKVD circular derided as the "mechanical"
registration of suspect population cohorts.[31] Central NKVD officials made
two substantial changes to the passport documents themselves in 1937
and 1938 in order to improve the ability of local NKVD administrations
to target suspect individuals: in late October 1937, the police began to add
photographs to all passports for the first time; and in April 1938, they
began to specify an individual's nationality on his or her passport document based on the documented ethnicity of the individual's parents, rather
than on his or her self-identification.[32]

Ezhov's goals were clear in the instructions issued to local NKVD
administrations: officers were explicitly instructed to concentrate on
identifying immigrants, fleeing kulaks, and other cohorts that were subject to repression when placing photographs in passports, and they were
told in April 1938, at the peak of the national operations, that it was
"impermissible to write in the passport of a German or a Pole that he is
Russian, Ukrainian, or Belorussian, even if he was born in the Russian,
Ukrainian, or Belorussian Republic."[33] Ezhov also tightened residence
restrictions in regime cities substantially in August and September 1937,
ordering the police to refuse to register individuals with two or more
sentences for any past infraction.[34] All these changes were designed to
uncover the "masked" enemies within the Soviet population, yet they
also reinforced the importance of the passport system in the daily law
enforcement activities of the urban police, who continued to rely on the
evidence of ethnicity, previous convictions, or past social status inscribed
in passport documents themselves, instead of the information gathered
by the covert registration and tracking systems associated with the passport system, to identify "dangerous" or "anti-Soviet" populations in their
areas.

Central complaints regarding the passport system largely disappeared
in late 1937 and early 1938, as the police concentrated on carrying out
Order 00447 (see chapter 6), but Ezhov returned to the issue in mid-1938
in conjunction with his attempts to improve covert policing techniques. In
June 1938, the center censured several *militsiia* administrations for sub-
standard registration procedures during the mass operations, complaining

that the local police had left thousands of registration cards out of the card catalogs, entirely ignored nationwide searches for particular suspects, and allowed tens of thousands of individuals, including ex-convicts, to come and go from major cities each month without registration.[35] Such complaints continued into the post-1938 era, because the November 1938 policy directives contained no concrete initiatives designed to improve registration or surveillance using the passport system. In December 1938, the center complained that local police were using their registration bureaus, which were in charge of maintaining the registration card catalogs, to record general population migration rather than to identify potential "criminal elements" or suspects who fled the police in other locales.[36] Surprise inspections in February 1939 in forty-two districts of the Moscow region uncovered 14,546 individuals living without registration and 95,807 individuals who had been registered locally but whose information had not been transmitted to the regional Central Address Bureau, which was responsible for checking all new registrations against lists of wanted criminals at large.[37] Similar complaints continued into 1940, with the center charging that the local police routinely issued passports to individuals not eligible for them, failed to collect passports from the dead, and failed to pay sufficient attention to apartment-block record keeping in major cities.[38] Constant censures of this sort did little to change the reality that local police administrations had neither the staff nor the expertise to use the passport system as a means of covert surveillance, preferring instead to simply check passports on the street and arrest individuals who could not produce the proper documents.

The Politburo attempted to respond to these difficulties in July 1938, as the operations against "criminal elements" drew to a close, by separating existing regime areas into two categories in order to reduce the number of individuals subject to full passport restrictions. The cities of Moscow, Leningrad, Kharkov, Baku, Sochi, and the 100-kilometer or 50-kilometer zones around them, plus border zones and several areas of particular military importance, were declared "special regime" locations, in which full restrictions remained in place. Residence restrictions were relaxed in all other regime locations, which included virtually all remaining urban areas, allowing individuals with previous convictions for several common crimes—including hooliganism, speculation and theft—to reside in these areas as long as the police determined that they did not present a "social danger."[39] This reform represented a genuinely moderate impulse on the part of the Politburo, driven especially by Vyshinsky's influence, but it was also an admission that the complexity of the passport system had overwhelmed the capacity of most local police administrations to use it in any way other than to support mass purges.

Even after this change, local police and Communist Party officials continued to clamor for inclusion in the list of regime areas in order to deal with ex-convicts and "criminal elements." Although the center was less willing to accord regime status to new locations than it had been in 1935 and 1936, the number of regime areas nonetheless continued to climb, reaching 635 cities and districts, plus border zones and zones around the most important cities, by mid-1940.[40] The NKVD leadership adamantly opposed the use of mass arrests during the expansion of the passport system after 1938, but the line separating expansion from mass repression was thin. When Murmansk was added to the list of regime cities in September 1939, for example, the local police were instructed to target "suspect elements, especially Finns, Estonians, and other foreigners; individuals administratively exiled in the past; those sentenced for counterrevolutionary crimes; Trotskyites; S[ocialist] R[evolutionarie]s; Mensheviks; and individuals involved in anti-Soviet activities." Beria forbade the police in Murmansk to allow the operation to assume a "mass character" and ordered them to implement regime restrictions "without creating a stir [*bez shuma*] and without unnecessarily frightening people," but he also authorized the local NKVD administration to arrest 500 to 700 individuals and send their cases to the NKVD Special Board for sentencing—a blatant contradiction and a return to the practices of 1937 and 1938.[41]

The passport restrictions regarding ex-convicts began to harden again as well. In May 1939, the NKVD reversed its earlier practice of issuing regime passports to individuals whose past sentences had been lifted by amnesty from the Soviet government, subjecting hundreds of thousands of average citizens, especially peasants who benefited from the amnesties promoted by Vyshinsky between 1936 and 1938, to permanent banishment from regime areas once again.[42] The creation of the two "regime" categories was prompted by concerns that the passport system was unnecessarily restrictive—a conclusion obvious even in the midst of the mass operations—yet the long-standing connections between the passport system, urban policing, and issues of national security were far stronger than the Politburo's attempts to rein in mass arrests after November 1938.

The nature of the passport system also ensured that extrajudicial punishment, flatly forbidden by the November 1938 directives, would quickly reemerge in policing practices in 1939 and 1940. The police lost all rights to sentence passport violators through their own police troikas at the end of the mass operations. Instead, punishments for passport violations that surpassed simple monetary fines were meted out by the courts, following the requirements of Article 192a of the Criminal Code of the Russian Republic. This change caused tremendous problems for local police and criminal justice administrations, because the court system was simply incapable of handling the hundreds of thousands of passport violations registered by the police in regime areas in a given year and because the code made no provisions for punishing first-time offenders in regime areas, as long as they possessed valid nonregime passports. In January 1940, USSR justice commissar Nikolai Rychkov brought the issue to the attention of the Sovnarkom, arguing that most violations of the passport system in the post-1938 period went essentially unpunished because the Criminal Code allowed for only relatively moderate punishment, even for second offenders.[43] When queried by the Sovnarkom for the opinion of the NKVD, the assistant commissar of internal affairs, V. V. Chernyshov, made plain the resentment harbored by top police officials regarding the loss of extrajudicial sentencing powers for passport offenders and "socially harmful elements." He suggested that individuals without passports who engaged in begging, thievery, or prostitution, and who were connected with the criminal milieu, should receive lengthy sentences in labor camps, and he recommended that the code specify two years of imprisonment for any second violation on the part of individuals with no employment or "defined place of residence."[44]

Vyshinsky, flexing his muscles in his new position as deputy chair of the Sovnarkom, refused to authorize a change to the Criminal Code, but in April 1940 the NKVD issued its own instructions on the matter, ordering the local police to repress passport violators while avoiding the court system but still carefully obeying the letter of the law. First-time violators were fined, even for the most petty cases, and those without demonstrated employment or places of residence were ejected from the city in question within twenty hours—a process that technically involved no sentencing and hence could be carried out by individual officers without turning to the courts. A second offense brought the court system into the process; individuals without a place of residence or employment were sentenced to two years of imprisonment, while those who proved a place of residence but were unemployed were transferred to the court system under Article 35 of the Criminal Code, which allowed for the judicial banishment of "socially harmful elements" for up to three years.[45] Article 35, as we have seen, served as the basis for the legal definition of "harmful elements" in the 1920s but had fallen out of use in the 1930s, as the police gained the right to sentence this category of offenders using extrajudicial means. Its reappearance in the post-1938 period suggests that the definitions of "social danger" that guided the police in the mid-1930s were spreading to the court system, and that the police continued to target cohorts of urban criminals and marginalized individuals in much the same way that they had before the mass operations, despite their nominal loss of extrajudicial sentencing powers.[46]

Finally, in August 1940, the USSR Justice and Internal Affairs commissariats agreed that judicial hearings for all nonpayers of fines for passport violations could be heard by the courts without the presence of the police officer issuing the fine. This simplified procedure created what were in essence extrajudicial hearings, because the officer was usually the only witness involved in the case and no proper legal procedures could be followed by judges hearing the cases.[47] The police may have lost the technical capacity to sentence passport violators and "socially dangerous elements" in November 1938, but the Soviet criminal justice system quickly adjusted to allow them to continue to repress "criminal" and "harmful elements" in much the same manner as they had for most of the 1930s.

The trend toward harsher restrictions on the mobility of suspect individuals and ex-convicts culminated in late 1940, with a second major restructuring of the passport system. All existing regime areas were again divided into two categories. "Regime I" locales included eleven particularly important cities, plus the entire Moscow region; the 100- and 50-kilometer zones around Leningrad and Kiev; zones along the external USSR border; and several districts in the south with particular strategic importance. "Regime II" locales included sixty-nine specific urban areas and numerous southern and eastern districts.[48] Regime I areas remained off limits to the same categories subject to previous "special regime" rules, including virtually all ex-convicts, refugees, and individuals without proper work invitations; Regime II areas were forbidden only to individuals guilty of political crimes and several important public-order crimes, now including, in contrast to the relatively moderate July 1938 regulations, speculation and repeat hooliganism.[49]

This two-tiered system acquiesced to certain realities of migration and work patterns in the USSR. For example, new instructions omitted the troublesome requirements that seasonal laborers be recruited through official labor organizations and show proof of living space before migrating to most regime cities. In sum, however, the changes signaled a return to the kind of strict quarantine of urban areas that had defined Soviet policing in the mid-1930s.[50]

Local *militsiia* administrations treated the imposition of the new system, which was carried out in conjunction with an exchange of the five-year passport documents handed out in 1935, as an opportunity to return to wholesale purges of unwanted individuals from their jurisdictions. The central instructions regarding the exchange were inconsistent, ordering the police to carry it out without reverting to a "mass campaign" but also ordering the police in Regime I areas to purge their locales of individuals with past criminal sentences, those who might be hiding from the police or using a fake passport, or any individuals who maintained connections with the criminal milieu.[51] Local officers went far beyond these guidelines, requesting additional staff to set up ad hoc distribution centers and turning the exchange into the same kind of campaign that had characterized the passport system in prior years.[52]

The restrictiveness of the passport system in the last months before World War II was also plainly visible in the fate of "special settlers" and their children. As we have seen in chapter 6, Vyshinsky and Ezhov agreed in early 1937, in conjunction with discussions of the USSR Constitution, that individuals exiled to special settlements would remain ineligible to move until mid-1939, at which point they would be allowed to move within their home regions; a year later, they were to gain the right to move to other regions of the USSR. The Politburo raised the issue of resettled individuals as the mass operations drew to a close, and in late October 1938 it resolved to allow the children of banished or exiled parents—the least-threatening group of "special settlers"—to receive passports and leave settlements or places of exile once they reached sixteen years of age, as long as they had not committed any crimes while in exile. Yet this absolution was only partial; these young adults were permanently forbidden to live in regime cities, making it impossible to seek education or employment in virtually all the USSR's urban areas.[53] The NKVD, furthermore, implemented the policy in a way that undermined the original intent of the instruction, ordering the local police in January 1939 to issue passports only to those children of settlers who were over sixteen at the moment of the issuance of the order and who had definite work or education plans at specific destinations, instead of making the practice automatic for all children in settlements as they reached the age of sixteen.[54] This practice was not changed until a year later, when it was protested by Pankratev to Molotov; under pressure from Vyshinsky, the NKVD eventually relented in January 1940, but the restriction against moving to regime locations remained in place.[55] Although some 80,000 children of special settlers received restricted passports in the prewar years, the overall move should be understood—in comparison with earlier amnesties of peasant populations and in contrast to pre-1937 debates on the ultimate fate of special settlers in general—as part of an overall hardening of Soviet policy regarding exiled populations after 1938.[56]

The special settlers themselves received no such exceptions from their onerous residence restrictions in the post-1938 period, notwithstanding the 1937 agreement between Ezhov and Vyshinsky. According to NKVD reports, once the mass operations were complete, numerous settlers began once again to claim the right to geographic mobility promised to them in the 1936 USSR Constitution, even though the existing regulations prohibited any and all migration by special settlers. Local passport police responded by sending such individuals back to their settlements or to labor camps.[57] Pankratev attempted in late March 1940 to soften these restrictions, appealing to Vyshinsky regarding individuals who were transferred to special settlements from the Gulag and labor colony system as part of the 1933 "clearing" of prison populations (see chapter 3). Pankratev argued that many of these individuals had been serving specific sentences of three or five years, handed down by the courts or extrajudicial bodies, when they were moved to the special settlements, after which they were considered equivalent in all respects to that of the larger category of "kulak" special settlers and hence fastened permanently to the settlements. The result, he argued, was what he termed a "strange situation" in which individuals, sentenced to specific terms in camps or colonies, faced lifelong sentences in settlements "without any sort of hope for release" and social isolation "until [their] last day."

After several months of delay, Vyshinsky declined Pankratev's suggestion that these individuals be freed from further incarceration, instructing the NKVD sometime after late May 1940 to maintain the existing regulations that required all settlers to remain in their locations of exile permanently, including those sentenced to specific sentences for specific crimes.[58] The special settlers became a permanent, hereditarily defined cohort, which was deemed incapable of rehabilitation and demanded total separation from Soviet society. Central definitions of this category were certainly genealogical, if not precisely genetic, showing that Stalin's famous dictum that "children should not suffer for the sins of their fathers" had substantial limits in the period after 1938.

Aggressive police responses to adult beggars and nomadic Gypsies in 1940 make clear the persistent tendency of the Stalinist regime to control "social danger" by restricting geographic mobility. The Sovnarkom received requests in late 1940 from justice, Procuracy, and Moscow Communist Party officials for a new law, and a corresponding police campaign, against homeless populations in major Soviet cities, which were reportedly growing as a result of harvest difficulties and a lack of sufficient police attention to the problem. Justice and police officials alike pointed to the existence of "professional" criminals among homeless populations and generally agreed that homeless individuals who "resisted" educational or welfare interventions should be subject to extrajudicial repression. In his December 1940 opinion on the matter, for example, Viktor Bochkov, who replaced Pankratev as USSR procurator in mid-1940, argued that most homeless adults in regime areas were healthy and fit to work, and that their refusal to do so identified them as "socially dangerous" (*opasnye*) individuals who should be swept off the streets and sentenced to terms in labor camps by the NKVD Special Board—an institution that had been explicitly restricted to hearing political cases by the November 1938 instructions that halted the mass operations.[59]

NKVD directives regarding beggary in late 1940 drew the same conclusions, charging that beggars were predominantly "declassed elements, alcoholics, loafers and others who do not want to work honestly" and that homeless populations were rife with "criminal elements," escapees from labor camps, or exiled "kulaks" attempting to avoid arrest. The Sovnarkom approved no new legislation on beggary in 1940, but the police responded vigorously to the issue nonetheless, within the boundaries of the passport system. Local police arrested beggars who lacked proper passport documents and sent them to the courts, where they were subject to sentences of two years in a labor camp for lack of defined place of residence, or charged as "harmful elements" under Article 35 of the Criminal Code for lack of employment, both per the April 1940 passport instructions. Because virtually all beggars fell into both categories, the police had ample legal justification to use the passport system to purge urban areas of them, even without specific authorization to use extrajudicial sanctions in the process.[60]

The police in Central Asia followed a virtually identical approach when incarcerating Gypsy populations (identified only as *tsygany* in NKVD documents) in 1940. The instructions issued to the police in 1940 regarding the passport system, discussed above, specifically included "nomadic Gypsies" on the list of the population cohorts that were to be ejected from both Regime I and II areas.[61] In late November 1940, the assistant procurator of the Uzbek Republic complained to the USSR Procuracy that the local NKVD administrations were applying this restriction incorrectly to the nomadic Gypsies who set up encampments every winter in Central Asia. The police arrested the Gypsies as soon as they appeared in areas covered by the regime restrictions and, rather than simply expelling them, sent them to court, citing their lack of employment or defined place of residence, which, under the April 1940 regulations, subjected them to two-year prison sentences. The regulations on beggars, argued the procurator, could have only been intended to apply to "declassed, vagrant elements" and not to the entire nomadic Gypsy population of Central Asia. In addition, the police usually arrested only men, leaving women and children to fend for themselves and pushing these families into destitution. If left unchecked, the procurator argued, this practice would eventually result in the incarceration of all Gypsies in labor camps. "If," he added, "the traditional lifestyle of Gypsies has become a crime, then it seems to me that a special legal instruction on this topic is necessary." If, on the contrary, a "historical mistake" was responsible for the situation, he suggested that the center add a notation to the passport instructions exempting Gypsy populations from such treatment.[62]

Molotov considered the procurator's questions in December 1940 and ordered the NKVD to cease arresting Gypsies for simple passport violations, subjecting them only to fines for first infractions. Gypsy populations, however, remained ineligible for regime passports, and second offenses were grounds for arrest.[63] The Gypsies were prosecuted, in the minds of both the central and local police officials, because of their inherent geographic mobility and "lack of defined place of residence," both of which functioned as direct markers of criminality by the end of the 1930s.

Speculation and Extrajudicial Repression, 1937–1940

Of all the problems faced by the Soviet police after 1938, shortages of consumer goods, lines in front of state retail stores, and widespread speculation in individual items were the most public, the most ubiquitous, and the most challenging to the notion that the USSR had reached "socialism" under Stalin's guidance. Barely a year after the record harvest of 1937, poor agricultural conditions and structural deficiencies in the Soviet trade system plunged the USSR into another cycle of goods deficits and the frantic attempts by trade officials to cope with the rampant speculation that accompanied them. As in years past, the Politburo responded to these problems with a combination of economic measures and overt police repression, directing the NKVD to bring order to retail trade with a series of campaigns against speculation in open air markets and—a new approach in 1939 and 1940—against lines themselves. These campaigns required the participation of the entire criminal justice system, and they involved many of the techniques of the "campaign of vigilance" against Soviet elites in 1936 and 1937, especially show trials of cases deemed particularly instructive. In practice, however, they primarily relied on police sweeps of urban areas and extrajudicial forms of repression, beginning with simple fines handed out by the police to line-standers and culminating, by 1940, in overt extrajudicial repression carried out by the NKVD's Special Board.

Police responses to speculation suffered substantially during the mass operations. Attention to the problem among top police officials disappeared almost altogether in the summer of 1937, reemerging only when the fall harvest and procurement campaigns once again brought the reality of shortages to the attention of economic planners. Although the fall of 1937 saw record harvests in most areas of the country, inefficiencies in the system of retail distribution produced isolated shortages nonetheless, as in Rostov, where the police reported in early November that thousands of people stood in lines overnight, waiting for major retail stores to open in the morning.[64] The explanations for these difficulties proffered by central NKVD officials focused almost entirely on the narrative tropes prevalent during the mass operations: shortages were the result of "organized" speculation carried out by "wreckers" who purposefully created "artificial" problems in the Soviet retail trade sector.[65] Such rhetoric was useless to local officers, who knew full well that speculation was, in the main, the product of individual buying and selling, often by collective farmers pouring into cities in search of goods not available in the countryside.[66] As a result, local police made every effort in 1937 and 1938 to handle petty speculation with administrative measures, arresting only the most egregious violators and subjecting the vast majority of offenders, most of whom were average Soviet citizens, to warnings or simple monetary fines.[67] This practice reduced the amount of effort expended by local police administrations to control speculation—an eminently rational strategy, given the demands of the mass operations—but it also ensured that the police, by the end of 1938, were entirely accustomed to handling petty speculation with extrajudicial means.[68]

Speculation became a major issue again in the fall of 1938, as provisioning difficulties in major cities marked the beginning of a third major wave of shortages of consumer goods in the 1930s. Central justice and police administrations reacted in the spirit of the mass operations, demanding that local officials uncover "Trotskyite-Bukharinite spies" in trade organizations and apply the law of August 22, 1932, which required a minimum sentence of five years for cases of speculation, to all individuals found guilty at court.[69] Although local police and justice officials responded aggressively to this campaign in late 1938, repeated complaints from justice and trade organizations regarding shortages and massive lines in the retail trade sector made it clear that systemic distribution problems, rather than the mere existence of "wreckers" in the trade sector, were the root cause of these problems.[70]

The effects of shortages on the fabric of urban life were, in any case, impossible to ignore. Exceptionally long lines began to appear in Moscow in early 1939, forming as soon as the stores closed for the evening and stretching by morning to sometimes thousands of people, who dozed in courtyards and alleyways while maintaining their place in the queue. The Moscow police estimated that only 15 to 30 percent of the people in lines were city residents; the rest were "professional" buyers, residents of the surrounding area, or line-standing "specialists" who would save a place overnight for a fee of 20 to 30 rubles.[71]

Local trade agencies complained that the police were unwilling to control these lines for consumer goods, often simply breaking up the lines altogether and ordering citizens to disperse until morning or, in some cases, actually organizing overnight queues at locations slightly removed from storefronts and then leading customers to stores in the morning. A Soviet Control Commission report, sent to Molotov in mid-1939, likewise noted that the police had halted any attempts to prevent lines in December 1938, citing Procuracy instructions regarding the end of the mass operations and the prohibition of all extrajudicial repression. According to the report, local police issued no fines and confiscated no purchased goods, limiting their activity instead to organizing queues and attempting to maintain order until stores opened in the morning.[72] Lines had been a staple feature of the Soviet urban landscape since trade restrictions were lifted in 1935, but the size, composition, and ubiquity of lines in major cities gave credence to the idea that petty speculation, and even the existence of the lines themselves, were responsible for the trade imbalances that caused widespread shortages of nearly all consumer goods in 1938 and 1939.

These problems in the trade sector were discussed by top Communist Party officials in early 1939, provoking a major campaign in April and May that not only targeted speculation but also made standing in lines itself an offense. On April 5, 1939, the Sovnarkom prohibited the formation of lines in Moscow in front of stores that sold manufactured goods. The *militsiia* was ordered to disperse lines before the stores opened, to hand out minimum fines of 100 rubles "on the spot" (*na meste*) to individuals who disturbed public order in lines, and to charge particularly egregious violators of public order with hooliganism and send their cases to court. Petty speculators were to be exiled from Moscow under the passport regime, with more serious cases handed over to the courts. Court and Procuracy officials were ordered to process cases of speculation in under five days, to stage show trials of serious cases for the edification of the Moscow population, and to prosecute the chairs of rural soviets for the widespread practice of providing collective farmers with documents that allowed them to travel to Moscow to purchase consumer goods.[73]

The Moscow police had little difficulty fulfilling these orders, using passport sweeps to expel non-Muscovites standing in line and controlling hooliganism and other types of disorder with fines or arrests. The novel task of controlling lines directly did require certain adjustments, based on trial and error. The Moscow police initially prohibited lines altogether, with the result that unruly crowds threw themselves at storefronts once the doors were opened, but the police quickly changed their policy to allow for queuing up thirty minutes before opening time, resulting in more orderly formation of lines each morning. Within days, the police reported that the lines had dropped from thousands of people to several hundred, most of whom were city residents. Judicial officials also reported that show trials, now a staple part of the educative portion of policing campaigns, were a success; between April 5 and 27, thirteen such show trials were staged in workers' clubs in Moscow, with roughly 700 workers attending.[74] The Politburo, in response to this perceived success, expanded the campaign in May to Leningrad, where the police likewise had little difficulty carrying it out.[75]

The ease with which the police swept speculators and hooligans from the streets of Moscow and Leningrad during these campaigns overwhelmed the court system and underscored the structural difficulties caused by the post-1938 abolition of extrajudicial punishments. Most cases in Moscow were not heard by the courts in the requisite five days after they were delivered by the police; in fact, more than a hundred judges in Moscow

Peoples' Courts were not even informed of the April 5 order by the Justice Commissariat until several days after the campaign began. The Moscow Procuracy suffered from the same kind of inefficiency, failing to complete its required processing of the cases quickly enough to meet the five-day deadline.[76] Most cases took between five and fifteen days to pass through the court system, with a substantial number taking more than thirty days— this despite the fact that the police forwarded only the most serious cases to court, handling the vast majority with fines or the passport system.[77] The antispeculation campaign of early 1939 proved to the Politburo that police pressure on lines was a viable way to control the outward manifestations of endemic goods shortages, but it called into question the viability of the complete elimination of extrajudicial repression of nonpolitical crimes from the Soviet criminal justice system.

The regime's response in early 1939 to problems of shortages, lines, and speculation in major Soviet cities was only a hint of what was to follow later in the year. A poor harvest in the fall of 1939, along with the economic stresses of the Russo-Finnish War, compounded existing food deficits and produced some of the worst shortages in the Soviet Union since the devastating famine of 1932–33. Manufactured items and food goods were virtually absent from retail stores in major cities, while conditions in the countryside verged on disaster, forcing collective farmers to slaughter their cattle for lack of feed, as they had in 1932 and 1933.[78]

Central Communist Party officials were well apprised of the situation and were not particularly sanguine about the ability of simple police action to improve it. The procurator of the Republic of Bashkiria, for example, reported to the center in December 1939 that shortages in the city of Ufa had produced huge lines for bread and bread products, many stretching to 3,000 people. Customers in Ufa, who stood in lines for up to twenty-four hours, did not suffer the situation lightly, ignoring the possibility of retribution by the NKVD in order to vent "unhealthy attitudes and utterances" and, in some cases, smashing windows and breaking down the doors of the restricted food stores that served party or soviet employees.[79]

In January 1940, the Soviet Control Commission reported that the situation in most cities had reached a crisis point. The new year began with shortages of some bread products, but within days many stores were out of bread products altogether.[80] A. V. Liubimov, the USSR trade commissar, reported the same information to Politburo member Anastas Mikoyan in late January, suggesting that the Politburo restrict bread sales to closed shops and cafeterias in factories and other state institutions in order to prevent speculation.[81] The Politburo attempted to respond to the crisis by forbidding sales of bread products in rural locations and by creating restricted retail outlets for employees of defense-related industries and the military, but Stalin held firm on the issue of rationing to the general public in order to protect "free" Soviet retail trade.[82]

The Politburo responded to this situation much as it had in 1939, ordering local police and justice agencies to increase pressure on speculators and providing local police administrations with new powers to mete out punishments on their own authority. The police in Moscow and Leningrad were ordered to levy fines of 100 rubles on individuals merely traveling to these two cities in order to purchase manufactured goods, as well as those who violated norms of public order. Serious cases of speculation, and acts of hooliganism in lines, were again to be sent to the courts for harsher punishments. Individuals who purchased more than twice the standard norm per person of a given product were subject to immediate confiscation of property and the same 100-ruble fine; repeat offenders could be arrested for violation of the rules of trade (Article 105). The Politburo insisted that the police categorize individuals who purchased items with "intent to resell" as speculators (Article 107), opening the door to prison sentences for individuals buying and selling single items. The courts were again to hear cases within five days of arraignment; the procurators, for their part, were to review the cases on the same day that they arrived from the police and, as in 1939, prepare a series of show trials for public consumption.[83]

As in 1939, the *militsiia* in Moscow and Leningrad dispersed the lines with little difficulty and reduced the flow of goods from these two cities to nearby collective farms. Beria, for example, reported to Molotov that, between January 20 and 25, the Moscow police confiscated 82,948 kilograms of manufactured goods from 5,355 purchasers who were leaving the city by rail. Beria deemed these successes positive enough to warrant expanding the order to Kiev, Kharkov, Riazan, Kalinin, Saratov, and a dozen others major cities, a position supported by both Liubimov and Mikoyan.[84] Once the Politburo approved the expansion, the local police in other urban areas immediately petitioned for inclusion on the list of cities under these regulations, much as they had lobbied for regime passport status earlier in the decade. The Politburo was generally willing to comply, although several localities were still pointedly refused the right to deal with speculators with these abbreviated extrajudicial procedures. By mid-1940, a campaign that had been exceptional in 1939 had spread to nearly four dozen major Soviet cities, in practice making the November 1938 prohibition of extrajudicial punishment obsolete in nearly all major urban areas in the USSR.[85]

Such widespread extrajudicial prerogatives, although certainly not as severe as the punishments meted out by the police in previous years, gave the police little incentive to turn to the court system at all during these campaigns against petty economic crime. In most areas of the USSR, the police formally arrested and sent to court only a fraction of the individuals they detained for speculation in early 1940: 17 percent in the Ivanovo region, 25 percent in the Novosibirsk region, and 37 percent in the entire Ukrainian Republic.[86] Local police chiefs offer no real defense of their actions. The head of the *militsiia* in the Armenian republic, for example, explained that many of his local police chiefs in 1940 were responding to pressure to increase the quality of investigative materials in cases sent to court by refusing to prosecute cases of speculation: "Evidently they decided to arrest [*privlekat'*, specifically to arrest and begin judicial proceedings] absolutely nobody for speculation, thinking that doing so would be easier [*tak budet' spokoinee*]."[87]

In May 1940, the Sovnarkom largely acquiesced to the difficulties inherent in carrying out this campaign through the court system, and to the recalcitrance of the local police to participate in judicial hearings, by authorizing local *militsiia* administrations to forward cases of speculation at open air markets directly to the NKVD Special Board for sentencing to terms in prisons or labor camps.[88] This change contributed to a substantial increase in arrests from 1939 to 1940. The number of individuals arrested for speculation (Article 107) in the USSR climbed from just under 27,000 in 1939 to over 41,000 in 1940; in sum, nearly 80,000 people were detained for speculation in 1940, just under 30,000 in the first half of 1941.[89] The available archival information makes it impossible to determine how many of those detained, but not formally arrested, were subject to extrajudicial punishment by the Special Board, or were fined or released; but overall trends in extrajudicial sentencing in 1940 and 1941 suggest that those individuals who were detained specifically for speculation, as opposed to violating rules of trade, likely experienced harsher punishments than a fine.[90] With the decision to allow the Special Board to sanction speculators, Stalin left behind the central tenet of the November 1938 regulations that ended the mass operations, and he signaled that the police, rather than the Procuracy, was once again in charge of controlling crime and social disorder in the most important Soviet cities.

The reemergence of extrajudicial responses to speculation and other petty economic crimes in the post-1938 period was the result, in part, of Stalin's impatience with the kind of legal reforms promoted by Vyshinsky throughout the 1930s. Stalin never demonstrated any principled adherence to the idea that a "conservative" approach to the law could promote social stability or the compliance of the Soviet population with the regime's policy demands. He was willing, in 1940 no less than in 1936 or 1937, to turn to overt repression of "threatening" behaviors once they became pressing enough to intrude on the deliberations of the Politburo. Police responses to speculation in 1939 and 1940, however, also emerged from the inability of the court system, still reeling from the effects of the Stalinist terror, to shoulder its part of the burden of the campaigns. Although the court system remained fully involved in the repression of speculation, as show trials and high conviction rates in 1939 and 1940 attest, police responses to petty speculation in the years before World War II played a larger role in shaping the regime's overall response to the problem.

These police responses to economic crime also helped to complete the conceptual changes, begun under Yagoda earlier in the decade, regarding the threat posed by the petty reselling of consumer goods to the Soviet economic system. Traveling to cities to purchase scarce consumer goods, selling individual items purchased legally in state retail stores, standing in lines for hours to purchase goods, or reserving a place in the queue—itself a valuable commodity by 1940—were all basic aspects of Soviet life by the prewar years, yet they were also behaviors that central NKVD officials could identify as the final link in a long chain of purchasing and selling that supposedly connected the large-scale thief, embezzler, or "Trotskyite-Bukharinite agent" with the Soviet consumer. Local police remained generally unconcerned, in practice, with the "sources" of speculation or the covert investigation techniques that, according to central NKVD officials, could eradicate them. For local officers, focusing on petty reselling and line standing was a far more profitable method of controlling the public manifestations of Soviet trade deficiencies, one that reflected the institutional capacities of local NKVD administrations as well as the propensity of the local police to target groups rather than individual offenders.[91] Central policymakers fully understood that the local police dealt with speculation in ways that best suited local conditions, using tactics that targeted individual speculators through extrajudicial means but ignoring central calls to improve the covert surveillance of the "criminal milieu."[92] On the eve of the war, "mass operations" and extrajudicial repression were again a central part of the regime's attempts to control economic crime at all levels of Soviet society.

Hooliganism, Juvenile Delinquency, and Preparations for War, 1940–1941

In the final year before the outbreak of World War II, Stalin took several draconian steps that were intended to increase labor discipline and repress urban crime in preparation for the possibility of conflict with Nazi Germany. The threat of war had influenced Stalin's approach to policing and public order since the mid-1930s, as we have seen, but the initiation of hostilities on the European continent in 1939, and the disastrous course of the Russo-Finnish War, convinced him that further steps were necessary in order to force Soviet society at large to obey the policy dictates of the regime.

Therefore, in June 1940, the Politburo criminalized the most prevalent of labor infractions, making quitting without the permission of factory management punishable by two to four months in prison and making absenteeism or tardiness to work punishable by six months of compulsory labor (mandatory labor at one's place of employment, with a pay deduction of 25 percent). In July, the regime launched a campaign against production of defective goods, raising the punishment for such crimes to eight years in prison. In August, Stalin launched campaigns against hooliganism and against petty theft in economic institutions, setting a minimum punishment of one year in prison for all offenders. Finally, in late 1940 and early 1941 Stalin initiated a series of measures aimed at juvenile delinquency in urban areas, criminalizing truancy in certain categories of trade schools and, in May 1941, lowering the age of criminal responsibility for juvenile offenders to fourteen for all crimes not already subject to the twelve-year limit by Stalin's edict of April 7, 1935 (see chapter 4).

The campaigns against labor violations and theft in factories, though massive, were not primarily police matters. Carried out by factory administrations themselves, they were designed not only to force compliance but also to educate the Soviet workforce, with the court system serving as the arena for adjudication and public display of the process. The campaigns against hooliganism and delinquency, on the contrary, were the responsibility of the police. Urban *militsiia* administrations were already engaged by 1940 in large-scale campaigns against passport violations and speculation, as discussed above, but Stalin's interventions regarding hooliganism and juvenile delinquency brought long-standing police approaches to both issues back to the forefront of Soviet criminal justice, returning the issue of "socially harmful" population cohorts to the center of police activity in the months before the war.

By the end of the mass operations, police in urban areas relied almost exclusively on extrajudicial sanctions in order to control hooliganism and other petty public-order crimes—not only police troikas and the passport system, but also the far more widespread system of administrative fines, which by the mid-1930s operated with little or no oversight from justice agencies or local soviets. Most cases of petty hooliganism had been handled outside the court system since the late 1920s, with fines levied by the individual officers themselves. Such fines were, in theory, adjudicated by three-person administrative commissions created in city- or district-level soviets, but local *militsiia* administrations had gradually encroached on these commissions in the early 1930s, and by mid-decade the local *militsiia* chiefs themselves approved fines for hooliganism of up to 100 rubles as a matter of course.[93] The local police in the mid-1930s made vigorous use of the sentencing capacity afforded them by the fining system, in conjunction with their extrajudicial abilities to sentence passport violators and socially harmful elements directly to labor camps, in order to control urban social disorder without resorting to the court system.[94]

This tendency only accelerated after mid-decade, as many local soviets abolished the commissions completely, in flagrant contradiction to existing legislation; the police levied fines for hooliganism at will on those Soviet citizens who violated norms of public order but did not merit, in the opinions of local officers, harsher forms of repression by the courts or police troikas as "socially harmful elements."[95] Local police administrations issued administrative fines for often serious hooliganistic acts during the mass operations of 1937 and 1938 as well, usually with little concern for the procedural requirements of the process, in order to avoid the minimal bureaucratic difficulties inherent in the system of extrajudicial troikas.[96] All forms of hooliganism, both petty and serious, were subject to extrajudicial repression during the mass operations; the decision to turn to a fine, an NKVD troika, or the court system rested entirely with the individual policeman on patrol.

These trends continued in the post-1938 era. Although the November 1938 instructions did not specifically address the issue of fines, numerous reports on the implementation of these instructions criticized the propensity of the local police to levy substantial fines, especially for hooliganism, without the involvement of administrative commissions. A major study of fines in Moscow, produced for Kalinin by the Information and Statistics Department of the USSR Supreme Soviet in early 1939, complained that the police routinely qualified minor disturbances as hooliganism and issued substantial fines to average citizens for offenses as petty as public drunkenness or standing in lines for scarce consumer goods. A fine for hooliganism, furthermore, usually entailed the requirement to appear at the local police station for registration by the Detective Department as a "hooliganistic element." The widespread use of fines, according to the report, thus increased the tendency of local officers to identify large sectors of the urban population as recidivists or "harmful elements" under police surveillance (*na uchet*).[97]

Central discussions of fining in 1939 and 1940 focused on the idea that these abuses contradicted the promotion of "socialist legality" in the post-1938 period, a term that explicitly linked the policy shifts of November 1938 with the instruction of May 8, 1933, on arrests and the "clearing" of prisons. A series of investigations by the Soviet Control Commission in April and May 1939, for example, concluded that fining practices violated "socialist legality" because prosecutorial supervision was totally absent and because fines were essentially "extrajudicial" forms of punishment.[98] Some discussion took place at the center in 1939 and 1940 concerning the idea of abolishing the rights of the police to collect fines altogether and shifting the adjudication of all fines to the court system. Yet such a step would have overwhelmed the struggling court system with millions of additional cases and was never a serious possibility.[99] Fines were a constituent part of urban policing by the late 1930s, so entrenched in daily practices that they were impervious to the reforms that accompanied the end of the Stalinist terror.

Central anxiety regarding hooliganism in the prewar years was amplified by concerns about youth criminality, an issue that, as in the mid-1930s, combined concrete threats to Soviet urban life with symbolic threats to the Soviet system. Numerous observers within the Soviet criminal justice and welfare systems reported substantial increases in juvenile delinquency in the late 1930s, concentrating on particularly "threatening" manifestations of juvenile crime, such as hooliganism, murder, and rape. This trend began in late 1936 and early 1937, as the food shortages of that difficult winter produced almost immediate increases in reported levels of child homelessness in major Soviet cities. Central officials, still touting the

successes of the 1935 campaign against homelessness, reported only tim-
idly that homelessness was again on the rise, but they focused more aggressively on perceived increases in juvenile delinquency and crime.[100]
Even Ezhov, upon taking over the NKVD, was surprised to find that juvenile delinquency was again a major problem in urban areas and that the
capacities of the police, especially the juvenile detention system, to deal
with the problem were limited.[101]

Ezhov, however, paid little systematic attention to the issue of juvenile
crime in 1937 and 1938, even though reports from the NKVD and welfare
agencies warned that levels of delinquency continued to climb, especially
among the "recidivist" core of delinquents that had repeatedly escaped
from orphanages or NKVD juvenile labor colonies.[102] The NKVD instead
focused most of its attention during the mass operations on the question
of the children of repressed parents, generally attempting to place them in
closed orphanages or NKVD juvenile labor colonies for those deemed
"socially dangerous."[103] The problems inherent in administering the expanding juvenile colony and labor camp systems were of course substantial in 1937 and 1938, but debates between NKVD and child welfare
officials in December 1937 led not to fundamental reforms but to an expansion of the NKVD's juvenile labor colony system.[104] The issue of delinquency itself was of secondary importance to the NKVD in 1937 and
1938; the police spent little time with the issue before the mass operations
were complete.

Urban police administrations returned to the issue of delinquency with
force after November 1938, reporting substantial increases in the numbers
of school-age children apprehended on city streets and focusing in particular on manifestations of "socially dangerous" criminality among youth.
Nationwide, the police detained more than 33,000 juveniles under the age
of sixteen for criminal offenses in 1939 and sent just over 29,000 of them
to court; almost two-thirds of those detained were suspected of theft, although hooliganism and banditry were prevalent as well.[105] Police and
Communist Party officials argued vigorously that juvenile delinquency
threatened the basic social structure of Soviet cities. The police in Moscow, for example, reported in late 1939 that young males, under the age
of twenty-five and poorly served by cultural and political organizations,
were responsible for the majority of the most widespread and troublesome
crimes, including thefts of all sorts, hooliganism, and robbery of people
who were drunk in public. Just over 15 percent of the crimes committed
in Moscow from August to October 1939 were reportedly the work of

children under the age of sixteen; nearly half were the work of youths under twenty-five. Although the Moscow police claimed that homelessness was a comparatively minor problem compared with previous waves of juvenile homelessness in the 1930s, delinquency was more closely connected than it had been in the past to recidivism among a core of "socially dangerous" youth.[106]

Furthermore, reports on juvenile crime in 1939 and early 1940 stressed the organized nature of many of the crimes committed by youth, arguing that theft and hooliganism were often committed by semiorganized gangs, sometimes coordinated by "socially harmful elements" or young adult recidivists.[107] Moscow police recommended that the courts mete out harsher sentences to address the problem, if necessary sentencing recidivist offenders without defined places of residence as "socially harmful elements" under Article 35 of the Criminal Code.[108] Nationwide trends were similar, as central NKVD and Procuracy officials reported notable increases in levels of delinquency across the USSR in late 1939 and began to press for expanded repressions against youth offenders, especially those guilty of hooliganism and similar public-order crimes.[109] By the spring of 1940, NKVD, justice, welfare, and party officials at all levels were pressing for a new campaign against youth criminality and urban hooliganism. Local police administrations, for their part, were prepared to respond with whatever means, judicial or extrajudicial, that were made available to them.[110]

These general concerns regarding policing and public order in 1940 provided the context for Stalin's decision to launch a major campaign against hooliganism in 1940. His determination to force discipline on the Soviet labor force in the face of looming war, and the popular response to criminalization of common labor infractions in June 1940, provided him with immediate justification. According to discussions at the July 1940 Central Committee Plenum, employees who wanted to leave their jobs but were prohibited from doing so by the edict of June 26, 1940, often reacted with foot dragging, work slowdowns, and petty disruptions that were grounds for firing yet not serious enough to provoke a response from the criminal justice system. Petty hooliganism and small-scale theft on the shop floor were particularly prevalent, and both were usually punished with firing and, at worst, a fine. Stalin responded to reports of this kind of low-level resistance to his edict with another, on August 10, 1940, which set a minimum judicial punishment of one year of imprisonment for theft and hooliganism in state economic institutions.[111] The August edict also responded to the chorus of complaints regarding public order in Soviet cities by targeting hooliganism in public places with the same punishment.[112] Hooliganism and theft on the shop floor remained the responsibility of factory administrations, but by expanding the edict to include public hooliganism, Stalin ensured a vigorous response from the criminal justice system, especially the police.

The local police were more than willing to take advantage of the abbreviated procedural requirements stipulated by Stalin's August edict and to send a substantial number of individuals to the court system during this campaign.[113] In the first ten days of the operation, the police nationwide forwarded 2,850 cases of hooliganism to the court system, compared with 610 cases of petty theft forwarded by the police and factory administrations.[114] The police response was so vigorous, in fact, that it immediately overwhelmed the abilities of local justice organizations to process the cases sent to them; by September 1, according to the USSR Procuracy, the courts in the Russian and Ukrainian republics faced a backlog of 1,912 cases of hooliganism out of 6,830 cases forwarded to them by the police, despite the creation of special "duty chambers" (*dezhurnye kamery*) in major cities to handle the abbreviated hearings, and despite the requirement that all cases be heard by the courts within forty-eight hours.[115] Local justice officials, under substantial pressure in the post-1938 period to produce high rates of convictions, often responded to this situation by qualifying even serious cases of hooliganism as simple hooliganism (Article 74-1 of the Criminal Code), rather than aggravated hooliganism (Article 74-2), in order to avoid the more cumbersome procedures associated with proving and sentencing the more serious charge. Nonetheless, central justice officials complained throughout the campaign that hearings of cases at court were delayed by "red tape" (*volokita*) well beyond the required forty-eight hours.[116]

Local police responded to these perceived inefficiencies within the judicial system, as they had in years past, by taking numerous procedural shortcuts during the campaign and by dealing with hooliganism through extrajudicial channels whenever possible. Procuracy reports from mid-1940 complained that the police often issued administrative fines, sometimes above the 100 rubles allowed by statute, instead of forwarding cases to the courts, even when the accused had a criminal record or previous arrests. Once criminal proceedings were initiated, local police often halted cases in progress and transferred them to administrative commissions or local police chiefs for the imposition of fines, especially when it became clear, in the process of preparing cases for adjudication, that the evidence gathered by the police was insufficient, or too poorly prepared, to support a conviction at court.[117] Local officers were particularly lax with aspects of investigative procedure that pertained only to the court system; the police often appeared at crime scenes and simply wrote down names, often based on incorrect information provided by witnesses. Courts in major cities, under pressure to provide high levels of convictions during the campaign, often convicted individuals on the basis of this evidence despite its obviously poor quality.[118]

Ultimately, the campaign against hooliganism launched by the August 1940 edict targeted precisely those categories of petty offenders that the police had identified as particularly threatening in previous years, rather than members of the workforce who were attempting to evade the June 1940 edict on labor infractions. A summary of the first four months of the judicial portion of the campaign, forwarded by the USSR Justice Commissariat to Georgii Malenkov in early December, stressed that the police and courts had targeted hooliganism in public areas such as streets, parks, workers' clubs, and stores, much of which took place under the effects of alcohol. Most hooligans were under thirty-five years of age—over 75 percent in Moscow—and the vast majority were men.[119] The police and courts alike paid particular attention, as in the months before the campaign began, to hooligans with previous criminal records, connections to the criminal milieu, or other characteristics of "social harmful elements."[120] These campaigns produced drastic increases in judicial sentences for hooliganism. By November 1, 1940, the police nationwide had sent 107,440 cases of simple hooliganism alone to the courts under the edict, compared with 39,304 sentences handed out by the courts for both simple and aggravated hooliganism in the first six months of the year; more than 95 percent of these cases had been heard and sentenced by November 1, almost all to terms of incarceration.[121]

The judicial aspects of the campaign trailed off quickly, however, as rates of conviction dropped in the last months of 1940 and central justice officials began to send signals in early 1941 that the campaign was over.[122] Despite the relatively brief duration of the campaign, the overall effect was substantial; by January 1941, individuals sentenced for hooliganism made up 10 percent of the population of Soviet labor camps.[123] Post-1938 restrictions on extrajudicial sentencing notwithstanding, the 1940 campaign against hooliganism ultimately matched those earlier in the decade, in scope and severity, both because the court system was capable and willing to mete out harsher sentences than it had in previous years and because the local police aggressively targeted the same "dangerous" population cohorts that had been central to daily police work for the previous several years.

Widespread concerns among Communist Party and criminal justice officials about the effects of crime among youth on Soviet urban life, already visible in the antihooliganism campaign, prompted a similar campaign against juvenile delinquency in late 1940 and early 1941. Local police and Procuracy officials continued to report in 1940 and early 1941 that levels of violent, threatening juvenile crime were on the rise, even as levels of homelessness decreased; in particular, they stressed increases in delinquency among children who were in school but were poorly supervised by parents, educational institutions, and welfare agencies. The police reported in 1940 that most of the juveniles swept off the streets were guilty of acts of hooliganism and "mischief" (ozorstvo), with substantial numbers detained for theft or violations of traffic laws as well; most of those sent to court were charged with theft, hooliganism, and bodily injury. Procuracy reports also stressed increasing levels of recidivism among these unsupervised juveniles, complaining that that the courts sentenced the majority of children found guilty to probation; most simply returned to their criminal activity upon release.[124] The police focused in particular on hooliganism among juvenile urban offenders in the last half of 1940, responding to the ongoing campaign against adult hooliganism, and by early 1941 the police and courts alike were regularly arresting and sentencing juveniles for hooliganism, even though the crime was not included in the 1935 edict on juvenile crime and the practice of sentencing juveniles by analogy had been specifically prohibited in the pre-1938 period.[125]

These widespread concerns about violent, often organized hooliganistic activity among school-age youth prompted Stalin, in December 1940, to expand the campaign against labor infractions to include certain categories of trade and industrial schools. The resulting campaign against truancy and hooliganism among this group of students simultaneously addressed the issues of "unsupervisedness" (beznadzornost') and youth hooliganism, further blurring the distinction between the two.[126] These trends led directly to Stalin's decision, in late May 1941, to lower the age of criminal responsibility to fourteen years for all crimes, retaining a lower limit of twelve for those crimes listed in the 1935 edict and for actions that caused train wrecks (the latter added in early December, as a separate edict, due to Stalin's notion that juveniles were responsible for specific acts of "wrecking" on the rail system).[127] Although Soviet judges continued to resist the pressure to sentence children of twelve and thirteen to any sort of deprivation of freedom, the courts were willing to hand out relatively long prison sentences to older juveniles who, according to the police, were the source of a substantial amount, if not most, of the low-level urban disorder in the post-1938 period.[128]

Police responses to juvenile delinquency and hooliganism played a crucial role in the reemergence, after the November 1938 reforms, of long-standing patterns of police activity regarding "threatening" urban population cohorts. The 1940 campaigns against labor infractions, the most visible of Stalin's prewar attempts to instill discipline in Soviet society after the disruptions of the mass operations, were initially conceptualized as confrontations with the Soviet laboring masses rather than as attempts to purge Soviet society of "harmful" individuals or hooligans. Police responses to Stalin's 1940 campaign against hooliganism, however, were imbued with the same criminology that targeted "hooliganistic" offenders as part of the larger cohort of "socially harmful elements" throughout the 1930s. In carrying out these campaigns, the police made aggressive use of the Soviet judicial system, itself in the midst of a sea change in sentencing practices; by 1941, the police could count on the courts to sentence almost all the hooligans forwarded to them to lengthy sentences of imprisonment.[129] Yet in terms of police activity, the course of the judicial campaign was of secondary importance; individual officers controlled the eventual type of punishment that a particular offender would face, and they dealt with a substantial number of hooligans by fining them or confiscating their passports. Ultimately, police actions regarding hooligans and youthful offenders in urban areas in 1939 and 1940 directly replaced the extensive extrajudicial actions against "socially harmful elements" that dominated urban police work in the mid-1930s.

Conclusion

The mass operations of 1937 and 1938 had little effect on the basic contours of the Stalinist policing system. In many ways, they reinforced the tendency of local and central police officials alike to understand crime and social disorder in terms of threatening population contingents that had to be controlled and, ultimately, suppressed. Although this particular kind of working criminology corresponded closely to Stalin's understanding of the threats posed to Soviet society by marginal, national, "kulak," or otherwise "anti-Soviet" population "contingents," it did little to improve the ability of local police administrations to maintain order or to deal with the most pressing contradictions within the Stalinist economic and social systems in the late 1930s.

Certain failures of the Stalinist policing system were plainly visible to the Communist Party leadership in Moscow, even during the mass operations. Central officials correctly identified poor covert work, a lack of consistent attention to investigations, and the tendency of the local police to use administrative shortcuts to avoid the bureaucratic shortcomings of the Soviet judicial system as major impediments to the kind of police system that could both promote social cohesion among the Soviet population and control the criminal subcultures that were emerging as a constituent part of Soviet society. The major campaigns against urban crime in 1939 and 1940 only strengthened those policing tactics that relied on overt and often extrajudicial approaches to controlling social disorder, including the passport system, administrative fines, and widespread purges of urban areas.

Yet the entire edifice of the Soviet policing and judicial system, including such disparate structures as the internal passport system and the juvenile welfare system, was itself responsible for many of the contradictions within the Soviet system that made maximally repressive options not only possible but increasingly desirable to the center. Police approaches to speculation, juvenile delinquency, hooliganism, and passport violations in the post-1938 period all had the effect of expanding police understandings of "social danger" far beyond the core group of recidivists, professional criminals, and passport violators that had been the object of Soviet policing in the mid-1930s. These criminological ideas regarding "social harm" were brought to bear on ever larger parts of the (supposedly "noncriminal") Soviet population after 1938. Truant children, labor violators, line-standers searching for scarce consumer goods, and suspect individuals who wished to move from their home locations all shared in the characteristics of "socially harmful elements" and hence all became less and less distinguishable from the "threatening" population cohorts that the police had repressed as a matter of policy in years past.

By the end of the 1930s, neither class nor ethnicity played a primary role in the definitions of "alien" or "enemy" population cohorts held by the local police. Rather, the sociological schemas that supported policing practices regarding "dangerous" and "harmful" cohorts across the 1930s, including the passport system, had created new criminological categories, which by 1941 were as concrete as earlier categorizations based on class.[130] These definitions became absolute in the period after the mass operations; the vigorous debates in the mid-1930s regarding the ultimate status of "socially harmful elements," special settlers, and ex-convicts within Soviet society were largely settled by 1941 in favor of the complete and permanent isolation of such groups. By the beginning of World War II, police approaches to "harmful" populations had expanded to cover, conceptually, the entire Soviet population.

Conclusion

Indeed: abstraction is one of the modern mind's principal powers. When applied to humans, that power means effacing the face: whatever marks remain of the face serve as badges of membership, the signs of belonging to a category, and the fate meted out to the owner of the face is nothing more yet nothing less either than the treatment reserved for the *category* of which the owner of the face is but a *specimen*. . . . Genocide differs from other murders in having a *category* for its object.
　　—Zygmunt Bauman, *Modernity and the Holocaust*[1]

Terror is the realization of the law of movement; its chief aim is to make it possible for the force of nature or of history to race freely through mankind, unhindered by any spontaneous human action. As such, terror seeks to "stabilize" men in order to liberate the forces of nature or history.
　　—Hannah Arendt, *The Origins of Totalitarianism*[2]

Categorization and state violence are inextricably linked in the modern era. This is hardly a novel idea; it has long been a central tenet of critical theory, even before it became one the of most prevalent academic approaches to understanding state violence in the post-Foucauldian 1980s and 1990s. Yet the process of defining, categorizing, and shaping populations does not function in abstraction; to the contrary, it is the concrete product of the individual actions taken by the individual representatives of the state. The Soviet police officers of the 1920s and 1930s strove to control crime and social disorder by defining and controlling population cohorts, rather than by controlling specific social behaviors or the individuals who engaged in them. By the mid-1930s, policing practices had so reified these cohorts, referred to by central and local police officials alike as "contingents," that sociological definitions of "harmful elements," "dangerous elements," or "kulak elements" had replaced earlier notions of social categorization based on Marxist notions of class. These definitions of "threatening" cohorts served as the ideological and practical basis for mass repression, and mass murder, by the Stalinist regime.

This book has focused on this history of the Soviet policing system, both civil and political, for precisely this reason: the concrete bureaucratic practices of the Soviet police system, as it emerged in the early 1930s, generated the Stalinist approach to the categorization, control, and repression of population "contingents." Nascent understandings of the importance of population contingents existed well before the Stalin era, both in the military agencies that carried out "full cleansings" of "enemy aliens" during World War I and the Russian Civil War and in the fields of law, criminology, and policing science in the 1920s. Yet these ideas became a coherent set of policing practices only when they were internalized by individual officers, in the context of the forced social transformation carried out during Stalin's "revolution from above." The Stalinist police system that emerged from the First Five-Year Plan period concentrated almost exclusively on the identification and repression of "socially dangerous" and "socially harmful elements," carried out by extrajudicial repression and supported by the internal passport system, as its basic mode of law enforcement and social control. The OGPU's takeover of all policing in the early 1930s made it more likely that such approaches would dominate the Soviet policing system, because the OGPU's institutional culture was more steeped in them than was that of its chief rival, the Russian NKVD. Even so, the OGPU's takeover did not make this outcome inevitable. It was the role of the OGPU and the *militsiia* in carrying out the collectivization and dekulakization drives that brought these concepts to the center of the practices with which the Stalinist state attempted to maintain order and control its populations.

The eradication of undesirable and suspect groups within the Soviet population required not only the creation of a modern bureaucratic police system capable of carrying out such a task; it also required the internalization by members of that bureaucracy of an understanding of these individuals as abnormal, antisocial, and inherently anti-Soviet. These categories were neither Marxist nor, like the eliminationist racism of the National Socialist regime, biological. They were in a true sense sociological, based on a gradual accumulation of understandings of "threatening" population groups derived from years of specific governmental practices carried out by the local police. "Criminal contingents," "dangerous elements," "homeless elements," "kulak elements," "speculative elements," and many others were, in the minds of individual police officers, concrete character types, identifiable by a set of objective characteristics that were, by the mid-1930s, far more predictive of the realities of crime and Soviet social order than were earlier categorizations based on class. Even ethnicity, an increasingly important marker of membership in or exclusion from the "Soviet" polity in the 1930s, functioned as only one of several characteristics of "national elements"—sometimes directly, as in the case of the "German contingent," and sometimes less so, as in the ascription of "threatening" geographic mobility to Gypsy populations in Central Asia in the months before World War II. As we have seen, the Stalinist regime called upon its police system at several points in the 1930s to impose the full extent of its organizational and repressive power on the Soviet population. At these moments—especially in 1937 and 1938—particularly local understandings of "threatening" or "dangerous" populations augmented the categorizations of "anti-Soviet" individuals promoted by the central police and Communist Party officials. The result was the widespread application of deadly state violence to the Soviet population by a police system that was eminently capable of transforming abstract categorization into concrete repressive action.

* * *

My account of Stalinist policing challenges several accepted notions regarding the nature of Stalinist repression in the 1930s. One conclusion is clear: the roots of the Stalinist policing system in the statecraft of the late Tsarist era, the Civil War, and the New Economic Policy (NEP) period make it impossible to speak of a moderate Leninist socialism that was obliterated by a historically illegitimate Stalinist dictatorship—the latter understood as "Asiatic," Marxist, Great Russian, or simply genocidal. Stalinist repression was an inherent possibility in the Bolshevik system from the start; indeed, "full cleansings" of populations deemed a threat to national security preceded the Bolsheviks' rise to power. That this approach to state security became dominant in the 1930s is not a historical aberration but a product of the history of the Russian and Soviet state in the long era of political and social upheaval stretching from 1905 to 1941.

Nonetheless, Stalinist repression was the specific outcome of Stalin's rise to power. The Stalinist terror of 1937–38 began not, as is so often assumed, with the political assassination of Sergei Kirov in late 1934; it began with Stalin's decision to force the collectivization of agriculture and, in the process, to "eliminate kulaks as a class." These campaigns to transform the Soviet countryside, which irreversibly cemented Stalin's rejection of the NEP-era compromise between Soviet society and the Bolshevik regime, are the point at which the entire Soviet policing system began to take on the vision of social transformation that informed the OGPU's plans for "social engineering" in the late 1920s. Even though precursors to the mass operations of 1937 and 1938 are plainly visible in the transformational violence carried out by the Cheka during the Civil War, the collectivization drive is the point at which these ideas of "cleansing" society of all "threatening," "dangerous," or otherwise alien individuals began to dominate the Soviet policing system itself. Hence it was the "revolution from above," and the agricultural campaigns in particular, that set the pattern for Stalinist policing for the rest of the 1930s.

By the same token, no period of moderation in Stalinist repression in the mid-1930s separated the upheavals of collectivization and dekulakization from the mass repressions of 1937 and 1938. Repression was a constituent part of Soviet statecraft by the mid-1930s. The police relied on overt repression to remove "threatening" ethnic or social cohorts from the Soviet body politic and to shape the Soviet society that remained, defining protected Soviet spaces ("regime" areas) and "affixing" populations, both suspect and loyal, to their social and geographic locations in the Soviet polity. The steps taken by the Politburo to moderate repression in the mid-1930s, such as the "clearing" of prisons in 1933 and the temporary reduction in the extrajudicial sentencing powers of the political police that occurred with the creation of the USSR NKVD in 1934, were little more than attempts by Stalin to use alternating cycles of moderation and repression—by the mid-1930s, often following the planting and harvest seasons like clockwork—to improve the response of local officials to his policy demands.

The end of the mass operations in November 1938 likewise produced little fundamental change in the Stalinist policing system. The years 1937–38 cannot be seen simply as the denouement of the social and political transformations that Stalin began in the late 1920s—in the words of one influential account, a "monstrous postscript" to the First Five-Year Plan—that led to the stabilization of a more conservative Stalinist state system in the years before World War II.[3] To the contrary, the Soviet policing system was as dynamic in the years just before the beginning of

World War II as it had been for the previous decade. Campaigns against hooliganism, speculation in consumer goods, and passport violations in major Soviet cities all produced the same kind of "mass operations" that defined policing before 1938, despite the specific attempts by Lavrentii Beria, the head of the NKVD after 1938, to prevent this outcome.[4] World War II only reinforced the importance of mass repression in Soviet administration, increasingly directed at cohorts of "national elements" as nationality took a larger role in defining the Soviet body politic. The Soviet policing system was entirely dependent on repression throughout the 1930s; and this structural reality did not end—indeed, could not have ended—with the end of the mass operations in late 1938.

I have also traced the gradual expulsion of popular participation from Soviet policing during the 1930s. Participation and social activism were a crucial part of the vision of decentralized and spontaneous policing activity inherited by the early Bolshevik police from the revolutionary years, and they were central to the vision of a socialist civil policing system promoted by the civil police leaders within the Russian NKVD in the 1920s. Even the top leaders of the OGPU promoted a kind of "popular" participation in Soviet policing as they took control of the *militsiia* in the early 1930s, encouraging officers to cultivate daily contact with the population and solicit denunciations in order to make Soviet society more transparent to the state. Yet these utopian visions were overwhelmed in the 1930s by the demands of state administration in the face of massive social upheaval, and they were abandoned in the mid-1930s in favor of more insular—and effective—means of social categorization and social control. The mass operations of 1937 and 1938, in particular, were police actions, carried out by the state against a conceptually separate Soviet society; they entailed little of the popular mobilization and popular violence characteristic of the first great wave of Stalinist repression, the dekulakization drive. Participation in policing became, after the mid-1930s, merely an echo of the initial populist vision of policing in the early Soviet period.

This is not to say that the top policymakers and policymaking bodies, including Stalin himself, exercised anything approaching absolute power over local police administrations, much less over the Soviet population as a whole. Several of the most repressive policies promulgated by the regime in the realm of criminal justice in the 1930s—including some that are assumed to be Stalin's personal creations, such as the campaign to eliminate "kulaks as a class," or the repression of juvenile lawbreakers in 1935—emerged from the middle levels of the police bureaucracies themselves.

Ultimately, however, the key to understanding the Stalinist regime is not to be found in the mobilization of "democratic" impulses within the Soviet population. To the contrary, the most important factor explaining Stalinist repression remains the institutional, social, and cultural history of the Stalinist state itself.[5]

*   *   *

This book has located the Stalinist regime firmly in the context of modern European approaches to criminal justice and social control.[6] Many of the reforms promoted by top OGPU officials as they took control of civil policing after 1930 were explicitly modeled on what they took to be the most advanced methods of European law enforcement: urban constables created to bridge the persistent gap between the state and the populace, surveillance and registration systems to identify "dangerous elements" as they attempted to enter protected Soviet spaces, and overlapping card catalogs to track suspects as they moved across the USSR. The Stalinist police system was also motivated by an inherently modern vision of social transformation, one that mixed a millenarian drive to reshape Russian society along Marxist lines with the power of modern states to effect economic, political, and especially cultural change among the populations under their control. The drive of the Stalinist police system to categorize and control population "contingents" represents the Soviet variant of what Michel Foucault has called "biopolitics"—a range of administrative and intellectual practices dedicated to defining and shaping populations that James Scott has more recently dubbed "high modernism" and Zygmunt Bauman has described with the now-popular metaphor of the "gardening state."[7] Recent accounts of state violence in the USSR have correctly pointed out the propensity of the late Tsarist and early Bolshevik regimes to "garden" their populations; the violent population mobilizations of World War I and the Russian Civil War, and the drives of the Tsarist and early Bolshevik states to "cleanse" their polities of "alien elements," show that these regimes were fully engaged in the kind of violent modern statecraft characteristic of what is often termed "population politics."[8]

Yet it was the failure, rather than the success, of these overtly modernist visions of Soviet policing and population control that supplied one of the core mechanisms of Stalinist repression. The vision of "preventive policing" (*profilakticheskaia rabota*) held by top OGPU officials as they attempted to reform the *militsiia* in the early 1930s represents a clear manifestation of modern "biopolitics" in the concrete practices of the Stalinist police. Top OGPU officials envisioned a Soviet *militsiia* that would be fully engaged in the surveillance of the Soviet population, the prophylactic removal of "dangerous elements" from the body politic, and the constructive measuring and "affixation" of individuals to their place in the emerging Stalinist polity. By the mid-1930s, however, Soviet police officers had internalized an ethos of preventive policing based not on modern modes of covert surveillance, nor on the internalization by individual Soviet citizens of the categories into which the Stalinist regime intended to force the Soviet population, but rather on mass administrative purges of suspect population cohorts that relied on external markers of "social danger," such as passport documents, geographic location, and membership in population cohorts that were defined exclusively, and often secretly, by the police.[9]

The creation of this particularly Stalinist "biopolitics" did not occur within the professions on which Foucault, and virtually all commentators on the topic after him, have focused: criminologists, doctors, psychologists, and jurists.[10] These professions did generate knowledge about inherently "criminal" population cohorts in the late Tsarist and early Soviet periods, but such ideas did not run deep in the policing or criminal justice bureaucracies of the 1920s. In the early 1930s, these criminologists and jurists lost the leading role in generating criminological knowledge, as OGPU officials were transferred into detective departments and charged with interpreting, classifying, and ordering Soviet social reality. They did so not on the basis of categories developed by professional criminologists, but on the basis of highly schematic social categorizations provided to them by top Communist Party and police officials and, just as important, on the basis of their experiences with local police activity during Stalin's "revolution from above." Police officers themselves—poorly trained, often with little experience, operating in particularly local contexts that had little in common with the worlds inhabited by their intellectual and administrative superiors—played the primary role in generating the criminological knowledge that supported the Stalinist mass repression of the 1930s. The rough understandings of the nature of social disorder that were generated by these local police officers, which focused on the role of "socially dangerous elements" in all forms of crime, in turn shaped central approaches to social control and brought the repression of "socially dangerous elements" to the forefront of regime policy by the mid-1930s. This book, though firmly in the tradition of recent scholarship that calls attention to the particularly modern nature of state projects to categorize, shape, and repress populations, rejects the idea that these modernist templates can explain the emergence of mass repression in Stalin's Soviet Union.

* * *

The Stalinist regime deserves to be termed totalitarian. Models of totalitarianism have long been out of favor in Soviet studies, in part because the more popular variants of this model were often overly simplistic in their Orwellian accounts of a Soviet society bereft of personal and social connections and utterly dominated by the communist regime. The most compelling accounts of totalitarianism, however, were never so shallow. In particular, Hannah Arendt's analysis of modern dictatorships continues to offer much to scholars of the USSR. Arendt argued that totalitarian dictatorships emerged from the political and social dislocations of the early twentieth century, including world war, international depression, and the rise of modern mass politics. These totalitarian regimes used political violence ("terror") to promote unitary politico-historical goals, promising to overcome these dislocations by carrying out the "laws" of history or of nature: the triumph of the "Aryan race" over the supposedly degenerate remainder of the human species, the triumph of the proletariat over the international bourgeoisie, or the elimination of liberal politics altogether in favor of an illiberal, apolitical, classless modern society.

Notions of historical necessity and the overcoming of mere politics pervaded the political culture of the Stalinist policing system. The police strove to shape early Soviet society into a Stalinist vision of "socialism"— for example, casting urban disorder as a problem of "peasant mentalities" and banishing it from urban Soviet spaces, or casting violent crime and economic malfeasance as the products of recidivist "socially harmful elements" and removing this cohort from society altogether. The police at all levels created conceptual schemas with which they attempted to reorder Soviet reality in accordance with the idea that Stalin's regime could actually bring "socialism" to the USSR in the 1930s. In the process, they created interlocking bureaucratic and conceptual structures that were designed to remove those strata of the population that did not correspond to this vision. The internal passport system, for example, was inseparable from the idea of the "socially harmful elements" who could be controlled by it.

The police engaged in repeated purges of these strata from Soviet society in the 1930s, beginning with the "elimination of kulaks as a class" early in the decade and culminating in the attempt to remove "anti-Soviet elements" from society "once and for all" in 1937 and 1938.

Yet Stalinist policing strategies were not merely exclusionary. Systems of population registration and surveillance (e.g., "regime" passport restrictions) operated on the Soviet population as a whole, forcing all Soviet citizens into sociological categories and affixing them to their proper social and geographic locations in the Soviet polity. The overall goal of this set of policing imperatives was the creation of a unitary Soviet society: the elimination from the Soviet body politic of all criminal, marginal, and "anti-Soviet" cohorts and their replacement with a single unitary cohort of *Soviet* citizens. This drive to replace the multiplicity of human experiences with a single organizing principle is the essence of Arendt's definition of totalitarianism, and it is the essence of the Stalinist police system.

This is not to say that Soviet society was in fact totalitarian under Stalin. Arendt's account focused on the appeal of illiberal regimes to European populations disillusioned with the promises of liberal democracies, based as they are on deliberative political institutions and pluralistic political life. Totalitarian societies, in her view, were unified by the dominant ideology proffered by the state, eliminating the need for individual responsibility and active citizenship in favor of passive participation in the whole.[11] Although parts of this account correspond perfectly to the early Soviet experience, the last three decades of Soviet historiography have made it impossible to speak of the total domination of Soviet society by the Bolshevik regime. Nor did the Stalinist regime exercise control, as in Arendt's model, by randomly terrorizing the Soviet population; soviet state violence was often chaotic, but it was never random, neither in the initial years of the Stalin revolution nor during the mass operations of 1937 and 1938.[12] Despite the immense power of the Stalinist state to apply violence to the populations under its control, vast realms of Soviet experience, especially peasant and national subcultures, remained entirely outside the purview of "Bolshevik culture." Ultimately, the ability of the Bolsheviks to refashion the residents of the former Tsarist Empire into Soviet citizens was decidedly limited, even before the Soviet system began its slow decline toward collapse in the second half of the twentieth century.[13]

* * *

Bauman is correct in arguing that abstraction is one of the definitive characteristics of modern states, and that the process of casting individuals, "through exclusion, deportation, and confinement," into abstract categories is central to the forms of state violence that underpin modern mass repression. The modern drive to categorize, however, becomes murderous only in the context of modern totalitarian regimes. I have argued that the forms of abstraction that led to mass repression in the USSR emerged from the concrete bureaucratic practices of the Stalinist policing system itself. These modes of coercion were the product of the specific forms of policing and social control that made Stalin's "revolution from above" possible, and they became murderous not because they were a vehicle for understanding and categorizing the population but because they were turned toward the goal of refashioning the Soviet polity in pursuit of Stalin's overarching goal of state security. The Stalinist state employed repressive violence in the 1930s in order to stabilize, to categorize, and to "fix in place" (*zafiksirovat'*) Soviet populations precisely so that the state could, in Arendt's words, "race freely" through them. The state's goal, however, was not limited to an abstract notion of creating a classless society through the expulsion of all "anti-Soviet elements" from the Soviet body politic. The police employed deadly violence to force Soviet society into the form of a well-ordered polity that could be understood and controlled by the regime. That this goal of subjecting the entirety of Soviet society to the sociological categorizations produced by the operation of the state was only imperfectly accomplished in the 1930s (or at any time in the Stalin period) does not invalidate the goal itself. In this goal, the Soviet policing system was both totalitarian and inherently modern.

A Note on Sources

Scholars who began their careers studying the Soviet Union before its collapse likely have little sense of what it was like to come into the field in the midst of the "archival gold rush" of the 1990s. After a few scant years of Russian language instruction as an undergraduate and a semester in Leningrad in early 1991, I found myself, a young graduate student, living in Moscow and enjoying access to archival collections undreamt of only a decade before. The materials of the Politburo, the NKVD, the *militsiia*, the Procuracy, and the USSR Council of People's Commissars were all open to scholars, including parts of these collections formerly designated "secret," access to which had been so restricted that they did not even appear in publicly available finding aids. My introduction to archival research involved sifting through the most sensitive of documents, ranging from the individual case files of repressed individuals to personal communications between top figures in the Communist Party. I became an expert at deciphering comments scrawled, sixty years before, across documents marked "top secret," and in recognizing the handwriting of Stalin, Vyshinsky, and Molotov; I became accustomed, sitting in the cramped and stuffy reading rooms of the "formerly secret" portions of the NKVD and Sovnarkom archives, to having helpful archivists drop stacks of files on the table in front of me with the suggestion that I might find "something or other interesting" in them. I considered all this completely normal, a standard part of what it meant to do historical research on the topic of Stalinism in the 1930s. Memoirs, newspapers, Soviet legal journals: these were valuable preparation for my research, but my real education in the nature of Stalinism came from the tens of thousands of pages of archival documents that I, like most members of my scholarly cohort, read voraciously—documents often unrelated to my research topic but so fascinating that I could hardly tear myself away. This book was shaped almost entirely by my encounter with the post-Soviet archives, and hence the nature of the materials I consulted, their limitations as well their strengths, deserves some discussion.

Nearly all the archival collections consulted for this book are located in Moscow—a result of the extreme centralization of the Soviet state, as well as of my goal to write a book that examined the understandings of crime held by individuals at the highest levels of the Stalinist regime. The State Archive of the Russian Federation holds massive collections of documents produced by and for central-level police and justice agencies: the 1920s-era Internal Affairs Commissariat, the Central Militsiia Administration of the early 1930s, the post-1934 USSR NKVD, the USSR and Russian Justice commissariats, and the USSR Procuracy. Certain portions of these collections are highly organized—thematic codifications of circulars issued by the USSR NKVD, for example, or compendiums of the circulars issued by the USSR Procuracy for every year of its existence—but most are arranged simply by obvious topics noticed by the archival staff, by the individual to which they were sent, or by the year in which they were produced. Such materials pertain to every imaginable aspect of Soviet criminal justice—budgets, hiring practices, weekly or monthly reports from judicial or police agencies sent to the center as a matter of course, special reports generated at the periphery to respond to some policy initiative or another launched by the Politburo—and they speak to the difficulties of administering state bureaucracies across a nation as complex as the USSR.

These archival materials make it clear that gathering information was a formidable task for policymakers in Moscow. Imperfect transmission of information to the center—often purposefully imperfect, as local officials attempted to hide their own deficiencies or to shape the policies that they knew would be generated on the basis of the information they were providing—meant that central criminal justice officials often made policy decisions in the absence of reliable information from the periphery. Central police and justice officials fully understood this situation, and hence they cultivated information flows that provided as much locally produced data as they could extract from their bureaucracies. The archives of USSR-level criminal justice agencies are therefore full of materials produced at the lowest levels of the bureaucracies that they controlled: reports from individual procurators, weekly accounts of police activities produced by a single police precinct in a midsized Soviet city, or individual case files sent to the center for review. These collections make it possible for the researcher to trace the formation of policy at the center and its transmission down the bureaucratic hierarchies of the Soviet state, as well as the myriad methods by which local officials attempted to mold central policies to their benefit. The biases of these materials are evident to the careful researcher, but the nature of information exchange between center and periphery is part of any story of Soviet governance, including the present one.

This book also relies on extensive collections of documentation produced by the ruling bodies of the Communist Party and the Soviet state: the Political Bureau and the Organizational Bureau of the Communist Party, held in the Russian State Archive of Social-Political History, and the Russian and USSR-wide Councils of People's Commissars (Sovnarkom) and Central Executive Committees, held in the State Archive of the Russian Federation. These institutions served as arenas in which policy conflict was debated and often settled before it was passed upward to Stalin for final approval. The location of such debates changed throughout the Stalin period. In the 1920s, they often occurred within the Central Executive Committee and Russian-level Sovnarkom, but by the early 1930s, most policy formulation took place within the context of the USSR Sovnarkom, in conversations between the individual leaders of increasingly powerful USSR-level commissariats. Commissions of the Politburo served as the debating ground for many policy decisions related to Soviet criminal justice throughout the 1930s as well, often in tandem with commissions created under the auspices of the Sovnarkom. Proponents of competing policy initiatives brought to bear on these debates the information gathered from their own bureaucratic hierarchies—be they local police, justice, finance, welfare, or party officials—allowing the historian an unparalleled glimpse into the decisionmaking process at the highest level of the Stalinist system as well as a picture of the conflicts between the constituent parts of the Soviet state at the local level. In addition, information gathered by party and state institutions dedicated to checking on the sprawling bureaucracies that administered the country—the Worker-Peasant Inspectorate (Rabkrin), the Commission for Party Control, and the Commission for Soviet Control—provide investigative accounts of virtually every aspect of Soviet governance in the 1930s, including the activities of the civil and political police. This book is not a history of Soviet bureaucracies, yet the historian who is willing to take the time to understand how these complex bureaucracies interacted is rewarded with a source base far richer than that produced by criminal justice agencies alone.

I also worked extensively in the city and regional archives in Moscow, which provide a more detailed picture of policing in the capital of Stalin's USSR. Issues of crime and social order in Moscow were central to the policy decisions of the regime in the 1930s, often intruding into the deliberations of the Politburo itself. These local materials hence provide an opportunity to compare the understandings of crime and social order held by top police and Communist Party officials with those held by the officers in charge of maintaining order on the streets of the largest city in the USSR. The archives of the Moscow party organization were largely inaccessible regarding issues of policing and repression, but the state archives at the Moscow regional and city levels contain extensive collections that touch on all aspects of Soviet criminal justice. Much of my understanding of police responses to issues like juvenile delinquency and homelessness, speculation, hooliganism, and controlling the demographic mobility of "socially dangerous" population cohorts comes from my study of policing in Moscow. Such information is undoubtedly not representative of policing in every city in the USSR, but police activity in major urban areas, including Moscow, had the most influence on central policy formulation.

For all of the tens of thousands of pages of archival records consulted for this book, my source base contains glaring insufficiencies, often produced by uneven access to collections held by state and former-party archives. The records of the Soviet political police before 1934 are held by the Russian Federal Security Service (the successor to the KGB) rather than by the State Archive of the Russian Federation; they have been accessible only to select scholars, usually Russians or in some cases Westerners who have concluded lucrative research and publishing arrangements with archives and individuals strapped for funding in the post-Soviet era. The materials from the collections of the Central Militsiia Administration, produced between 1930 and 1934, are held in the State Archive of the Russian Federation and form the basis of many of the arguments found in the early chapters of this book. Similar materials for the period after 1934, unfortunately, are located within the collections of the USSR NKVD, held by the State Archive of the Russian Federation but made available only to select scholars. I was lucky enough to conduct a good portion of my research for this book in the late 1990s, when access to such collections was relatively liberal. Access to materials on Soviet criminal justice, especially the police, contracted substantially after the turn of the decade, as much as from a general sense among archivists of the changing atmosphere regarding "state secrets" under the government of Vladimir Putin (a former Chekist) as from any specific changes in archival regulations. A portion of the materials consulted for this book are hence no longer available, especially those in the collections of the USSR NKVD and the Central Militsiia Administration held by the State Archive of the Russian Federation.

This general contraction of archival access was mitigated somewhat by the publication of numerous collections of archival documents in the late 1990s and early 2000s, which are devoted to topics as wide ranging as Stalinist repression in the countryside, the structure of the NKVD, and the regime's responses to juvenile delinquency and homelessness. I make extensive use of several of these collections, especially in my analysis of the mass operations in chapter 6. I list them below in the bibliography in the section titled "Published Archival Documents, Memoirs, and other Primary Sources."

Throughout the chapter notes that follow below, these archives are cited: Gosudarstvennyi Arkhiv Novosibirskoi Oblasti, the State Archive of the Novosibirsk Region (hereafter GANO); Gosudarstvennyi Arkhiv Rossiiskoi Federatsii, the State Archive of the Russia Federation (hereafter GARF); Rossiiskii Gosudarstvennyi Arkhiv Noveishei Istorii, the Russian State Archive of Contemporary History (hereafter RGANI); Rossiiskii Gosudarstvennyi Arkhiv Sotsial'no-Politicheskoi Istorii, the Russian State Archive of Socio-Political History (hereafter RGASPI); Tsentral'nyi Arkhiv Obshchestvennykh Dvizhenii Moskvy, the Central Archive of Social Movements of Moscow (hereafter TsAODM); and Tsentral'nyi Gosudarstvennyi Arkhiv Moskovskoi Oblasti, the Central State Archive of the Moscow Region (hereafter TsGAMO). In the citations for the materials from these archives, these abbreviations are used: fond (f.), opis (op.), delo (d.), and list (l., i.e., page).

Notes

Introduction

1. Aleksandr I. Solzhenitsyn, *The Gulag Archipelago 1918–1956: An Experiment in Literary Investigation, I–II* (New York: Harper & Row, 1974), 68.

2. GARF, f. 7523, op. 65, d. 557, l. 53.

3. Arrests of "national elements" initially involved a different sentencing process, termed the "album procedure," which retained a minimal amount of supervision by central police and justice authorities in Moscow and did not involve specific quotas for arrests or executions. This system was abandoned in mid-1938 in favor of the demonstrably more efficient troikas. See chapter 6 for a full discussion of these sentencing procedures.

4. By "the present purge," Trotsky meant the Communist Party purge, which began in 1936 and was in full swing before he completed his pamphlet in late August 1937. Leon Trotsky, *Stalinism and Bolshevism: Concerning the Historical and Theoretical Roots of the Fourth International* (New York: Pioneer Publishers, 1937), 17.

5. Leon Trotsky, *The Revolution Betrayed: What Is the Soviet Union and Where Is It Going?* (New York: Harcourt Brace, 1937).

6. Roy Medvedev, *Let History Judge: The Origins and Consequences of Stalinism* (New York: Alfred A. Knopf, 1972), 234–39. Medvedev's revised edition, published at the end of the Gorbachev era, contained no changes to his analysis of 1937 and 1938. Roy Medvedev, *Let History Judge: The Origins and Consequences of Stalinism* (New York: Columbia University Press, 1989), 449–55. For a similar account, see Isaac Deutscher, *Stalin: A Political Biography* (New York: Oxford University Press, 1949), 345–85.

7. Robert Conquest, *The Great Terror: Stalin's Purge of the Thirties* (London: Macmillan, 1968), 282–87. Even in his 1990 "reassessment," in which he argues that mass repressions were expanded by the NKVD on the direct orders of the Politburo in 1937 and 1938 and entailed arrest quotas, Conquest relies on the metaphor of the "snowball" to explain the expansion of purges to society at large and argues that mass arrests with population at large were prompted by Stalin's desire to ensure that all possible political opposition within the country was eliminated. Robert Conquest, *The Great Terror: A Reassessment* (New York, Oxford: Oxford University Press, 1990),

NOTES TO PAGES 5–6

256–61. Neither Conquest nor Medvedev mentions the July and August 1937 Polit-buro orders that launched the mass operations, despite the fact that heavily revised editions of their books appeared in the very last years of the Gorbachev era.

8. Merle Fainsod, *Smolensk under Soviet Rule* (Cambridge, Mass.: Harvard University Press, 1958; Boston: Unwyn Hyman, 1989), 165–72, 232–37; page citations are to the reprint edition. Similarly, Zbigniew Brzezinski posits an analytical difference between "purge" and "terror" but ultimately fails to differentiate these processes sufficiently, casting Stalinist purges as an ever-expanding set of denunciations and arrests in Communist Party, state, military, and economic bureaucracies. Zbigniew Brzezinski, *The Permanent Purge: Politics in Soviet Totalitarianism* (Cambridge, Mass.: Harvard University Press, 1956), 65–97.

9. For the best introduction to these historiographic trends, see the exchanges between several leading historians in the field in *Russian Review* 45, no. 4 (1986), and 46, no. 4 (1987).

10. For representative examples, see Gabor T. Rittersporn, "The State against Itself: Social Tensions and Political Conflict in the USSR, 1936–1938," *Telos* 41 (1979): 87–104; Roberta Manning, *Government in the Soviet Countryside in the Stalinist Thirties: The Case of Belyi Raion in 1937*, Carl Beck Papers in Russian and East European Studies no. 301 (Pittsburgh: Russian and East European Studies, University of Pittsburgh, 1984); Lewis H. Seigelbaum, *Stakhanovism and the Politics of Productivity in the USSR, 1935–1941* (Cambridge: Cambridge University Press, 1988), esp. 248–59; Robert W. Thurston, "Fear and Belief in the USSR's 'Great Terror': Response to Arrest, 1935–1939," *Slavic Review* 45, no. 2 (1986): 213–34.

11. For the most important examples, see J. Arch Getty, "Party and Purge in Smolensk," *Slavic Review* 42, no. 1 (1983): 60–79; J. Arch Getty, *The Origins of the Great Purges: The Soviet Communist Party Reconsidered, 1933–1938* (Cambridge: Cambridge University Press, 1985); and Gabor Rittersporn, *Simplifications staliniennes et complications sovietiques: Tensions socials et conflicts politiques en URSS 1933–1953* (Paris: Editions des Archives Contemporaines, 1988), reprinted in English as *Stalinist Simplifications and Soviet Complications: Social Tension and Political Conflict in the USSR, 1933–1953* (Chur: Harwood Academic Publishers, 1991).

12. E.g., see Roberta Manning, "The Great Purges in a Rural District: Belyi Raion Revisited," *Russian History/Histoire Russe* 16, nos. 2–4 (1989): 409–33; J. Arch Getty, "The Politics of Repression Revisited," David L. Hoffmann, "The Great Terror on the Local Level: Purges in Moscow Factories, 1936–1938," Robert Thurston, "The Stakhanovite Movement: Background to the Great Terror in the Factories, 1935–1938," and William Chase and J. Arch Getty, "Patterns of Repression among the Soviet Elite in the Late 1930s: A Biographical Approach," all in *Stalinist Terror: New Perspectives*, ed. J. Arch Getty and Roberta Manning (Cambridge: Cambridge University Press, 1993); Hiroaki Kuromiya, "Stalinist Terror in the Donbas: A Note," *Slavic Review* 50, no. 1 (1991): 157–62; and Sheila Fitzpatrick, "Workers against Bosses: The Impact of the Great Purges on Labor-Management Relations," in *Making Workers Soviet: Power, Class, and Identity*, ed. Lewis H. Siegelbaum and Ronald Grigor Suny (Ithaca, N.Y.: Cornell University Press, 1994), 311–40. Even Dmitry Volkogonov's wide-ranging biography of Stalin followed these long-standing conventions, despite the unparalleled archival access afforded the author by his position in the USSR Ministry of Defense. Volkogonov argued that Stalinist repression reached "mass proportions" only gradually, as repressions within the Communist Party widened to encompass

broader sectors of the population; he failed to mention mass operations at all. Dmitry Volkogonov, *Stalin: Triumph and Tragedy* (New York: Grove Weidenfeld, 1991).

13. Only a handful of studies before the mid-1990s questioned the connection between the Communist Party purges and mass repression. E.g., see Roberta Manning, "The Soviet Economic Crisis of 1936–1940 and the Great Purges," in *Stalinist Terror*, ed. Getty and Manning, 116–41, which argues that the economic turndown that began in 1936 was in some measure a cause of the purges. For further discussion of Manning's thesis, see chapter 6.

14. *Trud*, no. 88, 4 June 1992. Similar documents were published *Moskovskie Novosti*, no. 25, June 21, 1992. These documents appeared in the public sphere in conjunction with legal challenges to Boris Yeltsin's 1991 decision to outlaw the Communist Party. The Yeltsin government amassed a massive amount of evidence from Soviet archives that was intended to prove that the Communist Party was not merely a political party but the ruling structure of a totalitarian regime; these documents eventually became the archival collection held in RGANI, fond 89. For a guide to these materials, see Lora Soroka, *Fond 89: Communist Party of the Soviet Union on Trial: Archives of the Communist Party State, Guide to the Microfilm Collection in the Hoover Institution Archives* (Stanford, Calif.: Hoover Institution Press, 2001).

15. Many of these initial findings were discussed by J. Arch Getty, Gabor T. Rittersporn, and Viktor Zemskov, "Victims of the Soviet Penal System in the Pre-War Years: A First Approach on the Basis of Archival Evidence," *American Historical Review* 98, no. 4 (1993): 1017–49.

16. E.g., see Manning's attempt to insert the mass operations into her narrative about the Communist Party purges in Belyi *raion* in her "Great Purges in a Rural District," esp. 191–93. See also Robert W. Thurston, *Life and Terror in Stalin's Russia, 1923–1941* (New Haven, Conn.: Yale University Press, 1996), esp. 59–106, which reiterates his earlier arguments to the effect that Stalin struck at perceived enemies "almost incoherently" in 1937 and 1938 and that average Soviet citizens did not fear the activities of the NKVD.

17. J. Arch Getty and Oleg V. Naumov, *The Road to Terror: Stalin and the Self-Destruction of the Bolsheviks, 1932–1939* (New Haven, Conn.: Yale University Press, 1999), 468–81, esp. 480–81. The Politburo orders that launched the mass operations do not pertain to Getty's study of the Communist Party purges, and his conclusions that the mass operations were a "blind rage and panic" that took place "without negotiating or defining who was to be involved" are incorrect, as chapter 6 will show. Likewise, James R. Harris, in a study of purging in the Urals region published well after information about the mass operations had become available, follows Getty's line almost entirely, focusing on bureaucratic tensions within the region and casting the decision of the center to demand expanded repressions in mid-1937 as the mere "match" to the more powerful "powder-keg" of tensions within local party and state bureaucracies. James R. Harris, "The Purging of Local Cliques in the Urals Region, 1936–7," in *Stalinism: New Directions*, ed. Sheila Fitzpatrick (London: Routledge, 2000), 262–85, esp. 279–80.

18. Chief among these historians was Gabor Rittersporn, whose attempts at synthesis in the late 1990s are some of the most path-breaking accounts of the nature and origins of mass repression in the field. Gabor T. Rittersporn, "Extra-Judicial Repression and the Courts: Their Relationship in the 1930s," in *Reforming Justice in Russia, 1864–1996*, ed. Peter H. Solomon Jr. (Armonk, N.Y.: M. E. Sharpe, 1997), 207–27;

Gabor T. Rittersporn, "'Vrednye elementy,' 'opasnye men'shinstva' i bol'shevistskie trevogi: massovye operatsii 1937–1938 gg. i etnicheskii vopros v SSSR," in *V sem'e edinoi: Natsional'naia politika partii bol'shevikov i ee osushchestvlenie na Severo-Zapade Rossii v 1920–1950-e gody*, ed. Timo Vihavainen and Irina Takala (Petroza-vodsk: Izdatel'stvo Petrozavodskogo universiteta, 1998), 99–122.

19. In addition to Rittersporn, "'Vrednye elementy,'" see Terry Martin, "The Origins of Soviet Ethnic Cleansing," *Journal of Modern History* 70, no. 4 (1998): 813–62.

20. The post-1991 literature on Stalinist repression in the Russian language is vast, but the work of Oleg Khlevniuk stands out as both exceptionally well grounded in archival research and as particularly focused on the nature of Stalin's power. Oleg Khlevniuk, *1937-i g.: Stalin, NKVD i sovetskoe obshchestvo* (Moscow: Respublika, 1992); Oleg Khlevniuk, *In Stalin's Shadow: The Career of "Sergo" Ordzhonikidze*, ed. Donald J. Raleigh (New York and London: M. E. Sharpe, 1995); Oleg Khlevniuk, *Politburo: Mekhanizmy politicheskoi vlasti v 1930-e gody* (Moscow: ROSSPEN, 1996); Oleg Khlevniuk, "Stalin as Dictator: The Personification of Power," in *Stalin: A New History*, ed. Sarah Davies and James Harris (Cambridge: Cambridge University Press, 2005); and Oleg Khlevnyuk, "The Objectives of the Great Terror, 1937–38," in *Soviet History, 1917–53: Essays in Honour of R. W. Davies*, ed. Julian Cooper, Maureen Perrie, and E. A. Rees (London: Palgrave Macmillan, 1995), 158–76.

21. For the most important examples, see the essays in *Repressii protiv poliakov i pol'skikh grazhdan*, ed. L. S. Eremina (Moscow: Zven'ia, 1997); and in *Nakazannyi narod: Repressii protiv rossiiskikh Nemtsev*, ed. I. L. Shcherbakova (Moscow: Zven'ia, 1999), especially the works by N. V. Petrov, N. G. Okhotin, and A. B. Roginskii. For examples of this work in English, see Marc Jansen and Nikita Petrov, *Stalin's Loyal Executioner: People's Commissar Nikolai Ezhov, 1895–1940* (Stanford, Calif.: Hoover Institution Press, 2002); and Nikita Petrov and Arsenii Roginskii, "The 'Polish Operation' of the NKVD, 1937–1938," in *Stalin's Terror: High Politics and Mass Repression in the Soviet Union*, ed. Barry McLoughlin and Kevin McDermott (Houndsmills, U.K.: Palgrave Macmillan, 2003), 153–72. For a history of Memorial, see Nanci Alder, *Victims of Soviet Terror: The Story of the Memorial Movement* (Westport, Conn.: Praeger, 1993).

22. In addition to the works by Rittersporn, cited above, see David R. Shearer, "Crime and Social Disorder in Stalin's Russia: A Reassessment of the Great Retreat and the Origins of Mass Repression," *Cahiers du Monde russe* 39, nos. 1–2 (1998): 119–48; David R. Shearer, "Social Disorder, Mass Repression, and the NKVD during the 1930s," *Cahiers du Monde russe* 42, nos. 2–4 (2001): 505–34; David R. Shearer, "Modernity and Backwardness on the Soviet Frontier: Western Siberia during the 1930s," in *Provincial Landscapes: Local Dimensions of Soviet Power, 1917–1953*, ed. Donald J. Raleigh (Pittsburgh: University of Pittsburgh Press, 2001), 194–216; and David R. Shearer, "Elements Near and Alien: Passportization, Policing, and Identity in the Stalinist State, 1932–1952," *Journal of Modern History* 76, no. 4 (2004): 835–81. See also Paul M. Hagenloh, "Socially Harmful Elements and the Great Terror," in *Stalinism*, ed. Fitzpatrick, 286–308.

23. The most important recent works include Jansen and Petrov, *Stalin's Loyal Executioner*; Oleg V. Khlevniuk, *The History of the Gulag: From Collectivization to the Great Terror*, trans. Vadim A. Staklo and ed. David Nordlander (New Haven, Conn.: Yale University Press, 2004); Wendy Z. Goldman, *Terror and Democracy in*

the Age of Stalin: The Social Dynamics of Repression (Cambridge: Cambridge University Press, 2007); and David R. Shearer, *Policing Stalin's Socialism: Repression and Social Order in the Soviet Union, 1924–1953* (New Haven, Conn.: Yale University Press, 2009).

24. The phrase comes from Robert C. Tucker, *Stalin in Power: The Revolution from Above, 1928–1941* (New York: W. W. Norton, 1990).

25. The phrase comes from George Leggett, *The Cheka: Lenin's Political Police* (Oxford: Clarendon Press, 1981), chap. 7. See also Lennard D. Gerson, *The Secret Police in Lenin's Russia* (Philadelphia: Temple University Press, 1976); and Robert Conquest, *Inside Stalin's Secret Police: NKVD Politics 1936–1939* (Stanford, Calif.: Hoover Institution Press, 1985).

26. The most important post-1991 studies of the structure of the early Soviet political police have been conducted by Nicolas Werth. See Nicolas Werth, "L'OGPU en 1924: Radiographie d'une institution à son niveau d'étiage," *Cahiers du Monde russe* 42, nos. 2–4 (2001): 397–422; and Nicolas Werth, "A State against Its People: Violence, Repression, and Terror in the Soviet Union," in *The Black Book of Communism: Crimes, Terror, Repression*, ed. Mark Kramer (Cambridge, Mass.: Harvard University Press, 1999), 33–268. On surveillance in the early Soviet period, see Peter Holquist, " 'Information Is the Alpha and Omega of Our Work': Bolshevik Surveillance in Its Pan-European Context," *Journal of Modern History* 69, no. 3 (1997): 415–50.

27. The most important of these accounts were written before the collapse of the USSR. See Tsuyoshi Hasegawa, "The Formation of the Militia in the February Revolution: An Aspect of the Origins of Dual Power," *Slavic Review* 32, no. 2 (1973): 303–22; and Neil Weissman, "Policing the NEP Countryside," in *Russia in the Era of NEP: Explorations in Soviet Society and Culture*, ed. Sheila Fitzpatrick, Alexander Rabinowitch, and Richard Stites (Bloomington: Indiana University Press, 1991), 174–91. Louise I. Shelley, *Policing Soviet Society: The Evolution of State Control* (London: Routledge, 1996) is not a serious addition to the literature on policing under Stalin, although it contains important discussion of the era after World War II.

28. The standard Soviet-era history of the *militsiia*, which is largely accurate but incomplete, is N. A. Shchelokov, ed., *Istoriia Sovetskoi Militsii* (Moscow: Akademiia MVD, 1977). The most important post-1991 studies of the *militsiia* are V. I. Vorontsov et al., *Organy i Voiska MVD Rossii: Kratkii Istoricheskii Ocherk* (Moscow: Ob"edinennaia redaktsiia MVD Rossii, 1996); A. V. Borisov et al., *Politsiia i Militsiia Rossii: Stranitsy Istorii* (Moscow: Nauka, 1995); and especially Aleksandr Iakovlevich Malygin, "Gosudarstvenno-pravovoi status militsii RSFSR v period provedeniia Novoi Ekonomicheskoi Politiki (20-e gody)," doktorskaia dissertatsiia, Akademiia MVD RF, 1992.

29. One important exception to this trend is the recent PhD dissertation by George Lin, which concentrates on institutional conflict between the political police and the civil police in the 1920s. George Lin, "Fighting in Vain: The NKVD RSFSR in the 1920s," PhD dissertation, Stanford University, 1997.

30. For the most important accounts see Holquist, " 'Information Is the Alpha and Omega of Our Work,'"; Peter Holquist, *Making War, Forging Revolution: Russia's Continuum of Crisis, 1914–1921* (Cambridge, Mass.: Harvard University Press, 2002); Peter Holquist, "State Violence as Technique: The Logic of Violence in Soviet Totalitarianism," in *Landscaping the Human Garden: Twentieth-Century Population Management in a Comparative Framework*, ed. Amir Weiner (Stanford, Calif.: Stanford

University Press, 2003); Eric Lohr, *Nationalizing the Russian Empire: The Campaign against Enemy Aliens during World War I* (Cambridge, Mass.: Harvard University Press, 2003); Amir Weiner, "Introduction: Landscaping the Human Garden," in *Landscaping the Human Garden*, ed. Weiner, 1–18; Joshua A. Sanborn, *Drafting the Russian Nation: Military Conscription, Total War, and Mass Politics, 1905–1925* (De Kalb: Northern Illinois University Press, 2003); and David L. Hoffmann, *Stalinist Values: The Cultural Norms of Soviet Modernity, 1917–1941* (Ithaca, N.Y.: Cornell University Press, 2003).

31. The most influential examples include Detlev J. K. Peukert, *The Weimar Republic: The Crisis of Classical Modernity* (New York: Hill and Wang, 1992); Zygmunt Bauman, *Modernity and the Holocaust* (Ithaca, N.Y.: Cornell University Press, 1989); James C. Scott, *Seeing Like a State: How Certain Schemes to Improve the Human Condition Have Failed* (New Haven, Conn.: Yale University Press, 1998); and, although less often cited, Michel Foucault, "The Birth of Biopolitics," in *Ethics: Subjectivity and Truth*, by Michel Foucault, ed. Paul Rabinow and trans. Robert Hurley (New York: New Press, 1994), 73–79.

32. Peter Holquist, "Violent Russia, Deadly Marxism? Russia in the Epoch of Violence, 1905–21," *Kritika: Explorations in Russian and Eurasian History* 4, no. 3 (2003), 651–52; Holquist, "State Violence as Technique," 20, 44.

33. Other scholars have challenged this "modernist" interpretation as well, based on concrete examinations of the workings of the Soviet policing system: see Shearer, "Elements Near and Alien," 835–81, esp. 877–80; and Terry Martin, " 'Registration' and 'Mood': OGPU Information Reports and the Soviet Surveillance System," paper presented at the conference "La police politique en Union soviétique, 1918–1953," Maison des Science de l'Homme, Paris, May 25–27, 2000.

34. The existence of these campaigns, overlooked in virtually all major accounts of Stalinist repression in the 1930s, contradicts the generally accepted understanding of the mid-1930s as a period of relative moderation of Stalinist violence between the upheavals of collectivization and the Stalinist terror of 1937 and 1938. This idea is most associated with the concept of the "Great Retreat," a term coined by the émigré political scientist Nicholas Timasheff to describe a "retreat" from radicalism in the mid-1930s in the realm of cultural and social policy. Nicholas Timasheff, *The Great Retreat: The Growth and Decline of Communism in Russia* (New York: E. P. Dutton, 1946).

35. "SVE" stands for "sotsial'no-vrednye elementy"; this category of offenders was also referred to as "sotsvredniki" by the local police.

Chapter 1

1. V. I. Lenin, *State and Revolution* (New York: International Publishers, 1932), 74–75; emphasis in the original.

2. V. N. Khaustov, V. P. Naumov, and N. S. Plotnikov, eds., *Lubianka: Stalin i VChK-GPU-OGPU-NKVD—Ianvar' 1922–dekabr' 1936* (Moscow: Mezhdunarodnyi fond "Demokratiia," 2003) (hereafter Khaustov, Naumov, and Plotnikov, *Lubianka 1922–1936*), 113.

3. Lenin, "April Theses," originally published in *Pravda*, no. 26, April 7, 1917; trans. in *Collected Works*, by V. I. Lenin, vol. 24 (London: Laurence and Wishart, 1964), 21–24.

4. For discussion of the centrality of the concept of the "well-ordered police state" in Tsarist administrative practice, see Marc Raeff, *Understanding Imperial Russia: State and Society in the Old Regime*, trans. Arthur Goldhammer (New York: Columbia University Press, 1984).

5. For the early evolution of the Tsarist police system, see V. I. Vorontsov et al., *Organy i Voiska MVD Rossii: Kratkii Istoricheskii Ocherk* (Moscow: Ob'edinennaia redaktsiia MVD Rossii, 1996), 41–63; and Scott J. Seregny, "The Nedel'shchik: Law and Order in Muscovite Russia," *Canadian-American Slavic Studies* 9, no. 2 (1975): 168–78. For police in the eighteenth century, see John Le Donne, "The Provincial and Local Police under Catherine the Great, 1775–1796," *Canadian Slavic Studies* 4, no. 3 (1970): 513–28.

6. Neil Weissman, "Regular Police in Tsarist Russia, 1900–1914," *Russian Review* 44, no. 1 (1985): 46–47. On Alexander II's reform efforts in the area of policing, see Robert J. Abbott, "Police Reform in the Russian Province of Iaroslavl, 1856–1876," *Slavic Review* 32, no. 2 (1973): 292–302.

7. Weissman calls this step the "first serious attempt by the tsarist state to establish a direct presence in the village." Weissman, "Regular Police," 50.

8. In 1900 the Tsarist government dedicated only 1,582 constables and 6,874 sergeants to the entire rural population of the Russian Empire, some 90 million people. Weissman, "Regular Police," 48–49.

9. For Alexander II's attempts to reduce the administrative responsibilities of police during the Great Reforms, see Abbott, "Police Reform," 296–99.

10. On police reform in the second half of the nineteenth century, see Clive Emsley and Barbara Weinberger, eds., *Policing Western Europe: Politics, Professionalism, and Public Order, 1850–1940* (Westport, Conn.: Greenwood Press, 1991).

11. Jennifer Davis, "Urban Policing and Its Objects: Comparative Themes in England and France in the Second Half of the Nineteenth Century," in *Policing Western Europe*, ed. Elmsley and Weinberger, 1–17.

12. The Ministry of Finance was the only other central ministry to have extended its hierarchy below the district level by 1905. See Weissman, "Regular Police," 56–57.

13. Robert W. Thurston, "Police and People in Moscow, 1906–1914," *Russian Review* 39, no. 3 (1980): 325–27.

14. Frederic S. Zuckerman, *The Tsarist Police in Russian Society, 1880–1917* (London: Macmillan, 1996), esp. chaps. 2, 9, and 10; Peter Holquist, "Violent Russia, Deadly Marxism? Russia in the Epoch of Violence, 1905–21," *Kritika: Explorations in Russian and Eurasian History* 4, no. 3 (2003): 627–52, esp. 631–36.

15. Zuckerman, *Tsarist Police*, chap. 13.

16. Eric Lohr, *Nationalizing the Russian Empire: The Campaign against Enemy Aliens during World War I* (Cambridge, Mass.: Harvard University Press, 2003), chap. 5, esp. 123–29, 152–54.

17. For a discussion of the merits of treating the period from 1914 to 1921 as a coherent epoch in Russian history, see Peter Holquist, *Making War, Forging Revolution: Russia's Continuum of Crisis, 1914–1921* (Cambridge, Mass.: Harvard University Press, 2002), introduction, esp. 2–6.

18. Zuckerman, *Tsarist Police*, 239–40.

19. Ibid., 245–47.

20. Tsuyoshi Hasegawa, "The Formation of the Militia in the February Revolution: An Aspect of the Origins of Dual Power," *Slavic Review* 32, no. 2 (1973): 305–7;

and Tsuyoshi Hasegawa, "Crime and Police in Revolutionary Petrograd, March 1917–March 1918: Social History of the Russian Revolution Revisited," *Acta Slavica Iaponica* 13 (1995): 8–9.

21. See Rex Wade, *Red Guards and Workers' Militias in the Russian Revolution* (Stanford, Calif.: Stanford University Press, 1984).

22. Hasegawa, "Crime and Police," 17.

23. Ibid., 26–28.

24. A. V. Borisov et al., *Politsiia i Militsiia Rossii: Stranitsy Istorii* (Moscow: Nauka, 1995), 95–96; Hasegawa, "Crime and Police," 28–29; Vorontsov et al., *Organy i Voiska MVD Rossii*, 216–17.

25. The head of the Moscow Detective Department, P. K. Marshalk, took no active political stance in October and retained his position until May 1918, when he fled the country. Aleksandr Dugin, "Organy moskovskoi gorodskoi militsii," kandidatskaia dissertatsiia, Gosudarstvennyi Istoriko-Arkhivnyi Institut, Moscow, 1988, 36–41.

26. The Bolsheviks abolished the municipal police administrations in the Petrograd and Moscow regions only in December 1917 and January 1918, respectively. Hasegawa, "Crime and Police," 28–29.

27. Vorontsov et al., *Organy i Voiska MVD Rossii*, 183.

28. Ibid., 217–18.

29. Ibid., 218–20.

30. I use the term *militsiia* to refer to the Soviet civil police after the middle of 1918. By this time the trend toward professionalization was clear, and the term "militia" is no longer applicable. The term *militsiia* is intended, therefore, to convey the bureaucratic stability of the organization and is used interchangeably with "civil police" for the rest of this book.

31. Dugin, "Organy moskovskoi gorodskoi militsii," 43–45.

32. The NKVD subdepartment in charge of the *militsiia*, in fact, was subordinate to the Department of Local Governance (Otdel mestnogo upravleniia) until October 1918. Little research has been done on this important function of the NKVD in the first few years after 1917. See Vorontsov et al., *Organy i Voiska MVD Rossii*, 219.

33. My argument here supports the thesis presented by Sheila Fitzpatrick, "The Civil War as a Formative Experience," in *Bolshevik Culture: Experiment and Order in the Russian Revolution*, ed. Abbott Gleason, Peter Kenez, and Richard Stites (Bloomington: Indiana University Press, 1985).

34. Petrovskii, along with Kamenev and Bukharin, was critical of the unrestricted repressions carried out by the Cheka in the fall of 1918 and was removed when such complaints were countered by Dzerzhinskii, with Lenin's support. Nicolas Werth, "A State against Its People: Violence, Repression, and Terror in the Soviet Union," in *The Black Book of Communism: Crimes, Terror, Repression*, ed. Mark Kramer and trans. Jonathan Murphy (Cambridge, Mass.: Harvard University Press, 1999), 79.

35. Ibid., 74–78; the quotation is on 77.

36. According to Peter Holquist, many of the officers in the Red Army who directed these repressive campaigns were graduates of Imperial military schools, products of the same milieu that produced campaigns against Jews and Germans during the Great War. Peter Holquist, "State Violence as Technique: The Logic of Violence in Soviet Totalitarianism," in *Landscaping the Human Garden: Twentieth-Century Population Management in a Comparative Framework*, ed. Amir Weiner (Stanford, Calif.: Stanford University Press, 2003), 25–9 (the quotation is on 25); Holquist, "Violent Russia," 645–46.

37. The Cheka likely relied on the technical expertise of a substantial number of former white-collar employees of the Tsarist political police—bookkeepers, experts in fingerprinting, or cryptographers—but Chekists themselves were almost never hold-overs from the Tsarist police, emerging instead from the contexts of underground revolutionary activity and Civil War. Zuckerman, *Tsarist Police*, 247–51.

38. The phrase came from Aleksandr Olminsky, a Bolshevik of long standing who was part of the group that criticized the actions of the Cheka in late 1918. Werth, "State against its People," 74–76; the quotation is on 79.

39. Holquist, *Making War*, 232–36.

40. Most internal surveillance functions were transferred to the Cheka by the end of the war, but such tasks remained only a small portion of the work of the Bolshevik political police well into the 1920s. Stuart Finkel, "An Intensification of Vigilance: Recent Perspectives on the Institutional History of the Soviet Security Apparatus in the 1920s," *Kritika* 5, no. 2 (2004): 308–9.

41. Aleksandr Iakovlevich Malygin, "Gosudarstvenno-pravovoi status militsii RSFSR v period provedeniia Novoi Ekonomicheskoi Politiki (20-e gody)," doktorskaia dissertatsiia, Akademiia MVD RF, 1992, 86. On eugenics in the early Soviet period, see Loren R. Graham, "Science and Values: The Eugenics Movement in Germany and Russia in the 1920s," *American Historical Review* 82, no. 5 (1977): 1133–64, esp. 1150–57.

42. E.g., Krylenko campaigned as late as 1929 for a radically simplified criminal code containing only three basic sections: socially harmful (*vrednye*), socially dangerous (*opasnye*), and especially socially dangerous acts. Krylenko envisioned specific punishments for only the first category; those guilty of "dangerous" or "especially dangerous" crimes would be isolated from society until they were rehabilitated or shot, respectively. Malygin, "Gosudarstvenno-pravovoi status," 85–86, 95. See also Robert Sharlet, "Pashukanis and the Withering Away of the Law in the USSR," in *Cultural Revolution in Russia, 1928–1931*, ed. Sheila Fitzpatrick (Bloomington: Indiana University Press, 1978), 169–89.

43. The idea of inherent criminality was widespread among detectives and policing scientists in Western countries in the early twentieth century. E.g., in Weimar Germany, detectives within the Criminal Police, who were steeped in the Enlightenment traditions of their university-educated milieu, believed that stringent "preventive" measures against the roughly 8,000 to 9,000 "professional" recidivists that they identified nationwide could eliminate virtually all urban crime. Patrick Wagner, "Operating on the Body of the Nation: Racist Criminal Politics and Traditional Policing in Nazi Germany," paper presented at the Australasian Association for European History, Twelfth Biennial Conference, Perth, July 5–9, 1999; Patrick Wagner, *Volksgemeinschaft ohne Verbrecher: Konzeptionen und Praxis der Kriminalpolizei in der Zeit der Weimarer Republik und des Nationalsozialismus* (Hamburg: Christians, 1996).

44. Malygin, "Gosudarstvenno-pravovoi status," 87–88.

45. N. A. Shabel'nikova, *Militsiia dal'nego vostoka Rossii: 1922–1930 gg.* (Vladivostok: Izdatel'stvo Dal'nevostochnogo universiteta, 2000), 187–88.

46. On Dzershinskii's concept of political power and the Cheka during the Civil War, see Werth, "State against Its People," 57–59, 67–69.

47. Malygin, "Gosudarstvenno-pravovoi status," 274.

48. Dugin, "Organy moskovskoi gorodskoi militsii," 49–50.

49. Vorontsov et al., *Organy i Voiska MVD Rossii*, 230.

50. Ibid., 223–24. The term "Industrial Militsiia" is a translation of the Russian Vedomstvennaia Militsiia, which translates literally as "departmental police" (i.e., police attached to a specific area of economic administration, e.g., retail supply, metallurgical production). Although some of these officers guarded nonindustrial economic institutions (grain distribution centers, collective farms, etc.) the vast majority of them guarded individual factories, construction sites, or distribution centers; hence the term "Industrial Militsiia" is most appropriate to the function of the organization.

51. George Lin, "Fighting in Vain: The NKVD RSFSR in the 1920s," PhD dissertation, Stanford University, 1997, 13; Vorontsov et al., *Organy i Voiska MVD Rossii*, 229.

52. Vorontsov et al., *Organy i Voiska MVD Rossii*, 225.

53. Ibid., 222; Dugin, "Organy moskovskoi gorodskoi militsii," 47, 51–52.

54. Iain Lauchlan, *Russian Hide and Seek: The Tsarist Secret Police in Petersburg, 1906–1914* (Helsinki: Finnish Literature Society, 2002), 109–12.

55. Werth, "State against Its People," 108–14.

56. For the most important account, see Stephen F. Cohen, *Bukharin and the Bolshevik Revolution: A Political Biography, 1888–1938* (New York: Alfred A. Knopf, 1973).

57. For discussion of repressions in the Don region, see Holquist, *Making War*, chap. 6. For a general discussion of repression connected with the transition to the NEP, see Finkel, "Intensification of Vigilance," 299–320, esp. 302–4.

58. Werth, "State against Its People," 113–18.

59. For the early history of the Soviet criminal justice system, see Peter H. Solomon Jr., *Soviet Criminal Justice under Stalin* (Cambridge: Cambridge University Press, 1996), 17–48.

60. A telegram to Dzerzhinskii from his assistant, I. S. Unshlikht, dated January 29, 1922, referred to "the draft of Kamenev-Stalin, with which Il'ich agrees"; the proposal called for the abolishment of the Cheka, the creation of a GPU within the NKVD RSFSR, and the removal of all administrative sentencing power from the political police. Malygin, "Gosudarstvenno-pravovoi status," 115–17.

61. George Leggett, *The Cheka: Lenin's Political Police* (Oxford: Clarendon Press, 1981), 339–42.

62. For copies of the relevant orders, see Khaustov, Naumov, and Plotnikov, *Lubianka 1922–1936*, 14–22.

63. Ibid., 22–23.

64. Ibid., 41–42, 784–85 n. 13.

65. Malygin, "Gosudarstvenno-pravovoi status," 118.

66. Dzerzhinsky resisted this change, correctly arguing that it would undermine much of the central authority that the NKVD had built up during the war and make policemen employees of local soviets rather than of the central NKVD. Malygin, "Gosudarstvenno-pravovoi status," 33, 283–84; Lin, "Fighting in Vain," 17–19.

67. Lin, "Fighting in Vain," 12–16; and Michael Jakobson, *Origins of the Gulag: The Soviet Prison-Camp System, 1917–1934* (Lexington: University of Kentucky Press, 1993), 67–69.

68. Malygin, "Gosudarstvenno-pravovoi status," 284–85; Lin, "Fighting in Vain," 32–53.

69. Neil Weissman, "Policing the NEP Countryside," in *Russia in the Era of NEP: Explorations in Soviet Society and Culture,* ed. Sheila Fitzpatrick, Alexander Rabinowitch, and Richard Stites (Bloomington: Indiana University Press, 1991), 179, 183–84.

70. The NKVD attempted to co-opt these local forms of policing in the 1920s by organizing them into volunteer detachments connected to an individual policeman. See GARF, f. 1235, op. 72, d. 340, l. 14ob, for a short summary of popular participation in the late 1920s. See also Weissman, "Policing the NEP Countryside," 182.

71. Lin, "Fighting in Vain," 68; Vorontsov et al., *Organy i Voiska MVD Rossii*, 241.

72. See I. A. Kondaurov, i dr., *Moskovskaia krasnoznamennaia militsiia* (Moscow: Iuridicheskaia literature, 1988), 100–7, and Dugin, "Organy Moskovskoi gorodskoi militsii," 135–56.

73. Vorontsov et al., *Organy i Voiska MVD Rossii*, 237.

74. E.g., in 1924 only 1.7 percent of the staff of the elite detective departments in the Russian Republic had prerevolutionary policing experience, notwithstanding the dire need for such experience in this highly skilled and technical area of policing. Vorontsov et al., *Organy i Voiska MVD Rossii*, 236–38.

75. Vorontsov et al., *Organy i Voiska MVD Rossii*, 232–33.

76. Werth, "State against Its People," 134.

77. Finkel, "Intensification of Vigilance," 310; Nicolas Werth, "L'OGPU en 1924: Radiographie d'une institution à son niveau d'étiage," *Cahiers du Monde russe* 42, nos. 2–4 (2001): 397–422.

78. Werth, "State against Its People," 135; Finkel, "Intensification of Vigilance," 309.

79. Leggett, *The Cheka*, chap. 7.

80. Malygin, "Gosudarstvenno-pravovoi status," 281–82. The original "Minus Six" cities were Moscow, Leningrad, Kharkov, Odessa, Rostov na Donu, and Kiev. Lin, "Fighting in Vain," 85.

81. Khaustov, Naumov, and Plotnikov, *Lubianka 1922–1936*, 23; Malygin, "Gosudarstvenno-pravovoi status," 281.

82. Malygin, "Gosudarstvenno-pravovoi status," 87. For more on the drafting of the Criminal Code of 1922, see Solomon, *Soviet Criminal Justice under Stalin*, 27–34.

83. GARF, f. 3316, op. 12, d. 29, ll. 5–7.

84. Republic-level OGPU special boards were authorized to exile individuals who were "suspected of committing banditry, robbery, or brigandage . . . in the case of lack of sufficient evidence to send the case to the court system"; those "without defined employment and not engaged in productive labor, in particular: (1) professional gamblers; (2) card-sharks and hucksters; (3) proprietors of any sort of criminal lair or houses of indulgence [brothels]; (4) dealers of cocaine, morphine, santonine, liquor, moonshine and other alcoholic beverages without the proper authorization; (5) speculators on the black market, regarding whom there is evidence of particular maliciousness or connections with the criminal milieu; (6) individuals who are socially dangerous due to their past activities, specifically: those who have not less than two sentences (*obvinitel'nye prigovory*) or four arrests (*privody*) for suspicion of property crimes or infringement against individuals or their dignity (hooliganism, solicitation of prostitution, pimping, etc.)." For the full text of this order, see A. I. Kokurin and N. V. Petrov, *Lubianka: VChK-OGPU-NKVD-NKGB-MGB-MVD-KGB 1917–1960* (Moscow: Mezhdunarodnyi fond "Demokratiia," 1997), 179–80.

85. GARF, f. 3316, op. 64, d. 21, ll. 10–17.

86. Lin, "Fighting in Vain," 77–88; Malygin, "Gosudarstvenno-pravovoi status," 291–92.

87. E.g., a resolution at a 1926 convention of regional NKVD chiefs suggested that local *militsiia* officials should have the right banish any individuals who had been

indicted, either in judicial or extrajudicial order, three times or more for any of fourteen enumerated crimes and who maintained contacts with the criminal underworld.
This suggestion was ignored by the Politburo. Malygin, "Gosudarstvenno-pravovoi
status," 94.

88. Werth, "State against Its People," 138–40. On banditry arising from state and
social instability in the Far East, see Shabel'nikova, *Militsiia dal'nego vostoka Rossii*,
212–18.

89. Shabel'nikova, *Militsiia dal'nego vostoka Rossii*, 216–17.

90. Malygin, "Gosudarstvenno-pravovoi status," 286–90.

91. Lin, "Fighting in Vain," 26–32, 45–50; the quotation is on 47 (emphasis in the
original). For several of the original documents related to the conflict, see Khaustov,
Naumov, and Plotnikov, *Lubianka 1922–1936*, 87–91.

92. Khaustov, Naumov, and Plotnikov, *Lubianka 1922–1936*, 113, 793 n. 46. See
also Werth, "State against Its People," 136.

93. Werth, "State against Its People," 135.

94. Malygin, "Gosudarstvenno-pravovoi status," 199–201.

95. See also Dzerzhinskii's October 1923 letter to Stalin in *Lubianka 1922–1936*,
ed. Khaustov, Naumov, and Plotnikov, 81–82.

96. Procuracy officials estimated that two-thirds of the 7,000 individuals sentenced to exile in Siberia by mid-1927, e.g., were speculators, currency traders, con-
trabandists, or other small-scale criminals. Victor Danilov, Roberta Manning, and Lynne
Viola, eds., *Tragediia sovetskoi derevni: Kollektivizatsiia i raskulachivanie, 1927–
1939—Dokumenty i materialy, V 5–ti tt. T.1, Mai 1927–noiabr' 1929* (Moscow:
ROSSPEN, 1999), 780 n. 58, citing GANO f. r-20 op. 2, d. 135, l. 13–14.

97. For a perceptive discussion of the cultural and legal bases of this campaign,
see Anne E. Gorsuch, *Youth in Revolutionary Russia: Enthusiasts, Bohemians, Delinquents* (Bloomington: Indiana University Press, 2000), esp. 167–76.

98. Malygin, "Gosudarstvenno-pravovoi status," 291.

99. Gorsuch, *Youth in Revolutionary Russia*, 175.

100. Weissman, "Policing the NEP Countryside," 186–88. For a full discussion of
fining in early Soviet criminal justice, see Peter H. Solomon Jr., "Criminalization and
Decriminalization in Soviet Criminal Policy, 1917–1941," *Law and Society Review* 16,
no. 1 (1981–82): 9–43.

101. Courts sentenced "dangerous elements" under the auspices of Article 35 of
the 1926 Criminal Code of the Russian Soviet Federated Socialist Republic. For a
translation of this article in English, see Oleg V. Khlevniuk, *The History of the Gulag:
From Collectivization to the Great Terror*, trans. Vadim A. Staklo and ed. David Nordlander (New Haven, Conn.: Yale University Press, 2004), 364–65.

102. For a full discussion of these debates, see Solomon, *Soviet Criminal Justice
under Stalin*, 17–48.

103. Malygin, "Gosudarstvenno-pravovoi status," 292; Werth, "State against Its
People," 140–41.

Chapter 2

1. GARF, f. 374, op. 27, d. 1923, l. 40.

2. GARF, f. 9415, op. 5, d. 488, ll. 59–60.

3. Winston S. Churchill, *The Second World War, Volume IV: The Hinge of Fate* (Boston: Houghton Mifflin, 1985), 446–48. For a discussion of the utility of this source, see Michael Ellman, "Churchill on Stalin: A Note," *Europe-Asia Studies* 58, no. 6 (2006): 965–71.

4. GARF, f. 9401, op. 1, d. 4157, ll. 203, 205. These figures come from a 1953 Ministry of Internal Affairs report summarizing the work of the political police in the period after the Civil War. I am indebted to Gabor Rittersporn for making this document available to me. This report is available in an English translation by Oleg V. Khlevniuk, *The History of the Gulag: From Collectivization to the Great Terror*, trans. Vadim A. Staklo and ed. David Nordlander (New Haven, Conn.: Yale University Press, 2004), 288–91.

5. Aleksandr Iakovlevich Malygin, "Gosudarstvenno-pravovoi status militsii RSFSR v period provedeniia Novoi Ekonomicheskoi Politiki (20-e gody)," doktorskaia dissertatsiia, Akademiia MVD RF, 1992, 201.

6. Nicolas Werth, "A State against Its People: Violence, Repression, and Terror in the Soviet Union," in *The Black Book of Communism: Crimes, Terror, Repression*, ed. Mark Kramer and trans. Jonathan Murphy (Cambridge, Mass.: Harvard University Press, 1999), 33–268; citation here to 140.

7. GARF, f. 3316, op. 64, d. 603, l. 3; GARF, f. 3316, op. 64, d. 604, ll. 1–7. The OGPU mounted another wave of repression of urban homeless adults and beggars in February 1930, sentencing them as "dangerous elements" to exile, banishment, or terms in concentration camps. GARF, f. 1235, op. 141, d. 789, l. 2.

8. Malygin, "Gosudarstvenno-pravovoi status," 293–94.

9. GARF, f. 3316, op. 64, d. 118, ll. 1–4.

10. GARF, f. 3316, op. 64, d. 244, ll. 1–2; GARF, f. 3316, op. 64, d. 483, l. 7. The Politburo rejected the OGPU's concurrent request to apply the same additional three years of banishment to individuals who had served three-year terms of banishment, effectively doubling their sentences using administrative means. GARF, f. 3316, op. 64, d. 483, l. 13.

11. The instruction applied to individuals convicted for one of a specific list of serious nonpolitical crimes (Articles 74, 104, 155, 162, 165, 166, 173, and 175 (pt. 2 and 3) of the Criminal Code) and who maintained continued contact with the criminal underworld, or those with one sentence and three arrests, or three separate sentences, in the previous five years for any crimes listed in the code. Procuracy officials estimated that the instruction would apply to some 8,000 inmates in the NKVD prison system in the RSFSR; some 9,200 individuals were eventually sentenced under its auspices. GARF, f. 3316, op. 64, d. 866, ll. 1–7, 11–12; Malygin, "Gosudarstvenno-pravovoi status," 103.

12. For detailed discussion of this order, see Peter H. Solomon Jr., "Soviet Penal Policy, 1917–1934: A Reinterpretation," *Slavic Review* 39, no. 2 (1980): 195–217.

13. E.g., see the argument by Iagoda and Prokof'ev in October 1927 that speculators were among the major causes of ongoing difficulties in provisioning in urban areas and should be dealt with by administrative measures. Danilov, Victor, Roberta Manning, and Lynne Viola, eds., *Tragediia sovetskoi derevni: Kollektivizatsiia i raskulachivanie, 1927–1939—Dokumenty i materialy, V 5–ti tt. T. 1, Mai 1927–noiabr' 1929* (Moscow: ROSSPEN, 1999) (hereafter Danilov, Manning, and Viola, *Tragediia sovetskoi derevni*, t. 1), 100–2.

14. Danilov, Manning, and Viola, *Tragediia sovetskoi derevni*, t. 1, 136, 200–2, 206–8, 231.

15. Ibid., 233–36.

16. For documents related to a 1929 campaign against urban speculation that underscore this conceptual division, see Danilov, Manning, and Viola, *Tragediia sovetskoi derevni*, t. 1, 680–81, 683–84, 691, 697, 700.

17. For surveys of the collectivization and dekulakization drives, see V. P. Danilov and S. A. Krasil'nikov, eds., *Spetspereselentsy v Zapadnoi Sibiri, 1930–vesna 1931 g.* (Novosibirsk: Nauka, 1992); N. A. Ivnitskii, "Kollektivizatsiia i raskulachivanie v nachale 30-x godov," in *Sud"by Rossiiskogo Krest'ianstva*, ed. Iu. N. Afanas'ev (Moscow: RGGU, 1996), 249–95; and the introduction to *Tragediia sovetskoi derevni: Kollektivizatsiia i raskulachivanie, 1927–1939—Dokumenty i materialy, V 5–ti tt. T. 3, Konets 1930–1933*, ed. Victor Danilov, Roberta Manning, and Lynne Viola (Moscow: ROSSPEN, 2001).

18. Lynne Viola, *The Role of the OGPU in Dekulakization, Mass Deportations, and Special Resettlement in 1930*, Carl Beck Papers in Russian and East European Studies no. 1406 (Pittsburgh: Russian and East European Studies, University of Pittsburgh, 2000), 5–7.

19. In contrast to previous instructions on the subject, cases regarding kulaks that demanded "particular haste," according to this instruction, could be processed through the Special Board rather than the court system. Danilov, Manning, and Viola, *Tragediia sovetskoi derevni*, t. 1, 714–16, 732.

20. Ibid., 742.

21. Viola, *Role of the OGPU*, 12–16.

22. Ibid., 16–17.

23. For examples of *militsiia* activity in support of these campaigns, see Victor Danilov, Roberta Manning, and Lynne Viola, eds., *Tragediia sovetskoi derevni: Kollektivizatsiia i raskulachivanie, 1927–1939—Dokumenty i materialy, V 5–ti tt. T. 2, Noiabr' 1929–Dekabr' 1930* (Moscow: ROSSPEN, 1999), 102, 144–45, 158–61, 182–83.

24. Lynne Viola, "The Other Archipelago: Kulak Deportations to the North in 1930," *Slavic Review* 60, no. 4 (2001): 730–55, esp.736–37; Lynne Viola, "The Aesthetic of Stalinist Planning and the World of the Special Villages," *Kritika: Explorations in Russian and Eurasian History* 4, no. 1 (2003): 119–20.

25. For typical examples, see TsGAMO, f. 267, op. 1, d. 1, l. 477, for an account of a rural precinct inspector in the Moscow region who responded to a protest of some one hundred women in March 1930 who were demanding the return of their cattle from the local collective farm; Danilov, Manning, and Viola, *Tragediia sovetskoi derevni*, t. 1, 661–63, for a similar account from the Armavirskyi region (*okrug*), in which some 1,000 to 1,500 peasants assembled to protest the seizure of cattle and repulsed all attempts by local officials to regain control of the situation, succumbing only to a detachment of OGPU troops; and Tracy McDonald, "A Peasant Rebellion in Stalin's Russia: The Pitelinskii Uprising, Riazan 1930," in *Contending with Stalinism: Soviet Power and Popular Resistance in the 1930s*, ed. Lynne Viola (Ithaca, N.Y.: Cornell University Press, 2002).

26. Viola, "Other Archipelago"; Viola, *Role of the OGPU*, 28–31, 35–37. *Militsiia* officers themselves served as ready source of recruits for these detachments, a policy that central NKVD officials condemned but were powerless to control; see GARF, f. 9415, op. 5, d. 474, l. 16. For an account of workers' brigades, see Lynne Viola, *Best Sons of the Fatherland: Workers in the Vanguard of Soviet Collectivization* (New York: Oxford University Press, 1987).

27. On campaigns against the "disenfranchised" and small-scale traders in the late 1920s, see Golfo Alexopoulos, *Stalin's Outcasts: Aliens, Citizens, and the Soviet State, 1926–1936* (Ithaca, N.Y.: Cornell University Press, 2003), 20–31, esp. 24–25.

28. Viola, *Role of the OGPU*, 21.

29. Less than a quarter of all NKVD employees were classed as workers in 1930, while 60 percent were peasants and 15 percent were white collar (*sluzhashchie*). White-collar employees were overrepresented in detective departments, while peasants dominated in the lower ranks of both the regular *militsiia* and Industrial Militsiia. GARF, f. 374, op. 27, d. 1923, ll. 27–34; GARF, f. 1235, op. 141, d. 910, ll. 37–39; GARF, f. A-406, op. 25, d. 326, ll. 5–21; GARF, f. 1235, op. 141, d. 910, ll. 1–43.

30. Although women had worked in small numbers in detective departments as early as the Civil War, local resistance to this change was immediate, even in major cities. The Moscow police administration refused to hire women for general police duties for over a year after the order was promulgated, acquiescing only after substantial pressure from NKVD authorities. GARF, f. 374, op. 28, d. 3054, l. 192ob; GARF, f. 1235, op. 141, d. 910, l. 35.

31. E.g., see various comments by the OGPU about the behavior of the local police in the Riazan region in 1929 in *Riazanskaia derevnia v 1929–1930 gg.: Khronika golovokruzheniia—Dokumenty i materialy*, ed. L. Viola, T. McDonald, S. V. Zhuralev, A. N. Mel'nik (Moscow: ROSSPEN, 1998), 50, 115, 190–91. See also complaints from the police chief of the Lower Volga Territory regarding provisioning difficulties and corruption in July 1930 in GARF, f. 1235, op. 141, d. 703, ll. 1–1ob.

32. One such central report states, e.g., that the rape of prostitutes was "extremely common": "[It] takes place everywhere and all the time, in Red Corners and in working offices, on the tables in station houses, in the streets, on boulevards, in open air markets, etc. . . . In the Orenburg *militsiia*, all the officers make use of prostitutes, from the Chief of the regional administration to the junior officer." GARF, f. 374, op. 28, d. 3054, l. 193ob.

33. See GARF, f. A-406, op. 25, d. 326, l. 17, e.g., for a 1928 report from the Russian Justice Commissariat that estimated that in most regions of the Russian Republic no more than 25 to 30 percent of cases sent to the courts by the *militsiia* were sufficiently investigated to support a trial. On the participation of Soviet judicial agencies in the industrialization and collectivization drives, see Peter H. Solomon Jr., *Soviet Criminal Justice under Stalin* (Cambridge: Cambridge University Press, 1996), 81–110.

34. GARF, f. 374, op. 28, d. 3054, l. 192.

35. Beloborodov was ousted for his role as one of the signatories of Trotsky's "Declaration of the 46" in 1923; he was subjected to internal exile from 1927 until 1930, after which his Communist Party membership was restored and he worked in low-level positions until he was arrested in 1936 and executed in 1938. George Lin, "Fighting in Vain: The NKVD RSFSR in the 1920s," PhD dissertation, Stanford University, 1997, 68–69, 123–24, 173.

36. Ibid., 127–29, citing *Sovetskoe stroitel'stvo* 8 (1928): 60–69; GARF, f. 3316, op. 64, d. 539, ll. 1–8.

37. See GARF, f. A-406, op. 25, d. 326, ll. 5–21, for a copy of the Rabkrin report, which was printed in seventy-six copies and distributed to state officials at the level of the Russian Republic.

38. Six hundred policemen were purged in the Central Black Earth region; in the Middle Volga region, 565 of 4,190 policemen who were reviewed were purged. GARF, f. 374, op. 28, d. 3054, l. 189.

39. Lin, "Fighting in Vain," 127–36.

40. *2-i vserossiiskii S"ezd administrativnykh rabotnikov: Stenograficheskii otchet* (Moscow: Narodnyi kommissariat vnutrennykh del, 1929), 18–19. The Russian term is *militseiskaia sistema*, which I translate as "militia system" because the idea of a popular militia most closely corresponds to the intended nature of the reform.

41. Aleksandr Dugin, "Organy moskovskoi gorodskoi militsii," kandidatskaia dissertatsiia, Gosudarstvennyi Istoriko-Arkhivnyi Institut, Moscow, 1988, 173–74.

42. GARF, f. 9415, op. 5, d. 474, l. 60.

43. GARF, f. 1235, op. 72, d. 340, ll. 17–32; GARF, f. 374, op. 27, d. 1923, l. 33.

44. GARF, f. 1235, op. 72, d. 340, l. 17.

45. GARF, f. A-406, op. 25, d. 388, ll. 5, 9–11. The issue was discussed in at least two meetings of representatives from Rabkrin, the OGPU, and the NKVD; for the transcript of one, see ibid., ll. 12–49. The Russian Sovnarkom supported this plan in February 1930, resolving to reorganize the NKVD and asking that the Politburo issue instructions to that effect. Lin, "Fighting in Vain," 135–37.

46. See Michael Jakobson, *Origins of the Gulag: The Soviet Prison-Camp System, 1917–1934* (Lexington: University of Kentucky Press, 1993), 124–25. Peter Solomon makes the case that economic concerns were paramount to the creation of the Gulag system in Solomon, "Soviet Penal Policy."

47. GARF, f. A-406, op. 25, d. 388, l. 17.

48. GARF, f. 374, op. 27, d. 1923, ll. 3, 6–7; RGASPI, f. 17, op. 3, d. 781, l. 1.

49. Lin, "Fighting in Vain," 150–56. The NKVD also had support from Kalinin, who generally opposed the self-aggrandizing moves of the OGPU. See GARF, f. 3316, op. 64, d. 539, ll. 2–8.

50. Viola, *Role of the OGPU*, 33–36.

51. L. Kosheleva et al., *Pis'ma I. V. Stalina V. M. Molotovu, 1925–1936 gg.* (Moscow: Rossiia molodaia, 1995), 215 n. 2.

52. Ibid., 214.

53. The duties of the NKVD regarding communal services (*khoziaistvo*) were transferred to a newly created communal services administration within each republican Sovnarkom. This part of the split of duties was relatively unimportant. See A. V. Borisov et al., *Politsiia i Militsiia Rossii: Stranitsy Istorii* (Moscow: Nauka, 1995), 140–41; and RGASPI, f. 17, op. 162, d. 9, l. 57.

54. Tolmachev was arrested in 1932, served a three-year sentence, and then returned to low-level work until he was again arrested in 1937 and executed in 1939. Lin, "Fighting in Vain," 172–74.

55. GARF, f. 374, op. 27, d. 1923, ll. 12–14, 19, 43, 35–37.

56. Ibid., l. 40.

57. RGASPI, f. 17, op. 3, d. 804, l. 1; RGASPI, f. 17, op. 3, d. 805, l. 1; RGASPI, f. 17, op. 3, d. 806, l. 16; RGASPI, f. 17, op. 162, d. 9, l. 71. Despite vigorous protests from the OGPU, the Justice Commissariat gained control not only over the NKVD's prison and labor colony systems but also over administration of compulsory labor (*prinudrabota*). See GARF, f. A-406, op. 25, d. 388, ll. 12–49; and GARF, f. 374, op. 27, d. 1923, l. 19. See also Jakobson, *Origins of the Gulag*, 122–23.

58. GARF, f. 1235, op. 141, d. 418, ll. 1–3; or GARF, f. 5446, op. 12a, d. 1141, ll. 61–63. The Politburo's decision to retain the appearance of control by local Soviets,

and the creation of republic-level police administrations within the state bureaucracy, were intended only to ensure that the new institutional structure outwardly corresponded to the USSR Constitution, which explicitly gave republics the right to control civil police activity within their borders. Borisov et al., *Politsiia i Militsiia Rossii*, 140–42.

59. New official instructions for the *militsiia* were published on May 25, 1931, as "Instructions Regarding the Workers' and Peasants' Militsiia" (*Polozhenie o RKM*), *SZ SSSR* no. 33 (May 31, 1931), Article 247, pp. 429–37. See also Borisov et al., *Politsiia i Militsiia Rossii*, 252–53; and GARF, f. 9415, op. 5, d. 476, ll. 248–50.

60. GARF, f. 9415, op. 1, d. 1, l. 21; V. I. Vorontsov et al., *Organy i Voiska MVD Rossii: Kratkii Istoricheskii Ocherk* (Moscow: Ob'edinennaia redaktsiia MVD Rossii, 1996), 246–47; GARF, f. 5446, op. 12a, d. 1141, ll. 64–69.

61. GARF, f. 9415, op. 1, d. 1, l. 18; GARF, f. 9415, op. 3, d. 3, ll. 6–6ob.

62. Nationwide figures for the purge are not available, but dismissals were substantial. Three hundred policemen were purged from the *militsiia* of Bashkiria, or 10 percent of the total staff. A total of 830 policemen were purged from the Lower Volga Territory, including 10 chiefs of district-level administrations; 40 more district chiefs were demoted but allowed to keep their jobs. In the Urals, 1,233 policemen were purged, 220 of whom were members of the officer corps. GARF, f. 9415, op. 5, d. 474, ll. 1–2, 3-5; GARF, f. 1235, op. 141, d. 910, ll. 22–21.

63. *SZ SSSR* no. 84 (December 31, 1932), Articles 518–19, pp. 824–25.

64. For a detailed description of the relationship between the *militsiia* and OGPU at the local level, see GARF, f. 1235, op. 141, d. 910, ll. 23–24.

65. E.g., one detective from the Republic of Georgia complained to his superiors: "Up to this point [May 1931] we have not received any sort of directives [from the central leadership in Moscow]. We've received no instructions, no textbooks. . . . In general, guidance from the center for the territories and regions has been very weak." GARF, f. 9415, op. 5, d. 475, l. 95.

66. A typical circular sent from the Central Militsiia Administration to local police in August 1931 complained that, despite orders sent in May of that year requesting statistical summaries of covert work by August 1, not a single police administration had sent the requested information to the center; see GARF, f. 9415, op. 5, d. 474, l. 69. See also GARF, f. 9415, op. 5. d. 474, l. 38; GARF, f. 9415, op. 3, d. 3, l. 49.

67. See GARF, f. 1235, op. 72, d. 340, ll. 1–6, for a report on precinct inspectors in the countryside in 1932–34.

68. GARF, f. 9415, op. 1, d. 2, l. 11; GARF, f. 1235, op. 141, d. 910, l. 15; GARF, f. 9415, op. 3, d. 3, ll. 78–79.

69. GARF, f. 9415, op. 5, d. 475, ll. 84–100, esp. 85.

70. The order for new uniforms can be found in GARF, f. 9415, op. 1, d. 1, ll. 51–55ob, complete with a description of the new uniforms and the rules for wearing them. On the delays, see ibid., ll. 149–50.

71. GARF, f. 1235, op. 141, d. 910, l. 39–40.

72. In 1930, for example, in five surveyed territories and regions of the Russian Republic, 1,015 policemen began work after receiving formal training while 899 policemen with previous training left for other jobs. GARF, f. 1235, op. 141, d. 910, ll. 39–37. In a final affront, police who quit for better work often took their precious uniforms with them, especially in the countryside; GARF, f. 9415, op. 3, d. 3, ll. 66–77.

73. According to one report, as of July 1, 1932, 23.3 percent of policemen were Communist Party members, 6.2 percent were Komsomol members, and 70.5 percent were nonparty; 21.2 percent were workers, 64.9 percent were peasants in various social and economic categories, and 13.9 percent were white-collar workers. The worker contingent was relatively stable, having grown 1.5 percent in 1931. GARF, f. 9415, op. 3, d. 3, ll. 26–27.

74. OGPU officials reported that the Industrial Militsiia were particularly prone to leave their jobs without returning their official police identification and were more prone to graft and theft in general than the regular *militsiia*, both because industrial policemen tended not to be career officers and because they had close contact with valuable goods. The OGPU carried out a general purge of the membership of the Industrial Militsiia in October 1931. I have found no information regarding the results of the purge in accessible Russian archives. GARF, f. 9415, op. 3, d. 9, l. 48; GARF, f. 9415, op. 1, d. 1, ll. 173–73ob; GARF, f. 9415, op. 5, d. 474, ll. 79a–80.

75. GARF, f. 9415, op. 5, d. 491, l. 9; GARF, f. 9415, op. 3, d. 3, ll. 26–28.

76. Central OGPU officials were well aware of the tendency of local police to use physical force and to violate norms of procedure when making arrests. A September 1931 order from Usov, the head of the *militsiia*, complained that local policemen often beat people they arrested to loss of consciousness, especially drunks. He condemned policemen who used physical methods during interrogation as "class-alien elements" and "holdovers from the Tsarist period." GARF, f. 9415, op. 1, d. 1, ll. 134–35.

77. E.g., a typical 1932 report from the Moscow region noted that in the Reutovskii district ten former kulaks, traders, and other "class-alien elements" worked in the *militsiia*; nepotism and theft of both public and private property were common, and drunken policemen fired indiscriminately on workers, raped arrested women, and even murdered drunks in local jails. In the Ramenskii district, a "Trotskyite group" reportedly controlled the local *militsiia* administration, openly promoting anti-Soviet agitation at rural meetings. GARF, f. 9415, op. 5, d. 491, ll. 8–9.

78. GARF, f. 9415, op. 3, d. 3, l. 83.

79. Police used the term "operational" (*operativnyi*) to describe both the style of policing and the name of the department that carried it out. Although I retain the term in the name of the Operational Department, the phrase "covert policing" makes more sense in English.

80. As the attempt to reintegrate the new Operational Department into the civil policing hierarchy failed quickly, as discussed below, the name was changed back to the Detective Department (*Ugolovnyi rozysk*), and the organization retained its separate status from the regular *militsiia*. For simplicity's sake, I will refer to individual officers in these departments as "detectives" throughout.

81. In a meeting of the heads of republic-level operational departments in late May 1931, Usov noted that no internal functional division existed within the OGPU between "outward order and operational questions" and that this division should be eliminated in the *militsiia*; he referred to these changes as the "operativization" of the *militsiia*. GARF, f. 9415, op. 5, d. 475, ll. 3–5. See also ibid., ll. 12, 21–23, 30–31.

82. The "Battle with Banditry" Department handled banditry, brigandage, armed robbery, murder and attempted murder, serious bodily injury, and aggravated hooliganism; crimes against individuals, including bodily injury, rape, and destruction of property; and arson, cattle rustling, resistance and insults to authority, and illegal

possession of weapons. The Economic Department (EKO) duplicated the policing functions of the Economic Department of the OGPU almost exactly, dealing with embezzlement, bribe taking, systematic theft in state institutions, the misuse of state property, spoilage of goods, disruption of labor discipline, hooliganism on the shop floor, and "all criminal acts bordering on wrecking." The Property Crimes Department (IPR, or *Imushchestvennoe prestuplenie*) handled economic crimes against individuals rather than state institutions, including theft, fraud, and swindling, as well as with less serious crimes that acquired political overtones if committed by "professional criminal elements," including pimping, maintaining criminal hideouts, sexual crimes, speculation, unarmed robbery, and thievery. Ibid., ll. 112–13.

83. Operational department administrations in localities were divided only into operational and secret-informational subdepartments. Scientific-technical duties, including the study of crime trends and gathering statistics, were assumed to be the duties of the local administrations as a whole. GARF, f. 9415, op. 5, d. 474, ll. 34–37, 112–14. See also the circular defining the structure and duties of the new Operational Department in ibid., ll. 33–38a.

84. GARF, f. 9415, op. 5, d. 488 ll. 74–75; GARF, f. 9415, op. 5, d. 491, l. 4.

85. This disengagement with undercover methods was viewed as an abject failure of policing by OGPU officials in the 1930s, but in the NEP era it was point of honor for the NKVD leadership as they stressed the essential differences between their organization and the OGPU. For example, Tolmachev, upon taking control of the NKVD in 1928, specifically instructed his investigators to cease all contact with the criminal underworld because such contact was characteristic of the conspiratorial nature of Tsarist police. Vorontsov et. al,, *Organy i Voiska MVD Rossii*, 244–45. See also GARF, f. 9415, op. 5, d. 475, l. 56.

86. Instructions to local detectives specified the categories of people to be recruited as informants: municipal employees who "know well the individuals living in a particular location and their style of life," prostitutes, truck drivers, taxi drivers, shoe shiners, handicraft workers, street and market vendors, etc.; employees of tea houses, bars, restaurants, hotels, motels, and other servants; people who worked in white-collar jobs in Soviet factories and concerns; and finally, individuals who have "previously been arrested by the O[perative] D[epartment] and due to their previous criminal activity are connected to the professional criminal world and therefore are able to provide valuable information." GARF, f. 9415, op. 5, d. 488, ll. 12–41, esp. 19. See also GARF, f. 9415, op. 5, d. 475, l. 57; GARF, f. 9415, op. 5, d. 491, ll. 18–22; GARF, f. 9415, op. 5, d. 475, l. 114; GARF, f. 9415, op. 5, d. 488, l. 24.

87. GARF, f. 9415, op. 5, d. 491, ll. 26–29; GARF, f. 9415, op. 5, d. 488, ll. 74–76.

88. GARF, f. 9415, op. 5, d. 488, l. 65.

89. GARF, f. 9415, op. 5, d. 475, ll. 58–59, 119, 121–22; GARF, f. 9415, op. 5, d. 482, ll. 38–40.

90. GARF, f. 9415, op. 5, d. 475, ll. 56–57, 119.

91. Ibid., l. 7.

92. Ibid., ll. 12, 56; GARF, f. 9415, op. 3, d. 3, ll. 6ob–9.

93. GARF, f. 9415, op. 3, d. 3, ll. 8ob–9.

94. GARF, f. 9415, op. 5, d. 491, l. 12. Another report noted with alarm that the Moscow Procuracy was more involved with directing undercover operations at the district level than were police administrations. Ibid., ll. 6–17.

95. GARF, f. 9415, op. 5, d. 476, ll. 69–70; GARF, f. 9415, op. 5, d. 486, l. 76.

96. E.g., the police in the Moscow region (not including the city itself) counted 11,171 registered informants at the end of 1932, mostly volunteers, who were supervised by district-level detectives. A tally of the work of 6,807 of these informants showed that they provided 7,383 denunciations for the first six months of 1932 but that these denunciations resulted in only 578 solved cases. The head of the regional Operational Department, furthermore, refused to vouch for even these figures, because they were based on self-reported statistics from only 80 of the roughly 146 district police administrations in the region and included informants who provided no useful information or had moved out of a particular area. GARF, f. 9415, op. 5, d. 491, ll. 1–5. See also ibid., l. 29, for a similar report from the Moscow region (excluding the city itself) that counted 10,455 registered informants at the end of December 1932, plus some 721 "connectors" (*sviazisti*, paid full-time police employees put in place only in November) and 332 "group leaders" (*gruppovodi*), which nonetheless produced only 6,121 instances of "reception of agent denunciations" during the fourth quarter of 1932.

97. GARF, f. 9415, op. 3, d. 3, l. 62–63. Local police, in their own defense, stressed the overwhelming difficulties involved in maintaining informant networks and the pressure on local detectives to solve crimes rather than work with informants. In the Moscow region, the two to four detectives serving each district were already overwhelmed with investigations of crimes and the registration and study of criminals. GARF, f. 9415, op. 5, d. 491, l. 28.

98. E.g., a September 1932 report states that only fifty professional full-time operatives (*razvedchiki*) served the detective departments of the city of Moscow. At these levels, according to the report, staff were so overworked that the backlog of assignments surpassed five or six days, after which the ability of operatives to gain information about crimes already committed was severely limited. The Moscow police leadership requested that the number of paid operatives in the city be doubled, arguing that paid spying had proven to be the most effective covert means of uncovering crimes. GARF, f. 9415, op. 5, d. 491, ll. 24–25.

99. A 1932 budget for the Moscow region (not including the city) allotted 160,000 rubles for "secret-operational expenses" to support a paid staff of forty-four undercover employees, including one plenipotentiary and forty-three assistants who were identified as "operatives" (*razvedchiki*). Ibid., l. 2. The budget set aside 85,080 rubles for paid undercover agents, at 160 rubles per month for the operatives and 210 rubles for the plenipotentiaries, plus 37,730 rubles for the maintenance of the undercover network—generally payments to informants.

100. E.g., see the response by central OGPU officials to an optimistic report on the state of informant activity in the Moscow region in late 1932, which stated that the "report sent in on the agent work of the Operational Department of URKM MO [Moscow Police Administration] completely fails to reflect the reality of the situation in this area of activity." The response noted the abysmal number of denunciations and cases solved on the basis of denunciations, concluding that the situation "suggests that a large portion of the undercover network is not fit for work." Ibid., ll. 26–27.

101. In Moscow, e.g., roughly 700 inspectors patrolled the city by 1934, one for every 5,000 residents. GARF, f. 5446, op. 15a, d. 1130, ll. 1–10; GARF, f. 9415, op. 5, d. 488, ll. 57–60.

102. See GARF, f. 9415, op. 5, d. 488, ll. 70–72, for a description of the role of stewards in the covert work of both the *militsiia* and the OGPU in 1932. In late 1934 the political police chief, Iagoda, requested that stewards be put in charge of public

order on streets in the major cities, initially Moscow and Leningrad, and that they be officially subordinated to the *militsiia*. GARF, f. 5446, op. 16a, d. 1270, l. 26.

103. In addition to the quotation at the beginning of this chapter, see GARF, f. 9415, op. 5, d. 488, ll. 59–61. In the countryside, where administrative means were limited, this ideal was muted. Precinct inspectors were expected to begin undercover work by amassing a group of voluntary informants in each rural locality they visited, but they were still responsible for so large an area that any daily use of such informants was impossible.

104. E.g., at an Operational Department conference in May 1931, police officials stressed the idea of unifying the investigative and outward work of the *militsiia* in the position of the precinct inspector. GARF, f. 9415, op. 5, d. 475, l. 111.

105. GARF, f. 9415, op. 5, d. 476, l. 248; GARF, f. 5446, op. 13a, d. 1314, ll. 2–5, 10.

106. Lazar Kaganovich, in a speech delivered to Moscow police officials in August 1932, stressed that the *militsiia* was not capable of maintaining order in the city without the assistance of "genuinely conscious" proletarians, communists, and non-party members who lent their "social activism" [*obshchestvennaia samodeiatel'nost'*] to the task. RGASPI, f. 81, op. 3, d. 151, ll. 7–8.

107. GARF, f. 9415, op. 5, d. 488, l. 67. The response of one OGPU official who was attending the conference at which the inspector levied this complaint is revealing regarding the practices of the political police. The OGPU chief lambasted the inspector for his complaints, saying that the inspector had barely begun to work but was already complaining about lack of materials: "Comrade K. has gone as far as saying that it's time for the precinct inspectors to have safes [in which to keep their materials], which inspectors presumably will strap to their backs [and make their rounds], while we [the OGPU] have behind us fifteen years of experience with this sort of work and our officers [*sotrudniki*], who have informer networks of several dozen people, carry their materials around in their pockets. . . . In the course of our work, the GPU writes down instructions as little as possible, allowing the officers to arrive at methods and techniques of contact themselves, such as how to communicate with informants and so on, because you can't come up with instructions that would cover everything, and because the more you gather up in terms of instructions, the less effectively you will do your job." Ibid., l. 70.

108. E.g., a set of 1932 instructions from the Western Siberian Territory states that, even though as a rule all contact with the informant network was the responsibility of the Operational Department, in individual cases precinct inspectors who had proven to be reliable could be put in charge of contact with informers who were not connected to the criminal milieu. Ibid., l. 23.

109. GARF, f. 9415, op. 3, d. 3, ll. 32, 63.

110. E.g., in the Dmitrovskii district of the Moscow region, the authorities investigated three Brigade cells and uncovered eleven members with previous criminal convictions. In one *militsiia* administration in the city of Kazan', the Brigade cell was reportedly made up of "criminal elements and children of fifteen to sixteen years of age" who systematically robbed arrested individuals. In the Moscow region as a whole, not including the city, in the first half of 1934, at least 1,493 criminal cases were brought against Brigade members who committed some 5,289 criminal acts. All from GARF, f. 9415, op. 1, d. 11, ll. 49–51.

111. *Na boevom postu*, vol. 12, November 20, 1932.

112. The Moscow Night Patrols apprehended 4,031 individuals between April 1 and May 7, 1931, including 1,993 hooligans, 1,464 "socially dangerous elements," and 574 people "directly committing or preparing to commit crimes." GARF, f. 9415, op. 5, d. 481, ll. 49, 60–62.

113. *Na boevom postu*, vol. 13, December 1, 1932.

114. GARF, f. 9415, op. 5, d. 481, ll. 61–63.

115. See TsGAMO, f. 792, op. 6, d. 967, for numerous reports on the 1935 antihooliganism campaign in Moscow that singled out the Brigades as a source of problems.

116. GARF, f. 9415, op. 5, d. 475, ll. 28–34. For a history of the institute, see Peter H. Solomon Jr., "Soviet Criminology: Its Demise and Rebirth, 1922–1963," *Soviet Union* 1, no. 2 (1974): 122–40.

117. The institute continued to produce and publish research into the mid-1930s, but its very existence became an issue in the expanding conflict between the OGPU and the justice agencies, and its influence on the day-to-day activities of the police declined substantially. GARF, f. 9415, op. 5, d. 474, ll. 33–34, and GARF, f. 374, op. 27, d. 1923, l. 40.

118. E.g., in 1931 Usov instructed a conference of regional police chiefs to "search for the political essence of every group of [criminal] bandits"; although the actions of certain individuals might be purely criminal, he argued, at the current time criminal bands were comprised predominantly of kulaks or "former people" and hence they should be treated as political offenders. GARF, f. 9415, op. 5, d. 475, l. 6; GARF, f. 9415, op. 5, d. 476, ll. 1–3.

119. One such swindler, after committing a series of thefts and scams in Moscow in 1929, moved to Leningrad and continued the same line of work, obtaining fake identification and taking a job as a bank teller, which enabled him to embezzle some 1,000 rubles through an accounting scam. From there he moved to Vladikavkaz, obtained a fake Komsomol card, and again took a job at a bank, embezzling over 1,500 rubles. The police report from which this example is drawn, a typical six-month police report on crime during the first half of 1931, includes numerous similar examples. GARF, f. 9415, op. 5, d. 477, ll. 46–47.

120. Ibid., ll. 52–53; GARF, f. 9415, op. 5, d. 476, ll. 181–216.

121. GARF, f. 9415, op. 5, d. 475, l. 6.

122. Residents of and visitors to urban areas were required to register with apartment-block officials, hotel operators, or other responsible individuals, who were in turn required to register even temporary city residents with local *militsiia* administrations. The regime expanded this system by making universal identity cards available (though not obligatory) to the population in 1927. See Mervyn Matthews, *The Passport Society: Controlling Movement in Russia and the USSR* (Boulder, Colo.: Westview Press, 1993), 17–21.

123. NKVD officials in Moscow maintained a similar catalog of important criminals at large across the USSR, but local police usually tailored their own systems to meet local needs, making impossible any coordination across jurisdictions or at the national level. GARF, f. 9415, op. 5, d. 475, l. 76.

124. The system of exile exhibited some of the same problems. Prisoners were usually convoyed to their places of exile by convoy troops, but they were sometimes told to exile themselves and report to the local *militsiia* or OGPU station upon their arrival. Local police were then responsible for cataloging and controlling the movements of these incarcerated populations. Ibid., l. 82.

125. GARF, f. 9415, op. 5, d. 474, ll. 17–17ob.

126. Ibid., l. 43.

127. Ibid., l. 115.

128. GARF, f. 3316, op. 64, d. 1188, ll. 1–1ob.

129. The OGPU also requested that all dekulakized peasants and special settlers be banned *permanently* from entering major cities. Central Communist Party officials rejected this suggestion. Ibid., ll. 2–3.

130. GARF, f. 9415, op. 1, d. 2, ll. 18–18ob.

131. This list applied to sentences handed down by the court system; the OGPU in this period generally preferred to issue sentences of exile to specific locations, although it remained authorized to issue sentences of banishment. GARF, f. 9415, op. 5, d. 474, ll. 83–84. The local police continued to refer to the punishment as "Minus Ten" for the next several years.

132. GARF, f. 9415, op. 5, d. 475, l. 75–77.

133. Each recidivist was to have a card with his photograph on the front and a physical description; the reverse of the card was to have information necessary for covert work against him (or, more rarely, her). These cards were kept in the Registration Bureau, and when *militsiia* operatives on the street reported that such an individual had appeared in the area, the card was to be transferred to the Detective Department for action. Ibid., l. 79.

134. Ibid., l. 126; ibid., ll. 80–81; GARF, f. 9415, op. 1, d. 1, l. 29.

135. GARF, f. 9415, op. 5, d. 475, l. 77. See also GARF f. 9415, op. 5, d. 476, l. 224ob.

136. See GARF, f. 9415, op. 5, d. 483, l. 34. For discussion of the practice, see Terry Martin, " 'Registration' and 'Mood': OGPU Information Reports and the Soviet Surveillance System," paper presented at the conference "La police politique en Union soviétique, 1918–1953," Maison des Science de l'Homme, Paris, May 25–27, 2000.

137. GARF, f. 9415, op. 5, d. 475, ll. 86, 126.

138. GARF, f. 9415, op. 5, d. 476, l. 224. See also GARF, f. 9415, op. 3, d. 3, l. 63, and GARF, f. 9415, op. 5, d. 475, l. 75.

Chapter 3

1. O. V. Khlevniuk, R. U. Davies, A. P. Kosheleva, E. A. Rees, and L. A. Rogovaia, eds., *Stalin i Kaganovich: Perepiska, 1931–1936 gg.* (Moscow: ROSSPEN, 2001), 235; emphasis in the original.

2. RGASPI, f. 81, op. 3, d. 151, ll. 8–10.

3. Victor Danilov, Roberta Manning, and Lynne Viola, eds., *Tragediia sovetskoi derevni: Kollektivizatsiia i raskulachivanie, 1927–1939—Dokumenty i materialy, V 5–ti tt. T. 3, Konets 1930–1933* (Moscow: ROSSPEN, 2001) (hereafter Danilov, Manning, and Viola, *Tragediia sovetskoi derevni*, t. 3), 233. According to statistics generated by the USSR Ministry of Internal Affairs in 1953, 20,201 individuals were sentenced to death by the OGPU in 1930, 10,651 in 1931. GARF, f. 9401, op. 1, d. 4157, l. 203.

4. For a complete description of the OGPU takeover of the special settlement system, see Lynn Viola, *The Unknown Gulag: The Lost World of Stalin's Special Settlements* (Oxford: Oxford University Press, 2007), 114–31.

5. Danilov, Manning, and Viola, *Tragediia sovetskoi derevni*, t. 3, 9–12; Viola, *Unknown Gulag*, 30–32.

6. Nicolas Werth, "A State against Its People: Violence, Repression, and Terror in the Soviet Union," in *The Black Book of Communism: Crimes, Terror, Repression*, ed. Mark Kramer and trans. Jonathan Murphy (Cambridge: Harvard University Press, 1999), 171.

7. RGASPI, f. 17, op. 162, d. 10, l. 108.

8. V. N. Khaustov, V. P. Naumov, and N. S. Plotnikov, eds., *Lubianka: Stalin i VChK-GPU-OGPU-NKVD—Ianvar' 1922–dekabr' 1936* (Moscow: Mezhdunarodnyi fond "Demokratiia," 2003) (hereafter Khaustov, Naumov, and Plotnikov, *Lubianka 1922–1936*), 276; GARF, f. 9401, op. 1, d. 4157, l. 203.

9. The OGPU arrested 331,544 individuals in 1930, 479,065 in 1931, and 410,433 in 1932. The number of cases adjudicated by the OGPU declined over the same period, from 208,069 in 1930 to 141,919 in 1932, reflecting central demands that the court system, rather than OGPU troikas, hear as many cases as possible, but this trend did not constrain the actions of the OGPU in the first instance. GARF, f. 9401, op. 1, d. 4157, l. 203.

10. GARF, f. 9415, op. 1, d. 1.77; RGASPI, f. 17, op. 162, d. 10, l. 127. See Khaustov, Naumov, and Plotnikov, *Lubianka 1922–1936*, 275–76, 280. For recent accounts that argue that these changes represented a fundamental policy reversal, see Stephen G. Wheatcroft, "Towards Explaining the Changing Levels of Stalinist Repression in the 1930s: Mass Killings," in *Challenging Traditional Views of Russian History*, ed. Stephen G. Wheatcroft (Basingstoke, U.K.: Palgrave Macmillan, 2002), 122–23; and Stephen G. Wheatcroft, "Agency and Terror: Evdokimov and Mass Killing in Stalin's Great Terror," *Australian Journal of Politics and History* 53, no. 1 (2007): 34–37.

11. Local police and justice officials usually participated in these arrests, but at times local soviet or Communist Party officials continued to arrest peasants on their own authority, often seizing property for communal or personal use. E.g., see Danilov, Manning, and Viola, *Tragediia sovetskoi derevni*, t. 3, 230–31.

12. E.g., as late as January 1932, the Central Militsiia Administration complained that local *militsiia* officers ignored the Politburo restrictions on arresting technical specialists, arresting local engineering or technical staff for problems in production that were the normal result of calculated risk rather than negligence. Local police (generally detectives, in these instances) were ordered to coordinate more closely with the OGPU on such cases, bringing charges against specialists and managers only with the agreement of local OGPU administrations. GARF, f. 9401, op. 12, d. 135, doc. 104. Documents in this particular file (*delo*) are not numbered by page, as is customary in Russian archives, but simply by document number; references to them are hereafter given as such.

13. GARF, f. 9415, op. 5, d. 474, ll. 58–59.

14. GARF, f. 9415, op. 3, d. 3, l. 50.

15. Danilov, Manning, and Viola, *Tragediia sovetskoi derevni*, t. 3, 15–17.

16. For discussions of economic crime, flight from collective farms and peasant responses to shortages, see GARF, f. 9415, op. 5, d. 485, ll. 51–56; GARF, f. 9415, op. 5, d. 485, ll. 57–61; Danilov, Manning, and Viola, *Tragediia sovetskoi derevni*, t. 3, 277–82; and, especially, the lengthy report from the OGPU's Secret-Political Department in ibid., 318–54.

17. E.g., see Danilov, Manning, and Viola, *Tragediia sovetskoi derevni*, t. 3, 396–97, 420–27.

18. For a recent account of the changes in Soviet agriculture in the early 1930s that are often termed a "Neo-NEP," see R. W. Davies and S. G. Wheatcroft, "The Soviet Famine of 1932–33 and the Crisis in Agriculture," in *Challenging Traditional Views of Russian History*, ed. Wheatcroft, 69–91, esp. 78–79.

19. For the edict, see *SZ SSSR* no. 56 (July 1, 1932), Article 298, 459–61; for materials of the Politburo Commission that discussed the edict and the Central Committee letter, see RGASPI, f. 81, op. 3, d. 43.

20. Almost none of the extensive discussion of these instructions by the Politburo commission charged with drafting them touched on the OGPU or *militsiia* in any way, focusing instead on the tendency of local state officials to form local troikas, courts, "headquarters," etc., instead of sending individuals through the court or police systems as required by law. Only late in the draft documents are the police even mentioned at all, and the drafts only instruct the Procuracy to strengthen supervision of arrests carried out by the *militsiia* and the OGPU. RGASPI, f. 81, op. 3, d. 43, ll. 33–42. For a recent account that mistakenly places this edict in the context of restrictions on extrajudicial sentencing, see Francesco Benvenuti, "The 'Reform' of the NKVD, 1934," *Europe-Asia Studies* 49, no. 6 (1997): 1037–38.

21. Justice officials were critical of the activities of the police, especially of sentencing mistakes committed by extrajudicial institutions during the dekulakization drive, but this was a pose that central justice officials, especially Krylenko and Vyshinskii, adopted quite consistently throughout the 1930s, even during periods in which they called for aggressive participation by justice officials in state-supported campaigns. See, among numerous examples, GARF, f. 8131, op. 37, d. 20, for a lengthy report from the Procuracy regarding OGPU activity in 1931, esp. ll. 6–12.

22. Khaustov, Naumov, and Plotnikov, *Lubianka 1922–1936*, 807 n. 97.

23. The Politburo singled out Communist Party members who participated in economic crimes as particularly deserving of harsh punishment. Khaustov, Naumov, and Plotnikov, *Lubianka 1922–1936*, 309–10.

24. GARF, f. 9415, op. 5, d. 485, ll. 51–58.

25. OGPU actions against theft on railways peaked in May 1932; in numerical terms, the OGPU arrested and sentenced substantially more individuals in May 1932 than in August, when Stalin called attention to hooliganism and theft on railways (see below). Khaustov, Naumov, and Plotnikov, *Lubianka 1922–1936*, 318–19.

26. Danilov, Manning, and Viola, *Tragediia sovetskoi derevni*, t. 3, 20–21.

27. Khaustov, Naumov, and Plotnikov, *Lubianka 1922–1936*, 808 n. 100, citing *Stalin i Kaganovich: Perepiska, 1931–1936 gg.*, ed. O. V. Khlevniuk, R. U. Davies, A. P. Kosheleva, E. A. Rees, and L. A. Rogovaia (Moscow: ROSSPEN, 2001), 243.

28. For a published copy of the law on theft, see Danilov, Manning, and Viola, *Tragediia sovetskoi derevni*, t. 3, 453; for the edict on speculation, which was approved by the Politburo on August 13, see Khaustov, Naumov, and Plotnikov, *Lubianka 1922–1936*, 316; and *SZ SSSR*, no. 65 (September 5, 1932), Article 375, 628.

29. Danilov, Manning, and Viola, *Tragediia sovetskoi derevni*, t. 3, 477–78.

30. The OGPU sent out Circular 530 on August 15, which I have not been able to find in the archives, and followed up with a directive from September 16, which was approved by the Politburo and from which I draw this discussion. See Danilov, Manning, and Viola, *Tragediia sovetskoi derevni*, t. 3, 481.

31. Ibid., 481–82. The Politburo repeated this order later in the campaign, in late November 1932, in almost exactly the same terms. Ibid., 557.

32. Notably, even the OGPU reported that 4,343 of the sentences handed down by its own extrajudicial bodies were for less than five years (a punishment that was absolutely disallowed by the August 7 edict, even for the courts). Some 7,661 individuals received sentences of between five and ten years, while 2,052 were sentenced to death, notwithstanding the fact that the death sentence was to be, according to the edict, the standard punishment for this offense. Khaustov, Naumov, and Plotnikov, *Lubianka 1922–1936*, 417–19.

33. Ibid., 425–26.

34. Peter H. Solomon Jr., *Soviet Criminal Justice under Stalin* (Cambridge: Cambridge University Press, 1996), 115–8. See also the USSR Supreme Court report on the August 7 Law in GARF, f. 3316, op. 64, d. 1254, ll. 14–16.

35. Danilov, Manning, and Viola, *Tragediia sovetskoi derevni*, t. 3, 489.

36. The report covers both the city and the Leningrad region. Detectives also reported on a number of "representative" cases of theft and speculation that were solved in August, all of which concerned accounting scams, bribery, and the systematic theft and resale of state property. GARF, f. 9415, op. 5, d. 486, ll. 69–72, 76.

37. GARF, f. 9415, op. 3, d. 3, ll. 50–51.

38. Danilov, Manning, and Viola, *Tragediia sovetskoi derevni*, t. 3, 732. For complaints from police officials in the Western Siberian Territory from late 1933 along the same lines, see GARF, f. 5446, op. 14a, d. 762, ll. 7–8. For a nationwide assessment from the Supreme Court, see GARF, f. 5446, op. 14a, d. 755, ll. 2–4.

39. Danilov, Manning, and Viola, *Tragediia sovetskoi derevni*, t. 3, 731. The OGPU leadership complained in November 1933 that even the network of state farms and rural provisioning concerns that were set up in 1932 and 1933 to provide for the *militsiia* itself were overrun with speculators and class-alien elements, who preferred to make profits dealing in the police's supply chain rather than supply their procurement needs. GARF, f. 9401, op. 12, d. 135, doc. 111.

40. E.g., see the OGPU report from Kazakhstan from December 1932 in Danilov, Manning, and Viola, *Tragediia sovetskoi derevni*, t. 3, 564–66.

41. GARF, f. 1235, op. 141, d. 1510, l. 2.

42. GARF, f. 9415, op. 3, d. 3, ll. 14–15. On the influx of peasants into Soviet urban life in the 1930s, see Moshe Lewin, *The Making of the Soviet System: Essays in the Social History of Interwar Russia* (New York: Pantheon Books, 1985); and David L. Hoffmann, *Peasant Metropolis: Social Identities in Moscow, 1929–1941* (Ithaca, N.Y.: Cornell University Press, 1994).

43. E.g., see the late 1932 discussions of policing in GARF, f. 9415, op. 3, d. 3, ll. 6–7.

44. GARF, f. 5446, op. 13a, d. 1320, ll. 6–8.

45. *Na boevom postu*, vol. 9, 1932. See also discussions of flophouses in Moscow in GARF, f. 9415, op. 5, d. 476, l. 266.

46. GARF, f. 9415, op. 3, d. 3, ll. 54–56.

47. Solomon estimates that 90 percent of cases of hooliganism in 1932 were processed in administrative procedure by the police, and that the number of individuals sentenced by courts and police for hooliganism in 1932 was four times the number in 1926. Solomon, *Soviet Criminal Justice under Stalin*, 136.

48. RGASPI, f. 81, op. 3, d. 51, l. 4.

49. Khlevniuk et al., *Stalin i Kaganovich*, 260.
50. Khaustov, Naumov, and Plotnikov, *Lubianka 1922–1936*, 316–17.
51. GARF, f. 9415, op. 5, d. 486, l. 62.
52. GARF, f. 1235, op. 141, d. 1395, l. 14. Not surprisingly, Krylenko, as head of the Justice Commissariat, disagreed with this proposal, arguing that it violated all existing legislation on punishments as it bypassed both judicial and extrajudicial sentencing procedures. GARF, f. 1235, op. 141, d. 1395, ll. 11–11ob.
53. Khaustov, Naumov, and Plotnikov, *Lubianka 1922–1936*, 343–44.
54. Enukidze, the head of the Central Executive Committee, personally crossed out Iagoda's request that OGPU troikas be allowed to sentence the more dangerous among these "hooliganistic elements" to execution, but he approved the right of the OGPU to sentence these categories of explicitly nonpolitical offenders in extrajudicial order. GARF, f. 3316, op. 64, d. 1356, ll. 1–3.
55. Important accounts of both periods include Margaret K. Stolee, "Homeless Children in the USSR, 1917–1957," *Soviet Studies* 40, no. 1 (1988): 64–83; Alan Ball, *And Now My Soul Is Hardened: Abandoned Children in Soviet Russia, 1918–1930* (Berkeley: University of California Press, 1984); Wendy Goldman, *Women, the State, and Revolution: Soviet Family Policy and Social Life, 1917–36* (Cambridge: Cambridge University Press, 1993); Peter H. Juviler, "Contradictions of Revolution: Juvenile Crime and Rehabilitation," in *Bolshevik Culture: Experiment and Order in the Russian Revolution*, ed. Abbot Gleason, Peter Kenez, and Richard Stites (Bloomington: University of Indiana Press, 1985); Jennie A. Stevens, "Children of the Revolution: Soviet Russia's Homeless Children (*Besprizorniki*) in the 1920s," *Russian History* 9, nos. 2–3 (1982): 242–64; and Rene Bosewitz, *Waifdom in the Soviet Union: Features of the Subculture and Re-education* (Frankfurt: Peter Lang, 1988).
56. Stolee, "Homeless Children," 66–68.
57. Solomon, *Soviet Criminal Justice under Stalin*, 198.
58. GARF, f. 1235, op. 141, d. 1146, l. 7; GARF, f. 9415, op. 5, d. 478, ll. 260–63; GARF, f. 9415, op. 5, d. 478, l. 65a. See also Goldman, *Women, the State, and Revolution*, 306.
59. GARF, f. 1235, op. 141, d. 408, l. 8; Ball, *And Now My Soul Is Hardened*, 176–78. Stolee concurs that the wave of homelessness that wracked the nation in the 1920s had largely subsided by 1930. Stolee, "Homeless Children," 71.
60. Reports from Moscow from the spring and summer of 1931 did not note any major increase in either homelessness or delinquency, but by August 1931 police officials began reporting notable increases in homeless children in the city and predicted further increases into the fall and winter. In August, the Moscow police estimated that there were 1,200 to 1,500 homeless children on the street at any given time. GARF, f. 9415, op. 5, d. 478, ll. 181–82, 186–88.
61. E.g., the welfare authorities in Kazakhstan warned Molotov in February 1932 of a "tremendous increase" in child homelessness, estimating that there were then roughly 44,000 homeless children in the republic and predicting an increase to 50,000 by the end of the year. GARF, f. 5446, op. 14a, d. 551, ll. 11–12.
62. Bubnov and Semashko, in an appeal sent directly to Molotov and Stalin in October 1932, deplored conditions in orphanages and argued that the situation regarding homeless children in general was perilous. The existing budget assignment of thirty-five kopeks a day for the provisioning of a single child in an orphanage, they wrote, was "obviously insufficient"; they added that "in the majority of localities, even

these starvation norms are not fulfilled." Most orphanages were without meat, sugar, and flour, and in some localities lacked a sufficient quantity of bread. GARF, f. 5446, op. 14a, d. 551, ll. 9–10.

63. Welfare agencies attempted to respond to the situation in part by expanding apprenticeship programs in the industrial and agricultural sectors. By April 1933, over 60,000 older homeless children had been placed in industrial, craft, or technical schools. GARF, f. 5446, op. 15a, d. 515, l. 2.

64. GARF, f. 9415, op. 5, d. 478, ll. 45–50.

65. One police report called "characteristic" the case of the detention center in the city of Sverdlovsk, in which the children in 1931 "destroyed the facility, beat and drove away the pedagogical staff, stole the property of the center and broke the windows." GARF, f. 9415, op. 5, d. 478, l. 252ob.

66. Central police officials claimed as early as 1931 that the overall situation would not improve unless recidivist juvenile offenders were placed in closed juvenile camps or, if necessary, directly into the camp system of the OGPU. GARF, f. 9415, op. 5, d. 478, ll. 182–83, 253; GARF, f. 9415, op. 3, d. 3, ll. 55–57.

67. GARF, f. 9415, op. 5, d. 478, l. 45. See also GARF, f. 9415, op. 5, d. 476, ll. 152–53.

68. GARF, f. 9415, op. 5, d. 479, l. 31.

69. Well over 40 percent of the juveniles apprehended by police in 1931 and 1932 had been detained previously: 17 to 19 percent once, 12 percent twice, and 14 to 15 percent three or more times. Most were apprehended for petty crimes, usually simple theft in public places. GARF, f. 9415, op. 5, d. 479, ll. 31, 251ob.

70. GARF, f. 9415, op. 5, d. 478.l81. In May 1932 Vul' reported that more than 60 percent of the 6,910 juveniles detained by the Moscow police in the first five months of the year were classed as "socially dangerous elements." GARF, f. 9415, op. 5, d. 478, l. 49.

71. GARF, f. 9415, op. 5, d. 478, ll. 181–82.

72. Roughly 95 percent of the juveniles detained by police in the early 1930s were boys. GARF, f. 9415, op. 5, d. 479, l. 28; GARF, f. 9415, op. 5, d. 478, ll. 251–53.

73. Juvenile detention centers were transferred from the Commissariat of Education to the *militsiia* in 1930. Moscow police created a central detention center in the former Danilov monastery in 1931, to which all homeless boys between the ages of three and sixteen years of age were sent after being apprehended by city police. GARF, f. 9415, op. 5, d. 478, ll. 45–50.

74. GARF, f. 9415, op. 5, d. 478, ll. 184, 186–88. See also Goldman, *Women, the State, and Revolution*, 320–21, for a discussion of these sweeps in 1931.

75. GARF, f. 9415, op. 5, d. 478, l. 183.

76. Ibid., ll. 45–46.

77. In the second half of 1932 police reported that, based on reports from 18 territories, they detained 26,230 juveniles in the second half of 1931, and 11,202 in the first quarter of 1932 (15 territories reporting). Of the 26,000 juveniles detained in the second half of 1931, 13,500 were detained in Moscow proper and 2,000 more in the region. GARF, f. 9415, op. 5, d. 479, ll. 29–30.

78. GARF, f. 9415, op. 5, d. 478, l. 114.

79. The territorial police chief suggested at the end of his report that repeat juvenile offenders be exiled to labor colonies created for the purpose, without a specific length of sentence, and freed only upon their rehabilitation. Ibid., ll. 59–61. Likewise,

police in the North Caucasus Territory in early 1933, repeating the charge that most homeless children had escaped repeatedly from orphanages, suggested that a "closed factory-school" be organized in each major urban area to deal with juvenile criminals; ibid., ll. 8–9.

80. GARF, f. 9415, op. 5, d. 479, ll. 42–43. Detective Department chiefs, at planning meeting in late 1932, made largely the same point, arguing that ongoing problems with escapes from orphanages should be handled by creating a new system of correctional labor institutions, resembling the child labor communes of the OGPU but administered by the *militsiia*, for juvenile offenders who were "difficult to rehabilitate." GARF, f. 9415, op. 3, d. 3, ll. 65–66.

81. Bubnov and Krylenko estimated that 200,000 children lived in orphanages in the Russian Republic in April 1933, 24,000 of whom were in orphanages for "socially neglected" children. Their estimate was several months behind and did not account for the massive expansion of homeless children that began in the winter of 1932–33. GARF, f. 5446, op. 15a, d. 515, l. 2.

82. No definitive estimates exist of the number of homeless children in the early 1930s, but documents related to the work of police organizations and orphanages make it clear that this wave was of the same order of magnitude as the first, i.e., in the millions. One former homeless child remembered the winter of 1932–33, when the Caucasian town in which he lived was overrun by masses of starving peasants from the countryside, as follows: "Waifs from all parts of Russia streamed to the south in the hope of finding food in the once-fertile region. Those who had joined the ranks of the waifs in the past two years were mostly the children of peasants who had been arrested, deported or starved to death by the forced collectivization." Nicholas Voinov, *The Waif* (New York: Pantheon Books, 1955), 50, cited in Stolee, "Homeless Children," 72–73.

83. Nearly 65 percent of children in the orphanage system in 1933 claimed that they had been forced onto the streets because of poor living conditions or death of their parents. GARF, f. 5446, op. 26, d. 18, ll. 201–2.

84. These figures come from reports complied in 1934. GARF, f. 5446, op. 26, d. 18, ll. 195–95ob.

85. Danilov, Manning, and Viola, *Tragediia sovetskoi derevni*, t. 3, 670.

86. GARF, f. 5446, op. 28, d. 18, ll. 195, 201.

87. Individuals sentenced as "dangerous elements" in 1931 received three years in a camp if they were deemed recidivists with five to ten previous convictions, or to exile or banishment in other cases. GARF, f. 8131, op. 37, d. 20, l. 41; GARF, f. 9401, op. 1, d. 4157, l. 203.

88. Krasilkov complained only that local police tended to expand the definition of "dangerous elements" to include individuals that had prior convictions but had since left the criminal world and become gainfully employed. GARF, f. 8131, op. 37, d. 20, ll. 41–42.

89. GARF, f. 9415, op. 5, d. 486, ll. 59–60, 74. For similar reports from Sverdlovsk in 1932, see GARF, f. 9415, op. 5, d. 488, ll. 62–63.

90. E.g., central OGPU officials sent a circular to local administrations in early August 1932 complaining that individuals who had served time in labor camps or exile were often unable to find stable employment upon release and were therefore arrested by local police; as ex-convicts, they fell under the statute on "dangerous elements" if they could not prove permanent employment and place of work. According to the circular, many such individuals desired work but fell under the influence of

professional criminals and declassed elements and became hardened criminals themselves. GARF, f. 9415, op. 5, d. 482, ll. 22–23.

91. Circular No. 858/52, *Glavnaia Inspektsiia RKM pri OGPU*, October 9, 1932. GARF, collection of documents; private communication from Aleksandr Malygin, Akademiia MVD RF.

92. Terry Martin, " 'Registration' and 'Mood': OGPU Information Reports and the Soviet Surveillance System," paper presented at the conference "La police politique en Union soviétique, 1918–1953," Maison des Science de l'Homme, Paris, May 25–27, 2000.

93. The exact date of the beginning of the operation is unclear in the documents, but the operation had been under way for several months by November. Of the 3,712 individuals ejected by the Registration Bureau, 3,287 were men and 425 women; 2,278 were previously "registered" by the Registration Bureau, 506 had previous arrests (*privody*), 502 had one previous sentence, 192 had two sentences, and 229 had 3 or more previous sentences. GARF, f. 9415, op. 5, d. 486, ll. 20–21. For comparable figures from August 1932, see GARF, f. 9415, op. 5, d. 486, ll. 78–79.

94. GARF, f. 8131, op. 37, d. 19, doc. 1 (pages unnumbered).

95. GARF, f. 9415, op. 3, d. 3, ll. 55–57.

96. Ibid., ll. 62–66. OGPU officials noted in 1932 that local police often subjected this category of "harmfuls" to the same extrajudicial sanctions as those deemed "dangerous," legal differences notwithstanding. By the early 1930s, central police officials used the terms "harmful" and "dangerous" interchangeably and often mistakenly, as in the December 1932 OGPU circular from the *GIM pri OGPU* to local police ordering them to carefully follow the requirements for identifying "harmful" elements when sending their cases to the OGPU Special Board for adjudication; the criteria listed by the circular (two past convictions or four arrests, etc.) clearly apply to "dangerous" elements by statute. GARF, f. 9415, op. 3, d. 3, l. 143.

97. GARF, f. 9415, op. 5, d. 482, ll. 24–27.

98. The majority of the Category I criminals were identified as "professional swindlers [*moshenniki*] of all sorts" (1,175) or "active professional thieves of all categories" (1,356); only 53 were deemed "former recidivists not engaged in useful labor and maintaining contacts with the criminal underworld," which was the only group that strictly conformed to the technical definition of "socially dangerous elements." Of the 5,009 individuals listed as Category II criminals, subject to deportation, over 3,000 were identified as "declassed and socially-parasitic elements (prostitutes, beggars, etc.)," 632 as "still-active recidivist hooligans," and 300 as "former professional criminals who have employment but retain contact with the criminal underworld." GARF, f. 9415, op. 5, d. 478, ll. 6–7.

99. Ibid., ll. 7–9.

100. For Iagoda's plan to create a massive special settlement system in 1933 to serve as the backbone of the Gulag system, see Khaustov, Naumov, and Plotnikov, *Lubianka 1922–1936*, 399–406. Iagoda suggested that the OGPU be authorized to send to the special settlements, in addition to deported peasants, all individuals arrested in conjunction with the passport distribution campaign and all prisoners sentenced to five years or less by the OGPU, excluding the "especially socially dangerous" among them. Ibid., 400. See also Viola, *Unknown Gulag*, 149.

101. For the most complete discussions of the passport system, see Mervyn Matthews, *The Passport Society: Controlling Movement in Russia and the USSR* (Boulder,

Colo.: Westview Press, 1993); David R. Shearer, "Elements Near and Alien: Passporti-zation, Policing, and Identity in the Stalinist State, 1932–1952," *Journal of Modern History* 76, no. 4 (2004): 835–81, esp. 840–44; and Gijs Kessler, "The Passport System and State Control over Population Flows in the Soviet Union, 1932–1940," *Cahiers du Monde Russe* 42, nos. 2–4 (2001): 477–504.

102. The police were instructed to conduct this task in a controlled, rational manner, and to refrain from engaging in any "mass operations" against dekulakized peasants in their localities without explicit approval from local OGPU administrations. GARF, f. 9415, op. 5, d. 482, l. 78.

103. Ibid., l. 59ob.

104. This commission, which included several representatives from the OGPU, met several times in early December, eventually producing recommendations that were forwarded to the Politburo on December 14. See Khaustov, Naumov, and Plot-nikov, *Lubianka 1922–1936*, 339, for the November 25 Politburo instruction creating the commission.

105. For drafts of the legislation under consideration by the commission, see GARF, f. 3316, op. 64, d. 1227, ll. 2–41.

106. Ibid., ll. 42–51.

107. RGASPI, f. 81, op. 3, d. 93, ll. 25–40. See RGASPI, f. 81, op. 3, d. 93, l. 24, for a note in Stalin's own hand stating "it's necessary to hurry with the passport system."

108. *SZ SSSR* no. 84 (December 31, 1932), Article 516–17, 821–23.

109. *SZ SSSR* no. 3 (January 28, 1933), Article 22, 20–23.

110. *SZ SSSR* no. 84 (December 31, 1932), Article 516–17, 821.

111. GARF, f. 9401, op. 12, d. 137, ll. 59–60ob.

112. *SZ SSSR* no. 3 (January 28, 1933) Article 22 (paragraph 20), 23.

113. *SZ SSSR* no. 28 (May 11, 1933), Article 168, 304–6; originally published on April 29, 1933, in *Izvestiia TsIK SSSR i VTsIK*, no. 112.

114. Stalin's position was made clear by his decision to send "commissions" to the countryside in late 1932, headed by major political functionaries such as Molotov, Kaganovich, and Iagoda, in order to force grain collection at any cost to local peasant populations, and by his decision to allow local OGPU troikas to pronounce death sen-tences in cases of counterrevolutionary activity by peasants during the harvesting cam-paign. Danilov, Manning, and Viola, *Tragediia sovetskoi derevni*, t. 3, 28; RGASPI, f. 17, op. 162, d. 14, ll. 17, 61.

115. Danilov, Manning, and Viola, *Tragediia sovetskoi derevni*, t. 3, 634–35.

116. Ibid., 32–33, citing N. A. Ivnitskii, *Kollektivizatsiia i raskulachivanie (nach-alo 30-x godov)* (Moscow: N.p., 1994), 204.

117. Although the Politburo initially expected distribution of passports to all urban residents to be complete by the end of 1933, the operation continued until at least mid-1934. The schedule was officially revised in late March, ordering that most of the passport distribution process take place by the end of 1933, with the exception of parts of the Central Asian republics and a handful of autonomous regions, which would be complete no later than the fall of 1934. GARF, f. 3316, op. 64, d. 1227, ll. 113–13ob.

118. Ibid., ll. 77, 84.

119. This is according to a ten-day report from on the progress of passport distri-bution by Prokof'ev, the head of the GURKM pri OGPU. Ibid., l. 83.

120. GARF, f. 5446, op. 14a, d. 740, l. 89. The published instructions call for the completion of passport distribution in the three initial cities by April 15, but the

operation stretched on for at least an additional six weeks. A top-secret compilation of instructions on the passport system, printed for the police in 1935, changed the completion date in the reprint of the original published instructions to June 1, 1933. Likewise, the original printed instructions called for the completion of registration in these areas by May 1, whereas the 1935 reprint changed the text to read June 15, 1933. Police officials, it is worth noting, were not above changing even their own supposedly secret documentation to avoid admitting past inconsistencies. GARF, f. 9401, op. 12, d. 137, ll. 58–59.

121. GARF, f. 5446, op. 14a, d. 740, l. 71.

122. The figure of 27 million includes 12,006,987 regime and 14,942,572 nonregime passports for the entire Russian Republic at the end of passport distribution, except the Kara-Kalpak, Iakut, and Kazakh autonomous republics, which had not yet been passportized. GARF, f. 1235, op. 141, d. 1650, l. 31.

123. Central instructions stated clearly, for example, that only ex-convicts who had been sentenced to terms of deprivation of freedom were to be expelled. The instructions additionally specified minimum sentences for certain crimes, below which individuals who had served those terms were not subject to expulsion—two years for bribery of state officials (Article 118 of the Criminal Code), for example, and one year for swindling (Article 169). GARF, f. 9401, op. 12, d. 137, ll. 59–61.

124. GARF, f. 1235, op. 141, d. 1650, ll. 30-31. In Magnitogorsk, where passport distribution began on February 25, police reported that they had arrested some 1,500 "parasitic elements" before the process even began and that 500 "kulaks, dekulakized peasants, and individuals not connected with production" fled the city every day. GARF, f. 3316, op. 64, d. 1227, ll. 90–91.

125. GARF f. 3316, op. 64, d. 1227, l. 80; GARF, f. 1235, op. 141, d. 1650, ll. 27–29. Unfortunately, the report gives no suggestion of how many people were coming into these cities versus how many were leaving.

126. GARF, f. 3316, op. 64, d. 1227, l. 105; GARF, f. 1235, op. 141, d. 1517, ll. 12–14. "Excesses" in the other direction were common as well; local police officials could be easily persuaded to issue passports to individuals not eligible for them, whether because of bribery, personal favor, or family relations. Central officials, however, reported that local police were generally inclined to err on the side of refusal. GARF, f. 3316, op. 64, d. 1227, l. 104.

127. For numerous examples of these abuses, see GARF, f. 1235, op. 141, d. 1517, ll. 13, 16–20ob; GARF, f. 3316, op. 64, d. 1227, ll. 101ob, 102, 104–7; GARF, f. 3316, op. 64, d. 1227, ll. 115–20, 121–28; and GARF, f. 3316, op. 64, d. 1619, l. 78.

128. The center was well aware of the ambiguities inherent in implementation of written instructions. One report at the USSR Central Executive Committee level noted that, along with written instructions, the police chiefs often gave "verbal instructions" to local officials to deny passports to all "former people," regardless of their legal status. GARF, f. 3316, op. 64, d. 1227, ll. 101–2.

129. Each of the newly created passport departments (stoly) in Moscow, furthermore, was headed by an officer of the OGPU Operative Department, further ensuring close cooperation between political and civil police. OGPU administrations were instructed to follow all individuals currently under surveillance as they were ejected from a given city, placing them under surveillance in their new places of residence. Coordinated surveillance across the USSR was difficult, even for the OGPU, and hence this instruction increased the propensity of Moscow OGPU administrations to

arrest rather than expel individuals under surveillance. GARF, f. 9401, op. 12, d.137, ll. 1–2.

130. Ibid., ll. 202–4.

131. GARF, f. 1235, op. 141, d. 1650, ll. 6–26, esp. 19–22.

132. The police also refused, as of August 1934, to register passports for 178,000 individuals who attempted to migrate to regime cities after the distribution process was complete; almost 103,000 of these cases occurred in Moscow. It is worth noting that the individuals who were ejected from regime cities appear on absolutely none of the existing statistical compilations of convicted populations, as they were neither sentenced by courts nor by OGPU troikas. They were, however, effectively subject to banishment from all regime areas. GARF, f. 1235, op. 141, d. 1650, ll. 27–35.

133. GARF, f. 1235, op. 141, d. 1650, l. 27.

134. GARF, f. 5446, op. 14a, d. 745, l. 1.

135. GARF, f. 5446, op. 14a, d. 762, ll. 3, 9.

136. GARF, f. 9415, op. 3, d. 3, ll. 66–68.

137. Ibid., ll. 80–81; GARF, f. 3316, op. 64, d. 1501, ll. 1–2.

138. *SZ SSSR* no. 84 (December 31, 1932), no. 518–19, pp. 824–25.

139. GARF, f. 9415, op. 3, d. 3, ll. 17–19, 27–28.

140. The OGPU leadership transferred nearly 250 *militsiia* officers from central to peripheral police administrations in the first nine months of 1932. Ibid., ll. 17–25; GARF, f. 9415, op. 5, d. 483, l. 32.

141. GARF, f. 5446, op. 14a, d. 762, l. 11ob.

142. Ibid., l. 7. In early 1933, the OGPU leadership estimated that, of the 1,205 individual administrative districts in the Russian Republic, 1,001 had four or fewer full-time policemen assigned to them, and 140 of those had no permanent police representation at all. GARF, f. 3316, op. 64, d. 1423, l. 7.

143. GARF, f. 1235, op. 141, d. 910, l. 11.

144. GARF, f. 9401, op. 12, d. 126, l. 222.

145. The center actually sent out two separate orders to this effect. GARF, f. 9415, op. 3, d. 3, l. 3; ibid., ll. 83–87.

146. The center estimated in April 1933 that the Commissariat of Heavy Industry employed some 100,000 hired guards; the Commissariat of Trade, 65,000; and Light Industry, 20,000. GARF, f. 5446, op. 14a, d. 755, ll. 3–4.

147. The creation of Political Departments (*politotdely*) in Machine Tractor Stations and state farms in 1933 was a direct attempt to deal with the failures of the August 1932 edict to protect collective farm property from theft and with the inability of local *militsiia* administrations to have any impact on the situation. Central commentators in 1933 claimed that OGPU policing systems in Machine Tractor Stations, along with the OGPU Transport Department teams that protected railroads, were the only effective means of preventing theft in the countryside. GARF, f. 5446, op. 14a, d. 755, ll. 2–3.

148. Ibid., ll. 1, 5, 6–11.

149. For recent examples, see Wheatcroft, "Towards Explaining the Changing Levels of Stalinist Repression," 126–27; Gabor T. Rittersporn, "Extra-Judicial Repression and the Courts: Their Relationship in the 1930s," in *Reforming Justice in Russia, 1864–1996*, ed. Peter H. Solomon Jr. (Armonk, N.Y.: M. E. Sharpe, 1997), 210; Benvenuti, "'Reform' of the NKVD," 1040. For discussion of influence of the May 8 Instruction on the work of justice agencies, see Solomon, *Soviet Criminal Justice under Stalin*, 124–26, 161–63.

150. For representative examples, see GARF, f. A-406, op. 25, d. 173, ll. 88–104; and GARF, f. A-406, op. 25, d. 173, ll. 73–82.

151. E.g., a series of such checks by Rabkrin officials in the Ivanov region in late 1932 resulted in the immediate release of 776 individuals who were being held without ongoing investigation. GARF, f. A-406, op. 25, d. 173, ll. 88–104, esp. 94.

152. Prokof'ev noted that police jails generally had absolutely no provisions for holding prisoners for more than a few days—no kitchens, and no staff or facilities for sanitation needs—and were often physically unsuitable as well; short-term prisons were set up in whatever shelter was available but was deemed unsuitable for normal habitation, including churches, barns, or the half-underground mud shelters common in the countryside. GARF, f. 3316, op. 64, d. 1423, ll. 1–1ob.

153. Ibid., ll. 4–5.

154. The OGPU's suggestions for improving this situation focused, not surprisingly, on restricting the ability of justice agencies to force police to house individuals under court or Procuracy investigation. The OGPU also proposed that Justice Commissariat prisons be forced to accept prisoners from the *militsiia*, and that the *militsiia* be freed from any requirements to convoy prisoners or carry out any other instructions from local justice officials. Ibid., ll. 2–12.

155. Khaustov, Naumov, and Plotnikov, *Lubianka 1922–1936*, 399–406. Stalin noted on his copy of the document that a "clearing" of prisons was necessary, but it is impossible to tell when he read Iagoda's suggestions and made the notation. Nonetheless, the notation makes it clear that Stalin understood the clearing of prisons to be directly connected with possibility of expanded special settlements.

156. RGASPI, f. 17, op. 162, d. 14, l. 66.

157. In a sign of dissatisfaction with the judicial system, the Politburo forbade investigators to hold in jails all individuals under investigation for nonserious crimes, although it somewhat blunted the force of the order by excluding an extensive list of crimes from this restriction, including nearly all the offences that were the focus of the various campaigns of the period. The Politburo also specifically ordered local state organizations of the various republics to increase the number of *militsiia* officers, a move that suggests that reduction of levels of policing was not the point. RGASPI, f. 17, op. 162, d. 14, ll. 89–92.

158. Ibid., l. 96; V. P. Danilov and S. A. Krasil'nikov, eds., *Spetspereselentsy v zapadnoi Sibiri, 1933–1938* (Novosibirsk: EKOR, 1994), 76–78, 264 n. 3. Special settlements were officially termed "labor settlements" from 1934 to 1944, after which the nomenclature reverted to special settlements. This book will continue to use the terms "special settlers" and "special settlements" for the sake of consistency.

159. GARF, f. 9415, op. 3, d. 6, ll. 2–2ob; GARF, f. 5446, op. 15a, d. 1073, l. 18.

160. Krylenko noted as well that provisions were provided nationwide for only 350,000 inmates and demanded that places of confinement be properly supported. GARF, f. 5446, op. 14a, d. 745, ll. 8–8ob. Krylenko's figures, in fact, were conservative; OGPU estimates of the number of prisoners in police and justice prisons, including open labor colonies, on May 10, 1933, totaled 769,966 individuals, of whom 415,000 were incarcerated in the prison system of the Justice Commissariat. GARF, f. 5446, op. 15a, d. 1073, l. 29. The March 1933 order on clearing prisons had in fact resulted in a reduction the number of individuals in OGPU prisons (87,655 on April 10; 63,165 on May 10) and in *militsiia* prisons (227,259 on April 10; 187,867 on May 10) but had no effect on the number of people in the custody of the Justice Commissariat (519,024 on April 10; 518,934 on May 10). Ibid., l. 31.

161. RGASPI, f. 17, op. 162, d. 14, l. 123.

162. Danilov, Manning, and Viola, *Tragediia sovetskoi derevni*, t. 3, 671.

163. This decision, then, represented a slight loss for Iagoda, who originally suggested that the new OGPU special settlements house *all* inmates sentenced to five years or less (a suggestion that would have certainly solved the problem of overcrowding in the Justice Commissariat's prison system but that was resisted by Krylenko). The OGPU was, however, instructed to send any "particularly socially dangerous" individuals, sentenced to between three and five years, to its hard labor camps. The order was approved by the Sovnarkom SSSR on April 20, 1933, no. 775-146s; see GARF, f. 7523, op. 65, d. 165, l. 1. See also Danilov and Krasil'nikov, *Spetspereselentsy v zapadnoi Sibiri, 1933–1938*, 15–22.

164. For the May 7 decisions, see Khaustov, Naumov, and Plotnikov, *Lubianka 1922–1936*, 435–40. For a published version of May 8 Instruction, see Danilov, Manning, and Viola, *Tragediia sovetskoi derevni*, t. 3, 746–50. For the original, see RGASPI, f. 17, op. 163, d. 981, ll. 229–38.

165. The instruction set specific maximums for further peasant deportations, broken down by region and totaling 12,000 families (presumably for the 1933 calendar year, although the instruction does not specify). Danilov, Manning, and Viola, *Tragediia sovetskoi derevni*, t. 3, 748.

166. See Solomon, *Soviet Criminal Justice under Stalin*, 162–63.

167. For complaints from the OGPU itself regarding the propensity of local *militsiia* officers to send baseless cases to troikas, see GARF, f. 9415, op. 3, d. 3, ll. 140–42.

168. In addition, the instructions were vague enough in this area to allow further conflict between justice and police organizations over their implementation. See GARF, f. 5446, op. 14a, d. 757, ll. 24–32, for an exchange between Krylenko and Prokof'ev, direct at Molotov and Stalin, over the Procuracy's right to control several categories of OGPU investigation.

169. Danilov, Manning, and Viola, *Tragediia sovetskoi derevni*, t. 3, 749–50.

170. GARF, f. 5446, op. 15a, d. 1073, ll. 15, 20–20ob, 21–22.

171. Ibid., ll. 32–35.

172. The Politburo issued instructions on July 5 regarding individuals to be sent to the newly created labor colonies in Kazakhstan and Western Siberia; in addition to the 124,000 individuals already exiled to these camps, the Politburo authorized the OGPU to send 426,000 more, including the 12,000 kulak families (48,000 individuals) in areas of complete collectivization that represented the total allowable deportations for the rest of 1933, as outlined in the May 8 instruction, and 133,400 kulaks currently in places of confinement who had been sentenced to between three and five years of deprivation of freedom and who were "released" from prisons under the May 8 instruction, plus their families, for a total of 378,000 individuals. RGASPI, f. 17, op. 162, d. 15, ll. 2, 14. The directive was then promulgated as a Sovnarkom order on August 21; see Danilov and Krasil'nikov, *Spetspereselentsy v zapadnoi Sibiri, 1933–1938*, 26–27.

173. Local Communist Party officials had requested this right in March, before the new special settlements had even become fully operational, but the Politburo had declined. RGASPI, f. 17, op. 162, d. 15, l. 2. See Danilov and Krasil'nikov, *Spetspereselentsy v zapadnoi Sibiri, 1933–1938*, 86–87, 285 n. 46, for communications from the Party Committee in the Western Siberian Territory on the subject.

174. RGASPI, f. 17, op. 162, d. 15, l. 27. The May 8 instruction made no mention of OGPU troikas; troikas were mentioned only in the May 7 Politburo decision noted above.

175. The latter was a particularly cynical move, given that the regime had recently announced with great fanfare the completion of the canal and the amnesty of the most diligent among the labor convicts that had built it. RGASPI, f. 17, op. 162, d. 15, ll. 17, 23.

176. Both forms of punishment remained available to police: "Minus 30" and exile without defined compulsory labor were options for passport troikas, OGPU troikas, and the OGPU's Special Board. For the police themselves, however, the punishments of banishment and exile were largely superfluous, because refusal of a regime-city passport was in effect lifetime banishment. GARF, f. 9415, op. 3, d. 6, ll. 4–5ob.

177. In mid-May OGPU officials reported that some 3,000 "recidivist teenagers" were slated to be transferred to the new special settlements in Siberia; Danilov and Krasil'nikov, *Spetspereselentsy v zapadnoi Sibiri, 1933–1938*, 85.

178. Experiences with this cohort of criminals in Western Siberia throughout June and July 1933 were so characterized by disease and starvation that several local OGPU officers were censured or arrested for their role in failing to properly provision these inmates. See Danilov and Krasil'nikov, *Spetspereselentsy v zapadnoi Sibiri, 1933–1938*, 16, 83–85, 86–87, 89–90, 106, 116.

179. As late as November 1933, the OGPU reiterated to local officials the policy that able-bodied violators of the passport system, including their families, were to be sent to the special settlement system. GARF, f. 9401, op. 12, d.137, l. 205.

180. RGASPI, f. 17, op. 162, d. 15, l. 30.

181. According to Communist Party officials in the Western Siberian Territory in late October 1933, roughly 100,000 individuals were deported to the special settlements by late October 1933, rather than the 500,000 initially approved by the Politburo. By late January 1934, that number had been revised upward to almost 132,000, although only roughly 72,000 still remained in special settlements; the remainder either fled or perished. Eventually, in April 1934, Iagoda responded to these difficulties by ordering police to cease sentencing "urban declassed elements" to special settlements, sending them to the labor camp system instead. Danilov and Krasil'nikov, *Spetspereselentsy v zapadnoi Sibiri, 1933–1938*, 56, 101, 118–19, 287–88 n. 50.

182. Khlevniuk et al., *Stalin i Kaganovich*, 246.

Chapter 4

1. GARF, f. 9401, op. 12, d. 137, ll. 65–66ob.

2. GARF, f. 9401, op. 12, d. 135, doc. 119, ll. 2, 5.

3. See Peter H. Solomon Jr., *Soviet Criminal Justice under Stalin* (Cambridge: Cambridge University Press, 1996), part III: "The Conservative Shift," esp. 154–56; Nicholas Timasheff, *The Great Retreat: The Growth and Decline of Communism in Russia* (New York: E. P. Dutton, 1946).

4. RGASPI, f. 17, op. 162, d. 15, l. 161. Similarly, the Politburo in early January 1934 authorized the OGPU to expel 2,000 "declassed elements" from Kharkov to labor colonies and labor camps, noting specifically that this expulsion should talk place in small groups of 80 to 100 individuals rather than as a large-scale operation. RGASPI, f. 17, op. 162, d. 15, l. 164.

5. RGASPI, f. 17, op. 3, d. 937, l. 28. For the Sovnarkom version of this order, see GARF, f. 5446, op. 15a, d. 1130, l. 11. Prokofev became an assistant head of the

USSR NKVD in July 1934, suggesting that Stalin's decision to remove him was either tactical or quickly reversed.

6. RGASPI, f. 17, op. 3, d. 937, l. 1.

7. Solomon, *Soviet Criminal Justice under Stalin,* 156, 162, citing Stalin, "Otchetnyi doklad XVII s'ezdu partii o rabote TsK VKP(b)," January 26, 1934, in Stalin, *Voprosy Leninizma,* 11th ed. (Moscow: N.p., 1952), 517.

8. GARF, f. 5446, op. 15a, d. 1130, ll. 12–12ob.

9. RGASPI, f. 17, op. 3, d. 939, l. 2; V. N. Khaustov, V. P. Naumov, and N. S. Plotnikov, eds., *Lubianka: Stalin i VChK-GPU-OGPU-NKVD—Ianvar' 1922–dekabr' 1936* (Moscow: Mezhdunarodnyi fond "Demokratiia," 2003) (hereafter Khaustov, Naumov, and Plotnikov, *Lubianka 1922–1936*), 509.

10. Solomon, *Soviet Criminal Justice under Stalin,* 161–62. Rittersporn also explicitly makes the argument that judicial reform progressed in a dialectical fashion in the 1930s in Gabor T. Rittersporn, "Extra-Judicial Repression and the Courts: Their Relationship in the 1930s," in *Reforming Justice in Russia, 1864–1996,* ed. Peter H. Solomon Jr. (Armonk, N.Y.: M. E. Sharpe, 1997).

11. GARF, f. 5446, op. 15a, d. 1130, ll. 12–12ob. For a published version, see Khaustov, Naumov, and Plotnikov, *Lubianka 1922–1936,* 487–89. Akulov, overshadowed by Vyshinskii in most accounts of the Soviet judiciary, was an active participant in these debates, and his position in the Communist Party and as former deputy head of the OGPU gave him additional clout in what were often bitter conflicts. For an assessment of Akulov as a "quiet figurehead" serving under the leadership of Vyshinskii, see Solomon, *Soviet Criminal Justice under Stalin,* 161.

12. Krylenko, who was named a member of the above commission but was unable to attend the first meeting, sent a letter to Kaganovich outlining his concerns on March 17. Krylenko suggested as well that a unionwide NKVD was unnecessary, a position that must have only annoyed Stalin, for whom the question was settled. Khaustov, Naumov, and Plotnikov, *Lubianka 1922–1936,* 508–9.

13. Ibid., 512, 814 n. 129.

14. Krylenko recommended that Stalin turn over the entire penal system to the new NKVD, judicial functions at the periphery to the USSR Supreme Court, and all prosecutorial functions to the rival USSR Procuracy. In this suggestion, Krylenko was playing a somewhat dangerous game of brinkmanship, arguing that the logical outcome of current trends in criminal justice was the redundancy of his own organization and that the Politburo should take that route if so intended. His real goal was to reassert some control over criminal justice for his Justice Commissariat vis-à-vis Vyshinskii and the ascendant USSR Procuracy. Ibid., 492–93.

15. In creating this commission, the Politburo noted that the idea of abolishing the Justice Commissariat "does not merit discussion"; hence Krylenko won his exercise in brinkmanship, although his organization remained on the defensive throughout these debates. RGASPI, f. 17, op. 3, d. 942, l. 2.

16. Francesco Benvenuti, "The 'Reform' of the NKVD, 1934," *Europe-Asia Studies* 49, no. 6 (1997): 1037–38, esp. 1041–43.

17. The July 10 instructions that accompanied the announcement of the new USSR NKVD detailed the structure of this new system of courts (*kollegiia*), which were set up within USSR and republican Supreme Courts, territorial and regional courts, and various levels of transport courts. The instructions called for the transfer of 1,000 cadres to the Procuracy, including 200 OGPU officers that were to staff the new judicial

kollegii. A. I. Kokurin and N. V. Petrov, *Lubianka: VChK-OGPU-NKVD-NKGB-MGB-MVD-KGB 1917–1960* (Moscow: Mezhdunarodnyi fond "Demokratiia," 1997) (hereafter, Kokurin and Petrov, *Lubianka: VChK-KGB, 1917–1960*), 185–86; RGASPI, f. 17, op. 3, d. 948, l. 95.

18. The creation of this system of courts also suggests that the basic idea that the July 1934 reforms of the NKVD eliminated the extrajudicial sentencing capacity of the OGPU should be reconsidered. In one series of orders in September 1934, the NKVD transferred 225 specific NKVD officers, by name, to work on the special courts at the Supreme Court of the Russian Soviet Federated Socialist Republic (RSFSR), various regional courts, war tribunals, certain city courts, rail courts, and water-transport courts. GARF, f. 9401, op. 1a, d. 5, ll. 43–48, 61–62, 67–68, 76–78. See RGASPI, f. 17, op. 21, d. 3057, l. 6, for a similar order pertaining to the creation of new collegiums (*kollegii*) within the Moscow regional and city courts, to be staffed by Procuracy and OGPU officials. I do not have complete figures for the number of OGPU/NKVD officers transferred to these positions in 1934, but available documentation makes it clear that the staffing the new collegiums with Procuracy and OGPU officers was the norm. These transfers began a process of intermingling of judicial and police systems that is discussed for the post-1938 period in Rittersporn, "Extra-Judicial Repression and the Courts"; this process, in my view, began substantially earlier.

19. Khaustov, Naumov, and Plotnikov, *Lubianka 1922–1936*, 515. Ezhov's appointment to the commission on judicial affairs in late March signaled the beginning of his involvement in the Soviet criminal justice system. Ezhov took an active role in this discussion, and it is evident that he was working at odds with Iagoda. On April 8, for example, he forwarded to Stalin his recommendations for the NKVD *nomenklatura* associated with the Politburo and Orgburo, noting that his suggestions were based on the new structure of the NKVD proposed by Kaganovich's commission and that he had not spoken to Iagoda about them. Ibid., 214.

20. Ibid., 516.

21. Ibid., 530–31; and RGASPI, f. 17, op. 3, d. 946, l. 65.

22. GARF, f. 8131, op. 38, d. 5, ll. 7–8. As harsh as these policies were, enforcement was often more severe. The Politburo had to follow up in late July with an order that instructed the police not to send Red Army soldiers caught riding freight cars to labor camps for six months, nor to apply the instruction to workers or collective farmers with no previous criminal record. RGASPI, f. 17, op. 3, d. 949, l. 29.

23. Akulov responded immediately (and essentially correctly) with a note stating that Iagoda's position was that the Procuracy did not have the right to take any effective action regarding passport seizures, yet the Sovnarkom declined to make any policy changes. GARF, f. 5446, op. 15a, d. 1094, ll. 1–13.

24. For published copies of these instructions, see Kokurin and Petrov, *Lubianka: VChK-KGB, 1917–1960*, 183–86.

25. GARF, f. 9401, op. 1a, d. 5, ll. 41–42ob.

26. Khaustov, Naumov, and Plotnikov, *Lubianka 1922–1936*, 558, 564. Although Iagoda's general request for troikas was rejected, Stalin did authorize at least one regional NKVD administration, in the West Siberian Territory, to promulgate death sentences, under the direction of the regional Communist Party boss, during September and October 1934. O. V. Khlevniuk, A. V. Kvashonkin, L. P. Kosheleva, and L. A. Rogovaia, eds., *Stalinskoe Politburo v 30-e gody: Sbornik dokumentov* (Moscow: AIRO-XX, 1995), 65. See RGASPI, f. 89, per. 73, doc. 41, for a list of relevant Politburo

decisions. Stalin may have also approved a similar process for the NKVD in Cheli-abinsk, although the record is inconclusive. O. V. Khlevniuk, R. U. Davies, A. P. Ko-sheleva, E. A. Rees, and L. A. Rogovaia, eds., *Stalin i Kaganovich: Perepiska, 1931–1936 gg.* (Moscow: ROSSPEN, 2001), 511–12.

27. The Special Board was made up of the commissar of internal affairs (or one of his assistants, in his absence), his assistant USSR NKVD chief, the NKVD chief of the Russian Republic, the head of the USSR *militsiia*, and the head of the NKVD in the republic in which the sentence was processed. A representative from the USSR Procuracy had the right to attend meetings and protest decisions. RGASPI, f. 17, op. 3, d. 954, ll. 8, 38.

28. GARF, f. 5446, op. 15a, d. 1172, l. 11.

29. Ibid., ll. 5–6. Akulov responded on April 20 with a note to Leplevskii stating that Iagoda's suggestions were in line with his thoughts but that the issue should be addressed in the context of the creation of the NKVD. Ibid., l. 7. Krylenko's com-ments in March to the effect that all prisoners sentenced to deprivation of freedom should be transferred to the OGPU, discussed above, also suggest that Iagoda was generally correct in his presentation of the issue.

30. GARF, f. 5446, op. 15a, d. 1095, ll. 1–2. See GARF, f. 5446, op. 15a, d. 1172, l. 1, for a note from May 15 to the effect that the issue was tabled at the Sovnarkom level because it was to be settled by the Politburo commissions.

31. Iagoda noted that the Moscow-Volga Canal project and OGPU labor camps at-tached to the Transbaikal and Ussuriiskyi railroad construction camps were alone ex-periencing a shortage of 140,000 laborers. GARF, f. 5446, op. 15a, d. 1172, ll. 2–3.

32. Khaustov, Naumov, and Plotnikov, *Lubianka 1922–1936*, 544–45. Krylenko complained of personal affront from Iagoda, who refused to send to him a copy of the draft instructions and told him that the Central Committee would "call him in" when it wanted his opinion.

33. Khaustov, Naumov, and Plotnikov, *Lubianka 1922–1936*, 547–48.

34. See RGASPI, f. 17, op. 3, d. 953, ll. 50, 100. For NKVD instructions regarding the transfer, see GARF, f. 9401, op. 1a, d. 5, ll. 65–65ob.

35. GARF, f. 9401, op. 12, d. 137, ll. 65–65ob.

36. Iagoda made numerous concrete policy demands, including transfers of Com-munist Party members and Red Army soldiers to *militsiia* positions to improve per-sonnel, and he ordered local police to shift to supporting the passport system more aggressively in both regime and nonregime cites, using not only the new article of the Criminal Code created to punish passport violators (Article 192-a) but also by maxi-mizing the use of large fines for passport violators. GARF, f. 9401, op. 12, d. 135, doc. 14; and GARF, f. 9401, op. 12, d. 137, ll. 67–68ob.

37. RGASPI, f. 17, op. 3, d. 945, l. 55.

38. The order placing Kaganovich at the head of this commission specifically re-ferred to Stalin's charges in January and to Iagoda's February response to the Polit-buro. RGASPI, f. 17, op. 3, d. 948, l. 44.

39. GARF, f. 5446, op. 15a, d. 1071, ll. 3–4.

40. RGASPI, f. 17, op. 3, d. 954, l. 26.

41. The discussion of this issue by Chubar's commission was already under way by this point, and this commission had already broached the idea of lowering the age of criminal responsibility (see below).

42. GARF, f. 5446, op. 16a, d. 1270, ll. 18–22.

43. Ibid., ll. 5–7.
44. Ibid., ll. 8–10.
45. GARF, f. 9415, op. 3, d. 9, ll. 33–34. To support this change, in mid-March the Central Executive Committee instructed all republic-level state administrations to press local officials to insist that individuals living in nonpassportized areas obtain one-year passports from local police officials before traveling to passportized areas. The Central Executive Committee repeated the order in September, singling out the propensity of village soviets to provide illegal certificates to peasants, who attempted to use them in cities in place of the proper short-term passports. GARF, f. 9401, op. 12, d.137, ll. 63–63ob. The police extended this order in mid-April to apply to individuals sent by industrial or state concerns to regime cities on assignment (*v komandirovku*); even high-level state functionaries were to be denied registration and ejected from regime cities within twenty four hours if they did not possess a passport before arrival. GARF, f. 9415, op. 3, d. 9, l. 58.
46. GARF, f. 9415, op. 3, d. 9, l. 43.
47. In addition, police in nonregime locations were instructed to award passports to all individuals who were eligible for them but, for whatever reason, did not receive them in the process of the initial distribution, including all individuals released from prisons. Ibid., ll. 64–65.
48. GARF, f. 1235, op. 141, d. 1650, ll. 27–28. See also the exceptionally critical report complied in late June 1934 by the Commission for Soviet Control regarding deficiencies in the passport system in the cities of Magnitogorsk and Stalino, which was sent to the Sovnarkom and read by Chubar', in GARF, f. 5446, op. 26, ch. II, d. 16, ll. 22–24.
49. GARF, f. 9401, op. 12, d. 137, ll. 58, 61.
50. GARF, f. 9415, op. 3, d. 9, l. 44; GARF, f. 1235, op. 141, d. 1650, l. 27.
51. GARF, f. 9415, op. 3, d. 8, ll. 23–25.
52. Ibid., ll. 56–57.
53. In 1933, according to central reports, 45,755 individuals escaped from penal institutions, of which only 28,370 were eventually recaptured; the rest returned to restricted areas and "again engaged in criminal activities," many appearing on construction sites and in major industrial factories. GARF, f. 9401, op. 1a, d. 5, ll. 36–36ob.
54. GARF, f. 9401, op. 12, d. 137, l. 62. Published in *SZ SSSR* no. 49 (October 8, 1934): 707.
55. Peasants were likely responding to the memories of the Tsarist passport system, which required a peasant to carry paperwork whenever he or she traveled; they were also likely attempting, in what was already a particularly Soviet response, to prepare for any eventuality, given the rapidly changing situation in the countryside. GARF, f. 9401, op. 12, d. 135, doc. 114; and GARF, f. 9401, op. 12, d. 137, l. 231. Published in *Tragediia sovetskoi derevni: Kollektivizatsiia i raskulachivanie, 1927–1939—Dokumenty i materialy, V 5–ti tt. T. 4, 1934–1936*, ed. Victor Danilov, Roberta Manning, and Lynne Viola (Moscow: ROSSPEN, 2002) (hereafter Danilov, Manning, and Viola, *Tragediia sovetskoi derevni*, t. 4), 354.
56. GARF, f. 5446, op. 16a, d. 1307, ll. 2–3.
57. Ibid., l. 4.
58. The local police expelled individuals from rural areas who arrived after April 15, 1935, without passports, much as they had expelled individuals in urban areas during the passport distribution process. GARF, f. 9401, op. 12, d. 137, ll. 237–37ob; see also Danilov, Manning, and Viola, *Tragediia sovetskoi derevni*, t. 4, 411–12.

59. It is worth noting, in this context, that passports were issued to peasants who lived near Machine Tractor Stations and to those who were members of state farms (*sovkhozy*); preventing their migration away from the farms was obviously not at issue in issuing them passports.

60. Golfo Alexopoulos, *Stalin's Outcasts: Aliens, Citizens, and the Soviet State, 1926–1936* (Ithaca, N.Y.: Cornell University Press, 2003), 148–49, 168–69.

61. Of a total of 31,364 individuals whose rights were restored as a result of the May 1934 measures, Berman reported, only 7,857 remained in the areas of their resettlement. GARF, f. 9479, op. 1s, d. 29, ll. 12–14.

62. Ibid., ll. 15–18.

63. Ibid., l. 10.

64. GARF, f. 9401, op. 12, d. 137, l. 236.

65. Akulov, once again, played a major role in opposing this change. As of April 16, 1935, the NKVD maintained that all criminal contingents that were sentenced to special settlements (*trudposelki*) should remain there permanently, and Akulov maintained that the issue should be considered by the Central Executive Committee. The available archival record suggests, somewhat inconclusively, that Berman's request was either rejected or postponed by the consideration of the new Criminal Code in 1935 (see below). GARF, f. 9479, op. 1s, d. 30, ll. 1–5.

66. GARF, f. 9479, op. 1s, d. 29, ll. 19–24.

67. On regime responses to the Kirov murder, see Lesley Rimmel, "Another Kind of Fear: The Kirov Murder and the End of Bread Rationing in Leningrad," *Slavic Review* 56, no. 3 (Fall 1997): 481–99; and I. A. Kondakova, " 'Provesti ochistky Leningrada kampaneiskim putem': Dokumenty AP RF o vysylke 'byvshikh liudei.' 1935–1936 gg.," *Istoricheskii Arkhiv*, no. 2 (2003): 104–22.

68. For the idea of "cultured" trade, see Julie Hessler, *A Social History of Soviet Trade: Trade Policy, Retail Practices, and Consumption, 1917–1953* (Princeton, N. J.: Princeton University Press, 2004), 197–247.

69. GARF, f. 9415, op. 3, d. 9, ll. 1–2.

70. GARF, f. 5446, op. 15a, d. 1073, ll. 187–88.

71. Ibid., l. 186.

72. RGASPI, f. 17, op. 3, d. 947, l. 3.

73. The regime began to apply substantial administrative and financial pressure to individual farmers in mid-1934 in order to force individuals back into the collective farm system. Danilov, Manning, and Viola, *Tragediia sovetskoi derevni*, t. 4, 11–14.

74. More than half of all cases of theft in the areas specifically investigated by the commission had not been subject to any sort of police or court investigation. GARF, f. 7511, op. 1, d. 74, ll. 3–26.

75. All grain brought to rural bazaars was seized by the police and given to grain procurement officials, but peasants caught bringing grain and bread products to market for sale were simply returned to their collective farms for informal hearings at a comrades' courts; only second offenders were subject to trial within the criminal justice system. GARF, f. 9401, op. 12, d. 135, doc. 113; GARF, f. 5446, op. 15a, d. 1073, ll. 116–17.

76. After the Party Plenum, the Council of Labor and Defense (known as STO) took up the question of speculation, recommending on July 23, 1934, that Bel'skii, Grin'ko, Antipov, Iagoda, and Molotov form a working commission to deal with the issue. The Sovnarkom then entered the debate and on August 1 created a commission under the leadership of Rudzutak, including Bel'skii, Prokof'ev, Mironov, and several

others, to work up draft instruction on speculation and bring it to the Sovnarkom on August 16. GARF, f. 5446, op. 15a, d. 1071, ll. 3–4. The relationship between these commissions is not clear from available archival documentation, but the Sovnarkom commission eventually generated policy recommendations that were acted on by the Politburo.

77. Ibid., ll. 13, 14–14ob.

78. Iagoda's policy suggestions were characteristically harsh: he suggested that the NKVD be accorded the right to fine petty speculators on the spot up to 500 rubles and to confiscate their property, with substitution of three months of compulsory labor for those unable to pay, and that the parents of juveniles caught speculating be subject to fines of 300 rubles or one month of compulsory labor. Ibid., ll. 16–21, 23.

79. Ibid., l. 1. The Sovnarkom removed the issue from consideration in early October 1934. The Finance Commissariat was unsatisfied and attempted again to press the issue at the end of October. R. Levin, the assistant commissar of finance of the Russian Republic, sent a request to Molotov for reconsideration of the question of speculation, noting that speculation remained a pressing concern for trade officials and that Rudzutak's commission had arrived at a series of concrete measures that would improve the matter if implemented. The Sovnarkom again declined to act, and Levin was informed that Rudzutak had officially removed the question from consideration. Ibid., l. 57.

80. See Danilov, Manning, and Viola, *Tragediia sovetskoi derevni*, t. 4, 314–30, for discussions of the rationing system at the plenum.

81. Ibid., 347, 931 n. 103.

82. See David L. Hoffmann, *Stalinist Values: The Cultural Norms of Soviet Modernity, 1917–1941* (Ithaca, N.Y.: Cornell University Press, 2003), 131–37, for a discussion of Stalin's vision of "socialist" trade in 1934 and 1935.

83. Elena Osokina, *Za fasadom "stalinskogo izobiliia": Raspredelenie i rynok v snabzhenii naseleniia v gody industrializatsii, 1927–1941* (Moscow: ROSSPEN, 1999), 180–82. Osokina stresses the limited nature of the Politburo's decision to abolish the rationing system; "free trade" in bread was not the goal, insofar as the Politburo never imagined that peasants themselves would market their own bread products to the population in any substantial quantities. The goal, rather, was unlimited trade *within* the state retail system.

84. GARF, f. 8131, op. 38, d. 6, ll. 12–14; GARF, f. 5446, op. 26, d. 34, ll. 32–34; GARF, f. 5446, op. 16a, d. 295, l. 10ob; GARF, f. A-461, op. 8s, d. 1, ll. 6–7. The USSR Procuracy repeated the call for a "differentiated" approach to speculation in mid-June; in particular, under no circumstances, argued the Procuracy, were workers to be charged for selling their personal items, such as shoes or individual items of clothing. GARF, f. 8131, op. 12, d. 2, ll. 102–2ob.

85. GARF, f. 8131, op. 38, d. 6, ll. 36–37.

86. Although issues of taxation and revenue played a role in these discussions, such issues cut both ways. Local soviets reportedly saw markets as a major source of income and were unwilling to clamp down on illegal trade. A complaint by a Finance Commissariat tax collector in Khar'kov was direct on this issue, challenging local police who he believed were overzealously repressing speculation: "If you clear out all the speculators, then we won't have anybody to tax." GARF, f. 5446, op. 16a, d. 404, ll. 11–17.

87. Osokina, *Za fasadom*, 183.

88. GARF, f. 5446, op. 16a, d. 404, ll. 4–10.

89. Iagoda identified family members of poorly paid white-collar employees, or white collar employees themselves, as the urban social group most likely to stand and line for long periods of time in order to purchase goods for resale. GARF, f. 5446, op. 18a, d. 904, ll. 4–5.

90. GARF, f. 9401, op. 12, d. 137, ll. 65, 66ob.

91. *Na boevom postu* 7 (1934): 1.

92. Glazkov, "Vernee i tverzhde udar po khuliganstvu," *Za sots. zakonnost'*, no. 5 (1935): 24; A. Gertsenzon, "Organy iustitsii v bor'be s khuliganstvom," *Za sots. zakonnost'*, no. 2 (1935): 16–17; L. Vul', "Khuliganstvo v Moskve i bor'ba s nim," *Za sots. zakonnost'*, no. 8 (1935): 18–21.

93. According to a mid-1935 USSR Procuracy report, judicial convictions for hooliganism in the years 1932–34 did not conform to the overall trend of substantial reductions in sentencing levels after 1933. GARF, f. 5446, op. 16a, d. 295, l. 5. Figures for judicial convictions for hooliganism in the Russian Republic are: 1932 (first half), 69,947; 1932 (second half), 55,064; 1933 (first half), 46,663; 1933 (second half), 41,287; 1934 (first half), 46,221; 1934 (second half), 52,277. I am unable to find any republic-level data on fines for hooliganism for the early 1930s. See below for fines in Moscow in 1934.

94. E.g., an investigation of two precincts in Moscow in late 1934 showed that 88 percent of fines handed out for hooliganism went to workers. TsGAMO, f. 792, op. 6, d. 980, ll. 84–84ob. For similar figures, see TsGAMO, f. 792, op. 6, d. 981, ll. 2–3.

95. TsGAMO, f. 792, op. 6, d. 980, ll. 48–50.

96. TsGAMO, f. 792, op. 6, d. 967, ll. 54–54ob; *Sbornik prikazov i tsirkuliarov Upravleniia RK militsii Moskovskoi oblasti*, no. 6 (1933): 5–6; RGASPI, f. 17, op. 21, d. 3057, l. 52; TsGAMO, f. 792, op. 6, d. 980, ll. 35–47.

97. TsGAMO, f. 792, op. 6, d. 981, ll. 28–30; ibid., l. 65. See also TsGAMO, f. 792, op. 6, d. 980, l. 143. Some sense of the relative scale of administrative and judicial punishment for hooliganism can be had from comparing these figures with the total of just under 98,000 judicial sentences for hooliganism in the entire RSFSR for the year 1934. However, due to difficulties in accounting practices and the inability of the police to track individuals once they had been fined, the majority of these fines were not actually collected. Numerous reports from Moscow agree that the number of fines collected hovered in the range of 40 percent for all fines handed out. E.g., see TsGAMO, f. 792, op. 6, d. 981, ll. 25–27, 65.

98. GARF, f. 5446, op. 16a, d. 1270, ll. 18–19.

99. Leplevskii insisted, however, that a one-month limit should be placed on pretrial incarcerations. GARF, f. 5446, op. 16a, d. 1270, ll. 5–10.

100. GARF, f. 5446, op. 16a, d. 1359, ll. 39–40. Vyshinskii claimed in a report on the work of the USSR Procuracy for January and February 1935 that a nationwide meeting of procurators on March 23 had discussed the issue of raising penalties for hooliganism and sent a corresponding request to the Sovnarkom, which responded by issuing the March decree on hooliganism. This self-aggrandizing account corresponds perhaps to the letter but hardly to the spirit of the archival record. GARF, f. 5446, op. 16a, d. 295, l. 12ob.

101. E.g., the Moscow regional Procuracy issued a circular on February 11 instructing local officials to improve the processing of cases on hooliganism, speeding cases through trial as quickly as possible and making sure that malicious hooliganistic acts were qualified under the Criminal Code as Article 74-2 (malicious hooliganism),

which required a sentence of deprivation of freedom, rather than Article 74-1 (simple hooliganism), which allowed for fines or compulsory labor. TsGAMO, f. 792, op. 6, d. 968.138. On March 10 the Moscow regional court repeated many of the same orders, adding that local judges should qualify as many cases as possible as banditry rather than as malicious hooliganism. TsGAMO, f. 792, op. 6, d. 968, l. 137.

102. Vul', "Khuliganstvo v Moskve," 20.

103. In Ukraine, furthermore, the Transport Department of the NKVD was still authorized, as of mid-February 1935, to sentence hooligans on railways using a troika that was created for the antihooliganism campaign in June 1934. GARF, f. 8131, op. 38, d. 5, ll. 7–8.

104. During the first three months of 1935, the police in Moscow's forty-ninth precinct investigated 59 cases of malicious hooliganism, sending 42 individuals to court and halting seven cases, and it fined 475 individuals for simple hooliganism. In the same period, the police sent 81 individuals to the Moscow NKVD troika for sentencing, 62 of whom were classified as "dangerous elements" and 19 as malicious hooligans. In the fourth quarter of 1934, the same precinct sent 88 individuals to the NKVD troika as "dangerous elements" and 5 as "hooligans," compared with 410 subject to fines. These statistics show, at a minimum, that the Moscow police sentenced individuals using troikas in the months after the creation of the NKVD in mid-1934, and that they sentenced individuals specifically for hooliganism (neither of which are provided for by any of the central regulations on the NKVD). TsGAMO, f. 792, op. 6, d. 967, ll. 63, 70. I have no material on this topic from locations other than Moscow, leaving open the possibility that Moscow was unique in this regard.

105. *Pravda*, no. 71 (March 13, 1935): 6.

106. All cases were to be tried by the special collegiums instead of the regular Peoples' Court system. RGASPI, f. 17, op. 3, d. 961, l. 21; ibid., l. 59; RGASPI, f. 17, op. 3, d. 962, l. 17; GARF, f. 8131, op. 38, d. 6, ll. 32–33, 34, 39–40.

107. *SZ SSSR* no. 18 (1935), Article 141, p. 248. For new NKVD regulations on weapons associated with this campaign, see GARF, f. 9401, op. 12, d. 135, doc. 117.

108. See A. Gertsenzon, "Organy iustitsii v bor'be s khuliganstvom," *SZ*, no. 2 (1935): 15; N. Aleksandrovskii, "Prokuratura i pechat' v bor'be s khuliganstvom," *ZSZ*, no. 5 (1935): 34–35 (quotation on 35); B. Utevskii, "Ispravitel'no-trudovye uchrezhdeniia v bor'be s khuliganstvom," *ZSZ*, no. 5 (1935): 29–30.

109. GARF, f. 3316, op. 64, d. 1619, l. 39.

110. GARF, f. 9401, op. 12, d. 135, doc. 119, esp. pp. 2, 5. In June the Politburo issued a related decision on the repression of banditry, and in early July the USSR Procuracy added specific instructions regarding banditry in Turkmenistan, reportedly caused by both border-crossers from Afghanistan and Iran and by internal bandits who stole cattle and attacked and robbed collective farms. RGASPI, f. 17, op. 3, d. 965, l. 1; GARF, f. 5446, op. 16a, d. 1359, l. 99.

111. E.g., see TsGAMO, f. 792, op. 6, d. 968, ll. 98–99, 129.

112. The NKVD issued a directive titled "Ob usilenii repressii za khuliganskie deistviia" at roughly the same time as the March 1935 law was promulgated. Unfortunately I have no statistical evidence regarding the total number of individuals sentenced extrajudicially under this directive, but it is clear that extrajudicial sentencing was an option for the police. See TsGAMO, f. 792, op. 6, d. 968, l. 125. E.g., the police in the Egor'evskii district of the Moscow region, in the first five months of 1935, removed and sent to the NKVD troika 31 "socially dangerous elements," compared

with 59 individuals sent to court, 19 sentenced directly by police to corrective labor for malicious hooliganism, and more than 660 fined for simple hooliganism. Almost 400 of those fined were classed as workers. TsGAMO, f. 792, op. 6, d. 968, l. 129–30. The police in Serpukov sent 60 individuals to the Moscow regional NKVD troika in the period of the campaign. TsGAMO, f. 792, op. 6, d. 968, ll. 125–28. Finally, see TsGAMO, f. 792, op. 7, d. 814, l. 1, for a report from the twenty-third *militsiia* administration in Moscow that states the police during the first half of 1936 sent 88 individuals to court for hooliganism while meting out 905 fines for the same offence. The report makes no mention of extrajudicial sentencing, because the police by that time were fully authorized to sentence "dangerous" elements using UNKVD (*militsiia*) troikas as a matter of course (see below).

113. TsGAMO, f. 792, op. 6, d. 968, l. 131; TsGAMO, f. 792, op. 6, d. 967, ll. 52–61. The brigades were reanimated in the Khrushchev period, with many of the same problems. See Louise I. Shelley, *Policing Soviet Society: The Evolution of State Control* (London: Routledge, 1996), 44–45.

114. TsGAMO, f. 792, op. 6, d. 968, ll. 181–200, 28–29.

115. See ibid., ll. 28–29, 127–28.

116. GARF, f. 3316, op. 64, d. 1620, ll. 1–56, esp. 10–11. For similar complaints from the USSR Procuracy, see GARF, f. 5446, op. 16a, d. 295, ll. 11–12.

117. Of the total 1,263 sentences meted out for banditry by the Special Collegium of the RSFSR Supreme Court in the first half of 1935, 601 were death sentences; in the first nine months of 1935, banditry (Articles 59-3 and 167) accounted for more than 20 percent of the caseload of the collegium, second only to counterrevolutionary crimes. GARF, f. A-428, op. 3, d. 3, ll. 1, 10–15. Lower (regional and line) courts in the RSFSR meted out 337 death sentences for these crimes in 1935 (246 in the first half, 91 in the second), 224 of which were approved by the Supreme Court; lower courts issued only 15 death sentences for these crimes in January and February 1936, suggesting that levels of executions had fallen to "normal" levels. GARF, f. A-428, op. 3, d. 17, ll. 1–2.

118. Judicial cases of hooliganism in the RSFSR increased from a low of some 41,000 in the second half of 1933 to just under 66,600 cases in the second half of 1935. Of a total of 441,848 sentences handed out by courts in the RSFSR in the first half of 1935 (with only 1,684 of 2,224 districts reporting, a substantial omission), 52,095 were for hooliganism. Prison or labor camp sentences rose from only 10 percent of all cases heard in the second half of 1933 to 42 percent in the first half of 1935. GARF, f. A-461, op. 8s, d. 1, ll. 1–2, 6–7; RGASPI, f. 17, op. 120, d. 171, ll. 50–51. Peter Solomon shows that the proportion of custodial sanctions meted out by judges for hooliganism continued to rise for the rest of the decade, reaching nearly two-thirds at its peak in 1939. Solomon, *Soviet Criminal Justice under Stalin*, 225.

119. GARF, f. 9401, op. 12, d. 135, doc. 133.

120. Hooliganism in these areas dropped from a total of just under 6,300 individuals detained in October 1935 to just over 6,100 in September 1935 and just over 5,400 in October 1935, although the latter decline was likely as related to the coming of colder months as to any specific actions on the part of the police. Armed robberies declined over the same period from 412 to 132 to 104, while unarmed robberies dropped from 1,419 to 563 to 557. GARF, f. 9401, op. 12, d.135, doc. 146. Although judicial and police statistics regarding levels of criminal activity must be approached with extreme care, there is little question that police campaigns against violent crime

caused a major drop in these behaviors in this period. See also GARF, f. 3316, op. 64, d. 1619, ll. 41–42, for a Procuracy report, written by Antonov-Ovseenko, that concurs that sharp declines in violent crime were the result not only of increased judicial repression of hooligans, thieves, recidivists, and escapees from penal institutions but also strict observance of the internal passport system in major urban areas.

121. GARF, f. 5446, op. 18a, d. 904, l. 2. In a March 1936 report, Iagoda estimated that incidences of armed robbery had declined by 45 percent in comparison with 1934 levels; unarmed robbery by 46 percent, theft of cattle by 55 percent, "qualified" theft by 32 percent, and even simple theft (a crime generally resistant to the kinds of large-scale campaigns carried out by police in 1935) by 17 percent. GARF, f. 9401, op. 12, d. 135, doc. 31. See TsGAMO, f. 792, op. 6, d. 968, ll. 125–28, for a similar assessment from the *militsiia* chief in Serpukhov, in the Moscow region, in mid-June 1935.

122. GARF, f. 9401, op. 12, d. 135, doc. 31.

123. Central Communist Party officials estimated that by 1934 some 43,500 children had been placed in foster care on collective farms; farms were paid 300 rubles a year for each child. The planned transfer of 15,000 older children to industrial jobs, or the placement of an additional 19,000 in foster homes, could not make up for the shortfall of spaces in late 1933, especially considering the need to place additional children in the system in 1934. GARF, f. 5446, op. 26, d. 18, ll. 195ob–196.

124. See the April 1934 Central Committee report on homelessness and delinquency, signed by M. Epshtein, the assistant commissar of education of the Russian Republic, in GARF, f. 5446, op. 26, d. 18, ll. 185–206. The specific charge that criminal acts by juvenile delinquents between the ages of twelve and sixteen years generally went unpunished is the earliest evidence that I have found that points to the eventual lowering of the age of criminal responsibility to twelve in April 1935.

125. GARF, f. 5207, op. 3, d. 33, ll. 10–11.

126. GARF, f. 5446, op. 16a, d. 1359, ll. 131–32; GARF, f. 5207, op. 3, d. 33, ll. 8–8ob.

127. RGASPI, f. 17, op. 3, d. 945, l. 55.

128. For these commission materials, see GARF, f. 5207, op. 3, d. 33, ll. 33–41, 59–61.

129. GARF, f. 5446, op. 26, d. 18, ll. 32–41. Bel'skii had suggested a one-time campaign as part of the first set of commission discussions in June, estimating that roughly 50,000 homeless children currently wandered the streets of major cities and presenting a detailed plan for a one-time sweep of homeless children across the USSR that was designed to eliminate the problem entirely. Ibid., ll. 1–4. Chubar's decision to include this recommendation was likely related to the need to prepare for the upcoming October holidays, which by this point always included a sweep of homeless children from the streets of major cities; it may have also been a response to the obvious increase in prestige and political power enjoyed by the NKVD, whose leaders had been pressing for harsher policies toward juveniles for months.

130. RGASPI, f. 17, op. 3, d. 953, l. 6. It should be remembered that in mid-October the Politburo transferred the Justice Commissariat's penal institutions to the NKVD, overriding Chubar's suggestion that special closed colonies be created for juvenile recidivists under the former.

131. GARF, f. 1235, op. 141, d. 1647, ll. 27–29.

132. GARF, f. 5207, op. 3, d. 32, l. 15. Krylenko, indignant not only that local police and welfare officials violated existing restrictions on sentencing juveniles but

also that the Justice Commissariat was neither consulted nor even notified about the campaign until after it was carried out, protested the action to the Russian Executive Committee. But his complaint was rejected entirely, making clear that a reformulation of existing judicial regulations regarding juveniles was well under way. GARF, f. 1235, op. 141, d. 1647, ll. 24–24ob, 25–26.

133. GARF, f. 5446, op. 16a, d. 1270, l. 25.

134. Both officials also generally agreed that individuals found guilty of drawing children into criminal activity should face five years' deprivation of freedom; the NKVD suggested, in addition, that parents of delinquents should be responsible for up to a year of compulsory labor. Ibid., ll. 7, 10.

135. RGASPI, f. 17, op. 3, d. 956, l. 4; RGASPI, f. 17, op. 3, d. 957, l. 5.

136. GARF, f. 5207, op. 3, d. 32, l. 38; GARF, f. 5446, op. 26, d. 50, l. 1. Although the conditions that led to homelessness affected boys and girls alike, central policy discussions ignored homeless girls almost entirely, focusing instead on the social danger presented by boys. Girls almost never figured into police discussions about urban disorder and crime; when they did appear, their situation was usually discussed in terms of criminal punishments for individuals bringing children into criminal activity, especially prostitution. For a note from Vyshinskii to Semashko to the effect that the same pressures of lack of space and funding afflicted the small network of orphanages for "difficult to rehabilitate" girls, see GARF, f. 5207, op. 3, d. 33, ll. 8–8ob.

137. GARF, f. 3316, op. 64, d. 1612, ll. 2–8.

138. GARF, f. 5446, op. 26, d. 50, l. 1.

139. GARF, f. 3316, op. 64, d. 1612, l. 2; GARF, f. 5446, op. 26, d. 50, l. 2.

140. For successive drafts and comments from commission members, see GARF, f. 3316, op. 64, d. 1612, ll. 16–20, 27–33 (Semashko's comments), 34–42, 78–90; and GARF, f. 5446, op. 26, d. 50, l. 64. Semashko and Krupskaia sent separate notes to the commission for discussion, challenging many of the conclusions reached by the majority. Krupskaia was adamantly opposed to increasing the role of courts and police in juvenile affairs; her suggestions focused almost exclusively on social and cultural services for children and mothers, and on expanded foster care programs in collective farms for children currently in orphanages. GARF, f. 3316, op. 64, d. 1612, ll. 21–26; also published in *Deti GULAGa, 1918–1956*, ed. S. S. Vilenskii, A. I. Kokurin, G. V. Atmashkina, and I. Iu. Novichenko (Moscow: Mezhdunarodnyi fond "Demokratiia," 2002), 174–76.

141. Commission members attempted to influence Stalin directly as well, as in the case of a telegram sent by Voroshilov to Stalin, Molotov, and Kalinin on March 19, 1935. Voroshilov's telegram was prompted by a story in the March 15 issue of *Rabochaia Moskva* regarding violent juvenile crime in Moscow; he ended his vitriolic comments by asking, "I don't understand why these scoundrels shouldn't be shot. Do we really have to wait until they grow up and become serious brigands?" Khlevniuk et al., *Stalinskoe Politburo v 30-e gody*, 144–45. Benvenuti mistakenly assumes that Voroshilov's telegram initiated the process that led to the edict of April 7, 1935; the archival record makes it clear that the opinion expressed by Voroshilov, who was a member of the Kalinin commission, was well within the range of suggestions presented by commission members in early 1935. Benvenuti, "'Reform' of the NKVD," 1048.

142. RGASPI, f. 17, op. 3, d. 962, ll. 5, 57. For a published copy, see Vilenskii et al., *Deti GULAGa*, 182–83, or *Sovetskaia Iustitsiia* 13 (1935): 11. Solomon argues that the edict on juvenile crime was "Stalin's personal creation." Although Stalin was the ultimate arbiter of the conflicts between upper-level Communist Party and state

functionaries, in this instance he was responding to suggestions put forth by commission members. The instruction he chose to promulgate was substantially harsher than the proposal forwarded to him by the commission, but it corresponded to suggestions proposed by NKVD representatives on the commission from at least mid-1934. Solomon, *Soviet Criminal Justice under Stalin*, 200–1.

143. The fact that the crimes listed in the decree did not correspond exactly to sections of the Criminal Code caused substantial confusion among even central justice officials. E.g., the RSFSR Supreme Court ruled in November 1935 that the principle of analogy did not apply in cases regarding juveniles and that juveniles could only be prosecuted under the April 7 instructions for the exact crimes on the list; the USSR Supreme Court overruled this ruling in December, instructing local judicial officials to prosecute juveniles for crimes that entailed "violence or bodily injury," such as hooliganism (Article 74); likewise, theft that was accomplished by means of "swindling" (Article 169) could subject juveniles between the ages of twelve and sixteen to criminal responsibility for the latter rather than the former. GARF, f. A-461, op. 8s, d. 73, l. 23. This instruction opened the door for judicial prosecutions of crimes that carried harsh sentences, such as banditry; more important, this kind of flexibility in the judicial sphere could only have increased the likelihood that police would make the same decisions.

144. Solomon, *Soviet Criminal Justice under Stalin*, 198.

145. Vyshinsky, who was not a member of the Kalinin commission but was privy to its deliberations, moved even before the April 7 decision was made, sending a circular to local Procuracy officials on March 31 that berated them for allowing courts to issue lenient sentences for serious juvenile crimes and ordered them to send concrete suggestions for policy changes to him by April 25. GARF, f. 8131, op. 12, d. 2, ll. 48–48ob. This circular was discussed at a meeting of USSR Procuracy officials in late March. Solomon, *Soviet Criminal Justice under Stalin*, 201. As with the case of hooliganism, once Vyshinskii realized that a substantial policy change was likely, he issued this instruction in advance of the actual Politburo decision to make it seem like his organization had initiated the change. See also RGASPI, f. 17, op. 21, d. 3058, l. 199.

146. Juvenile courts had plainly been the preference of many of the participants in the Kalinin commission and had been promoted by justice officials outside the commission debates in March, but the Politburo edict of April 7 stated only that juveniles committing the crimes listed be sent to a "criminal court." The Procuracy circular made no reference to the list of crimes provided by the April 7 edict, instructing local officials to create juvenile courts to hear "cases regarding juvenile delinquents." The circular hence represents an attempt to add detail to the April 7 instructions and to override the recommendations of the Kalinin commission, still pending at the Politburo level at this point, that these cases be heard by three-person panels headed by a judge. GARF, f. 8131, op. 37, d. 54, l. 1, or GARF, f. 8131, op. 12, d. 2, l. 53; Solomon, *Soviet Criminal Justice under Stalin*, 200.

147. GARF, f. 5446, op. 26, d. 50, ll. 100–10, esp. 100.

148. GARF, f. 3316, op. 64, d. 1612, ll. 74–76, 92; RGASPI, f. 17, op. 3, d. 9631, l. 4; Vilenskii et al., *Deti GULAGa*, 183–87.

149. RGASPI, f. 17, op. 3, d. 964, ll. 50, 115.

150. GARF, f. 5446, op. 18a, d. 847, ll. 12–16.

151. GARF, f. 9401, op. 1a, d. 7, ll. 3, 5, 8. For an exchange between Vyshinskii and Iagoda in mid-1936 on this issue that was decided in favor of the latter, see GARF, f. 5446, op. 18a, d. 847, ll. 3–9ob.

152. Iagoda expected an additional influx of 30,000 homeless children by the end of 1936 as a result the promulgation of the 1935 laws. GARF, f. 5446, op. 16a, d. 591, ll. 21–22.

153. RGASPI, f. 17, op. 3, d. 964, l. 50.

154. RGASPI, f. 17, op. 3, d. 962, l. 32. For the Procuracy/Supreme Court circular sent to local officials, see GARF, f. 8131, op. 38, d. 6, ll. 47–47a; for a follow-up circular sent a month later that suggests that local court officials were still wary of the idea of abolishing amelioration for juvenile offenders, see GARF, f. 8131, op. 37, d. 54, l. 4. For further discussion of the death penalty and juvenile offenders, see Solomon, *Soviet Criminal Justice under Stalin*, 202–3.

155. GARF, f. 8131, op. 37, d. 54, l. 5, or GARF, f. 8131, op. 38, d. 7, l. 57. And, in July 1936, when Vyshinskii forwarded to Stalin and Molotov a report of a criminal band of juveniles, all between the ages of fifteen and eighteen, who had systematically raped schoolgirls in Western Siberia and had been sentenced to various punishments, he was not asking for approval. The two "ringleaders" had both been born in 1920 and, as sixteen-year olds, were no longer juridically "juveniles"; hence the death sentences for banditry handed down by the Special Collegium of the territorial (*krai*) court required no higher review. GARF, f. 8131, op. 37, d. 72, l. 71. For a different interpretation of this document, see Solomon, *Soviet Criminal Justice under Stalin*, 202–3.

156. E.g., Stolee relates Alexander Orlov's claim that Stalin ordered the political police to shoot homeless children interfering with rail transport and that mass executions and other "administrative measures" led to a solution of the problem "in the true Stalinist spirit"; she notes that this and other claims of this nature are "as yet unsubstantiated." Margaret K. Stolee, "Homeless Children in the USSR, 1917–1957," *Soviet Studies* 40, no. 1 (1988): 64–83, esp. 74, citing Alexander Orlov, *The Secret History of Stalin's Crimes* (New York: Random House, 1953) and Robert Conquest, *The Great Terror: A Reassessment* (New York: Oxford University Press, 1990). Orlov's accusation is not supported by any archival evidence and is, in my opinion, completely false.

157. GARF, f. 9401, op. 1a, d. 7, l. 57; GARF, f. 9401, op. 12, d. 135, doc. 120. Iagoda was, as usual, aware of the possibility of "excesses," and he ordered local police not to arrest children for inconsequential acts of theft committed by first-time offenders, including theft of candy from stores, fruit from orchards, or vegetables from individual gardens. All arrests under the April 7 instructions were to be approved by the local police chief personally. GARF, f. 9401, op. 1a, d. 7, l. 65.

158. E.g., an investigation by the Committee for Party Control of the children's cells in local *militsiia* stations in Moscow in 1936 turned up numerous cases such as: "Apprehended one Victor Ryzhkov, nine years old . . . because he 'ran up on a roof and got his kite'; and 'Vova Krutov, ten years old, apprehended for aimless wandering in a bread store.'" GARF, f. 5207, op. 3, d. 37, ll. 41–48. The Party Control Commission report from which these examples are drawn states that such examples could be repeated tens of times for each police precinct investigated. See also TsGAMO, f. 792, op. 6, d. 1031, ll. 10–18.

159. Police were also authorized to begin administrative procedures against the parents of juveniles who committed crimes not listed in the April 7 instruction, releasing children to these parents but fining them up to 200 rubles. GARF, f. 9401, op. 12, d. 135, doc. 120.

160. *Sovetskaia Iustitsiia* 25 (1935): 6; GARF, f. 9401, op. 1a, d. 7, l. 99.

161. GARF, f. 3316, op. 64, d. 1619, l. 88ob. For a similar report from the RSFSR Supreme Court stating that police handled virtually all the investigations, and that neither the Procuracy nor local education or welfare officials participated in any meaningful way, see GARF, f. 5207, op. 3, d. 31, l. 39.

162. GARF, f. 9401, op. 1a, d. 7, l. 65.

163. GARF, f. 5207, op. 3, d. 31, ll. 48, 36; GARF, f. 3316, op. 64, d. 1619, ll. 88–89ob.

164. A compilation of statistics on juveniles age twelve to eighteen years sentenced between 1935 and 1938, from the files of the USSR Procuracy and based on statistics gathered by the Justice Commissariat of the USSR, lists the following sentences for the USSR (not including the Tadzhik SSR) (from GARF, f. 8131, op. 37, d. 533, l. 201):

	Age 12–16	Age 16–18	Total
First half of 1935	1,403	27,213	28,616
Second half of 1935	5,322	23,702	29,024
First half of 1936	7,887	21,793	29,680
Second half of 1936	7,114	17,116	24,260
First half of 1937	7,915	13,921	21,866
Second half of 1937	9,319	13,661	22,980
First half of 1938	9,952	13,361	23,313
Second half of 1938	10,214	14,879	25,093

165. According to a July 1936 report from the RSFSR Supreme Court, courts in the year following the May 7 edict heard 3,170 cases regarding juvenile offenders, sentencing 18,426 individuals (17,262 juveniles and 1,164 adults). Of the juveniles, an estimated 43.5 percent (7,513) were between the ages of twelve and sixteen years of age; the majority of juveniles were sentenced for theft (over 82 percent of those between twelve and sixteen). GARF, f. 5207, op. 3, d. 31, ll. 45–48. Judges in 1935 meted out custodial sentences to only 53.5 percent of offenders under the age of sixteen. Solomon, *Soviet Criminal Justice under Stalin*, 206.

166. J. Arch Getty, Gabor T. Rittersporn, and Viktor Zemskov, "Victims of the Soviet Penal System in the Pre-War Years: A First Approach on the Basis of Archival Evidence," *American Historical Review* 98, no. 4 (1993): 1017–49, esp. 1026. Juveniles not convicted of crimes but still serving time in the colonies were not, as Getty, Rittersporn, and Zemskov suggest, predominantly children of arrested parents; such children were generally sent to orphanages if under the age of fourteen years (if between fourteen and sixteen, they were indeed been sent to labor colonies, if relatives could not be found to care for them). It should also be noted that statistics based on official (though secret) figures for labor colonies underestimate the number of juveniles actually serving time in them. Local penal officials generally maintained the fiction that juveniles under sixteen years of age were sent only to special colonies for youths; Gulag officials were wary of reporting the existence of a large population of underage children in their adult labor colonies. See GARF, f. 5446, op. 18a, d. 847, ll. 3–8.

167. A total of 73,458 juveniles passed through NKVD detention centers in the second half of 1935, 125,220 in 1936, and 121,123 in the first eight months of 1937. Most of these children had been apprehended by the police (201,139) or by railroad administrations (42,088, over 17,000 from the first six months of 1935 alone); 16,800

by "social organizations" such as the Komsomol; and only 29,498 by welfare and educational organizations, which had been in charge of sweeping children off the streets before May 1935. GARF, f. 1235, op. 141, d. 2032, ll. 9–30, esp. 26–30.

168. GARF, f. 5446, op. 18a, d. 904, ll. 5–6.

169. The Moscow Children's Department of the *militsiia* reported that, while in 1936 some 15,243 homeless children passed through the Danilov detention center, the number dropped to 9,055 in 1937 and only 2,250 for the first half of 1938. GARF, f. 5207, op. 3, d. 39, l. 32. See also GARF, f. 1235, op. 141, d. 2032, ll. 1–6, for a report from Semashko to the Soviet Central Executive Committee in January 1937 in which he claimed that the problem of homelessness had been completely solved and "there are now no homeless children on the streets of [our] cities."

170. Cases of theft by juveniles, according to Iagoda, fell from 7,538 in the second quarter of 1935 to 5,501, 4,256, and 3,960, respectively, in the following quarters; hooliganism from 1,771 to 924, 674, and 691; and unarmed robbery from 517 to 245 to 125 to 87. Homeless and delinquent children picked up by the police fell steadily from 30,466 in July 1936 to 18,672 in December. Iagoda added that 60 percent of these children were unsupervised rather than homeless, and that 30 percent of the homeless children picked up in early 1936 had escaped from orphanages. GARF, f. 5446, op. 18a, d. 904, ll. 5–7.

171. GARF, f. 5207, op. 3, d 31, ll. 61–62.

172. The police delivered 125,220 children to NKVD detention centers in 1936 and 121,123 in the first eight months of 1937. GARF, f. 1235, op. 141, d. 2032, ll. 9–30, esp. 26–30. For similar accounts, see GARF, f. 5207, op. 3, d. 39, l. 32, for levels of delinquency in Moscow between 1936 and 1938, and GARF, f. 5207, op. 3, d. 37, l. 47, for a Commission for Party Control (KPK) report in Moscow on juvenile affairs for the first seven months of 1936 that lists a total of 41,499 children picked up by the police and brought to police stations, of whom 4,429 were homeless and 1,731 were lost. See also GARF, f. 5207, op. 3, d. 37, ll. 65–69, for an investigation of juvenile affairs in Moscow that found that police detained a total of 69,243 children in 1936, 15,243 of whom were taken to the Danilov detention center; of those sent to the center, 5,417 were guilty of theft and 5,352 were picked up for begging, while cases sent to court were listed as predominantly qualified theft, hooliganism, swindling, murder, and sexual crimes, suggesting that police in Moscow at least were interpreting the April 7 edict rather liberally by 1936.

Chapter 5

1. GARF, f. 9401, op. 12, d. 135, doc. 133.

2. Ibid., doc. 31. NKVD Order 00192 in May 1935 created regional police troikas authorized to sentence "socially harmful elements" to five years in labor camps; see below.

3. For the structure of the USSR NKVD, see V. N. Khaustov, V. P. Naumov, and N. S. Plotnikov, eds., *Lubianka: Stalin i VChK-GPU-OGPU-NKVD—Ianvar' 1922–dekabr' 1936* (Moscow: Mezhdunarodnyi fond "Demokratiia," 2003) (hereafter Khaustov, Naumov, and Plotnikov, *Lubianka 1922–1936*), 543–44.

4. N. V. Petrov and K. V. Skorkin, *Kto rukovodil NKVD, 1934–1941: Spravochnik* (Moscow: Zven'ia, 1999), 104. Bel'skii headed the *militsiia* until August 1937.

5. GARF, f. 5446, op. 16a, d. 1270, ll. 1–3. Pay for police in the countryside, however, lagged behind the levels desired by the center throughout the mid-1930s, and Iagoda continued to complain in the mid-1930s that not all members of the *militsiia* officer corps were paid as well as corresponding officers of the UGB.

6. The Politburo approved the creation of a Central Inspectorate of border guards, internal troops, and the *militsiia* in December 1934, naming N. M. Bystrykh as its head; the body was abolished in late 1936. RGASPI, f. 17, op. 3, d. 955, l. 58; Petrov and Skorkin, *Kto rukovodil NKVD*, 46; GARF, f. 9401, op. 12, d. 126, ll. 294–95.

7. GARF, f. 9401, op. 12, d. 135, doc. 119.

8. E.g., see the relationships between UGB and the *militsiia* officers corps presented by Mikhail Shreider, *NKVD iznutri: Zapiski Chekista* (Moscow: Vozvrashchenie, 1995).

9. Iagoda chastised NKVD chiefs in early 1935, e.g., for paying little attention to the *militsiia*. Some 29,000 of a total of 180,000 policemen (including the Industrial Militsiia) were censured in 1934 for dereliction of duty, 8,000 of whom were sent to military tribunals for punishment; Iagoda charged that local NKVD chiefs used punishment in place of training, an approach that produced high rates of labor turnover and suicide. GARF, f. 9401, op. 12, d. 135, doc. 119. In addition, Iagoda censured and removed the *militsiia* chief of the Tadzhik republic in early January 1935 for the poor overall state of police work in the republic. GARF, f. 9401, op. 12, d. 135, doc. 18.

10. Labor turnover among lower ranks was still in the range of 40 percent across the USSR, and higher in individual locations. GARF, f. 9401, op. 12, d. 137, l. 65ob; GARF, f. 9401, op. 12, d. 135, doc. 26; GARF, f. 9401, op. 12, d. 135, doc. 24.

11. Ibid., doc. 117.

12. *Na boevom postu*, vol. 9 (1934): 1.

13. GARF, f. 9401, op. 12, d. 135, doc. 26.

14. The Politburo transferred funding for all police activity to the central (USSR) budget with the creation of the USSR NKVD. Iagoda added the issue of the Industrial Militsiia to these deliberations, and in October 1934 the Sovnarkom, citing budgetary pressures, resolved that the USSR budget would pay only for a restricted number of Industrial Militsiia administrations serving union-level organizations, such as the USSR Commissariat of Heavy Industry. The Sovnarkom ordered the NKVD to review existing contracts and reduce the size of the Industrial Militsiia as much as possible, forcing those institutions to replace police coverage with their own hired guards. GARF, f. 5446, op. 16a, d. 1270, l. 36; GARF, f. 9401, op. 12, d. 135, doc. 15; GARF, f. 9415, op. 3, d. 8, ll. 15–17.

15. The 1935 plan called for 28,381 officers to guard 925 specific institutions instead of the 1934 level of 64,595 officers guarding 1,904 institutions. The Commissariat of Heavy Industry was the largest single benefactor of *militsiia* labor power both before and after the reorganization, with 31,360 officers in 1934 and 11,566 in 1935; agricultural harvest and planting organizations occupied a distant second place. GARF, f. 5446, op. 16a, d. 1270, ll. 31–32.

16. GARF, f. 9415, op. 3, d. 8, ll. 49, 55; GARF, f. 9401, op. 12, d. 135, doc. 115.

17. GARF, f. 5446, op. 18a, d. 618, l. 20.

18. GARF, f. 9401, op. 12, d. 135, doc. 133.

19. For examples from Moscow, see TsGAMO, f. 792, op. 7, d. 814, l. 1; and ibid., ll. 148–49.

20. Ibid., ll. 100–102.

21. GARF, f. 9401, op. 12, d. 135, doc. 119, ll. 8–9.

22. Investigators estimated that in the first four months of 1935 only 30 percent of the registered informants in Moscow provided any information at all, and that a number of district police administrations had not received a single report from undercover informants. GARF, f. 9401, op. 12, d. 135, doc. 26.

23. Ibid., doc. 119.

24. See GARF, f. 5446, op. 16a, d. 1262, ll. 2–3; and GARF, f. 9401, op. 12, d. 137, l. 148. Vyshinskii protested the former circular immediately, but the archival record suggests that the Sovnarkom declined to move on his complaint in light of the impending discussion of revisions to the Criminal Code, which never occurred. The instructions remained in force until Vyshinskii's successful attempt to limit the scope of the passport system in this area in early 1936.

25. E.g., in late March 1935, Iagoda revoked the exception that allowed passports to be awarded to longtime natives of a particular regime city who were otherwise ineligible to live in regime cities (retirees, dependents of authorized individuals, et al., who were also deprived of voting rights, were "former people," had no ongoing employment, etc.). Although instructions to local police warned them not to turn the process of ejecting these people into a "one-time mass campaign," the proximity of the 1935 campaigns against urban crime and the purges of Leningrad in the wake of the Kirov murder made purges the likely outcome. GARF, f. 9401, op. 12, d. 137, l. 135. See also Khaustov, Naumov, and Plotnikov, *Lubianka 1922–1936*, 613–17, esp. 617, for documents relating to the purges of Leningrad that show recalcitrance on Iagoda's part; Iagoda's failure to support this purge may have played a role in his eventual replacement as head of the NKVD.

26. RGASPI, f. 17, op. 3, d. 968, l. 33; or GARF, f. 5446, op. 57, d. 37, l. 67. The local police were instructed not to allow the exchange to assume the character of a "mass operation," but the sheer size of the exchange made it unlikely that the local police would be able to accomplish the operation without some recourse to campaign-style activities. GARF, f. 9401, op. 12, d. 137, ll. 140–40ob, 149–54. See TsGAMO, f. 792, op. 7, d. 689, ll. 20–21, and GARF, f. 5446, op. 18a, d. 616, l. 144, for complaints about incompetence, corruption, and severe shortages of blank passport documents during the exchange.

27. In 1935, Iagoda ordered local police to maintain comprehensive catalogs of all authorized residents in their areas and to send notice to other police jurisdictions when a resident moved from one regime city to another. Central NKVD officials compiled nationwide list of individuals refused regime passports, expecting that local officers would compare the passports of in-migrants to the list in order to identify individuals ejected from other regime locales. By 1936, 359 specific urban areas with populations of 20,000 or more were required to maintain continually updated card catalogs of registered passports. GARF, f. 9415, op. 3, d. 9, ll. 43, 53; GARF, f. 9401, op. 12, d. 137, ll. 98–99; GARF, f. 9401, op. 12, d. 137, ll. 160–65; GARF, f. 5446, op. 18a, d. 618, l. 29.

28. See GARF, f. 9401, op. 12, d. 233, ll. 484–501, for a copy of this article of the Russian Soviet Federated Socialist Republic (RSFSR) criminal code (192a), added in July 1934, that was distributed to local police administrations.

29. The mere existence of passport troikas in 1934 and early 1935 contradicts the essence of the Politburo decision in mid-1934, taken in conjunction with the formation of the USSR NKVD, which supposedly eliminated all extrajudicial sentencing capacity of the police, with the exception of the Special Board. It also contradicts nearly all

scholarly accounts of extrajudicial sentencing in this period, which generally agree that local sentencing power of the NKVD was eliminated in 1934 as a part of a "moderate" set of moves on the part of the Politburo. These passport troikas had jurisdiction only over regime areas and thus did not represent a general right to administrative sentencing by the NKVD; they were approved on a case-by-case basis, as were other troikas in 1933 and early 1934.

30. GARF, f. 9401, op. 12, d. 137, l. 81.

31. This charge comes from a complaint about the passport system sent to Molotov by Vyshinskii and was essentially the same complaint that Akulov had leveled at the OGPU in early 1934 (see above). GARF, f. 5446, op. 18a, d. 845, ll. 24–26.

32. GARF, f. 5446, op. 18a, d. 904, l. 10. The report does not contain information on extrajudicial sanctions, likely because the jurisdiction of "police troikas" extended to passport violators after mid-1935 (see below).

33. Antonov-Ovseenko noted that passport troikas most often handed out sentences to labor camps or special settlements, and that just under 3,000 individuals were "sent to back to their homelands" by Moscow police as part of campaigns against beggary in early 1935, without any sort of administrative hearing at all, including 929 juveniles as part of the antihomelessness campaign. GARF, f. 3316, op. 64, d. 1619, ll. 79–80ob.

34. E.g., see the booklet of passport instructions distributed to local policemen early 1935 in GARF, f. 9401, op. 12, d. 137, ll. 78–98.

35. GARF, f. 1235, op. 141, d. 1650, l. 28. Passport officials in nonregime cities were often more restrictive than statutes allowed. E.g., Iagoda scolded local administrations in April 1935 for refusing to issue passports to individuals who completed sentences in labor camps, banishment, or exile, complaining that such decisions disrupted the rehabilitation of ex-convicts and set them "back on the path of crime." GARF, f. 9401, op. 12, d. 137, l. 51.

36. The police were specifically instructed not to make any such notations on an individual's passport itself, nor were they even supposed to tell these individuals that they were under surveillance, in order to preserve the covert nature of the system. GARF, f. 9401, op. 12, d. 137, l. 83.

37. For a detailed description of the process of surveillance (*nadzor*), both by the GUGB and the *militsiia*, see GARF, f. 5446, op. 16a, d. 1252, ll. 5–26. The GUGB maintained a parallel system of surveillance for individuals sentenced to exile for crimes investigated by the political police; see chapter 6 for a discussion of the effectiveness of that system in the mid-1930s.

38. GARF, f. 9401, op. 12, d. 137, ll. 160–65, 250–50ob, 272–73; GARF, f. 9401, op. 12, d. 135, doc. 130.

39. In March 1934, the Politburo ordered local OGPU administrations to carry out purges of "socially dangerous elements" in urban areas and sentence them to terms in labor camps using the Special Board. This order, referred to as "Telegram 80," is referenced in NKVD documents in 1935 but is unavailable in the Russian archives. "Dangerous elements" apprehended under its auspices were technically sentenced by the Special Board under the applicable article of the Criminal Code (in the RSFSR, Article 7-35, which had been in existence since the mid-1920s but was used only infrequently by extrajudicial sentencing bodies prior to 1934). GARF, f. 9401, op. 12, d. 137, l. 67ob.

40. See GARF, f. 8131, op. 38, d. 6, ll. 29–29ob, for a copy of Akulov's complaint.

41. The police troikas were comprised of a regional NKVD chief, a regional *militsiia* chief, and the head of whatever police administration made a given arrest. This definition of "harmful elements" did not entail a specific number of detainments (*privody*, technically not an arrest, which in the Soviet criminal justice system signaled the beginning of judicial proceedings), as did previous versions of these instructions; a single previous detainment was sufficient. Procuracy instructions regarding supervision of police troikas stressed that local procurators were to pay special attention to proof of past detainments and current contact with the criminal milieu, both of which were widely abused by local police. See GARF, f. 8131, op. 38, d. 6, ll. 61–64.

42. E.g., Vyshinskii refrained from criticizing the work of the police troikas in an exchange with Iagoda and Molotov regarding police activity in 1935, despite the fact that he disagreed with Iagoda on virtually all issues related to extrajudicial sanction in this period. GARF, f. 5446, op. 18a, d. 904, ll. 12, 16.

43. E.g., Iagoda rejected a request from Communist Party officials in the East Siberian Territory in mid-1935 to grant regime status to the city of Sretensk and several surrounding rural areas, which were supposedly overrun by dekulakized peasants and other expellees from the nearby eastern border zone. Even though Kliment Voroshilov, the defense commissar, supported the request in order to protect military garrisons in the area, Iagoda demurred, arguing that rural areas not adjacent to the Soviet border did not merit regime status. GARF, f. 5446, op. 16a, d. 1291, ll. 1–4.

44. GARF, f. 9401, op. 12, d. 135, doc. 146; GARF, f. 9401, op. 12, d. 233, ll. 497–501; GARF, f. 5446, op. 24a, d. 32, ll. 1–17.

45. The term most often used to describe the removal of harmful elements from cities was the bureaucratic "removal" (*iz"iatie*); the term "purge" (*chistka*) was used less frequently and usually appeared in internal correspondence between Communist Party and police leaders rather than in instructions to local police.

46. GARF, f. 9401, op. 12, d. 135, doc. 147.

47. These figures must be treated with great care. The exact figures are 119,159 and 141,318 individuals identified as being sentenced by "troikas" in 1935 and 1936, respectively, by a report created in 1953 by the First Special Section of the Ministerstvo vnutrennikh del (MVD) USSR. The only standing troikas in operation in 1935 and 1936 were the police (*militseiskie*) troikas. GARF, f. 9401, op. 1, d. 4157, l. 203. The figure for 1935 roughly agrees with the estimate presented by Iagoda in early 1936 that police troikas sentenced 122,796 individuals in 1935 for criminal offenses during ongoing "purges of cities"; see Khaustov, Naumov, and Plotnikov, *Lubianka 1922–1936*, 744.

48. Determining exactly how many individuals were detained in the USSR by police as "harmful elements" in 1935 and 1936 is difficult, given available archival documentation. According to internal NKVD calculations complied in late 1935, of the 265,720 individuals swept off the streets as "SVEs" by November 1, 1935, 84,903 (32 percent) were sentenced by the police troikas, 65,274 of whom received sentences to labor camps (of over three years by necessity, but usually five years); 97,920 were transferred to justice organizations; and 64,483 received "other" methods of administrative punishment (usually expulsion from regime cities under the passport system). Individual totals for the months of September and October 1935 show that 39 and 36 percent, respectively, of the individuals detained in the USSR as socially harmful elements in those months were sentenced by police troikas. Taking the most conservative percentage (39 percent) and applying it to the total number of individuals sentenced by police troikas in 1935 and 1936, we can surmise that police swept off the streets

almost 306,000 individuals in 1935 and over 362,000 individuals in 1936. Assuming that the ratio in 1936 of individuals swept off the streets to those sentenced matched that of the months up to November 1935 (32 percent) would result in the figures of more than 372,000 individuals in 1935 and some 442,000 individuals in 1936. The truth likely lies somewhere in the middle. All from GARF, f. 9401, op. 12, d. 135, doc. 147; and GARF, f. 9401, op. 1, d. 4157, l. 203.

49. In 1934, the courts sentenced only a quarter of those found guilty to any kind of deprivation of freedom; in 1935, 37 percent (many of which were political cases handled by the new Special Collegia system after the creation of the USSR NKVD); for the next several years, roughly 40 percent. Peter H. Solomon Jr., *Soviet Criminal Justice under Stalin* (Cambridge: Cambridge University Press, 1996), 222–29. Police troikas sentenced to terms in labor camps 84 and 79 percent of the total sentenced in September and October 1934, respectively, and 66 percent of the total up to November 1, 1935, suggesting that the trend was toward harsher sentencing by the troikas toward the end of the year. GARF, f. 9401, op. 12, d. 135, doc. 147.

50. GARF, f. 8131, op. 38, d. 5, ll. 91–92. E.g., see the December 1934 report from the Special Department of the USSR Procuracy, which was responsible for oversight of all issues relate to the GUGB, charging that the police troika in the Kuibyshev Territory handed out "standard" sentences of terms in labor camps and colonies to socially harmful elements, never using sentences of exile or banishment; the report also claims that employees of the Detective Department often sent completely fabricated case files to the troikas, which were approved without further consideration. GARF, f. 8131, op. 38, d. 7, ll. 75–77.

51. In 1936, the labor camps incarcerated 103,513 "socially harmful elements" and 104,826 individuals convicted of political crimes. Gabor T. Rittersporn, "Extra-Judicial Repression and the Courts: Their Relationship in the 1930s," in *Reforming Justice in Russia, 1864–1996*, ed. Peter H. Solomon Jr. (Armonk, N.Y.: M. E. Sharpe, 1997), 212, 215. The number of "harmful elements" continued to climb and reached 285,831 by 1939 (or some 22 percent of individuals in the camps); J. Arch Getty, Gabor T. Rittersporn, and Viktor Zemskov, "Victims of the Soviet Penal System in the Pre-War Years: A First Approach on the Basis of Archival Evidence," *American Historical Review* 98, no. 4 (1993): 1017–49, esp. 1032.

52. See Khaustov, Naumov, and Plotnikov, *Lubianka 1922–1936*, 587, 819–20 n. 153.

53. GARF, f. 3316, op. 64, d. 1620, ll. 1–56.

54. The Politburo appointed Vyshinskii general procurator of the USSR on March 3, 1935, after resolving to move Akulov to the position of head of the USSR Central Executive Committee (TsIK) in order to replace Avel Enukidze, who fell under Stalin's suspicion in early 1935 and was transferred, also on March 3, to the Transcaucasian TsIK. RGASPI, f. 17, op. 3, d. 960, ll. 12, 25, 66. Many commentators see Akulov's transfer as a demotion and as the first step toward his arrest two years later, yet he continued to participate in top-level debates regarding the criminal justice system in mid-1935, and the position of head of TsIK was no secondary post. For a summary of existing explanations of the end of Akulov's career, see Solomon, *Soviet Criminal Justice under Stalin*, 247.

55. Vyshinskii's only real attack in this response was aimed at what he called lenient sentencing practices of the Supreme Court of the Russian Republic. GARF, f. 8131, op. 37, d. 59, ll. 55–73; or GARF, f. 3316, op. 64, d. 1620, ll. 57–75.

56. Individual peasants not in collective farms were not eligible for the amnesty. RGASPI, f. 17, op. 3, d. 969, ll. 24–25.

57. Victor Danilov, Roberta Manning, and Lynne Viola, eds., *Tragediia sovetskoi derevni: Kollektivizatsiia i raskulachivanie, 1927–1939—Dokumenty i materialy, V 5–ti tt. T. 4, 1934–1936* (Moscow: ROSSPEN, 2002), 9–10. The amnesty specifically did not apply to "recidivists" or individuals convicted of counterrevolutionary and antistate crimes, or those guilty of "systematically" failing to fulfill their quotas in various agricultural campaigns. Ibid., 533.

58. RGASPI, f. 17, op. 3, d. 974, l. 173; Solomon, *Soviet Criminal Justice under Stalin*, 128–29.

59. RGASPI, f. 17, op. 3, d. 965, ll. 39, 75; GARF, f. 5446, op. 57, d. 36, ll. 178–79.

60. RGASPI, f. 17, op. 120, d. 171, ll. 12–20.

61. Krylenko attempted to preempt the criticism of the investigation in a letter to the Central Committee in mid-August, but his arguments were ignored by Stalin, who had already lost trust in the justice commissar and had begun the process of removing him from office. RGASPI, f. 17, op. 120, d. 171, ll. 1–11. Krylenko's position was further weakened by the discussions of the new Soviet Constitution, which began on Stalin's orders in mid-1935 and focused on the relative positions of the Procuracy, Justice Commissariat, and Supreme Court in the criminal justice system. By early 1936, Vyshinskii had defeated his rival and secured a reorganization of the Soviet judiciary that placed the Procuracy at the head of a more centralized Soviet criminal justice system, sealing the fate of Krylenko's Justice Commissariat and, in the process, of Krylenko himself. See Solomon, *Soviet Criminal Justice under Stalin*, 179–82, esp. 180.

62. RGASPI, f. 17, op. 120, d. 171, l. 61.

63. Marc Jansen and Nikita Petrov, *Stalin's Loyal Executioner: People's Commissar Nikolai Ezhov, 1895–1940* (Stanford, Calif.: Hoover Institution Press, 2002), 22–28.

64. Iagoda's omission from the committee suggests that his decline was well under way. RGASPI, f. 17, op. 120, d. 244, l. 36.

65. RGASPI, f. 17, op. 120, d. 244, ll. 1–21, 22–35. The figure of 25 percent refers to only the first half of 1935, but the report suggests that the proportion would be roughly the same for the second half of the year.

66. For examples of these "special reports," see RGASPI, f. 17, op. 120, d. 171, ll. 68–89, 169–79, 180–90.

67. RGASPI, f. 17, op. 114, d. 741, ll. 137–75. For numerous drafts of the letter, see RGASPI, f. 17, op. 120, d. 244 and 171.

68. On May 20, 1936, Piatnitskii forwarded to Ezhov and Andreev a "corrected draft, according to your instructions, of the closed letter to party organizations regarding the work of courts and procuracy-investigative administrations." RGASPI, f. 17, op. 120, d. 24, ll. 55–75. Neither was satisfied, and Piatnitskii, Ezhov, and Andreev traded corrections and drafts through the months of May and June.

69. RGASPI, f. 17, op. 120, d. 244, ll. 89–118.

70. Solomon, *Soviet Criminal Justice under Stalin*, 192.

71. GARF, f. 8131, op. 37, d. 70, ll. 103–8ob; also in Khaustov, Naumov, and Plotnikov, *Lubianka 1922–1936*, 742–44.

72. GARF, f. 8131, op. 37, d. 70, ll. 138–42; also in Khaustov, Naumov, and Plotnikov, *Lubianka 1922–1936*, 744–47. Iagoda did note that police troikas sentenced

nearly 123,000 "criminals elements" in 1935 as part of ongoing "purges of cities," but he did not dwell on this cohort, as Vyshinskii had not mentioned it specifically.

73. GARF, f. 8131, op. 37, d. 70, ll. 134–36ob; also in Khaustov, Naumov, and Plotnikov, *Lubianka 1922–1936*, 748–50. Vyshinskii's response does mention the sentencing of "harmful elements" as evidence that the sentencing practices of the Special Board indeed did influence overall penal populations in the mid-1930s. He was correct, but none of his suggestions focus on reducing the size of this group of detainees.

74. For a detailed discussion of Krylenko's complaints, see Sarah Davies, "The Crime of 'Anti-Soviet Agitation' in the Soviet Union in the 1930's," *Cahiers du Monde russe* 39, nos. 1–2 (1998): 157.

75. GARF, f. 8131, op. 37, d. 71, ll. 127–33.

76. Agranov referred an NKVD order from August 1935 specifically prohibiting verbatim transcription of offensive and anti-Soviet statements in case files. GARF, f. 5446, op. 18a, d. 849, l. 1–4.

77. Khaustov, Naumov, and Plotnikov, *Lubianka 1922–1936*, 742, 750.

78. Molotov had approved the request on April 1 and forwarded it to the Politburo for discussion, although the archival record shows that he rejected the attached request to authorize the Special Board to sentence individuals to compulsory psychiatric treatment. No direct record of the Politburo's response is available, but the Sovnarkom documentation bears a note from Valerian Mezhlauk stating that the issue, per Molotov's order, was removed from consideration a week later. GARF, f. 5446, op. 17, d. 313, ll. 125–27.

79. The total number of individuals sentenced for counterrevolution agitation in 1936 was just over 32,000—a large number, to be sure, but substantially fewer than the more than 141,000 "harmful elements" and passport violators sentenced by the police troikas in the same year. GARF, f. 9401, op. 1, d. 4157, l. 203.

80. On March 15, the Politburo issued an instruction, suggested by Vyshinskii, which removed language from passport regulations that automatically banished from regime areas family members of individuals who were ineligible for passports. RGASPI, f. 17, op. 3, d. 976, l. 17. Vyshinskii may have taken this decision as a signal that further changes were possible.

81. GARF, f. 5446, op. 18a, d. 845, ll. 24–26.

82. GARF, f. 5446, op. 16a, d. 1270, ll. 23–32.

83. Vyshinsky, when asked for his opinion on the issue in mid-December, had no objection, suggesting only that the Procuracy be involved in working up the necessary instructions. GARF, f. 5446, op. 18a, d. 845, ll. 31–33, 34.

84. Ibid., ll. 28–30; GARF, f. 8131, op. 37, d. 71, ll. 118–20.

85. Vyshinskii suggested that a notation reading "Issued on the Basis of Point 11 of Sovnarkom Instruction No. 861" be placed in the passports of any individuals who were forbidden to live in regime areas because of a sentence of any kind. GARF, f. 5446, op. 18a, d. 845, ll. 19–20ob; GARF, f. 8131, op. 37, d. 71, ll. 116–17ob. In making this suggestion, Vyshinskii was consistent with his earlier statement, made in December 1935, that he had no objections to such a notation on principle; his attempt to limit the instructions to ex-convicts was part of his ongoing attempt to protect certain categories of censured individuals, such as *lishentsy*, from further legal and social stigmatization. On March 29, for example, he wrote to the Politburo asking that it consider publishing an order to the effect that individuals should not be rejected for work solely on the basis of their social position, previous judgments, loss of voting rights, or the same regarding their parents. GARF, f. 8131, op. 37, d. 71, l. 58.

86. Iagoda also claimed, somewhat ingenuously, that Procuracy officials already exercised the right to protest the confiscation of passports by individual officers, a statement that was technically true but meaningless in practice, because individuals whose passports were confiscated were immediately expelled from the city in question and hence were unable to bring a protest to a local procurator. GARF, f. 5446, op. 18a, d. 845, l. 15–18.

87. GARF, f. 5446, op. 17, d. 314, ll. 173–76; RGASPI, f. 17, op. 3, d. 980, ll. 24, 122. The instruction also updated certain language in the original 1933 passport instructions that had lost both practical and theoretical meaning by 1936. E.g., the category of "kulaks and fleeing dekulakized" was removed, and the original instruction that refused passports individuals who migrated to regime areas after January 1, 1931, without an official labor invitation, was revised to simply state that all individuals migrating to regime areas without an invitation were prohibited from receiving passports. GARF, f. 5446, op. 17, d. 314, l. 173.

88. GARF, f. 9401, op. 12, d. 137, ll. 156–59. David Shearer mistakenly concludes that the Politburo decision restricted the use of notations to the passports of ex-convicts. The notation approved by the Politburo read "Issued on the Basis of point No. 11 of Sovnarkom Resolution No. 861 from April 28, 1933." Point No. 11 of that resolution refers not to ex-convicts but to all individuals refused passports in regime areas. The wording of the Politburo resolution itself makes this meaning clear as well. Shearer's argument that Iagoda intended to place such a notion on passports held by all individuals in nonregime areas, rather than just those held by individuals not eligible for regime passports, is not supported by the documentation; the idea would have been pointless insofar as it failed to differentiate between individuals who were eligible to move to regime areas and those who were not. David R. Shearer, "Elements Near and Alien: Passportization, Policing, and Identity in the Stalinist State, 1932–1952," *Journal of Modern History* 76, no. 4 (2004): 835–81, esp. 864–69.

89. Vyshinskii's one victory in this exchange—the reduction in the list of crimes that resulted in rejection from regime cities—was less important than the other changes. The crimes omitted by the new regulations were more pertinent to the late-NEP era than the mid-1930s: Article 59-5, refusal to serve in home front reserves by individuals excused from military service on the basis of religious motives; 59-12, hard-currency violations; 101, home brewing; 102, bootlegging; and 104, the sale of cocaine. These crimes were included in the original passport instructions in 1933 in order to purge cities of "former" people of various kinds, and their removal from the instructions in 1936 was of little concern to Iagoda. On the contrary, nearly all crimes important to urban police in 1936 remained: Article 74-2, malicious hooliganism; 107, speculation; all forms of theft more serious than simple pocket theft; the law of August 7, 1932; murder and several other violent crimes; and all serious state and political crimes contained in the earlier instruction. GARF, f. 9401, op. 12, d. 137, ll. 158–59.

90. GARF, f. 5446, op. 18a, d. 904, ll. 4–5.

91. Ibid., l. 15ob.

92. The Moscow police chief, Vul, responded to the criticisms by noting that the market was also served by a number of undercover officers (although, as we have seen, this system was hardly effective in 1936) and that he was "not in a position to do anything else." TsGAMO, f. 792, op. 7, d. 689, ll. 5–6.

93. Elena Osokina, *Za fasadom "stalinskogo izobiliia": Raspredelenie i rynok v snabzhenii naseleniia v gody industrializatsii, 1927–1941* (Moscow: ROSSPEN,

1999), 203–5. According to reports from the NKVD Economic Department, illegal rationing by local officials did continue in certain areas through the end of 1936. Khaustov, Naumov, and Plotnikov, *Lubianka 1922–1936*, 776–78.

94. RGASPI, f. 17, op. 3, d. 978, l. 2.

95. GARF, f. 5446, op. 57, d. 42, ll. 124–31.

96. Ibid., ll. 164–66. The language regarding repeat offenders closely corresponded to understandings of speculation held by the police themselves; arresting all individuals for selling items at inflated prices would have been impossible. For the working up of the instructions, which originally included language referring to the August 1932 law on speculation and subjected a much broader group of resellers to Article 107, see GARF, f. 8131, op. 37, d. 72, ll. 134–35, 141–42.

97. GARF, f. 5446, op. 22a, d. 178, ll. 171–72.

98. Ibid., l. 282.

99. Most sentences were handed down in Moscow, where the police troika sentenced 2,152 individuals while the courts sentenced 630, 111 of which were for Article 107 and 519 for Article 105. GARF, f. 8131, op. 37, d. 73, l. 19.

100. Jansen and Petrov, *Stalin's Loyal Executioner*, 38–42.

101. RGASPI, f. 17, op. 120, d. 171, l. 169–79.

102. GARF, f. 5446, op. 17, d. 314, ll. 181–83; RGASPI, f. 17, op. 3, d. 980, ll. 23, 119.

103. GARF, f. 8131, op. 37, d. 72, l. 173; GARF, f. 5446, op. 18a, d. 856, ll. 1–3. Iagoda's argument was characteristic of the NKVD's approach to policing by 1936, which assumed that any contact with expelled "contingents" would cause increases in crime.

104. GARF, f. 8131, op. 38, d. 10, ll. 19–21.

105. Jansen and Petrov, *Stalin's Loyal Executioner*, 49–51.

106. Ibid., 54–56.

Chapter 6

1. V. N. Khaustov, V. P. Naumov, and N. S. Plotnikov, eds., *Lubianka: Stalin i Glavnoe upravlenie gosbezopasnosti NKVD, 1937–1938* (Moscow: Mezhdunarodnyi fond "Demokratiia," 2004) (hereafter Khaustov, Naumov, and Plotnikov, *Lubianka 1937–1938*), 359; emphasis in the original.

2. As reported to Vyshinskii by the mother of the arrested individual. GARF, f. 8131, op. 37, d. 132, ll. 6–10.

3. The choice of name for the waves of Stalinist repression in 1937 and 1938 is crucial to any analysis of the period. Following Robert Conquest's terminology, many Western historians refer to the period as the "Great Terror." In Russian the period is often called the "Ezhovshchina," or the "era of Ezhov." Both terms are misleading, the former because it suggests that the goal of Stalinist repression in 1937 and 1938 was to terrorize the population as a whole, and the latter because it suggests that Ezhov had more influence on the unfolding repressions than he did. This and the following chapter will use more specific terms to refer to the separate processes under discussion but will occasionally refer to the entire process as the "Stalinist terror" or the "terror" for convenience.

4. This metaphor comes from titles of Ginzburg's classic memoirs, which have become the basis of the most widespread understanding of Stalin's purges. Eugenia

Semyonovna Ginzburg, *Journey into the Whirlwind*, trans. Paul Stevenson and Max Hayward (New York: Harcourt Brace Jovanovich, 1975); and Eugenia Semyonovna Ginzburg, *Within the Whirlwind*, trans. Ian Boland (New York: Harcourt Brace Jovanovich, 1981).

5. For a full account of Ezhov's early career, see Marc Jansen and Nikita Petrov, *Stalin's Loyal Executioner: People's Commissar Nikolai Ezhov, 1895–1940* (Stanford, Calif.: Hoover Institution Press, 2002), 1–29.

6. RGASPI, f. 671, op. 1, d. 118, ll. 9–10. According to Ezhov, the NKVD as of early 1936 maintained roughly 270,000 general informants (*osvedomiteli*), who were unpaid and generally did not have regular contact with the political police. To control this large and unwieldy group of informants, local NKVD administrations appointed the more qualified among them as "residents," each of whom coordinated the work of ten regular informants. Ezhov estimated that there were 27,650 residents in the USSR. NKVD officers interacted exclusively with these individuals, rather than directly with informants among the population, a practice that, according to Ezhov, severely reduced the quality of information that reached the NKVD. Local NKVD administrations also maintained separate "special informants" who reported on political opposition and counterrevolutionary crime, generally in economic institutions. These special informants were far fewer in number than the general informants: in an early draft of his report to Stalin, Ezhov claimed that there were some 2,000 special informants in Leningrad, although in later drafts he changed that claim to read "several thousand" in Leningrad and up to 40,000 to 50,000 in other regions. Finally, the NKVD maintained a much smaller network of paid agents, numbering in the hundreds in a given region. Ibid., ll. 3–10, 25–32.

7. Ibid., ll. 28, 31–32, 44–46.

8. Ezhov's investigation included a verification of the staff of the entire Leningrad NKVD. Some 298 of the 2,747 NKVD agents who were investigated were removed, 137 of whom were sent to work in the camp system as punishment; 590 of the 3,050 *militsiia* officers who were investigated were removed, 141 of whom were likewise sent to work in the camp system but 438 of whom were simply fired. RGASPI, f. 671, op. 1, d. 118, ll. 44–46. On Ezhov's role in the Communist Party purges, see Jansen and Petrov, *Stalin's Loyal Executioner*, 31–51.

9. Ezhov recommended just before his appointment as head of the NKVD that Stalin expand investigations against the Rightists, and he suggested to the Politburo just after that several thousand Trotskyites be executed and several thousand more be exiled as part of the Politburo decision "On the Attitude to Counterrevolutionary Trotskyite-Zinovievist Elements." Jansen and Petrov, *Stalin's Loyal Executioner*, 51, 56–57.

10. Vladimir Nikolaevich Khaustov, "Deiatel'nost' organov gosudarstvennoi bezopasnosti NKVD SSSR (1934–1941 gg.)," doktorskaia dissertatsiia, Akademiia FSB RF, Moscow, 1997, 119–20.

11. GARF, f. 9401, op. 12, d. 126, ll. 304–5; GARF, f. 9401, op. 12, d. 135, document 119. I find no evidence that Iagoda's removal as head of the NKVD had anything to do with his position, positive or negative, on the issue of separating the work of the regular and political police.

12. The Counterintelligence Department was renamed the Third Department as part of this reorganization. N. V. Petrov and K. V. Skorkin, *Kto rukovodil NKVD, 1934–1941: Spravochnik* (Moscow: Zven'ia, 1999), 32.

13. The new Speculation Department was also charged with combating "petty wrecking" (*mel'koe vreditel'stvo*) in Soviet economic institutions, a category of crime

that defies easy categorization as either political or criminal. GARF, f. 9401, op. 12, d. 126, ll. 23–26. In early May, in order to elevate the importance of the OBKhSS within local police administrations, Ezhov removed them from local detective departments and created separate speculation departments within local police administrations, subordinated directly to the central NKVD Speculation Department in Moscow. Ibid., l. 28.

14. On Iagoda's attempts to enhance the work of the political police in suppression of "counterrevolutionary" hooliganism and crime on railroads in 1935, see Petrov and Skorkin, *Kto rukovodil NKVD*, 40 n. 2.

15. The Politburo approved a force of 21,500 rail police but planned for full staffing only on January 1, 1939. The remainder of the Transport Department of the State Security Administration, along with a newly organized department within State Security (the Eleventh) dealing with water transport and communications, handled all strictly political crimes. Khaustov, Naumov, and Plotnikov, *Lubianka 1937–1938*, 113; Petrov and Skorkin, *Kto rukovodil NKVD*, 41.

16. Ezhov also began a process of improving Party representation within the NKVD, restructuring the Party apparatus within NKVD administrations and subordinating Party cells within local administrations directly to central and territorial Party bodies rather than to central NKVD agencies. This change increased the extent to which local NKVD branches reported directly to central Party authorities, rather than to central NKVD officials. RGASPI, f. 17, op. 114, d. 624, l. 10. This move was consistent with Ezhov's overall plans for the NKVD, but the extent to which it succeeded is open to further research.

17. See James Morris, "The Polish Terror: Spy Mania and Ethnic Cleansing in the Great Terror," *Europe-Asia Studies* 56, no. 5 (2004): 751–66, esp. 758–59; and Terry Martin, "The Origins of Soviet Ethnic Cleansing," *Journal of Modern History* 70, no. 4 (1998): 846–52.

18. Khaustov, Naumov, and Plotnikov, *Lubianka 1937–1938*, 116; Jansen and Petrov, *Stalin's Loyal Executioner*, 73.

19. See, e.g., Ezhov's February 1937 report to Stalin on the existence of foreign intelligence agents in the West Siberian Territory, in which he warned that Polish intelligence agents were actively organizing counterrevolutionary groups in Novosibirsk to carry out diversionary acts against the transport system and to foment rebellion in the event of war. Khaustov, Naumov, and Plotnikov, *Lubianka 1937–1938*, 92–94.

20. Khaustov, Naumov, and Plotnikov, *Lubianka 1937–1938*, 100, 103.

21. See Stalin's speech to the Plenum in Khaustov, Naumov, and Plotnikov, *Lubianka 1937–1938*, 95–109, esp. 96, 98–99.

22. For discussion of Ezhov's appearance at the Plenum, and the orchestrated NKVD reports supporting him, see Jansen and Petrov, *Stalin's Loyal Executioner*, 59–60.

23. Khaustov, Naumov, and Plotnikov, *Lubianka 1937–1938*, 639 n. 18.

24. RGASPI, f. 17, op. 3, d. 986. ll. 4, 24. This action represented a qualitative expansion of the sentencing power of the NKVD, as such cases were generally heard by military tribunals or by judicial collegiums prior to this time. The Special Board also retained the existing right to sentence socially dangerous elements to five years (spelled out again in the Politburo decision), which continued to be exercised through police (UNKVD) troikas.

25. Bel'skii was promoted to assistant chief of the NKVD in early November 1936 and remained the head of the *militsiia* until August 1937; he was removed in April

1938 as part of as part of Beriia's rise to power. Petrov and Skorkin, *Kto rukovodil NKVD*, 104.

26. GARF, f. 5446, op. 18a, d. 618, ll. 18–30.

27. See Elena Osokina, *Za fasadom "stalinskogo izobiliia": Raspredelenie i rynok v snabzhenii naseleniia v gody industrializatsii, 1927–1941* (Moscow: ROSSPEN, 1999), 195–201. Osokina argues that the regime chose to intervene in 1936 in order to protect the collective farm system, rather than the peasantry itself, from the effects of famine.

28. Roberta Manning, "The Soviet Economic Crisis of 1936–1940 and the Great Purges," in *Stalinist Terror: New Perspectives*, ed. J. Arch Getty and Roberta Manning (Cambridge: Cambridge University Press, 1993), 123; Osokina, *Za fasadom*, 203–5; Victor Danilov, Roberta Manning, and Lynne Viola, eds., *Tragediia sovetskoi derevni: Kollektivizatsiia i raskulachivanie, 1927–1939—Dokumenty i materialy, V 5–ti tt. T. 4, 1934–1936* (Moscow: ROSSPEN, 2002) (hereafter Danilov, Manning, and Viola, *Tragediia sovetskoi derevni*, t. 4), 913–14.

29. A Commission for Soviet Control (KSK) report from March 1937 on speculation in Kuibyshev region, for example, complained that police arrested speculators in open air markets after little investigation; courts, as a result, could sentence individuals transferred to them only to "violation of norms of trade" (Article 105), giving them short terms of compulsory labor or relatively minor fines, when better investigative practices on the part of police might have allowed judges to prove intent to speculate and resulted in harsher sentences. GARF, f. 5446, op. 26, d. 102, ll. 5–6.

30. A circular sent by Vyshinskii to local procurators in February contained typical demands that local officials increase repression against "all manner of speculative and wrecking elements, who disrupt the organization of trade in bread products." GARF, f. 5446, op. 22a, d. 178, l. 179.

31. The possibility that the abolition of the category of *lishentsy* would provoke mass confusion at the local level was not lost on central officials during the original discussion of the Constitution. Krylenko, well aware of the bureaucratic difficulties associated with such a fundamental change, proposed a blanket amnesty of all individuals sentenced to deprivation of voting rights for criminal infractions before the date of the promulgation of the Constitution (December 5, 1936) simply so that local judicial officials could avoid the onerous task of compiling lists of individuals who were to remained disenfranchised. See Golfo Alexopoulos, *Stalin's Outcasts: Aliens, Citizens, and the Soviet State, 1926–1936* (Ithaca, N.Y.: Cornell University Press, 2003), 170–76. Although Krylenko's fears were well founded, his suggestion was flatly rejected, as it would have entailed the lifting of residence restrictions on hundreds of thousands of ex-convicts, something neither Ezhov nor Stalin was willing to allow.

32. See, e.g., the request for guidance sent Molotov from the Communist Party committee of the Orenburg region on March 31, 1937, in GARF, f. 5446, op. 20a, d. 931, l. 3.

33. V. P. Danilov and S. A. Krasil'nikov, eds., *Spetspereselentsy v zapadnoi Sibiri, 1933–1938* (Novosibirsk: EKOR, 1994), 70–72. Vyshinsky, writing for the Procuracy in April 1937, noted simply that the previous regulations regarding special settlers remained in force and that the Constitution did not give individuals in special settlements the right to leave. Krestnitskii, Krylenko's assistant, made the point even more pointedly in a note sent to Molotov at the same time, stating that Article 135 pertained only to the right to participate in elections and had "no relationship whatsoever to the question of exile or banishment of a given citizen." GARF, f. 5446, op. 20a, d. 931, ll. 1–2, 5–6.

34. Likewise, the reduction in 1936 in the number of crimes that resulted in automatic banishment from all regime cities, which had resulted from Vyshinskii's challenge to Iagoda on the issue (as discussed in chapter 5), was limited in practice by the NKVD's refusal to issue any kind of blanket application of these new regulations. Rather, the NKVD in June 1937 set up a single three-person commission to review all requests nationwide for change of passport status from any ex-convicts who were now eligible for regime passports and who, encouraged by the Constitution, had the resolve to apply for them. GARF, f. 9401, op. 12, d. 137, l. 173.

35. See, e.g., the NKVD reports in Danilov, Manning, and Viola, *Tragediia sovetskoi derevni*, t. 4, 868–74, 900–4, 906–11. The problem of food shortages eased substantially in the fall of 1937 due to record harvest levels, but by that time Stalin had already made the decision to launch the waves of mass repression that would engulf the USSR in 1937 and 1938. Roberta Manning makes a compelling argument that the Terror was in some measure a response to the economic difficulties experienced by the regime in 1936 and 1937. All available evidence suggests that the famine of 1936 and 1937, and the regime's understanding of the response of collective farmers to it, was not central to Stalin's actual decision to launch mass repression. That existing archival evidence does not support the idea that economic concerns were central among Stalin's conscious reasons for launching the Terror does not invalidate Manning's argument that economic issues played a role in the overall context that made mass repression more likely. See Manning, "The Soviet Economic Crisis."

36. GARF, f. 3316, op. 64, d. 1978, ll. 1–30.

37. Oleg Khlevnyuk, "The Objectives of the Great Terror, 1937–38," in *Soviet History, 1917–53: Essays in Honour of R. W. Davies*, ed. Julian Cooper, Maureen Perrie, and E. A. Rees (London: Palgrave Macmillan, 1995), 168–69.

38. For a detailed description of these *Izvestiia* articles, which appeared on March 15, 18, and 20, see Sheila Fitzpatrick, *Everyday Stalinism: Ordinary Life in Extraordinary Times: Soviet Russia in the 1930s* (Oxford: Oxford University Press, 1999), 78–79.

39. GARF, f. 5446, op. 22a, d. 69, ll. 6–9, 12, 25. The rather timid tone of the request was unusual for Vyshinskii, suggesting that he was taking pains to maintain good relations with Ezhov and that he was unsure of his political position vis-à-vis the new head of the NKVD.

40. Ibid., ll. 44–47.

41. Ibid., ll. 23–24, 21–22.

42. Ibid., ll. 29–33.

43. This view, although it has a long history in Soviet studies and even among participants in the events in question, was revived by Oleg Khlevniuk in the mid-1990s and instantly attained the status of something like the new orthodox position among specialists on Stalin's terror, both because of the clarity of Khlevniuk's argument and his unparalleled access to Russian archives. See Khlevnyuk, "Objectives of the Great Terror," 172–74. For an earlier version of this thesis that focuses on purges of Communist Party, state, and military elites in preparation for war, see Isaac Deutscher, *Stalin: A Political Biography* (New York: Oxford University Press, 1949).

44. Peter H. Solomon Jr. terms this process the "campaign of vigilance." Peter H. Solomon Jr., *Soviet Criminal Justice under Stalin* (Cambridge: Cambridge University Press, 1996), 235–44.

45. For detailed descriptions of these purges, see Jansen and Petrov, *Stalin's Loyal Executioner*, 60–61, 66–70.

46. A stenogram of Ezhov's speech at this plenum was either never taken or was destroyed, but a lengthy summary of his theses was prepared for the meeting and has been preserved. Jansen and Petrov, *Stalin's Loyal Executioner*, 76–77; Victor Danilov, Roberta Manning, and Lynne Viola, eds., *Tragediia sovetskoi derevni: Kollektivizatsiia i raskulachivanie, 1927–1939—Dokumenty i materialy, V 5–ti tt. T. 5, 1937–1939, Kniga 1, 1937* (Moscow: ROSSPEN, 2004) (hereafter Danilov, Manning, and Viola, *Tragediia sovetskoi derevni*, t. 5), 306–8.

47. E.g., in the spring of 1937, the GUGB claimed to have uncovered large-scale terrorist, diversionary, and counterrevolutionary organizations in the Far-Eastern Territory, and to have arrested 170 individuals involved in a "fascist-terrorist" conspiracy that operated in several cities in the USSR. Khaustov, Naumov, and Plotnikov, *Lubianka 1937–1938*, 166–69, 219, 227–29.

48. Danilov, Manning, and Viola, *Tragediia sovetskoi derevni*, t. 5, 256–57.

49. The territorial Communist Party boss, R. I. Eikhe, had in fact reported at the February–March 1937 party plenum on the danger in Western Siberia from "inveterate enemies" among former party members and exiled kulaks, who would "attempt by all means to continue [their] struggle" against Soviet power; the NKVD had been engaged in sentencing supposed counterrevolutionaries within these exiled populations from at least 1936. Khlevnyuk, "Objectives of the Great Terror," 160; Danilov, Manning, and Viola, *Tragediia sovetskoi derevni*, t. 5, 596 n. 39. For discussion of policing in Western Siberia, see David R. Shearer, "Modernity and Backwardness on the Soviet Frontier: Western Siberia during the 1930s," in *Provincial Landscapes: Local Dimensions of Soviet Power, 1917–1953*, ed. Donald J. Raleigh (Pittsburgh: University of Pittsburgh Press, 2001), 194–216; and David R. Shearer, "Elements Near and Alien: Passportization, Policing, and Identity in the Stalinist State, 1932–1952," *Journal of Modern History* 76, no. 4 (2004): 835–81, esp. 856–57.

50. RGANI f. 89 perechen' 73, d. 48 l. 1. See also Khaustov, Naumov, and Plotnikov, *Lubianka 1937–1938*, 232.

51. Stalin's decision to entrust the sentencing of cases of counterrevolutionary rebellion in Western Siberia to an NKVD troika was not by itself surprising, given the geographic isolation of the area. Western Siberia had been exceptional in terms of extrajudicial sanction throughout the mid-1930s; e.g., the Politburo authorized the NKVD to mete out extrajudicial sentences of execution using a troika, headed by Eikhe, in 1934, at a time when such troikas had been abolished in conjunction with the creation of the USSR NKVD. RGANI f. 89, per. 73, document 41.

52. This telegram is published in Khaustov, Naumov, and Plotnikov, *Lubianka 1937–1938*, 234–35. The telegram was followed by NKVD operational circular no. 266, which instructed regional NKVD administrations to prepare estimates of kulaks and criminals, broken down into the two categories, for submission to Ezhov for approval. The NKVD circular added that local police were to register kulaks and criminals who had illegally fled incarceration, in addition to those that had served their sentences; this addition could only have been interpreted by local police as an order to uncover new enemies among marginalized populations, as any individuals who were known to have been fugitives would have been arrested immediately and hence would not have been subject to mere registration prior to this order. Khaustov, Naumov, and Plotnikov, *Lubianka 1937–1938*, 644 n. 34, and Danilov, Manning, and Viola, *Tragediia sovetskoi derevni*, t. 5, 319. Politburo materials make it clear that Stalin intended local party bodies to be in charge of this operation and that NKVD administrations were to follow their

lead, but at the same time, Stalin's initial instructions made no provisions for sentencing procedure for those who were to be exiled, simply instructing the NKVD to supervise the operation. See also Jansen and Petrov, *Stalin's Loyal Executioner*, 90–93, who argue that the party was ultimately in charge of the mass repressions of 1937–38.

53. David Shearer, following Oleg Khlevniuk, argues that Stalin's fear of a "fifth column," based on his readings of reports on the Spanish Civil War, was central to his decision to repress marginal populations in mid-1937. David Shearer, "Social Disorder, Mass Repression, and the NKVD during the 1930s," *Cahiers du Monde russe* 42, nos. 2–4 (2001): 505–34, esp. 530–31. This argument is certainly correct, yet it explains Stalin's general concern with rebellion and insurgency rather than his specific decision to launch repression against "kulaks and criminal elements" in early July 1937. Local concerns with the connection between marginal contingents and rebellion during war, which became common in the summer of 1937, were the product of central discussion of the same issue (which, as noted above, was widespread from at least early 1937) rather than the cause of Stalin's decision in July; these conceptual connections had been made at the center well before the summer of 1937.

54. RGANI, f. 89, per. 73, d. 47–150, are all Politburo entries regarding orders sent to localities during the mass operations. These estimates have been summarized and thoroughly analyzed by Rolf Binner and Marc Junge, "Wie der Terror 'gross' wurde: Massenmord und Lagerhaft nach Befehl 00447," *Cahiers du Monde russe* 42, nos. 2–4 (2001): 557–614.

55. RGANI, f. 89, per. 73, d. 49; *Trud*, June 4, 1992, 1; Binner and Junge, "Wie der Terror 'gross' wurde," 599–602; Danilov, Manning, and Viola, *Tragediia sovetskoi derevni*, t. 5, 320–22.

56. Khaustov, Naumov, and Plotnikov, *Lubianka 1937–1938*, 241–42; RGANI, f. 89, per. 73, d. 50, l. 1.

57. Khaustov, Naumov, and Plotnikov, *Lubianka 1937–1938*, 645 n. 34. Prior to the start of the mass operations, such targets would have been arrested by the NKVD but ultimately sentenced by regional courts or military tribunals; the distinction between summary repression and proper (if preordained) legal procedure was clear for Mironov in reference to these cases.

58. Danilov, Manning, and Viola, *Tragediia sovetskoi derevni*, t. 5, 327.

59. Ibid., 602 n. 59; Jansen and Petrov, *Stalin's Loyal Executioner*, 83–85. Because no stenographic record of this conference exists, this account is based primarily on the testimony of NKVD officials, especially Mironov, after their arrests in 1938 and 1939, and hence must be treated with care. Nonetheless, this account is entirely consistent with Ezhov's general line regarding "foreign elements" and the NKVD in the preceding months.

60. The Politburo reduced execution quotas for twenty of the forty regions that sent in estimates, increased quotas for seventeen regions, and left three the same. Many increases were simply rounded up to the even fifty or hundred, although in a few cases the Politburo decided on substantial increases in areas where the estimates were comparatively low; decreases were generally more substantial. Binner and Junge, "Wie der Terror 'gross' wurde," 595–607. These figures are not exhaustive, because several locations may have sent in estimates that are not available in the archives, but they are complete enough to draw the above conclusions.

61. The existing documentation regarding these quotas does not support further inferences regarding Stalin's targets. Some of the quotas approved by the Politburo in

early July did not contain separate estimates of kulaks and criminals, and the revised quotas approved by the Politburo in late July, as communicated in Order 00447, did not differentiate between kulaks and criminals (although some of Ezhov's successive communications maintained this distinction).

62. N. Okhotin and A. Roginskii, "Iz istorii 'nemetskoi operatsii' 1937–1938 gg.," in *Nakazannyi narod: Repressii protiv rossiiskikh Nemtsev*, ed. I. L. Shcherbakova (Moscow: Zven'ia, 1999), 35–75, esp. 35–36, 38. For the original Politburo decision, see Khaustov, Naumov, and Plotnikov, *Lubianka 1937–1938*, 250–51, 647 n. 43. A major expansion of border zones is relevant in this context as well: on July 17, the Sovnarkom approved the expansion of strict border-zone passport restrictions to numerous districts near the Soviet border in Armenia, Azerbaidzhan, Turkmenistan, Uzbekistan, and Tadzhikistan and ordered the NKVD to expel suspect elements from these areas. GARF, f. 5446, op. 57, d. 49, ll. 77–78.

63. See Okhotin and Roginskii, "Iz istorii 'nemetskoi operatsii,'" 37–38, for a particularly clear formulation of this connection.

64. Stalin's concern with the "German operation" may have delayed the launching of the operation against kulaks and criminals, which was originally scheduled to begin on July 28. Several NKVD chiefs in remote regions commenced arrests on that date, likely assuming that the previous schedule remained in force. Jansen and Petrov, *Stalin's Loyal Executioner*, 86–87.

65. This document, first published in the Russian newspaper *Trud* on June 4, 1992, has since been published in part by Arch Getty and Oleg V. Naumov, *The Road to Terror: Stalin and the Self-Destruction of the Bolsheviks, 1932–1939* (New Haven, Conn.: Yale University Press, 1999), 473–80; and in full, by Khaustov, Naumov, and Plotnikov, *Lubianka 1937–1938*, 272–81.

66. Junge and Binner, "Wie der Terror 'gross' wurde," 606; Khaustov, Naumov, and Plotnikov, *Lubianka 1937–1938*, 277.

67. J. Arch Getty's argument that the telegram of July 3 was sent in response to pressure on the Politburo from local Communist Party officials regarding the threat from "kulaks" and religious figures to upcoming Soviet elections is not supported by the available evidence. Getty argues that, because the electoral law was published in *Pravda* on July 2, the July 3 telegram should be seen as a "compromise" offered to local party leaders: "In return for forcing the local party leaders to conduct an election, Stalin chose to help them win it by giving them license to kill or deport hundreds of thousands of 'dangerous elements.'" J. Arch Getty, "'Excesses Are Not Permitted': Mass Terror and Stalinist Governance in the Late 1930s," *Russian Review* 61, no. 1 (2002): 126. The July 3 telegram said nothing about "dangerous elements," a category of individuals that the NKVD had been actively sentencing to labor camps since 1935. Neither of the two categories targeted by Stalin's telegram had the right to vote. As we have seen above, dekulakized peasants were not allowed to leave their locations of special settlement, even after their terms were completed, and they were guaranteed the right to vote only within those settlements. Likewise, ex-convicts who had served sentences for even moderately serious crime remained deprived of voting rights under the 1936 Soviet Constitution. Central and local concerns over the influence of various groups of "former people" on the election did play a role in the unfolding of the mass operations, as we will see, but there is no evidence that it played a role in Stalin's decision in early July to launch them. In any case, in October 1937 Stalin simply called off the contested elections and allowed only one candidate for each position, while the

mass operations that allegedly made them possible were under way. There is no reason to believe that he would have deemed it necessary to execute several hundred thousand people in order to "win" these elections.

68. For an analysis of the changes in the pending campaign between July 2 and July 30 that comes to the conclusion that Stalin was forced against his own wishes to expand the operations beyond the categories listed in the July 2 telegram, either by Ezhov or by regional party secretaries, see Getty, "'Excesses Are Not Permitted,'" 128–29. Getty's assertion that "Stalin may not have been the one most eager to once again launch a campaign-style operation" (p. 116) contradicts the available evidence, and it is inconsistent with Stalin's demonstrated propensity to turn to mass operations in times of crisis in the decade prior to 1937.

69. J. Arch Getty argues, to the contrary, that the mass operations of 1937 and 1938 are best understood as a "blind terror" and as evidence of a "deep-seated insecurity" on the part of the Politburo regarding its ability to rule the country. Contextualizing the mass operations in the long-term history of Soviet policing, rather than the concurrent party purges, calls this conclusion into question. Getty and Naumov, *Road to Terror*, 468–69, 480–81.

70. J. Arch Getty's contrary argument that "the time of mass NKVD arrests was clearly on the wane" in the mid-1930s is based on skewed reporting of the statistics in the documents that he cites. Getty writes that "each year from 1933 to 1936, the number of both political and non-political arrests [according to the document in question, for cases initiated by the NKVD] declined," and that the same period saw a threefold decrease in arrests for political crimes (Article 58), from 283,029 in 1933 to 91,127 in 1936, and a fivefold decrease in arrests for nonpolitical offenses, from 222,227 in 1933 to 40,041 in 1936. Getty, "'Excesses Are Not Permitted,'" 121. This document, which is a compilation of the cases investigated by the Cheka, OGPU, and NKVD from 1921 to 1953 that was prepared by the First Special Department of the USSR Ministry of Internal Affairs, contains information that directly contradicts Getty's conclusion. Although arrests did in fact decline in the period in question, arrest was a procedural step that was often taken only when a case was sent through the court system (including the system of Military Tribunals and the Special Collegiums created to hear cases investigated by the political police); cases that were sentenced extrajudicially, by the police (UNKVD) troikas, did not necessarily require a formal arrest. Hence, according to the document, the number of individuals *sentenced* in cases investigated by the NKVD fell drastically from 1933 (239,664) to 1934 (78,999), undoubtedly as a response to the May 1933 directive on halting arrests and clearing prisons, but then climbed to 267,076 in 1935 and 274,670 in 1936. The absolute and relative numbers of those sentenced to prison or labor camps on cases investigated by the NKVD followed the same pattern; after a drop from 138,903 in 1933 to 59,451 in 1934, the number climbed to 185,846 in 1935 and 219,418 in 1936—higher than that of any year after 1921. Furthermore, the table includes the figures for individuals sentenced by the NKVD police troikas for 1935 and 1936 (119,159 and 141,318, respectively), showing that the "fivefold" decline in nonpolitical arrests cited by Getty, though technically true for arrests, is a mischaracterization of the data. These statistics do not support Getty's contention that mass operations were "on the wane" in the mid-1930s; as we have seen in previous chapters, they were not. GARF, f. 9401, op. 1, d. 4157, ll. 201–3, 205; Oleg V. Khlevniuk, *The History of the Gulag: From Collectivization to the Great Terror*, trans. Vadim A. Staklo and ed. David Nordlander (New Haven, Conn.: Yale University Press, 2004), 288–89.

71. Petrov and Roginskii make much the same point in their article on the "Polish operation." N. V. Petrov and A. B. Roginskii, "Pol'skaia operatsiia" NKVD 1937–1938 gg.," in *Repressii protiv poliakov i pol'skikh grazhdan* (Moscow: Zven'ia, 1997), 22–23.

72. These general figures do not include all executions or sentences in 1937–38 but refer only to estimates of individuals sentenced during specific mass operations by extrajudicial bodies. See further discussion of these statistics in note 176 below.

73. The mass operations that were carried out under the auspices of NKVD Order 00447 will be referred to from this point forward as "operations against anti-Soviet elements" to differentiate them from the "national operations." Some Western and Russian historians have begun to refer to these operations as "the kulak operations"; e.g., see the introduction to Danilov, Manning, and Viola, *Tragediia sovetskoi derevni*, t. 5, 45; and Getty, " 'Excesses Are Not Permitted,' " 115. This nomenclature appeared only occasionally in police and Communist Party usage at the time. Politburo documents almost always referred to these operations either as "operations of repression of criminals, kulaks, and other anti-Soviet elements" or as "operations of repression of anti-Soviet elements," and most NKVD documents followed suit.

74. See Jansen and Petrov, *Stalin's Loyal Executioner*, 85–86, for discussion of these operational conferences in late July in the Western Siberian Territory.

75. The West Siberian NKVD reported that analogous situations existed in other grain administrations in the region, reminding us that Vyshinsky's efforts to amnesty convicts in the mid-1930s were hardly the final word on the matter. GANO, f. 4, op. 34, d. 4, ll. 51–64. I am grateful to David Shearer for making available to me all the documents from GANO cited in this book.

76. Danilov, Manning, and Viola, *Tragediia sovetskoi derevni*, t. 5, 338.

77. See the full text of the order in Khaustov, Naumov, and Plotnikov, *Lubianka 1937–1938*, 272–81, esp. 277–78.

78. Given the current state of Russian archives, research on the actions of operative groups is virtually impossible. For a short description of the operational sectors, see Jansen and Petrov, *Stalin's Loyal Executioner*, 85–86.

79. NKVD Circular 61, dated August 7, 1937, ordered police to transfer to NKVD troikas all ongoing cases involving armed or aggravated robbery, recidivists specializing in theft of personal items in public (e.g., purse snatchers and pocket thieves), robbery of individuals who were drunk, sale and purchase of stolen property, or maintenance of criminal "lairs"; all recidivists who were caught after escaping from places of confinement; and all criminal-recidivists who had not severed connections with the criminal milieu, had no permanent employment and were not engaged in socially useful labor, even if at the moment of their arrest they had not committed any specific crime. Such language was of course familiar to local police, as it duplicates the definition of "harmful elements" contained in the legislation creating both the NKVD Special Board and police (UNKVD) troikas in 1935. D. I. Bogomolov and A. Ia. Razumov, *Leningradskii martirolog 1937–1938*, vol. 1 (Saint Petersburg: RNB, 1995), 47–48.

80. GARF, f. 9401, op. 12, d. 126, l. 48. Operational groups on railways, it bears repeating, were hardly new. Stalin had ordered the same thing in 1932 in conjunction with his campaign against theft of socialist property; see chapter 3.

81. Danilov, Manning, and Viola, *Tragediia sovetskoi derevni*, t. 5, 349–52.

82. GARF, f. 8131, op. 37, d. 132, ll. 1–39. See also GARF, f. 7523, op. 65, d. 557, ll. 26–31, for a similar case from Moscow in November 1937, the Procuracy

review of which makes clear that the charge of "connection with the criminal milieu" was often little more than an excuse to arrest and sentence all ex-convicts in a given area.

83. Vyshinskii's review of the case in 1938 noted that, given the fact G. was indeed a collective farmworker and had a record of conscientious labor, there was no grounds to consider her a "socially harmful element." The case seems to have been resolved in G.'s favor sometime after July 1938, when the NKVD Special Board agreed to release her with one year's probation. GARF, f. 7523, op. 65, d. 557, ll. 33–33a. See also GARF, f. 7523, op. 65, d. 563, l. 40, for a case from July 1938, in which Leningrad police arrested a sixteen-year-old girl in one of the retail stores of the Gostinyi Dvor department store with eight rubles in her pocket. She confessed to stealing the money; although she was enrolled in school and had a valid passport and residence registration, she maintained "connections with criminal milieu" in the form of a boyfriend suspected of theft himself. The regional police (UNKVD) troika hence sentenced her to three years in a labor camp on July 15, 1938. The case was protested by Kalinin to the Procuracy and seems to have been dismissed in April 1939.

84. GARF, f. 8131, op. 37, d. 146, ll. 172–73. In addition, the Procuracy report noted that NKVD administration in Grozny routinely transferred cases of people already serving terms in the Grozny prison, for both political and nonpolitical crimes, to the NKVD troikas, charging them with anti-Soviet agitation and sentencing them to death. Ibid., 174–76.

85. The final phrase, of course, refers to the exact provisions of NKVD Circular 61, discussed above, which authorized NKVD campaigns against criminal elements in the absence of specific crimes. The reference to Frinovskii's order was unlikely to help the assistant chief's situation in 1940, after Frinovskii himself had been arrested. GARF, f. 8131, op. 37, d. 131, l. 36.

86. All from ibid., ll. 36–39. The documentation does not clarify the article of the criminal code under which K. was sentenced to death.

87. See Danilov, Manning, and Viola, *Tragediia sovetskoi derevni*, t. 5, 365, for an NKVD report from the Western region which notes that, by September 15, the political police (UGB) had arrested 5,414 individuals, while the *militsiia* had arrested 4,333; the NKVD troika during the same period sentenced 2,335 individuals, while the police (UNKVD) troika sentenced 2,256.

88. See GARF, f. 5446, op. 22a, d. 179, ll. 158–59, for an example of a regional police troika that sentenced individuals under the auspices of Article 107 (speculation) during the mass operations, even though police troikas were technically limited to sentencing "socially harmful elements" and passport violators.

89. See, e.g., Danilov, Manning, and Viola, *Tragediia sovetskoi derevni*, t. 5, 339, for a suggestion from the NKVD of the Western region that all Category II cases of criminals be heard by police troikas, which did not operate under any quota limits in these years.

90. See Jansen and Petrov, *Stalin's Loyal Executioner*, 109, for the figure of 200,000 sentences from UNKVD troikas from 1937 and 1938; for the figure of 400,000, see N. G. Okhotin and A. B. Roginskii, " 'Bol'shoi terror': 1937–1938—Kratkaia khronika," *30 oktiabria* no. 74 (2007): 1, 3–7. The latter figure is, in my view, likely more accurate. Jansen and Petrov's statement that police troikas sentenced individuals to two years of deprivation of freedom is a mistake (perhaps a clerical error); police troikas were authorized to sentence to up to five years and, in practice,

often sentenced above that amount in 1937 and 1938. For a memoir account of the activities of the police troikas during 1937 and 1938 that, somewhat dubiously, stresses the separation of police troikas from the work of the GUGB, see Mikhail Shreider, *NKVD iznutri: Zapiski Chekista* (Moscow: Vozvrashchenie, 1995), esp. 71 n. 1, for a discussion of police troikas. Note that Shreider incorrectly attributes the creation of police troikas to Ezhov. We have no additional information on the categories of individuals sentenced by the police troikas in 1937 and 1938. Because the NKVD troikas tended to apply Article 58 to most of its victims, we have no way of knowing how many individuals were sentenced by NKVD troikas under Article 58 but were actually picked up for other reasons, such as passport violations. Statistics compiled at the end of the mass operations list 157,694 individuals arrested in 1937 and 45,183 in 1938 by the NKVD for "other" crimes (neither political crimes nor membership in any specific political or ethnic group), but it is impossible to correlate the two categories on the basis of existing documentation. Khaustov, Naumov, and Plotnikov, *Lubianka 1937–1938*, 659–60 n. 78.

91. Danilov, Manning, and Viola, *Tragediia sovetskoi derevni*, t. 5, 338–39. Also see the report from the NKVD chief of the Ordzhonikidze region, who noted that a portion of the total of 2,203 individuals arrested in his area as of August 11 were participants in fascist, Socialist-Revolutionary, or sectarian groups but identified most simply as "kulaks" or "criminal elements." He made no attempt to justify these arrests with reference to any large-scale, unified counterrevolutionary conspiracy. Danilov, Manning, and Viola, *Tragediia sovetskoi derevni*, t. 5, 340–41.

92. Khaustov, Naumov, and Plotnikov, *Lubianka 1937–1938*, 338–39.

93. GARF, f. 7523, op. 65, d. 557, ll. 41–45.

94. Danilov, Manning, and Viola, *Tragediia sovetskoi derevni*, t. 5, 38–43, 259–68.

95. For successive Politburo orders regarding show trials from August 3, August 31, and September 10, see, respectively, Khaustov, Naumov, and Plotnikov, *Lubianka 1937–1938*, 298; GARF, f. 5446, op. 22a, d. 178, ll. 35–36; and Khaustov, Naumov, and Plotnikov, *Lubianka 1937–1938*, 344–45. In terms of scale, the show trials paled beside the operations against "anti-Soviet elements" in the countryside; see Danilov, Manning, and Viola, *Tragediia sovetskoi derevni*, t. 5, 512–17, for a USSR Procuracy report that puts the number of individuals arrested by mid-December in trials related to grain collection and cattle administrations at just over 5,600, with just under 2,000 executed—a substantial part of the rural elite, but statistically a minor part of the work of the NKVD in 1937.

96. GANO, f. 4, op. 34, d. 4, ll. 6–8, 16. For a similar example, see the relatively mundane report from the Stalingrad region in Danilov, Manning, and Viola, *Tragediia sovetskoi derevni*, t. 5, 273–74; compare this to the more strident summary report from the GUGB, which blamed shortages on "counterrevolutionary and wrecking activities in the countryside of kulak, religious-sectarian and other anti-Soviet elements," in ibid., 274–78.

97. E.g., Ezhov's reports to Stalin on the progress of the mass operations in August and early September repeatedly made the connection between the repression of "anti-Soviet elements" on collective farms and the improvement of the grain collection campaign in the fall of 1937. Khaustov, Naumov, and Plotnikov, *Lubianka 1937–1938*, 338–40.

98. GANO, f. 4, op. 34, d. 4, ll. 9–10. See Danilov, Manning, and Viola, *Tragediia sovetskoi derevni*, t. 5, 365, for a similar report from the Western region from

mid-September, which claims that "Rightist-Trotskyite" conspiracies made up of state and Communist Party elites strove to disrupt agricultural campaigns by protecting "kulaks" in the collective farm system.

99. GANO, f. 4, op. 34, d. 4, ll. 16–28, esp. 16, 22–23, 25.

100. GARF, f. 9401, op. 12, d. 135, doc. 153.

101. On August 1, 1937, Bel'skii clarified the working relationship between the UGB and the *militsiia* by authorizing local UGB operative departments, which were in charge of the actual arrests carried out in the mass operations, to issue instructions directly to *militsiia* precincts and to call meetings with precinct inspectors in order to coordinate police activities in support of the mass operations. GARF, f. 9401, op. 12, d. 137, ll. 175–76.

102. The central *militsiia* leadership reissued instructions regarding the work of the Brigades in October 1937. GARF, f. 9401, op. 12, d. 126, l. 79; GARF, f. 9401, op. 12, d. 135, l. 80.

103. NKVD investigators in the Turkmen republic simply fabricated case files as well, often relying on "staff witnesses" to provide testimony regarding individuals already under arrest or, more directly, calling "witnesses" who did not speak Russian and entering into case files whatever details they desired. GARF, f. 8131, op. 37, d. 145, ll. 56–58, 67.

104. E.g., see the NKVD report from the Ordzhonikidze Territory in Danilov, Manning, and Viola, *Tragediia sovetskoi derevni*, t. 5, 341–42, which refers to denunciations as evidence of peasant support for the repressions; GARF, f. 8131, op. 37, d. 145, ll. 25, 27, for a complaint from Mikhail Pankrat'ev, the USSR Procurator after June 1939, regarding troika decisions on the Dalstroi area that condemned dozens of individuals on the basis of a single denunciation; and ibid., ll. 68–70, for cases of mass denunciation under torture in the Turkmen republic. The extensive Procuracy report on the mass operations in the Turkmen republic, in ibid., ll. 46–84, suggests that denunciations from the public at large played little role in the mass operations in the area.

105. Local show trials in the fall of 1937 have been the subject of analysis by Sheila Fitzpatrick, Michael Ellman, and Roberta Manning. Both Ellman and Manning overestimate the extent to which these trials involved the rural population in the direct selection of targets for the mass operations. The regional show trials were intended to create support for the "campaign of vigilance" and, just as important, to ensure that the repressions taking place in the countryside did not disrupt the 1937 harvest and grain-procurement campaigns. Stalin's August 3 order calling for regional show trials says nothing about the mass operations, even though it was addressed to Communist Party secretaries at the regional, territorial, and republican levels—the same levels that received the orders to plan for and begin mass operations in the preceding weeks. All three orders instead call for a mobilization of popular support for campaigns to "tear out by the roots" wreckers from among state and party officials in agricultural institutions—elite categories that were not primarily targeted by the mass operations. Michael Ellman, "The Soviet 1937–1938 Provincial Show Trials Revisited," *Europe-Asia Studies* 55, no. 8 (2003): 1305–21, esp. 1310–12; Roberta Manning, "Politicheskii terror kak politicheskii teatr. Raionnye pokazatel'nye sudy 1937g. i massovye operatsii," in *Tragediia sovetskoi derevni*, ed. Danilov, Manning, and Viola, t. 5, 51–70; Sheila Fitzpatrick, "How the Mice Killed the Cat: Scenes from the Great Purges in the Russian Provinces," *Russian Review* 52, no. 3 (1993): 299–320. See also Danilov, Manning, and Viola, *Tragediia sovetskoi derevni*, t. 5, 394–517, for extensive documentation

on these show trials, none of which suggests any connection between the trials and mass operations under way at the same time.

106. Danilov, Manning, and Viola, *Tragediia sovetskoi derevni*, t. 5, kn. 1 (1937), 344.

107. Local NKVD administrations followed "peasant moods" regarding the repressions closely. E.g., reports from Western Siberia noted that collective farmers greeted the operations of removals of kulak elements positively and claimed that, in those areas where repression was accompanied with "mass-political explanatory work," farmers responded by increasing labor productivity and discipline. GANO, f. 4, op. 34, d. 4, l. 27. According to Jansen and Petrov, the mass operations met active resistance in only a handful of areas in the North Caucasus. Jansen and Petrov, *Stalin's Loyal Executioner*, 102.

108. Vladimir Nikolaevich Khaustov, "Razvitie sovetskikh organov gosudarstvennoi bezopasnosti: 1917–1953 gg.," *Cahiers du Monde russe* 42, nos. 2–4 (2001): 361–62. Stalin himself personally approved the arrests and execution of extensive lists of high-level Communist Party and state functionaries, including all in the Central Committee *nomenklatura* (those party officials appointed directly by the Central Committee); such cases were generally forwarded to military tribunals, judicial collegiums, or the NKVD Special Board rather than to local NKVD troikas. See also Jansen and Petrov, *Stalin's Loyal Executioner*, 72, 91–92.

109. Khaustov, Naumov, and Plotnikov, *Lubianka 1937–1938*, 400–1, 427, 649 n. 51.

110. RGANI f. 89, per. 73, d. 108, ll. 1–2; Khaustov, Naumov, and Plotnikov, *Lubianka 1937–1938*, 415–16; Binner and Junge, "Wie der Terror 'gross' wurde," 595.

111. Danilov, Manning, and Viola, *Tragediia sovetskoi derevni*, t. 5, 327. For examples of regional NKVD administrations in the Western Siberian Territory and the Ordzhonikidze Territory making substantial numbers of arrests before August 5, see Danilov, Manning, and Viola, *Tragediia sovetskoi derevni*, t. 5, 340–41.

112. By the beginning of October the West Siberian NKVD administration reported that 11,374 individuals had been sentenced under Order 00447, including 6,513 to execution, even though the quota of 5,000 executions remained in effect. The remaining 1,513 individuals were being held, according to the report, until the regional NKVD received approval for an increased quota, which occurred only in mid-October. Danilov, Manning, and Viola, *Tragediia sovetskoi derevni*, t. 5, 340, 377–78, 604 n. 63.

113. The Omsk territorial NKVD had sent in rather low estimates to the Politburo in early July but was given quotas of 1,000 Category I and 2,500 Category II arrests by Order 00447. The NKVD chief who had submitted the low estimates was removed by Ezhov in mid-July; his replacement was evidently more willing to comply. See Danilov, Manning, and Viola, *Tragediia sovetskoi derevni*, t. 5, 344, 604 n. 65; Khaustov, Naumov, and Plotnikov, *Lubianka 1937–1938*, 322, 325, 330; Binner and Junge, "Wie der Terror 'gross' wurde," 602; and Jansen and Petrov, *Stalin's Loyal Executioner*, 89.

114. Ezhov instructed local NKVD chiefs to seek his personal approval before sending any Category II sentences to camps or prisons, so that the central Gulag administration could rationally plan the distribution of prisoners. This demand was hardly illogical, given the level of chaos in the distribution and movement of penal populations in the early 1930s. Khaustov, Naumov, and Plotnikov, *Lubianka 1937–1938*, 277.

115. Ibid., 337–43.

116. For a particularly clear example, see the description of the mass operations by the NKVD chief of the Ordzhonikidze Territory in early August as a process of arresting "all formerly repressed kulaks and criminals," in Danilov, Manning, and Viola, *Tragediia sovetskoi derevni*, t. 5, 340.

117. These figures are computed from NKVD totals for each separate national operation. Petrov and Roginskii, "Pol'skaia operatsiia," 33.

118. Khaustov, Naumov, and Plotnikov, *Lubianka 1937–1938*, 299, 301–3.

119. See Khaustov, Naumov, and Plotnikov, *Lubianka 1937–1938*, 302. See also Nicolas Werth, "The Mechanism of a Mass Crime: The Great Terror in the Soviet Union, 1937–1938," in *The Specter of Genocide: Mass Murder in Historical Perspective*, ed. Robert Gellately and Ben Kiernan (Cambridge: Cambridge University Press, 2003), 231–37, for a summary in English of current research on the national operations.

120. On these deportations, see Morris, "Polish Terror," 758–60.

121. Francine Hirsch, *Empire of Nations: Ethnographic Knowledge and the Making of the Soviet Union* (Ithaca, N.Y.: Cornell University Press, 2005), 294.

122. Even in Moscow, the counterintelligence department of the NKVD, which was responsible for surveillance of foreigners and those suspected of spying and which carried out most arrests in 1937 and 1938, did not maintain accurate enough records of Polish émigrés to target them effectively and hence sought information from other NKVD departments, or from other Soviet institutions, in order to attempt to identify individuals with connections to foreign powers. See Morris, "Polish Terror," 760–61.

123. Khaustov, Naumov, and Plotnikov, *Lubianka 1937–1938*, 303–21.

124. Ibid., 366–68, 650–51 n. 56. The Kharbin region had been a destination for anti-Bolshevik forces during the Civil War and contained a substantial population of Russians in the 1920s and 1930s, making it a potential source of anti-Soviet conspiracies in the minds of NKVD officials. Svetlana V. Onegina, "The Resettlement of Soviet Citizens from Manchuria in 1935–36: A Research Note," *Europe-Asia Studies* 47, no. 6 (1995): 1043–50.

125. See Khaustov, Naumov, and Plotnikov, *Lubianka 1937–1938*, 325–26, 376, 464, 468–69; Jansen and Petrov, *Stalin's Loyal Executioner*, 96–97.

126. Khaustov, Naumov, and Plotnikov, *Lubianka 1937–1938*, 345–47. The Orenburg NKVD requested an increase of its original Category I quota of 1,500 to 3,500, which was approved by Stalin on August 28.

127. Ibid., 352–59.

128. Jansen and Petrov, *Stalin's Loyal Executioner*, 96.

129. Khaustov, Naumov, and Plotnikov, *Lubianka 1937–1938*, 649 n. 50.

130. Ibid., 323–24; emphasis in the original.

131. Ibid., 331–32.

132. Ibid., 404–14.

133. Mikhail Shreider identifies Gorbach as particularly aggressive in his approach to the mass operations and underscores Gorbach's personal ties to Ezhov and Frinovskii. Shreider, *NKVD iznutri*, 86–95.

134. Danilov, Manning, and Viola, *Tragediia sovetskoi derevni*, t. 5, 256–57.

135. For a full description of these organizations and NKVD actions against them in Western Siberia, see Danilov, Manning, and Viola, *Tragediia sovetskoi derevni*, t. 5, 596–97 n. 39.

136. For successive reports from Western Siberia, see Khaustov, Naumov, and Plotnikov, *Lubianka 1937–1938*, 361–62, 365–66, 381–82, 423–24, 427–28,454–66, 461–62, 653 n. 66; see also Danilov, Manning, and Viola, *Tragediia sovetskoi derevni*, t. 5, 377–81.

137. By October 5, the NKVD troika in Western Siberia had approved a total of 10,820 executions in both the "ROVS" and "anti-Soviet elements" operations, 9,525 of which had already taken place—nearly twice the quota of 4,960 provided in conjunction with Order 00447. GANO, f. 4, op. 34, d. 26, ll. 10–14; reprinted in Danilov, Manning, and Viola, *Tragediia sovetskoi derevni*, t. 5, 378–81.

138. Danilov, Manning, and Viola, *Tragediia sovetskoi derevni*, t. 5, 597 n. 40. The West Siberian Territory was divided into the Novosibirsk and Altai regions in September 1937, with individual ROVS and Order 00447 troikas for each. For the sake of readability, I will continue to refer to both regions collectively as "Western Siberia" for the remainder of the chapter, and I will report arrest and execution figures together for the two regions.

139. For a recent discussion of the total mortality associated with Stalin's terror, see Michael Ellman, "Soviet Repression Statistics: Some Comments," *Europe-Asia Studies* 54, no. 7 (2002): 1151–72.

140. Danilov, Manning, and Viola, *Tragediia sovetskoi derevni*, t. 5, 605 n. 73.

141. For NKVD orders regarding the elections, which instructed local police to ensure that no counterrevolutionary slogans, placards, or leaflets were distributed during the campaign, see GARF, f. 9401, op. 12, d. 135, doc. 152. At the October Central Committee Plenum, at least one regional Communist Party secretary, from the Archangel region, noted that he had requested an increase in his execution quota specifically in order to deal with counterrevolutionaries among special settlers in the area in preparation for the upcoming elections. Danilov, Manning, and Viola, *Tragediia sovetskoi derevni*, t. 5, 382–83. See also ibid., 519–26, for several examples from November 1937 of regional NKVD administrations reporting on the "danger" posed to the election campaign by "anti-Soviet elements."

142. At least one regional NKVD chief made explicit its assumption that the operations were to end in early December and that no repressions would be allowed after that point, requesting on November 20 an additional quota of 1,000 executions in advance of the approaching end of the operations. Khaustov, Naumov, and Plotnikov, *Lubianka 1937–1938*, 433. In sum, the Politburo approved 141,000 additional sentences, including 73,000 executions, in November and December. Danilov, Manning, and Viola, *Tragediia sovetskoi derevni*, t. 5, 605–6 n. 73.

143. Danilov, Manning, and Viola, *Tragediia sovetskoi derevni*, t. 5, 387–93. In addition, the categories of sentences most associated with the operations against "anti-Soviet elements" were concentrated in 1937: 234,301 individuals sentenced for counterrevolutionary agitation in 1937, 57,366 in 1938; 157,694 sentenced for "other" (mostly nonpolitical) crimes in 1937, and 45,183 in 1938. Petrov and Roginskii, "Pol'skaia operatsiia," 30; Khaustov, Naumov, and Plotnikov, *Lubianka 1937–1938*, 659–60 n. 79.

144. The initial signal for this change came in early December 1937, when the Politburo resolved that individuals not be fired from their jobs because members of their families had been arrested for counterrevolutionary crimes. The decision was issued as a Sovnarkom USSR resolution on January 10, 1938. RGASPI, f. 17, op. 3, d. 994, l. 56; GARF, f. 5446, op. 57, d. 53, l. 27. See Jansen and Petrov, *Stalin's Loyal*

Executioner, 124–30, for discussion of the plenum and of the halting of Communist Party purges in 1938.

145. According to Jansen and Petrov, Ezhov did note at the conference that these operations were by nature limited, arguing that NKVD troikas "should not exist outside of time and space" and that "someone has to be repressed, someone has to be shot; so the question is about quotas." Jansen and Petrov, *Stalin's Loyal Executioner*, 133.

146. Khaustov, Naumov, and Plotnikov, *Lubianka 1937–1938*, 467–68. The largest additional quotas pertained to Ukraine (6,000/1,000), the Far Eastern Territory (8,000/2,000), and Moscow (4,000/500).

147. Roughly 600,000 individuals had been arrested as of January 31, 1938. Okhotin and Roginskii, "Iz istorii 'nemetskoi operatsii,'" 60, 74 n. 32. At least two regional NKVD administrations that had been left off the list immediately requested additional quotas to deal with "anti-Soviet elements" that were already under arrest or surveillance, suggesting that local NKVD chiefs were still influencing the nature and duration of the campaigns in 1938. Khaustov, Naumov, and Plotnikov, *Lubianka 1937–1938*, 470–71.

148. Okhotin and Roginskii, "Iz istorii 'nemetskoi operatsii,'" 60. Jansen and Petrov draw the same conclusion; see *Stalin's Loyal Executioner*, 89, 132.

149. The circular complained that the regional procurator, furthermore, did not exercise any supervision over the process, generally signing the troika decisions after the fact without even reading them. GARF, f. 5446, op. 22a, d. 179, ll. 185–86. Such orders were difficult to enforce: as late as March 27, 1939, central Procuracy officials complained that the revision of sentences handed down by the Gor'kii police troika was stalled and had produced no fundamental results. GARF, f. 8131, op. 38, d. 37, ll. 1–2ob.

150. GARF, f. 5446, op. 22a, d. 179, ll. 169–70. See also ibid., ll. 158–59, for a complaint from Vyshinskii regarding the police troika in the Odessa region, which he claimed regularly sentenced individuals for crimes outside of its competence, including anti-Soviet agitation and speculation.

151. Solomon, *Soviet Criminal Justice under Stalin*, 252–56. As part of this attempt to reassert control over police investigations, Vyshinskii also reorganized the Procuracy at the regional and republican levels, creating a hierarchical system of special departments of the Procuracy in mid-May 1938 that was responsible for supervision of both the political police and the *militsiia* and that reported directly to the USSR Procuracy. GARF, f. 5446, op. 22a, d. 179, ll. 173–74. See also GARF, f. 8131, op. 37, d. 232, ll. 178–83, for a report from the procurator of the Saratov region detailing the difficulties faced by justice officials as they attempted to regain some amount of control over criminal prosecutions in the spring of 1938.

152. "Prikaz NKVD no. 00319 ot 21 maia 1938 g. c ob"iavleniem 'Instruktsii troikam NKVD po rassmotreniiu del ob ugolovnykh i deklassirovannykh elementakh i o zlostnykh narusheliakh polozheniia o pasportakh.'" GARF (location unknown); private communication from Aleksandr Malygin, Akademiia MVD RF.

153. GARF, f. 5446, op. 22a, d. 179, l. 46.

154. Khaustov, Naumov, and Plotnikov, *Lubianka 1937–1938*, 652 n. 62.

155. As of January 10, 10,150 individuals had been arrested under the auspices of the "German operation," out of an eventual total of 56,787. Okhotin and Roginskii, "Iz istorii 'nemetskoi operatsii,'" 63. Fewer than 45 percent of those repressed as Poles in 1937 and 1938 were arrested in 1937, fewer than 20 percent of those arrested as

"German elements"; the proportion was substantially less for the remaining ethnicities targeted by the national operations. Khaustov, Naumov, and Plotnikov, *Lubianka 1937–1938*, 659–60 n. 78. These statistics must be treated with care, because it was not customary for NKVD officials to record the ethnicities of those swept up in the national operations in 1937, but the overall trend is clear.

156. Khaustov, Naumov, and Plotnikov, *Lubianka 1937–1938*, 468–69, 654 n. 71.

157. Ibid., 657–58 n. 74.

158. Jansen and Petrov, *Stalin's Loyal Executioner*, 135–36.

159. See, in addition to the analyses by Okhotin and Roginskii, and Petrov and Roginskii, the description of the tactics used to fill quotas in the Ivanovo region in Shreider, *NKVD iznutri*, 71–72; and Werth, "Mechanisms of a Mass Crime," 236.

160. Khaustov, Naumov, and Plotnikov, *Lubianka 1937–1938*, 659 n. 78; Jansen and Petrov, *Stalin's Loyal Executioner*, 136. This deception, according to one commentator, came to light only because the regional NKVD administration criticized the actions of Frinovskii at the center regarding the albums, suggesting that such practices were likely more widespread. Okhotin and Roginskii, "Iz istorii 'nemetskoi operatsii,'" 71.

161. Khaustov, Naumov, and Plotnikov, *Lubianka 1937–1938*, 517, 538, 544–46.

162. For a full discussion of the inefficiencies of the album procedure in 1938, see Petrov and Roginskii, "Pol'skaia operatsiia," 159–62.

163. Albums in Moscow were sent back to localities for immediate consideration by the special troikas. For a copy of this order, see Khaustov, Naumov, and Plotnikov, *Lubianka 1937–1938*, 549. Special troikas were created at the republican and territorial levels, with the exception of Ukraine, Kazakhstan, and the Far Eastern Territory, where they were authorized in each region.

164. This intent was made clear days later, when Stalin authorized an exception for the NKVD in Belorussia, which had carried out a wave of arrests of "Polish elements" in August on the direct orders of Ezhov; Stalin authorized the special troika in Belorussia to sentence all individuals arrested before September 1, maintaining all other aspects of the order. Khaustov, Naumov, and Plotnikov, *Lubianka 1937–1938*, 550.

165. NKVD Operative Sectors had collected information on ethnicity, as a rule, only after May 1938. Petrov and Roginskii, "Pol'skaia operatsiia," 166–70.

166. The cases of 2,711 individuals were returned to police administrations for more investigation or for transfer to the court system, and 137 individuals were set free. Okhotin and Roginskii, "Iz istorii 'nemetskoi operatsii,'" 62.

167. Petrov and Roginskii, "Pol'skaia operatsiia," 31, 37–38; Okhotin and Roginskii, "Iz istorii 'nemetskoi operatsii,'" 62, 70–71. We unfortunately have no comparable figures for the other nationalities.

168. Petrov and Roginskii, "Pol'skaia operatsiia," 31.

169. E.g., in the Crimea, some 770 people were shot on November 28 and 29 under the explicit orders of the NKVD chief, who reportedly participated personally in the majority of these executions. Jansen and Petrov, *Stalin's Loyal Executioner*, 165. Likewise, NKVD officials in Smolensk continued to execute individuals in custody after the issuance of the November instructions but falsified their paperwork to hide their tardiness. Roberta Manning, "Massovaia operatsiia protiv 'kulakov i prestupnikh' elementov: Apogei Velikoi Chistki na Smolenshchine," in *Stalinizm v rossiiskoi provintsii: Smolenskie arkhivnye dokumenty v prochtenii zarubezhnykh i rossiiskikh istorikov*, ed. E. V. Kodin (Smolensk: N.p., 1999), 239–41. See GARF, f. 8131,

op. 37, d. 145, ll. 25, 27, for a similar complaints that the NKVD chief of Dalstroi added ninety-six cases to the protocol of a troika meeting, without the knowledge of the other members, in November 1938.

170. Jansen and Petrov, *Stalin's Loyal Executioner*, 146–52.

171. Khaustov, Naumov, and Plotnikov, *Lubianka 1937–1938*, 562; RGASPI, f. 17, op. 3, d. 1002, l. 37.

172. Khaustov, Naumov, and Plotnikov, *Lubianka 1937–1938*, 606.

173. The instructions, however, provided numerous exceptions to these rules, especially for NKVD administrations at the periphery. For the instructions in English, see Getty and Naumov, *Road to Terror*, 531–37.

174. Khaustov, Naumov, and Plotnikov, *Lubianka 1937–1938*, 612–17, 618–22. It should be noted that these instructions made no mention of the category of "socially dangerous elements," which had been part of the board's responsibility since its creation.

175. After helping to draft the resolution that ended the mass operations, which was approved by the Politburo on November 17, Ezhov was forced to resign as head of the NKVD; Beriia officially took his place on November 25. RGASPI, f. 17, op. 3, d. 1003, ll. 25, 34–35.

176. Okhotin and Roginskii, "Iz Istorii 'nemetskoi operatsii,'" 69; Petrov and Roginskii, "Pol'skaia operatsiia," 33. These figures correspond with those reported in a summary of police activity in the Stalin period created by the First Special Department of the MVD in 1953, which lists 1,101,433 cases sentenced by troikas, and 681,692 death sentences handed down in cases investigated by the political police (not necessarily by troikas) in 1937 and 1938. GARF, f. 9401, op. 1, d. 4157, l. 202; or A. I . Kokurin and N. V. Petrov, *GULAG (Glavnoe upravlenie lagerei), 1917–1960* (Moscow: Materik, 2000), 433. These figures do not, in my estimation, include the between 200,000 and 400,000 sentences meted out by the police troikas in 1937 and 1938. These statistics should be taken only as guidelines, and they do not include the crimes prosecuted by the *militsiia* and sentenced under the court system during these two years, which is probably in the range of 2 million, or roughly 200,000 individuals deported from border regions in 1937 and 1938 without troika hearings, or sentences of execution meted out in cases initiated by the Procuracy. The total number of executions carried out in 1937 and 1938 is likely in the range of 700,000. The slightly higher estimates for sentences and executions for the operations associated with Order 00447 come from the latest research of scholars at Memorial: Okhotin and Roginskii, " 'Bol'shoi terror,'" 1, 3–7.

177. The idea that Stalinist repression in 1937 and 1938 reversed several years of moderate policy initiatives is central to nearly two decades of "revisionist" explanations of the "Great Purges," which claim that the purges were a reaction by the regime to its own failure to gain control over local Communist Party and state officials in the period of the "Great Retreat." The programmatic version of this thesis was advanced by J. Arch Getty, *Origins of the Great Purges: The Soviet Communist Party Reconsidered, 1933–1938* (Cambridge: Cambridge University Press, 1985).

178. Social activism played a major role in most accounts of the "Great Terror" produced between the 1970s and 1990s, in part because the social historians that dominated the field intentionally focused on this topic. Scholars have returned to these questions in the last several years, building on the insights of earlier accounts in order to provide more complex interpretations of the genesis and nature of the Stalinist

terror in 1937 and 1938. The best examples include Cynthia V. Hooper, "Terror from Within: Participation and Coercion in Soviet Power, 1924–1964," PhD dissertation, Princeton University, 2003; and Wendy Goldman, *Terror and Democracy in the Age of Stalin: The Social Dynamics of Repression* (Cambridge: Cambridge University Press, 2007). Neither study, however, sustains an argument regarding the relationship between social activism and the mass operations, rather than the purges of the Communist Party or of industrial elites. For a recent survey of existing studies of the mass operations that concurs with the conclusion that popular participation played little or no role, see Barry McLoughlin, "Mass Operations of the NKVD, 1937–8: A Survey," in *Stalin's Terror: High Politics and Mass Repression in the Soviet Union*, ed. Barry McLoughlin and Kevin McDermott (Houndsmills, U.K.: Palgrave Macmillan, 2003), 118–52, esp. 143–44.

179. These arguments have been advanced most forcefully by J. Arch Getty, " 'Excesses Are Not Permitted' "; by Getty and Naumov, *Road to Terror*, and by Robert W. Thurston, *Life and Terror in Stalin's Russia, 1923–1941* (New Haven, Conn.: Yale University Press, 1996).

180. Jansen and Petrov, *Stalin's Loyal Executioner*, 133. See note 145 above.

Chapter 7

1. Excerpts from the first two points of Beriia's Instruction to local NKVD administrations, "On Methods for Carrying Out the Instruction of the Sovnarkom and the Central Committee of November 17, 1938," issued on November 26, 1938. V. N. Khaustov, V. P. Naumov, and N. S. Plotnikov, eds., *Lubianka: Stalin i Glavnoe upravlenie gosbezopasnosti NKVD, 1937–1938* (Moscow: Mezhdunarodnyi fond "Demokratiia," 2004) (hereafter Khaustov, Naumov, and Plotnikov, *Lubianka 1937–1938*), 613.

2. Complaint from the Assistant Procurator of the Uzbek Republic, Rybin, to Stalin, Molotov, and USSR Procurator Viktor Bochkov, dated November 25, 1940. GARF, f. 5446, op. 24a, d. 4, l. 25.

3. For the most programmatic statement of this thesis, see Peter H. Solomon Jr., *Soviet Criminal Justice under Stalin* (Cambridge: Cambridge University Press, 1996), 256–60.

4. E.g., see GARF, f. 8131, op. 15, d. 80, ll. 16–17, from the Crimea; and the numerous communications in GARF, f. 8131, op. 15, d. 80.

5. GARF, f. 9401, op. 12, d. 135, doc. 69; GARF, f. 5446, op. 22a, d. 179, ll. 60–61; GARF, f. 8131, op. 38, d. 35, ll. 12–13. Ezhov requested 11,000 additional policemen in late September 1937 to cope with these problems, including 3,000 to transport prisoners to and from courts, troikas, or places of confinement, and 4,000 to deal with the duties of local *militsiia* administrations in carrying out mass arrests. GARF, f. 5446, op. 20a, d. 965, ll. 5–13. As with Ezhov's earlier request for more officers (see chapter 6), the Sovnarkom rejected the proposal, ordering the NKVD to increase *militsiia* staff levels by filling the 12,273 vacant spaces (*nekomplekt*) within existing budgetary guidelines rather than requesting funding for additional officers. GARF, f. 5446, op. 20a, d. 965, l. 1.

6. GARF, f. 5446, op. 57, d. 49, ll. 75–76; GARF, f. 5446, op. 17, d. 327, l. 136; GARF, f. 5446, op. 57, d. 49, l. 116.

7. Khaustov, Naumov, and Plotnikov, *Lubianka 1937–1938*, 608. A 1939 investigation of the mass operations in the Turkmen Republic likewise concluded that neither the political police nor the *militsiia* possessed the capacity to target "anti-Soviet elements" using covert surveillance techniques. GARF, f. 8131, op. 37, d. 145, ll. 51–52.

8. GARF, f. 5446, op. 22a, d. 130, ll. 9–14, 15–20.

9. Ibid., l. 22; ibid., l. 3. Neither figure includes Industrial Militsiia officers under the control of the NKVD, which had shrunk to a negligible number by 1938; see ibid., ll. 4–4ob. Although reliable statistics on the political police are difficult to find, that institution likely expanded comparably in the era of the mass operations. According to budget figures from the USSR Sovnarkom, the GUGB employed 32,742 full-time officers in late 1936, including 7,930 at the center, 23,211 "operative employees," 1,334 members of the *militsiia* officer staff, and 267 local commanders of fire departments and registration departments (ZAGS). GARF, f. 5446, op. 17, d. 326, ll. 2–3.

10. Vladimir Nikolaevich Khaustov, "Deiatel'nost' organov gosudarstvennoi bezopasnosti NKVD SSSR (1934–1941 gg.)," doktorskaia dissertatsiia, Akademiia FSB RF, Moscow, 1997, 124. This plan was based on instructions first given to Ezhov at the January–February 1937 Central Committee Plenum; the delay was caused by Stalin's decision that mass operations were to take precedence over NKVD reform.

11. Ibid.; GARF, f. 9401, op. 12, d. 126, l. 104.

12. Khaustov, "Deiatel'nost' organov gosudarstvennoi bezopasnosti," 125.

13. Khaustov, Naumov, and Plotnikov, *Lubianka 1937–1938*, 607–11.

14. Ibid., 613. For a full discussion of the influence of the November 1938 orders on the Soviet judicial system, see Solomon, *Soviet Criminal Justice under Stalin*, 256–66; and Gabor T. Rittersporn, "Extra-Judicial Repression and the Courts: Their Relationship in the 1930s," in *Reforming Justice in Russia, 1864–1996*, ed. Peter H. Solomon Jr. (Armonk, N.Y.: M. E. Sharpe, 1997).

15. Khaustov, Naumov, and Plotnikov, *Lubianka 1937–1938*, 663 n. 91; Marc Jansen and Nikita Petrov, *Stalin's Loyal Executioner: People's Commissar Nikolai Ezhov, 1895–1940* (Stanford, Calif.: Hoover Institution Press, 2002), 192.

16. TsAODM, f 3, op. 50, d. 75, ll. 82–84, 89–92.

17. Khaustov, Naumov, and Plotnikov, *Lubianka 1937–1938*, 663–64 n. 92. For more on the relationship between the Party and the NKVD during the mass operations, see Khaustov, "Razvitie sovetskikh organov gosudarstvennoi bezopasnosti," 360–63.

18. E.g., see Khaustov, Naumov, and Plotnikov, *Lubianka 1937–1938*, 625–28, 630, 664 n. 95.

19. This view is shared by Jansen and Petrov, *Stalin's Loyal Executioner*, 165–66.

20. Vyshinskii outlined these procedures in a communication to local procurators in January 1939, stressing that cases about which procurators and NKVD chiefs disagreed were to be forwarded to his office directly. GARF, f. 8131, op. 38, d. 36, l. 3. NKVD chiefs were instructed as well in mid-January 1939 to consider protests forwarded to them by the Procuracy and to send notice to the NKVD center in Moscow regarding cases they agreed were unfounded. GARF, f. 8131, op. 38, d. 41, l. 2. In October, the procurators were allowed to petition for reduced sentences as well as complete amnesty, but the responsibility for the ultimate decision was shifted from regional NKVD chiefs to the Special Board in Moscow. GARF, f. 8131, op. 38, d. 39,

ll. 4–4ob. These procedures, unmistakably ad hoc when compared with the work of previous one-time and standing amnesty commissions, could have resulted only in a handful of reversals or reductions of troika sentences.

21. For examples of high-level police chiefs making positive determinations in 1939 regarding protests filed by the Procuracy in cases of harmful elements, see GARF, f. 7523, op. 65, d. 562, l. 28; and GARF, f. 7523, op. 65, d. 563, l. 40.

22. E.g., see GARF, f. 8131, op. 38, d. 37, ll. 1–2ob, 58–62; and ibid., ll. 40–41.

23. GARF, f. A-461, op. 8s, d. 25, ll. 30–37.

24. GARF, f. 8131, op. 37, d. 149, ll. 112–13ob. See also GARF, f. 7523, op. 65, d. 575, ll. 96–103, for an example of what must have been an common occurrence: because protests were forwarded to the NKVD rather than justice organizations for consideration, local NKVD officials responded by harassing or arresting the individuals submitting protests.

25. For a discussion of a futile attempt by several high-ranking Procuracy officials to restrict Beriia's expanding political influence by appealing to Andrei Zhdanov to replace Pankrat'ev with a more vigorous advocate for the judicial system, see Solomon, *Soviet Criminal Justice under Stalin*, 263–64.

26. The military procurator of the Moscow Military District in June 1940 complained to the USSR Procuracy that the NKVD Special Board had at some point in mid-March 1940 simply halted all consideration of protests of troika decisions, declining to approve even a single protest in the preceding three months. GARF, f. 8131, op. 37, d. 242, ll. 1–5.

27. GARF, f. 5446, op. 24a, d. 158, ll. 29–31.

28. According to Solomon, reversals of troika convictions in 1939 and 1940 likely numbered "no more than a few thousand." Solomon, *Soviet Criminal Justice under Stalin*, 259.

29. See GARF, f. 8131, op. 38, d. 36, for numerous Procuracy circulars complaining about the inability of local justice officials to meet the requirements of the November 17, 1938, instructions regarding the supervision of cases. For a discussion of the impact of Stalinist terror on Soviet judicial administrations, see Solomon, *Soviet Criminal Justice under Stalin*, 244–52.

30. GARF, f. 9401, op. 12, d. 137, ll. 175–76. In mid-August, the center completely reorganized the existing system of address bureaus and registration card catalogs, centralizing all existing organizations into 413 central address bureaus, which took over all registrations systems and card catalogs associated with the passport system. GARF, f. 9401, op. 12, d. 137, ll. 179–86.

31. This complaint comes from a late-August NKVD circular that provided examples of deficient investigative work in the Azov-Black Sea region in the initial weeks of the mass operations, including poor use of the passport system. GARF, f. 9401, op. 12, d. 135, doc. 76.

32. The police began to include photographs in all new passports issued after late October and to glue photographs into already existing passports; the process was to be completed in regime areas by January 1, 1939, and in all other areas by the beginning of 1940. RGASPI, f. 17, op. 3, d. 992, ll. 83, 160; GARF, f. 9401, op. 12, d. 137, ll. 306–6ob; GARF, f. 9401, op. 12, d. 135, doc. 88. Note that this change did not apply to border zones, where passports already contained photographs.

33. Khaustov, Naumov, and Plotnikov, *Lubianka 1937–1938*, 651–52 n. 61; GARF, f. 9401, op. 12, d. 233, l. 502. See also Francine Hirsch, *Empire of Nations: Ethnographic*

Knowledge and the Making of the Soviet Union (Ithaca, N.Y.: Cornell University Press, 2005), 293–97.

34. GARF, f. 9401, op. 12, d. 137, ll. 304–4ob. These instructions also mandated that local police, when processing applications for residence in regime cities, were to ignore the provisions of Article 55 of the Russian Soviet Federated Socialist Republic (RSFSR) Criminal Code, or corresponding codes of other republics, which stipulated that individuals who were sentenced for minor infractions but remained free of sentences for a period of three or six years, depending on the original infraction, were no longer considered "ex-convicts." For further restrictions on ex-convicts in regime areas in August and September 1937, see GARF, f. 9401, op. 12, d. 137, ll. 177–78, 193. Taken together, these changes represent a complete reversal of Vyshinskii's qualified triumph over Iagoda regarding the restrictiveness of the passport system in 1936 (see chapter 5).

35. For successive instructions on passports in mid-1938, see GARF, f. 9401, op. 12, d. 233, ll. 436–38, 473, 475–76, 478–78ob, 479–79ob.

36. To improve the system, the center ordered local police to focus on potential criminals in the registration process and, more fundamentally, to send information to the bureaus regarding any unknown individual moving to any area, even in rural districts not covered by the passport system. This order, for the first time, expanded the reach of the nationwide criminal registration system to rural areas of the USSR; it was intended to prevent criminal populations from fleeing to rural areas to escape central information surveillance systems. GARF, f. 9401, op. 12, d. 233, ll. 459–59ob.

37. GARF, f. 9401, op. 12, d. 233, ll. 394–94ob, 430.

38. For complaints from the center regarding the inability of local police to use the passport system as a means of covert surveillance in 1939 and 1940, see GARF, f. 9401, op. 12, d. 233, ll. 205–5ob, 243–43ob, 323–23ob, 325–25ob, 400–400ob, 415–16.

39. Regular regime locations were open to individuals convicted of speculation, hooliganism, and a handful of other prevalent petty-order crimes (Articles 73, 74, 107, 162, and 169 of the Criminal Code), but all other restrictions remained in place. The requirement that individuals migrate to regime areas only after receiving official invitations to employment was also abolished for second-level regime cities, eliminating a troublesome bureaucratic practice that was generally observed in the breach anyway. GARF, f. 9401, op. 12, d. 233, ll. 472–72ob. The elimination of required invitations for regular regime locations underscores the extent to which the passport system was not intended, nor did it function, as a way to keep peasants on collective farms in the 1930s.

40. GARF, f. 5446, op. 24a, d. 32, ll. 44–46.

41. GARF, f. 9401, op. 12, d. 233, l. 381. See also GARF, f. 5446, op. 24a, d. 953, ll. 76–79, for a similar request, declined by Vyshinskii among others, regarding the Aleksandrovskii district in Ivanovskaia region, which was located just outside of the 100-kilometer zone surrounding Moscow and hence was the location of substantial migration of exiles, many of whom actually worked within the zone.

42. An exception was maintained for individuals who could prove that immediate family members lived in the regime area in question, with whom they had lived before arrest. GARF, f. 9401, op. 12, d. 233, l. 424. This general change of policy toward convict and ex-convict populations is consistent with the abolishment by the NKVD in June 1939 of the practice of granting early release from labor camps for good behavior; henceforth, good work behavior was rewarded with additional food rations and

other incentives, whereas refusal to work was grounds for additional punishment, including execution. GARF, f. 7523, op. 65, d. 301, ll. 1–2.

43. Because the Criminal Code allowed for incarceration only in cases where a violator possessed no passport, most violations in regime locales were punishable only by a fine or, on the second offense, by six months of compulsory labor at one's place of employment (*prinudrabota*). The majority of cases heard in the post-1938 period by the courts pertained to precisely this category of individuals; e.g., for the three months of July to September 1939, police in the city of Moscow arrested 15,419 individuals for passport violations, of whom 14,799 had valid nonregime passports. GARF, f. 5446, op. 24a, d. 186, l. 6.

44. Ibid., l. 3.

45. Ibid., l. 9; GARF, f. 9401, op. 12, d. 233, ll. 262–62ob.

46. It should be remembered that the application of Article 35 entailed lifetime banishment from all regime areas, even after an individual served out his or her sentence for the crime, because Article 35 was one of the articles of the criminal code that was included in the regime restrictions.

47. GARF, f. 9401, op. 12, d. 233, l. 313.

48. Regime I locations included Moscow and the Moscow region; Leningrad and the surrounding 100-kilometer zone; Kiev and the surrounding 50-kilometer zone; Baku, Belostok, Grodno, L'vov, Sevastopol, and the Sevastopol military district; Murmansk, Sochi, and its district; Gagri and the Mineral'naia Voda health resorts; plus districts along the USSR border and several other "forbidden" military zones. GARF, f. 9401, op. 12, d. 233, ll. 217ob–218.

49. Ibid., l. 218ob. Regime II locations were off limits to all individuals who had convictions for all political crimes (Article 58 of the RSFSR Criminal Code), the August 7, 1932, law on theft, banditry (59-3), repeat hooliganism (74), speculation (107), murder (136), robbery (165 parts II and III), brigandage (167), or espionage (193–24).

50. GARF, f. 9401, op. 12, d. 233, l. 219. Little disagreement emerged between NKVD and justice officials regarding these changes, suggesting that the overall nature of the passport system was, by late in the decade, no longer a point of contention. For materials exchanged between Vyshinskii and Beriia in the process of working up the new passport instructions, see GARF, f. 5446, op. 24a, d. 32, ll. 1–73, esp. 21–46.

51. GARF, f. 9401, op. 12, d. 233, ll. 264–65, 300–300ob.

52. Ibid., ll. 202–2ob, 296–96ob.

53. The passports issued to these children received the standard notation prohibiting the bearer from residing in a regime area. For the Sovnarkom version of this order, see GARF, f. 5446, op. 57, d. 56, l. 70; or S. S. Vilenskii, A. I. Kokurin, G. V. Atmashkina, and I. Iu. Novichenko, eds., *Deti GULAGa, 1918–1956* (Moscow: Mezhdunarodnyi fond "Demokratiia," 2002), 308. See also GARF, f. 7523, op. 65, d. 303, for examples of this policy in practice in 1939 and 1940.

54. GARF, f. 5446, op. 23a, d. 288, l. 1; GARF, f. 9401, op. 12, d. 233, l. 431.

55. GARF, f. 5446, op. 23a, d. 288, ll. 3–7. For the January 1940 NKVD circular acquiescing to Pankrat'ev's criticism, see GARF, f. 9401, op. 12, d. 233, l. 330.

56. See Amir Weiner, *Making Sense of War: The Second World War and the Fate of the Bolshevik Revolution* (Princeton, N.J.: Princeton University Press, 2001), 147, for the number of passports issued to children of special settlers in the prewar period. Weiner's stress on possible redemption of children of special settlers is, in this instance,

highly misplaced, especially in comparison with peasant populations in general, which were accorded new freedoms by the 1940 passport reforms to migrate temporarily, even to regime cities, in search of work. For an account that stresses the impossibility of redemption for settlers in the post-1938 era, see Lynn Viola, *The Unknown Gulag: The Lost World of Stalin's Special Settlements* (Oxford: Oxford University Press, 2007), 167–81.

57. GARF, f. 7523, op. 65, d. 310, ll. 10–20, esp. 10–11. See also GARF, f. 7532, op. 65, d. 303, l. 2, for a March 1939 letter from Soviet officials in the Chkalovskii region regarding former wives of dekulakized male peasants, who were claiming in increasing numbers in the post-1938 period the right to move away from special settlements because they had divorced their husbands and remarried individuals who had not been dekulakized.

58. GARF, f. 7523, op. 65, d. 165, ll. 1–5; or GARF, f. 5446, op. 24a, d. 165, ll. 1–5.

59. GARF, f. 5446, op. 24a, d. 954, ll. 96–96ob.

60. Ibid., ll. 93–95, 97.

61. GARF, f. 9401, op. 12, d. 233, l. 7.

62. GARF, f. 5446, op. 24a, d. 4, l. 25.

63. Ibid., ll. 26–27.

64. Khaustov, Naumov, and Plotnikov, *Lubianka 1937–1938*, 425.

65. GARF, f. 9401, op. 12, d. 135, doc. 158. See also GARF, f. 9401, op. 12, d. 135, doc. 159, for similar instructions to local police regarding "wrecking" in bread production.

66. GARF, f. 5446, op. 57, d. 53, l. 199.

67. E.g., an investigation of select cases of individuals charged with Articles 107 and 105 in the first quarter of 1938 in Moscow found that, of 186 individuals sentenced for these crimes, 72 were workers and 56 were white-collar employees; only a handful were individual farmers or "declassed elements," the categories of people that, according to the general criminological outlook of central police officials, were responsible for most cases of speculation. GARF, f. 8131, op. 15, d. 89, l. 29.

68. In the first nine months of 1937, police across the USSR formally arrested and sent to court, or sent to their own troikas, only 17 percent of the people that were taken into custody for speculation; the rest were fined, banished, or simply released with a warning to leave the city in question. GARF, f. 9401, op. 12, d. 135, doc. 158. See also GARF, f. 8131, op. 15, d. 89, ll. 23–24; GARF, f. 5446, op. 57, d. 53, l. 199; and GARF, f. 9401, op. 12, d.135, doc. 161.

69. GARF, f. 5446, op. 22a, d. 179, ll. 95–96; GARF, f. 8131, op. 15, d. 89, ll. 52a–52l.

70. E.g., the police in Moscow sent 365 individuals to the court system for speculation between September and November 1938, 92 percent of whom were convicted; more than half those convicted received sentences of five years or more. GARF, f. 8131, op. 15, d. 89, ll. 146a–46e. For a mid-October 1938 censure of the Moscow Communist Party leadership by the Politburo for shortages of staple food items, which resulted in the removal of several district-level party secretaries, see RGASPI, f. 17, op. 3, d. 1002, l. 45. See also Julie Hessler, *A Social History of Soviet Trade: Trade Policy, Retail Practices, and Consumption, 1917–1953* (Princeton, N. J.: Princeton University Press, 2004), 235–43.

71. GARF, f. 5446, op. 23a, d. 1450, ll. 1, 13, 18–19.

72. Ibid., ll. 28–31, 60–64.

73. GARF, f. 5446, op. 57, d. 58, ll. 92–94. This Sovnarkom order, which was promoted most aggressively by Beriia, was issued after only three or four days of debate at the Politburo level. During the drafting process, Molotov expressed discomfort at Beriia's suggestion for show trials, crossing out this part of the draft in his working copy. The rather harsh suggestion that disruptive line-standers be charged with hooliganism was also added late in the drafting process, most likely on Stalin's initiative, because neither Molotov nor Beriia included it in his draft. GARF, f. 5446, op. 23a, d. 1450, ll. 19, 72–77.

74. See GARF, f. 5446, op. 23a, d. 1450 for numerous reports on the implementation of the new decrees. These examples taken from ll. 41–43, 49–51.

75. GARF, f. 5446, op. 57, d. 58, l. 140.

76. GARF, f. 5446, op. 23a, d. 1450, ll. 38–40.

77. GARF, f. 8131, op. 38, d. 37, l. 32; GARF, f. 5446, op. 23a, d. 1450, ll. 41–43.

78. E.g., see GARF, f. 8131, op. 37, d. 165, ll. 55–62.

79. GARF, f. 8131, op. 37, d. 145, l. 231.

80. The Soviet Control Commission also complained that the police limited their response to preventing the formation of lines instead of restricting access to Moscow and Leningrad. GARF, f. 5446, op. 24a, d. 2833, ll. 13–15.

81. Ibid., ll. 6–7.

82. On the regime's response to the 1939–40 crisis, see Elena Osokina, *Za fasadom "stalinskogo izobiliia": Raspredelenie i rynok v snabzhenii naseleniia v gody industrializatsii, 1927–1941* (Moscow: ROSSPEN, 1999), 206–18.

83. GARF, f. 8131, op. 38, d. 42, ll. 9–11.

84. Beriia noted, in addition, that Moscow police arrested and sent to court only 23 of these 5,355 individuals but fined 2,478 of them—another clear indication of the propensity of local police to avoid the court system after 1938, as well as a reminder of the fact that records of individuals arrested, much less those sentenced, represent a tiny fraction of people subject to police action throughout the 1930s. GARF, f. 5446, op. 24a, d. 2835, ll. 13–15. In the January 1940 report cited above, Liubimov suggested that the order on lines be expanded from Moscow and Leningrad to include a dozen other major cities. Mikoian agreed, adding two more cities to the draft in his own hand. GARF, f. 5446, op. 24a, d. 2833, ll. 6–7.

85. For numerous examples of localities requesting that they be added to the list of cities falling under the January 1940 speculation rules, see GARF, f. 5446, op. 24a, d. 2833. Areas that requested the right to deal with speculation in this manner but were refused included Ulan-Ude, Kovrov, Vladimir, Kineshma, Vychuga, and the Ivanovo region.

86. GARF, f. 9415, op. 5, d. 87, ll. 73–75.

87. Ibid., ll. 41–42.

88. The order, which contained general instructions to the Procuracy and Justice systems to increase judicial pressure on speculators as well, was issued by none other than Vyshinskii, and it applied both to speculation and violation of rules of trade (Articles 107 and 105). GARF, f. 5446, op. 24a, d. 167, ll. 1–2.

89. GARF, f. 9415, op. 5, d. 89, ll. 17–17ob.

90. The NKVD Special Board sentenced 45,768 individuals in 1938 and 13,021 in 1939; but in 1940, that number climbed again, to 42,912. It is likely that at least some

portion of these sentences were meted out to speculators and other nonpolitical offenders. The 1953 MVD report from which these figures are taken identifies the sentences meted out by the Special Board in 1939 and 1940 as pertaining to "counterrevolutionary" crimes, but this identification is inconsistent with the demonstrated activity of the Special Board in these years. It is also inconsistent with the information, provided in the report, that 29,534 individuals were sentenced to between three and five years for these crimes in 1939, and 43,684 in 1940; it is highly unlikely that the Special Board would have sentenced individuals to less than five years for any sections of Article 58, even after November 1938.

91. Numerous NKVD reports claim that local police administrations, especially speculation departments, continued to fail to control the "channels" of organized speculation to the extent desired by the center in 1939 and 1940. E.g., see the reports in GARF, f. 9415, op. 5, d. 87, esp. ll. 3, 7–14, 19–20, 22, 39–40, 43–46.

92. GARF, f. 5446, op. 24a, d. 2883, ll. 24–27a.

93. Local police chiefs understood this practice as "proper" administration and tended to stay within these limits, which were technically illegal but accepted by all involved parties; see TsGAMO, f. 792, op. 6, d. 981, l. 2.

94. E.g., in Moscow in 1934, the police levied an average of 250 fines a day for hooliganism, second only to 1,000 fines levied daily for traffic violations. Ibid., ll. 1–2.

95. In areas where the commissions existed in the middle and late 1930s, they usually met only to approve the fines handed down by local police chiefs after the fact. E.g., see TsGAMO, f. 792, op. 6, d. 980, l. 36; and GARF, f. 7511, op. 1, d. 225, ll. 17, 75.

96. An investigation in Moscow in late 1937 found that police routinely handed out fines for crimes like malicious hooliganism, even when committed by individuals with several past sentences for hooliganism or theft—a combination of past offenses that often resulted in sentencing to execution by an NKVD troika in 1937. Procuracy officials charged that such practices were widespread in all areas of the Russian Republic. GARF, f. 8131, op. 15, d. 47, ll. 1–13. For NKVD orders dated September 25, 1937, demanding that local police issue administrative fines according to existing legislation and to avoid arresting individuals for offenses punishable only by fines, see GARF, f. 9401, op. 12, d. 135, doc. 145.

97. The report estimated that police in Moscow, with 3.8 million residents, issued administrative fines to 10 percent of the adult population (231,552 individuals) in 1937 and to 14 percent of the adult population (312,741 individuals) in 1938, with proportions up to 20 percent noted in areas on the periphery of the city. Such figures did not include those fines levied "on the spot" (na meste), a procedure used mostly for traffic violations; the Moscow police issued such fines to more than 1.6 million individuals in 1937 and 1938. GARF, f. 7523, op. 65, d. 401, ll. 1–9.

98. See GARF, f. 7511, op. 1, d. 227, l. 2, for instructions to local Soviet Control Commission (KSK) organizations regarding these investigations; see GARF, f. 7511, op. 1, d. 227, ll. 13–18, for a KSK report on fines in the Novosibirsk region; see GARF, f. 7511, op. 1, d. 227, ll. 59–78, for a similar report on the Sverdlovsk region; and see GARF, f. 7511, op. 1, d. 227, ll. 118–24, for a compilation of results from several such investigations, all dated late April and early May 1939.

99. The idea of transferring fines to the court system was broached as early as April 1938, as Ezhov began his attempts to restructure the NKVD and rein in the operations against criminal elements; GARF, f. 5446, op. 22a, d. 38, l. 122. The Supreme Soviet report to Kalinin, cited above, recommended that adjudication of fines be

transferred to comrades courts or to trade union organizations for measures of "social" influence; GARF, f. 7523, op. 65, d. 401, l. 9. For discussions of the burdens that hearing only a portion of cases regarding fines, those involving nonpayment, placed on the court system in 1941, see GARF, f. 8131, op. 37, d. 544, ll. 149–55; and GARF, f. 5446, op. 25a, d. 7338, ll. 1–7.

100. N. A. Semashko, in a letter addressed to the Soviet Central Executive Committee in January 1937, requested that the Politburo create a commission, modeled on Kalinin's 1935 commission, to address the issue of delinquency; in mid-February 1937, he reported that the number of homeless children migrating to Moscow from the surrounding region had increased in the previous months and that the overall levels of homelessness had climbed again to levels characteristic of 1935. GARF, f. 1235, op. 141, d. 2032, ll. 1–6; GARF, f. 5207, op. 3, d. 37, ll. 52–52ob.

101. In March 1937, Ezhov sent an indignant request to Molotov for additional funding for juvenile labor colonies, estimating that the entire colony system had space for a maximum of 35,844 children but currently housed 37,913. Anything less than 50,000 spaces, he argued, would make it impossible for the NKVD to deal with the new influx of children swept off the streets as homeless or sentenced to colonies as lawbreakers during police actions in 1937. In addition, he asked for an immediate extension of 3.3 million rubles for the complete restructuring of the Tomskii juvenile labor colony, which currently held 6,000 juvenile offenders under inadequate conditions and with no program of work or rehabilitation; he complained that these children lived in extremely overcrowded conditions, slept two to a bed, and were employed in no useful activities. GARF, f. 5446, op. 20a, d. 944, ll. 99–100.

102. See the report on homelessness and delinquency in the post–May 1935 period, complied in November 1937 by the NKVD Department of Labor Colonies, in GARF, f. 1235, op. 141, d. 2032, ll. 9–30, 39–41, esp. 26–30; and GARF, f. 5207, op. 3, d. 42, ll. 2–3.

103. The regime generally did not send juveniles to labor camps along with their repressed parents. See Corinna Kuhr, "Children of "Enemies of the People" as Victims of the Great Purges," *Cahiers du Monde russe* 39, nos. 1–2 (1998): 209–20. For specific orders to the effect that children of repressed parents were to be sent, as a rule, to orphanages maintained by the Education Commissariat, see GARF, f. 5446, op. 57, d. 52, ll. 27–27ob; GARF, f. 5446, op. 22a, d. 178, l. 17; and GARF, f. 5446, op. 17, d. 328, l. 66.

104. Complaints from top justice and child welfare officials, especially Semashko and Kalinin, in late 1937 regarding the horrific conditions of overcrowding, hunger, boredom and escapes in orphanages and the NKVD's juvenile labor colony system led to the formation of a commission under the auspices of the Russian Central Executive Committee to address the problem. Kalinin was harshly critical of suggestions presented by the NKVD to expand the juvenile labor colony system, arguing that juvenile colonies, which he called "naked prisons," would produce only recidivist adult criminals. Ultimately the commission produced an instruction, issued by the Central Executive Committee in early February 1938, which ordered welfare agencies to accept children from police institutions but also approved the creation of additional NKVD colonies for "particularly socially neglected juvenile lawbreakers [and] disorganizers, who require a longer period of rehabilitation." See GARF, f. 1235, op. 141, d. 2032. ll. 31–32, 33, 35, 36–38, 39–41, 42–46, 47–52, 53–54; the final Instruction is found on ll. 55–57.

105. In 1939, the police apprehended 33,219 juveniles under the age of sixteen years for criminal offenses, of whom 29,234 were sent to court and 24,975 were eventually sentenced; many, perhaps up to 50 percent, would have been sentenced to probation. The most prevalent crimes among those detained were theft (22,090, or almost exactly two-thirds, including both simple and qualified theft), hooliganism (2,697 individuals), and banditry (2,205). Neither of the latter two crimes was listed in the 1935 instruction on juvenile homeless and delinquency and hence technically were not grounds for judicial sentencing, but police routinely arrested juveniles for such offenses anyway, usually maintaining that such crimes were committed in conjunction with actions listed in the instructions (e.g., hooliganism, if it also entailed "causing bodily injury"). The trend continued into the first half of 1940, when the courts sentenced 11,584 juveniles under the age of sixteen, 4,454 to deprivation of freedom. GARF, f. 8131, op. 37, d. 533, ll. 209–12. Another set of statistics shows 24,700 children under sixteen appearing in courts in 1938, 33,000 in 1939. J. Arch Getty, Gabor T. Rittersporn, and Viktor Zemskov, "Victims of the Soviet Penal System in the Pre-War Years: A First Approach on the Basis of Archival Evidence," *American Historical Review* 98, no. 4 (1993): 1017–49, esp. 1027.

106. According to the report, 40 percent of the cases of hooliganism in Moscow between August and October 1939 were committed by individuals, mostly men, under the age of twenty-five years, almost half by youth under twenty; 68 percent of armed robberies by individuals under twenty-five, well over half by youth under twenty; and 52 percent of reported thefts by individuals under twenty-five, with more than three-quarters committed by youths under twenty and more than a third by juveniles below the age of sixteen. GARF, f. 8131, op. 37, d. 533, ll. 230–58.

107. See, in addition to the Moscow-level and USSR-level police reports cited above, the report from the Leningrad Procuracy to the city Communist Party Committee regarding widespread instances of rape committed in Leningrad by groups of youth, in GARF, f. 8131, op. 37, d. 240, l. 26–31. See also GARF, f. 8131, op. 37, d. 533, ll. 65–70.

108. The report was prepared by the city's *militsiia* and Detective Department chiefs and delivered to Pankrat'ev in November 1939. Note that, on the cover letter to the report, Pankrat'ev wrote in his own hand a note dated December 12, 1939, to T. Tadevosian, the USSR procurator for juvenile affairs, instructing him to use the material in the report in the process of working up "a [or the] letter to the [C]entral [C]ommittee regarding crime among juveniles." GARF, f. 8131, op. 37, d. 533, l. 230.

109. A police report covering the USSR as a whole, compiled by the USSR-level Detective Department in December 1939, reiterated both the analysis and the suggestions of the Moscow report, recommending in addition that the 1935 instruction on delinquency and homelessness be expanded to subject juveniles below the age of sixteen years to criminal responsibility for the crimes of swindling, arson and hooliganism. GARF, f. 8131, op. 37, d. 533, ll. 171–80. See also GARF, f. 8131, op. 37, d. 533, ll. 219–29, and RGASPI, f. 17, op. 21, d. 3074, ll. 60–61, for similar examples. These suggestions were reiterated in a letter from Beriia and Pankrat'ev to Stalin and Molotov, sent on February 28, 1940, which outlined ongoing difficulties with juvenile delinquency and suggested that welfare and educational agencies be forced to confront the problem more aggressively but pointedly omitted any reference to expanded police or judicial actions against juvenile delinquents. Vilenskii et al., *Deti GULAGa*, 327–31.

110. Specific discussion of the need to raise judicial penalties for theft, related to ongoing campaigns against speculation and shortage in the consumer goods sector, were ongoing in 1940 as well. In late July 1940, Pankrat'ev recommended to the Sovnarkom that simple theft be punished with two years in prison, qualified theft with five years, and theft of state property with eight years. Pankrat'ev was opposed by Goliakov, chairman of the USSR Supreme Court, who argued that first-time offenders be limited to one-year sentences and that the maximum penalty for organized theft of state property not exceed five years. GARF, f. 5446, op. 24a, d. 158, ll. 79–84. For a complaint from the Moscow city Party Committee that hooliganism and theft were among the most important areas of activity that demanded additional attention from police, courts, and Procuracy officials in late February 1940, see GARF, f. 5446, op. 24a, d. 226, ll. 1–4, esp. 2.

111. Donald Filtzer, *Soviet Workers and Late Stalinism: Labour and the Restoration of the Stalinist System after World War II* (Cambridge: Cambridge University Press, 2002), 160–61.

112. For a full account of the judicial aspects of the campaign against labor infractions, see Solomon, *Soviet Criminal Justice under Stalin*, 299–328. See also GARF, f. 8131, op. 37, d. 348, ll. 147–49, for a Procuracy report, which was compiled just before the August 10 edict was issued, on hooliganistic responses to the June edict on labor infractions. The inclusion of hooliganism in public places in the August 10 edict was broached at the July Central Committee Plenum by Vyshinskii, but the idea was hardly Vyshinskii's own, because numerous commentators from the Procuracy and NKVD had recommended increasing judicial repression against hooligans in the preceding months.

113. This campaign involved some of the most drastic shortcuts in legal procedure in the post-1938 period. In the case of hooliganism, the police were authorized to forward short protocols directly to the courts, listing only basic information about the case; the courts were instructed to hear cases within forty-eight hours of the delivery of these police protocols. Likewise, cases of petty theft in which the offenders were "caught red-handed" (*zaderzhan s polichnym*) were formulated as protocols by the police or factory guards and sent directly to People's Courts, where they were to be heard in less than forty-eight hours. Only in cases that were serious enough to warrant punishment above the standard one year in prison was prosecutorial sanction necessary. Furthermore, sentences were to be carried out immediately after the court decision, regardless of the state of a prisoner's appeal. Solomon, *Soviet Criminal Justice under Stalin*, 328; GARF, f. A-461, op. 8s, d. 73, l. 3. This sentencing procedure was not technically "extrajudicial," yet for those sentenced under the auspices of the August edict, the distinction was academic.

114. Exactly 2,051 of these cases of hooliganism had been heard by the courts within the ten-day period, compared with 331 of the cases of theft. GARF, f. 8131, op. 37, d. 348, l. 150.

115. For comparison, courts in the same two republics faced a backlog of 915 cases of petty theft, out of a total of 2,338 cases, as of September 1; GARF, f. 8131, op. 37, d. 348, ll. 50–51. See also the complaint the RSFSR Procuracy that the court system in the fourth quarter of 1940 failed to meet the required two-day limit in 24 percent of cases of hooliganism and 35 percent of cases of petty theft; GARF, f. A-461, op. 8s, d. 73, ll. 30–33.

116. GARF, f. 8131, op. 37, d. 348, ll. 46–47, 64–72.

117. See ibid., ll. 44–49, 94; GARF, f. A-461, op. 8s, d. 73, ll. 21–22ob, 42–51; and GARF, f. 8131, op. 37, d. 347, ll. 12–24, esp. 13.

118. An investigation by the Moscow Procuracy regarding the activities of the police in December 1940 and January 1941 found that, of the 1,526 cases sent to People's Courts by the police in these two months, only 250 of them were investigated by the *militsiia*, including 87 that had been sent back to the police by the courts themselves for further investigation. Most of these cases rested on investigative materials that were not of high enough quality to support convictions, especially those cases that were not subjected to additional police investigation; nonetheless, of the 1,126 cases that were checked in detail by the Moscow Procuracy, 953 (85 percent) resulted in prison sentences of one year, while only 164 resulted in a verdict of not guilty; the remaining 9 were sentenced to probation. GARF, f. 8131, op. 37, d. 346, ll. 36–45. See also GARF, f. 8131, op. 37, d. 348, ll. 93–99, for a Procuracy report from one Moscow district that concluded that the duty chamber (*dezhurnaia kamera*) of the district People's Court that was set up to hear cases related to the August edict generally deferred to the *militsiia* and issued one-year sentences in nearly all cases forwarded to it.

119. GARF, f. 5446, op. 24a, d. 182, l. 156.

120. E.g., see the discussion of cases of particularly egregious hooliganism in the Russian Republic, all identified as recidivists, in GARF, f. A-461, op. 8s, d. 73, l. 43.

121. GARF, f. 5446, op. 24a, d. 182, ll. 158–59. Solomon estimates that prosecutions for hooliganism in 1940 were twice the number in 1939. Solomon, *Soviet Criminal Justice under Stalin*, 330.

122. Courts in the Russian Republic heard only 25,489 cases in October, compared with the peak of 40,590 cases in September. GARF, f. 5446, op. 24a, d. 182, ll. 155–56. See also Solomon, *Soviet Criminal Justice under Stalin*, 330.

123. Rittersporn, "Extra-Judicial Repression and the Courts," 219–20. No statistical evidence is available regarding the number of individuals subjected to administrative fines for hooliganism during the campaign. Given the realities of local police work in the late 1930s, it is unlikely that any nationwide or republic-wide statistics exist. On the basis of previous patterns of policing activity, fines would have been far more prevalent than the number of cases sent to court.

124. For successive Procuracy reports on the issue of delinquency, see GARF, f. 8131, op. 37, d. 533, ll. 28–29, 71–73, 73–74, 82, 259–63, 264–82, 285–300.

125. GARF, f. 8131, op. 37, d. 533, ll. 52–53, 74, 266–68. The USSR Procuracy officially approved the application of the August 10 edict on hooliganism, including the one-year minimum prison sentence, to juveniles between twelve and sixteen years of age when their hooliganistic activities were committed in conjunction with "violence" or "causing bodily injury," both of which were listed in the 1935 edict on juvenile homelessness and delinquency. GARF, f. 8131, op. 37, d. 348, ll. 163–64. Central officials also made exceptions to the letter of the law in this period regarding juveniles accused of crimes of state security. E.g., in early November 1940, Bochkov, the USSR procurator, responded to a query from the Ukrainian Procuracy regarding the question of whether juveniles who were engaged in counterrevolutionary activity could be charged under criminal law. Bochkov informed the republic-level procurator that the issue was under consideration and, until a decision was reached, children under the age of sixteen who were engaged in counterrevolutionary activity should be sentenced not by the court system but by the NKVD Special Board and sent to NKVD labor colonies. GARF, f. 8131, op. 37, d. 232, ll. 171–73.

126. Young students at these schools were subjected to arrest and criminal sanction for the same kinds of violations outlined in the June 1940 edict on labor infractions. For a mid-1941 report on the progress of this campaign, see Vilenskii et al., *Deti GU-LAGa*, 371–72. See also GARF, f. 8131, op. 37, d. 533, for numerous reports of police abuses of this new attendance law, especially ll. 48–50 and 7–10, regarding a case in the Kiev region in which local police arrested a group of seventh graders and held them for six days for skipping class.

127. This decision, which was promulgated on May 31, 1941, as an edict of the USSR Supreme Soviet, was supported by Vyshinskii, who provided an opinion to that effect to Stalin on May 19. GARF, f. 5446, op. 25a, d. 7351, ll. 47–48, 49. I am unable to determine precisely with whom the idea originated in a workable form, but the issue was under discussion within the USSR Procuracy from at least early May 1941. See GARF, f. 8131, op. 37, d. 533, ll. 181–82.

128. See Solomon, *Soviet Criminal Justice under Stalin*, 209–10, for a discussion of judicial sentences of juveniles in the post-1935 Stalin period. Solomon estimates that roughly the same number of juveniles were sentenced to custodial sanctions in 1940 as in 1914 (ca. 13,000–15,000). Solomon's discussion does not take into account the fact that juveniles were subject to extrajudicial repression by NKVD troikas during the mass operations and thereafter by the NKVD Special Board. No statistics are available regarding the number of children repressed using these means in the post-1938 period, but, given the anecdotal information cited above, they were likely not inconsequential. Gabor Rittersporn estimates that 55.7 percent of the more than 155,000 juveniles who received prison terms between April 1935 and 1940 were sentenced by various extrajudicial institutions of the NKVD rather than the courts; Rittersporn, "Extra-Judicial Repression and the Courts," 221.

129. Rittersporn argues that the judicial system by 1940 had taken on the ethos of the extrajudicial system; "Extra-Judicial Repression and the Courts," esp. 220–21.

130. On the connection between ethnicity and class in the creation of alien "contingents" in the 1930s, see Weiner, *Making Sense of War*, 138–49. Weiner's argument that redemption was possible in the prewar period is partially correct regarding "national elements," but only because the definitions of these cohorts that were prevalent in the prewar period, as argued above, were constructed in terms other than ethnicity.

Conclusion

1. Zygmunt Bauman, *Modernity and the Holocaust* (Ithaca, N.Y.: Cornell University Press, 2000; orig. pub. 1989), 227; emphasis in the original.

2. Hannah Arendt, *The Origins of Totalitarianism* (New York: Harcourt Brace, 1973; orig. pub. 1951), 465.

3. Sheila Fitzpatrick described the events of 1937 and 1938 as a "monstrous post-script" to the First Five-Year Plan in her synthesis of the Russian revolutionary era, published in 1982. Sheila Fitzpatrick, *The Russian Revolution* (New York: Oxford University Press, 1982), 3. Fitzpatrick's statement should not be taken as a whitewashing of Stalinist terror but as a claim that the events of 1937 and 1938 completed the radical social transformations that began in the late 1920s. Peter H. Solomon Jr., makes a compatible argument regarding the "reconstruction" of the Soviet criminal

justice system in the years preceding World War II. Peter H. Solomon Jr., *Soviet Criminal Justice under Stalin* (Cambridge: Cambridge University Press, 1996), 267–98.

4. On this point I disagree with David R. Shearer's recent argument that the regime did not apply policies of "mass social repression" to the geographic core of the empire after the end of the mass operations of 1937–38, reserving such policies for territories added to the USSR after 1939. David R. Shearer, "Elements Near and Alien: Passportization, Policing, and Identity in the Stalinist State, 1932–1952," *Journal of Modern History* 76, no. 4 (2004): 835–81, esp. 877.

5. This conclusion is in accord with the most important recent studies of Stalinist repression. In addition to the work of Oleg Khlevniuk cited above, see David R. Shearer's discussion of the Stalinist regime as a militarized "service state" in "Elements Near and Alien," 877–80.

6. The idea of a particularly Soviet "modernity" has produced much conflict within the field in the past decades. For a c itical response to this concept, see Terry Martin, "Modernization or Neo-Traditionalism? Ascribed Nationality and Soviet Primordialism," in *Stalinism: New Directions*, ed. Sheila Fitzpatrick (London: Routledge, 2000), 348–67. I am sympathetic to these criticisms, but nonetheless the "modern" nature of the OGPU project is plainly clear in the concrete forms of Soviet policing, especially in comparison with the policing systems of the Tsarist and NEP eras.

7. See Michel Foucault, "The Birth of Biopolitics," in *Ethics: Subjectivity and Truth*, ed. Paul Rabinow and trans. Robert Hurley (New York: New Press, 1994), 73–79; Zygmunt Bauman, *Modernity and the Holocaust* (Ithaca, N.Y.: Cornell University Press, 2000; orig. pub. 1989); and James C. Scott, *Seeing Like a State: How Certain Schemes to Improve the Human Condition Have Failed* (New Haven, Conn.: Yale University Press, 1998).

8. In addition to the works by Holquist, Hoffmann, and Weiner, cited above, see Peter Holquist, "To Count, to Extract, to Exterminate: Population Statistics and Population Politics in Late Imperial and Soviet Russia," in *A State of Nations: Empire and Nation-Making in the Age of Lenin and Stalin*, ed. Ronald Grigor Suny and Terry Martin (Oxford: Oxford University Press, 2001), 111–44.

9. The idea of internalization of modes of state domination has been the topic of numerous recent works on the USSR in the 1930s, the most compelling of which is Jochen Hellbeck, *Revolution on My Mind: Writing a Diary Under Stalin* (Cambridge, Mass.: Harvard University Press, 2006).

10. Scott speaks of the "bureaucratic intelligentsia, technicians, planners, and engineers"; Scott, *Seeing Like a State*, 96.

11. I draw here, in addition to Hannah Arendt's *Origins of Totalitarianism*, from Elisabeth Domansky's perceptive discussion of the connection between totalitarian regimes and totalitarian societies; Elisabeth Domansky, "The Transformation of State and Society in World War I Germany," in *Landscaping the Human Garden: Twentieth-Century Population Management in a Comparative Framework*, ed. Amir Weiner (Stanford, Calif.: Stanford University Press, 2003), 46–66.

12. The idea that totalitarian violence was inherently random formed a fundamental part of the definitions of totalitarianism posited by influential accounts of Stalinism and Nazism in the 1950s, most importantly, those of Arendt, in *The Origins of Totalitarianism*, and Zbigniew Brzezinski, *The Permanent Purge: Politics in Soviet Totalitarianism* (Cambridge, Mass.: Harvard University Press, 1956). This idea has survived to the current day, often appearing as an analytically unnecessary aside in accounts of

the 1930s by scholars whose work is far more complex than this simplistic idea. E.g., see comments about the random nature of Stalinist terror in the introduction to Sheila Fitzpatrick, *Everyday Stalinism: Ordinary Life in Extraordinary Times—Soviet Russia in the 1930s* (Oxford: Oxford University Press, 1999), 7; and Amir Weiner's conclusion, largely unrelated to the rest of his discussion, that the "randomness of Soviet terror" played a major role in the "cumulative radicalization of Soviet population policies," in Amir Weiner, "Nothing but Certainty," *Slavic Review* 61, no. 1 (2002): 53.

13. This conclusion contradicts several recent studies that stress the integrative nature of Soviet cultural practices. In addition to the work of Hellbeck, cited above, see especially Kotkin's idea of "speaking Bolshevik"; Stephen Kotkin, *Magnetic Mountain: Stalinism as a Civilization* (Berkeley: University of California Press, 1995). For a direct challenge to this interpretation, see Jeffrey J. Rossman, *Worker Resistance under Stalin: Class and Revolution on the Shop Floor* (Cambridge, Mass.: Harvard University Press, 2005).

Bibliography

Primary Sources

Archives

GANO (Gosudarstvennyi Arkhiv Novosibirskoi Oblasti, State Archive of the Novosibirsk Region), fond 4, Novosibirskii oblastnoi komitet KPSS, Novosibirsk Regional Committee of the Communist Party.

GARF (Gosudarstvennyi Arkhiv Rossiiskoi Federatsii, State Archive of the Russia Federation):

fond A-406, Narodnyi komissariat raboche-krest'ianskoi inspektsii (Rabkrin RSFSR), Commissariat of the Workers' and Peasants' Inspectorate of the Russian Republic.

fond A-428, Verkhovnyi Sud RSFSR, Supreme Court of the Russian Republic.

fond A-461, Prokuratura RSFSR, Procuracy of the Russian Republic.

fond 374, Narodnyi komissariat raboche-krest'ianskoi inspektsii (Rabkrin SSSR), Commissariat of the Workers' and Peasants' Inspectorate of the USSR.

fond 1235, Vserossiiskii tsentral'nyi ispolnitel'nyi komitet (VTsIK) RSFSR, All-Russian Central Executive Committee.

fond 3316, Tsentral'nyi ispolnitel'nyi komitet (TsIK) SSSR, Central Executive Committee of the USSR.

fond 5207, Detskaia komissiia pri VTsIK, Children's Commission attached to the All-Russian Central Executive Committee.

fond 5446, Sovet narodnykh komissarov (Sovnarkom) SSSR, Council of People's Commissars of the USSR.

fond 7511, Komissiia sovetskogo kontrolia pri SNK SSSR, Soviet Control Commission attached to the USSR Council of People's Commissars.

fond 7523, Verkhsovet SSSR, Supreme Soviet of the USSR.

fond 8131, Prokuratura SSSR, USSR Procuracy.

fond 9401, OGPU-NKVD-MVD SSSR.

fond 9415, Glavnoe upravlenie Militsii MVD SSSR, Central Police Administration of the USSR Ministry of Internal Affairs.

fond 9479, 4-yi spetsotdel MVD SSSR (Spetspereselenie), Fourth Special Department of the USSR Ministry of Internal Affairs (Special Resettlement).

RGANI (Rossiiskii Gosudarstvennyi Arkhiv Noveishei Istorii, Russian State Archive of Contemporary History), fond 89, Dokumenty po "delu KPSS," Documents related to the Communist Party of the Soviet Union on Trial.

RGASPI (Rossiiskii Gosudarstvennyi Arkhiv Sotsial'no-Politicheskoi Istorii, Russian State Archive of Socio-Political History):

fond 17, Tsentral'nyi komitet, Central Committee of the Communist Party of the USSR.

fond 81, Kaganovich, L. M.

fond 671, Ezhov, N. I.

TsAODM (Tsentral'nyi Arkhiv Obshchestvennykh Dvizhenii Moskvy, Central Archive of Social Movements of Moscow), fond 3, Moskovskii oblastnoi komitet KPSS, Moscow Regional Committee of the Communist Party.

TsGAMO (Tsentral'nyi Gosudarstvennyi Arkhiv Moskovskoi Oblasti, Central State Archive of the Moscow Region):

fond 267, Administrativnyi otdel Moskovskogo okruzhnogo ispolkoma, Administrative Department of the Moscow County Executive Committee.

fond 792, Gruppa partiinogo i sovetskogo kontrolia pri Moskovskom komitete VKP(b), Party and Soviet Control Group attached to the Moscow Party Committee.

Journals and Newspapers

Administrativnyi Vestnik (Moscow)
Moskovskie Novosti (Moscow)
Na boevom postu (Moscow)
Pravda (Moscow)
Sobranie zakonov i rasporiazhenii raboche-krest'ianskogo pravitel'stva SSSR (SZ SSSR)
Sotsialisticheskaia zakonnost' (SZ) (Moscow)
Sovetskaia iustitsiia (Moscow)
Trud (Moscow)
Za sotsialisticheskuiu zakonnost'(ZSZ)

Published Archival Documents, Memoirs, and Other Published Primary Sources

Bogomolov, D. I., and A. Ia. Razumov. *Leningradskii martirolog 1937–1938*. Vol. 1. Saint Petersburg: RNB, 1995.

Danilov, V. P., and S. A. Krasil'nikov, eds. *Spetspereselentsy v Zapadnoi Sibiri, 1930–vesna 1931 g*. Novosibirsk: Nauka, 1992.

———. *Spetspereselentsy v Zapadnoi Sibiri, 1933–1938*. Novosibirsk: EKOR, 1994.

Danilov, Victor, Roberta Manning, and Lynne Viola, eds. *Tragediia sovetskoi derevni: Kollektivizatsiia i raskulachivanie, 1927–1939—Dokumenty i materialy, V 5–ti tt. T. 1, Mai 1927–noiabr' 1929.* Moscow: ROSSPEN, 1999.

———. *Tragediia sovetskoi derevni: Kollektivizatsiia i raskulachivanie, 1927–1939: Dokumenty i materialy, V 5–ti tt. T. 2, Noiabr' 1929–Dekabr' 1930.* Moscow: ROSSPEN, 1999.

———. *Tragediia sovetskoi derevni: Kollektivizatsiia i raskulachivanie, 1927–1939— Dokumenty i materialy, V 5–ti tt. T. 3, Konets 1930–1933.* Moscow: ROSSPEN, 2001.

———. *Tragediia sovetskoi derevni. Kollektivizatsiia i raskulachivanie, 1927-1939: Dokumenty i materialy, V 5–ti tt. T. 4, 1934–1936.* Moscow: ROSSPEN, 2002.

———. *Tragediia sovetskoi derevni: Kollektivizatsiia i raskulachivanie, 1927–1939— Dokumenty i materialy. V 5-ti tt. T. 5. 1937–1939. Kniga 1. 1937.* Moscow: ROSSPEN, 2004.

Ginzburg, Eugenia Semyonovna. *Journey into the Whirlwind*, trans. Paul Stevenson and Max Hayward. New York: Harcourt Brace Jovanovich, 1975.

———. *Within the Whirlwind*, trans. Ian Boland. New York: Harcourt Brace Jovanovich, 1981.

Khaustov, V. N., V. P. Naumov, and N. S. Plotnikov, eds. *Lubianka: Stalin i VChK-GPU-OGPU-NKVD—Ianvar' 1922–dekabr' 1936.* Moscow: Mezhdunarodnyi fond "Demokratiia," 2003.

———. *Lubianka: Stalin i Glavnoe upravlenie gosbezopasnosti NKVD, 1937–1938.* Moscow: Mezhdunarodnyi fond "Demokratiia," 2004.

Khlevniuk, O. V., R. U. Davies, A. P. Kosheleva, E. A. Rees, and L. A. Rogovaia, eds. *Stalin i Kaganovich: Perepiska, 1931–1936 gg.* Moscow: ROSSPEN, 2001.

Khlevniuk, O. V., A. V. Kvashonkin, L. P. Kosheleva, and L. A. Rogovaia, eds. *Stalin-skoe Politburo v 30-e gody: Sbornik dokumentov.* Moscow: AIRO-XX, 1995.

Kokurin, A. I., and N. V. Petrov. *GULAG (Glavnoe upravlenie lagerei), 1917–1960.* Moscow: Materik, 2000.

———. *Lubianka: VChK-OGPU-NKVD-NKGB-MGB-MVD-KGB 1917–1960.* Moscow: Mezhdunarodnyi fond "Demokratiia," 1997.

Kondakova, I. A. "'Provesti ochistky Leningrada kampaneiskim putem': Dokumenty AP RF o vysylke 'byvshikh liudei.' 1935–1936 gg." *Istoricheskii Arkhiv,* no. 2 (2003): 104–22.

Kosheleva, L. et al. *Pis'ma I. V. Stalina V. M. Molotovu. 1925–1936 gg.* Moscow: "Rossiia molodaia," 1995.

Petrov, N. V., and K. V. Skorkin. *Kto rukovodil NKVD, 1934–1941: Spravochnik.* Moscow: Zven'ia, 1999.

Shreider, Mikhail. *NKVD iznutri: Zapiski Chekista.* Moscow: Vozvrashchenie, 1995.

2-i vserossiiskii S"ezd administrativnykh rabotnikov. Stenograficheskii otchet. Moscow: Narodnyi kommissariat vnutrennykh del, 1929.

Vilenskii, S. S., A. I. Kokurin, G. V. Atmashkina, and I. Iu. Novichenko, eds. *Deti GULAGa, 1918–1956.* Moscow: Mezhdunarodnyi fond "Demokratiia," 2002.

Viola, L., T. MacDonald, S. V. Zhuralev, A. N. Mel'nik, eds. *Riazanskaia derevnia v 1929–1930 gg. Khronika golovokruzheniia. Dokumenty i materialy.* Moscow: ROSSPEN, 1998.

Voinov, Nicholas. *The Waif.* New York: Pantheon Books, 1955.

Secondary Sources

Abbott, Robert J. "Police Reform in the Russian Province of Iaroslavl, 1856–1876." *Slavic Review* 32, no. 2 (1973): 292–302.

Alder, Nanci. *Victims of Soviet Terror: The Story of the Memorial Movement.* Westport, Conn.: Praeger, 1993.

Alexopoulos, Golfo. *Stalin's Outcasts: Aliens, Citizens, and the Soviet State, 1926–1936.* Ithaca, N.Y.: Cornell University Press, 2003.

Arendt, Hannah. *The Origins of Totalitarianism.* New York: Harcourt Brace & Co., 1973; orig. pub. 1951.

Ball, Alan. *And Now My Soul Is Hardened: Abandoned Children in Soviet Russia, 1918–1930.* Berkeley: University of California Press, 1984.

Bauman, Zygmunt. *Modernity and the Holocaust.* Ithaca, N.Y.: Cornell University Press, 2000; orig. pub. 1989.

Benvenuti, Francesco. "The 'Reform' of the NKVD, 1934." *Europe-Asia Studies* 49, no. 6 (September 1997): 1037–56.

Binner, Rolf, and Marc Junge, "Wie der Terror gross wurde: Massenmord und Lagerhaft nach Befehl 00447." *Cahiers du Monde russe* 42, nos. 2–4 (2001): 557–614.

Borisov, A. V., et al. *Politsiia i Militsiia Rossii: Stranitsy Istorii.* Moscow: Nauka, 1995.

Bosewitz, Rene. *Waifdom in the Soviet Union: Features of the Subculture and Reeducation.* Frankfurt: Peter Lang, 1988.

Brzezinski, Zbigniew. *The Permanent Purge: Politics in Soviet Totalitarianism.* Cambridge, Mass.: Harvard University Press, 1956.

Chase, William, and J. Arch Getty. "Patterns of Repression among the Soviet Elite in the Late 1930s: A Biographical Approach." In *Stalinist Terror: New Perspectives,* ed. J. Arch Getty and Roberta Manning. Cambridge: Cambridge University Press, 1993.

Churchill, Winston S. *The Second World War, Volume IV: The Hinge of Fate.* Boston: Houghton Mifflin, 1985.

Cohen, Stephen F. *Bukharin and the Bolshevik Revolution: A Political Biography, 1888–1938.* New York: Alfred A. Knopf, 1973.

Conquest, Robert. *The Great Terror: A Reassessment.* New York: Oxford University Press, 1990.

———. *Inside Stalin's Secret Police: NKVD Politics 1936–1939.* Stanford, Calif.: Hoover Institution Press, 1985.

Davies, R. W., and S. G. Wheatcroft. "The Soviet Famine of 1932–33 and the Crisis in Agriculture." In *Challenging Traditional Views of Russian History,* ed. Stephen G. Wheatcroft. Basingstoke, U.K.: Palgrave Macmillan, 2002.

Davies, Sarah. "The Crime of 'Anti-Soviet Agitation' in the Soviet Union in the 1930's." *Cahiers du Monde russe* 39, nos. 1–2 (1998): 149–68.

———. *Popular Opinion in Stalin's Russia: Terror, Propaganda and Dissent, 1934–1941.* Cambridge: Cambridge University Press, 1997.

Davis, Jennifer. "Urban Policing and Its Objects: Comparative Themes in England and France in the Second Half of the Nineteenth Century." In *Policing Western Europe: Politics, Professionalism, and Public Order, 1850–1940,* ed. Clive Emsley and Barbara Weinberger. Westport, Conn.: Greenwood Press, 1991.

Deutscher, Isaac. *Stalin: A Political Biography.* New York: Oxford University Press, 1949.

Domansky, Elisabeth. "The Transformation of State and Society in World War I Germany." In *Landscaping the Human Garden: Twentieth-Century Population Management in a Comparative Framework*, ed. Amir Weiner. Stanford, Calif.: Stanford University Press, 2003.

Dugin, Aleksandr. "Organy moskovskoi gorodskoi militsii." Kandidatskaia dissertatsiia, Gosudarstvennyi Istoriko-Arkhivnyi Institut, Moscow, 1988.

Ellman, Michael. "Churchill on Stalin: A Note." *Europe-Asia Studies* 58, no. 6 (2006): 965–71.

———. "The Soviet 1937–1938 Provincial Show Trials Revisited." *Europe-Asia Studies* 55, no. 8 (2003): 1305–21.

———. "Soviet Repression Statistics: Some Comments." *Europe-Asia Studies* 54, no. 7 (2002): 1151–72.

Emsley, Clive, and Barbara Weinberger, eds. *Policing Western Europe: Politics, Professionalism, and Public Order, 1850–1940*. Westport, Conn.: Greenwood Press, 1991.

Eremina, L. S., ed. *Repressii protiv poliakov i pol'skikh grazhdan*. Moscow: Zven'ia, 1997.

Fainsod, Merle. *Smolensk under Soviet Rule*. Cambridge, Mass.: Harvard University Press, 1958; Boston: Unwyn Hyman, 1989.

Filtzer, Donald. *Soviet Workers and Late Stalinism: Labour and the Restoration of the Stalinist System after World War II*. Cambridge: Cambridge University Press, 2002.

Finkel, Stuart. "An Intensification of Vigilance: Recent Perspectives on the Institutional History of the Soviet Security Apparatus in the 1920s." *Kritika* 5, no. 2 (2004): 299–320.

Fitzpatrick, Sheila. "The Civil War as a Formative Experience." In *Bolshevik Culture: Experiment and Order in the Russian Revolution*, ed. Abbott Gleason, Peter Kenez, and Richard Stites. Bloomington: Indiana University Press, 1985.

———. *Everyday Stalinism. Ordinary Life in Extraordinary Times: Soviet Russia in the 1930s*. Oxford: Oxford University Press, 1999.

———. "How the Mice Killed the Cat: Scenes from the Great Purges in the Russian Provinces." *Russian Review* 52, no. 3 (1993): 299–320.

———. *The Russian Revolution*. New York: Oxford University Press, 1982.

———. "Workers against Bosses: The Impact of the Great Purges on Labor-Management Relations." In *Making Workers Soviet: Power, Class, and Identity*, ed. Lewis H. Siegelbaum and Ronald Grigor Suny. Ithaca, N.Y.: Cornell University Press, 1994.

Foucault, Michel. "The Birth of Biopolitics." In *Ethics: Subjectivity and Truth*, ed. Paul Rabinow and trans. Robert Hurley. New York: New Press, 1994.

Frierson, Cathy. "Crime and Punishment in the Russian Village: Rural Concepts of Criminality at the End of the Nineteenth Century." *Slavic Review* 46, no. 1 (1987): 55–69.

Gerson, Lennard D. *The Secret Police in Lenin's Russia*. Philadelphia: Temple University Press, 1976.

Getty, J. Arch. "'Excesses Are Not Permitted': Mass Terror and Stalinist Governance in the Late 1930s." *Russian Review* 61, no. 1 (2002): 113–38.

———. *Origins of the Great Purges: The Soviet Communist Party Reconsidered, 1933–1938*. Cambridge: Cambridge University Press, 1985.

————. "Party and Purge in Smolensk." *Slavic Review* 42, no. 1 (1983): 60–79.

————. "The Politics of Repression Revisited." In *Stalinist Terror: New Perspectives*, ed. J. Arch Getty and Roberta Manning. Cambridge: Cambridge University Press, 1993.

Getty, J. Arch, and Oleg V. Naumov. *The Road to Terror: Stalin and the Self-Destruction of the Bolsheviks, 1932–1939*. New Haven, Conn.: Yale University Press, 1999.

Getty, J. Arch, Gabor T. Rittersporn, and Viktor Zemskov. "Victims of the Soviet Penal System in the Pre-War Years: A First Approach on the Basis of Archival Evidence." *American Historical Review* 98, no. 4 (1993): 1017–49.

Goldman, Wendy. *Terror and Democracy in the Age of Stalin: The Social Dynamics of Repression*. Cambridge: Cambridge University Press, 2007.

————. *Women, the State, and Revolution: Soviet Family Policy and Social Life, 1917–36*. Cambridge: Cambridge University Press, 1993.

Gorsuch, Anne E. *Youth in Revolutionary Russia: Enthusiasts, Bohemians, Delinquents*. Bloomington: Indiana University Press, 2000.

Graham, Loren R. "Science and Values: The Eugenics Movement in Germany and Russia in the 1920s." *American Historical Review* 82, no. 5 (1977): 1133–64."

Harris, James R. "The Purging of Local Cliques in the Urals Region, 1936–7." In *Stalinism: New Directions*, ed. Sheila Fitzpatrick. London: Routledge, 2000.

Hasegawa, Tsuyoshi. "Crime and Police in Revolutionary Petrograd, March 1917–March 1918: Social History of the Russian Revolution Revisited." *Acta Slavica Iaponica* 13 (1995): 1–41.

————. "The Formation of the Militia in the February Revolution: An Aspect of the Origins of Dual Power." *Slavic Review* 32, no. 2 (1973): 303–22.

Hessler, Julie. *A Social History of Soviet Trade: Trade Policy, Retail Practices, and Consumption, 1917–1953*. Princeton, N.J.: Princeton University Press, 2004.

Hirsch, Francine. *Empire of Nations: Ethnographic Knowledge and the Making of the Soviet Union*. Ithaca, N.Y.: Cornell University Press, 2005.

Hoffmann, David L. "The Great Terror on the Local Level: Purges in Moscow Factories, 1936–1938." In *Stalinist Terror: New Perspectives*, ed. J. Arch Getty and Roberta Manning. Cambridge: Cambridge University Press, 1993.

————. *Peasant Metropolis: Social Identities in Moscow, 1929–1941*. Ithaca, N.Y.: Cornell University Press, 1994.

————. *Stalinist Values: The Cultural Norms of Soviet Modernity, 1917–1941*. Ithaca, N.Y.: Cornell University Press, 2003.

Holquist, Peter. "'Information Is the Alpha and Omega of Our Work': Bolshevik Surveillance in its Pan-European Context." *Journal of Modern History* 69, no. 3 (1997): 415–50.

————. *Making War, Forging Revolution: Russia's Continuum of Crisis, 1914–1921*. Cambridge, Mass.: Harvard University Press, 2002.

————. "State Violence as Technique: The Logic of Violence in Soviet Totalitarianism." In *Landscaping the Human Garden: Twentieth-Century Population Management in a Comparative Framework*, ed. Amir Weiner. Stanford, Calif.: Stanford University Press, 2003.

————. "To Count, to Extract, to Exterminate: Population Statistics and Population Politics in Late Imperial and Soviet Russia." In *A State of Nations: Empire and Nation-Making in the Age of Lenin and Stalin*, ed. Ronald Grigor Suny and Terry Martin. Oxford: Oxford University Press, 2001.

————. "Violent Russia, Deadly Marxism? Russia in the Epoch of Violence, 1905–21." *Kritika: Explorations in Russian and Eurasian History* 4, no. 3 (2003): 627–52.

Hooper, Cynthia V. "Terror from Within: Participation and Coercion in Soviet Power, 1924–1964." PhD dissertation, Princeton University, 2003.

Ivnitskii, N. A. "Kollektivizatsiia i raskulachivanie v nachale 30-x godov." In *Sud"by Rossiiskogo Krest'ianstva*, ed. Iu. N. Afanas'ev. Moscow: RGGU, 1996.

Jakobson, Michael. *Origins of the Gulag: The Soviet Prison-Camp System, 1917–1934.* Lexington: University of Kentucky Press, 1993.

Jansen, Marc, and Nikita Petrov. *Stalin's Loyal Executioner: People's Commissar Nikolai Ezhov, 1895–1940.* Stanford, Calif.: Hoover Institution Press, 2002.

Juviler, Peter H. "Contradictions òf Revolution: Juvenile Crime and Rehabilitation." In *Bolshevik Culture: Experiment and Order in the Russian Revolution*, ed. Abbot Gleason, Peter Kenez, and Richard Stites. Bloomington: Indiana University Press, 1985.

Kessler, Gijs. "The Passport System and State Control over Population Flows in the Soviet Union, 1932–1940." *Cahiers du Monde Russe* 42, nos. 2–4 (2001): 477–504.

Khaustov, Vladimir Nikolaevich. "Deiatel'nost' organov gosudarstvennoi bezopasnosti NKVD SSSR (1941–1941 gg.)." Doktorskaia Dissertatsiia, Akademiia FSB RF, Moscow, 1997.

————. "Razvitie sovetskikh organov gosudarstvennoi bezopasnosti: 1917–1953 gg." *Cahiers du Monde russe* 42, nos. 2–4 (2001): 357–74.

Khlevniuk, Oleg. *1937-i g.: Stalin, NKVD i sovetskoe obshchestvo.* Moscow: Respublika, 1992.

————. *The History of the Gulag: From Collectivization to the Great Terror*, trans. Vadim A. Staklo and ed. David J. Nordlander. New Haven, Conn.: Yale University Press, 2004.

————. *In Stalin's Shadow: The Career of "Sergo" Ordzhonikidze*, ed. Donald J. Raleigh. Armonk, N.Y.: M. E. Sharpe, 1995.

————. *Politburo: Mekhanizmy politicheskoi vlasti v 1930-e gody.* Moscow: ROSSPEN, 1996.

————. "Stalin as Dictator: The Personification of Power." In *Stalin: A New History*, ed. Sarah Davies and James Harris. Cambridge: Cambridge University Press, 2005.

Khlevnyuk, Oleg (variant spelling). "The Objectives of the Great Terror, 1937–38," in *Soviet History, 1917–1953: Essays in Honour of R. W. Davies*, ed. Julian Cooper, Maureen Perrie, and E. A. Rees. London: Palgrave Macmillan, 1995.

Kondaurov, I. A. et al. *Moskovskaia krasnoznamennaia militsiia.* Moscow: Iuridicheskaia literatura, 1988.

Kotkin, Stephen. *Magnetic Mountain: Stalinism as a Civilization.* Berkeley: University of California Press, 1995.

Kuhr, Corinna. "Children of 'Enemies of the People' as Victims of the Great Purges." *Cahiers du Monde russe* 39, nos. 1–2 (1998): 209–20.

Kuromiya, Hiroaki. "Stalinist Terror in the Donbas: A Note." *Slavic Review* 50, no. 1 (1991): 157–62.

Lauchlan, Iain. *Russian Hide and Seek: The Tsarist Secret Police in Petersburg, 1906–1914.* Helsinki: Finnish Literature Society, 2002.

Le Donne, John. "The Provincial and Local Police under Catherine the Great, 1775–1796." *Canadian Slavic Studies* 4, no. 3 (1970): 513–28.

Leggett, George. *The Cheka: Lenin's Political Police.* Oxford: Clarendon Press, 1981.

Lenin, V. I. *Collected Works,* vol. 24. London: Laurence and Wishart, 1964.

———. *State and Revolution.* New York: International Publishers, 1932.

Lewin, Moshe. *The Making of the Soviet System: Essays in the Social History of Interwar Russia.* New York: Pantheon Books, 1985.

Lin, George. "Fighting in Vain: The NKVD RSFSR in the 1920s." PhD dissertation, Stanford University, 1997.

Lohr, Eric. *Nationalizing the Russian Empire: The Campaign against Enemy Aliens during World War I.* Cambridge, Mass.: Harvard University Press, 2003.

Malygin, Aleksandr Iakovlevich. "Gosudarstvenno-pravovoi status militsii RSFSR v period provedeniia Novoi Ekonomicheskoi Politiki (20-e gody)." Doktorskaia dissertatsiia, Akademiia MVD RF, 1992.

Manning, Roberta T. *Government in the Soviet Countryside in the Stalinist Thirties: The Case of Belyi Raion in 1937.* Carl Beck Papers in Russian and East European Studies no. 301. Pittsburgh: Russian and East European Studies, University of Pittsburgh, 1984.

———. "The Great Purges in a Rural District: Belyi Raion Revisited." *Russian History/ Histoire Russe* 16, nos. 2–4 (1989): 409–33.

———. "The Great Purges in a Rural District: Belyi Raion Revisited." In *Stalinist Terror: New Perspectives,* ed. J. Arch Getty and Roberta Manning. Cambridge: Cambridge University Press, 1993.

———. "Massovaia operatsiia protiv 'kulakov i prestupnikh' elementov: Apogei Velikoi Chistki na Smolenshchine." In *Stalinizm v rossiiskoi provintsii: Smolenskie arkhivnye dokumenty v prochtenii zarubezhnykh i rossiiskikh istorikov,* ed. E. V. Kodin. Smolensk, 1999.

———. "Politicheskii terror kak politicheskii teatr: Raionnye pokazatel'nye sudy 1937g. i massovye operatsii." In *Tragediia sovetskoi derevni: Kollektivizatsiia i raskulachivanie, 1927–1939—Dokumenty i materialy, V 5-ti tt. T. 5, 1937–1939, Kniga 1. 1937,* ed. Victor Danilov, Roberta Manning, and Lynne Viola. Moscow: ROSSPEN, 2004.

———. "The Soviet Economic Crisis of 1936–1940 and the Great Purges." In *Stalinist Terror: New Perspectives,* ed. J. Arch Getty and Roberta Manning. Cambridge: Cambridge University Press, 1993.

Martin, Terry. "Modernization or Neo-Traditionalism? Ascribed Nationality and Soviet Primordialism." In *Stalinism: New Directions,* ed. Sheila Fitzpatrick. London: Routledge, 2000.

———. "The Origins of Soviet Ethnic Cleansing." *Journal of Modern History* 70, no. 4 (1998): 813–62.

———. "'Registration' and 'Mood': OGPU Information Reports and the Soviet Surveillance System." Paper presented at the conference "La police politique en Union soviétique, 1918–1953," Maison des Science de l'Homme, Paris, May 25–27, 2000.

Matthews, Mervyn. *The Passport Society: Controlling Movement in Russia and the USSR.* Boulder, Colo.: Westview Press, 1993.

McDonald, Tracy. "A Peasant Rebellion In Stalin's Russia: The Pitelinskii Uprising, Riazan 1930." In *Contending with Stalinism: Soviet Power and Popular Resistance in the 1930s,* ed. Lynne Viola. Ithaca, N.Y.: Cornell University Press, 2002.

McLoughlin, Barry. "Mass Operations of the NKVD, 1937–8: A Survey." In *Stalin's Terror: High Politics and Mass Repression in the Soviet Union,* ed. Barry McLoughlin and Kevin McDermott. Houndsmills, U.K.: Palgrave Macmillan, 2003.

Medvedev, Roy. *Let History Judge: The Origins and Consequences of Stalinism.* New York: Columbia University Press, 1989; orig. pub. 1971.

Moine, Nathalie. "Passportisation, Statistique des Migrations et Contrôle de l'Identité Sociale." *Cahiers du Monde Russe* 38, no. 4 (1997): 587–600.

Morris, James. "The Polish Terror: Spy Mania and Ethnic Cleansing in the Great Terror." *Europe-Asia Studies* 56, no. 5 (2004): 751–66.

Okhotin, N., and A. Roginskii. "Iz istorii 'nemetskoi operatsii' 1937–1938 gg." In *Nakazannyi narod: Repressii protiv rossiiskikh Nemtsev*, ed. I. L. Shcherbakova. Moscow: Zven'ia, 1999.

Onegina, Svetlana V. "The Resettlement of Soviet Citizens from Manchuria in 1935–36: A Research Note." *Europe-Asia Studies* 47, no. 6 (1995): 1043–50.

Osokina, Elena. *Za fasadom "stalinskogo izobiliia": Raspredelenie i rynok v snabzhenii naseleniia v gody industrializatsii, 1927–1941.* Moscow: ROSSPEN, 1999.

Petrov, Nikita, and Arsenii Roginskii. "The 'Polish Operation' of the NKVD, 1937–1938." In *Stalin's Terror: High Politics and Mass Repression in the Soviet Union*, ed. Barry McLoughlin and Kevin McDermott. Houndsmills, U.K.: Palgrave Macmillan, 2003.

Petrov, N. V., and A. B. Roginskii. "'Pol'skaia operatsiia' NKVD 1937–1938 gg." In *Repressii protiv poliakov i pol'skikh grazhdan*, ed. L. S. Eremina. Moscow: Zven'ia, 1997.

Peukert, Detlev J. K. *The Weimar Republic: The Crisis of Classical Modernity.* New York: Hill and Wang, 1992.

Raeff, Marc. *Understanding Imperial Russia: State and Society in the Old Regime*, trans. Arthur Goldhammer. New York: Columbia University Press, 1984.

Rimmel, Lesley. "Another Kind of Fear: The Kirov Murder and the End of Bread Rationing in Leningrad." *Slavic Review* 56, no. 3 (1997): 481–99.

Rittersporn, Gabor T. "Extra-Judicial Repression and the Courts: Their Relationship in the 1930s." In *Reforming Justice in Russia, 1864–1996*, ed. Peter H. Solomon Jr. Armonk, N.Y.: M. E. Sharpe, 1997.

———. *Simplifications staliniennes et complications sovietiques: Tensions socials et conflicts politiques en URSS 1933–1953.* Paris: Editions des Archives Contemporaines, 1988. Published in English as *Stalinist Simplifications and Soviet Complications: Social Tension and Political Conflict in the USSR, 1933–1953.* Chur: Harwood Academic Publishers, 1991.

———. "The State Against Itself: Social Tensions and Political Conflict in the USSR, 1936–1938." *Telos* 41 (1979): 87–104.

———. "'Vrednye elementy,' 'opasnye men'shinstva' i bol'shevistskie trevogi: massovye operatsii 1937–1938 gg. i etnicheskii vopros v SSSR." In *V sem'e edinoi: Natsional'naia politika partii bol'shevikov i ee osushchestvlenie na Severo-Zapade Rossii v 1920–1950-e gody*, ed. Timo Vihavainen and Irina Takala. Petrozavodsk: Izdatel'stvo Petrozavodskogo universiteta, 1998.

Rossman, Jeffrey J. *Worker Resistance under Stalin: Class and Revolution on the Shop Floor.* Cambridge, Mass.: Harvard University Press, 2005.

Sanborn, Joshua A. *Drafting the Russian Nation: Military Conscription, Total War, and Mass Politics, 1905–1925.* De Kalb: Northern Illinois University Press, 2003.

Scott, James C. *Seeing Like a State: How Certain Schemes to Improve the Human Condition Have Failed.* New Haven, Conn.: Yale University Press, 1998.

Seigelbaum, Lewis H. *Stakhanovism and the Politics of Productivity in the USSR, 1935–1941*. Cambridge: Cambridge University Press, 1988.

Seregny, Scott J. "The Nedel'shchik: Law and Order in Muscovite Russia." *Canadian-American Slavic Studies* 9, no. 2 (1975): 168–78.

Shabel'nikova, N. A. *Militsiia dal'nego vostoka Rossii: 1922–1930 gg*. Vladivostok: Izdatel'stvo Dal'nevostochnogo universiteta, 2000.

Sharlet, Robert. "Pashukanis and the Withering Away of the Law in the USSR." In *Cultural Revolution in Russia, 1928–1931*, ed. Sheila Fitzpatrick. Bloomington: Indiana University Press, 1978.

———. "Stalinism and Soviet Legal Culture." In *Stalinism: Essays in Historical Interpretation*, ed. Robert C. Tucker. New York, 1977.

Shchelokov, N. A., ed. *Istoriia Sovetskoi Militsii*. Moscow: Akademiia MVD, 1977.

Shcherbakova, I. L., ed. *Nakazannyi narod: Repressii protiv rossiiskikh Nemtsev*. Moscow: Zven'ia, 1999.

Shearer, David R. "Crime and Social Disorder in Stalin's Russia: A Reassessment of the Great Retreat and the Origins of Mass Repression." *Cahiers du Monde russe* 39, nos. 1–2 (1998): 119–48.

———. "Elements Near and Alien: Passportization, Policing, and Identity in the Stalinist State, 1932–1952." *Journal of Modern History* 76, no. 4 (2004): 835–81.

———. "Modernity and Backwardness on the Soviet Frontier: Western Siberia during the 1930s." In *Provincial Landscapes: Local Dimensions of Soviet Power, 1917–1953*, ed. Donald J. Raleigh. Pittsburgh: University of Pittsburgh Press, 2001.

———. *Policing Stalin's Socialism: Repression and Social Order in the Soviet Union, 1924–1953*. New Haven, Conn.: Yale University Press, 2009.

———. "Social Disorder, Mass Repression, and the NKVD during the 1930s." *Cahiers du Monde russe* 42, nos. 2–4 (2001): 505–34.

Shelley, Louise I. *Policing Soviet Society: The Evolution of State Control*. London: Routledge, 1996.

Solomon, Peter H., Jr. "Criminalization and Decriminalization in Soviet Criminal Policy, 1917–1941." *Law and Society Review* 16, no. 1 (1981–82): 9–44.

———. *Soviet Criminal Justice under Stalin*. Cambridge: Cambridge University Press, 1996.

———. "Soviet Criminology: Its Demise and Rebirth, 1922–1963." *Soviet Union* 1, no. 2 (1974): 122–40.

———. "Soviet Penal Policy, 1917–1934: A Reinterpretation." *Slavic Review* 39, no. 2 (1980): 195–217.

Solzhenitsyn, Aleksandr I. *The Gulag Archipelago, 1918–1956: An Experiment in Literary Investigation, I–II*. New York: Harper & Row, 1973.

Soroka, Lora. *Fond 89: Communist Party of the Soviet Union on Trial—Archives of the Communist Party State, Guide to the Microfilm Collection in the Hoover Institution Archives*. Stanford, Calif.: Hoover Institution Press, 2001.

Stevens, Jennie A. "Children of the Revolution: Soviet Russia's Homeless Children (*Besprizorniki*) in the 1920s." *Russian History* 9, nos. 2–3 (1982): 242–64.

Stolee, Margaret K. "Homeless Children in the USSR, 1917–1957." *Soviet Studies* 40, no. 1 (1988): 64–83.

Thurston, Robert W. "Fear and Belief in the USSR's 'Great Terror': Response to Arrest, 1935–1939." *Slavic Review* 45, no. 2 (1986): 213–34.

———. *Life and Terror in Stalin's Russia, 1923–1941.* New Haven, Conn.: Yale University Press, 1996.

———. "Police and People in Moscow, 1906–1914." *Russian Review* 39, no. 3 (1980): 320–38.

———. "The Stakhanovite Movement: Background to the Great Terror in the Factories, 1935–1938." In *Stalinist Terror: New Perspectives*, ed. J. Arch Getty and Roberta Manning. Cambridge: Cambridge University Press, 1993.

Timasheff, Nicholas. *The Great Retreat: The Growth and Decline of Communism in Russia.* New York: E. P. Dutton, 1946.

Trotsky, Leon. *The Revolution Betrayed: What Is the Soviet Union and Where Is It Going?* New York: Harcourt Brace, 1937.

———. *Stalinism and Bolshevism: Concerning the Historical and Theoretical Roots of the Fourth International.* New York: Pioneer Publishers, 1937.

Tucker, Robert C. *Stalin in Power: The Revolution from Above, 1928–1941.* New York: W. W. Norton, 1990.

Viola, Lynne. "The Aesthetic of Stalinist Planning and the World of the Special Villages." *Kritika: Explorations in Russian and Eurasian History* 4, no. 1 (2003): 101–28.

———. *Best Sons of the Fatherland: Workers in the Vanguard of Soviet Collectivization.* New York: Oxford University Press, 1987.

———. "The Other Archipelago: Kulak Deportations to the North in 1930." *Slavic Review* 60, no. 4 (2001): 730–55.

———. *The Role of the OGPU in Dekulakization, Mass Deportations, and Special Resettlement in 1930.* Carl Beck Papers in Russian and East European Studies no. 1406. Pittsburgh: Russian and East European Studies, University of Pittsburgh, 2000.

———. *The Unknown Gulag: The Lost World of Stalin's Special Settlements.* Oxford: Oxford University Press, 2007.

Volkogonov, Dmitry. *Stalin: Triumph and Tragedy.* New York: Grove Weidenfeld, 1991.

Vorontsov, V. I., et al. *Organy i Voiska MVD Rossii: Kratkii Istoricheskii Ocherk.* Moscow: Ob"edinennaia redaktsiia MVD Rossii, 1996.

Wade, Rex. *Red Guards and Workers' Militias in the Russian Revolution.* Stanford, Calif.: Stanford University Press, 1984.

Wagner, Patrick. "Operating on the Body of the Nation: Racist Criminal Politics and Traditional Policing in Nazi Germany." Paper presented at the Australasian Association for European History, Twelfth Biennial Conference, Perth, July 5–9, 1999.

———. *Volksgemeinschaft ohne Verbrecher: Konzeptionen und Praxis der Kriminalpolizei in der Zeit der Weimarer Republik und des Nationalsozialismus.* Hamburg: Christians, 1996.

Weiner, Amir. "Introduction: Landscaping the Human Garden." In *Landscaping the Human Garden: Twentieth-Century Population Management in a Comparative Framework*, ed. Amir Weiner. Stanford, Calif.: Stanford University Press, 2003.

———. *Making Sense of War: The Second World War and the Fate of the Bolshevik Revolution.* Princeton, N.J.: Princeton University Press, 2001.

———. "Nothing but Certainty." *Slavic Review* 61, no. 1 (2002): 44–53.

Weissman, Neil. "Local Power in the 1920s." In *Reform in Modern Russian History*, ed. Theodore Taranovski. Washington, D.C.: Woodrow Wilson Center, 1995.

————. "Policing the NEP Countryside." In *Russia in the Era of NEP: Explorations in Soviet Society and Culture*, ed. Sheila Fitzpatrick, Alexander Rabinowitch, and Richard Stites. Bloomington: Indiana University Press, 1991.

————. "Regular Police in Tsarist Russia, 1900–1914." *Russian Review* 44, no. 1 (1985): 45–68.

Werth, Nicolas. "L'OGPU en 1924: Radiographie d'une institution à son niveau d'étiage." *Cahiers du Monde russe* 42, nos. 2–4 (2001): 397–422.

————. "The Mechanism of a Mass Crime: The Great Terror in the Soviet Union, 1937–1938." In *The Specter of Genocide: Mass Murder in Historical Perspective*, ed. Robert Gellately and Ben Kiernan. Cambridge: Cambridge University Press, 2003.

————. "A State against Its People: Violence, Repression, and Terror in the Soviet Union." In *The Black Book of Communism: Crimes, Terror, Repression*, ed. Mark Kramer and translated by Jonathan Murphy. Cambridge, Mass.: Harvard University Press, 1999.

Wheatcroft, Stephen G. "Agency and Terror: Evdokimov and Mass Killing in Stalin's Great Terror." *Australian Journal of Politics and History* 53, no. 1 (2007): 20–43.

————. "Towards Explaining the Changing Levels of Stalinist Repression in the 1930s: Mass Killings." In *Challenging Traditional Views of Russian History*, ed. Stephen G. Wheatcroft. Basingstoke, U.K.: Palgrave Macmillan, 2002.

Zuckerman, Frederic S. *The Tsarist Police in Russian Society, 1880–1917*. London: Macmillan, 1996.

Index